Related Titles by David Matsumoto

The Handbook of Culture and Psychology

Culture and Modern Life

Unmasking Japan: Myths and Realities of the Emotions of the Japanese

People: Psychology from a Cultural Perspective

Cultural Influences on Methods and Statistics

A World of Diversity video with student workbook and facilitator's guide

Culture and Psychology

People Around the World

SECOND EDITION

David Matsumoto

San Francisco State University

Wadsworth
Thomson Learning

Australia • Canada • Mexico • Singapore • Spain • United Kingdom • United States

Psychology Editor: *Marianne Taflinger*
Editorial Assistants: *Suzanne Wood, Rachael Bruckman*
Marketing Manager: *Jenna Opp*
Project Editor: *Tanya Nigh*
Print Buyer: *Mary Noel*
Permissions Editor: *Joohee Lee*
Production Service: *Scratchgravel Publishing Services*

Text Designer: *Anne Draus*
Copy Editor: *Margaret Tropp*
Cover Designer: *Roger Knox*
Cover Printer: *Custom Printing*
Compositor: *Scratchgravel Publishing Services*
Printer: *Custom Printing*

Printed in the United States of America
1 2 3 4 5 6 7   03 02 01 00 99

For permission to use material from this text,
contact us by
   Web: http://www.thomsonrights.com
   Fax: 1-800-730-2215
   Phone: 1-800-730-2214

Library of Congress Cataloging-in-Publication Data
Matsumoto, David Ricky.
   Culture and psychology : people around the world /
David Matsumoto.—2nd ed.
      p. cm.
   Includes bibliographical references and index.
   ISBN 0-534-35436-X (alk. paper)
   1. Ethnopsychology.   2. Personality and culture.
3. Intercultural communication. I. Title.

GN502 .M374 2000
155.8'2—dc21   99-051518

For more information, contact
Wadsworth/Thomson Learning
10 Davis Drive
Belmont, CA 94002-3098
USA
http://www.wadsworth.com

International Headquarters
Thomson Learning
International Division
290 Harbor Drive, 2nd Floor
Stamford, CT 06902-7477
USA

UK/Europe/Middle East/South Africa
Thomson Learning
Berkshire House
168-173 High Holborn
London WC1V 7AA
United Kingdom

Asia
Thomson Learning
60 Albert Street, #15-01
Albert Complex
Singapore 189969

Canada
Nelson Thomson Learning
1120 Birchmount Road
Toronto, Ontario M1K 5G4
Canada

To the memory of my dad and mom,
Paul and Mitsuno Matsumoto,
for their wonderful teachings and
the great family they gave me

About the Author

David Matsumoto is Professor of Psychology and Director of the Culture and Emotion Research Laboratory at San Francisco State University. He earned his B.A. from the University of Michigan and his M.A. and Ph.D. from the University of California, Berkeley. He has studied emotion, human interaction, and culture for 20 years and is a recognized expert in this field. He is the author of over 200 works on culture and emotion, including original research articles, paper presentations, books, book chapters, videos, and assessment instruments. He is the recipient of numerous awards, including the Conference Award from the Japanese Academy of Budo, the Excellence in Teaching Award from the Northern California Chapter of Phi Beta Kappa, and the Group Achievement Award from the National Aeronautics and Space Administration (NASA). He is a former G. Stanley Hall Lecturer for the American Psychological Association and has presented his work to scientific and lay audiences around the world.

Dr. Matsumoto is also very active in the world of the Olympic sport of judo, bringing his expertise in intercultural relations to this arena as well. In addition to being the head instructor of the East Bay Judo Institute in El Cerrito, California, he currently serves as the Program Director of Development for United States Judo, Inc., the national governing body of judo in the United States. He has coached and managed many senior and junior judo teams representing the United States in international competition and training. He has been team leader for the U.S. judo team at the 1995 World Championships in Chiba, Japan, the 1996 Summer Olympic Games in Atlanta, Georgia, and the 1997 World Championships in Paris, France.

Brief Contents

Preface   xv

1 An Introduction to Cross-Cultural Psychology   1

2 Understanding and Defining Culture   17

3 Culture and Self   53

4 Ethnocentrism, Stereotypes, and Prejudice   75

5 Evaluating Cross-Cultural Research   105

6 Culture and Basic Psychological Processes   137

7 Culture and Development   173

8 Culture and Gender   209

9 Culture and Physical Health   229

10 Culture and Mental Health   251

11 Culture and Emotion   271

12 Culture and Language   313

13 Culture and Nonverbal Behavior   337

14 Intercultural Communication   359

15 Culture and Personality   385

16 Culture and Social Behavior   403

17 Culture and Organizations   445

18 Conclusion: Implications for Mainstream Psychology and Everyday Life   489

References   507

Name Index   551

Subject Index   559

Contents

Preface   xv

 1 **An Introduction to Cross-Cultural Psychology**   **1**

What Psychology Is All About   2
The Creation of Knowledge and Truth in Science   3
Understanding the Process of Research in Psychology   4
Cross-Cultural Research and Psychology   8
The Impact of Cross-Cultural Psychology:
 Gaining a Multicultural Perspective   11
The Goal of This Book   14
Glossary   16

2 **Understanding and Defining Culture**   **17**

Why Is It Important to Define Culture?   17
The Use of the Term *Culture* in Everyday Language   18
A Definition of Culture   23
Pancultural Principles versus Culture-Specific Differences:
 Emics and Etics   35
An Introduction to Ethnocentrism and Stereotypes   37
Transforming Culture into a Measurable Construct   38

The Influence of Culture on Psychology   47
Conclusion   49
Glossary   50

3 Culture and Self   53

Culture and Concepts of Self   54
An Example of Different Cultural Conceptualizations of Self:
    Independent and Interdependent Selves   56
Critical Thinking and Evaluation of the Analysis
    of Independent and Interdependent Selves   66
Beyond Independent and Interdependent Self-Construals:
    Interrelated and Isolated Self-Concepts   70
Multicultural Identities   71
Conclusion   73
Glossary   73

4 Ethnocentrism, Stereotypes, and Prejudice   75

Ethnocentrism and Intergroup Attitudes   76
Stereotypes   83
Prejudice, Discrimination, and "Isms"   92
Going Beyond Prejudice and Discrimination   97
Conclusion   101
Glossary   102

5 Evaluating Cross-Cultural Research   105

Why It Is Important to Understand Cross-Cultural
    Research Methods   105
The Nature of Truth in Psychology and
    the Importance of Research   106
The Parameters and Conditions of Hypothesis-Testing Research   109
Special Issues in Cross-Cultural Research   115
Guidelines for Reviewing Cross-Cultural Research   130
Conclusion   134
Glossary   136

6 Culture and Basic Psychological Processes 137

Culture and the Biological Bases of Behavior 137
Culture and Perception 140
Culture and Cognition 147
Culture and Consciousness 157
Culture and Intelligence 161
Conclusion 171
Glossary 172

7 Culture and Development 173

Enculturation and Socialization 173
Culture and Psychological Processes in Development 193
Conclusion 204
Glossary 205

8 Culture and Gender 209

The Relationship of Gender and Culture
    to Mainstream Psychology 210
Some Definitions 211
Cross-Cultural Research on Gender 212
Conclusion 225
Glossary 226

9 Culture and Physical Health 229

Cultural Differences in the Definition of Health 230
Culture and Conceptions of the Body 231
Sociocultural Influences on Physical Health
    and Medical Disease Processes 232
Cultural Influences on Attitudes and Beliefs Related
    to Health and Disease 242
A Model of Cultural Influences on Physical Health 245
Cultural Differences in Dealing with Illness 246
Conclusion 249
Glossary 250

10 Culture and Mental Health 251

Defining Abnormality   252
Culture and the Assessment of Abnormal Behavior   261
Culture and the Treatment of Abnormal Behavior   264
Conclusion   269
Glossary   270

11 Culture and Emotion 271

The Importance of Emotion in Our Lives   271
Culture and Emotion Expression   272
Culture and Emotion Perception   282
Culture and the Experience of Emotion   290
Culture and the Antecedents of Emotion   298
Culture and Emotion Appraisal   301
Culture and the Concept and Language of Emotion   305
Conclusion   311
Glossary   312

12 Culture and Language 313

The Components of Language and Language Acquisition   314
Language Differences across Cultures   317
Language and Worldview: The Case for Linguistic Relativity   323
Language and Behavior: The Special Case of Bilingualism   330
Conclusion   335
Glossary   336

13 Culture and Nonverbal Behavior 337

What Are Nonverbal Behaviors?   337
Classifying the Functions of Nonverbal Behaviors   338
Verbal and Nonverbal Behaviors in Communication   340
Cultural Influences on Nonverbal Behaviors and
    Their Implications for Communication   343
Cross-Cultural Research on Nonverbal Behaviors   346

Applied Studies Examining Cross-Cultural
Differences in Nonverbal Behaviors   355
Conclusion   356
Glossary   357

14 Intercultural Communication   359

Defining Communication   360
The Components of Communication   360
The Role of Culture in the Communication Process   362
Intracultural versus Intercultural Communication   365
Toward Effective Intercultural Communication   373
Conclusion   382
Glossary   383

15 Culture and Personality   385

Defining Personality   386
Cross-Cultural Research on Personality   388
Culture and the Five Factor Model of Personality   394
The Measurement of Personality across Cultures   397
The Measurement of Personality to Assess Psychopathology
across Cultures   398
Culture and Indigenous Personalities   399
Conclusion   401
Glossary   402

16 Culture and Social Behavior   403

Culture and Ingroup/Outgroup Relationships   403
Culture, Person Perception, and Attractiveness   410
Culture and Interpersonal Attraction:
Love, Intimacy, and Intercultural Marriages   414
Culture and Attributions   421
Culture and Aggression   433
Culture and Conformity, Compliance, Obedience,
and Cooperation   436
Conclusion   441
Glossary   442

17 Culture and Organizations 445

Organizational Culture and Organizational Climate   446
Culture and Organizational Structure   448
Cultural Differences in Work-Related Values   449
Recent Research on Organizational Culture   458
Culture and the Meaning of Work   469
Culture, Motivation, and Productivity   470
Culture, Leadership, and Management Styles   473
Culture and Decision-Making Processes   476
Intercultural Issues Regarding Business and Work   479
Conclusion   485
Glossary   486

18 Conclusion: Implications for Mainstream Psychology and Everyday Life 489

Implications for Mainstream Psychology   490
Implications for Our Everyday Lives   495
Conclusion   503

References   507

Name Index   551

Subject Index   559

Preface

The Place of Culture in the Evolution of Mainstream Psychology

Since the publication of the first edition of *Culture and Psychology* just a few years ago, the importance of learning about culture and diversity is no longer debated in all areas, subfields, and specialties of psychology. Researchers' incorporation of culture as an important and defining variable has dramatically increased over the past few years, and practitioners are well aware of its contributions to behavior in applied settings ranging from psychotherapy to organizational consulting. Teachers continue to expand coverage of culture in their courses, balancing the great infusion of new information from contemporary research that involves culture with the diversity of thought, opinions, and backgrounds of an increasingly pluralistic student population. The number of cross-cultural courses offered by psychology departments has continued to rise. These movements have occurred not only across the United States at both the college/university and high school levels but internationally as well.

The past decade witnessed an explosion of new research in psychology that has incorporated culture. Many of these studies continue to be cross-cultural comparisons of various psychological phenomena, documenting similarities and differences across cultures in human behavior. Many newer studies, however, have gone beyond the mere documentation of differences to begin the all-important search for the mediators of those differences. Collectively, this literature has grown immensely in size, scope, and implications, contributing new knowledge, new ideas, new frameworks, and new ways of thinking.

Indeed, psychology—both mainstream and cross-cultural—is in an interesting state of evolution in method, thinking, and approach. More than at any other time, ideas and knowledge in psychology have become more flexible and pluralistic, attempting to encompass the fluidity of psychological truths as they vary across time, place, and context. Methods and concepts are increasingly borrowed from other disciplines, and contemporary studies involving culture are more sophisticated, complex, and precise than in the past. These changes only promise even further evolution of knowledge in psychology, bolstered in no small part by the contribution of culture to theories and research.

Improvements to This Edition

Doubles the content to capture this evolution of knowledge and to provide a full course in a single text. The second edition of *Culture and Psychology* captures the evolution in this field. The first change you will notice from the first edition is that the amount of material covered has increased dramatically, resulting in a second edition that is almost twice as large as the first. This change reflects the substantially larger literature in all areas of psychology and the importance this literature has acquired in those areas. (The first edition had 490 references; this edition contains more than 1,000.)

Synthesizes information about culture with knowledge from the mainstream literature. Another major improvement in this edition concerns the increased synthesis of that large literature with mainstream knowledge. When critically examined, the literature presented here forces us to reconsider the ways in which we understand psychology. Thus, you will find in this edition new ways of viewing, understanding, studying, and thinking about psychology and human behavior that did not exist in the previous edition.

Includes new chapters and a totally revised organization. This edition is also enhanced by other changes:

- A new structure of the book, with five introductory chapters that build baseline knowledge concerning the "foundations" of culture, twelve chapters that span various content areas of psychology, and a concluding chapter.
- The division of the single chapter on health in the first edition into two chapters in the second edition, one dealing with mental health and the other dealing with physical health.
- A new chapter on intercultural communication.
- A new chapter on culture and personality.
- New figures that reinforce the story of culture and psychology.

Includes major refinements in each chapter. Considerable refinements have been made to the individual chapters as well. Here are some of the highlights of the changes in each chapter:

- *Chapter 1:* This chapter was totally rewritten to discuss cross-cultural psychology from the standpoint of scientific philosophy, beginning with a big-picture perspective of what psychology is all about, the role of research in psychology, and how cross-cultural psychology tests limitations to knowledge based on research.
- *Chapter 2:* This chapter now incorporates new sections on the layperson's conceptions of culture; factors that influence culture; the relationships among culture, race, ethnicity, nationality, disability, and sexual orientation; and popular culture. It also includes a comprehensive review of culture definitions, as well as measurement techniques of culture.
- *Chapter 3:* This chapter includes an expanded theoretical discussion of the relationship between culture and self-concept, as well as new sections discussing the theoretical underpinnings of the Markus and Kitayama view, alternative views, and multicultural identities.
- *Chapter 4:* This chapter expands the discussion of stereotypes and the psychological attributes that contribute to them. It also includes new sections reviewing cross-cultural research that highlights the contribution of psychological factors on ethnocentrism; the content of stereotypes; new material on the role of affect; and prejudice, discrimination, and "isms."
- *Chapter 5:* This chapter was improved by including new material on the nature of research and truth in psychology, focusing on the concepts of validity, reliability, and replication; on being a consumer of research and the different types of research paradigms available in psychology; on the concept of equivalence, design, and the interpretation of findings; and on a handout presenting guidelines on how to review cross-cultural research.
- *Chapter 6:* This chapter includes new material on the relationship between culture and biology; face recognition; decision making; creativity; consciousness; and IQ, intelligence testing, and selection issues.
- *Chapter 7:* This chapter was completely reorganized to give readers a sense of the multiple factors that contribute to enculturation. It also includes new material on attachment; the process of enculturation; biological bases, attitudes, language, and other factors contributing to cross-national differences in math abilities; and the development of cultural identity.
- *Chapter 8:* This chapter now includes a new review of studies on gender stereotypes; gender differences in other psychological constructs; and how culture influences gender.
- *Chapter 9:* This chapter now includes new material on culture and conceptions of the body; psychosocial determinants of health and disease; IC and health; cultural discrepancies and health; eating disorders; suicide; and culturally sensitive treatment approaches. It also provides readers with a model of cultural influences on physical health.
- *Chapter 10:* This chapter was reorganized into three sections, including definition, assessment, and treatment. It includes new material on etic versus emic viewpoints in defining abnormality, somatization, culture-bound syndromes, psychiatric diagnoses, and clinical training.

- *Chapter 11:* This chapter has been improved by the incorporation of new material on emotional expression and perception, including a discussion of the current debate concerning the universality of emotion, emotion antecedents, emotional experience, and emotion appraisal.
- *Chapter 12:* This chapter incorporates new work in the discussion of culture and language lexicons, language pragmatics, the Sapir–Whorf hypothesis, bilingualism, and misperceptions about bilinguals.
- *Chapter 13:* This chapter includes more general discussion about the nature of nonverbal behaviors. It also includes new material on the importance of nonverbal behaviors in communication, other nonverbal behaviors not previously covered, and applied studies.
- *Chapter 14:* This is an entirely new chapter on intercultural communication, covering the definition and components of communication, the role of culture in the communication process, intracultural versus intercultural communication, and effective intercultural communication.
- *Chapter 15:* This is also an entirely new chapter on culture and personality, including cross-cultural research, the five-factor model of personality, and the measurement of personality.
- *Chapter 16:* This chapter has been substantially enlarged and improved by the inclusion of new research on ingroups and outgroups, attractiveness, love and marriage, attributions, nonacademic topics, aggression, and cooperation.
- *Chapter 17:* This chapter involves a reorganization of the material into two broad themes: organizational culture and work. It includes new material on organizational culture and climate, the measurement of organizational culture, practical applications of knowledge about organizational culture, work behaviors, decision making, negotiation, and international business.
- *Chapter 18:* This chapter was substantially enlarged by the inclusion of a large section on implications for mainstream psychology, the development of a model of intercultural growth and sensitivity, and advice for those who want to break into the field of cross-cultural psychology.

Summary of the improvements. As you can see from the descriptions above, this edition of *Culture and Psychology* reflects the breadth, scope, depth, and understanding of the influence of culture on human behavior as well as the intimate relationship between culture and psychology. It was written with a threefold purpose for its intended audience (students in cross-cultural psychology courses on both the undergraduate and graduate levels): first, to recast knowledge and truth in psychology in a different light, one that incorporates culture and context as important frameworks; second, to reflect the current evolution in thinking about human behavior in psychology; and, third, to highlight the importance of culture and its influence on people. I hope that you will share my enthusiasm as you read this book and challenge your mind and heart with its messages.

Acknowledgments

I have been fortunate to enjoy the collaboration of many scholars over the years who have helped forge my thinking about culture and psychology. They truly are too numerous to mention here individually, but to all with whom I have worked and published, I offer a collective statement of great appreciation for your hard work, kindness, and friendship over the years.

I am also forever indebted to my current and former students, lab assistants, and Visiting Scholars who have been a part of the Culture and Emotion Research Laboratory in the Psychology Department of San Francisco State University. In particular, I owe a remarkable debt of gratitude to Kristie Kooken, Charlotte Ratzlaff, Rebecca Ray, and Sachiko Takeuchi, who helped me teach cross-cultural psychology at San Francisco State University and who contributed countless hours of hard work and dedication to this course and to helping me refine my ideas about culture and psychology. I also give thanks to Sunita Paul and her team of workers who helped me tremendously in preparing the references for the final manuscript.

As in the past, the people at Wadsworth/Thomson Learning have done a marvelous job of working with me in a professional and courteous manner through all phases of this revision. In particular, my editor Marianne Taflinger has believed in my work for many years, and I am extremely grateful for the trust, respect, and friendship she has offered me. I would also like to extend my warmest appreciation to those who reviewed the second edition: Ali Banuazizi, Professor of Cultural Psychology, Boston College; Susan E. Dutch, Westfield State College; Grace Galliano, Kennesaw State University; Ron Jacques, Ricks College; Bill Hill, Kennesaw State College; Kenneth Keith, University of San Diego; Jennifer Abe-Kim, Loyola Marymount University; Richard Logan, University of Wisconsin–Green Bay; and Katherine Van Giffen, California State University–Long Beach.

My ability to bring together such a large and comprehensive review is no small tribute to the love and support I have always received from my family. Thank you, Sayaka, for being a great daughter to us; you are a source of great pride and joy in our lives. And thank you, Mimi, for being the best wife, mother, and partner in the whole wide world.

David Matsumoto

An Introduction to Cross-Cultural Psychology

Cultural diversity is one of the most important topics in the United States today. All of us are continually being thrust into an increasingly diverse world—at school, at work, and at home—and misunderstandings can lead to confusion and anger. Identifying yourself with a particular group may engender in yourself a feeling of protectionism for the group to which you belong. *Diversity* is a buzzword for "difference," and conflicts and misunderstandings often arise because of these differences.

Cultural diversity is American society's biggest challenge. Corporate America is attempting to address that challenge through workshops, seminars, and education in diversity throughout the workforce. The educational system has addressed diversity by hiring and retaining faculty of color and infusing material related to different cultures throughout the curriculum. Government has attempted to deal with diversity through policies such as equal employment opportunity, and affirmative action.

The challenges that face us in the names of cultural diversity and intercultural relations also represent our biggest opportunities. If we can meet those challenges and turn them to our favor, we can actualize a potential in diversity and intercultural relations that will result in far more than the sum of the individual components that comprise that diverse universe.

It is with this belief that this book was written—to meet the challenge of diversity and somehow turn that challenge into opportunity. Doing so is not easy. It requires each of us to take an honest look at our own cultural background and heritage, their merits and limitations. Fear, rigidity, and sometimes stubborn pride come with any type of honest assessment. Yet without that assessment, we cannot meet the challenge of diversity and improve intercultural relations.

In academia, that assessment brings with it fundamental questions about what is taught in our colleges and universities today. To ask how cultural diversity colors the nature of the truths and principles of human behavior delivered in the halls of science is to question the pillars of much of our knowledge about the world and about human behavior. From time to time, we need to shake those pillars to see just how sturdy they are. This is especially true in the social sciences, and particularly in psychology—the science specifically concerned with the mental and behavioral characteristics of people.

What Psychology Is All About

No field is better equipped to meet the challenge of cultural diversity than psychology. And in fact, psychology has met, and continues to meet, the challenge of culture through a subfield known as *cross-cultural psychology*. To get a better handle on what cross-cultural psychology is all about, it is important first to have a good grasp of what psychology is all about.

I see psychology as having two main goals. The first goal is building a body of knowledge about people. Psychologists seek to understand behavior when it happens, explain why it happens, and even predict it before it happens. Two aspects of psychology are important in achieving this goal: the conduct of psychological research and the creation of theoretical models of behavior. Research and theory go hand in hand in psychology.

The second goal of psychology involves taking that body of knowledge and *applying* it to intervene in people's lives, hopefully to make those lives better. Psychologists perform various important roles in pursuit of this goal: as therapists for individuals, families, and groups; as counselors in schools, universities, churches, and other community organizations; as trainers in businesses and work organizations; as consultants for police, lawyers, courts, sport organizations, athletes, and teams; and in a host of other applied professions. Psychologists work on the front lines, if you will, dealing directly with people to affect their lives in a positive fashion.

The two goals of psychology—creating a body of knowledge and applying that knowledge—are not mutually exclusive. Indeed, they share a close relationship, as well they should. Psychologists who are on the front lines do not work in a vacuum; they take what psychology as a field has collectively learned about human behavior and use that knowledge as a basis for their applications and interventions. This learning initially comes in the form of academic training of counselors, therapists, and consultants as they achieve academic degrees from universities. But it continues well after formal education has ended, through continuing education programs and individual scholarship—reviewing the literature, attending conferences, joining and participating in professional organizations. Thus, applied psychologists engage in a lifelong learning process that helps them to intervene in people's lives more effectively.

Likewise, psychologists who do research and create theories are cognizant of the practical and applied implications of their work. In fact, most researchers and theoreticians are well aware that the value of psychological theory and research is often judged by its practical usefulness in society (see, for example, Gergen, Gulerce, Lock, & Misra, 1996). Theories are often tested for their validity not only in the halls of science, but also in the streets, if you will, and they often have to be revised because of what happens in those streets.

Theory/research and application/intervention are thus the two goals of psychology as I, and many others, see them. While some psychologists may choose to focus on one or the other, it is important to remember that psychology as a collective whole seeks to achieve both. The two goals, and the close relationship between them, are important aspects of psychology in general. Cross-cultural psychology has a special meaning to mainstream psychology because of these goals.

The Creation of Knowledge and Truth in Science

Just how is knowledge created in psychology? Human behavior is at the heart not only of psychology, but also of many social sciences. It is also an important element in many other fields, including business, communication, economics, and even biology and chemistry. Although each of these disciplines takes a different approach and has a unique viewpoint for understanding human behavior, they all have at least one thing in common: reliance on formal, systematic, scientific research as the primary method by which knowledge is generated.

Each discipline has its own scientific approach and uses a unique paradigm and theoretical framework to understand and interpret data. Psychology, for instance, relies heavily on scientific research through interviews and laboratory experiments involving human participants to generate knowledge about how and why people behave as they do. Observational research, case studies, bibliographic studies, and surveys are also important research tools in psychology. Despite the differences in approaches, the goals are similar: to uncover information about individuals—that is, to generate knowledge. Researchers conducting psychological studies often attempt to interpret and understand their data on the level of the individual. This characteristic, among others, sets psychology apart from other social science disciplines concerned with human behavior.

All disciplines rely on scholarship and research at least to some degree to discover knowledge about the world and about human behavior. One of the elemental bases of research is the conduct of a study. In evaluating the knowledge obtained, it is important to be assured that the research—that is, the studies conducted on a particular topic—meets some minimal standards of scientific rigor. Strict adherence to scientific principles allows us to "trust" the information produced by a study. Indeed, if the methods of any study are compromised to the point that the results obtained in that study are biased, those results should not necessarily be believed, regardless of how attractive and personally appealing the results may be. Only when the methods used in a study meet objective and well-accepted standards for quality and rigor can the findings be accepted as making a statement about human behavior.

Knowledge is never generated in a single study. It is only when individual research findings are consistently repeated across studies that the field begins to believe that a finding can be generalized to many people. **Generalizations*** are comprised of truths or principles winnowed from multiple, systematic research efforts that are believed to be true for a larger group of people than those actually studied. In psychological research, consistent repetition of a finding across a number of studies is called **replication** of a result, and replication is an essential ingredient in the quest for truth about human behavior (see Figure 1.1).

It is incumbent on any serious student of human behavior, whether in psychology or any other field of social science, to be able to evaluate for him- or herself the basis of psychological knowledge—the truths and principles that the field of psychology collectively holds. As you can see from Figure 1.1, research—that is, individual studies—is the primary vehicle by which knowledge is created; thus, it is incumbent on serious students to understand the process of research and its contribution to knowledge. As studies are the backbone of research, it is also important to understand how studies are constructed and conducted, and how their methodological parameters influence the generation of facts that become psychological knowledge. Indeed, it does no good for us to merely accept truths or principles of psychology; we should harbor a healthy degree of skepticism about these truths, and about the processes by which they were generated. This skepticism—critical thinking, if you will—is at the heart of the scientific process, in psychology and in other fields. For these reasons, it is important to understand how studies are conducted, the relationship between research and theory, and the relationship between the methods used in a study and the findings that are produced in that study. These findings collectively become psychological knowledge.

Understanding the Process of Research in Psychology

Research and Theory

All research starts from a theory. A **theory** is a model of human behavior—essentially, someone's guesses about how people are. Glancing at any psychology textbook quickly reveals that psychology offers many theories about many aspects of human behavior—theories of emotion, thinking, intelligence, language development, altruism, and so forth.

A theory is an organized and coherent set of facts and assumptions. Some facts and assumptions about people can be tested to see whether or not they are correct; these testable aspects of a theory are called **hypotheses**. Aspects of theories that remain untested constitute the **assumptions** of that theory.

***Boldface** terms are defined in the glossary at the end of each chapter.

Figure 1.1 The generation of knowledge, truth, and principles in psychology

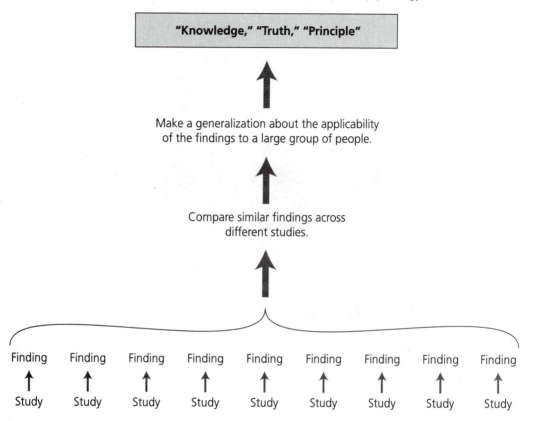

Hypotheses are tested by means of studies. An important feature of a testable hypothesis is that it must be falsifiable; that is, a study can show it to be incorrect if it is indeed incorrect, as well as correct if it is correct.

A study is designed to test specific hypotheses. Once completed, if it was conducted validly, the study will either confirm or disconfirm the hypotheses it was designed to test. If the study is not conducted validly, then it doesn't matter whether it confirms the hypotheses or not, because one cannot trust its results. The confirmed or disconfirmed hypotheses, in turn, inform the original theory from which they came, either reinforcing the theory or calling for its revision. This process is outlined in Figure 1.2.

Theories in psychology represent collections of facts organized in some way to produce models of human behavior. Research is the process by which the individual facts that comprise a theory are confirmed or disconfirmed. Thus, research is one of the building blocks of theories, and theories comprise what we know as psychological knowledge, truth, or principle.

Figure 1.2 The cyclical relationship between theory and research in psychology

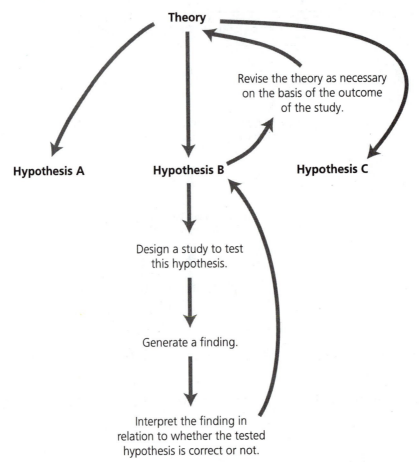

The Relationship between Methods and Knowledge

Because studies contribute to what we know as truth, we should recognize that truth is heavily dependent on how those studies were conducted. All studies are conducted under specific conditions, with certain methodological parameters decided upon by researchers. For example, researchers make decisions concerning the nature, number, and characteristics of the participants; the nature and type of instruments, materials, or tests; and the procedures by which participants will engage with the instruments and tests to produce data. Researchers also make decisions about how to manipulate and analyze their data. Once findings are produced, they make decisions about how to interpret those findings based on their hypotheses. These numerous parameters of any study are outlined in Figure 1.3. As discussed previously, the entire process begins

Figure 1.3 An overview of the process of research in psychology

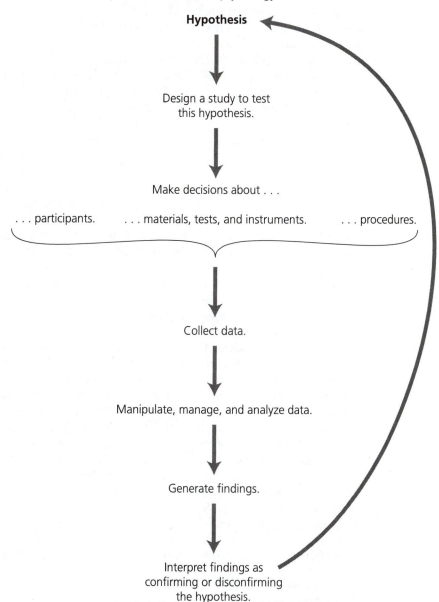

and ends with hypotheses, and these hypotheses, in turn, inform models of human behavior (theories).

As you can see from Figure 1.3, scientific research is not a process that occurs in a vacuum without human contact; quite to the contrary, it is heavily dependent on the conscious and deliberate decisions made by the person or persons conducting the research. Even theories and hypotheses are person driven, and thus are affected by the particular ways of thinking of their creators. Decisions made concerning how a study will be conducted form the basis for the parameters and conditions under which the research is conducted. Because data about people are gathered within this framework, *the knowledge generated by research is bounded by these artificial parameters; that is, the parameters of any study define the limitations of the knowledge generated in that study.*

If, for example, researchers ask participants to view an ambiguous stimulus and choose from a list of ten items what they think they see in the stimulus, the researchers will obtain a finding about a perception that is limited to the ten choices provided. Using that same methodology, a researcher can then study how such perceptions may be related to other phenomena, or how the perceptions reflected in those choices differ across cultural or gender groups. A considerable amount of time and effort can be expended conducting such studies and developing elaborate theoretical frameworks concerning how and why such perceptions exist and are maintained. What is too often forgotten is that the very nature of the data derived from this set of studies is dependent on the way those data were obtained in the first place. It may very well be the case, for example, that the perceptions reported by the study participants were simply the best alternatives available from the restricted list of ten items. Although it may be the case that participants' choices were close to their perceptions, it may also be true that the choices had little to do with their actual perceptions. Participants may have selected the least wrong choice available, but not necessarily one that matched their actual perceptions of the stimulus. If the participants had been allowed to say whatever came to their minds about the stimulus in an open-ended format, they might have provided entirely different data. Or if given different choices, they might have selected differently. Data obtained in any research project are dependent on the methods used by the researcher and the personal biases of the scientists who design and conduct those studies.

It follows, therefore, that if a researcher changes a methodological parameter in his or her study, that change may produce a change in the findings. Changing the nature of the tests administered, for example, or the time of day of administration, or the way in which data are analyzed may bring about differences in findings, even when studying the same topic. Changes in the characteristics of the participants may also bring about differences. This last relationship is a primary basis for cross-cultural research in psychology.

Cross-Cultural Research and Psychology

Most research on human behavior conducted in the United States involves American college or university students as study participants. The reasons are largely pragmatic. University faculty need to do research, for themselves as much as for the field, and the easiest population to access is often university student volunteers. Another reason why most American psychological research involves American university students has been a lack of concern about issues of diversity and its impact on theory and research, and quite frankly, some of the political ramifications of doing such research. As a result, the majority of the information and research you read about in textbooks and research articles in mainstream psychology is based on studies involving American college or university student participants or samples.

There is nothing wrong with such research, and the findings obtained from such samples are definitely true for those samples. These findings may be replicated across multiple samples, using different methodologies. In short, many findings may weather tests for scientific rigor that would normally render them acceptable as a truth or principle about human behavior. However, a basic question still remains: Is what we know as truth or principle about human behavior, which we have learned in our "traditional" or usual way, true for all people, regardless of gender, race, ethnicity, culture, class, or lifestyle? Again, this question has particular import when you consider the nature of the samples generally included in psychological research.

Cross-cultural research asks these questions about psychological truths and principles by examining and testing them in people of differing cultural backgrounds. In cross-cultural research, these questions are addressed quite simply—by including participants of more than one cultural background and then comparing data obtained across the cultural groups. This research approach is primarily concerned with examining how our knowledge about people and their behaviors from one culture may or may not hold for people from another culture.

Cross-cultural research can be understood in relation to mainstream academic psychology as a matter of **scientific philosophy**. This term refers to the logic underlying the methods used to conduct research and generate knowledge in psychology. As explained previously, knowledge depends on research to confirm or disconfirm hypotheses; research, in turn, involves a methodology designed to collect data that can falsify or support hypotheses. Methods involve many specific parameters, one of which includes decisions about the number and nature of the participants in the study. Cross-cultural research involves the inclusion of people of different cultural backgrounds—a specific type of change in one of the parameters of methodology.

What, then, is the difference between cross-cultural research and any other type of research that changes a parameter of a study? If we consider cross-cultural research from the standpoint of scientific philosophy, other studies that change other parameters of research—such as the specific tests or measures that are used, or the procedures by which data are collected—also raise important questions about the generalizability of findings. Changes can also occur in characteristics of the participants other than their cultural background, such as their socioeconomic class, age, gender, or place of residence. All these types of changes are important in relation to the philosophy underlying psychology's science. But the meaning of a study and its findings differs if it compares different cultures than if it compares different ways of measuring a variable, for example. This difference is related to what may be considered the *cross-cultural approach*.

The **cross-cultural approach** or perspective that cross-cultural research brings to mainstream psychology goes far beyond simple methodological

changes in the studies conducted to test hypotheses related to truth and knowledge. It is a way of understanding truth and principles about human behaviors
within a global, cross-cultural perspective. Cross-cultural research not only
tests similarities and differences in behaviors, thus expanding our knowledge
about people; it also tests possible limitations of our traditional knowledge by
studying people of different cultures. In its narrowest sense, cross-cultural research simply involves including participants from different cultural backgrounds and testing possible differences between these different groups of participants. In its broadest sense, however, the cross-cultural approach is
concerned with understanding truth and psychological principles as either **universal** (true for all people of all cultures) or **culture-specific** (true for some
people of some cultures).

Certainly, some truths must be true for all; we call those truths *universals.*
Still, there is much about the world and about human behavior that is true for
one culture but not for others. It may very well be the case, therefore, that even
though a finding is replicated in studies involving subjects from a given culture
and society, it is not true for another culture or society, and vice versa. Some
truths and principles, in this sense, are not absolutes; they are, in fact, culturally relative and culturally bound. And not only are the results of our research
bound by our methods and culture, but the very standards of care we use when
we evaluate the scientific rigor and quality of research are also bound by the
cultural frameworks within which our science occurs (Pe-Pua, 1989).

In the United States, psychology is segmented into specific topic areas, for
example, clinical, social, developmental, personality, and the like. Cross-cultural
psychology and cross-cultural approaches are not topic-specific. Cross-cultural
researchers are interested in a broad range of phenomena related to human behavior—from perception to language, child rearing to psychopathology. Cross-
cultural psychologists and cross-cultural research can be found in any specific
area or subdiscipline within psychology. What distinguishes a cross-cultural
approach from a traditional or mainstream approach, therefore, is not the phenomenon of interest but the testing of limitations to knowledge by examining
whether that knowledge is applicable to or obtainable from people of different
cultural backgrounds. The approach, not the topic, is what is important in
cross-cultural psychology.

For many years, cross-cultural research was never truly accepted as a serious and active subfield of psychology. Rather, cross-cultural studies were considered to be the domain of those few psychologists who had esoteric interests
in cultures far from mainstream psychology in the United States, or in ethnic
minority populations (see Betancourt & Lopez, 1993; Graham, 1992).

In the past few years, however, cross-cultural research in psychology has
gained newfound popularity. No doubt much of this popularity is due to the
current focus on cultural diversity and intergroup relations, and the increasing
diversity of the U.S. population. Increasing problems and tensions in intercultural relations, and a growing recognition of the limitations of the psychological literature, have also enhanced awareness of the need for a cross-cultural
approach.

In a much larger sense, however, an increased interest in cross-cultural psychology is a normal and healthy development, questioning the nature of the truths and principles amassed to date and searching for ways to provide an even more accurate picture of human behavior across people of different cultural backgrounds. As psychology has matured and such questions have been raised, many scientists and writers have come to recognize that much (but not all) of the research and the literature once thought to be universal for all people is indeed culture-bound. The increasing importance and recognition of cross-cultural approaches in the social sciences, and in psychology in particular, are reactions to this realization. Cross-cultural research and scholarship have had a profound impact on our understanding of truths and principles about human behavior.

In the cross-cultural psychological literature, two approaches to doing research have been especially effective and productive. In one, called a bottom-up approach (Betancourt & Lopez, 1993), researchers begin with a psychological phenomenon of interest observed when studying a particular culture, and then study it across many other cultures to examine and refine theories about it. In the second, called a top-down approach, researchers typically begin with a theory about behavior and incorporate aspects of culture in testing its limitations and broadening its domain. Both approaches have been used in cross-cultural psychology with great success, and have contributed widely to our understanding and knowledge of behavior across cultures.

Even without considering knowledge added using a cross-cultural approach, a great mass of information about people has already been developed. Indeed, an enormous body of information in the social sciences is considered as truth by American scientists, professors, and students. The comprehensiveness of most social science textbooks and the density of most course syllabi attest to the fact that there is a great deal out there to be learned. Why, you may ask, should it be necessary to go beyond information that currently exists?

The answer to this question lies in understanding the twofold impact of cross-cultural psychology on mainstream psychology—first, on psychological knowledge and theory, and second, on principles of application. Incorporating cross-cultural issues in our understanding of human behavior means asking some very basic, yet extremely important, questions both about the truths taught in classes across the United States today and about how they are applied to intervene in people's lives. Those questions are best addressed by a cross-cultural approach.

The Impact of Cross-Cultural Psychology: Gaining a Multicultural Perspective

Cross-cultural psychology has been an active subfield of psychology for many years now, and it has contributed much wonderful and important new information to psychological knowledge. Studies comparing people of different cultures actually date back almost 100 years. The International Association of

Cross-Cultural Psychology was founded in 1972. Its flagship journal, the *Journal of Cross-Cultural Psychology*, has been in existence since 1970, and has published many original research articles documenting similarities and differences between cultures. As the field embraces larger, broader-based definitions of culture (see Chapter 2), psychological studies on cultural diversity are more numerous today than ever before, spanning all the topics of psychology and appearing in mainstream as well as specialty academic journals. The impact of this growth in cross-cultural research on mainstream psychology has been enormous, and is related to both goals described earlier—the creation of knowledge, and the application of that knowledge.

On Psychological Truths: The Cultural Revolution in Psychology

Despite the wealth of knowledge that has already been gathered in mainstream psychology, it is vitally important to incorporate a cross-cultural approach into our knowledge and learning base. We need to examine whether the information we have learned (or will learn in the future) is applicable to *all* people of *all* cultures or only to *some* people of *some* cultures. Scientific philosophy suggests that we have a duty and an obligation to ask these questions about the scientific process and about the nature of the truths we have learned, or will learn, about human behavior.

Why is it important to ask, and answer, these questions? Clearly, the knowledge that is created in psychology should be accurate and descriptive of all people, not only people of a certain culture (or race, ethnicity, nationality, gender, or sexual orientation). For too many years, students and faculty alike in psychology have been handed information garnered from research that they have questioned as being truly applicable to themselves. Certainly, psychology instructors can learn and understand a theory and the research that supports it, and then teach it; likewise, students can learn and memorize these theories and facts. But the mere fact that people can teach and learn something does not mean that it accurately reflects all people, and students and faculty members alike have lamented about this issue for years.

The field of psychology has an obligation—to its teachers, students, practitioners, and especially all the people whose lives are touched by its knowledge—to produce accurate knowledge that reflects and applies to them. Cross-cultural research plays an important role in helping psychologists produce that accurate knowledge for all because it tests whether or not what is true for some is also true for others. If it is true for others, then we know that whatever findings were generated from the studies, and whatever theories or models of human behavior were supported by those findings, accurately describe many people. If findings from these studies suggest, however, that truth is relative—true for some but not necessarily true in the same way for others—then they suggest that we need to change our theories, adapt our models and our knowledge, so that they can incorporate those differences among people.

This is not an easy challenge for the field to embrace. As you will see throughout this book, and in almost any other contemporary resource in psychology, cultural diversity in findings and cultural differences in research are widespread and commonplace in all areas of psychology. These differences are forcing psychologists to take a good, hard look at their theories, and in many cases to call for revisions, sometimes major, in the way we have conceptualized many aspects of behavior. As a result, many psychologists see an evolution from cross-cultural psychology as a subfield to a **cultural psychology**, with culture incorporated as a necessary and important ingredient in mainstream psychology.

In cultural psychology, cultural similarities and differences in behavior—in thoughts, feelings, attitudes, opinions, motivations, and so on—are part of mainstream theories, not merely interesting side theories by those solely interested in culture. In some cases, incorporating culture as a standard part of any conceptual model in some cases may require only minor adjustments to the original theory; in most cases, however, the incorporation of culture requires fundamental and sometimes profound changes in the essence of those theories.

The incorporation of culture into mainstream psychology is, moreover, only part of the total picture of the move toward a cultural psychology. Much of current psychology as a science is a product of traditionally American and European ways of thinking about the mind, and about science. The entire scientific process and its products—the theories and models that summarize our understanding of human behavior—are themselves bound and limited by the cultural contexts in which they were derived and existed. These theories, and the procedures used to test them, may or may not have relevance to people in other cultures. Some authors have even argued that the move toward a cultural psychology should really be a move toward a *multicultural* psychology—one that incorporates the unique psychologies of the multitude of cultures around the world that may not be assimilable into a single psychology (Gergen, Gulerce, Lock, & Misra, 1996). Whether or not that position is accepted, current mainstream psychology clearly needs to move in this direction, finding ways to educate and be educated by other psychological approaches in other cultures.

The move from *cross-cultural* psychology to a *cultural* psychology involves basic changes in the way psychologists understand many aspects of human behavior. We are in the midst of this evolution in knowledge right now, making it a very exciting time for psychology.

In Our Own Lives and Interactions with Others

The field of psychology has an obligation to ensure that its knowledge is accurate and applicable for all people of all backgrounds not only for reasons of scientific philosophy, but also because of the second goal of psychology—to impact positively on people's lives. Psychologists use the body of knowledge they have built to intervene in people's lives. Research and theories in psychology are not simply shelved in libraries; rather, this knowledge forms the basis on which many psychologists intervene in people's lives as counselors, therapists, consultants, and in many other roles. Psychological theories are only as good as their applicability to people in their real lives (Amir & Sharon, 1987; Gergen et al., 1996). And because we touch people's lives, we have to get it right.

As we come more and more in contact with people from different cultural backgrounds, it becomes increasingly important to learn about universals and culture-specifics in our truths—that is, in the beliefs we hold about people and the way they are. More important, we need to use those universals and specifics to help us formulate guiding principles that can be used as resources in our relations with others. To be ignorant of such resources would render us inflexible in our ability to deal with those around us in a dynamic, ever diversifying world.

Yet the content that is produced in cross-cultural psychology is only half the picture. Indeed, one of the main contributions of cross-cultural approaches to applied psychology is the *process* it fosters in asking questions. Cross-cultural psychology has questions inherently built into its core, questions such as "Is what we know true for all people regardless of their cultural backgrounds?" "If not, under what conditions are they different?" "Under what contexts do differences occur, and why?" "What is it about culture that produces such differences?" "What factors other than culture, such as socioeconomic class, heredity, or environment, may contribute to these differences?"

The process of asking these and other important questions about human behavior lies at the core of cross-cultural psychology. The generation of these questions, the harboring of skepticism, and the inquisitive, voyaging nature of the cross-cultural approach together define its process. And this process is even more important than the content. Indeed, it is impossible to learn everything that has been discovered about enough topics in psychology spanning all the cultures of the world to be effective in intercultural situations in our everyday lives. It makes more sense, therefore, to learn about the process of asking those questions that define a cross-cultural approach, because it is the process that we can take with us to all areas of our lives.

This process is as much one of critical thinking as it is anything else. Cross-cultural approaches to psychology, in fact, can be understood as an extension of critical thinking. Improving one's thinking skills in this fashion will aid in everyday life, especially in an increasingly multicultural world.

The Goal of This Book

When we think of cultural diversity and intercultural relations in the United States, some of the most pressing concerns have to do with interethnic and interracial relations in our own states, cities, and communities. Although U.S. society has never been homogeneous, the diversity in the American population and culture is greater today than ever before. This diversity is due to many factors, including immigration trends, technological advances, and increasing global economic and social interdependence. This increasing diversity is not without its share of tension and struggle. Very few universities in today's world are totally free from intergroup conflict regarding issues of race, ethnicity, or culture. Congruent with such concerns, most students want to learn about cultural diversity as it relates to them within this perspective—that is, with a focus on ethnic and racial minorities and intergroup relations within the United States. Indeed, as you will discover in the remaining chapters of this book, a considerable number of studies conducted in the United States pertain to ethnic differences in a variety of behaviors.

This book has a broader perspective, however, focusing not only on those questions but also on work from other countries and cultures, providing students with a perspective on the United States and American culture in relation to the rest of the world. At the same time, much of the information and many of the principles learned in this process can be applied to better our understanding of ethnic and racial groups within the United States. Gaining a broader perspective on our own intracountry differences in relation to the rest of the world will take much of the "heat" off relationships among different groups here in this country. Oftentimes, the problems we think are huge because they are right in our faces seem smaller when we understand that they are part of a larger picture of cultural diversity that occurs throughout the world.

Even as we obtain a multicultural perspective, we need to realize that we in the United States have a special role with regard to how we deal with cultural diversity and intercultural conflict. The United States, more than many other countries, is a microcosm of the world, with people of many different cultures coexisting here, mirroring the world but on a smaller scale. The problems, issues, and pitfalls that face the entire world face us, and many of the problems we face are, or will be, faced by others in the future. How we address this challenge bodes well or ill not only for our own future, but for the larger global community within which we exist.

As we dive into cross-cultural research and psychology, we must realize that it is neither a panacea nor a utopia of human knowledge. Studying culture does not automatically make cultural conflicts disappear. Instead, studying culture and psychology should give us a better basis (1) to understand, (2) to respect and appreciate, and (3) to empathize with cultural differences when they occur. Liking these differences, or accepting them, is an entirely different question.

Cross-cultural research has its own limitations. Research examining ethnic and cultural differences among groups within the United States are typically not considered cross-cultural and have generally remained separate from the cross-cultural literature. The politics of looking at such differences within the United States has made relevant literature more difficult to assimilate. In cross-cultural research, it is much easier to find or conduct studies that compare Americans as a whole with Japanese or Germans than studies of African Americans versus European Americans or Hispanics versus Asians. The former studies often suffer because they assume that Americans are homogeneous in comparison to other cultural groups in other countries. The participants in such studies are usually middle-class Americans of European ancestry.

But these problems should not deter us from our quest for the truth about human behavior. Just as we need to take what we can from previous, culture-bound research, we must do the same with the cross-cultural literature. We must recognize the limitations and the parameters under which the information was derived and somehow build a foundation from little bits and pieces of information that will come together into a larger, coherent structure.

After all is said and done, what do I intend that you gain from this book? In challenging the traditional, I definitely do not mean to disregard its importance or the importance of the work that produced that knowledge; to do so would demonstrate a level of insensitivity that should have no place in our academic work. Instead, I seek to raise questions about the traditional, mainstream knowledge of human behavior. I want to know whether what we know of organizations, development, personality, emotion, communication, and many other aspects of human behavior is applicable to people of all cultural backgrounds. I want to challenge the traditional by seeking out answers to these questions in the cross-cultural literature. And if the research suggests that people are different from what is typically believed, I want to find better ways to understand those differences than are available today. I want to impart the flavor of the evolution in science and knowledge that is now occurring.

I offer this book to you as a way to understand, appreciate, respect, and feel cultural diversity and its influence on human behavior. In this book, there should be no right and wrong, no good and bad. In learning about others—in meeting the challenge of cultural diversity—our biggest challenge is within ourselves.

 # Glossary

assumption Component of a theory that cannot be tested empirically.

cross-cultural approach A viewpoint for understanding truth and principles about human behaviors across cultures.

cross-cultural research Any type of research on human behavior that compares specific behaviors across two or more cultures. This approach is primarily concerned with testing the possible limitations of knowledge gleaned from one culture by studying people of different cultures.

cultural psychology Mainstream psychology incorporating culture as an essential aspect.

culture-specific A research finding considered to be true for some people of some cultures but not for others.

generalization A research finding that is considered true for a larger group of people than those actually represented in the study or studies that produced the finding.

hypothesis A testable prediction or guess, generally derived from a theory, that can be either confirmed or disconfirmed empirically.

replication A consistent finding that is obtained across a series of studies involving different methodologies or samples.

scientific philosophy The need to evaluate truths and principles against the parameters under which those truths were obtained.

theory A proposed model of human behavior.

universal A research finding considered to be true for all people of all cultures.

Understanding and Defining Culture

Why Is It Important to Define Culture?

It is fashionable today in mainstream psychology, in both theoretical as well as empirical work, and in other social scientific disciplines, to talk about culture. As I mentioned in the last chapter, culture has quickly become one of the most important and pressing issues facing psychologists today. Unfortunately, however, many psychologists and laypersons alike use the words *culture, race,* and *ethnicity* interchangeably, as if they are all the same terms denoting the same concepts. In addition, people often use the word *culture* to describe people of different nationalities. Do these terms all refer to the same concept? While there is clearly some overlap among them, there are also important differences among these words and concepts. A recognition of these differences is important for a clearer and fuller understanding of cross-cultural research and its impact on psychological knowledge.

Before embarking on the task of learning about cultural influences on behavior, it is important and useful to tackle the question of what the word *culture* means. Differences observed across studies and theories in various psychological disciplines are often related to differences in the usage of culture not only as a theoretical or explanatory concept but also as an empirical construct in research. A researcher's definition of culture, whether explicit or implicit, ultimately has an impact on how he or she views culture as influencing people's lives; my own views are no exception. Thus, in presenting cross-cultural material as I do in this book, it is imperative to make explicit my own biases and definitions regarding the word *culture.*

The bulk of this chapter is thus devoted to defining culture. I will examine first how the term *culture* is used in everyday language, and assess the breadth of life it really refers to. After examining some previous definitions of culture, I will then discuss a definition of culture for this book. I will contrast this definition of culture with race, ethnicity, and nationality, and suggest that culture is what makes these terms important, especially in relation to understanding psychological similarities and differences among these social constructs. I will also suggest that the constructs of gender, sexual orientation, and disability can be understood in terms of culture as it is defined here. Later in the chapter, I will discuss ways in which psychologists have attempted to measure aspects of culture in their research, and what these measurement techniques mean to theory and empirical work. Finally, I will discuss how culture, along with other factors, affects psychology.

The Use of the Term *Culture* in Everyday Language

Common Usages of the Word *Culture*

We use the word *culture* in many different ways in everyday language and discourse. As mentioned earlier, sometimes we use the word *culture* to mean race, nationality, or ethnicity. For example, we often refer to people of African American ancestry as coming from African American culture, or Chinese people as coming from Chinese culture. But we also use the word *culture* to reflect trends in music and art, food and clothing, rituals, traditions, and heritage. In short, we use the word *culture* to refer to many different things about people—physical and biological characteristics, behaviors, music, dance, and other activities.

Kroeber and Kluckhohn (1952) and later Berry, Poortinga, Segall, and Dasen (1992) have described six general categories in which culture is discussed:

- *Descriptive* uses highlight the different types of activities or behaviors associated with a culture.
- *Historical* definitions refer to the heritage and tradition associated with a group of people.
- *Normative* uses describe the rules and norms that are associated with a culture.
- *Psychological* descriptions emphasize learning, problem solving, and other behavioral approaches associated with culture.
- *Structural* definitions emphasize the societal or organizational elements of a culture.
- *Genetic* descriptions refer to the origins of a culture.

These categories make it clear that we use the concept and term *culture* to describe and explain a broad range of activities, behaviors, events, and structures in our lives.

Used in the ways just described, culture has become increasingly fashionable in the United States in the past few years; we speak of cultural diversity, cultural pluralities, and multiculturalism in many areas of life, including school and the workplace. It is also important to recognize, however, that the word *culture* may have different meanings or emphases in other cultures. If you refer to culture in Japan, for instance, a Japanese person may think first of flower arranging or a tea ceremony rather than the aspects of culture we normally associate with the word. Likewise, while learning about culture in this book, it is important to remember that this view of culture is only one view, and other cultures may have other views. We should not forget that our studies of culture and the ways in which we understand cultural influences on behavior conceptually (this book included) all stem from a particular view of culture—one that is rooted in American thinking and science.

Because we use *culture* to refer to so many different things about life, it is no wonder that it generates so much confusion and ambiguity. We can get a better understanding of the complex nature of culture if we look at all the aspects of life referred to by the word *culture*.

Aspects of Life Touched on by Culture

Culture is used in so many different ways because it touches on many aspects of life. In an early work, Murdock, Ford, and Hudson (1971) described 79 different aspects of life that culture had something to do with. Barry (1980) rearranged this list into eight broad categories, which were also reported by Berry et al. (1992)

- General characteristics
- Food and clothing
- Housing and technology
- Economy and transportation
- Individual and family activities
- Community and government
- Welfare, religion, and science
- Sex and the life cycle

These broad categories make it very clear that culture is a complex concept embedded in many aspects of life and living. Some aspects involve material things, such as food and clothing; some refer to societal and structural entities, such as government organization and community structure; others refer to individual behaviors, to reproduction, or to organized activities, such as religion and science.

Culture, in its truest and broadest sense, cannot simply be swallowed in a single gulp (Malpass, 1993)—not in this book, not in a university course, not in any training program. Although I will attempt to bring you closer to a better understanding of what culture is and how it influences our lives, we must begin by recognizing and admitting the breadth and scope and enormity of culture. Culture cannot possibly be contained within the pages of a book or the confines of a university semester or quarter. Culture, in all its richness and complexity, is huge.

Laypersons' Conceptions of Culture

The way people understand and talk about culture in their everyday lives mirrors this complexity and richness. In a recent study (Matsumoto, Kasri, Milligan, Singh, & The, 1997), we asked 340 university undergraduates to define the word *culture;* to list and describe the culture most important to them; to list some attitudes, beliefs, opinions, or activities that demonstrate this culture; and to list and describe other cultures they knew about. All responses were coded into their most basic elements, and inspection of these elements revealed that the responses were just about as varied as the individual participants themselves. The coded elements were then categorized into higher-order categories, which included the following:

- Beliefs
- Characteristics
- Combinations
- Differences
- Education
- Environment
- Expressions
- Family
- History
- Hobbies
- Identity
- People
- Race
- Religion
- Rules
- Similarities
- Subgroups

When participants defined the word *culture,* they most often used the category Expressions, followed by History and Beliefs. When they listed the culture most important to them, however, they most often used the category Race. In describing attitudes, beliefs, opinions, or activities characteristic of their culture, they used Beliefs, Expressions, Religion, and Family most often. When describing other cultures, participants used Race most often.

These results suggest that people understand culture as a multifaceted construct, one that encompasses many, if not all, aspects of life, as discussed so far in this chapter. It is interesting, however, that race is used as a common *label* for culture. Although there is doubtless considerable overlap between race and culture, they are not necessarily one and the same. This relationship will be discussed further later in the chapter.

Culture as an Abstraction

Culture refers to so much of life and living, but culture itself cannot be seen or felt or heard or tasted. What is concrete and observable to us is not culture per se but differences in human behavior—actions, thoughts, rituals, traditions, and the like. We see the *manifestations* of culture, but we never see culture itself.

For example, look at the cultural differences in greeting behaviors. In American culture, we learn to shake hands when we greet others, and handshaking has become ritualistic and automatic for many of us. Yet people of other cultures have different ways of greeting people. People of some cultures, for example, greet each other with a slight bow of the head. Some cultures encourage this bow with hands together in front as in prayer. Some cultures encourage a bow from the waist with the face lowered out of sight. Some cultures engage only in an eyebrow flash. We can witness these actions, and many other behavioral manifestations of culture, and we *infer* that a cultural difference underlies these various behaviors—that the behaviors are different because the culture is different. Culture is used as an explanatory concept to describe the reason we see differences in behaviors such as greetings.

In this sense, culture is an abstract concept. We invoke the concept of culture to describe similarities among individuals within a group and differences between groups. We use the concept of culture as an explanatory construct to help us understand and categorize those within-group similarities and between-group differences. It is a theoretical or conceptual entity that helps us understand why we do the things we do and explains the differences in the behaviors of different groups of people. As an abstract concept, culture is a label.

The Cyclical and Dynamic Nature of Culture

But like many labels, culture has a life of its own. Just as similarities within groups and differences between groups give rise to culture as an abstract concept, that abstract concept feeds back on those behaviors, reinforcing our understanding of those similarities and differences. Culture, in whatever way we come to know it, helps to reinforce, promulgate, and strengthen the behavioral similarities and differences that produced it in the first place, producing a cycle of reciprocity between actual behaviors and our theoretical understanding of them as culture (see Figure 2.1).

This reciprocal relationship helps to explain why we are taught to do many things simply because "that is the way they have always been done and it is how they should be done." Learning to eat a certain way, with a certain etiquette, with certain foods, with certain utensils, in a certain order, simply because "that's the way things are done" is just one of many examples of how the abstract concept of culture drives behaviors. Engaging in those behaviors, of course, further reinforces these aspects of culture. It is in this fashion that culture and the actual behaviors culture describes share a close, intimate relationship. Although it may appear throughout this book that culture is an abstract theoretical concept that sits above people and mysteriously influences our behavior, that is not the case. As an explanatory concept that people have created, culture shares a close relationship with behaviors.

For this reason, changing behaviors will necessarily force a change in culture. Because culture is a concept we produce to help us explain actual behaviors, a discrepancy between behavior and culture produces tension in this relationship that often leads to a change in culture. Therefore, as your behaviors change during the course of your life, however slightly, these changes may be related to changes in culture within yourself and across people of the same generation. Differences in behaviors between younger and older generations surely signal differences in the underlying culture of these two groups and contributes to what we call the "generation gap."

In fact, there is always some degree of discrepancy between behaviors mandated by culture and the abstract concept of culture. That is, there is never a one-to-one correspondence across people in the behaviors mandated by an

Figure 2.1 Cycle of reciprocity: Observing, labeling, feedback, and reinforcing. When something is *labeled* culture, it *becomes* culture; then the culture reinforces the label.

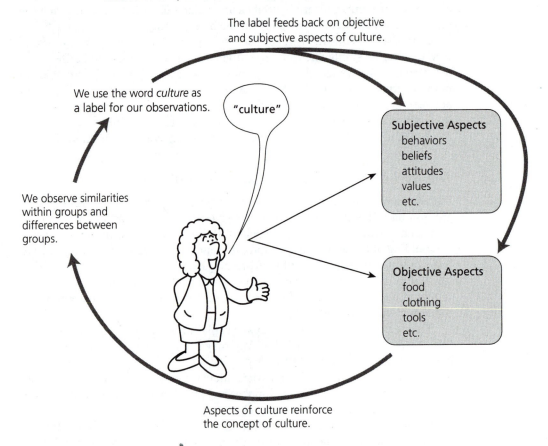

underlying culture and the actual behaviors that occur. Instead, there will always be some degree of discrepancy, however small, between behaviors and culture, despite their close and intimate relationship. Thus, there is always a dynamic tension in this relationship. In this sense, even as an abstract concept or principle, culture is never a static entity. It is always dynamic and changing, existing within a tensive relationship with the actual behaviors it is supposed to explain and predict. In fact, the degree of tension between culture as an underlying construct and the behaviors that it mandates may be an important aspect of culture itself. Some cultures may be characterized by a high degree of tension, whereas others may be characterized by relatively less tension. This difference in the degree of tension is most likely related to Pelto's (1968) distinction of tight versus loose societies.

A Definition of Culture

Previous Definitions of Culture

Over the past 100 years or so, many scholars have made explicit their and the field's definitions of culture. Although these definitions share many similarities, they sometimes exhibit important differences as well. Well over 100 years ago, for example, Tylor (1865) defined culture as all capabilities and habits learned as members of a society. Linton (1936) referred to culture as social heredity. Kroeber and Kluckholn (1952) defined culture as patterns of and for behavior acquired and transmitted by symbols, constituting the distinct achievements of human groups, including their embodiments in artifacts (p. 181). Rohner (1984) defined culture as the totality of equivalent and complementary learned meanings maintained by a human population, or by identifiable segments of a population, and transmitted from one generation to the next (pp. 119–120). Triandis (1972) contrasted objective aspects of culture, such as tools, with subjective aspects, such as words, shared beliefs, attitudes, norms, roles, and values. This distinction is also related to Kroeber and Kluckholn's (1952) concept of explicit and implicit culture; we will return to this distinction later in the chapter. Jahoda (1984) argued that culture is a descriptive terms that captures not only rules and meanings, but also behaviors. Some theorists have defined culture in terms of personality (Pelto & Pelto, 1975; Schwartz, 1978), and others as shared symbol systems transcending individuals (Geertz, 1973). Berry, Poortinga, Segall, and Dasen (1992) define culture simply as the shared way of life of a group of people (p. 1).

A few years ago, Poortinga (1990) offered an interesting and different definition of culture. Noting the tremendous range of possible behaviors a person might exhibit in any situation, and the fact that the actual behaviors used are typically limited, Poortinga attempted to distinguish among the various sources of constraints on people's behaviors: external or internal, distal or proximal. Mechanisms leading to internal constraints arising from distal sources involve genetic transmission; mechanisms leading to internal constraints arising from proximal sources involve cultural transmission. Likewise, mechanisms of external constraint from distal sources involve the ecological, socioeconomic, and historical context of behavior; mechanisms of external constraint from proximal sources involve situational contexts. Against this theoretical backdrop, Poortinga (1990) defined culture as "manifest in shared constraints that limit the behavior repertoire available to members of a certain socio-cultural group, in a way different from individuals belonging to some other group" (p. 6).

As this brief review indicates, many different attempts have been made to define and describe culture, perhaps as many as there are theorists and serious students of culture. A few years ago, Soudijn, Hutschemaekers, and Can de Vijver (1990) analyzed 128 definitions of culture in order to identify common dimensions among them. Their analysis revealed five semantic dimensions within which the definitions could be placed. These researchers argued, however, that instead of integrating all five dimensions into a single, cohesive definition of culture, students of culture should be free to emphasize specific dimensions to highlight particular concerns they may have about human behavior.

A Definition of Culture for This Book

Given the enormity of culture, the approach I have taken in researching the literature, conducting our own research program involving cross-cultural issues, and writing this book is to adopt a definition of culture that is most germane and relevant for understanding the influence of culture on individuals at different levels of analysis. Even with these parameters (constraints may be a better word), culture is a rather difficult concept to define formally. I define **culture** as *a dynamic system of rules, explicit and implicit, established by groups in order to ensure their survival, involving attitudes, values, beliefs, norms, and behaviors, shared by a group but harbored differently by each specific unit within the group, communicated across generations, relatively stable but with the potential to change across time.* Let's examine some of the key components of this definition.

Dynamic.   Culture, as an abstract concept, describes average, mainstream tendencies; it cannot describe all behaviors of all people in any culture. Thus, there will always be some degree of discrepancy, however small, between behaviors and culture. This discrepancy creates a dynamic tension as mentioned earlier. In this sense, culture is not static. It is always dynamic and changing, existing within a tensive relationship with the actual behaviors it is supposed to explain and predict. In fact, this degree of tension may be an important aspect of culture itself. Some cultures may be characterized by a high degree of tension, whereas others may be characterized by relatively less.

System of rules.   Culture does not refer to any single behavior, rule, attitude, or value. It refers, instead, to the entire system of these constructs. In this sense, culture is like a syndrome, as noted by Triandis (1994), involving a constellation of separate but interrelated psychological components. I prefer the metaphor system rather than syndrome, however. Syndrome implies a core element with manifestations emanating from it, not unlike a disease pathogen with symptomatology, whereas system focuses on the functional, working relationship among the various components.

Groups and units.   Culture exists on multiple levels—across individuals within groups, and across groups within a larger group (such as a business corporation). This definition of culture, therefore, is applicable at multiple levels of analysis. When applied to a group of individuals, the units are specific individuals within the group. This is probably the most common usage. But other levels of analyses are also possible. For example, a large corporation often comprises multiple departments or sections. The company as a whole will have a system of rules—both official company policy (explicit) and the unofficial way things are done (implicit)—that constitutes that company's organizational culture. In this context, the group may be the company as a whole, and the units the various sections or departments within it.

To ensure their survival.   The system of rules that comprise culture exists essentially to ensure survival of the group. These rules also allow for units within the group to coexist with one another, providing a framework for social order instead of the potential chaos of a free-for-all. They also allow for groups and units to balance the needs of the group's survival with the desires, wishes, and needs of the unit, taking into account the larger social context and resources at hand. This concept is related to Poortinga's (1990) definition, discussed earlier, involving constraints on behavior.

Attitudes, values, beliefs, norms, and behaviors.   This definition of culture does not refer to tools, homes, utensils, or other physical objects, although these too are important artifacts of culture. It does not refer to physical or necessarily observable attributes, such as skin color, facial morphology, and the like. It does not refer to citizenship or living space within a particular area or region. Rather, it focuses on ideas, attitudes, values, beliefs—the contents of the mind of each and every individual who lives in that culture. Not only do these aspects of culture exist in people's minds, but they also exist as a social consciousness above and beyond individuals. The behaviors that are shared are indeed observable and are often seen in rituals or common, automatic behavior patterns that arise because of shared cultural values and behavioral norms. These elements collectively constitute the subjective aspects of culture (Triandis, 1972), as opposed to the objective aspects (discuss further later in the chapter). Without seeking to diminish the importance of the objective elements of culture, we deem the subjective elements more important for our understanding of cultural influences on behavior.

Shared by a group.   Sharing refers to the degree to which individuals within a particular group have or hold the same value, attitude, belief, norm, or behavior. It does not necessarily refer to sharing in the physical sense; rather, this sharing refers to a psychological sharing of an attribute among members of the culture.

Harbored differently by each specific unit.   As noted earlier, culture describes average, mainstream tendencies of a group of units; it does not describe accurately all aspects of behavior for all units in the group. Individual units will harbor that culture's values, beliefs, behaviors, and the like, to differing degrees; that is, they will exhibit individual differences in their adherence or conformity to culture. The recognition of individual differences in culture forms one of the bases for understanding the limitations of stereotypes, and is also related to Pelto's (1968) classification of tight versus loose societies.

Communicated across generations, relatively stable.   Fads that come and go, even though they have a life of their own and are shared by many people at any one time, are not necessarily considered culture in the sense used here. Instead, culture is that system of rules that is durable, relatively stable over time, and hence especially important in helping units within the group. Core aspects of the system of rules are transmitted across generations. (The distinction between culture and popular culture is discussed later in the chapter.)

But with the potential to change across time.   Despite the relative stability of culture, however, it is never static. As described earlier, culture is a dynamic entity, always in a tensive relationship with the behaviors, attitudes, values, beliefs, and norms it is supposed to describe. Units change over time, and because culture exists in a reciprocal relationship with its components, the tension allows for the possibility that culture itself may change over time. Change is inevitable when the system described by culture no longer accurately describes the mainstream average tendency of the group. We have been witness to drastic cultural changes over the past 30 years in the American culture, as well as in other cultures (such as Japan's). We are witness today to the changes taking place in many of the former Soviet bloc cultures of Eastern Europe.

This definition of culture is similar to many previous definitions, especially with regard to the sharing of psychological attributes and characteristics, and the communication of cultural elements across generations. It differs from previous definitions primarily in its broader concept of units within groups—not only groups of individuals but also groups of groups. Thus, it enables us to understand culture in social structures and societies with multiple levels, such as individuals within a family, families within communities, communities in regions, and regions in countries; or individuals within a section, sections within departments, departments within organizations, and organizations within an international community. Culture can be described at all of these levels of analysis, referring to individuals, groups, and social structures.

This definition of culture is "fuzzy," in that it provides no hard-and-fast rules to determine what a culture is or who belongs to that culture. Culture is a sociopsychological construct, a sharing across people of psychological phenomena such as values, attitudes, beliefs, and behaviors. What defines members of the same culture is whether they share these psychological phenomena. What distinguishes members of one culture from another is the absence of these shared phenomena.

What Kinds of Factors Influence Culture?

Cultures help to ensure the survival of groups and individuals by balancing the needs of the individuals and groups with the resources available to meet those needs. This is generally true whether we are talking about primitive cultures with few resources and limited technology or the modern, urban societies that exist in many countries of the world today. Given the necessity to survive, cultures help to select behaviors, attitudes, values, and opinions that may optimize the tapping of resources to meet survival needs. Thus, as suggested by Poortinga (1990), out of all the myriad behaviors possible in the human repertoire, cultures help to focus people's behaviors and attention on a few limited alternatives in order to maximize their effectiveness given their resources and their environment.

Several factors affect this balancing act, and all of them influence culture in one way or another. For example, the environment in which the culture exists will influence the nature of that culture. A land void of natural resources may encourage teamwork and community spirit among its members, and interrelationships with other groups that have abundant resources, in order to survive. These needs and relationships would foster certain psychological characteristics and attributes that complemented teamwork, community spirit, and interdependence. In a land with abundant resources, however, a society would have less need for such values and attitudes, and they would be less important in its culture.

Population density also affects culture. Societies with higher population densities may require greater social order in order to function effectively. These societies may encourage hierarchy and groupism, with related psychological attributes, more than societies with relatively less population density.

Affluence is associated with culture. It has been shown to be related not only to a cultural dimension known as individualism (Hofstede, 1980, 1983), but also to national characteristics in emotionality (Wallbott & Scherer, 1988). As societies become more affluent, they are more able to obtain resources with less reliance on others, fostering these types of psychological characteristics.

Technology also affects culture. Communication technology (such as cellular phones and electronic mail), for example, brings with it its own brand of communication culture, in which rules regarding interactions and interpersonal engagement seem to change rather rapidly. The widespread use of computers has brought with it the ability to work independently, loosening the reliance on others to get work accomplished and the need to interact with co-workers. These types of changes have the potential to bring about changes in psychological functioning and behavior, which, in turn, lead to changes in culture.

Climate is yet another factor that affects culture. Groups that live near the equator, in hot, humid, and tropical areas, will exhibit a lifestyle that is very different from that of groups living in temperate or arctic zones, with seasonal changes and weather extremes. Differences in climate will affect the clothes people wear, the types of foods they eat, storage and container systems for food supplies, health (infectious and parasitic diseases tend to be more frequent in hotter climates), and many other facets of living. People in hotter climates may be more lethargic, and may tend to organize their daily activities more around shelter, shade, and temperature changes that occur during the day. People who live nearer the poles may organize their lives around available sunlight. All of these factors are likely to influence people's attitudes, beliefs, and behaviors, and hence their culture.

Culture as an Individual as Well as a Social Construct

We often speak of the culture of a group as if it were a single, unitary concept equally applicable to all members of the group. When we speak of Middle Eastern culture, for example, we tend to assume that all people with roots in the Middle East are relatively homogeneous with regard to some psychological trait, characteristic, or behavior. This assumption is also prevalent in cross-cultural research. When a study compares people from the United States, Brazil, and Puerto Rico, the implicit assumption is that individuals within the groups are relatively homogeneous. (I will discuss this topic more fully in Chapter 5.) At some level, of course, culture is relevant for all members of the group that comprise that culture. But the definition of culture adopted in this book suggests something more than a single, unitary concept that is inflexible across individuals. The definition of culture used here suggests that culture is as much an individual, psychological construct as it is a social construct. To some extent, culture exists in each and every one of us individually as much as it exists as a global, social construct. Individual differences in culture can be observed among people in the degree to which they adopt and engage in the attitudes, values, beliefs, and behaviors that, by consensus, constitute their culture. If you act in accordance with those shared values or behaviors, then that culture resides in you; if you do not share those values or behaviors, then you do not share that culture.

While the norms of any culture should be relevant to all the people within that culture, it is also true that those norms will be relevant to different degrees for different people. It is this interesting blend of culture in anthropology and sociology as a macroconcept and in psychology as an individual construct that makes understanding culture difficult but fascinating.

Our failure in the past to recognize individual differences in constructs and concepts of culture has undoubtedly aided in the formation and maintenance of stereotypes. Stereotypes are generalizations about the culture of a group of people that we impose on all individuals within that group. (Chapter 4 provides a more complete discussion of this topic.) Stereotypes often contain a grain of truth. But they are also often wrong because individuals within a group may not all share its cultural values and norms to the same degree.

Culture versus Personality

The fact that there can be individual differences within a culture raises questions about the difference between culture and personality. If culture exists as a psychological phenomenon, and if different people harbor it to different degrees, then aren't we really talking about personality and not culture? The fact that I have defined culture as a sociopsychological phenomenon does indeed blur the distinction between culture and personality. Many personality traits are sociopsychological in nature. Treating culture as an abstract phenomenon, not based on physical characteristics or national citizenship, contributes to this ambiguity, as does the notion that culture can be different for different people.

Many attributes shared across members of a cultural group are psychological in nature and are common referents in discussions of personality as well.

Nonetheless, there are important distinctions between this definition of culture and what is traditionally considered personality. First, culture is a conglomeration of attributes that are shared with other members of a cultural group. Although there may be individual differences in the degree to which members of a cultural group harbor those attributes, most members of the group do share the attribute. This is not necessarily true for personality traits, which by definition refer to individual differences in traits across people and not to differences in the degree to which an attribute is shared.

A second important aspect of culture is stability, as defined by cross-generational education and transmission of cultural values and behaviors. Parents, extended families, and peers serve as human socialization and enculturation agents across generations, ensuring that rituals, customs, beliefs, and norms are communicated to younger generations in much the same way as they were learned before. Schools, businesses, government agencies, laws, and the like serve as institutional agents in enculturation and fill the same role toward similar outcomes as do human agents. Consequently, there is a great deal of consistency in culture over time (despite the ever-present tension between culture and behavior). Such continuity is not necessarily true for personality traits. Personality is usually discussed in terms of traits or attributes of individual people within their own lifetimes.

A final distinction between culture and personality revolves around the idea of culture as a macroconcept, a social phenomenon. As discussed earlier, not only does culture exist in each and every individual, but it also exists as a social phenomenon, a label depicting the programmed patterns of life we have learned and become accustomed to. As a social label, culture has a life of its own, reinforcing the behaviors it influences. These behaviors then feed back onto the social label of culture, so that the label is reinforced as well. Culture thus has a cyclical nature between its properties as a social label and the individual behaviors of its members. Concepts of personality do not share commonality with social labeling, nor with the cyclical nature of a social label (although it can be said that a personality label can cycle with individual behaviors).

Culture and Diversity

I have provided a *functional* definition of culture—one that is based on the functioning of psychological processes, rather than on social categories or constructs. Given that definition, I believe that many categories and descriptions of people can be considered as cultural groups. These categories include some that are typically associated with culture, such as race, ethnicity, and nationality, but they also include others not usually associated with culture, such as gender, sexual orientation, and disability. Not only are people who belong to these groups similar in terms of the defining characteristic, such as their sex, sexual orientation, or race; I believe that members of these social groups also share something else—a culture—and that their underlying culture is one of the most important features of these individuals. Their culture makes them unique and diverse, especially in relation to their psychology.

Culture and race.   Race is not culture, although many people use the terms interchangeably (as in the Matsumoto et al. study described earlier). Two people of the same race may be very similar or very different in their cultural dispositions, and in their actual behaviors, thoughts, and feelings. It is true that many people of the same racial heritage may share the same socialization processes and thus be **enculturated** in similar ways. When we speak of a Hispanic culture or an African American culture or an Asian culture, our conceptions of those groups may be quite accurate. But it is also true that there need not be a one-to-one correspondence between race and culture. Just because you are born a certain race does not necessarily mean you adopt the culture that is stereotypic of that race. Culture is learned behavior; race is not.

In fact, although we use the term *race* as if we all know what we are talking about, there is actually considerable controversy surrounding it. Many contemporary scholars suggest that there are three major races—Caucasoid, Mongoloid, and Negroid—but past studies of the origins of race have proposed as many as 37 different races (Yee, Fairchild, Weizman, & Wyatt, 1993). Although laypersons typically use skin color, hair, and other physical characteristics to define race, most physical anthropologists use population gene frequencies.

Regardless of which biological or physical characteristics one uses to define race, the very concept of race is much less clear-cut than previously believed (Lewontin, Rose, & Kamin, 1984). Some authors have suggested that the distinctions among races are arbitrary and dubious at best (Zuckerman, 1990). Even studies of genetic systems, including blood groups, serum proteins, and enzymes, have shown considerably more within-group than between-group variation, suggesting that racially defined groups are actually more similar than different.

There is even controversy about the origins of race. Prevalent theories posit a common ancestor originating in Africa 200,000 years ago, whose descendants then migrated to other parts of the world. Evidence for these theories comes from physical anthropology and archeology. Other theories and apparently conflicting sets of evidence, however, suggest that humans may have existed in multiple regions of the world as far back as 2,000,000 years ago, and that intermixing among regions occurred (Wolpoff & Caspari, 1997).

Many psychologists and other social scientists today would agree that race is more of a social construction than a biological essential. Hirschfield (1996), for example, suggests that people have a natural propensity to create categories, especially those dealing with human characteristics (see also the discussion of stereotypes in Chapter 4). Because easily identifiable physical characteristics are often used in this category-formation process, "race" becomes central to these folk theories, and thus gains cognitive and social meaning and importance.

Race as a social construction raises a number of other problems. Category boundaries among the socially constructed races are ambiguous and vary with social context (Eberhardt & Randall, 1997; Davis, 1991; Omi & Winant, 1994). And because race is a social construction, people of different societies and cultures differ in their definitions of race. In some cultures, race is a continuum along a dimensional scale, not a categorical or nominal entity (Davis, 1991). Many Brazilians believe that race is not heritable, and varies according to economic or geographic mobility (Degler, 1971, reported in Eberhardt & Lynn, 1997). In some countries, socioeconomic mobility is associated with changes in perceptions of physical properties such as skin color and hair texture (Eberhardt & Lynn, 1997).

I agree with many others (for example, Betancourt & Lopez, 1993; Zuckerman, 1990) that the study of psychological differences between races is of little scientific and practical use without a clear understanding of the underlying causes of the similarities and differences observed. These causes will necessarily involve culture, as defined in this book, because culture as a functional psychological phenomenon determines what is psychologically meaningful and important for different races, whether race is defined as a biological essential or a social category. Culture is what gives race its meaning, and it is culture that psychologists should be concerned with.

Culture and ethnicity.   Ethnicity is another term that is used interchangeably with race and culture. It is most widely used to describe different groups of peoples in the United States, and appears to include concepts of both race and culture. Examples of categories that are typically referred to as ethnic groups include African Americans, Asians and Pacific Islanders, Latinos, and Native Americans. Thus, ethnicity is generally used in reference to groups characterized by a common nationality, geographic origin, culture, or language (Betancourt & Lopez, 1993). The concept of ethnicity is derived from the Greek word *ethnos*, meaning people of a nation or tribe.

Psychologists usually use ethnicity as a category to describe differences among people—reporting, for example, ethnic differences in learning styles, emotion, or parenting. When ethnicity is used only as a category, however, the outcome can be more destructive than constructive. Although information about ethnic differences on a broad range of psychological phenomena can be useful, such information by itself does not explain the nature of the relationship between ethnicity and psychology. Exactly what variables related to ethnicity account for psychological differences among individuals and groups of individuals? The use of ethnicity (or race, for that matter) as a categorical descriptor does little to address this important concern. Put simply, just knowing the ethnicity (or race, or nationality) of a person does little to explain psychological outcomes in cognition, emotion, motivation, or health (Phinney, 1996).

Given the limitations of ethnicity as a category descriptor, it is incumbent on psychologists to go beyond mere use of ethnic labels to explain individual and group differences in psychology. Phinney (1996) has outlined three key aspects of ethnicity that deserve further attention: cultural norms and values; the strength, salience, and meaning of ethnic identity; and attitudes associated with minority status. I agree, of course, with the emphasis on culture as an underlying determinant of psychological functioning. Culture makes ethnic group differences meaningful, and psychologists should focus on it, as well as the other two aspects outlined by Phinney (1996), in understanding and describing ethnicity.

Culture and nationality.   Nationality in its strictest sense refers to a person's country of origin. People of many different ethnicities in the United States, for example, would simply be referred to as American. Likewise, a person from France is French, from Japan, Japanese.

Nationality is yet another grouping variable that is often used interchangeably with culture. It is not uncommon, for example, for people to speak of French culture, German culture, Chinese culture, and even American culture. That is, in our language, we often equate nationality with culture.

Nowhere is this clearer than in cross-cultural research. In many cross-cultural studies, researchers obtain data from samples in different countries. When they find differences between the samples, they interpret the differences as a function of culture, not country. That is, researchers often assume that culture underlies country.

It may not be a bad assumption to make. Certainly, different countries and nationalities are associated with different cultures as we understand them. And this method of understanding culture and doing research has had its place in the history of cross-cultural psychology.

But such practices are not without their share of problems. Nationality per se is not culture. Just because a person is from France, for example, does not necessarily mean that he or she will act in accordance with what we would consider the dominant French culture or with our stereotypes of French people. Just as culture does not necessarily conform to race or racial stereotypes, culture does not necessarily conform to nationality or citizenship. One's passport does not necessarily determine one's cultural values.

Equating nationality with culture is also problematic in that it ignores the possibility of multiple and equally important cultures coexisting within a nation. To assume that everyone from the United States harbors the values, attitudes, and opinions of the "dominant" American culture (whatever that is) would be to ignore the multiple cultures that exist within this country. Such multiculturalism probably exists in many countries.

Again, as with race and ethnicity, what is important about nationality in relation to psychology is not citizenship per se, but the underlying cultural attitudes and values that affect individual and group psychology. It is incumbent on psychologists to go beyond describing national differences and calling them culture, to examine what aspects of functional psychological culture contribute to national differences in various areas of psychological functioning.

Culture and gender.   As will be discussed in more detail in Chapter 8, psychologists draw important distinctions between the terms *sex* and *gender*. *Sex* refers to the biological and physiological differences between men and women, the most obvious being the anatomical differences in the reproductive systems of men and women. Accordingly, the term *sex roles* is used to describe the behaviors and patterns of activities men and women may engage in that are directly related to their biological differences and the process of reproduction (such as breastfeeding). In contrast, *gender* refers to the behaviors or patterns of activities that a society or culture deems appropriate for men and women. These behavior patterns may or may not be related to sex and sex roles, although they oftentimes are. *Gender role* refers to the degree to which a person adopts the gender-specific and appropriate behaviors ascribed by his or her culture.

Describing and understanding psychological gender differences, then, requires us to go beyond the biological, anatomical, or physiological differences between men and women. Gender differences arise because of differences in the psychological cultures transmitted to men and women. Gender differences are thus cultural differences, and men and women can be said to belong to different cultures. Of course, they may also belong to a larger culture (such as a national culture), and their gender cultures may coexist within the larger culture. This is yet another example of how culture can be understood on multiple levels of analysis, as the definition of culture presented earlier in the chapter suggests.

Culture and disability.   Persons with disabilities differ from those without in that they share some type of physical impairment in their senses, limbs, or other parts of their bodies. Although the lay public has generally viewed the main distinction of persons with disabilities as the physical impairments they have, a growing body of work in psychology has found important sociopsychological characteristics of disability as well (for example, Clymer, 1995; Hughes & Paterson, 1997; Marks, 1997). Persons with disabilities are first and foremost people, of course, sharing the same feelings, ways of thinking, and motivations as everyone else. Beyond that, however, they also share some unique ways of thinking and feeling that may be specific to the fact of their impairment. To the extent that they share certain unique psychological attitudes, opinions, beliefs, behaviors, norms, and values, they share a unique culture.

In recent years, a number of authors have begun to describe the culture of disability (for example, Rose, 1995; Slee & Cook, 1994). These works highlight the unique psychological and sociocultural characteristics of this group of people, refocusing our attention on a broader picture of the person in understanding the psychological characteristics of persons with disabilities. Seen in this light, psychological studies involving participants with disabilities can be viewed as yet another example of cross-cultural studies, as they involve comparisons not only of the presence or absence of impairment, but of more important conditions of culture.

Culture and sexual orientation.   People form different sexual relationships with others, and the type of persons with whom they form such relationships constitutes a major aspect of their sexual orientation. Often, we tend to view these relationships as the sole or major defining characteristic of a person's sexual orientation. Yet one of the most important aspects of any sexual orientation—whether straight or gay, mono or bi—is the particular psychological aspects and characteristics that are shared by and unique to each orientation. These distinctive psychological characteristics may indeed be cultural, as defined in this chapter. In fact, understanding shared psychological attributes among people sharing the same sexual orientation as cultural (for example, gay culture) has become not only fashionable in recent years, but well accepted in psychology (Abramson & Pinkerton, 1995; Suggs & Miracle, 1993).

The common thread to all the discussions in this section is that people are often grouped on the basis of shared characteristics that are oftentimes visible or otherwise easily identifiable (race, ethnicity, nationality, sex, disability, or sexual orientation). While there may or may not be objective bases underlying these classifications or groupings, we cannot forget that they are important social constructs and categories. We use these groupings as mental categories, as Hirschfeld (1996) has suggested with race. Problems occur, however, when we consider these mental categories as endpoints in and of themselves, instead of as gatekeepers to important sociopsychological—that is, cultural—differences (and similarities) among the categories. Thus, it is important to recognize that one of the most important features of each of these social categories is its underlying culture—that unique set of shared attributes that influence its members' psychologies.

Is culture the only important underlying feature of these social groupings? Of course not. There may be a host of other factors, personal and social, psychological and biological, innate and environmental, that affect the psychologies and behaviors of these, and all, individuals. Culture is not the only factor, although it is probably a very important one, in understanding individuals. The interaction between culture and social categories—such as race, nationality, disability, or sexual orientation—is a challenge for future research to uncover. For now, it is important to recognize that culture is one of the most important factors that gives each of these social categories its unique psychological meaning, and it is culture that many psychologists should be concerned with.

Culture and Popular Culture

From time to time, it is fashionable to refer to fads that come and go as "culture." This type of culture is also referred to as "popular culture" by the mass media and in everyday conversation. Popular culture generally refers to trends in music, art, and other expressions that become popular among a group of people.

Certainly, popular culture and culture as I have defined it share some similarities—perhaps most important, the sharing of an expression and its value by a group of people. However, there are also important differences. For one, popular culture does not necessarily involve sharing a wide range of psychological attributes across various psychological domains. Culture, as defined in this chapter, involves a *system* of rules that cuts across attitudes, values, opinions, beliefs, norms, and behaviors. Popular culture may involve sharing in the value of a certain type of expression, but does not necessarily involve a way of life.

A second important difference concerns cultural transmission across generations. Popular culture refers to values or expressions that come and go as fads or trends within a few years. Culture, however, is relatively stable over time and even across generations (despite its dynamic quality and potential for change).

Thus, although culture and popular culture have some similarities, there are important differences as well. The cross-cultural literature in psychology, and the culture described in this book, is the culture defined in this chapter, not popular culture (although the psychology of popular culture is a topic well deserving of consideration).

Pancultural Principles versus Culture-Specific Differences: Emics and Etics

One way of conceptualizing principles in cross-cultural studies is by using the concepts of *emics* and *etics*. As introduced in Chapter 1, these terms define the tension that often exists when studying cultures and cultural differences. **Etics** refer to those aspects of life that appear to be consistent across different cultures; that is, etics refer to universal or pancultural truths or principles. **Emics** in contrast, refer to those aspects of life that appear to differ across cultures; emics, therefore, refer to truths or principles that are culture-specific. These terms originated in the study of language (Pike, 1954), with phonetics referring to aspects of language and verbal behaviors that are common across cultures, and phonemes referring to aspects of language that are specific to a particular culture and language. Berry (1969) was one of the first to use these linguistic concepts to describe universal versus culturally relative aspects of behavior.

The concepts of emics and etics are powerful because of their implications for what we may know as truth. If we know something about human behavior that we regard as a truth, and it happens to be an etic (that is, universal) trait, then the truth as we know it is truth for all, regardless of culture. However, if that something we know about human behavior and regard as truth happens to be an emic (that is, culture-specific) trait, then what we regard as truth is not necessarily what someone from another culture regards as truth. In fact, these truths may be quite different. In this sense, truth may be relative, not absolute. This definition of truth should force us all to reconsider what we believe to be true.

Cross-cultural studies provide many examples of emics and etics. Indeed, one of the major goals of the study of cultures is to uncover exactly which aspects of human behavior are emic traits and which are etic traits. One fundamental and important point to remember when studying cultural differences in people and across cultural groups is that both etics and emics will be present.

Most cross-cultural psychologists would agree that there are just as many, if not more, emics as there are etics. That is, people of different cultures actually do differ with respect to most aspects of human behavior. In some sense, this is not surprising. Each culture evolves in its own distinctive way to "manage" human behaviors in the most efficient and appropriate fashion to ensure survival. The options chosen will differ depending on population density, availability of food and other resources, affluence, and other factors. To the extent that each culture must meet different needs in the physical and social environment, each culture will develop different ways to address those needs. These choices are expressed as emic aspects by people within that culture.

Nonetheless, there are probably more similarities among people from different cultures than we might think, especially at the level of intention and goodwill. These similar underlying constructs can have many behavioral manifestations, which is what we observe in everyday discourse and what we therefore tend to focus on in our thinking about culture and diversity.

Etics and emics, then, refer to the tension between universal and culture-specific truths about the world. In other books and other classes, you may hear these constructs discussed in terms of universality versus cultural relativity. Some people may also suggest that these poles are captured in the issue of nature versus nurture. Nature refers to the influence of biology and genetic heredity, whereas nurture refers to the influence of the environment and learning in the origin of psychological traits. In my thinking, however, equating nature with universality is problematic, for the simple reason that psychological traits that are universal may be universal because of culture-constant learning rather than biological destiny. So, there is not necessarily a one-to-one correspondence between biology and universality.

Regardless of the terminology used, it is important to recognize that these ideas represent opposite poles with regard to human behavior, with universality at one pole and cultural relativity at the other. Unfortunately, when we polarize important concepts, there is a tendency to take an either-or approach to understanding differences. When observing behaviors and trying to interpret them, we often try to put them into either the etic or the emic category. This categorization process itself may be culture bound; searching for the one category in which to classify some behaviors may actually reflect a Western, or rather an American, way of thinking. This way of thinking may have its roots in the American individualistic cultural value of searching for uniqueness in ourselves, a search that is generalized to other objects and events in the environment.

Another way of thinking may be more productive for understanding cultural influences on human behavior. Instead of considering whether any behavior we observe is etic or emic, we can ask how that behavior can be both etic (or universal) and emic (or culturally relative) at the same time. Perhaps some parts or aspects of that behavior are etic, and other parts are emic.

For example, suppose you are having a conversation with a person from a culture different from yours. While you talk to this person, you notice that she does not make eye contact with you when she speaks and does not look at you when you speak. On the few occasions when she does look your way, her gaze is quickly averted somewhere else when your eyes meet. From your cultural background, you may interpret that she does not feel very positive about you or your interaction. You may even begin to feel put off and reject any attempts at future interaction. You may not feel trusting or close to her. But she may come from a culture in which direct gazing is discouraged or seen a sign of arrogance or disrespect. She may be avoiding eye contact not because of any negative feelings but out of deference and politeness to you. Of course, these behavioral differences have real and practical implications in everyday life; think about this scenario occurring in a job interview, in a teaching/learning situation at an elementary school, at a business negotiation, or even in a visit with your therapist.

If we examine this behavior in terms of etic–emic polarity, we will undoubtedly come to the conclusion that gaze behavior must be a cultural emic; that is, cultures have different rules regarding the appropriateness of gazing at others when interacting with them. But let's ask ourselves another question: Is there any aspect of this behavior that can be described as etic? The answer to this question may lie in the causes or roots of the cultural differences. In the example described here, your partner wanted to show deference or politeness to you. Thus, she enacted gaze behaviors that were dictated by her cultural background in accordance with the underlying wish to be polite. If you are an American with the same wish for politeness, your culture dictates a different gaze pattern—that you look your partner straight in the eye when talking and show interest and deference by looking directly at her when she speaks. It is only the outward behavior manifestation that differs between the representatives of these two cultures; the underlying reason is exactly the same. Thus, while the outward behaviors we can observe may rightly be called emic, the inner attributes that underlie those behaviors may in fact be etic.

The same process can be applied to arguments concerning nature versus nurture—that is, the influence on behavior of biological and genetic factors versus environment and learning. In the past, many people have polarized this argument to suggest that psychological traits must be one or the other. Perhaps it would be more fruitful to consider the *relative* influence of biology *and* learning in understanding behavior—that is, the biological and genetic predispositions toward certain types of learning, and the underlying physiological and anatomical correlates of that learning.

Etics and emics can coexist in relation to human behavior. Our understanding of cultures and cultural influences on behavior will be vastly improved if we avoid the tendency to compartmentalize behaviors into one or the other category and, instead, search for ways in which any given behavior actually represents both tensions.

An Introduction to Ethnocentrism and Stereotypes

The existence of many emics, or cultural differences, is not in itself problematic. Potential for problems arise, however, when we attempt to interpret the meaning underlying or producing those differences. Because we all exist in our own cultures with our own cultural backgrounds, we tend to see things through that background. Culture acts as a filter, not only when perceiving things but also when thinking about and interpreting events. We may interpret someone else's behavior from our own cultural background and come to some conclusion about that behavior based on our own beliefs about appropriate behavior. Our interpretation may be wrong, however, if the behavior we are judging originates from a different cultural orientation than our own. In some cases (more often than we think), we may be way off in our interpretation of other people's behavior.

We do not always have the ability to separate ourselves from our own cultural background and bias in order to understand the behavior of others. This type of resistance forms the basis of **ethnocentrism**—viewing and interpreting the behavior of others through our own cultural filters. All people need to be aware of these biases in seeking to understand the behavior of others of different cultural backgrounds.

Ethnocentrism is closely related to another important topic, stereotypes. **Stereotypes** are generalized attitudes, beliefs, or opinions about people who belong to cultures other than our own. Stereotypes may be grounded in fact but are often combinations of fact and fiction about people from a particular cultural group. Stereotypes are handy in giving people some basis for judging, evaluating, and interacting with people of other cultures—an outline or framework of some sort—but they can be very dangerous and damaging when people adhere to them inflexibly and apply them to all people of that cultural background, without recognizing the possibly false basis of the stereotype or individual differences within that culture.

We often find that we are different from people of other cultures, either through research or through our everyday interactions and experiences. Our discovery of these differences can have severe and serious negative consequences. The potential for misuse occurs when value dichotomies such as good/bad, right/wrong, and superior/inferior are attached to behaviors of others that differ from our own expectations of appropriate behavior. Emics, etics, ethnocentrism, and stereotyping are all important concepts to learn about and remember when trying to understand the behavior of others. Indeed, Chapter 4 on intergroup relations is devoted exclusively to these topics. As you progress and learn more about cultural similarities and differences, it is important to have some idea of the potential pitfalls in this endeavor. Needless to say, making premature value judgments and maintaining an inflexible ethnocentric attitude are not conducive to progress in this field.

Transforming Culture into a Measurable Construct

One of the challenges that has faced cross-cultural psychology throughout its history has been how to conceptualize culture in theories of human behavior, and how to measure it in research. Historically, when researchers studied cultures, they generally adopted one of two approaches: ethnography or cross-culture comparison. **Ethnographies** are in-depth examinations of a single culture that typically involve immersion of a researcher in that culture for an extended period of time. **Cross-cultural comparisons** generally involve sampling individuals from at least two cultural groups, measuring some behavior of interest in both groups, and comparing the behaviors between those groups. Ethnographies have been common in anthropology, cross-cultural comparisons in psychology and, to a lesser extent, sociology. In recent years, there has been an interesting merging of research approaches across disciplines, with an increasing number of scientists adopting comparative techniques for use in single-culture immersion research and comparative researchers adopting qualitative ethnographic methods to bolster their traditional quantitative approach.

One of the major concerns in cross-cultural comparisons has been how researchers define and measure culture in their research. Most cross-cultural studies **operationalize** culture as country. Samples from the United States, Japan, Germany, and France usually constitute the cross-cultural sample. Most studies are not actually cross-country studies, but cross-city studies (for example, San Francisco versus Tokyo versus Frankfurt versus Paris). Also, many samples are really samples of convenience, meaning that the researcher has a friend at a university in one of these cities who will collect data for the project. Because many studies are conducted this way, researchers often have to resort to stereotype, impression, or anecdote to interpret observed differences. Thus, despite the fact that thinking about cultures has progressed steadily over the years, the way in which researchers generally study culture has not. In short, there has been a discrepancy between how theorists talk about culture and its effects on human behavior and how researchers actually study it in their research.

Fortunately, the gap between theory and method with regard to culture is closing fast, thanks to recent developments not only in the measurement of culture but in conceptualizations of it that make it amenable to measurement. Needless to say, these developments have major positive impacts not only empirically in cross-cultural research but also theoretically on cross-cultural theories and models of behavior.

Reducing Culture from an Abstract, Fuzzy Construct to Specific, Finite Elements

As described earlier in this chapter, culture in all its enormity and complexity is an extremely large construct that really describes many aspects of a people's way of life. One of the ways previous writers have begun to get a handle on culture is to separate aspects of culture into two components: objective and subjective elements (Triandis, 1972; also see explicit and implicit culture in Kroeber & Kluckhohn, 1952). **Objective elements of culture** are the physical manifestations of culture, things that we can actually see and touch, such as clothing, artifacts, utensils, foods, and architecture. **Subjective elements of culture** are all those aspects that we cannot see and touch but we know exist, such as social norms, customs, attitudes, and values. It is the subjective aspects of culture that most psychologists are interested in, and that are most consonant with the definition of culture proposed earlier in this chapter.

Cross-cultural psychologists have characterized the subjective elements of culture in two ways: by domain and by dimension. *Domain* refers to specific sociopsychological characteristics that are considered to be meaningful outcomes, products, or constituents of culture, including attitudes, values, beliefs, opinions, norms, customs, and rituals. *Dimension* refers to general tendencies that affect behavior and reflect meaningful aspects of cultural variability. Figure 2.2 summarizes this reduction of culture from a large, abstract, fuzzy concept to subjective domains and dimensions.

Finally, subjective domains and dimensions of culture can exist both socially—that is, across individuals within groups—and individually, within each member of a cultural group. To the extent that subjective domains and dimensions of culture can be identified on the individual level, they can be *measured* in psychological research. Research on the various domains of psychology—attitudes, values, beliefs, and the like—has been standard fare for psychologists for many years. The real challenge for cross-cultural psychology, then, has been to identify meaningful dimensions of cross-cultural variability on which the

Figure 2.2 "Reducing" culture to domains and dimensions

domains may vary, and to develop psychometrically valid and reliable ways of assessing these dimensions within these domains.

To the extent that such assessment procedures can be developed, cross-cultural researchers will be able to specify exactly what it is about culture that they think influences behavior, and why. They will be able to measure those dimensions and domains in their research and assess directly the contribution of those domains and dimensions to the behaviors of interest. Should such measures of culture exist, then we can break free, to some degree at least, from the lock that stereotypes and anecdotes, derived from a reliance on country and race definitions, have on cross-cultural research. The trick, again, is to find meaningful dimensions of cultural variability with which to assess the psychological domains in individuals.

The Search for Meaningful Dimensions of Cultural Variability

Many scholars have searched for meaningful dimensions of culture and have provided a number of alternatives. Probably the best-known dimension of cultural variability is **individualism–collectivism** (IC). Anthropologists, sociologists, and psychologists alike have used this dimension to explain differences between cultures (Hofstede, 1980; Kluckholn & Strodtbeck, 1961; Mead, 1961; Triandis, 1972). IC refers to the degree to which a culture encourages, fosters, and facilitates the needs, wishes, desires, and values of an autonomous and unique self over those of a group. Members of individualistic cultures see themselves as separate and autonomous individuals, whereas members of collectivistic cultures see themselves as fundamentally connected with others (Markus & Kitayama, 1991a). In individualistic cultures, personal needs and goals take precedence over the needs of others; in a collectivistic culture, individual needs are sacrificed to satisfy the group.

Numerous other dimensions of cultural variability have been proposed. Mulder (1976, 1977) and later Hofstede (1980, 1984), used the dimension of **power distance** (PD)—the degree of inequality in power between a less powerful individual (I) and a more powerful other (O). Matsumoto (1991) suggested a slightly modified version of PD called **status differentiation** (SD)—the degree to which cultures maintain status differences among their members. Hofstede (1980, 1984) also proposed **uncertainty avoidance** (UA)—the degree to which cultures develop institutions and rituals to deal with the anxiety created by uncertainty and ambiguity—and **masculinity** (MA)—the degree to which cultures foster traditional gender differences among their members. Pelto (1968) suggested classifying cultures along a dimension of **tightness**—that is, their degree of internal homogeneity. Hall (1966) suggested that cultures can be differentiated along a dimension of **contextualization**: High-context cultures foster differential behaviors according to the specific context within which the behavior occurs; low-context cultures minimize differences in behavior due to context.

Most of the cross-cultural research and theorizing on the psychological dimensions of culture, however, has focused on individualism–collectivism. Research over the years has focused on its definition, attributes, geographic distribution around the world, consequences for interpersonal and intergroup relations, and applications (see Triandis, 1995, for a comprehensive review of this construct). Thus, IC may be taken as the prime example of an attempt to identify a meaningful dimension of cultural variability and to develop ways of measuring its influence in various psychological domains. At the same time, it is important to recognize that this focus on IC may represent a bias among American researchers, working and thinking in an American system, studying a concept so important to American culture—individualism—and its counterpart, collectivism.

Theoretical work on individualism–collectivism.

A considerable body of literature demonstrates the theoretical relevance and empirical utility of the IC concept. Cultural dimensions such as IC are advantageous to theory and research because they can be used to predict and interpret cultural differences without relying on stereotypes, personal anecdotes, or impressions. Also, there is congruence in the conceptual understanding of IC among cross-cultural researchers around the world (Hui & Triandis, 1986). One of the best-known studies of IC was conducted by Hofstede (1980, 1984), who analyzed data from a questionnaire assessing IC tendencies among employees in an international corporation with sites in more than 50 countries. Each country was rank-ordered by the degree to which people endorsed IC values. The United States, Australia, and Great Britain were the most individualistic; Colombia, Venezuela, and Pakistan were the most collectivistic (see Table 2.1).

Triandis, Bontempo, Villareal, Asai, and Lucca (1988) suggest that cultural differences on IC are related to differences in self–ingroup versus self–outgroup relationships. (See Brewer & Kramer, 1985; Messick & Mackie, 1989; and Tajfel, 1982, for reviews of the ingroups–outgroups classification.) Individualistic cultures tend to have more ingroups. Because numerous ingroups are available to individuals, members are not strongly attached to any single ingroup. Members of these cultures tend to drop out of groups that are too demanding, and their relationships within their groups are marked by a high level of independence or detachment. In collectivistic cultures, depending much more on the effective functioning of groups, a member's commitment to an ingroup is greater. Collectivists keep stable relationships with their ingroups no matter what the cost and exhibit a high level of interdependence with members of their groups. I will discuss this topic more fully in Chapter 16 on social behavior.

Triandis, Leung, Villareal, and Clack (1985) suggest that IC orientations for individuals are both setting-specific and group-specific. They argue that collectivism must be viewed as a syndrome relating to interpersonal concern rather than as a unitary disposition. The results from a subsequent study on IC values in the United States, Japan, and Puerto Rico (Triandis et al., 1988) support this position.

Table 2.1 IC Scores across Countries in Hofstede's Study

Country	Actual IDV	Country	Actual IDV
U.S.A.	91	Argentina	46
Australia	90	Iran	41
Great Britain	89	Brazil	38
Canada	80	Turkey	37
Netherlands	80	Greece	35
New Zealand	79	Philippines	32
Italy	76	Mexico	30
Belgium	75	Portugal	27
Denmark	74	Hong Kong	25
Sweden	71	Chile	23
France	71	Singapore	20
Ireland	70	Thailand	20
Norway	69	Taiwan	17
Switzerland	68	Peru	16
Germany (F.R.)	67	Pakistan	14
South Africa	65	Colombia	13
Finland	63	Venezuela	12
Austria	55	Mean of 39 countries (HERMES)	51
Israel	54		
Spain	51	Yugoslavia (same industry)	27
India	48		
Japan	46		

Work goal scores were computed for a stratified sample of seven occupations at two points in time. Actual values and values predicted on the basis of multiple regression on wealth, latitude, and organization size.

Source: G. Hofstede, *Culture's Consequences: International Differences in Work-Related Values,* p. 158. Copyright © 1980 Sage Publications. Reprinted by permission of Sage Publications, Inc.

Empirical work on individualism–collectivism. Many studies demonstrate the utility of IC in explaining cultural differences in behavior. For example, IC has been used to predict cultural differences in the expression, perception, and antecedents of emotion (Gudykunst & Ting-Toomey, 1988; Matsumoto, 1989, 1991; Wallbott & Scherer, 1988). Another study (Gudykunst et al., 1992) used IC to examine cultural differences in self-monitoring and communication outcomes in ingroup and outgroup relationships in four cultures. In the same vein, a study by Lee and Boster (1992) demonstrated the differential effects of speech rate on perceptions of speaker credibility in individualistic and collectivistic cultures.

Georgas (1989, 1991) used the IC dimension to explain changes in family values in Greece. He found that the current transition of Greece from an agriculture- and trade-based society with an extended family system to an industrialized, service-oriented society "is accompanied by the rejection of collectivistic values and the gradual adoption of individualist values" (p. 90).

Hamilton, Blumenfeld, Akoh, and Miura (1991) compared teaching styles in American and Japanese elementary classrooms. American teachers directed their instruction toward individuals during both full class instruction and private study time. Japanese teachers, however, consistently addressed the group as a collective. Even when children were working individually, the Japanese teachers checked to make sure all of the children were working on the same task.

Leung (1988) used IC to compare the United States and Hong Kong on conflict avoidance. People rating high on collectivism were more likely to pursue a dispute with a stranger, and Leung concluded that the cultural differences found were consistent with previous conceptualizations of IC.

These works highlight the importance of individualism–collectivism in conceptualizing, predicting, and explaining cultural similarities and differences. A number of researchers have even gone beyond identifying the IC concept in understanding cultural differences—they have developed ways of measuring it.

Measuring IC. One of the best-known attempts to measure IC comes from Hofstede's (1980, 1984) previously mentioned study of IBM employees in 50 countries. His survey consisted of 126 questions clustered around four major themes: satisfaction, perception, personal goals and beliefs, and demographics. Hofstede's IC measurement method, however, was not designed to generate scores for individuals; rather, the unit of analysis was the country. His study, therefore, was an *ecological* rather than individual analysis of culture. In comparative research, it is important to have a measure of IC on the level of the individual because we deal with a relatively small number of people in a cultural sample. By examining the influence of culture at the individual level, we can characterize a psychological culture underlying the samples in our research and examine its influence on other aspects of human behavior.

Triandis (1995) reviewed 20 studies that designed and tested different scales to measure IC on the individual level. (Some of these works are outlined briefly here; interested readers are directed to Triandis, 1995, Appendix, for a comprehensive review and discussion of method.) By far the most concerted effort has been that of Triandis and his colleagues. These attempts have resulted in the use of a number of different scales across a number of studies. Hui (1984, 1988), for example, developed the INDCOL scale to measure an individual's IC tendencies in relation to six collectivities (spouse, parents and children, kin, neighbors, friends, and coworkers and classmates). Respondents indicate their agreement with statements describing key IC concepts—such as sharing, decision making, and cooperation—in relation to each target collective. Scores are then summed across items within each collective, and then across collectives to generate a General Collectivism Index (GCI). Later, Triandis et al. (1985) used items from the INDCOL and further broadened them by adding scenarios and other ratings. Triandis et al. (1986) used items from Hui (1984), Triandis et al. (1985), and items suggested by colleagues in other cultures to measure IC. Triandis et al. (1988) used items from the INDCOL and U.S.-originated emic items to measure IC.

Triandis, McCusker, and Hui (1990) used a multimethod approach to measuring IC that represented an evolution not only in thinking about IC but also in method. These researchers viewed IC as a cultural *syndrome* that includes values, beliefs, attitudes, and behaviors (see also Triandis, 1996); they treated the various psychological domains of subjective culture as an entire collective rather than as separate aspects of culture. Their multimethod approach included ratings of the social content of the self, perceptions of homogeneity of ingroups and outgroups, attitude and value ratings, and perceptions of social behavior as a function of social distance. Participants were classified as either individualist or collectivist on the basis of their scores on each method. On the individual level, Triandis refers to individualism and collectivism as **idiocentric** and **allocentric** tendencies, respectively (Triandis et al., 1986).

Most recently, Triandis and his colleagues (Singelis, Triandis, Bhawuk, & Gelfand, 1995) have developed measures that include items assessing a revised concept of individualism and collectivism they call horizontal and vertical individualism and collectivism, representing yet further advances in the conceptual understanding of IC. In *horizontal collectivism,* individuals see themselves as members of ingroups in which all members are equal. In *vertical collectivism,* individuals see themselves as members of ingroups, which are characterized by hierarchical or status relationships. In *horizontal individualism,* individuals are autonomous and equal. In *vertical individualism,* individuals are autonomous but unequal.

The work of other writers (reviewed in Triandis, 1995) covers a broad range of psychological constructs in their assessment of IC, including attitudinal, value, and norm ratings, self-perceptions, and independent and interdependent self-construals. While these works offer researchers a number of alternatives for IC assessment, Triandis' multimethod system and his latest efforts in assessing horizontal and vertical IC are by far the most advanced and sophisticated assessment tools available. These measures assess IC tendencies in different psychological domains, combining IC tendencies across a wide range of phenomena into a single measurement technique.

It is also important, however, to be able to measure IC tendencies across different contexts as well different psychological domains. No single score can capture context-specific tendencies, either in terms of their conceptual implications or empirical applications. Indeed, as Triandis et al. (1988) have pointed out, IC should vary in different social contexts. People act differently depending on whom they are interacting with and the situation in which the interaction is occurring. A person may have collectivistic tendencies at home and with close friends and individualistic tendencies with strangers or at work, or vice versa. If a culture fosters collectivistic tendencies within self–ingroup relationships, it is unlikely that it will foster those same tendencies to the same degree in self–outgroup relationships. If it did, the meaning of collectivism, as defined by the ingroup–outgroup distinction, would be contrary to the fundamental definition of collectivism. This view of IC suggests the value of generating context-specific scores on IC rather than producing single scores collapsed across contexts. This view of IC also suggests that IC tendencies on the individual level should be understood as profiles of IC tendencies across contexts rather than as single scores that globally summarize IC tendencies.

Matsumoto and his colleagues (Matsumoto, Weissman, Preston, Brown, & Kupperbusch, 1997) have developed a measure of IC for use on the individual level that assesses context-specific IC tendencies in interpersonal situations. Their measure, called the IC Interpersonal Assessment Inventory (ICIAI), includes a list of 25 items compiled from previous work on IC by Triandis and colleagues (1990), Hui (1984, 1988), and Schwartz and Bilsky (1987). The items are described in general value terms (for example, obedience to authority, social responsibility, sacrifice, loyalty) rather than by specific statements tied to single actions. Universal values, such as love and security, are not included, based on Schwartz's (1990) assertion that those "maturity" values serve both individualists and collectivists. The 25 items are presented in relation to four social groups of interactants: (1) family, (2) close friends, (3) colleagues, and (4) strangers. These four groups were selected based on their collective differences and the supposition that they maximized context-specific differences in a manageable number of contexts. All the items are rated twice, once in terms of general values as guiding principles for each person's behaviors and a second time in terms of the frequency of actual behaviors (see the box "Sample Items from the Individualism–Collectivism Interpersonal Assessment Inventory"). This measure has been used to demonstrate IC differences across different countries as well as across different ethnic groups within the United States.

The ICIAI and Triandis and colleagues' multimethod assessment techniques described earlier represent major advances for cross-cultural research and our understanding of the influence of cultural dimensions of variability on human behavior. Being able to measure IC, or any other cultural dimension, on the individual level is advantageous for a variety of reasons. First, it allows us to characterize the IC nature of different groups, and to examine the relative importance of I or C in those groups. Triandis and his colleagues have administered their measures of IC to samples in different cultures and countries around the world, and on the basis of these data, have been able not only to characterize the cultures as relatively I or C, but also to estimate the proportion of the population in each of these cultures with primarily I or C tendencies at the individual level. Second, measurement of IC allows for an important methodological check in our research. Using such measures, researchers no longer have to assume that the groups in their studies are I or C; they can demonstrate it empirically. Third, given individual differences in IC within samples, IC scores can be used as covariates in appropriate analyses. Differences between groups can be tested with the effects of IC statistically controlled.

Sample Items from the Individualism–Collectivism Interpersonal Assessment Inventory (ICIAI)

Below is a list of general descriptions of behavior. We want to know how important you believe each is as a *value* in relation to four social groups. Consider each of the descriptions as a general, hypothetical value. Also, consider the value separately in each of the four social groups. Please tell us how important each is in terms of being a *guiding principle* for you, regardless of whether you actually find yourself in these situations. Please make an attempt to answer each item.

Please use the following rating scale when giving your answers. Write the appropriate number in the space provided for each of the four social groups.

NOT IMPORTANT AT ALL						VERY IMPORTANT
0	1	2	3	4	5	6

	Family	Friends	Colleagues	Strangers
To comply with direct requests from	_____	_____	_____	_____
To maintain self-control toward	_____	_____	_____	_____
To share credit for accomplishments of	_____	_____	_____	_____
To share blame for failures of	_____	_____	_____	_____
To sacrifice your goals for	_____	_____	_____	_____
To sacrifice your possessions for	_____	_____	_____	_____
To compromise your wishes in order to act together with	_____	_____	_____	_____
To maintain harmonious relationships among	_____	_____	_____	_____

Source: Matsumoto, Weissman, Preston, Brown, & Kupperbusch, 1997.

The Influence of Culture on Psychology

How can we understand the influence of culture on psychology? Clearly, with the distinctions I have drawn here, cultures are learned phenomena. Newborns have no culture (although they may very well have biological and temperamental dispositions to learning certain cultural tendencies; see Chapter 7 on development). As children grow older, they learn specific behaviors and patterns of activities appropriate and inappropriate for their culture, and they either adopt or reject those cultural values and mores.

Berry and his colleagues (1992) have suggested that the model presented in Figure 2.3 describes how cultural practices can affect psychology. In this model, three factors—the ecological environment, the sociopolitical context, and biology—all affect cultural practices. These cultural practices, in turn, influence psychological characteristics and traits. As Berry and colleagues (1992) rightly point out, culture is not the only factor influencing psychology; biology and the sociopolitical context influence individual psychologies as well. I would suggest that a host of other factors also influence psychology, including familial and community characteristics, cultural identity, affluence, and the like.

An important point to remember is that the factors involved in understanding culture and psychology, as outlined in Figure 2.3, are not static or unidimensional. Indeed, the entire system is dynamic and interrelated; it feeds back on and reinforces itself. As mentioned earlier in this chapter, there is a continual tension between individual behaviors within any culture and the cultural labels that are used to describe them. Cultural changes occur when the cultural labels no longer describe a majority of the individuals within that culture; thus,

Figure 2.3 Framework for examining relationships among contextual variables and gender differences in behavior.

Source: Cross-Cultural Psychology: Research and Applications, by J. W. Berry, Y. H. Pootinga, M. H. Segall, and P. R. Dasen, p. 58. Copyright © 1992 Cambridge University Press. Reprinted with permission of Cambridge University Press.

psychological characteristics influence culture as well. As a result, the system is not linear, with influences going in a single direction; it acquires a life of its own. And the life of this system is reinforced by the glue we know as culture.

Conclusion

Culture is an elusive, abstract concept that forms the basis for much of our understanding of life. It is the sum of all the learned ways of living that have been carried down from one generation to the next in the form of rituals, tradition, heritage, and behaviors. Culture is the set of programmed responses that we and our ancestors before us have learned to adapt to our environment and to others around us in daily living. It is, in effect, the software of our minds.

While culture is one of the most important influences on our lives, it is probably the least thought of. We do not think about our culture every day, and we do not necessarily see culture. We see manifestations of our cultural heritage and that of others—the similarities and differences—around us all the time, yet we do not readily stop to think about culture on a sociopsychological level. Because culture is invisible, we often latch onto other, more readily observable concepts to help us explain and understand people's behaviors. We may resort to using race or nationality to help us talk about behaviors that are affected by culture. These concepts are easier for us to use because they are observable; our minds can deal with this type of information more easily.

But focusing on the visible rather than the invisible has its limitations. By focusing solely on visible constructs such as race or nationality to explain cultural differences, we lock ourselves into a pattern of understanding the world—a worldview—that is doomed to fail. Neither race nor nationality can explain the richness of the concept we know as culture. If we try to pigeonhole all of human behavior into fixed categories, we will find that much about life does not fit. Stereotypes and images cannot, and perhaps should not, cover the complexity of culture as a psychological phenomenon.

In the United States, it seems that there are two extremes when people talk about culture. On the one hand, some people are desperately seeking culture—trying to find their roots, heritage, and tradition. On the other hand, some people consider culture as a foreign and irrelevant concept. To these individuals, culture is something that refers to groups and is shunned by many who reject the notion that groups can influence their behavior. American culture is characterized by a great deal of tension between culture–behavior relationships and the values related to concepts of culture.

Regardless of how we think about culture in our conscious, everyday lives, we cannot ignore the fact that much of our behavior is steeped in a tradition of culture, our own culture. For many people who reject the notion of culture, it is probably safe to say that their culture does not embrace notions of cultural heritage, but challenges traditions and the past. Interestingly enough, in challenging and rejecting culture, these people are indeed living their cultural mores and values.

The task of understanding culture, and understanding cultural influences on our own behavior, is not an easy one. Remember that whenever you evaluate cultural influences, whether of your own or another culture, you look at those influences through your own cultural "eyes." An invisible filter exists that always influences how we perceive and evaluate things, regardless of whether we are aware of it or not. You are reading this text right now with that filter on and evaluating what I have to say through that filter. We make judgments about ourselves and others that are biased, even though we are absolutely convinced that we are unbiased in making those judgments. For example, you may believe that you are rather interdependent or collectivistic, not independent and individualistic, and that your behaviors take social relations into account much more than your peers' do. However, the culture in which you live may be, as a whole, more independent and individualistic than other cultures. While you are relatively interdependent within your own culture, you may still be very independent when viewed in comparison to the rest of the world. And yet you may absolutely believe that you are interdependent, because you cannot see the implicit standard of your own culture in relation to the standard provided by the rest of the world (see also Kitayama & Markus, in press–b).

As you work through the rest of this book, it is important to consider the evidence provided about how cultures affect behaviors. But it is also important to pause and remember that we are thinking about these differences from the viewpoint of our own cultural biases and internal, implicit standards. Many years ago, Durkheim (1938/1964) wrote, "air is no less heavy because we do not detect its weight" (p. 5). Likewise, water is no less important to fish because they may not be aware of its existence. Culture is that air for us as water is for the fish.

 Glossary

allocentric Collectivistic tendencies on the individual level.

contextualization A cultural dimension: the degree to which cultures foster differential behaviors according to the specific context within which those behaviors occur.

cross-cultural comparisons A method of research that involves sampling individuals from at least two different cultural groups, measuring some behavior of interest in both groups, and comparing the behaviors between those groups.

culture The set of attitudes, values, beliefs, and behaviors shared by a group of people, but different for each individual, communicated from one generation to the next.

emics Aspects of life that appear to differ across cultures; truths or principles that are culture-specific.

enculturation The process by which individuals learn and adopt the ways and manners of their culture.

ethnocentrism Viewing and interpreting the behavior of others through one's own cultural filter.

ethnographies In-depth examinations of a single culture that typically involve immersion of a researcher in that culture for an extended period of time.

etics Aspects of life that appear to be consistent across different cultures; universal or pancultural truths or principles.

idiocentric Individualistic tendencies observed on the individual level.

individualism–collectivism (IC) A dimension along which cultures vary: the degree to which a culture encourages, fosters, and facilitates the needs, wishes, desires, and values of an autonomous and unique self over those of a group. In individualistic cultures, personal needs and goals take precedence over those of others; in a collectivistic culture, personal needs are sacrificed to satisfy the group.

masculinity A cultural dimension: the degree to which cultures foster traditional gender differences among their members.

objective elements of culture Physical manifestations of culture; things we can actually see and touch, such as clothing, artifacts, utensils, foods, and architecture.

operationalize The way in which a research variable is defined and measured.

power distance A dimension along which cultures vary: the degree to which cultures foster or maintain inequality in power among people.

status differentiation A cultural dimension: the degree to which cultures maintain status differences among their members.

stereotypes Generalized attitudes, beliefs, or opinions about people identified with or belonging to particular groups or cultures.

subjective elements of culture Aspects of culture that we cannot see and touch but we know exist, such as social norms, customs, attitudes and values.

tightness A cultural dimension: the degree of homogeneity within a culture.

uncertainty avoidance A cultural dimension: the degree to which cultures develop institutions and rituals to deal with the anxiety created by uncertainty and ambiguity.

3

Culture and Self

Although culture is generally considered a macrolevel construct, it operates both on the social level and on the personal and individual level, as discussed in Chapter 2. All of us operate in our worlds as individual agents of culture, bringing our implicit, underlying psychological culture to every situation, context, and interaction. We bring this culture to school, work, and meetings with our friends and family. It is a basic part of our selves.

Because culture plays such a major role in shaping our sense of self and identity, it has a pervasive influence on all our behaviors across all contexts. It is imperative that we go beyond the material presented in Chapter 2 that defined culture and examine how culture comes to play such a dominant role in shaping our core sense of self. Then we can explore how that sense of self, fundamentally interrelated with culture, affects our feelings, our thinking, and our motivations. Our sense of self, also known as *self-concept* or *self-construal,* is an important guide to understanding our own behavior as well as understanding and predicting the behavior of others.

In this chapter, we will examine the importance of the concept of self in explaining cultural differences in behaviors and psychological traits. We will explore some examples of different cultural conceptualizations of self, uncovering the consequences of these different conceptualizations for different aspects of behavior. We will also review some of the most recent work on culture and self that challenges previous assumptions about their relationship. We will also discuss the relevant and timely topic of bicultural identity, a topic that has gained importance because of the increasing number of people in all societies who are multicultural. Much of what is described in this chapter serves as a backdrop for material presented in the rest of the book, and thus forms a foundation for understanding and appreciating cultural diversity.

Culture and Concepts of Self

One of the most powerful and pervasive concepts in the social sciences is the **self-concept**. Scholars have wondered and written about the "self" for many years. We may not consciously think about our self very much, yet how we understand or construe our sense of self is intimately and fundamentally tied to how we understand the world around us and our relationships with others in that world. Whether conscious or not, our concept of self is an integral and important part of our lives.

Think about some descriptions of yourself. You may believe you are an optimist or a pessimist, extroverted or introverted. We use these labels as shorthand descriptions to characterize ourselves. Suppose a young woman tells you she is "sociable." An array of underlying meanings are attached to this one-word description. Descriptive labels such as this usually imply (1) that we have this attribute within us, just as we possess other attributes such as abilities, rights, or interests; (2) that our past actions, feelings, or thoughts have close connections with this attribute; and (3) that our future actions, plans, feelings, or thoughts will be controlled or guided by this attribute and can be predicted more or less accurately by it. In short, if someone describes herself as "sociable," we know that her concept of self is rooted in, and supported and reinforced by, a rich repertoire of specific information concerning her own actions, thoughts, feelings, motives, and plans. The concept of her self as "sociable" may be central to her self-definition, enjoying a special status as a salient identity (Stryker, 1986) or self-schema (Markus, 1977).

A sense of self is critically important and integral to determining our own thoughts, feelings, and actions, and to how we view the world and ourselves and others in that world, including our relationships with other people, places, things, and events. In short, our sense of self is at the core of our being, unconsciously and automatically influencing our every thought, action, and feeling. Each individual carries and uses these internal attributes to guide his or her thoughts and actions in different social situations. A noted anthropologist, Clifford Geertz (1975), described the self as "a bounded, unique, more or less integrated motivational and cognitive universe, a dynamic center of awareness, emotion, judgment, and action organized into a distinctive whole and set contrastively both against other such wholes and against a social and natural background" (p. 48).

These assumptions about the meaning and importance of self are especially relevant within an American psychological framework that is rooted in an individualistic way of thinking. In an individualistic culture, the self is seen as a bounded entity consisting of a number of internal attributes, including needs,

Figure 3.1 A model of how culture influences actions, behaviors, thoughts, and feelings indirectly through self-concepts

abilities, motives, and rights. As people grow up within a certain cultural milieu, that cultural milieu shapes, bounds, and molds their sense of self so that the self-concept "makes sense" within that cultural milieu. If self-concepts are important integrators and organizers of all our psychological traits, characteristics, and behaviors, and if culture shapes and molds our sense of self, then we can conclude that culture shapes and molds our behaviors, thoughts, and feelings indirectly via our self-concepts (see Figure 3.1).

Because cultures differ, it then follows that *different cultures produce different self-concepts in their members, and these different self-concepts, in turn, influence all other aspects of individual behaviors.* That is, what people actually mean and understand as the self is dramatically different in different cultures. The sense of self we define in a predominantly individualistic American culture is not necessarily the same sense of self as that defined by other cultures, especially collectivistic ones. These differences in self-concepts occur because different cultures are associated with different systems of rules of living, and exist within different social and economic environments and natural habitats. The different demands that cultures place on individual members mean that individuals integrate, synthesize, and coordinate their worlds differently. In short, they have fundamentally different self-concepts.

Just as our own sense of self has a powerful influence on our lives, so the sense of self of people in other cultures influences their lives just as profoundly. Our self-concepts may be totally different from those of another culture. Yet, we do not think about these differences often because we are not very aware of our own sense of self and how much it influences our behavior. "Self" is an important, abstract concept that helps us understand much of our psychological composition. But, because it is an abstract concept, we are not always cognizant of its influences in ourselves, let alone in others. We only see these differences in the clashes that occur when people with different senses of self interact.

By raising the possibility that your own concept of self may not make much intuitive sense to people of other cultures, I don't want to imply that students or experts in social psychology from other cultures fail to understand the notion of self as a theoretical concept in social psychology. To the contrary, they certainly can and do understand "self" as a theoretical construct. Yet the nature of their understanding is very different from that of Americans. People from other cultural backgrounds may understand Western concepts of self in the same way many Americans understand four-dimensional space. That is, they may understand the concept on a theoretical or cognitive level but have almost no experiential basis for that understanding. They don't feel that understanding emotionally.

Recently, Markus and Kitayama (1991b) used these notions to describe two fundamentally different senses of self, contrasting the Western or individualistic construal of self as an independent, separate entity with a composite construal of self more common in many non-Western, collectivistic cultures, in which the individual is viewed as inherently connected or interdependent with others and inseparable from a social context. They illustrated how these divergent forms of self are tied to differences in what people notice and think about, what they feel, and what motivates them (Markus & Kitayama, 1991b). Of course, all cultures cannot be pigeonholed into one of these two categories, but we can use these categories by way of example to highlight the relationship among culture, self, and psychology summarized in Figure 3.1. However, they need to be applied flexibly if we are to understand different cultures and, more important, different people on their own bases rather than forcing them into conceptual categories based on theory alone.

An Example of Different Cultural Conceptualizations of Self: Independent and Interdependent Selves

An Independent Construal of Self

In the United States, standing out and asserting yourself is a virtue: "The squeaky wheel gets the grease." American politicians routinely credit their success to self-confidence, trusting their instincts, and the ability to make decisions and stick by them. In many individualistic cultures like ours, there is a strong belief in the separateness of individuals. The normative task in these cultures is to maintain the independence of the individual as a separate, self-contained entity.

In American society, many of us have been socialized to be unique, to express ourselves, to realize and actualize the inner self, and to promote our personal goals. These are the tasks the culture provides for its members. These cultural tasks have been designed and selected throughout history to encourage the independence of each separate self. With this set of cultural tasks, our sense of self-worth or self-esteem takes on a particular form. When individuals successfully carry out these cultural tasks, they feel satisfied about themselves, and self-esteem increases accordingly. Under this **independent construal of self**, individuals focus on personal, internal attributes—individual ability, intelligence, personality traits, goals, or preferences—expressing them in public and verifying and confirming them in private through social comparison. This independent construal of self is illustrated graphically in Figure 3.2(a). Self is a bounded entity, clearly separated from relevant others. Note that there is no overlap between the self and others. Furthermore, the most salient self-relevant information (indicated by bold Xs) relates to attributes thought to be stable, constant, and intrinsic to the self, such as abilities, goals, and rights.

Figure 3.2 **(a)** Independent construal of self; **(b)** interdependent construal of self

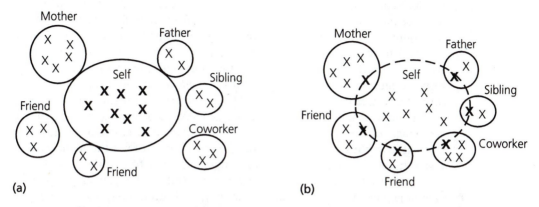

Source: "Culture and the Self: Implications for Cognition, Emotion, and Motivation," by H. Markus and S. Kitayama, 1991. *Psychological Review, 98,* pp. 224–253. Copyright © 1991 American Psychological Association. Reprinted by permission of the authors.

An Interdependent Construal of Self

Many non-Western, collectivistic cultures neither assume nor value overt separateness. Instead, these cultures emphasize what may be called the "fundamental connectedness of human beings." The primary normative task is to fit in and maintain the interdependence among individuals. Individuals in these cultures are socialized to adjust themselves to an attendant relationship or a group to which they belong, to read one another's minds, to be sympathetic, to occupy and play their assigned roles, and to engage in appropriate actions. These cultural tasks have been designed and selected throughout history to encourage the interdependence of the self with others.

Given this construal of the self, self-worth, satisfaction, and self-esteem can have very different characteristics from those familiar to us. The self-esteem of those with interdependent construals of the self may depend primarily on whether they can fit in and be part of a relevant ongoing relationship. Under this construal of self, individuals focus on their interdependent status with other people and strive to meet or even create duties, obligations, and social responsibilities. The most salient aspect of conscious experience is intersubjective, rooted in finely tuned interpersonal relationships. The **interdependent construal of self** is illustrated graphically in Figure 3.2(b). The self is unbounded, flexible, and contingent on context. Note the substantial overlapping between the self and relevant others. The most salient aspects of the self (shown by bold *X*s) are defined in relationships—that is, those features of the self related to and inseparable from specific social contexts. This does not mean that those with interdependent selves do not have any knowledge of their internal attributes, such as personality traits, abilities, and attitudes. They clearly do. However, these internal attributes are relatively less salient in consciousness and thus are unlikely to be the primary concerns in thinking, feeling, and acting.

Because of their collectivistic nature, many Asian cultures foster interdependent construals of self. In these cultures, if you stand out, you will most likely be punished: "The nail that sticks up shall get pounded down." In Japan, for example, political rhetoric sounds very different from that in the United States. A former vice prime minister of Japan once said that in his 30-year career in national politics he had given the most importance and priority to interpersonal relations. Similarly, "politics of harmony" was the sound bite a former Japanese prime minister used to characterize his regime in the 1980s.

Of course, considerable variation on independent versus interdependent construals of the self also occur within a single culture. People of different ethnicities within a culture, for example, may have different tendencies with regard to independent versus interdependent self-construals. Men and women may have different self-construals. Even within ethnic and gender groups, considerable variation in self-construals may, and often does, occur (Gilligan, 1982; Joseph, Markus, & Tafarodi, 1992). These intracultural differences are also important when considering cultural differences. In this chapter, I will describe general tendencies associated with independent and interdependent self-construals, acknowledging the limitations in representation within groups.

Consequences for Cognition, Motivation, and Emotion

Different concepts of self between cultures contribute to substantial cross-cultural differences in a variety of areas and behaviors. In this section, I will show how the two construals of the self affect our thinking, our feelings, and our behaviors. Cognitive, emotional, and motivational processes can vary dramatically with the construal of the self shared by a cultural group, and these variations have major implications for behavior.

Consequences for self-perception.
Different construals of self have different consequences for how we perceive ourselves. With an independent construal of self, one's internal attributes such as abilities or personality traits are the most salient self-relevant information. These internal attributes should be relatively less salient for those with interdependent selves, who are more likely to think about the self in particular social relationships (for example, "me" with family members, "me" with my boyfriend) or in specific contexts ("me" in school, "me" at work).

Several studies (Bond & Tak-Sing, 1983; Shweder & Bourne, 1984) have supported these notions. In these studies, subjects wrote down as many of their own characteristics as possible. Subjects typically generated several types of responses. One response type was the abstract, personality-trait description of the self, such as "I am sociable." Another response type was the situation-specific self-description, such as "I am usually sociable with my close friends." Consistent with our knowledge of independent and interdependent selves, these studies show that American subjects tend to generate a greater number of abstract traits than do Asian subjects. These findings confirm that people with an independent construal of self view their own internal attributes, such as abilities or personality traits, as the most salient self-relevant information. Internal attributes are relatively less salient for those with interdependent selves, who are more likely to think about the self in particular social relationships or contexts.

These findings, of course, do not mean that Americans have more knowledge about themselves than Asians do, or vice versa. Because the most salient information about self for the interdependent selves is context-specific, these individuals generally find it difficult or unnatural to state anything in abstract, noncontextual terms. Instead, those with interdependent selves are culture bound to define themselves in relation to context.

Consistent with this analysis, Triandis and colleagues (see Triandis, 1989, for a review) have shown that individuals from interdependent cultures (for example, China, Japan, and Korea) generate many more social categories, relationships, and groups to which they belong. Indeed, in a study done in the People's Republic of China, as many as 80% of all the responses given to the self-description task were about their memberships in a variety of different groups. Dhawan, Roseman, Naidu, Komilla, and Rettek (1995) reported similar tendencies in self-perception in a study comparing American and North Indian participants.

Another recent study by Bochner (1994) compared self-perception statements made by Malaysian, Australian, and British participants. The responses were coded according to whether they were idiocentric, allocentric, or group self-references, and weighted according to the order in which they were reported. As predicted, Malaysians produced more group and fewer idiocentric references. This is a strong indication that specific relationships are very important for self-definition in this culture. The data from this study also indicated that cultural variations in self-concept are not categorically different across cultures; that is, all people seem to identify themselves according to both personal attributes and group membership. Rather, what differentiates among people in different cultures is the relative salience of either type of self-reference when describing oneself.

The studies cited so far suggest that interdependent selves find it difficult to describe themselves in terms of abstract internal attributes; that is, they find it artificial and unnatural to make abstract statements such as "I am sociable" without specifying a relevant context. Whether a person is sociable or not depends on the specific situation. If this interpretation is correct, then interdependent people should be comfortable describing themselves in terms of abstract internal attributes *once a context has been specified.*

Cousins (1989) has provided evidence to support this analysis. He asked American and Japanese respondents to write down who they were in various specific social situations (for example, at home, in school, or at work). This instruction supposedly helped respondents to picture a concrete social situation, including who was there and what was being done to whom. Once the context was specified, the Japanese respondents actually generated a greater number of abstract internal attributes (for example, I am hardworking, I am trustworthy,

I am lazy) than did the Americans once the context was specified. American respondents tended to qualify their descriptions (I am more or less sociable at work, I am sometimes optimistic at home). It was as if they were saying "This is how I am at work, but don't assume that this is the way I am everywhere." With this more contextualized task, the Americans may have felt awkward providing self-descriptions because their self-definitions typically are not qualified by specific situations.

Consequences for social explanation.   Self-construals also serve as a **cognitive template** for interpreting the behaviors of other people. (This process is related to the material on cultural differences in attributions in Chapter 16.) Those with independent selves assume that other people will also have a set of relatively stable internal attributes such as personality traits, attitudes, or abilities. As a result, when they observe another person's behavior, they draw inferences about the actor's internal state or disposition that supposedly underlies and even caused that behavior.

Research done primarily in the United States supports these claims. For example, when subjects read an essay supporting Fidel Castro in Cuba (Jones & Harris, 1967), they inferred that the author must have a favorable attitude toward Castro. Furthermore, such dispositional inferences occur even when obvious situational constraints are present. The subjects in this study inferred a pro-Castro attitude even when they were explicitly told that the person was assigned to write a pro-Castro essay and no choice was given. The subjects ignored these situational constraints and erroneously drew inferences about the author's disposition. This bias toward inference about the actor's disposition even in the presence of very obvious situational constraints has been termed **fundamental attribution error** (Ross, 1977).

Fundamental attribution error may not be as robust or pervasive, however, among people of interdependent cultures, who share assumptions about the self that are very different from those in Western cultures. This self-construal includes the recognition that what an individual does is contingent on and guided by situational factors. These individuals are more inclined to explain another's behavior in terms of the situational forces impinging on the person rather than internal predispositions.

Miller (1984) examined patterns of social explanation in Americans and Hindu Indians. Both Hindu and American respondents were asked to describe someone they knew well who either did something good for another person or did something bad to another person. After describing such a person, the respondents were asked to explain why the person committed that good or bad act. American respondents typically explained the person's behavior in terms of general dispositions (for example, "She is very irresponsible"). The Hindus, however, were much less likely to offer dispositional explanations. Instead, they tended to provide explanations in terms of the actor's duties, social roles, and other situation-specific factors (see also Shweder & Bourne, 1984).

Some writers (Lively & Bromley, 1973) have suggested another explanation for these results, based on Piaget's theory of intellectual development. In a nutshell, Piaget (1952, 1954) suggested that humans go through various stages of intellectual development, generally proceeding from "concrete operations" to higher stages of "abstract operations" (see Chapter 7 for a full discussion). Using this theory as a framework, some theorists have suggested that non-Western people (such as the Hindu Indian adults in the study just described) are less developed intellectually than American adults. As a result, the Indians used situation-specific, concrete terms whereas Americans used more abstract trait terms in social explanations.

This explanation, however, smacks of ethnocentricity. Whenever we characterize other cultures in a way that places them in an inferior position to our own, we have to be careful. Indeed, the theory may reflect our desire to see ourselves in a favorable light. In this case, differences in self-construal can account for why Indians may not seek to explain social behaviors in abstract terms, even if they are fully capable of abstract reasoning. They find it unreasonable or unnatural to explain others' and their own behaviors in abstract dispositional terms. Still, are there data that rule out differences as a function of cognitive ability?

Fortunately, Miller (1984) collected data from people of different social classes and educational attainment and showed that the Indian tendency toward situation-specific explanations did not depend on these factors. Thus, it is very unlikely that the situational, context-specific thinking common among Indians was due to an inability to reason abstractly. Instead, the context-specific reasoning common in India seems to be due primarily to the cultural assumption of interdependence that is very salient in the Hindu culture. Given the interdependent construal of self, the most reasonable assumption to be made in explaining another's behavior is that this behavior is very much constrained and directed by situation-specific factors.

Consequences for achievement motivation.   Western literature on motivation has long assumed that motivations are internal to the actor. A person's motives to achieve, affiliate, or dominate are salient and important features of the internal self—features that direct and energize overt behaviors. With an alternative, interdependent self-construal, however, social behaviors are guided by expectations of relevant others, felt obligations to others, or the sense of duty to an important group to which one belongs. This point is best illustrated by achievement motivation.

Achievement motivation refers to a desire for excellence. Such a desire, in this broad sense, is found quite widely across cultures (Maehr & Nicholls, 1980). In the current literature, however, desire for excellence has been conceptualized in a somewhat more specific manner—as individually or personally based rather than socially or interpersonally rooted. In two classic works in this area (Atkinson, 1964; McClelland, 1961), the desire for excellence is closely linked with an individual's tendency to push him- or herself ahead and actively strive for and seek individual successes. This notion of achievement, in fact, is congruent with the independent construal of the self widely shared in Western culture.

From an alternative, interdependent frame of reference, however, excellence may be sought to achieve broader social goals. These social forms of achievement motivation are more prevalent among those with an interdependent construal of the self. Interdependent selves have ever-important concerns that revolve around fully realizing the individual's connectedness with others. Thus, the nature of achievement motivation in these groups is quite different from that among those with independent construals of the self.

Yang (1982) distinguished between two forms of achievement motivation: individually oriented and socially oriented (compare Maehr & Nicholls, 1980). Individually oriented achievement is commonly found in Western cultures such as the United States. It is for the sake of "me" personally that the individual strives to achieve. In Chinese society, however, socially oriented achievement is much more common. According to this form of achievement, the individual strives to achieve for the sake of relevant others such as family members. A Chinese student, for example, may work hard to gain admission to a prestigious university and then eventually to a top company. Behaviorally, there may be no difference between this Chinese individual and an American who also strives to succeed both in school and at work. In the Chinese case, however, the ultimate goal may not be advancement of his or her personal career but rather a goal that is more collective or interdependent in character. Interdependent goals may include enhancing his or her family's social standing, meeting a felt expectation of family members, or satisfying his or her sense of obligation or indebtedness to the parents who have made enormous sacrifices to raise and support the student. In other words, the Chinese student's desire to achieve is much more socially rooted and does not necessarily reflect his or her desire to advance the quality or standing of "me" personally.

Supporting this notion, Bond (1986) assessed levels of various motivations among Chinese individuals and found that the Chinese show higher levels of socially oriented rather than individually oriented achievement motivation. Yu (1974) reported that the strength of the achievement motive in China is positively related to familism and **filial piety**. In fact, filial piety is a major social construct in many cultures influenced by Confucian and Buddhist teachings and philosophy, which tend to be more collectivistic than individualistic. In such cultures, those most strongly motivated to excel also take most seriously their duties and obligations to family members, especially to parents.

A similar observation has been reported in Japan. K. Doi (1982, 1985) asked Japanese college students 30 questions designed to measure tendencies to persevere and pursue excellence (achievement tendency). An additional 30 questions measured desires to care for and be cared for by others (affiliation tendency). The results suggested a very close association between achievement motivation and affiliation, with those high in achievement also high in affiliation. These findings are in stark contrast to many Western findings, which indicate that these two dimensions of motivation are typically unrelated (for example, Atkinson, 1964). Both the Chinese study and the Japanese study indicate that achievement in those cultures is closely related to people's social orientation of being connected and interdependent with important others in their lives.

Consequences for self-enhancement and -effacement. Since James (1890), psychologists have repeatedly demonstrated what appears to be an extremely powerful motive to have a positive view of self. As early as 4 years of age, American children think they are better than most others. Wylie (1979) found that American adults typically consider themselves to be more intelligent and more attractive than average. In a national survey of American students, Myers (1987) found that 70% of the students thought they were above average in leadership ability; with respect to the ability to get along with others, 0% thought they were below average, and 60% thought they were in the top 10%. This tendency to *underestimate* the commonality of an individual's desirable traits has been called the **false uniqueness effect.** This effect appears to be stronger for males than for females in the United States (Joseph et al., 1992). It is one clear method of enhancing self-esteem. But is it true for people of different cultures?

Maintaining or enhancing the self may assume a different form for those with interdependent construals of self. For them, positive appraisals of the inner attributes of self may not be strongly linked with overall self-esteem or self-satisfaction. Instead, overall self-esteem or self-satisfaction are more likely to be derived from fulfilling roles of interdependence with others.

Overall esteem or satisfaction about the self within an interdependent framework may result from the recognition that the individual is performing well in the cultural tasks of belonging, fitting in, engaging in appropriate action, promoting others' goals, maintaining harmony, and so on. It may also derive from the individual's capacity to regulate and coordinate his or her inner personal thoughts and feelings so they fit into the pursuit of interdependence with others. For the interdependent self, viewing oneself as unique or different would be unnecessary to maintain a sense of self-worth because the inner attributes of self contributing to an individual's perceived uniqueness are less self-defining. Being unique is undesirable, akin to being the nail that sticks up, because it isolates the person from the ever-important relationship.

In an initial examination of cultural variation in the tendency to see the self as different from others, Markus and Kitayama (1991a) administered questionnaires containing a series of false uniqueness items to Japanese and American college students. The questions took the form "What proportion of students in this university have higher intellectual abilities than you?" The questionnaire items were from one of three categories: abilities (intellectual, memory, and athletic), independence (independent, hold more strongly to their own view), and interdependence (more sympathetic, more warmhearted).

The data are summarized in Figure 3.3. The most striking aspect of these data is the marked difference between the Japanese and the American students in their estimations of their own uniqueness. American students assumed that only 30% of people on average would be better than themselves on various traits and abilities. The Japanese students, however, showed almost no evidence of this false uniqueness. In most cases, they claimed that about 50% of students would be better than they are. You might suspect that these results occurred because the Japanese students tended to use 50% as their preferred answer. This was not the case; the variability in the data was virtually identical for both

Figure 3.3 Estimates of the percentage of people who are better than oneself in three categories of behavior

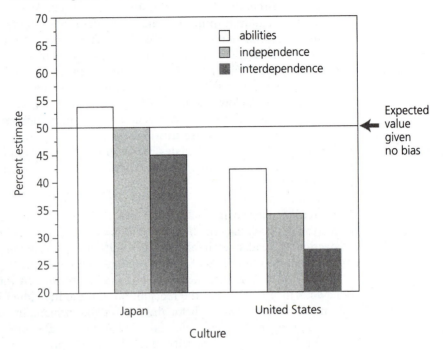

Source: Data from H. R. Markus and S. Kitayama, "Cultural Variation in Self-Concept." In G. R. Goethals and J. Strauss (Eds.), *Multidisciplinary Perspectives on the Self* (New York: Springer-Verlag, 1991).

Americans and Japanese. This finding is typical and predictable for such a sample of college students evaluating themselves free of the need to establish their own uniqueness.

Consequences for the social connotation of emotion. Emotions can be classified into those that encourage independence of the self from others and those that encourage interdependence with others (Kitayama, Markus, & Matsumoto, 1995). Some emotions, such as pride or feelings of superiority, occur when you have accomplished your own goals or desires or have confirmed desirable inner attributes, such as intelligence and wealth. The experience of these emotions tends to verify those inner attributes. Similarly, some negative emotions, such as anger or frustration, result primarily when your own internal attributes, such as goals or desires, are blocked or interfered with. In both cases, your inner attributes are made salient and contrasted against the relevant social context. These emotions tend to separate or disengage the self from social relationships and to promote the perceived independence of the self from those relationships. Kitayama, Markus, and Matsumoto (1995) have called these types of emotions **socially disengaged emotions.**

Other positive emotions, such as friendly feelings and feelings of respect, result from being part of a close, more or less communal, relationship. Once experienced, they further encourage this interpersonal bond. Some types of negative emotions, such as feelings of indebtedness or guilt, act in a similar manner. These emotions typically result from failure to participate successfully in an interdependent relationship or from doing some harm to the relationship. They motivate the individual to restore harmony in the relationship by compensating for the harm done or repaying the debt. These behaviors further engage and assimilate the self in the relationship and enhance the perceived interdependence of the self with relevant others. These emotions can be called **socially engaged emotions**.

All people experience both types of emotions, but people with interdependent self-construals may experience them differently from people with independent self-construals. Socially engaged emotions may be more intense and internalized for interdependent selves, whereas those with independent self-construals may experience socially disengaged emotions more intensely and internally.

Consequences of social connotation and indigenous emotions.   Although many emotions are common across cultures, others are unique to particular cultures (Russell, 1991). Such culture-specific emotions are called **indigenous emotions**. Several anthropological studies have suggested that the socially engaged emotions just described are salient in some non-Western cultures to a degree that is unheard of in the West. Lutz (1988), who studied the emotions of people in the Micronesian atoll of Ifaluk, found that an emotion known as *fago* is central to this culture. According to Lutz, *fago* can be roughly described as a combination of compassion, love, and sadness. This emotion is likely to motivate helping behaviors and to create and enhance close interpersonal relationships. In our terminology, *fago* is a highly socially engaged emotion. A contrasting emotion, *ker*, described as a combination of happiness and excitement, is perceived as "dangerous, socially disruptive" (p. 145). Ifaluk people regard *ker* as a highly socially disengaged emotion.

A similar analysis has been applied to another non-Western culture. T. Doi (1973) has suggested that the emotion *amae* is pivotal in understanding the Japanese culture. *Amae* refers to a desire or expectation for others' indulgence, benevolence, or favor. According to Doi, its prototypic form can be found in the mother–infant relationship, whereby the infant feels a desire for "dependency" on the mother and the mother provides unconditional care and love to the infant. This prototype is subsequently elaborated to an adult form of *amae*, which is much more differentiated and sophisticated and is applicable to nonkin relationships, such as work relationships between a supervisor and his or her subordinates. Subordinates may feel *amae* toward the supervisor for his or her favor and benevolence. Reciprocal feelings on the part of the supervisor increase and consolidate the affectionate bond between them. A lack of reciprocation can lead to negative emotions on both sides. As in the Ifaluk concept of *fago*, social engagement seems to define this emotion for the Japanese culture.

These anthropological studies fit well with the two construals of the self described here. For people with interdependent self-construals, public and intersubjective aspects of the self are elaborated in conscious experience; for those with independent selves, private and more subjective aspects are highlighted. Compare Figures 3.2 and 3.3. Because social connotation is a relatively public and intersubjective aspect of emotion, it is especially salient in the emotional experience of non-Western, interdependent people in collectivistic cultures. By contrast, in Western, individualistic cultures that foster independent senses of self, the more internal, private aspects of emotion, such as good and bad feelings or moods, may be more salient (Kleinman, 1988). This is true even though people of individualistic cultures recognize the social connotations of different emotions.

Consequences for happiness. *Happiness* refers to the most generic, unqualified state of feeling good. Terms such as *relaxed, elated,* and *calm* are used to describe this generic positive state. People across cultures share the general notion of happiness as defined in this way (Wierzbicka, 1986). However, the specific circumstances of happiness, and the meanings attached to it, depend crucially on the construal of the self as independent or as interdependent. Evidence suggests that people experience this unqualified good feeling when they have successfully accomplished the cultural task of either independence or interdependence.

Kitayama, Markus, Kurokawa, and Negishi (1993) asked both Japanese and American college undergraduates to report how frequently they experienced different emotions, including three types of positive emotions. Some terms used to describe the emotions were generic, such as *relaxed, elated,* and *calm.* Others had more specific social connotations, either socially engaged (such as *friendly feelings, feelings of respect*) or disengaged (*pride, feelings of superiority*). An interesting cross-cultural difference emerged when correlations among these three types of emotions were examined (see Figure 3.4).

For the Americans students, generic positive emotions were associated primarily with the socially disengaged emotions. That is, those who experienced the emotions that signal success in cultural tasks of *independence* (socially disengaged emotions such as pride) were most likely to feel "generally good." This pattern was completely reversed among the Japanese students. Those who experienced the emotions that signal success in cultural tasks of *interdependence* (socially engaged emotions such as friendly feelings) were most likely to feel "generally good." The exact meanings or connotations of "feeling good" are shaped through culture and are linked very closely with the cultural imperatives of independence (in the United States) and interdependence (in Japan).

Critical Thinking and Evaluation of the Analysis of Independent and Interdependent Selves

As described earlier in this chapter, there is little doubt that culture influences our sense of self which, in turn, affects many other aspects of our psychological characteristics and behaviors. The work of Markus and Kitayama (1991b)

Figure 3.4 Cultural differences in the correlation between general positive feelings and socially engaged versus disengaged emotions in the United States and Japan

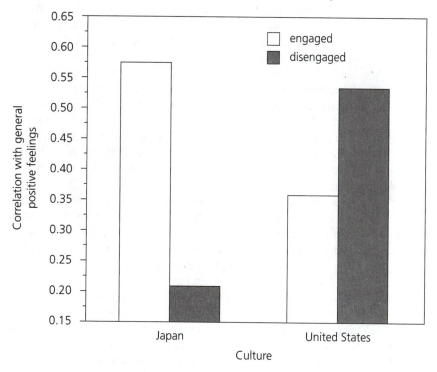

Source: Data from S. Kitayama, H. R. Markus, M. Kurokawa, and K. Negishi, *Social Orientation of Emotions: Cross-Cultural Evidence and Implications* (unpublished manuscript, University of Oregon, 1993).

reviewed here has been very influential in the field. It offers a prime example of how self-concepts may differ across cultures and provides a conceptual framework within which to understand the influence of culture on self. Their approach has the additional advantage of synthesizing and integrating a wide variety of cross-cultural research findings related to self-perceptions, social explanations, motivation, and emotion. The notions of independent versus interdependent self-construals make intuitive sense, permitting their easy acceptance in cross-cultural as well as mainstream psychology.

A scholarly evaluation of their theory, however—or any theory, for that matter—must go beyond merely asking whether or not it "makes sense" and whether or not the outcomes predicted by the theory occur. A more difficult, and more needed, level of analysis is to examine the assumptions underlying the theory and provide direct evidence in support of those assumptions. Without such support, it cannot be known in any true sense whether the predicted outcomes (as in self-perception) are occurring because of the theoretical framework (independent versus interdependent selves) or because of some other factors. That is, the framework needs to be supported in and of itself, rather than through its predicted outcomes.

For example, studies comparing Asians and Americans were used to support the notion of independent versus interdependent self-construals. However, when differences between these groups are attributed to different self-construals, and these self-construals are related to individualism and collectivism, at least two major assumptions are being made: (1) that Asians have interdependent self-construals, whereas Americans have independent self-construals; and (2) that Asians are collectivistic and Americans are individualistic. Without ascertaining empirically that these two assumptions are valid, it is impossible to assert that the observed differences are due to cultural differences of self-construals, and not to other differences such as geography, social class, or diet. The only way to address these concerns is to examine them empirically.

One of the hindrances to research examining the first assumption has been the lack of a psychometrically valid and reliable way to measure self-construals on the individual level. Luckily, however, Singelis and his colleagues (Singelis, 1994; Singelis & Sharkey, 1995) have developed such a measure, and have used it in two studies testing self-construals of people of different ethnic groups at the University of Hawaii. In both studies, they found that Asian Americans were more interdependent than European Americans, while European Americans were more independent than Asian Americans. These findings are consistent with Markus and Kitayama's claims concerning Asian and non-Asian differences in self-construal, albeit among ethnic groups within the United States. However, in another study using the same scale, with American and Japanese nationals (Carter and Dinnel, 1997), the Japanese were found to be more independent than the Americans. Studies on other cultural groups also report no differences in independent versus interdependent self-responses (Watkins & Regmi, 1996), questioning the generalizability of that assumption.

A recent study by Dabul, Bernal, and Knight (1995) provides another interesting twist on these findings. These researchers conducted open-ended interviews calling for self-descriptors from Mexican and Anglo American adolescents. When total scores derived from coding were used, they found that Mexican Americans described themselves more allocentrically than did Anglo Americans, whereas idiocentric self-descriptors were more important for Anglo Americans. When these scores were corrected for frequency of usage, however, the differences disappeared. Not only do these findings raise further questions about the validity of the assumption, they also highlight the possible influence of different methods of research and data analysis on the findings.

The second assumption—that Asians are collectivistic and Americans are individualistic—also has major problems. As described in Chapter 2, a host of measurement techniques are now available to assess individualistic and collectivistic tendencies on the individual level. These measures have been used quite extensively over the past few years, and their results generally do not support the stereotype of Asian, and particularly Japanese, collectivism. For example, when Matsumoto and colleagues (1997) measured IC tendencies using their IC

Interpersonal Assessment Inventory, they found that Americans were more collectivistic than Japanese. In a follow-up study, Matsumoto, Kudoh, and Takeuchi (1996) showed that within Japan, older working adults (average age 40) were more collectivistic than Japanese university undergraduates, suggesting that the stereotype of Japanese collectivism may have been appropriate in the past but is questionable today.

Carter and Dinnel (1997) have reported similar findings. They administered Yamaguchi's (1994) collectivism scale, Triandis' collectivistic values index (Triandis et al., 1990), Singelis's (1994) self-construal scale, and a host of individual and collective self-esteem measures to American and Japanese participants. Contrary to their expectations, they found that collectivism was more characteristic of Americans than Japanese, and that independent self-construals were more characteristic of Japanese than Americans (contrary to Singelis's findings on Asian Americans versus European Americans). Carter and Dinnel (1997) found no difference between the Americans and Japanese on collective self-esteem.

In yet another study, Kashima and colleagues (1995) administered a number of collectivism and allocentrism scales to participants in Australia, mainland United States, Hawaii, Japan, and Korea. Koreans and Japanese did score higher than mainland Americans and Australians on collectivism, whereas the latter scored higher on scales related to agency and assertiveness. These findings are consistent with previous notions of cultural differences among these groups. However, on a scale measuring interpersonal relatedness, mainland American women scored highest, followed by Australian women, Hawaiian women, Korean men, Hawaiian men, Australian men, and mainland American men. Unexpectedly, Japanese men and women scored lowest on this scale.

Recently, Takano and Osaka (1997) reviewed ten other studies comparing Americans and Japanese on individualism–collectivism measures. They reported that two studies on conformity and five questionnaire studies found no differences between samples from the two countries. Two experimental studies on cooperation and one questionnaire study found that Japanese were more individualistic than Americans. The only study that found Japanese respondents to be more collectivistic than Americans was Hofstede's (1980) original study (described in Chapter 2), in which Individualism was defined without a collectivistic component.

Taken together, these studies highlight the difficulty of accepting the validity of the two assumptions underlying Markus and Kitayama's (1991b) conceptual framework regarding independent versus interdependent self-construals. Aside from the studies cited in this section, the most crucial test of these assumptions would be a simultaneous assessment of IC tendencies on the group level and self-construals on the individual level *within the same participants in the same study*. Without such an assessment, we cannot assert with any confidence that these proposed factors, and no others influenced the data outcome. This study, unfortunately, does not exist.

Where does this leave us? I believe that Markus and Kitayama's (1991b) original conception of independent versus interdependent self-construals is an important one that has made a major contribution to the field, increasing our awareness of the influence of culture on self and thus on individual behaviors. I agree with the notion of independent versus interdependent self-construals, but strongly believe that it is incumbent on its proponents to test the crucial underlying assumptions. It may be that these types of self-construals do exist but their underlying bases are related to something other than individualism and collectivism. Future research needs to elucidate this matter more directly.

Beyond Independent and Interdependent Self-Construals: Interrelated and Isolated Self-Concepts

Actually, the concept of independent versus interdependent selves is not unlike other dualities of self and human nature proposed throughout the history of psychology, including Freud's (1930/1961) union with others versus egoistic happiness, Angyal's (1951) surrender and autonomy, Balint's (1959) ocno-philic and philobatic tendencies, Bakan's (1966) communion and agency, Bowen's (1966) togetherness and individuality, Bowlby's (1969) attachment and separation, Franz and White's (1985) individuation and attachment, Stewart and Malley's (1987) interpersonal relatedness and self-definition, and Slavin and Kriegman's (1992) mutualistic and individualistic urges (all cited in Guisinger & Blatt, 1994). Many theorists, including Doi (1973), Kim and Berry (1993), and Heelas and Lock (1981) have noted the difference between con-ceptualization of self in mainstream American psychology and in other cul-tures. Sampson (1988) has referred to the sense of self in mainstream ap-proaches as *self-contained individualism*, contrasting it with what he termed *ensembled individualism*, in which the boundary between self and others is less sharply drawn and others are part of oneself.

Guisinger and Blatt (1994) suggest that mainstream American psychology has traditionally placed greater importance on self-development, stressing au-tonomy, independence, and identity, over the development of interpersonal re-latedness. They also suggest, however, that evolutionary pressures of natural selection have fostered two basic developmental approaches—one involving self-definition as described in mainstream psychology, the other focusing on the development of interpersonal relatedness. They cite evidence from observa-tional research as well as social biology to support their claims that coopera-tion, altruism, and reciprocation are aspects of self-development equally as im-portant as autonomy and individual definition. Moreover, they suggest that these dual developmental processes are not mutually exclusive, as they are of-ten depicted. Rather, they are fundamentally and basically intertwined—that the development of a mature sense of self in one aspect depends, in part, on the development of a mature self in the other.

More recently, Niedenthal and Beike (1997) have carried these concepts a step further, proposing the existence of both interrelated and isolated self-concepts. Whereas previous theories of self distinguished different types of self on the level of personality, motivation, and culture, their view focuses on the level of cognitive representation. Specifically, they suggest that "some concepts derive their meaning through mental links to concepts of other people, whereas other concepts of self have an intrinsic or cognitively isolated characterization" (p. 108). Like Guisinger and Blatt (1994), they suggest that these concepts exist not as dichotomies, but rather as interrelated dualities. Referring mainly to the cognitive structures characteristic of these two tendencies, Niedenthal and Beike (1997) suggest that individuals represent the self with a variety of more or less interrelated structures at the same time, and that one person can have separate interrelated and isolated self-concepts in the same domain.

These recent developments in notions of self, incorporating issues of relatedness into mainstream conceptions of autonomy and individuality in a coherent system of dualism, have many far-reaching implications for our understanding of culture and self. If these dualities coexist, cultures may emphasize both types of self-construal rather than only one. Moreover, the relative importance of one sense of self may differ in different contexts, and cultures may influence these relativities as well. Future research needs to examine the simultaneous duality of these aspects of self across contexts and cultures to create a clearer picture of the relationship between culture and self, and of how culture influences individual behaviors via self.

Multicultural Identities

The term *cultural identity* refers to individuals' psychological membership in a distinct culture. As culture is a psychological construct—a shared system of rules—it is conceivable that people not only have a single cultural identity, but in some circumstances, two or more such identities. These multicultural identities are becoming increasingly commonplace in today's world, with borders between cultural groups becoming less rigid, increased communication and interaction among people of different cultural groups, and more intercultural marriages. If culture is defined as a psychological construct, the existence of multicultural identities suggests the existence of multiple psychocultural systems of representations in the minds of multicultural individuals.

In fact, a small but important number of studies have begun to document the existence of such multiple psychological systems in multicultural individuals. Oyserman (1993), for example, conducted four studies testing Arab and Israeli Jewish students in Israel. While social, collectivistic types of identities had long been considered central to many cultures of that region, Oyserman suggested that these cultures would include considerable individualistic aspects as well, given the history of the region and the influence of the British. In her studies, participants completed a battery of tests including assessments of individualism, collectivism, public and private self-focus, and intergroup conflicts. Across all four studies, the results indicated that individualism as a worldview was related to private aspects of the self and to distinguishing between self and others, while collectivism was related to social identities, public aspects of the self, and increased awareness of intergroup conflict. Both cultural groups endorsed both types of cultural tendencies, suggesting that members of these groups use both individualistic and collectivistic worldviews in organizing perceptions of self and others.

Another study by Oyserman and her colleagues (Oyserman, Gant, & Ager, 1995) also supported the existence of multiple concepts of self. In this study, they examined the effects of multiple, contextualized concepts of the self on school persistence in European American and African American youths. They found that different self-concepts were predictive of achievement-related strategies for European Americans and African Americans. More important, balance between different achievement-related self-construals predicted school achievement, especially for African American males.

Other studies have documented a *cultural reaffirmation* effect among multicultural individuals living in multicultural societies. For example, Kosmitzki (1996) examined monocultural and bicultural Germans and Americans, who made trait-attribute ratings of themselves, their native cultural group, and their adoptive cultural group. Compared with monoculturals, bicultural individuals identified more closely with their native culture, evaluated it more positively, and evaluated the two cultures as less similar to each other. In short, the bicultural individuals appeared to endorse even more traditional values associated with their native culture than did native monocultural individuals in those native cultures.

This curious finding is well supported in other studies as well. For example, Matsumoto and colleagues (1997) did a study in which they compared ratings of collectivistic tendencies in interpersonal interactions of Japanese Americans with those of Japanese nationals in Japan. They found that the Japanese Americans were more collectivistic than the Japanese nationals in the native culture. A study comparing Korean Americans and Korean nationals on the same measure (Lee, 1995) found similar results. Sociological studies involving immigrants to the United States, including China, Japan, Korea, and the Philippines, also suggest that the immigrant groups in the United States from other Asia–Pacific countries appear to be more traditional than the native cultures from which they came (for example, Takaki, 1998). Anecdotally, strong cultural traditions, customs, heritage, and language seem to continue among Chinese American immigrant populations throughout the United States.

What may account for such findings? I would speculate that when immigrant groups arrive in the United States, they bring with them the culture of their native group *at that time*. As they are immersed within a multicultural society, the stress of multicultural life in a different world contributes to the cultural reaffirmation effect, as documented by Kosmitzki (1996) and others. The immigrant group thus crystallizes its sense of culture—the one they brought with them at the time—and it is this psychological culture that is communicated across generations of immigrant groups. As time passes, the native culture itself may undergo change, but the immigrant group continues to transmit the original cultural system they brought with them. After some time, if you compare the immigrant group with the native cultural group, you will find that the immigrant group actually conforms more to the original cultural stereotype than does the native group, because the immigrant culture has crystallized while the native culture has changed. Thus, while individual members of immigrant groups often grow up with multicultural identities, the identity of their native culture is often one of long-standing tradition and heritage.

Conclusion

Culture is a macrolevel social construct that identifies the characteristics and attributes we share with others. But culture also influences the very core nature of our beings as individuals. Because culture shapes and colors our experiences, behaviors, attitudes, and feelings, it helps mold our fundamental sense of self—our self-concept, self-construals, and self-identities. Culture influences these core aspects of our sense of self, and we carry these self-construals with us in all aspects of life. Whether at work, at school, having fun, or interacting with other people, we take our culture and our culture-bound sense of self with us. These self-construals help us understand the world around us and others in it, and guide us and our behaviors in ways we are not always aware of.

Because culture influences core aspects of the self, I thought it was necessary to understand its importance and pervasiveness before studying other cultural influences on behavior. Indeed, the information discussed in this chapter will have an impact on all the remaining information presented in this book. I hope you can carry this information with you as we continue our journey to learn how culture influences behavior.

Glossary

achievement motivation A desire for excellence.

cognitive template A logical framework that serves as the basis for understanding ourselves and others.

false uniqueness effect The tendency for individuals to underestimate the commonality of desirable traits and to overestimate their uniqueness.

filial piety A sense of duty and obligation to family members, especially parents. This sense is especially strong in Asian and other collectivistic cultures.

fundamental attribution error A tendency to explain the behaviors of others using internal attributions but to explain one's own behaviors using external attributions.

independent construal of self A sense of self that views the self as a bounded entity, clearly separated from relevant others.

indigenous emotions Emotions relatively specific to particular cultures.

interdependent construal of self A sense of self that views the self as unbounded, flexible, and contingent on context. This sense of self is based on a principle of the fundamental connectedness among people.

self-concept The way in which we understand or construe our sense of self or being.

socially disengaged emotions Emotions that tend to separate or disengage the self from social relationships and to promote the perceived independence of the self from those relationships.

socially engaged emotions Emotions that lead to behaviors that engage and assimilate the self in social relationships and enhance the perceived interdependence of the self with others.

Ethnocentrism, Stereotypes, and Prejudice

In dealing with cultural differences in thoughts, opinions, attitudes, and behaviors, as you will in the rest of this book, it is easy to develop cognitive or emotional reactions to the material, to make generalizations and negative stereotypes of others, and even to prejudge those differences and the people who engage in those behaviors before you truly understand their basis. These processes and reactions are commonplace in the world today, and the terms *ethnocentrism, stereotypes, prejudice,* and *discrimination* are often used to describe them. Unfortunately, the terms are often used without being clearly understood, in ways that actually foster the problems they are supposed to clarify.

Some of today's most pressing social issues concern these processes—both domestically within the United States, because of our increasingly diverse and multicultural society, and internationally, as borders between countries and cultures become increasingly permeable as a result of advances in transportation, technology, and business. You cannot pick up a newspaper or magazine or turn on the television news without seeing a story about problems related to ethnocentrism or racial or national stereotypes. These problems range from doing business internationally to violence and wars based on racial or ethnic differences. These issues promise to become even more salient in the future as technology brings the diverse cultures of the world ever closer together.

My biases in this chapter are twofold. First, meaningful discussion about these topics is impossible without first defining them thoroughly. Many differences of opinion arise, in fact, not out of disagreement over the meaning or importance of these terms in our everyday lives but over differences in definitions. For this reason, it is important to place those definitions on the table, at least as "working definitions," to be used in discussions as we encounter the cultural differences presented in the rest of the book.

Second, defining these terms leads to a better understanding of how they are created, how they are maintained, and how they might be changed. Certainly, changes are possible without conscious awareness and deliberate cognitive understanding. But the goal of this book is to analyze processes related to cultural similarities and differences, and to understand the contribution of psychology to those processes. This understanding can also provide a basis for change.

A great deal has been written about these topics in the social science literature, particularly in disciplines such as sociology and ethnic relations. In this chapter, I will borrow from the existing literature in psychology to develop a psychological explanation of the processes associated with ethnocentrism, stereotypes, prejudice, and discrimination. The first part of the chapter deals with ethnocentrism, building upon our earlier definition of culture and suggesting that ethnocentrism is a normal consequence of learning the ways of society and culture in everyday life. In this view, we are all ethnocentric; the important question is whether we recognize it or not.

The second part of the chapter deals with stereotypes—positive as well as negative stereotypes, and stereotypes about one's own group as well as other groups. As with ethnocentrism, I believe that stereotypes are inevitable consequences of everyday psychological functioning, building upon other psychological processes that we all use in our daily lives. Again, the issue is not whether or not we harbor stereotypes, but whether or not we recognize them *and* their limitations.

The third part of the chapter deals with prejudice, discrimination, and a host of "isms" (such as racism), using the previous material on ethnocentrism and stereotypes to understand them. While ethnocentrism and stereotypes are inevitable psychological processes, prejudice and discrimination are not (although not all writers agree, as we shall see). We will discuss the nature of these processes, and how they develop.

Finally, the chapter ends with a discussion of how we can go beyond prejudice and discrimination in our dealing with cultural differences. Not only is this discussion important as a basis for engaging effectively with the rest of the material in this book; it is also important in our everyday lives. Although these topics have been addressed elsewhere, it is most often from a social or cultural perspective. One of the overall goals of this chapter is to examine the contribution of not only social but also psychological factors in the creation and maintenance of all these processes, as well as the interaction between culture and psychology.

Ethnocentrism and Intergroup Attitudes

Different Definitions of Ethnocentrism

One of the fundamental concepts concerning intergroup relations is ethnocentrism. This term is often used in a negative way, defined as the *inability* to view others in a manner outside of your own cultural background. A related definition of ethnocentrism would suggest a tendency to judge people of other groups, societies, or lifestyles according to the standards of one's own ingroup or culture, oftentimes viewing outgroups as inferior (for example, see Healey, 1998; Noel, 1968). Because many people talk about ethnocentrism in such negative terms, much related discussion centers around the need to "rid" ourselves of ethnocentrism.

But can we really rid ourselves of ethnocentrism? A different analysis of this problem suggests not; in fact, it suggests that ethnocentrism is a normal psychological function and an inevitable part of our lives. Indeed, although this word is often used in a way that carries negative connotations, it need not have these connotations. I define **ethnocentrism** as *the tendency to view the world through one's own cultural filters*. With this definition, and knowledge about how we acquire those filters, it follows that just about everyone in the world is ethnocentric. That is, everyone learns a certain way of behaving, and in doing so, learns a certain way of perceiving and interpreting the behaviors of others. It is in this way that we first perceive and make interpretations about others, and is a normal consequence of growing up in society. In this sense, ethnocentrism per se is neither bad nor good; it merely reflects the state of affairs—that we all have our cultural filters on when we perceive others.

Ethnocentrism as a Normal Consequence of Socialization and Enculturation

As we grow up, we learn many rules about how to behave. These rules form the basis of culture. Culture consists of the many rules concerning the regulation and control of our behavior via socially appropriate channels. For example, we learn that "big boys don't cry" and "You don't scratch yourself in public." As these rules shape our behavior, we learn that many rules come with sanctions for transgressing them. If a boy cries in public, for example, he may be ridiculed by his friends or family; he may be called a sissy or some other name.

When we are very little, these rules must be constantly reinforced in us. Our parents, friends, teachers, and other agents of socialization continually remind us of the rules. Many of these rules are also transmitted and reinforced by organizations and institutions. All of these lessons contribute to the process of enculturation discussed in Chapter 7. As we get older, we need to be reminded less and less about these rules. We begin to act upon them with less and less conscious effort.

During adolescence, many people believe, we begin to rebel against the rules. We begin to question authority and the rules that authority dictates to us. We begin to seek out new ways and rules of behavior. We search for "ourselves." This process is related to Erikson's stage of "identity versus role confusion" (discussed in Chapter 7). After adolescence, however, many people seem to come back to their roots, to the ways and rules with which they were brought up. Oftentimes, this happens after college or university life, when a person needs to step out into the workforce and relearn the rules of society. By this time, we have learned how to act according to those rules. Generally, no one around us needs to remind us of the rules as our parents, teachers, and friends did when we were little. Indeed, not only will we have internalized the rules of behavior by the time we are adults, but we will have learned them so well that we can act according to those rules automatically without thinking very much about them. Many of these rules make up what we know as our culture—the conglomeration of learned rules about how to behave. To the extent that we share these rules about behavior with others, we share a certain culture with them.

But rules of behavior are not the only things we learn as we grow. We also learn how to perceive others, how to interpret the behaviors of others, and how to make judgments of those behaviors. Because we share a set of rules with a certain group of people, we develop a set of expectations about the kinds of behaviors people should exhibit. That is, we implicitly learn that the rules with which we were raised and that are true for us must also be true for others who share the same cultural heritage. This tacit knowledge need not be spoken each time we, as adults, operate on that knowledge. It is similar to communication between two computers that have the same basic operating system and "speak" the same language.

Not only do we have certain expectations about people's behaviors, but we also have learned patterns of judgments about those behaviors. We have emotional reactions associated with those expectations and judgments that range from acceptance and pleasure to outrage, hostility, and frustration. When we interact with someone of our own cultural background, we interact using the same "ground rules." Whatever discussions or negotiations we have will be held above and beyond those ground rules, because we both implicitly and tacitly share them. Thus, there is an underlying current of acceptance about those ground rules as we interact (even though we may or may not like the specific content of the interaction).

When we observe or interact with people who engage in transgressions to what we view as "normal" or "socially appropriate," however, we have negative reactions. We become upset or frustrated or annoyed because we have learned that those types of behaviors are not appropriate, and negative emotions have become associated with that learning. Of course, these types of reactions will be more common when interacting with people of different cultural backgrounds, because they operate with different ground rules. But these reactions often occur when interacting with people of our own cultural heritage as well.

Oftentimes our emotional reactions lead us to make judgments about others. When the behaviors we observe are what we would normally expect in a given situation, we make an implicit judgment that the person is a member of our culture or that the person is engaging in socially appropriate behavior. We may consider the individual to have been socialized "well" into our culture; they are "good." But when the behavior we observe is what we do not expect, we begin to question that person. Oftentimes, we interpret the behavior to mean that the person is "bad" or "stupid" or "had a bad upbringing." At the very least, there is uncertainty and ambiguity.

Often we make these judgments of good and bad, right and wrong, without a second thought. Indeed, why should we give those judgments second thought? The judgments are often rooted in our upbringing since childhood, and are the only types of judgments we have learned to make. As such, they are colored by our emotions, which serve as guidelines in helping us form opinions about ourselves and others.

Thus, as we become enculturated, not only do we learn how to act, but we also learn how to perceive and interpret how other people act. Our learning is associated with strong emotions of acceptance or rejection, with moral judgments of good or bad, right or wrong, and with judgments of personality. These rules of perceiving and interpreting form the basis for our own "filters" that we use in seeing the world. As we become more and more enculturated, we add more layers to those filters. These filters have lenses that allow us to perceive the world in a certain way, from a certain angle, or through a certain color. By the time we are adults, we share the same filters, with the same prescription and color filtering, with other people in our cultural group. It is as if we all purchased a camera filter with the same properties. We have these filters on all the time, so that by the time we are adults we hardly notice they are there. They become part of our self, inseparable and invisible. They are a normal part of our psychological composition because of the way we were socialized and enculturated. Culture exists in each and every individual as a set of psychological rules, attitudes, values, and beliefs, and strong associations exist between those rules and our emotions and judgments of morality and personality.

Recognizing One's Own Ethnocentrism

Given that we are all ethnocentric to some degree, an important issue is whether or not we are aware of that ethnocentrism. Some people are well aware that they relate to others and to diversity through the cultural filters of their own particular lifestyle and culture. They understand that the way they perceive and interpret others and the world around them is only one way of doing so, that other interpretations exist, and that their interpretations may not be accurate in relation to the actual *intent* of the actors producing the differences they perceive. Other people are not aware that they relate to diversity with their cultural filters on; they believe that their way of perceiving and interpreting the world is the only way of perceiving and interpreting. Such people do not recognize the existence of other possible interpretations, nor the possibility that they themselves may be wrong. The question, therefore, is not whether ethnocentrism exists, but whether or not people recognize that they *are* ethnocentric.

It is important to consider ways to develop flexibility when interacting with others, while at the same time accepting our own ethnocentrism. The work of several researchers (for example, Bochner, 1982; Boucher, Landis, & Clark, 1987; Brislin, 1993) suggests a number of ways to attain this flexibility. First, it is important to know how our own culture filters reality, distorting, rotating, and coloring images so we see things a certain way. Second, it is important to recognize and appreciate the fact that people of different cultural backgrounds have different filters that produce their own distortions, rotations, and coloring of reality, and that their version of reality will seem as real and valid to them as ours is to us. Third, while knowledge of our own and other people's cultures and their influences on the filtering process is a necessary condition to gaining flexibility, it is not sufficient. We have to learn to deal somehow with the emotions, judgments of morality, and judgments of personality that are associated with our ethnocentrism and cultural filters. I am not suggesting that our potential negative reactions are not valid; what I am suggesting is that we must give ourselves a chance to go beyond those reactions and try to learn about other people's viewpoints. In doing so, we may have to force ourselves to take a crash course on cultural filters from different cultures and superimpose them over our own filters so we can come closer to seeing the world from another person's vantage point. Above all, this process means learning to put our emotional reactions and moral judgments on hold, however briefly, even though we have learned them so well that they are generally automatic.

All of this requires a substantial degree of learning and effort. These new filters are superimposed over and above our existing cultural filters, not substituted for them. Our own cultural filters become a permanent and fixed part of ourselves (although it is true that because they are learned we are constantly modifying them as we go along). We do not get rid of our own filters when learning to be flexible; we learn ways to add onto them to help us see things from different perspectives. We don't necessarily lose ourselves in this process—a realistic fear of many people—rather, we gain new skills and knowledge.

I think of this entire package of events as **flexible ethnocentrism**. It is important to realize that flexible ethnocentrism does not mean you must accept or like the other viewpoint. Some may argue, for example, that the criminal mentality constitutes a culture in itself. You can engage in flexible ethnocentrism to attempt to understand the criminal culture and viewpoint; accepting or liking it, however, is another matter entirely.

The alternative to this process of gaining flexibility is **inflexible ethnocentrism**. This term refers to the traditional notion of ethnocentrism as an inability to go beyond one's own cultural filters in interpreting the behavior of others. Inflexible ethnocentrism may arise from ignorance of the processes necessary to gain a different cultural viewpoint, or from a refusal to engage in such a process. It is important to differentiate between ethnocentrism as a general process applicable to people of all cultures, and the flexible or inflexible use of that ethnocentrism in positive or negative ways.

If you ask people which type of ethnocentrism they have, most will probably say they are flexible. But people's subjective judgments of themselves and their own abilities are tempered by culture as well (as in the false uniqueness effect discussed in Chapter 3). The best indicator of the type of ethnocentrism a person has is his or her actual interpretations of the behaviors of others. A person who interprets the behavior of someone from a different cultural background solely from his or her own perspective, attaching value statements such as "They are terrible" or "That's why people hate them," is reacting inflexibly. Those who interpret behavior from a flexible ethnocentric viewpoint are likely to use qualifying statements such as "That's the way they have learned to do things" or "We can't judge that right or wrong from our perspective."

As you were reading this section, you had your own cultural filters on. Most people have one of two types of reactions to this section. One type acknowledges these types of ethnocentrism (the "mm-hmm" and "ah-hah" reaction). The other type questions what was described in this section (the "Is that really true?" reaction). Which type of reaction did you have? Which type of ethnocentrism do you think you operate with?

The Contribution of Psychological Factors to Ethnocentrism and Intergroup Attitudes

More than three decades ago, Campbell and Levine (1965; cited in Seelye & Brewer, 1970) suggested that a number of psychological factors contribute to ethnocentrism. (In terms of the previous discussion, I believe all the studies cited in this section defined ethnocentrism as the inflexible type.) On the individual level, they cited variables such as ingroup loyalty, ethnocentric hostility, authoritarianism, rigidity, self-esteem, and extent or frequency of contact with outgroup members. They tested the relationship between these variables and acculturation in a study of Americans who were living in Guatemala. Data were collected in open-ended interviews that covered many aspects of daily life, as well as attitudes, opinions, beliefs, and behaviors. They then related all of the variables collectively to acculturation to Guatemalan life. They concluded that "actual contact with the Guatemalan culture, especially to the extent that it increases the individual's sense of security within the new culture and reduces his commitment to the original ingroup, has more impact on adaptation to the culture than attitudinal variables" (p. 154). Their findings suggest the important role of emotion, self, and values in the formation of ethnocentrism discussed earlier in this chapter, as well as their role in developing flexibility in one's ethnocentrism.

Other studies, however, suggest that exposure to differences can lead to negative attitudes and emotions. Vrij and Winkel (1994), for example, showed Dutch police officers slides of either black (Surinamer) or white (Dutch) actors, supposedly being interrogated about a crime, and asked for their impressions. In addition to skin color and appearance, the researchers manipulated accent, fluency, and speech style to correspond to either the Surinamer or Dutch individual. The results indicated that speech style and fluency of the Surinamers were both related to more negative impressions of nervousness, unpleasantness, and suspiciousness. Thus, differences evoked more negative attitudes than did similarities.

Likewise, Bochner and Osako (1977) presented Hawaiian Japanese, Japanese, and Australian participants with a slide depicting either a Japanese or a Caucasian couple. The participants were asked to describe how the couples were similar. The responses were then scored for the presence or absence of ethnic or racial references involving skin color, race, outgroups, or physiognomy. The Australians described the Japanese but not the Caucasians in ethnic terms, while the Japanese described the Caucasians but not the Japanese in ethnic terms. The Hawaiian Japanese used ethnic terms equally in describing both couples. These findings suggest that people use stereotypic ethnic terms and *ethnic role salience* when describing others perceived as outgroup members—that is, those who are different from themselves. These results also confirm the analysis of ethnocentrism presented earlier.

That ethnocentrism and intergroup attitudes are highly dependent on sociocultural factors was also supported in a study of anti-Semitism in Quebec, Canada (Sniderman, Northrup, Fletcher, Russell, & Tetlock, 1993). The researchers conducted a telephone survey of 2,084 respondents, 60% of whom also completed and mailed back a questionnaire. English- and French-speaking respondents were asked five questions in their native language about their attitudes toward Jews. Their responses were then correlated with responses from corresponding samples in Quebec on relevant personality, political, and sociocultural variables. The French-speaking Canadians were more likely to agree with negative characterizations of Jews, and less likely to agree with positive characterizations, than were English-speaking Canadians. These differences were correlated with the French-speaking participants' support for conformity as a value, and not correlated with personality or political variables. These findings were interpreted to suggest that Quebecers are more likely to distrust and dislike people who are different, and fear that too much freedom to differ can threaten an orderly society.

In yet another study, Greek Canadians were questioned about their attitudes toward culture and language maintenance; economic and cultural security, measured by their own family's economic situation, perceived economic standing of own group, anticipated own group survival, and perceived social status of own group; social distance to seven other Canadian ethnic groups; trait attribution; and ethnocentrism (Lambert, Mermigis, & Taylor, 1986). The Greek Canadians clearly viewed their own group most positively—as hardworking, intelligent, law-abiding, and the like. They also preferred social contacts within their own group over those with people of other groups. Interestingly, the security variables relating to economic and social status and group survival were positively correlated with positive evaluations of other groups, and with closeness on social distance measures. Again, these findings highlight the importance of emotions, self, and values in the maintenance of ethnocentrism and the development of flexible ethnocentrism.

These studies are indicative of the psychological factors that contribute to ethnocentrism, and to the recognition (or lack thereof) of one's own ethnocentric attitudes. Because ethnocentrism is so often discussed in negative terms, and not as an inevitable consequence of enculturation and socialization as defined earlier, many readers may have difficulty accepting the premise that ethnocentrism is a normal part of everyday psychological functioning. Yet some degree of ethnocentrism is essential to social order and cohesion. Without such implicit positive evaluations of one's own cultural ways, there would be no reason to observe norms of behavior and laws of society, or to work together with others in daily life. Thus, ethnocentrism plays an important role and function, helping to hold society and culture together. A larger question concerns how we can become more flexible in our use of our ethnocentrism, a topic to which we will return at the end of this chapter. First, however, we turn our attention to a closely related psychological construct, stereotypes.

Stereotypes

Definition and Types of Stereotypes

Stereotypes are generalized images that we have about groups of people, particularly about their underlying psychological characteristics or personality traits. Common, everyday parlance suggests that stereotypes are "bad." But, as with ethnocentrism, the situation is not that simple.

First, stereotypes can be either positive or negative. For example, a common positive stereotype is that Asians are hardworking, the "model minority." Another positive stereotype is that Germans are industrious and scientifically minded. Thus, although many stereotypes are negative, we should not forget that stereotypes can also be positive.

Second, stereotypes can be generally true or completely false. Stereotypes based on some degree of "factual" observation are called *sociotypes* (Triandis, 1994). But stereotypes can also be totally baseless. Because stereotypes can be perpetuated without direct observation of the behaviors of others, some stereotypes have no factual connection to the target group. Even when we convince ourselves that a stereotype is based on direct observations, we have to question the validity of those observations and the interpretations based on them because of the cultural and psychological biases inherent in those processes.

Finally, people hold stereotypes about their own groups as well as about other groups. Stereotypes about one's own group are called *auto-stereotypes,* while stereotypes about other groups are called *hetero-stereotypes.* In fact, there is often a considerable degree of overlap between a group's auto-stereotypes and the hetero-stereotypes that others hold about that group. Iwao and Triandis (1993), for example, asked Japanese and American undergraduates to respond to three scenarios describing conflicts among individuals and to rate stereotypes of Americans and Japanese. When respondents from the two different cultures were similar in their interpretations of an episode, the relationship between auto- and hetero-stereotypes was high; when they were dissimilar in their interpretations, the relationship was low. The Japanese viewed themselves as passively accepting inconsistencies between their public and private selves, acting according to group norms, whereas Americans tried to reduce the discrepancy between their private and public selves. Similarities between auto-stereotypes held by people about their own group and hetero-stereotypes about that group held by others have also been reported by Nichols and McAndrew (1984) and Walkey and Chung (1996).

Not only do we have auto- as well as hetero-stereotypes, but auto-stereotypes are just as variable as hetero-stereotypes. In one study (Nichols & McAndrew, 1984), for example, four groups of students—Americans in the United States, Americans living in Spain, Spaniards, and Malays—rated their stereotypes of Spanish, Malaysian, and American college students using seven pairs of bipolar adjectives. The results indicated unanimous or near unanimous agreement across the four groups on some stereotypes, and large disagreements on others. More important, the variability in auto-stereotypes was comparable to the variability in stereotypes of others, both within and across groups.

Thus, stereotypes can be either positive or negative, generally true or totally false, and held about one's own group as well as about other groups. Understanding not only a definition of stereotypes but the different ways in which they can manifest themselves is important to understanding their role in intergroup relations and improving those relationships.

The Content of Stereotypes

A number of studies spanning many years have examined the content of stereotypes. In one of oldest and most often cited studies, Katz and Braly (1933) involved undergraduates at Princeton University. In this study, the students were given a list of adjectives and were asked to select those they considered representative of ten different racial/ethnic groups. The 12 traits most frequently assigned to each group by the students are shown in Table 4.1.

This study was followed up on the same university campus in 1951 and again in 1967 (Karlins, Coffman, & Walters, 1969). The researchers found a number of surprising changes over the years, both in stereotypes and in the willingness to ascribe stereotypic traits to the various groups. Other researchers have conducted similar studies of American university students, using similar methodologies (for example, Clark & Person, 1982; Wood & Chesser, 1994).

These studies, and others like them (for example, Nichols & McAndrew, 1984; Smith, Griffith, Griffith, & Steger, 1980), used perhaps the most common approach to measuring stereotypes—providing participants with a list of adjectives describing psychological traits or characteristics and asking them to select those they considered representative of the target groups specified. More recent studies, however, have used more sophisticated methods and data analysis techniques to examine the possible psychological factors or dimensions that underlie such ratings. For example, Forgas and O'Driscoll (1984) asked participants from two cultures, Australia and Papua New Guinea, to give similarity ratings between pairs of 20 different countries. These similarity ratings were then subjected to a multidimensional scaling procedure that reduced the ratings to a limited number of underlying dimensions. The researchers found that three dimensions summarized the ratings for both cultural groups: European/non-European, communism/capitalism, and development (underdeveloped/developed). Although there were some differences between the two groups in the relative importance of each of these dimensions, both groups were similar in that the same dimensions described their ratings of the 20 countries.

Table 4.1 The Twelve Traits Most Frequently Assigned to Various Racial and National Groups by 100 Princeton Students

Traits	Frequency	Traits	Frequency	Traits	Frequency
Germans		Very religious	29	Aggressive	20
Scientifically minded	78	Industrious	21	Straightforward	19
Industrious	65	Extremely nationalistic	21	Practical	19
Stolid	44	Superstitious	18	Sportsmanlike	19
Intelligent	32	Quarrelsome	14		
Methodical	31	Imaginative	13	**Chinese**	
Extremely nationalistic	24	Aggressive	13	Superstitious	34
Progressive	16	Stubborn	13	Sly	29
Efficient	16			Conservative	29
Jovial	15	**English**		Tradition-loving	26
Musical	13	Sportsmanlike	53	Loyal to family ties	22
Persistent	11	Intelligent	46	Industrious	18
Practical	11	Conventional	34	Meditative	18
		Tradition-loving	31	Reserved	17
Italians		Conservative	30	Very religious	15
Artistic	53	Reserved	29	Ignorant	15
Impulsive	44	Sophisticated	27	Deceitful	14
Passionate	37	Courteous	21	Quiet	13
Quick-tempered	35	Honest	20		
Musical	32	Industrious	18	**Japanese**	
Imaginative	30	Extremely nationalistic	18	Intelligent	45
Very religious	21	Humorless	17	Industrious	43
Talkative	21			Progressive	24
Revengeful	17	**Jews**		Shrewd	22
Physically dirty	13	Shrewd	79	Sly	20
Lazy	12	Mercenary	49	Quiet	19
Unreliable	11	Industrious	48	Imitative	17
		Grasping	34	Alert	16
Negroes		Intelligent	29	Suave	16
Superstitious	84	Ambitious	21	Neat	16
Lazy	75	Sly	20	Treacherous	13
Happy-go-lucky	38	Loyal to family ties	15	Aggressive	13
Ignorant	38	Persistent	13		
Musical	26	Talkative	13	**Turks**	
Ostentatious	26	Aggressive	12	Cruel	47
Very religious	24	Very religious	12	Very religious	26
Stupid	22			Treacherous	21
Physically dirty	17	**Americans**		Sensual	20
Naïve	14	Industrious	48	Ignorant	15
Slovenly	13	Intelligent	47	Physically dirty	15
Unreliable	12	Materialistic	33	Deceitful	13
		Ambitious	33	Sly	12
Irish		Progressive	27	Quarrelsome	12
Pugnacious	45	Pleasure-loving	26	Revengeful	12
Quick-tempered	39	Alert	23	Conservative	12
Witty	38	Efficient	21	Superstitious	11
Honest	32				

Source: Katz & Braly, 1933.

Walkey and Chung (1996) recruited Chinese and European adolescents living in New Zealand, and asked them to rate both Chinese and Europeans on 21 pairs of adjectives. Before conducting any data analyses, the researchers subjected the ratings to a procedure known as factor analysis, which identifies the psychological factors underlying the ratings and reduces the ratings to a smaller number of factors. Two factors emerged from the data: work ethic, and social versus individual control. Both groups rated the Chinese as high on work ethic and moderate on individual versus social control. Both groups also rated the Europeans less positively on work ethic and more individually rather than socially controlled.

These last two studies exemplify more recent approaches to identifying and examining the content of stereotypes that people hold about themselves and others. Williams and Best (1994) used a similar approach in their research on gender stereotypes across countries and cultures (reported in Chapter 8), reducing 300 adjectives to a much more manageable and interpretable three scales. These approaches enable us to gain a better insight into the psychological structure of stereotypes in the people's minds and allow for improved research on this issue for years to come. Forgas and O'Driscoll (1984), for example, extended their findings by correlating the three underlying dimensions with demographic variables to see how the structure of stereotypes is associated with factors such as age, gender, and socioeconomic status. These approaches provide a much better understanding of stereotypes than previously offered in the literature.

The Development of Stereotypes: A Psychological Analysis

Stereotypes are products of normal, everyday psychological processes that lead, naturally and inevitably, to the formation and maintenance of stereotypes. To understand how stereotypes are developed and maintained, therefore, it is important to have a basic understanding of the psychological processes on which they are built. These processes include *selective attention, appraisal, concept formation and categorization, attributions, emotion,* and *memory*—all of which should be familiar to you from your introductory psychology classes. They are also discussed elsewhere throughout this book (for example, perception and memory in Chapter 6, emotion in Chapter 11, categorization of colors in Chapter 12, and appraisal in Chapter 11). Here I limit the discussion to a basic presentation of these principles as they relate specifically to stereotypes.

Selective attention.   Psychologists agree that the amount of stimulation we receive through our senses is too much for us to process and make sense of in our everyday lives. There is no way in which we can attend to all the signals and stimuli we receive from the world. Thus, we pick and choose which stimuli to attend to (for example, the words on this page, the voice of someone talking to you) and the sensory modalities or channels by which we will attend to them (for example, sight or hearing). This process is called **selective attention**. Generally studied by psychologists interested in perception, selective attention refers to the process by which we filter out many of the stimuli that bombard our senses, thus receiving a more meaningful, finite amount of information that we can then process. Because our sensation and perceptual systems have limited capacities, that is, we must learn ways to limit the amount of information we actually receive and process. Inherent in this selection process is a certain degree of bias. The cocktail party phenomenon illustrates this selection process: People can often hear their own names across the room at a party even though myriad other sounds are occurring at the same time.

Appraisal.   When we witness events or situations or engage with others, we are constantly appraising those stimuli (compare Lazarus, 1991). **Appraisal refers to the process by which we evaluate the relevance of stimuli in terms of their meaning to our lives.** On the basis of the appraisal process, we have emotional reactions, then make decisions concerning appropriate behavioral responses, which Lazarus (1991) refers to as *coping*. The process of appraisal is relevant to stereotypes because it provides a psychological mechanism by which we actively operate on incoming stimuli and process them in terms of their meaning to us.

Concept formation and categorization.   In our everyday lives, we encounter a multitude of stimuli—objects in the environment, people we meet, things we hear or say—and it is literally impossible for us to keep track of them all. That is, as our minds create mental representations of all of the people, places, events, situations, and activities with which we engage, it is impossible to represent all of these stimuli as single, independent units of information. Thus, we develop concepts by which we can mentally represent these events, situations, places, and people so that our minds can deal with them. A **concept** is a mental category we use to classify events, objects, situations, behaviors, or even people with respect to what we perceive as common properties.

We form concepts so that we can evaluate information, make decisions, and act accordingly. (Cultures differ on exactly what these common properties may be; this matter is discussed more fully in Chapter 6.) We use these common properties to aid us in classification or **categorization**, which refers to the process by which psychological concepts are grouped together. It is far easier and more efficient to create concepts or categories of information, and to evaluate and act on those categories than it is to process each individual item. In psychology, the study of concept formation involves examining how people classify or categorize events, objects, situations, and people into concepts.

Concept formation and categorization provide us with a way to organize the diversity of the world around us into a finite number of categories. Those categories, in turn, are based on particular properties of the objects that we perceive or deem to be similar in some psychologically meaningful way. For example, we may classify all objects of a certain color together, all types of facial expressions representing a particular emotion together, and so on. Once such concepts have formed, we can access the individual stimulus through the category, and gather information about that stimulus based on that category.

There are a variety of theories about how concept formation occurs. However, what is most germane to our discussion here is recognition of the existence of concepts and their general utility in organizing the world around us.

Attribution.   One common characteristic of people is a felt need to explain, in our own minds, the causes of events and behaviors. **Attribution** refers to this process by which we infer the causes of our own and other people's behavior. (This process was mentioned in Chapter 3 and will be discussed in more detail in Chapter16.)

Attributions serve important functions in our lives. They allow us to organize information in psychologically meaningful ways. This psychic organization is necessary at the very least because of the sheer number of events that occur around us. Some research has shown that attributions are related to control and that people who desire control are more likely than others to make attributions (Burger & Hemans, 1988). Attributions also help people to accommodate new information about their world and help resolve discrepancies between new and old ways of understanding the intentions and behaviors of others (Snyder & Higgins, 1988).

Emotion.   Emotions are an integral and important part of our normal, everyday lives. Emotions are important motivators of our behaviors, telling us to run when we are afraid and fight when we are angry (Tomkins, 1962, 1963). Emotions are important readout devices (Buck, 1984), telling us how we are interpreting the events and situations around us at a moment's notice. Emotions are also important interpersonal markers, informing us about the status of our relationships with others.

In the past decade, Forgas and his colleagues have reported an interesting and important line of research on the role of emotion in person perception, intergroup discrimination, and stereotype judgments. This research suggests the existence of mood-congruent bias in such judgments of others. In one study, for example, Forgas and Moylan (1991) induced happy, sad, or neutral moods in participants who then formed impressions about Asians or Caucasians interacting with same-race or other-race partners. Participants who were happy had more positive judgments of the target persons; participants who were sad had more negative judgments. In addition, the *degree* of influence of mood on judgment was larger when the participants were judging mixed-race dyads. On the basis of these and similar findings (for example, Forgas & Bower, 1987; Forgas & Fiedler, 1996), Forgas has suggested that the role of emotion or mood in these types of judgments may be greatest when participants engage in *substantive* processing, which requires them to select, learn, and interpret novel stimuli and to relate this information to preexisting knowledge (for a review of this affect infusion model, see Forgas, 1992, 1994).

By the same token, Forgas (1994) suggests that stereotype judgments of others are probably the least affected by emotion or mood, because these judgments involve a *direct* access strategy—the direct retrieval of preexisting information. Although this notion has not been tested directly, Forgas (1994) cites some evidence to support this claim (for example, Salovey & Birnbaum, 1989; Schwarz, Strack, Kommer, & Wagner, 1987; Srull, 1983, 1984). These studies, however, did not test two issues about emotion that I believe are important to the stereotypic judgment process. One concerns the warding off of negative emotion brought about by the mismatch of expectations due to one's cultural filters and the reality of differences. The second concerns the positive emotions of the stereotyping process that reinforce those processes and the sense of self that contains it. Thus, it would appear that emotion plays a much more important role in the stereotyping process than is elucidated by current research.

Memory.   Memory refers to our ability to remember past events, actions, people, objects, situations, learned skills, and so forth. It also refers to how we store such information. Psychologists generally differentiate among three subtypes of memory and memory-related processes: *sensory memory,* the initial coding of memory-related stimuli; *short-term memory,* the "working" memory that serves as an intermediary between sensory and long-term memory (Baddeley & Hitch, 1974); and *long-term memory,* the storage and retrieval of information over long, sometimes indefinite periods of time.

    Semantic memory is a special type of long-term memory for rules, ideas, and general concepts about the world, including other people; it is usually based on generalizations or images about events, experiences, and learned knowledge. Semantic memory can also be based on verbal knowledge communicated from one person to the next without any basis in actual experience or interaction with the target of the memory. It refers to knowledge that is gathered over a long period of time and continually modified or reinforced as the individual engages with related facts, events, or experiences (Bahrick & Hall, 1991). These properties of semantic memory make it especially relevant to our understanding of stereotypes.

Putting it all together.   All of the psychological processes discussed here interact to make stereotypes an inevitable aspect of our psychological life. Actually, as general categories of mental concepts, stereotypes are invaluable aids, helping us keep information about the world organized in our mental representations. We have such categorical representations about many objects in the world, and there is no way we could keep track of the world without them. Categorical representations of people happen to be called *stereotypes.*

    As a special type of category—that is, having to do with people—stereotypes are important in helping us interact effectively with, or act as a hindrance to, others in our world. The problem is that it is relatively easy for negative stereotypes to develop, because our own cultural upbringing, cultural filters, and ethnocentrism create a set of expectations in us about the behaviors and traits of others. When we observe people from a different cultural background, we are often exposed to behaviors, activities, or situations that do not match our initial expectations based on our own cultural backgrounds.

These observations can lead to negative attributions about the causes of those events, or the underlying intentions or psychological characteristics of the actors being observed. Because such events are unexpected, they often require what Forgas (1994) would call substantive processing, which is the type of processing most affected by induced emotion. If the emotion induced at the time is negative, which is a natural reaction to our witnessing something outside of our expectations, then that negative emotion will be more likely to contribute to negatively valenced attributions about the other person. Such negatively valenced attributions can form the core of a mental concept that may then be placed in a category of such people. This negative attribution will also have a reinforcing effect on the value and expectation system that began the process. The result is a negative stereotype.

Once developed, stereotypes are easily reinforced. Our expectations change according to our stereotypes. We may selectively attend to events that appear to support our stereotypes, ignoring, albeit unconsciously, events and situations that challenge those stereotypes. Our negative attributions may be reenacted, thus reinforcing the negative stereotypes held as categorical representations of that group of people.

Even when we attend to events that are contrary to our stereotypic beliefs, we often come up with unique attributional processes to convince ourselves that our stereotype is correct. We may suggest that the observed event was a fluke, or that the person observed was not a good representative of the group to which the stereotype applies. Such dismissals can occur quickly, with little conscious thought or effort, and are resistant to infusion of emotion at the time.

To suggest that our attention, attributional, and emotional processes may be biased is nothing new. Indeed, I have made this point throughout the first few chapters of this book, and will return to it in later chapters as well. These and other psychological processes make up an integrated psychological system that we know of as our sense of self or self-concept. The core concept underlying the entire discussion in this section is that these psychological processes are all biased so as to reinforce that self-concept. Our emotions, attributions, and attention processes are all constructed so as to help us reinforce the cultural knowledge we have learned from many years of enculturation and socialization. Even the content of our stereotypes probably serves to reinforce our sense of self; as we confirm those stereotypes, we are reinforcing that self-concept.

Thus, stereotypes are an integral and important part of a complete package of psychological processes that constitute our sense of self and self-concept. They are intimately tied to our emotions, values, and core self, and as such, are difficult to change once we acquire them. Yet other factors, too, contribute to the formation and maintenance of stereotypes.

Other Contributing Factors

Stereotypes may develop from several different sources. One, as we have seen, is ethnocentrism. When we observe the behavior of others, we perceive that behavior and make interpretations (attributions) about underlying causes based on rules we have learned from our own cultural upbringing. Those interpretations serve as mental categories or concepts that help us organize and assimilate information about people. As we grow up, we may selectively attend to particular behaviors and even ignore the existence of evidence or behaviors to the contrary, reinforcing the mental categories we have created. These categories are stored as verbal labels in long-term memory and play a major role in the way we interact with the world. All of these processes may be influenced by personal preference, cultural factors, and the like, and all are open to errors in the processing of information. Because of the cyclical nature of the interaction between basic psychological processes and our culturally based ethnocentrism, these processes form a feedback loop, reinforcing errors and creating and maintaining mental categories of people we come to know as stereotypes.

Stereotypes may also be created and perpetuated in individuals merely by communication of verbal labels from generation to generation, with no actual interaction with the people who are the target of the stereotype (Brislin, 1993). Stereotypes can be created and reinforced by television, movies, magazines, and other media. Stereotypes may be formed through limited exposure to members of the target group or to exposure based on a "biased" sample. Thus, stereotypes can be formed and reinforced in a person on the basis of very limited exposure, or no exposure at all, to the target group. The complex interplay of these external factors with our own cultural and psychological processes make stereotypes a difficult problem to deal with.

Sometimes a stereotype is a product of our own observation of something we have interpreted as negative. Because of our need to classify information about people and to verify such classifications based on selective attention and memory processes, we often associate our interpretations with inferred traits of the target person, generalize those traits to observable, *identifiable characteristics* of that person (for example, skin color), and then make a *generalizable statement* that can be used to describe all people sharing that identifiable characteristic. Thus, we come up with statements such as "Blacks, or Japanese, or Hispanics, or Jews are ————." To be sure, many stereotypes are associated with groups whose defining characteristics are not visible—such as lawyers or homosexuals—and these stereotypes are equally limiting, intense, and resistant to change.

Whether positive or negative, stereotypes are generally limiting and potentially discriminatory. This is so because stereotypes as mental categories of people tend to take on a life of their own. Rather than using stereotypes as "best guess" generalizations about a group of people, which we then adjust based on interactions with specific individuals, we often use stereotypes as a rigid set of assumptions about all people of that group, regardless of individual differences or evidence to the contrary. Data (that is, actual observed behavior) that might seem to challenge the stereotype will be "massaged" to the point where they can be used to support the stereotype. Data that cannot be reinterpreted to support the stereotype will simply be discarded as random chance occurrences. Stereotypes used in this way become more and more entrenched because all our experiences serve to reinforce the stereotype, regardless of how true or false it is.

Stereotypes exist, even in the most pluralistic of people. What is important is how we go beyond them, using them only as basic guides to interacting with people of other cultural backgrounds. As guides, stereotypes are not written in stone but give us ideas, impressions, or images of people that can be used for an initial encounter, after which they can be discarded or reinforced depending on the exact nature of the interaction and behavior observed.

There is a fine line between using a generalization as a guide and using a stereotype to vindicate your personal view of the world. Vindicating your view of the world by using stereotypes rigidly and inflexibly allows you only a limited view of the world, its people and events. Vindicating your view of the world by using stereotypes inflexibly also provides a framework within which prejudice and discrimination are likely to occur.

Prejudice, Discrimination, and "Isms"

Prejudice

Although ethnocentrism and stereotypes are normal and inevitable consequences of daily psychological functioning and enculturation into society, they often form the basis of limited and detrimental patterns of thinking about, and dealing with, others in the world. These processes are called prejudice, discrimination, and a host of terms ending with the suffix -ism.

Prejudice refers to the tendency to *prejudge* others on the basis of their group membership. That is, prejudiced people think about others solely in terms of their stereotypes. The term *prejudice* is often used to describe the tendency to think of others in a negative way, based on a negative stereotype. But just as stereotypes can be both positive and negative, so too can people be prejudiced in both positive and negative ways.

Although ethnocentrism and stereotypes are normal and inevitable consequences of psychological functioning, prejudice is not. Prejudice results solely from an individual's inability to realize the limitations in his or her ethnocentric and stereotypic thinking. Those individuals who realize that they have stereotypes, that their stereotypes may or may not be accurate, and that stereotypes never describe all the members of any group, are less likely to be prejudiced. Those who do not recognize the limitations in their ethnocentric and stereotypic thinking, and who do not even recognize that their ethnocentrism and stereotypes exist, will be more likely to exhibit prejudicial thinking about themselves as well as others.

Prejudice can have two components: a cognitive (thinking) component, and an affective (feeling) component. Stereotypes form the basis of the cognitive component of prejudice—the stereotypic beliefs, opinions, and attitudes one harbors toward others. The affective component comprises one's personal feelings toward other groups of people. These feelings may include anger, contempt, resentment, or disdain, or even compassion, sympathy, and closeness. Although the cognitive and affective components are often related, they need not be, and may actually exist independently of each other within the same person. That is, a person may have feelings about a particular group of people without being able to specify a stereotype about them; and a person may have stereotypic beliefs about others that are detached from their feelings.

Discrimination

Most social scientists make a distinction between prejudice and discrimination. Whereas prejudice involves stereotypic cognitions and/or feelings about groups of people, **discrimination** typically refers to the unfair treatment of others based on their group membership. That is, the difference between prejudice and discrimination is the difference between thinking/feeling (prejudice), on the one hand, and doing (discrimination), on the other.

Like stereotypes and prejudice, discrimination can include preferential or positive treatment as well as deferred or negative treatment. If one harbors positive stereotypes about a group of people and is prejudiced in their favor, for example, one may engage in behaviors that actively promote or enhance individual members of that group solely on the basis of their group membership. Of course, discrimination is often negative, resulting in unfair, less favorable treatment of others. The important issue in defining discrimination revolves around the concept of fairness and treatment based on group membership.

Although prejudice and discrimination are often linked, they need not be. Merton (1968) highlighted the ways in which prejudice and discrimination may be related to each other in any single person. Those who are unprejudiced may or may not discriminate, and those who discriminate may or may not be prejudiced.

Prejudice and discrimination are processes that occur on the individual level. When similar processes occur on the group or organizational level, they are known as various –isms and institutional discrimination.

"Isms" and Institutional Discrimination

Racism, classism, and sexism are just a few of the many examples of the prejudicial thoughts and feelings that can be harbored by large groups of people about other groups based on their biological, sociological, or psychological characteristics. The particular characteristic used is generally attached to the -*ism* suffix. Thus, racism is group-based prejudicial thought based on race, classism is prejudice based on social class, and sexism is prejudice based on sex.

Although prejudice can be either positive or negative in content, -isms are usually negative and derogatory, used to justify inferior status on the part of the people being characterized. While the term *prejudice* describes preferential thoughts and feelings held by an individual, -isms are used to describe prejudices that are held by one group of people about another. As such, they generally constitute systems of ideas, beliefs, and opinions held by a large group of people, and are often woven into the social and cultural fabric of that group.

Thus, they constitute an ideology, and as such, can be communicated from one generation to the next, much as other elements of culture are communicated (see Healey, 1998).

Institutional discrimination is discrimination that occurs on the level of a large group, society, organization, or institution. It is unequal or unfair patterns of behavior or preferential treatment of people by a large group or organization solely on the basis of group membership. These patterns of treatment may or may not be conscious and deliberate. Allegations concerning such institutional discrimination are all around us in the daily news, involving the educational system, places of business and work, the legal and criminal justice systems, and professional sports.

One of the most immediate and controversial issues regarding possible institutional discrimination concerns affirmative action policies in admissions to colleges and universities. At the time of this writing, for example, California has voted to repeal affirmative action admissions procedures in the University of California system. Proponents of the repeal point to data suggesting that, despite many years of affirmative action policies for underrepresented populations, there has been no real change in the numbers of people from these groups being educated because many drop out or fail. They also point to the cost of remedial education needed to compensate for poor academic preparation, detracting from the university's ability to provide quality education to those students who were admitted based on non–affirmative action criteria.

On the other side, opponents of the repeal point to their own data suggesting that affirmative action policies were working to educate far greater numbers of individuals from underrepresented groups. They suggest that other problems, such as the need for remediation, merely highlight the other racist and discriminatory programs and policies of the university system and society as a whole.

This debate promises to continue for years to come, in California and throughout the United States. As we as a population engage in these debates, it is important to study both sides of the issue, leaving our individual prejudices aside, and to weigh the pros and cons of any proposed policy changes with an open mind. In doing so, we need to keep in mind all of the possible ramifications of such policies, not only in terms of their overt consequences for education, but also in terms of their social and psychological consequences.

A recent study by Maio and Esses (1998) throws an interesting light on this subject. These authors examined the degree to which knowledge about affirmative action policies may produce negative perceptions about people who benefit from such policies. They presented participants with a fictitious editorial describing an unfamiliar group in a positive manner. In one condition, the editorial indicated that the group benefited from affirmative action policies; in another condition, there was no mention of such benefit. When affirmative action was mentioned, participants expressed less favorable perceptions of and attitudes toward the group. The participants even expressed less favorable attitudes toward immigration by the group, and toward immigration in general.

These findings highlight the need for us, as psychologists and concerned citizens of the world, to gather as much data as possible about social and psychological consequences of programs and policies related to allegations of -isms or institutional discrimination and to become fully educated and informed about issues.

Origins of and Factors Contributing to Prejudice

Social scientists have been concerned for many years about the factors that contribute to the origin and maintenance of prejudice and discrimination. By far the most common theories involve issues of intergroup conflict and power. In general, these theories (see review in Healey, 1998) suggest that the competition that naturally occurs among groups in any society—whether for power, prestige, status, or wealth—produces prejudicial and discriminatory thoughts, feelings, and actions among both those in power (the "haves") and those without (the "have-nots"). Such prejudice and discrimination on both sides, but especially on the part of the haves, can serve as a justification to exploit the have-nots. As such prejudice and discrimination require an identifying variable or characteristic to which they can become attached, race, ethnicity, or social class is often used as that marker (see also Mirande, 1985; Moore, 1988).

Another argument that has gained attention in recent history is that prejudice and discrimination are inevitable outcomes of social biology and evolution (see, for example, van der Berghe, 1981). This argument suggests that sentiments about ethnicity and race are logical extensions of kinship sentiment—that is, the favoring of kin over nonkin. Kinship sentiments are biologically and evolutionarily functional, increasing the likelihood of one's own genes being transmitted to future generations. Because racial and ethnic groups can be viewed as extensions of kin, these sentiments may predispose people to behave more favorably to such kin. If kinship sentiments do apply to ethnicity and race, this argument continues, prejudice and discrimination may indeed be fundamental and inevitable.

Other factors have also been suggested as contributing to the origin and maintenance of prejudice and discrimination. Some theories focus on social and cultural factors, suggesting that society promotes ideological prejudice and institutional discrimination in order to impose inferior status on some groups. This inferior status, in turn, reinforces the ideological prejudice and institutional discrimination, which themselves further reinforce the inferior status. Children growing up in such societies, whether as members of the "inferior" or the "superior" group, become enculturated in these ways of thinking, feeling, and acting, which become a part of their own operating culture, thus ensuring the reenactment of this cycle of exploitation.

A study by Hampel and Krupp (1977) highlights the importance of cultural factors over other social and political factors in maintaining prejudicial stereotypes. This study assessed prejudicial attitudes in three samples of participants: Britons in England; Caucasian, English-speaking South Africans;

and Caucasian, Afrikaans-speaking South Africans. Attitudes were assessed about racial minorities in England (for the British sample), and about the Bantu in South Africa. The results indicated that English-speaking South Africans were more similar in their attitudes to Britons in England than to the Afrikaans-speaking South Africans, even though the latter group shared the same social and political environment. Two earlier studies involving South African high schoolers (Orpen, 1971a, 1971b) also confirmed the strong relationship between adherence to cultural norms among English-speaking South Africans and prejudicial attitudes, above and beyond the existence of personality variables thought to contribute to prejudice.

Other theories have focused on aspects of personality that contribute to the formation and maintenance of prejudice and discrimination. Of particular note is the work on the relationship between authoritarian personality and prejudice (Adorno, 1950, cited in Healey, 1998). This work suggests that prejudicial thoughts and feelings and discriminatory behaviors are an integral part of authoritarian personalities, and that people with such personalities in fact require prejudicial thoughts and feelings to function effectively in their lives and in society.

More recent research, however, suggests a more precise relationship between authoritarianism and prejudice. Verkuyten and Hagendoorn (1998), for example, conducted two studies that examined the interaction of self-categorization, authoritarian personality, ingroup stereotypes, and prejudicial attitudes. Participants were instructed to focus on themselves either as unique individuals (personal identity condition) or as members of a larger group (national identity condition). They also completed an authoritarian personality questionnaire, provided data about their stereotypes regarding their own group, and rated three different outgroups in terms of prejudicial attitudes. The results indicated that authoritarian personality predicted prejudicial attitudes only when the participants focused on their personal identities. When participants focused on their national identities, their ingroup stereotypes predicted their prejudicial attitudes, but individual differences on the authoritarian measure did not. These findings suggest that personality variables may be salient only when the reference for prejudicial thought is oneself as an individual, and not as a member of a larger group.

Recent research is also beginning to explore the bases of institutional racism and discrimination. Jeanquart-Barone and Sekaran (1996), for example, tested employees of a national, predominantly minority, organization. Participants provided data on perceived racism in their organization, supportiveness of the climate at work, perceived supervisory discrimination, general supervisory support, procedural justice, and indoctrination—the degree to which the employees' values meshed with those of the organization. The results indicated that the last five variables were all significant predictors of institutional racism. In particular, supportive climate was negatively correlated with racism; that is, higher levels of a supportive climate were associated with decreased perceptions of institutional racism. Perceived supervisory discrimination, in contrast, was positively correlated with institutional racism.

Which of these factors is responsible for prejudice and discrimination, both on the individual and group levels? The answer, of course, is all of them—intergroup power conflicts, sociobiology, sociocultural history, personality, and others. There is no single cause of prejudice and discrimination—which is why they plague so many societies of the world today, and why it is often so difficult to work through these issues. Still, it is important to try, especially as we continue in the rest of this book to uncover differences around the world in psychology and behavior.

Going Beyond Prejudice and Discrimination

Recognizing One's Own Ethnocentrism and Stereotypic Thinking

While ethnocentrism and stereotypes may be inevitable, there is a fine but important distinction between them and prejudice and discrimination. Whether people "cross the line" between prejudicial and nonprejudicial thought depends, first, on whether they recognize their own ethnocentrism, and stereotypic thoughts. Individuals who are unaware of the inevitably ethnocentric basis of their own worldviews will not likely be able to recognize that other worldviews are possible. Likewise, individuals who are unaware of the stereotypic biases in their thoughts, attitudes, and opinions will not be able to recognize that those attitudes cannot accurately describe all the individuals with whom they come in contact. Without recognizing one's own ethnocentrism and stereotypic thinking, one cannot develop empathy in another person's viewpoint and worldview. And empathy, as we will see at the end of this book, is the key to true intercultural sensitivity.

Only those individuals who realize that ethnocentrism and stereotypic thoughts are normal and inevitable psychological processes have the ability to recognize the limitations inherent in those processes. Recognizing one's own ethnocentrism makes it possible to recognize the existence of a separate, and potentially different, ethnocentrism in others. Likewise, recognizing the stereotypic attitudes in one's own thinking enables one to recognize the limits and fallibility of stereotypes. Thus, a major first step in moving beyond prejudice and discrimination is to increase awareness of ethnocentrism and stereotypes, their inevitability and their inherent limitations.

Working to Reduce Prejudice

Because prejudicial attitudes are based on fixed and rigid stereotypes, methods to reduce prejudicial thought would necessarily include intervention on the level of those stereotypes. If the first step is to recognize the existence of stereotypes, the next step is to recognize their inherent limitations:

1. Stereotypes are based on interpretations we produce based on our own cultural filters and background, or on communication from external sources.
2. Stereotypes are often associated with identifiable characteristics.
3. Stereotypes are generalizations about a group of people.

By examining each of these three points, we can find ways to use stereotypes more flexibly.

Our interpretations may be wrong, based on wrong facts or no facts. Our stereotypes are based on interpretations we have made about the underlying meaning, psychological characteristic, or personality trait of a person. These interpretations are based on the cultural rules we have learned that are applicable to ourselves and they are made about behavior observed through our own cultural filters. In some cases, stereotypes may not be based on facts at all, having simply been told to us by others or reinforced by the media.

Other people may engage in behavior we interpret to be rude or offensive, as viewed through our own cultural filters. In fact, that behavior may not have been intended as rude or offensive from the other person's viewpoint. Furthermore, the behavior we observed may not even be the behavior that actually occurred, because our cultural filters may have distorted our perceptions of it or because we selectively attended to parts of an action sequence but not the whole. Thus, it may be that our perceptions of the event and/or our interpretations of its underlying causes are incorrect. When interacting with people of a culture that is obviously different from our own, the potential for being mistaken is much larger than when interacting with someone of the same culture.

On the other hand, your interpretations may be correct, despite the fact that you and the other person come from different cultural backgrounds. It may be the case that the person was trying to be rude and offensive. You may actually be correct in your perceptions and interpretations—or you may not be. The point is that we don't really know. All we know is that we perceive events and behaviors and make interpretations about those events and behaviors based on our own cultural filters and rules. We may not know whether we are exactly correct in our perceptions and interpretations (although there are times when we are more sure of our interpretations than others). We usually believe that we are absolutely, entirely correct, because we interpret the world through our own cultural filters. But the very fact that we may be incorrect should make us more flexible in our assumptions about others and their behaviors. When we are mistaken in our judgments, the costs can be high, whether in business, love, or everyday relationships.

The characteristics we identify are often selected without reason. In creating stereotypes, we generally associate our images and impressions with identifiable characteristics of a group of people. Oftentimes, these characteristics are racial or ethnic; thus, we hear that African Americans, Asians, or Hispanics are a certain way. But race and ethnicity are not the only types of visible characteristics for which we have stereotypes. Stereotypes also exist about other observable, physical characteristics. Thus, we hear stereotypes about blondes or redheads. Sometimes stereotypes are formed on the basis of other characteristics that identify a group of people, such as lawyers, homosexuals, or politicians.

Why do we define our stereotypes according to characteristics that identify groups? The answer lies in basic psychological processes related to concept formation and categorization. With such categories, it is easier for us to summarize the wealth of information about the world around us. Indeed, it is impossible to keep track of all the possible information about people we come in contact with. One of the easiest ways to group or categorize is by observable, physical characteristics. Thus, it is easy to make generalizations or stereotypes on the basis of race, because racial differences are generally visible and easy to verify. Because they are easy to verify, such stereotypes can also be reinforced rather easily. Besides race, it is also easy to make stereotypes based on sex or class or occupation. Thus, we have stereotypes about men and women, rich and poor, lawyers, doctors, and many other groups.

This aspect of stereotypes highlights how they are limited. The important elements of stereotypes are not the characteristics we can see but the aspects of the person we cannot observe. It is this invisible aspect of people that produces differences and diversity in the first place; this invisible aspect is culture. Indeed, it is culture as a sociopsychological phenomenon, and not race, sex, class, or occupation, that produces differences in behavior. Learned patterns of behaviors, rituals, values, attitudes, and opinions produce behavior differences. Neither race, sex, class, nor occupation per se can produce such differences; culture can and does. Other authors writing on ethnic and race relations, including Steele (1990), Taylor (1992), Sowell (1983), and Steinberg (1989), have expressed the same idea in different ways. It is the central message of Martin Luther King's "I Have a Dream" speech.

Generalizations about a group may not describe any single individual within the group.   Stereotypes are generalizations about a group of individuals that share some identifiable characteristic. Aside from whether those generalizations are true, we must also realize that within any group there are considerable individual differences. For example, saying that African Americans, Asians, or Hispanics are ———, even if the generalization has some validity, doesn't mean that each and every African American, Asian, or Hispanic person you meet is ———. As with any other aspect of culture, there are bound to be individual differences in the degree to which any description of a culture or group of people applies to specific individuals within the group. Some people will indeed be rude and offensive; others will be polite and deferent. Some will be untrustworthy and devious; others will be totally trustworthy and forthright.

A stereotype, or any statement about a group of people, is *at best* merely a summary of a tendency of the group as a whole. (At worst, it reflects a generalization about a group of people that has no basis in fact and serves as an excuse for discrimination.) As with any summary, there are bound to be people that summary fits and those it doesn't fit. While group tendencies may differ substantially, individuals within those groups may or may not differ at all, depending on their individual placement within their respective groups.

We need to challenge the bases of group stereotypes and the generalizations underlying them. We need to recognize individual differences within groups and the fact that no stereotype can adequately describe all people within a certain group. Stereotypes are not likely to disappear. It is human nature to develop guidelines and to use categories and groups to store the wealth of information about people that we gain in our lives. We cannot ignore stereotypes, but we can realize their potential abuses and use them more wisely. Stereotypes should be used as guidelines for interaction, not as rigid and inflexible descriptors of people. We need to validate or invalidate stereotypes, not use them to vindicate ourselves. Only by understanding the bases for stereotypes can we begin the process of using them better.

Working to Reduce Discrimination

One of the most important aspects of the stereotypic thought process that contributes to discrimination is the emotions involved. As noted earlier, negative emotions are often infused in the stereotypic thought process, because negative emotions are likely consequences of mismatches between reality and one's expectations based on culture. As the research by Forgas and his colleagues suggests, these negative emotions may color the attributions people make about such mismatches and the other people involved, and these negative attributions may be precisely those that are committed to long-term memory. As stereotypic attitudes crystallize, this process becomes less affected by emotion infusion (direct access judgments), while positive emotions that occur because of a match between perceived reality and held stereotypes reinforce this system.

As negative emotions about outgroups and self-serving emotions reinforce stereotypic attitudes (prejudice), they serve as the primary motivators for behavior and action, and thus form the basis for discrimination. Again, the major difference between prejudice and discrimination is that discrimination involves external actions or behaviors against outgroup others, whereas prejudice involves internal thoughts or feelings. Once negative and self-serving emotions are activated, it may very well be human nature for people to regress in their level of critical and open thinking, to revert back to a more primitive cognitive style. Witness young children who get hurt or angry; once overcome by their emotions, their thinking reverts back to a more primitive level—a phenomenon known as *regression*. Adults are no different. Once we feel hurt or angry, it is only natural to revert to a more primitive way of thinking and to respond behaviorally by lashing out and treating others unfairly—in short, by discriminating against others.

It thus follows that one of the most important ways of working to reduce discrimination (in addition to recognizing our own ethnocentrism and stereotypes and thinking critically about the limitations of those stereotypes) is learning to control our emotions. We need to be able to regulate our negative emotions when they occur, as well as our positive, reinforcing emotions when they are challenged. Only if we can regulate such emotional processes in ourselves can we then engage in other critical thinking exercises, examining the possible biases in our thoughts, feelings, and actions and adjusting them accordingly. Without the ability to regulate emotions, such higher-order thought processes are impossible. We will discuss these processes in greater detail in the final chapter of this book.

⬚ Conclusion

Improving our understanding of ethnocentrism and stereotypes, and their contribution to prejudice and discrimination, is extremely important in today's world. Despite the steps we have taken in recent decades to close the gap between different groups of people, especially racial groups, the 1992 riots in Los Angeles and the recurring cries to "Buy American!" both speak to the strong and pervasive sentiments of group identification that can have negative or positive effects.

One of the first steps to improving our understanding of intergroup relations is improving our understanding of culture—notably, the influence of culture on basic psychological processes and the formation and maintenance of ethnocentrism and stereotypes. Improving our understanding of culture and its influences, however, is only one of many steps along the road. We need to search our own culture to discover the reasons these stereotypes have persisted and how our own culture may be fostered or facilitated by their maintenance. We need to recognize the existence of considerable individual variability within groups and cultures. We need to recognize the limitations of our own ethnocentrism, and of vindictive, limited stereotyping. By recognizing group and individual differences and by acknowledging rather than ignoring their influences, we are free to allow ourselves to engage with people on a common ground rather than prejudging their actions, behaviors, and reasons via stereotypes based entirely on our ground or theirs.

The study of culture reveals the importance of cultural background, upbringing, and heritage and their impact on our behaviors. Many of our behaviors as adults are not only shaped by culture but also draw their meaning from culture. Recognizing the important contributions of culture to actions, behaviors, and the reasons behind them helps us to understand, respect, and appreciate those differences when we observe them in real life.

This material is presented early in the book in order to familiarize you with these processes prior to your engaging with the material that follows. Undoubtedly, as you go on and engage with the rest of the book, you will discover many differences as well as similarities among people in their thoughts, feelings, actions, and behaviors. You will engage with that material with your ethnocentric cultural filters on, and through the lens of your stereotypic attitudes. Hopefully, because of the material presented in this chapter, you will be able to recognize your own ethnocentrism and stereotypic thinking as you engage with that material. Hopefully, you will be able to catch yourself if you start to cross the line from that ethnocentrism and those stereotypes to prejudice or discrimination. Hopefully, you will engage in critical thinking about some of the characteristics of those stereotypes, and regulate your emotional reactions.

Several studies over the years have highlighted the potential contribution of increased intercultural experiences to the reduction of inflexible ethnocentric attitudes, fixed stereotypes, prejudice, and discrimination (for example, Bochner & Perks, 1971; Vornberg & Grant, 1976). Many of these studies have focused on intercultural experiences gained by participants' traveling and living in cultures other than those in which they were enculturated. In that vein, it is my hope that you can engage with the rest of the material in this book as a sort of intercultural journey into the psychology of people of different cultural backgrounds. Hopefully, that experience can help increase your level of intercultural sensitivity.

And what are we to do if we are the victims of prejudice and discrimination? One of the first avenues of coping, based on the analyses presented in this chapter, is to recognize the limitations and origins of such thoughts, feelings, and actions in others. Unfortunately, in many instances we have little recourse concerning the limitations in others' thoughts or actions, as people will change only if they want to change. Recent research has also highlighted some attributional processes as well as psychological disengagement as important coping mechanisms for members of negatively stereotyped groups (Major, Spencer, Schmader, Wolfe, & Crocker, 1998; Moghaddam, Taylor, Lambert, & Schmidt, 1995).

The material in this chapter is some of the most difficult to write about because it is so emotionally charged. Almost everyone you talk with will have an opinion, sometimes a strong one, about these issues. These issues are so charged, in fact, that we become afraid to engage in what could be healthy discussion for fear of offending others or revealing supposed "biases" on our part. Although the material presented here is undoubtedly influenced by my own views, the most important point is that this presentation can serve as a springboard for healthy discussion about these most difficult topics. Whether you agree with the material presented here or not, I hope the interactions that result from the thoughts it stimulates will exhibit the type of tolerance for widely divergent opinions that the topic deserves.

Glossary

appraisal The process by which we evaluate the relevance of stimuli in terms of their meaning to our lives.

attribution The process by which we infer the causes of our own and other people's behavior.

categorization The process by which psychological concepts are grouped together.

concept A mental category we use to classify events, objects, situations, behaviors, or even people with respect to what we perceive as common properties.

discrimination The unfair treatment of others based on their group membership.

ethnocentrism The tendency to view the world through one's own cultural filters.

flexible ethnocentrism Ethnocentrism in which people can learn ways of putting on hold, however temporarily, their ethnocentrism and perceptions of and reactions to reality based on their cultural filters and interpret the behaviors of others from the others' perspective.

inflexible ethnocentrism Ethnocentrism that is characterized by an inability to go outside one's own perspective and view the behavior of others from the others' cultural perspective.

institutional discrimination Discrimination that occurs on the level of a large groups, society, organization, or institution.

prejudice The tendency to prejudge others on the basis of their group membership.

selective attention The process by which we filter out many of the stimuli that bombard our senses, thus receiving a more meaningful, finite amount of information that we can then process.

semantic memory A special type of long-term memory for rules, ideas, and general concepts about the world, including other people; it is usually based on generalizations or images about events, experiences, and learned knowledge.

stereotypes Generalized images we have about groups of people, particularly about their underlying psychological characteristics or personality traits.

5

Evaluating Cross-Cultural Research

Why It Is Important to Understand
Cross-Cultural Research Methods

This chapter discusses special issues specific to the conduct of cross-cultural research. This material is important to learn because the ability to read and understand cross-cultural research is an integral part of learning about the relationship between culture and psychology. It is a skill that is crucial to understanding and evaluating the work that will be presented in the remainder of the book. It is a skill that many of you will need in other parts of a course on cross-cultural psychology, such as conducting literature reviews and evaluating that literature. And it is a skill that many of you will need in your continued work in the field, conducting your own studies and evaluating those of others.

Not only is it important to be able to read and understand cross-cultural research; you also need to be able to evaluate it on its own merits. As active consumers of research in your everyday and academic lives, cross-cultural and mainstream, you need to approach reviewing research with a critical (but fair and open) mind and eye. You need to accept information or conclusions not because your teacher told it to you, or because you read about it in an abstract or discussion section of a paper. Instead, you need to be able to access the literature directly, read everything about a study from the theoretical framework and hypotheses through the methods of data collection and analysis to the interpretation of the findings, and make up your own mind as to whether you believe the findings are valid and reliable. You need to have established criteria for making those judgments, and you need to know which questions to raise when reviewing that research.

This chapter presents a set of relevant questions and criteria. Armed with this information, you will be able to read and evaluate cross-cultural research critically and systematically—research that will be presented in the remainder of the book, as well as other studies in this field. If some of you go on to conduct your own cross-cultural studies, these same questions and criteria can serve as guidelines for your own work, to ensure that your studies will produce valid and reliable information.

In this chapter, I will first review the place and importance of research in the production of knowledge in psychology, discuss our roles as consumers of that research, and briefly introduce different types of research approaches in psychology. Next, I will give a brief outline of the types of issues and decisions most researchers face in conducting hypothesis-testing studies. Then, I will discuss in detail the specific issues involved in cross-cultural research, from theory to method to data to interpretation. Finally, I will provide you with a chart that you can use to systematically review research on your own.

The Nature of Truth in Psychology and the Importance of Research

Validity, Reliability, and Replication

As we discussed in Chapter 1, psychology as a discipline relies on research to test theories and generate knowledge. Cross-cultural psychologists who are interested in generating knowledge about cultural diversity and its influences on human behavior are no different in that reliance. Research is the primary way all scientists generate reliable knowledge about the world.

Truth and principle in psychology are not generated easily. Instead, scientists infer truth from research only after research findings have met multiple sets of criteria for validity and reliability. **Validity** refers to the degree to which a finding, measurement, or statistic is accurate, or represents what it is supposed to. **Reliability** refers to the degree to which a finding, measurement, or statistic is consistent. If findings are not reliable or valid, they are not considered true.

The first set of criteria that a finding must meet applies to every study. As we will discuss below, every study is designed with a specific purpose in mind, and its methods are designed to achieve certain goals. The methods that are used to collect and analyze data must themselves meet specific criteria for validity and reliability in order for the findings that are generated from that study to be accepted by the scientific community.

A second set of criteria that a finding must meet applies to multiple studies on the same topic. No matter how well any single study is conducted, most scientists and scholars will not accept its results as a general truth or principle, because every study on human behavior is conducted under certain conditions or research parameters that limit the results obtained from that study. Scientists are interested in the robustness—the strength and consistency— of findings despite differences in the methods used to study them.

The concept that research findings may be limited to the parameters and conditions of the studies that generated them applies to all areas of psychology. The very existence of multiple measures of similar constructs (for example, self-concept, intelligence, personality) suggests the possibility that differences in methods can create differences in findings. Even the statistical procedures used to analyze data within a study comprise a parameter and condition of the findings, and findings may change when these procedures are changed. In one study on the relationship between expressive behavior and affective experience, for example, Ruch (1995) placed participants in one of three alcohol-consuming conditions, and showed them slides containing jokes or cartoons. Five different analytic procedures were employed, some involving within-subject analyses (analyzing data for each participant) and some involving between-subject analyses (analyzing data across participants). Findings were different for the two methods, with within-subject analyses producing the greatest indices of relationship between the expression behaviors and subjective experience.

Thus, for a research result about human behavior to be considered a truth, virtually the same study must be conducted repeatedly, with different participants, under different parameters and conditions. If a researcher obtains the same finding, despite having changed a number of parameters of the research, we can say that the findings are reliable—that is, they are consistent across studies. These studies may be conducted by the same researcher or research team, or by separate, independent researchers. In either case, when the same, or virtually the same, result is obtained, we call this repeated finding a **replication**. Only when findings are replicated will scholars and scientists start to believe that the findings say something about human behavior. Replicated findings form the basis for "truths" in academia and science. Truth, therefore, is heavily dependent on how the research was conducted.

Being a Consumer of Research

In addition to the scientists who actually do the research and conduct studies on human behavior, many teachers and students are active consumers of the research of others. They search for research relevant to their interests, read and evaluate the reports, and digest them well enough to communicate their cumulative results to others. Research, therefore, plays a major role not only in generating knowledge and testing ideas but also in communicating that knowledge to others. Many of you who read this book may never personally conduct a study in psychology, cross-cultural or otherwise. But almost all of you will be affected by research, and will have to review and evaluate research as part of your educational and professional careers.

To be an active, informed, and critical receiver of knowledge, you cannot simply read a study and accept its findings or claims solely because it was published. You need to be able to read, understand, and then evaluate all aspects of a study, from its theoretical framework and design to the nature of its statistical analyses and interpretation of findings. You need to be able to judge for yourselves whether you agree or disagree with the outcomes of the studies, and to formulate the reasons why you agree or disagree. In short, you need to be able to think critically about research in order to consume it properly, not just swallow it whole as if it were always true.

As an informed consumer of knowledge, if you read a study that employed what you believed were faulty methods and procedures, you wouldn't (and shouldn't) believe the results of that study, no matter how attractive or politically correct those results appear. On the other hand, if you found those methods and procedures to be problem-free and the data generated by those procedures believable, you would (and should) have confidence in the results. But to make these decisions, you need a working understanding of research methods and statistics, and of the general parameters and conditions under which most studies are conducted.

When reviewing research, you need to pay particular attention to two sections: Methods and Results (statistical analyses and findings). To the untrained eye, these sections of any research article are the most boring and seemingly irrelevant; many people skim or even skip them, concentrating instead on the "interesting stuff" in the introduction and discussion sections. But to the trained eye, the material in the Methods and Results sections is *the* most important aspect of any article. It is there that critical readers and evaluators must make their judgments about the validity and reliability of the procedures used and the findings reported.

Different Types of Research in Psychology

Psychologists actually engage in many different types of research, differentiated by their approach and the questions they address. For example, the case study (or $n = 1$ study) is a research paradigm often used in clinical studies examining the effects of treatment interventions in the lives of specific individuals. Biographic research is also generally done on specific individuals, often deceased; it may be conducted through written materials by and about the individuals, interviews with others who knew them, and the like. At the other end of the spectrum, survey research is an approach that polls large groups of individuals about their opinions, beliefs, and attitudes regarding consumer goods, political candidates, or a wide variety of issues.

In contrast to these approaches is a whole branch of research based on *hypothesis testing*. Research based on this approach seeks to (1) test a hypothesis generated from a theoretical framework and (2) generalize the findings of the study to a larger population. Hypothesis-testing studies are generally of two types: those that attempt to demonstrate the existence of a relationship among a set of variables, and those that attempt to demonstrate a cause–effect relationship between variables. These two types of studies are not the same, because the mere demonstration of a correlation between variables (for example, ice cream consumption and drowning) does not necessarily imply that one causes the other. Other variables may actually explain or cause the relationship (for example, summer brings hotter weather, which leads more people to eat ice cream and also leads more people to go swimming, which increases the frequency of drowning).

Although opinions differ on the value of different research approaches in psychology, my own belief is that they are all equally valuable. They use different methodologies because they ask different questions about different groups of people. They are all similar, however, in the sense that they are empirical—that is, they use methods and procedures that conform to certain scientific standards for validity and reliability. Although many people equate empirical with quantitative—research that involves numbers—I believe that qualitative research can also be empirical. The important question is whether or not the researchers have used methods and procedures that meet some criteria for validity and reliability.

Different approaches have different advantages and disadvantages. In general, case studies and biographic research provide richness and complexity with regard to the variables of interest and the lives of the individuals studied, which hypothesis-testing research tends to lack. On the other hand, hypothesis-testing research has the advantage of controlling for extraneous factors, isolating relationships among variables, and being generalizable to a larger population, which is not true of case studies and biographic research.

Much of the research in psychology, mainstream as well as cross-cultural, is of the hypothesis-testing type. The next section describes, in general terms, how such research is conducted. Although this material may be familiar to many of you who have had courses in research methodology or statistics, it reviews some basic issues and focuses in particular on the conscious and unconscious decisions researchers make in conducting research. This discussion, in turn, forms the basis for understanding and evaluating hypothesis-testing research in cross-cultural psychology.

The Parameters and Conditions of Hypothesis-Testing Research

All hypothesis-testing studies are conducted under specific conditions or research parameters. These conditions exist because it is impossible to study *all* people on *all* behaviors in a single study. Researchers thus need to narrow the focus of their study, and control for variables that are extraneous to their target variables of interest. These types of decisions create the conditions and parameters of a study, which in turn constitute its limitations. That is, the parameters and limitations of a study bound the knowledge that it generates.

If you ask researchers about the decisions they make in conducting a study, many will not be aware of just how many decisions are involved because many of them are automatic or made according to custom ("the way things are generally done" or "how another study did it"). In effect, psychological research and researchers have a culture of their own. As people gain more experience in conducting research and especially in thinking about how to conduct research, they become more aware of the many decisions involved. This section outlines some, but by no means all, of those decisions.

Decisions about the Theory and Hypothesis Being Tested

Hypothesis-testing studies are designed to test specific hypotheses and address specific questions. These hypotheses, in turn, are derived from psychological theories, or models of behavior. One of the first decisions researchers make when conducting a study concerns what theory they want to address, and what hypotheses they want to test. For example, a researcher may want to examine the hypothesis that boys in elementary school do better at a particular type of problem than girls, or that the number of people in a given area (population density) is related to certain types of health problems. These hypotheses may derive from theories that the researchers or others have formulated—suggesting, for example, that differential socialization practices for boys and girls lead to different academic aptitudes in school, or that the incidence of disease is a function of the number of people one comes in contact with.

Generally, researchers begin with a question they want to answer, then design a study to answer it. Conversely, every study, by its very nature, answers some question. Even if you do not know what question a researcher started out trying to answer, you should be able to surmise what that question was just by reading about what the study is trying to do. Sometimes, the question the researcher started out with is not actually addressed by the study conducted. Researchers may believe (and tell you in the Introduction) that their study is addressing a certain question or testing a certain hypothesis, but close inspection of their methods may reveal that the data collected do not exactly match that question or hypothesis.

Research questions and hypotheses should be closely related but sometimes this relationship is not as close as we would like. In all cases, however, researchers have some question they want to answer. Just what question to ask is the first decision a researcher makes.

Decisions about Methodology

Among the many decisions that must be made about methodology are those involved in choosing a basic approach, selecting participants, defining variables, and establishing research procedures.

The type of research paradigm to address the hypothesis.   Once researchers decide what question they want answered, the next step is to select a general research approach or **research paradigm** to answer it. Among the many types of research paradigms used in psychology are case studies, longitudinal research, experimental research, correlational research, and quasi-experimental research. Public health research may use an epidemiological approach to understanding the causes and nature of various health outcomes and diseases. Sociological research may use social markers and other institutions to delineate social changes and their impact on people. Anthropological research may use in-depth studies of single cultures, where researchers immerse themselves in the culture and try to learn everything about it (ethnographies). Research in economics and business may study the number and types of industries or look at changes in gross national products or other national economic indicators.

With so many research paradigms available, researchers need to choose the one that seems most appropriate to the question they want to answer. Often researchers do not give much thought to choosing an approach because certain paradigms are traditionally linked to certain questions. Nevertheless, the approach used to conduct the actual study is a decision made by the researcher, whether deliberately or by default. This decision, in turn, places certain conditions, restrictions, and limitations on the study and the information generated from it. The general research approach adopted defines the nature of the data obtainable as a result of these methods. The nature of these data, in turn, affects the kinds of results that can be reported and the interpretation and understanding of the phenomenon under study.

The participants.   In most studies on human behavior in psychology, the basic unit of analysis is a person (commonly referred to as a subject or participant). Different research paradigms, however, may use different units of analysis. Epidemiological surveys across countries, for example, may use country as the unit of analysis. Industries may be the unit of analysis in a study of the effects of different types of companies on the national economy. Much educational research involves classrooms as the unit of analysis. Deciding on the unit of analysis places a further condition on the nature of the data generated in the study.

Assuming that the person is the unit of analysis, as it is in most psychology research, it is obviously impossible to study all the people to whom we would like to apply our findings and principles of behavior. Thus, a researcher must decide how to limit the units of analysis in a study to a manageable and realistic size, and how to recruit them. The final group of units included in a study is commonly referred to as the **sample**, and the procedures researchers use in obtaining their sample is called the **sampling procedure**.

Most studies require that several decisions, not one, be made to achieve a workable number of units. For example, a researcher may decide to study human behavior. Of course, it is impossible to study everyone in the world. Thus, the researcher may decide to limit his or her samples to university students in the United States because they are the most easily accessible to the researcher, many of whom happen to be housed, supported, and employed by universities. Even then, a researcher cannot possibly survey all university students in the United States in one study. The decision often made by psychology researchers is to study university students enrolled in introductory psychology courses in a single university, for the simple reason that researchers can offer research participation as an alternative activity in partial fulfillment of class requirements. Even then, only a small number of the students enrolled in the course at one particular time will actually participate. Thus, what started out as a research question applicable to many or all people of the world ends up including only a small, specially chosen sample of a very limited nature. Most studies that have to do with human behavior must make similar types of limiting decisions, regardless of the unit of analysis. Those decisions, in turn, place conditions and limitations on the information obtained and its ultimate interpretation.

Conceptual and empirical definitions of variables.   In addition to decisions about samples, researchers make decisions about how to measure the variables they are interested in. The ways researchers decide to measure something is intimately related to the ways they *conceptually* define it. The way a variable is conceptually defined dictates how it should be measured. The method of measurement, in turn, places a limitation on the nature of the information obtained by that type of measurement. Conversely, every method of measurement defines the nature of what is being measured *by default*. That is, even if you don't know how a researcher conceptually defined something, you should be able to infer that definition from the way it is measured. In recent years, for example, researchers interested in intelligence have broadened their conceptual definition to include such things as musical, artistic, and other creative abilities, and physical, sport-type abilities. These changes in conceptual definition dictate changes in the ways these aspects of intelligence are measured.

How researchers conceptually define a variable (such as intelligence) reflects the way they understand that variable theoretically, and suggests a certain way of measuring that variable. This process of moving from concept to measure is known as **operationalization**. For example, researchers interested in studying intelligence need to have a conceptual definition about what they believe intelligence is. Most American psychologists studying intelligence in the past, for instance, believed that intelligence consists mainly of cognitive skills related to verbal, analytic, and problem-solving abilities. These researchers used methods such as the Wechsler Adult Intelligence Scale (WAIS) to measure intelligence. The WAIS has a total of 11 different types of tests, some verbal and some analytical. The verbal tests include vocabulary and reading comprehension, the analytical tests include jigsaw puzzle picture completion and a test in which subjects arrange a set of pictures so that they tell a story.

Issues of validity and reliability are of particular importance in the operationalization of variables. Researchers need to use measurement methods that have been shown to measure their variables of interest validly and reliably. Many years of effort and many studies are often necessary just to demonstrate the validity and reliability of a psychological measure before it can be used with confidence in hypothesis-testing research. Many researchers spend much of their careers validating measures so that not only they but others can use them. Validation research includes studies that show how the measure is related to other similar measures of that construct, and unrelated to dissimilar measures; how it predicts other constructs that it should predict; and how it provides the same finding in the same person across time, and within itself. Using measures that have amply demonstrated their validity and reliability enables researchers, and the consumers of their research, to know what they are measuring.

The specific tasks, questionnaires, or instruments (such as the WAIS) used to measure a variable place further conditions and limitations on the nature of the information gathered by that method. The data obtained using such measures may be obtainable only with those measures; other measures may produce different findings.

Environment, setting, and procedures. All research occurs in a particular environment and setting, and these factors are further conditions of the research. Many studies in psychology, for example, occur in laboratory settings. Participants may be asked to appear at a designated laboratory or experimental room where an experimenter explains the purpose and procedures of the experiment. The participants may view a movie screen, interact with a computer, or do a task, but this setting defines the environmental parameters under which the data are obtained.

Many studies of human behavior are observational in nature; that is, they involve experimenters recording their observations of certain types of behaviors in a particular setting. The setting may be the university student center, a home, a village, a shopping mall—just about anywhere. Wherever the research takes place, that setting defines an environmental condition under which the research is taking place, and this condition becomes a parameter and limitation of the data so obtained.

Researchers also decide the type of instructions to give to participants, the time of day to conduct the experiment, the books to look at to uncover historical or archival data, and so on. All of these decisions, regardless of the type of study or the unit of analysis, further define the conditions of the study. Many of these mundane decisions may be given little thought by some researchers, and even less by many consumers of the research. Nevertheless, they define the conditions and limitations under which data are obtained and knowledge is generated.

Decisions about Analyzing Data and Reporting Findings

Once researchers have conducted a study and collected their data, they need to analyze those data. The basic decisions about how the data will be analyzed should be made in conjunction with the original design of the study and its methods, not after the data have been collected.

More often than not, the need to do something with the quantitative data in psychological research leads us into the land of statistics. Statistics are used to manipulate data so that researchers can draw some meaning from the data. Simply counting the number of times a particular behavior occurs is a statistical manipulation. Finding the average number of times a response occurs is also a statistical manipulation. In some studies, the statistical manipulations can be quite complex, involving a multiple-step process with different types of outcomes. Names such as *analysis of variance, discriminant analysis, multiple regression,* and *correlation* abound in the research literature. But regardless of the name and complexity of the statistics, they all have the same purpose: to transform the data obtained in a study into something from which researchers can draw some meaning.

Researchers have many choices as to how to analyze their data. The most common statistics used in hypothesis-testing research can be grouped generally into two types. *Descriptive statistics* are those procedures that summarize or describe the data. Examples of descriptive statistics are means, standard deviations, and frequency distributions. *Inferential statistics* are those procedures that enable researchers to make inferences about the probable existence of differences between groups or conditions, or relationships among variables, in a larger population. Examples of inferential statistics are analysis of variance, chi-square, and correlation coefficient.

In addition to choosing appropriate statistical procedure, researchers make decisions concerning how they want to manipulate the data. For example, they can devise different ways of splitting their data files—using all or only parts of the data. They can choose to transform the data in certain ways, such as using difference scores instead of raw scores, or performing a mathematical transformation on their raw scores. They can even choose not to use any statistics at all and base their findings entirely on their own inferences about the data. The specific procedures researchers use to analyze data dictate how the data will be presented. This presentation, in turn, affects the types of meanings researchers and the consumers of that research draw from the data. Because methods of data analysis affect how the data are presented, they constitute yet another condition or limitation on research.

Decisions about Interpreting the Findings

In any study, be it psychological, sociological, or anthropological in nature, researchers need to draw conclusions on the basis of their data and findings. Because hypothesis-testing research is designed to examine specific hypotheses generated from specific theories, the conclusions should relate to the validity of the hypothesis and the meaning of that validity to the theory from which the hypothesis was generated.

Although the interpretations a researcher draws from a study will depend on the nature of the findings, a whole host of other factors also influence that interpretation—among them, prior findings, nonfindings, previous literature, and methodological constraints. Other factors worth noting include the researcher's own background and upbringing, and his or her particular theoretical biases and preferences. All interpretations are made under these conditions—that is, in the context of whatever viewpoint the researcher brings to the interpretation. These conditions form yet another constraint on the findings of a study.

To summarize, all of the myriad decisions that researchers must make in conducting their studies form the conditions and parameters of their research; these conditions and parameters, in turn, act as limitations on the findings. Because a finding is bound by the conditions under which it was produced, its generalizability to a larger population can only be demonstrated when it is replicated across multiple studies.

While these parameters and limitations are important in all types of research, cross-cultural research brings with it a number of special problems and issues. Building on the information presented here, the next section describes some of those issues.

Special Issues in Cross-Cultural Research

The Importance of Equivalence

Doing research in different cultures and comparing the results in one culture against those found in another brings with it its own set of special issues. Just as it is important for the informed and critical reader to understand some basic issues pertaining to all types of research, so it is important for consumers of cross-cultural research to have some understanding of the special issues that affect cross-cultural research.

One concept that is of crucial importance in the conduct and evaluation of cross-cultural research is that of equivalence. **Equivalence** in cross-cultural research can be defined as a state or condition of similarity in conceptual meaning and empirical method between cultures that allows comparisons to be meaningful. In its strictest sense, if any aspect of a cross-cultural study is not entirely equivalent in meaning or method across the cultures being compared, then the comparison loses its meaning. Lack of equivalence in a cross-cultural study creates the proverbial situation of comparing apples and oranges. If the theoretical framework and hypotheses have equivalent meaning in the cultures being compared, and the methods of data collection, management, and analysis have equivalent meaning, only then are the results from that comparison meaningful. Apples in one culture can be compared only to apples in another.

The issue of equivalence pertains to each of the specific aspects of conducting a study described in the previous section. The serious student of cross-cultural methodology will find that many of the "special" issues in cross-cultural research are really extensions of issues pertaining to all types of research, as the concept of equivalence in concept and method, validity and reliability in measurement are the same for all types of studies. Some issues, however, pertain solely to the conduct of research in different cultures and countries—among them, the issue of language comparability and translation, and the possibility of cultural response sets in the data. This section will give you a flavor of just what these issues are, to better equip you for reading, understanding, and evaluating cross-cultural research on your own.

The Nature of the Theory and Hypotheses Being Tested

As mentioned earlier, researchers decide what hypotheses to test based on some theoretical model. But especially in cross-cultural work, it is important to realize that people generate theories, which are therefore bound and influenced by the cultural framework of the theorist. How we think about people, interpersonal relationships, basic human nature, fate, luck, supernatural forces, and the like are all influenced by our culture. Thus, when psychologists create theories about human behavior, it is important to remember that the cultural framework of the people who create them binds those theories themselves.

It is, in fact, quite interesting to play with the idea that our own cultural framework and experiences influence our theories of behavior. Some people say, for example, that the thinking of people with PhDs and who were trained to do research in the United States or Europe may be bound by a sense of "logical determinism" and "rationality" that is characteristic of such formal and systematic educational systems. Others say that because we are so used to drawing two-dimensional theories of behavior on paper, that medium affects the way we think about people and psychology. It could be argued that other people of the world who have not been exposed to such an educational system, or who are not used to reducing their thoughts about the world onto a two-dimensional space, may not think in the same way. If this is the case, then a real question arises as to whether a theory created within a Western cultural framework is meaningful in the same ways to people who do not share that culture. If the theory is not meaningful in the same way, then it is not equivalent.

Similarly, researchers who formulate research questions and specific hypotheses have their own cultural upbringing and backgrounds, and hence their own biases. Whether good or bad, right or wrong, conscious or unconscious, these biases influence the types of questions we think are important and, thus, those questions we believe should be studied in cross-cultural research.

Will a hypothesis that we believe is important to test be important or meaningful in the same way to someone from a different cultural background? For example, suppose researchers want to examine cultural differences in how quickly people can solve maze-type puzzles presented to them on a computer. It might be interesting and relevant to conduct this type of study in the United States, Hong Kong, and France and compare the results of the American, Chinese, and French participants. But this study might not be as relevant to preliterate cultures such as those indigenous to New Guinea. If people from those cultures were asked to participate in the research, they might be afraid to go near that mechanical-looking contraption (the computer).

Or suppose researchers decided to study cultural differences in problem-solving ability in the United States and among tribespeople in Africa. One method might be to present subjects in both cultures with a device that had to be manipulated in some way to obtain a reward, such as money. The Americans might be able to approach this task and be successful at it. The tribespeople, however, might believe the task to be entirely meaningless, might view the contraption with fear, and might not care one bit about money! In contrast, if the problem-solving task were to track different animals by using scents and footprints, the tribespeople might respond very positively to the task. Imagine American subjects performing such a task!

As every hypothesis-testing study examines hypotheses that are generated from culture-bound theories, a major concern of cross-cultural research is the equivalence in meaning of the overall theoretical framework being tested, and the meaning and importance of the specific hypotheses being addressed. If these are not equivalent across the cultures participating in the study, then the data obtained from them are not comparable, because they mean different things. If, however, the theoretical framework and hypotheses are equivalent across the participating cultures, the study may be meaningful and relevant.

Clearly, researchers cannot simply decide on their own which questions are important to study across cultures and then impose these questions on people of other cultures. More often than not, the questions a researcher creates are assumed to be equally important and to have the same meaning in other cultures. This ethnocentric way of doing research cannot be avoided if the researcher single-handedly conducts the study without ascertaining the validity of his or her biases first. Involving cultural informants, such as a collaborator in each of the participating cultures, is a step in the right direction (although not always a definitive step, as they, too, may be influenced by their own cultural or educational background).

Issues in Cross-Cultural Research Methodology

Among the many methodological issues affecting cross-cultural research are those involving research design, definitions of culture, sampling, definition of variables, language barriers, and research procedures.

Design issues.   In cross-cultural research, by far the most prevalent type of hypothesis-testing study is one that compares two or more cultures on some psychological variable of interest. These studies generally examine whether the cultures in the study differ from each other on the variable, often with the hypothesis that one culture will have significantly higher scores on the variable than the other. While these studies merely show the existence of differences among cultures, they are important to the psychological literature because they test the limitations to knowledge generated in mainstream psychological research and help to advance our theoretical and conceptual thinking in all areas of psychology.

Another type of hypothesis-testing cross-cultural study is one that examines why cultural differences occur. These studies not only look for differences among cultures on their target variables, but also include measurements of other variables that they believe will account for those differences. Poortinga, van de Vijver, Joe, and Koppel (1987) have likened these types of studies to the peeling of an onion—layer after layer until nothing is left. These researchers view culture in the following way:

> In our approach culture is a summary label, a catchword for all kinds of behavior differences between cultural groups, but within itself, of virtually no explanatory value. Ascribing intergroup differences in behavior, e.g., in test performance, to culture does not shed much light on the nature of these differences. It is one of the main tasks of cross-cultural psychology to peel off cross-cultural differences, i.e., to explain these differences in terms of specific antecedent variables, until in the end they have disappeared and with them the variable culture. In our approach culture is taken as a concept without a core. From a methodological point of view, culture van be considered as an immense set of often loosely interrelated independent variables (cf. Segall, 1983, 1984; Strodtbeck, 1964). (p. 22)

These researchers suggest that culture as an unspecified variable should be replaced by more specific variables in order to truly explain cultural differences. These variables, called *context variables,* should be measured to examine the degree to which they can statistically account for cultural differences. Inferences about the nature of cultural differences can then incorporate the degree of contribution by the context variables. If the context variable included in any study does not account for all of the differences between cultures, then other context variables should be incorporated in subsequent research to account for more of the differences among cultures, until all the differences have been accounted for.

Although most hypothesis-testing cross-cultural research uses individual participants as the unit of analysis, some studies use countries or cultures as the unit of analysis. Data may be obtained from individuals in those cultures, but they are often summarized or averaged for each culture, and those averages are used as data points for each culture. Analyses based on this type of design are called *ecological-* or *cultural-level analyses,* in contrast to traditional individual-level analyses. Examples of such ecological-level analyses include Hofstede's (1980, 1983) studies of cultural values across 50+ cultures, Triandis et al.'s (1988) study of the relationship between individualism–collectivism and incidence of heart attacks in eight cultures, Matsumoto and Fletcher's (1994) study of the relationship between four cultural dimensions and incidence rates for six disease states, and Matsumoto's (1989) study of the relationship between cultural dimensions and judgments of emotion in 15 cultures.

There are important differences in the interpretations justified on the basis of ecological- versus individual-level research. A relationship between a cultural variable and a target variable (for example, individualism and the incidence of cardiovascular disease) on the ecological level does not necessarily mean that such a relationship exists on the individual level. The relationship may or may not exist on the individual level within the cultures studied, and if it does, it may or may not be in the same direction. (Also see Leung, 1989.)

Two non-hypothesis-testing types of research designs are worth noting here. The first is what may be called a cross-cultural validation study. These studies examine whether a measure of a psychological construct that was originally generated in a single culture is applicable, meaningful, and thus equivalent in another culture. These studies do not test a specific hypothesis about cultural differences; rather, they test the equivalence of psychological measures and tests for use in other cross-cultural comparative research. Although these types of studies are not as common as hypothesis-testing cross-cultural research, they serve an important purpose in investigating the cross-cultural applicability of many of the methodological techniques used in research.

The second type of research design is known as **ethnography**. These studies are conducted mainly by anthropologists, but also by some cross-cultural psychologists. They involve considerable fieldwork, with the researchers visiting and oftentimes living together with the people they are interested in studying. Being immersed in a culture for an extended period of time, these researchers learn firsthand the customs, rituals, traditions, beliefs, and ways of life of the culture to which they are exposed. Comparisons to other cultures are done on the basis of their own knowledge, experience, and education about their own and other cultures. This approach is not unlike the case study of individual lives, with cultures serving as the larger unit of analysis. As such, it shares many of the advantages of that approach, including the richness and complexity of the data obtained, as well as the disadvantages in terms of generalizability. These ethnographic studies make an important contribution to the field, complementing existing hypothesis-testing research on specific psychological variables.

Definitions of culture.   When cross-cultural researchers do a study, they may decide to gather data from, say, the United States, Germany, Japan, and India. That is, they gather data from different *countries*. Through their research methods, then, researchers often make the assumption that countries equal culture. However, most cross-cultural scholars define culture as the shared conglomeration of attitudes, values, behaviors, and beliefs communicated from one generation to the next via language. This definition of culture is subjective not objective, sociopsychological not biological.

Despite this definition of culture, cross-cultural researchers have lacked an adequate way of measuring this "sharing" of psychological characteristics in their research. Instead, they have relied on aspects of people that are easier to measure—typically, race (for example, black versus white), ethnicity (for example, Hispanic versus Asian American), or nationality (for example, American, Japanese, German, Brazilian). Although there is certainly overlap between culture and these other social constructs, reliance on these constructs can be problematic.

As noted in Chapter 2, a number of writers have pointed out the inadequacy of using race as a grouping variable in comparative research. Zuckerman (1990), for example, observed that there is more variability within racial groups than between them on such items as skin color, hair type and color, eye color, stature, head shape and size, facial features, and blood type. Further, none of these features are correlated with each other, and none can unequivocally distinguish among racial groups. He then went on to analyze cross-racial differences in temperament, crime, and personality and suggested that there are considerably more differences within groups than between them on these variables as well. Rather than working to help bridge gaps among people, Zuckerman (1990) concluded, psychological research using self-classification by participants into a racial grouping can actually undermine such attempts, allowing the findings from such research to foster racism instead. By reducing culture to race, these procedures promote stereotypic beliefs and opinions about people.

Scientists have tried to develop ways of measuring culture more directly on the individual and psychological levels. With the development of these new methodologies, researchers will no longer need to rely on participants' self-classification by race, ethnicity, or nationality. By actually measuring culture as a sociopsychological variable, researchers can ascertain empirically that the groups in their studies differ on the intended cultural variable, and can go further in investigating the degree to which these variables contribute to the differences between groups. Cross-cultural studies using these methods, however, are still the exception rather than the rule.

Most, if not all, of the studies conducted to date and presented in this book have measured culture by either race, ethnicity, or nationality. Still, we cannot and should not categorically dismiss these studies or their findings. They provide us with valuable information about possible cultural differences, because cultural differences do underlie countries. These studies alert us to the limitations to what we know and regard as truth based on research from mainstream academia. Thus, it is still important for us to consider these studies, but we must consider them with degree of caution because of the discrepancy between our definition of culture and the definition of culture used in the research. When we conduct research using these categories to classify people, we must do so with care concerning the presumed relationship between these categories and the underlying culture.

Besides the issue of how to measure culture, researchers must decide which cultures to include in a study. More often than not, cross-cultural researchers have studied cultures as a matter of convenience rather than on the basis of compelling theoretical, empirical, or practical questions. Technology has now advanced to the point where conducting a study almost anywhere has become possible for most people who want to do so. As the ease of such choices increases, however, it becomes even more incumbent on cross-cultural researchers to exercise those choices wisely, based on compelling reasons rather than convenience. Thus, the choice of cultures to include in a study and to compare becomes another dimension on which to evaluate cross-cultural research.

The participants: sampling adequacy. More often than not, it is assumed that a group of people who participate in a cross-cultural study (the sample) are "good" representatives of that particular culture. For instance, in the simplest cross-cultural research design, researchers obtain a sample of people in one culture, obtain data from them, and compare those data to data collected in another culture or to known values. Let's say a researcher obtained a sample of 50 Americans as part of a cross-cultural study. Are the 50 Americans adequate representatives of American culture? If they were recruited from Beverly Hills in California, would that be the same as recruiting 50 participants from the

Bronx in New York? Or 50 people from Wichita, Kansas? If the 50 participants were all of European descent, would they be an "adequate" sample? If not, what percentage of people of different racial and ethnic backgrounds would the researcher need to include? If the sample required 25% to be of African descent, does it matter which African Americans are included? What criteria can be used to decide whether the sample of 50 people are representative of American culture? What is "American" culture anyway?

The questions are endless, they are not easy to answer, and they pertain to any sample of participants in any culture. Cross-cultural researchers need to pay particular attention to issues of sampling in the conduct of their research. Aside from being unable (most of the time) to measure culture on a subjective level, cross-cultural research too often simply assumes that the participants in their studies are adequate representatives of their culture, whatever it is. This unrealistic and unacceptable assumption of homogeneity among group members can only serve to perpetuate stereotypic impressions and interpretations based on the findings. That is, when differences are found, researchers assume that the differences are "cultural" because they assume that the samples are representatives of culture. In reality, the differences a researcher finds in a study of the United States, Japan, Brazil, and Mexico may be the same as the differences that would be found in a study of Minneapolis, Los Angeles, Miami, and Newark!

The participants: noncultural, demographic equivalence. A different question involving sampling in cross-cultural research is whether the samples are equivalent in all possible ways except culture, so that a comparison among them is a comparison of culture and not something else. For the research to be methodologically sound, researchers need to make sure the samples they compare are somehow equivalent on noncultural variables. If they are not equivalent on demographic or other types of variables, then those variables on which they are not equivalent would serve as *confounds* in the study. For example, a researcher might compare two groups of subjects from two different cultures that are matched for age, education, and religion but differ in socioeconomic status (SES). Should differences be found between these two samples, it would not be clear whether those differences are due to the underlying cultural differences between the two samples or to differences in SES. SES would confound culture. Ensuring that cross-cultural samples are equivalent is not easy.

As another example, imagine comparing data from a sample of 50 Americans from Los Angeles with sample of 50 preliterate members of the Fore tribe in New Guinea. Clearly, the Americans and the Fore come from entirely different backgrounds—different socioeconomic classes, different educational levels, different social experiences, different forms of technology, and so on. How can you know that any differences, if found, are due to culture rather than other factors? Clearly, comparing data from a sample of respondents in a major international metropolis to data from members of a preliterate tribe with minimal outside contact is very difficult. Would we obtain similar differences if we studied different socioeconomic classes within the United States?

Although this example may be far-fetched, the question remains valid for more subtle differences in cross-cultural samples. How would you establish equivalence between a sample from Los Angeles and samples from Paris, Vienna, and Singapore? Cross-cultural researchers need to establish some basis of equivalence among their samples to make cultural comparisons meaningful. But often the samples differ on many noncultural dimensions as well as cultural ones. For example, in one study, Matsumoto and Assar (1992) compared judgments of facial expressions of emotion, using university students in the United States and India. Not only are there major cultural differences between the two groups; there are also religious, socioeconomic, and linguistic differences between them. Where does culture stop and the noncultural factors start? In many cases, differences in these noncultural, demographic characteristics are inextricably intertwined with culture, and cannot be eliminated or controlled in the study.

The real issue, therefore, is not whether the cultural groups also differ on noncultural demographic characteristics, but whether the researchers who conducted the study are aware of these differences. When differences are found on their target variables, researchers who are not aware of the noncultural demographic factors usually assume that the observed differences reflect cultural differences—which may not be the case. Researchers who are aware of demographic differences, however, will present data concerning their sample characteristics, engage in some formal statistical tests to examine the contribution of these characteristics to their variables of interest, and temper their interpretations according to what they find. As consumers of cross-cultural research, we need to be aware of such alternative interpretations of the data even when the researchers are not.

The conceptual and empirical definitions of variables. The question here is whether the conceptual meaning of variables and the way they are measured are equivalent across the cultures included in a study. Different cultures may conceptually define a construct differently, and/or measure it differently. Just because something has the same name in two or more cultures does not mean that it has the same meaning (Wittgenstein, 1953, cited in Poortinga, 1989), or that it can be measured in the same way. If a concept means different things to people of different cultures, or if it is measured in different ways in different cultures, then comparisons can be meaningless. It follows, therefore, that cross-cultural researchers need to be keenly aware of the issue of equivalence with regard to their conceptual definitions and empirical operationalization of the variables in their study.

Debate concerning cross-cultural studies of intelligence highlights these issues. As described earlier in this chapter, many researchers in the United States in the past have considered intelligence to consist mainly of verbal and analytical types of critical thinking skills. Tests (such as the WAIS) assessing these skills have been widely used in this research. This definition may have been fine for the United States, but a different culture may have a different conception of just what constitutes intelligence. For example, let's say a culture considers nobility of character and sincerity as markers of intelligence. If we test a sample of people from this culture on the WAIS and compare these data to American data, are we really studying cross-cultural differences in intelligence? Another culture may consider the ability to have smooth, conflict-free interpersonal relationships a marker for intelligence. Yet another culture may consider creativity and artistic abilities to be indices of intelligence. Would comparisons of WAIS data from all of these cultures constitute cross-cultural comparisons of intelligence? Of course, researchers may be interested in the specific traits being measured; the problem occurs when we interpret them as defining a concept of "intelligence" that is assumed to be true for everyone.

Even if a researcher can establish equivalence in the conceptual definition of a variable, the empirical operationalization of it is another question. Let's say, for example, that two cultures do indeed define intelligence in terms of verbal and analytic abilities, such as those measured by the WAIS. Now let's look at the exact ways by which the WAIS measures this definition of intelligence. If the test includes a question about American presidents, can we use the test in this study? Would it be fair to give subjects in France this test to measure their intelligence?

With regard to ability tests (such as intelligence and aptitude testing), some writers go as far as to suggest that such tests are inherently nonequivalent across cultures. Greenfield (1997), for example, argues that constructs such as intelligence and cognitive ability are inherently symbolic products of a culture. As such, the constructs and tests of it presuppose a certain cultural framework in order to be valid. Because these frameworks are not universally shared, cross-cultural comparisons of ability and intelligence are meaningless. A totally opposite viewpoint, however, is that concepts of intelligence, aptitudes, and abilities are shared across cultures, and thus comparable for research purposes.

Similar questions may arise concerning the equivalence in construct and operation of values. Peng, Nisbett, and Wong (1997), for example, have argued that common methods for assessing values, such as giving participants a list of values and asking them to rate them or rank them in order of importance, may not be valid across cultures. They suggest that such methods may be invalid because of cultural differences in the meanings of specific value items, and because some value judgments may be based on inherent social comparisons with others rather than on direct inferences about a private, personal value system. In order to investigate this possibility, these researchers examined four different value survey methods: the traditional ranking, rating, and attitude scaling procedures and a behavioral scenario rating method. The only method that yielded reasonable validity estimates was the behavioral scenario rating method, the most unorthodox of all the measures tested.

Questions concerning equivalence in construct and measurement of variables involve not only those measures that yield single scores, but extend also to methods involving multiple item measurement and multiple scale score computation. If a researcher, for example, uses a scale with 50 items that score to five different scales, questions arise as to whether each of the 50 items represents the construct equivalently in all cultures tested, and whether the five scales are equivalently represented in all cultures. As a statistical technique known as factor analysis is often used to derive scale scores from a larger pool of items on a measure, similar factor analytic results in all cultures being studied would be one way to assess the degree of equivalence across cultures, at least in the scale structure of the measure.

A simple way to illustrate these issues regarding equivalence of conceptual definitions and empirical methods is to use the analogy of a cross-cultural study on temperature. Let's say we are interested in conducting such a study between two cultures, A and B. The first question is whether both cultures have a concept of temperature, and whether it refers to the same thing in both cultures. If the answer is no, then it may be pointless to continue with a comparative study of temperature (although other study possibilities do exist). If the answer is yes, then the next question is how to measure it. If culture A measures temperature on the Celsius (C) scale, while culture B measures temperature on the Fahrenheit (F) scale, then clearly those methods of measuring temperature are not directly comparable. It is incumbent on the researchers to find a way to measure temperature that is equivalent in both cultures, and then to compare those scores.

Poortinga (1989) has suggested that when a measure has high content validity in all cultures being tested (it has been shown to mean the same thing in all cultures), and when the construct being measured is in a psychological domain that is similar or identical across cultures (such as color schemes or pitch scale for tones), valid comparisons are generally possible. When unobservable psychological traits and attributes are being measured, comparison may still be possible as long as equivalence in the conceptual meaning of the psychological domain and in its measurement has been established for all participating cultures. All other research situations, according to Poortinga (1989), preclude valid comparison across cultures.

Cross-cultural researchers have an obligation to demonstrate the cross-cultural validity of their measures on the level of item and scale in order to establish their equivalence for comparison. Researchers need to think critically about possible cultural differences in the conceptual definitions of different variables of interest in cross-cultural research; but researchers also have to examine *in detail* the exact methods they will use to measure those variables, down to the precise wording of individual items on the tests. Cultural differences in either the conceptual definitions of variables or their measurement are very common, and we need to be aware of these possibilities. Of all the issues involving cross-cultural equivalence, those concerning the validity and reliability of the conceptual meaning and methodological operationalization of variables are arguably the most crucial to any cross-cultural study.

Language and translation issues. Another issue in cross-cultural research is the linguistic equivalence of the research protocols. If you want to compare questionnaire responses of an American sample to those of a sample in Beijing, for example, you will need to have both English and Chinese versions of the questionnaire. How will you know if the questionnaires are equivalent? Cross-cultural researchers frequently use a procedure known as **back translation** to ensure equivalence in their research protocols (Brislin, 1970). Back translation involves taking the protocol in one language, translating it to the other language, and having someone else translate it back to the original. If the back-translated version is the same as the original, they can be considered equivalent. If it is not, the procedure is repeated until the back-translated version is the same as the original.

The concept underlying this procedure is that the end product must be a translation equivalent to the original version. This process serves to **decenter** the original language (Brislin, 1970, 1993), eliminating any culture-specific concepts of the original language. Through this process, culture-specific meanings and connotations are gradually eliminated from the research protocols, so that what remains is the closest linguistic equivalents in both languages. Because they are linguistic equivalents, successfully back-translated protocols are comparable in cross-cultural hypothesis-testing research.

But even if the words being used in the two languages are the same, there is no guarantee that those words have exactly the same meanings, with the same nuances, in the two cultures. A successful back translation gives the researcher protocols that are the closest linguistic equivalents in two or more different languages. However they still may not be exactly the same. In translating the English word *anger,* for example, we might indeed find an equivalent word in Russian or Swahili. But would it have the same connotations, strength, and interpretation in those languages as it does in English? It is very difficult to find exact translation equivalents of most words.

Such subtle differences are inherent and inevitable when doing cross-cultural research. Cross-cultural researchers need to be aware of issues of language equivalence so as not to confuse language differences with the cultural differences they want to test. "Perfect" equivalence between any two languages is unattainable, and this fact should be considered when evaluating cross-cultural research. The astute researcher and research consumer should be able to incorporate such subtle influences in their interpretations of the data.

The research environment, setting, and procedures. The issue of equivalence also applies to the environment, setting, and procedures used to collect data in different cultures. In many universities across the United States, students enrolled in introductory psychology classes are strongly encouraged to participate as research subjects in partial fulfillment of class requirements. U.S. students generally expect to participate in research as part of their academic experience, and many American students are "research-wise."

Customs differ in other countries. In some countries, professors simply collect data from their students or require them to participate at a research laboratory. In some countries, students may consider it a privilege rather than a chore or course requirement to participate in an international study. Thus, expectations about and experience with research participation may differ.

All the decisions researchers make in any other type of study are made in cross-cultural studies as well. But those decisions can mean different things in different countries. Laboratory or field, day or night, questionnaire or observation—all these decisions may have different meanings in different cultures.

Cross-cultural researchers need to confront these differences in their work, and establish procedures, environment, and setting that are equivalent across the cultures being compared. By the same token, consumers need to be aware of these possible differences when evaluating cross-cultural research.

Issues in Analyzing and Reporting Cross-Cultural Comparison Data

Although the major issues regarding equivalence in cross-cultural research are methodological, issues regarding data and data analysis are not devoid of such influence. In fact, one of the most important issues that researchers and consumers alike need to be aware of is the possibility of cultural response sets.

Cultural response sets. **Cultural response sets** are tendencies for members of a given culture to use certain parts of a scale when responding. Response sets pertain to cross-cultural findings, and not necessarily to the methods by which the study was conducted. If cultural response sets exist, any differences found among cultures may reflect these response tendencies rather than actual differences on the items the researcher intended to measure.

For example, suppose participants in the United States and Korea are asked to judge the intensity of a certain stimulus, using a 7-point scale. When examining the data, the researcher may find that Americans generally scored around 6 or 7, whereas Koreans generally scored around 4 or 5. The researcher may interpret these findings to mean that the Americans perceived more intensity in the stimulus than did the Koreans. But what if Koreans actually rate everything lower than Americans, not just this stimulus? What if they actually perceive a considerable degree of intensity in the stimulus but have a cultural tendency to use the lower part of the scale?

Cultural response sets may act in different ways. Members of collectivistic cultures may hesitate to use the extreme end points of a scale, consistent with a cultural reluctance to "stick out." Members of other cultural groups may be more inclined to use the endpoints. Bachman and O'Malley (1984), for example, found evidence of extreme response styles among African Americans, and Marin, Gamba, and Marin (1992) found similar evidence for Hispanics.

To the extent that these cultural differences result in different uses of response alternatives on questionnaires or interviews, they contribute to nonequivalence in the data, making valid comparisons difficult. Fortunately, statistical manipulations allow researchers to assess whether cultural response sets may be operating in a data set, and to deal with them if found. Researchers need to be aware of cultural response sets and the statistical techniques available to deal with them (see Matsumoto, 1994, for an introduction), and consumers of that research need to be similarly aware.

Other issues regarding data analysis. In testing cultural differences on target variables of interest, researchers often use inferential statistics such as chi-square or analysis of variance (ANOVA). These statistics compare the differences observed between the groups to the differences one would normally expect on the basis of chance alone, and then compute the probability that the results would have been obtained solely by chance. If the probability of obtaining the findings they did is very low (less than 5 %), then researchers infer that the findings did not occur because of chance—that is, that the findings reflect actual differences between the cultural groups from which their samples were drawn. This "proof by negation of the opposite" is at the heart of the logic underlying hypothesis testing and statistical inference.

Just because differences between group tendencies (such as means) are statistically significant, however, does not by itself give an indication of the degree of difference between the groups. Indeed, group means may be statistically different even though there is considerable overlap among the scores of the individuals comprising the two groups. To get an idea of the robustness of the significant differences between cultures, researchers need to go beyond inferential statistics to another class of statistics known as *effect size estimates*. Among the available statistics of this type are R^2, eta, omega, and d. Despite differences in detail, they all give the experienced reader some idea of the ratio of the between-group differences to the individual-level variation within each group. Without them, researchers and consumers often fall into the trap of interpreting significant group differences as differences between all members of the respective groups. With these statistics, however, researchers and consumers can have an idea of the degree to which the between-group cultural differences actually reflect the individuals tested, helping to break the hold of stereotypic interpretations based on group difference findings.

Cultural Influences on the Interpretation of Findings

Several issues are especially pertinent to interpreting findings obtained in cross-cultural research—among them, cause–effect versus correlational interpretations, the role of researcher bias and value judgments, and dealing with nonequivalent data.

Cause–effect versus correlational interpretations. In hypothesis-testing cross-cultural studies, cultural groups often are treated as independent variables in research design and data analysis, making these studies a form of quasi-experiment. It is important to remember, however, that the data from such studies are basically correlational in nature, and that inferences drawn from them can only be correlational inferences. For example, if a researcher compared data from the United States and Japan on social judgments and found that Americans had significantly higher scores on a person perception task, any interpretations of these data would be limited to the association between cultural membership (American or Japanese) and the scores. Cause–effect inferences (for example, being American causes one to have higher person perception scores) are unwarranted. For such causal statements to be justified, the researcher would have had to (1) create the conditions of the experiment (the cultural groups) and (2) randomly assign people to each of the conditions. These experimental conditions cannot apply in any study in which one of the main variables is cultural group. It makes no more sense to assume a causal relationship between cultural membership and a variable of interest than it does to assume such a relationship on the basis of sex, hair color, or height.

A related type of mistaken interpretation that cross-cultural researchers often make is to suggest specific reasons why cultural differences occurred, even though the specific reasons were never measured in the study. For instance, a researcher might take the significant American–Japanese differences found in the previous example and suggest that these differences occurred because of differences between individualism and collectivism in the two cultures. Unless the researchers actually measured individualism and collectivism in their study, found that the two cultures differed on it this dimension, and showed that it accounted for the cultural group differences on social judgments, the interpretation that this construct (IC) is responsible for the group differences is unwarranted. In fact, such interpretations about why a cultural group difference has occurred often appear in cross-cultural research articles, but they should be taken only as suggesting a possible context variable for further investigation. Problems arise when researchers and consumers assume that there is a relationship between the cultures and the context variable, and that the context variable actually accounts for the cultural differences. In accordance with Poortinga et al.'s (1987) earlier suggestions, I believe that these types of context variables need to be measured directly in cross-cultural research for such interpretations to be warranted.

Researcher bias and value judgments.　Just as culture can bias formulation of the research questions in a cross-cultural study, it can also bias the ways researchers interpret their findings. Most researchers will inevitably interpret the data they obtain (whether from questionnaires, responses to a task, or whatever) through their own cultural filters, and these biases can affect their interpretations to varying degrees.

For example, if the mean response for Americans on a rating scale is 6.0, and the mean for Hong Kong Chinese is 4.0, one interpretation is that the Americans simply scored higher on the scale. Another interpretation may be that the Chinese are suppressing their responses. This type of interpretation is common, especially in research with Asian samples. But how do we know the Chinese are suppressing their responses? What if it is the Americans who are exaggerating their responses? What if the Chinese mean response of 4.0 is actually the more "correct" one, and the American one is the one that is off? What if we surveyed the rest of the world and found that the overall mean was 3.0, suggesting that both the Chinese *and* the Americans inflated their ratings? In other words, the interpretation that the Chinese are suppressing their responses is based on an implicit assumption that the American data are "correct." I myself have made this sort of ethnocentric interpretation of research findings, in a study involving American and Japanese judgments of the intensity of facial expressions of emotion, without really giving much consideration to other possibilities (Matsumoto & Ekman, 1989). In later research (Matsumoto, Kasri, &

Kooken, in press), we were able to show that in fact the Americans exaggerated their intensity ratings of faces, relative to inferences about subjective experience of the posers—the Japanese did not suppress.

Examples such as this one are found throughout the cross-cultural literature. Anytime researchers make a **value judgment** or interpretation of a finding, it is always possible that this interpretation is bound by a cultural bias. Interpretations of good or bad, right or wrong, suppressing or exaggerating, important or not important, are all value interpretations that may be made in a cross-cultural study. And these interpretations may reflect the value orientations of the researchers as much as they do the cultures of the samples included in the study. As researchers, we may make those interpretations without giving them a second thought—and without the slightest hint of malicious intent—only because we are so accustomed to seeing the world in a certain way. As consumers of research, we may agree with such interpretations when they agree with the ways we have learned to understand and view the world, and we will often do so unconsciously and automatically.

Dealing with nonequivalent data. Despite the best attempts to establish equivalence in theory, hypothesis, method, and data management, cross-cultural research is often inextricably, inherently, and inevitably nonequivalent. It is impossible to create any cross-cultural study that means exactly the same thing to all participating cultures, both conceptually and empirically. What cross-cultural researchers often end up with are best approximations of the closest equivalents in terms of theory and method in a study.

Thus, researchers are often faced with the question of how to deal with nonequivalent data. Poortinga (1989) outlines four different ways in which the problem of nonequivalence of cross-cultural data can be handled:

1. *Preclude comparison.* The most conservative thing a researcher could do is not make the comparison in the first place, concluding that it would be meaningless.
2. *Reduce the nonequivalence in the data.* Many researchers take steps to identify equivalent and nonequivalent parts of their methods, and then refocus their comparisons solely on the equivalent parts. For example, if a researcher used a 20-item scale to measure anxiety in two cultures and found evidence for nonequivalence on the scale, he or she might then examine each of the 20 items for equivalence and rescore the test using only those items that are shown to be equivalent. Comparisons would then be based on the rescored items.
3. *Interpret the nonequivalence.* A third strategy is for the researcher to interpret the nonequivalence as an important piece of information concerning cultural differences.
4. *Ignore the nonequivalence.* Unfortunately, what many cross-cultural researchers end up doing is simply ignoring the problem, clinging to beliefs concerning scale invariance across cultures despite a lack of evidence to support those beliefs.

How researchers handle the interpretation of their data, given nonequivalence, depends on their experience and biases, and on the nature of the data and the findings. Because of the lack of equivalence in much cross-cultural research, researchers are often faced with many gray areas in interpreting their findings. Culture itself is a complex phenomenon, neither black nor white but replete with gray. It is the objective and experienced researcher who can deal with these gray areas, creating sound, valid, and reliable interpretations that are justified by the data. And it is the astute consumer of that research who can sit back and judge those interpretations relative to the data in their own minds and not be unduly swayed by the arguments of the researchers.

Guidelines for Reviewing Cross-Cultural Research

Students, teaching faculty, and researchers alike are all consumers of research. We all need to be able to pick up a research article published in a scientific journal in psychology and be able to read, understand, and evaluate it. We need these skills in order to know the literature, understand the state of knowledge in an area, write papers, plan research, and teach.

In this section, I provide a systematic way of evaluating cross-cultural research on your own. The summary sheet shown in Table 5.1 was created to highlight most of the important issues discussed in this chapter, listing in summary form all of the questions you need to ask about individual research articles that you read and review for your own course requirements, research projects, or interests. These guidelines apply specifically to hypothesis-testing cross-cultural research; they may be less pertinent to ethnographies and validation studies. As you address each of these questions (discussed in more detail below), you can simply circle Yes, No, or DK (don't know).

Photocopy this summary sheet and use it when conducting your literature reviews and evaluating articles. Remember, your goal is to judge for yourself the merits of individual studies in terms of their potential contribution to truth and knowledge in psychology.

Theory and Hypotheses

Earlier in this chapter, we discussed how all theories are generated within a certain cultural framework. Theories, and the hypotheses generated from theories, are therefore bounded by the cultural framework within which they originated. The issue raised in Questions 1 and 2 is whether the theory and hypotheses being tested are equivalent for all cultures participating in the study. In order to make this evaluation, you need to sit back and try to understand conceptually the theoretical framework being presented in the Introduction section of the article—its logic, premises, and assumptions—and then evaluate the cultural framework within which these premises and assumptions do and do not hold true.

Table 5.1 Summary Sheet for Evaluating Cross-Cultural Research

Author(s): _____

Title: _____

Journal: _____

Pub. Info.: _____

Theory and Hypotheses

1. Does the theory "make sense" for all the cultures
   being tested in the study? Why or why not?   Yes No DK

2. Are the hypotheses meaningfully equivalent for
   all participants?   Yes No DK

Methods

3. Is the design appropriate for the question being addressed?   Yes No DK

4. Are the subjects adequate representatives of their culture?   Yes No DK

5. Is culture operationalized according to sociopsychological
   constructs? If not, how is it operationalized?   Yes No DK

6. Are the subjects equivalent for comparison purposes—
   no other characteristics or demographic confounds?   Yes No DK

7. Are the concepts being measured equivalent in all
   cultures in the study?   Yes No DK

8. Do the scales, subscales, and items being used have the
   same reliability and validity characteristics in all cultures
   in the study?   Yes No DK

9. Are the scales/constructs contextualized meaningfully
   for all subjects?   Yes No DK

10. Do subjects come to the laboratory or complete testing
    procedures with equivalent expectations?   Yes No DK

11. Is procedural equivalence established across nuisance
    parameters of the study?   Yes No DK

12. Did the researchers establish linguistic equivalence in
    their methods and research protocols by using back-
    translation procedures?   Yes No DK

(continued on next page)

Table 5.1 Summary Sheet for Evaluating Cross-Cultural Research *(continued)*

Data and Analyses

13. Do subjects provide data on a level of measurement that is meaningful to them while at the same time equivalent across cultures?   Yes   No   DK

14. Are there cultural response sets operating in the data set?   Yes   No   DK

15. Do the researchers take adequate steps to check for cultural response sets, and control them if necessary?   Yes   No   DK

16. If cultural differences are found, do the researchers provide an index of the size of those differences (effect size statistics)?   Yes   No   DK

Interpretations and Conclusions

17. Are the interpretations of the findings bound by the cultural filters and biases of the researcher, or of the theories?   Yes   No   DK

18. Are the interpretations of cultural mediators justified in relation to how culture was operationalized in the study?   Yes   No   DK

19. Do the researchers make unwarranted cause–effect interpretations of the relationship between culture and their target variables?   Yes   No   DK

20. Do the researchers make value judgments based on the findings?   Yes   No   DK

21. Are the interpretations sufficiently tempered by awareness of the unconscious cultural processes that may have affected the research or theory?   Yes   No   DK

22. Are there sufficient methodological concerns to preclude any meaningful conclusions based on the data presented?   Yes   No   DK

Other Questions about the Study

23. How do the findings contribute to our knowledge with regard to cultural influences on the target variables of interest?

24. How would changes in any aspect of the methodology affect the outcomes of the study (for example, cultural or demographic backgrounds of the participants, methods of measuring key variables)?

25. Can the findings be used by some to foster stereotypes of members of the cultures represented in the study?

26. Can the findings be used by some to foster prejudice or discrimination against members of the cultures represented in the study?

Methods

Question 3 asks whether the design chosen by the researchers provides an appropriate way to test their hypotheses. Each of the concepts described in the hypothesis should be manipulated in some fashion in the study so that (1) the hypothesis can be falsified, and (2) if not falsified, rival hypotheses can be eliminated.

Questions 4, 5, and 6 bear on the issues of sampling adequacy and equivalence in noncultural demographic variables.

Questions 7 and 8 address the conceptual and empirical definitions of variables. Issues of cross-cultural validity may be addressed in other research, which should be cited.

Question 9 also relates to the conceptual and empirical definition of variables. In many cultures, questions about abstract psychological constructs are not very meaningful (see for example, the discussion regarding self-construals in Chapter 3). In these cultures, questions about psychological traits and characteristics make sense only if a specific context is provided (when you are at home, with friends in a public place, at work). If the cultures participating in the study are of this nature, then psychological data will only be meaningful if their measures are sufficiently contextualized.

Questions 10 and 11 bear on the issue of equivalence across cultures in the setting, environment, and procedures of the study.

Question 12 asks whether or not the researchers took care to establish linguistic equivalence in their protocols by employing back-translation procedures.

Data and Analyses

The issue raised in Question 13 is whether the scale of measurement provided to the participants is equivalent in all cultures being tested. Even though the concepts being tested are equivalent in all cultures, different scales may have different meanings for different cultures. Participants from one culture, for example, may not hesitate to give scalar ratings about their attitudes using a 7-point scale (1 through 7). Participants in another culture, however, may be unfamiliar with such scales, and unaccustomed to grading their responses in this way, preferring to respond in an open-ended fashion. If such differences exist, the data may be nonequivalent.

Questions 14 and 15 bear on the issue of cultural response sets.

Question 16 addresses the issue of calculating and presentating effect sizes when documenting group differences.

Interpretations and Conclusions

Questions 17, 20, and 21 address the possibility that researcher bias and value judgments may affect interpretations of the data.

Questions 18 and 19 focus on the nature of the interpretations—that is, cause–effect versus correlational.

Question 22 is an overall, summary question about the study as a whole. There is no such thing as a perfect, flawless study; every study will be compromised in some fashion, to some degree. The real question facing researchers and consumers of research is whether the limitations are sufficient to preclude drawing any meaningful conclusions about any part of the data, or whether some kind of conclusion is warranted despite the flaws or limitations. This evaluation is totally subjective, based upon your review and evaluation of all of the points discussed here, and the weight you give to each in relation to the possible contribution of the study and its findings to the literature.

Other Questions about the Study

In addition to questions that can be raised directly about the validity and reliability of the findings reported in a study, I have listed some questions that need to be raised with regard to what it all might mean. In conducting studies, researchers need to consider these important questions from the outset. Likewise, consumers need to ask difficult questions about the impact and ramifications of each study, not only in terms of the existing literature and current state of knowledge, but also in terms of potential applications of that knowledge, good and bad, by all types of consumers.

A Final Note about DK Responses

DK responses may have one of two meanings. The first is that you, the reader, do not have the skills or expertise necessary to make the evaluation called for. For example, you may not have sufficient background in statistics or theory to evaluate adequately the questions bearing on these issues. In these cases, there is little recourse except to continue learning in these areas in order to become more competent and proficient.

The second type of DK response, however, occurs when the study itself does not provide sufficient information on which to base an evaluation. These DK responses are much more problematic, because cross-cultural researchers have a responsibility to address most, if not all, of these points in some fashion in presenting their studies, even if only in a phrase or sentence or two. It is important for consumers to know that researchers were cognizant of the issues, and addressed them somehow. It is worse for the reader to be left hanging, not knowing whether the issues were addressed, because in the end such ambiguity is detrimental to the study's contribution to the literature, knowledge, and application.

✖ Conclusion

Research is the primary way in which scholars and scientists generate knowledge about the world. Knowledge discovered through the research process and found repeatedly across a number of studies is said to be replicated. Replicated findings and knowledge form the basis for what we know as "truth" about the world. It is this truth that is taught to you in schools and conveyed every day in the classroom and through your readings.

Truth and knowledge are bounded, however, by the conditions, parameters, and limitations of the studies that produced that knowledge. All studies are bounded in some fashion by these parameters, whether established through conscious decisions or by default. These limitations apply to all research in all social sciences, regardless of field or discipline. Researchers and consumers of research need to be aware of these conditions and parameters and how they limit the knowledge produced by research.

Cross-cultural research has its own special set of issues concerning the conditions and parameters of research. Many of these issues are merely extensions of general research issues into the cross-cultural arena. Other issues, however, are specific to cross-cultural research. To be a critical reader and evaluator of the cross-cultural research, you need to be alert to these issues.

The issues are so numerous, in fact, that you may well wonder whether *any* cross-cultural study can tell us anything. It is true that all studies have at least some imperfections, and every study has its limitations. But that does not necessarily mean we cannot learn something from that study. The real question is whether the flaws of a study so outweigh its procedures as to severely compromise the trust you might place in its data. If a study is so compromised by problems that you don't trust the data, you shouldn't believe it, whether it is cross-cultural or not. But if a study's problems are less serious, you should be able to glean information from it about cultural differences. If you can do this over a number of studies in an area, they might *cumulatively* or *collectively* say something about that area, even though any single study might not.

Despite all the inherent difficulties, cross-cultural research offers a number of exciting and interesting opportunities not available with traditional research approaches. Through cross-cultural research, we are able to test the limits and boundaries of our knowledge in psychology and about human behavior. We are able to push the envelope of knowledge and understanding about people in ways that are impossible with traditional research approaches. The cross-cultural enterprise itself offers a process by which scientists and laypersons from disparate and divergent cultures can come together and work toward common goals, thereby improving human relations across what otherwise may seem a considerable chasm. The findings from cross-cultural research offer scientists, scholars, and the public ways to further our understanding of human diversity that can serve as the basis for renewed personal and professional interrelationships and can help to focus public and social policy. Methodologically, cross-cultural studies offer researchers a way to deal with empirical problems related to the conduct of research, such as confounding variables present in traditional research approaches.

This process of evaluating the merits of each study in terms of the trust you would place in the data and then accumulating bits and pieces of information across the studies you trust is integral to learning about a field. In this chapter, I have tried to provide a solid basis for developing and practicing these skills.

The material presented in this chapter is just the tip of the iceberg. There are many excellent resources available, other than those cited throughout this chapter, that explain cross-cultural research issues to a greater level of specification for specialists in the field, including issues of methodology (for example, van de Vijver & Leung, 1997a, 1997b), interpretation (Leung, 1989), and data analysis (Leung & Bond, 1989; Matsumoto, 1994). It is this cumulative process that I myself went through in selecting studies and findings from the various fields of cross-cultural psychology to present to you in the remainder of this book. But don't take my word for it; you need to evaluate that research for yourself. It is a skill that takes practice in order to do well, but like many skills, it can be learned. As you read and evaluate the studies presented in this book and elsewhere, I hope you will find that, while cross-cultural research has its own problems and limitations, it has advantages and potentialities that far outweigh the difficulties.

Glossary

back translation A technique of translating research protocols that involves taking the protocol as it was developed in one language, translating it into the target language, and having someone else translate it back to the original. If the back-translated version is the same as the original, they are generally considered equivalent. If it is not, the procedure is repeated until the back-translated version is the same as the original.

cultural response sets Cultural influences on the use of response scales; the cultural tendency to use certain parts of a scale, irrespective of question content.

decenter The concept underlying the procedure of back translation that involves eliminating any culture-specific concepts of the original language or translating them equivalently into the target language.

equivalence A state or condition of similarity in conceptual meaning and empirical method between cultures that allow comparisons to be meaningful.

ethnography A type of study of a culture that involves in-depth immersion in the culture, often requiring the researcher to spend a consid-

erable amount of time learning the ways and customs of that culture.

operationalization The ways researchers conceptually define a variable and measure it.

reliability The degree to which a finding, measurement, or statistic is consistent.

replication Research findings that are repeatedly and consistently found across several studies.

research paradigm An approach to doing research that is characterized by particular methodologies that address certain types of research questions.

sample The final group of units that is included in a study.

sampling procedure The procedures researchers use in determining their sample.

validity The degree to which a finding, measurement, or statistic is accurate, or represents what it is supposed to.

value judgment An interpretation of data that involves attribution of a value, such as good or bad, right or wrong, based on one's own cultural framework.

6

Culture and Basic Psychological Processes

Just as atoms and molecules serve as the building blocks of matter, some psychological processes serve as the building blocks of other psychological constructs. In this chapter, we begin our exploration of cultural similarities and differences in psychology by examining the nature of those psychological building blocks.

We begin by exploring how people of different cultures may differ in the biological bases of their behavior. Next, we examine the relationship between culture and perception, focusing on research that has examined cultural differences in visual perception using optical illusions. After that, we examine the relationship between culture and cognition, including memory, face recognition, categorization, problem solving, decision making, and creativity. Then, we discuss the relationship between culture and consciousness, examining cross-cultural research on dreams, time perspective and orientation, and the perception of pain. We conclude by looking at the important topic of intelligence and what recent cross-cultural research has to say about this highly charged topic, as well as the difficult issues surrounding the use of intelligence and aptitude tests in selection for employment and admission to schools.

Culture and the Biological Bases of Behavior

One of the first topics you learn about in introductory psychology is the various biological—anatomical and physiological—systems that underlie human behavior. Among these basic systems are the brain and central nervous system;

the structure of the eyes, ears, and other sensory systems; the autonomic nervous system, including the sympathetic and parasympathetic nervous systems; and the skeletal muscular systems, including striated and smooth muscles.

This information is important to our understanding of psychological phenomena for several reasons. First, it grounds us in our understanding of exactly how we process sensory information—for example, how stimuli are perceived on our retinas, and how that stimulation is converted to neural signals that travel along the optic nerve to our brains and become acted upon. Second, it helps us to understand how psychological phenomena may be represented in the body. What happens when we are stressed out? How does our brain tell us to move our hand when it touches a hot object? Finally, it helps us understand the bodily functions underlying movements and behaviors.

Like much information presented in mainstream psychology, much of this information is presented as if it were the same for all people of all cultures. In fact, there is very little research that speaks directly to this issue. Most scientists who are expert in the biological bases of behavior will attest to the fact that all people seem to have the same structural anatomy. Certainly, people are amazingly similar in their structural (anatomical) and functional (physiological) functions, regardless of culture, race, or ethnicity.

But evidence from a variety of sources points to differences as well. These are not necessarily differences in structural anatomy. All people have eyes, ears, nose, and mouth; all people have a stomach, intestines, and a heart; all people have a spinal column, brain, and neurons. Rather, evidence suggests that people may differ in the relative sizes of these anatomical structures as well as their functional, physiological relationships, thereby implying differences in psychological and behavioral functioning.

The field of medicine has long been aware of individual differences in biological function and process. Medication can have vastly different effects on two individuals, as can disease processes and health-promoting behaviors. What accounts for these differences? Surely, some of them could be related to genetic or hereditary differences in precise biological composition. If so, these genetic differences may be related to selective evolutionary pressures that predisposed people to exhibit these biological characteristics. If such individual differences are not genetic in nature, they may have resulted from learning and environmental pressures early in life. In either scenario, learning and the environment play an important role in determining biological characteristics, highlighting the interaction between biology and lifestyle (see also Janicki & Krebs, 1998; Papousek & Papousek, 1997; Turner, 1993).

If the effects of learning and lifestyle exist on the group level, such effects may indeed be cultural. The field of anthropological medicine highlights these possible differences. For instance, we know that, at least in this country and culture, calcium plays an important role in the development of strong bones, and lack of calcium fosters the development of a potentially debilitating disease process known as osteoporosis. Osteoporosis, which can be detected by low levels of bone density measured in various areas of the body, increases the risk of fractures, especially among elderly women, which in turn can lead to major disruptions in lifestyle and even death. There are cultures in other parts of the world, however, where such relationships are not entirely true. Japanese women, for example, tend to have lower bone mineral densities, but have lower fracture rates than what would be expected based on baselines in this country. Mayan women of the Yucatan Peninsula also have low bone mineral densities, but low fracture rates. Such anecdotal evidence suggests that the functional relationships between minerals (calcium), bone density, and disease risk (fracture rates) may be mediated by lifestyle issues such as diet, exercise, social support, and other factors, all of which are important components of culture (see also work examining cultural differences in the menopause by Weber, 1997).

Closer to home, psychologists are becoming increasingly aware of the reciprocal relationship between biology and psychology. Early work on the biological bases of behavior was colored by the bias of searching for how biology "caused" psychology—that is, the assumption that our biological composition "caused" predispositions for certain behaviors. Important new research, in such fields as the biobehavioral factors related to violent behaviors and aggression (APS Observer, 1997), now shows that not only does physiology affect behavior, but experience alters physiology, even to the very structure and function of the brain. This new research suggests that early learning experiences and environmental factors may modify the effects of predisposing physiological factors and may actually change neurophysiological functioning. These environmental factors may include diet, trauma, and even types of parenting (see also Zahn-Waxler, Friedman, Cole, Mizuta, & Hiruma, 1996). If these effects are represented on the group level, as in most cultures, this opens the door to the possibility that cultural lifestyle practices influence biological composition, thereby affecting the biological bases of behavior.

Other areas of research also suggest such possibilities, as in the differential incidence of certain physical disease processes in people of different cultures, races, and ethnicities (see also the discussion on this topic in Chapter 9 on physical health). Some research has also documented racial differences in head size (to be discussed later in this chapter, along with the potential pitfalls of the methods and interpretations involved in that research). Research in the field of sports has documented racial differences in such variables as physique and stature, muscle size and length, and the speed of neural transmission. Cumulatively, all of these sources suggest that, even though all humans may be born with the same anatomical structures, there may be differences as well as similarities in the functional and physiological relationships among those anatomical structures. And these similarities and differences, if they exist, may be related to culture as defined so far in this book.

Before leaving this area of speculation, I would like to acknowledge the potential political difficulties in conducting research in this area and reporting the findings. Examining cultural differences in many areas of psychology can be a very touchy issue, especially with regard to such topics as morality, intelligence, and cooperative behaviors. The political ramifications of such research is compounded when the biological bases of these phenomena are studied. I believe such research is made more difficult because of (1) people's assumption that biology "causes" the psychology, (2) the improper reliance on race as a measure of culture, and (3) biases in the interpretation of the findings from such research for personal or political agendas. As a result, many good researchers stay away from potentially "hot" topics. It is my hope, however, that such research will be conducted by competent scientists sensitive to these issues, who can elucidate on the nature of similarities and differences in biological bases of behavior and the possible causes of such similarities and differences that may be rooted in culture, as defined through functional issues such as lifestyle, diet, and exercise. At the same time, the general public needs to be educated about these issues and their potential pitfalls, so that the attitudes surrounding the receipt of such information can be constructive for knowledge, not destructive for people.

Culture and Perception

Perception and Experience

Perception is the process of gathering information about the world through our senses. Before considering how culture affects our perceptions, we must first realize that regardless of culture, our perceptions of the world do not necessarily match the physical realities of the world, or of our senses. Consider visual perception. All of us have a **blind spot** in each eye—a spot with no sensory receptors, where the optic nerve goes through the layer of receptor cells on its way back toward the brain. But if you close one eye, you probably won't experience a hole in the world. There is no blind spot in our conscious perception, even though we have no receptors receiving light from one area of the eye. Our brains fill it in so it looks as if we see everything. It is only when something comes at us out of this spot that we get some idea that something is wrong with our vision in this particular location. Many of you may have performed a brief experiment in an introductory psychology course that illustrates the existence of the blind spot. The point here is that our perception of the world as "complete" does not match the physical reality of the sensation we receive through our visual system.

Everyday experiences with temperature and touch illustrate similar distortions in perception. Fill three bowls with water—one with hot water, one with ice water, and one with lukewarm water. If you put your hand in the hot water for a few seconds and then in the lukewarm water, the lukewarm water will feel cold. If you wait a few minutes, then put your hand in the ice water and then the lukewarm water, the lukewarm water will feel warm. The lukewarm water will not have changed its temperature; rather, it is our perception of the water that has changed (compare with Segall, 1979).

Once we begin to question our own senses, we want to know their limits. We want to know what influence our experiences and beliefs about the world have on what we perceive. We also want to know if other people perceive things the same as we do. If others do not see things as we do, what aspects of their experiences and backgrounds might explain those differences?

One thing we know about our perceptions is that they change. One way they change was noted in our perception of the temperature of the bowls of water. Our perceptions also change when we know more about a particular thing. We all have experienced seeing something complex, like a piece of machinery, for the first time. Can you remember the first few times you looked under the hood of a car? To those who don't now much about mechanics, the engine seems like one immense jumble. But for those who learn about the engine, it becomes familiar and differentiated into specific parts: a carburetor, an engine block, an alternator, and so forth. So, clearly, the way we "see" things changes with our experiences with them.

How might someone with a very different background "see" something that is very familiar to us? How might we "see" something that is very familiar to them and less so to us? A teacher visiting in Australia related an interesting anecdote that highlights these cultural differences in perception. She was teaching at a school for aborigine children in Australia and was trying to teach them to play a schoolyard game called "Who touched me?" In this game, everyone stands in a circle and the person who is "it" is blindfolded. Then another person from the circle quietly walks around the outside of the circle, touches the blindfolded person, and then returns to her or his place. The blindfold is removed, and the person who is "it" has to guess who touched him or her. The teacher found that the aborigine children didn't really want to play, but they cooperated because she was the teacher. Later, in the classroom, she found the students to be uncooperative and reluctant to try anything she suggested. They refused to make any effort to learn the alphabet. She began to think they were being stupid or naughty.

Later, to her surprise, she found out that the children thought *she* was the stupid one. Aborigine children can tell whose footprint is on the ground behind them with a casual glance. So the teacher had them playing a game that was completely silly to them; it was so easy as to make no sense at all as a game. When the children realized that the teacher couldn't tell people's footprints apart, they thought she was stupid and saw no point in paying attention to her. They just humored her so they wouldn't get into trouble, but they didn't take her or her ideas about what they should learn seriously.

Cultural Influences on Visual Perception

Most of what we know about cultural influences on perception comes from cross-cultural research on visual perception. Much of this excellent work has been based on testing differences in optical illusions by Segall, Campbell, and Hersokovits (1963, 1966). **Optical illusions** are perceptions that involve an apparent discrepancy between how an object looks and what it actually is. Optical illusions are often based on inappropriate assumptions about the stimulus characteristics of the object being perceived. One of the best-known optical illusions is the Mueller–Lyer illusion (see Figure 6.1). Research has shown that subjects viewing these two figures typically judge the line with the arrowheads pointing in as longer than the other line—even though the lines are actually the

Figure 6.1 The Mueller–Lyer illusion

Which line is longer? To most people the top line appears longer than the bottom line. The lines are actually identical in length.

Figure 6.2 The horizontal–vertical illusion

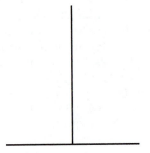

Which line is longer? To most people the vertical line appears longer than the horizontal line, although both lines are the same length.

same length. Another well-known illusion is the horizontal–vertical illusion (see Figure 6.2). When subjects are asked to judge which line is longer, they typically respond that the vertical line is longer—when, again, they are the same length. A third well-known example is the Ponzo illusion (see Figure 6.3). When subjects view this image, they typically report that the horizontal line closer to the origin of the diagonals is longer than the one away from the origin. Of course, they are the same length.

Several important theories have been developed to explain why optical illusions occur. One of these is the **carpentered world theory**, which suggests that people (at least most Americans) are used to seeing things that are rectangular in shape and unconsciously come to expect things to have squared corners. If we see a house from an angle and the light reflected off it does not form a right angle on the eye, we still perceive it as a house with square corners. In the Mueller–Lyer illusion, we tend to see the figures as having square corners that project toward or away from us. We know that things that look the same size to our eyes but are at different distances are actually different in size.

Figure 6.3 The Ponzo illusion

*Which horizontal line is longer? To most people the upper line
appears longer, although both are the same length.*

Therefore, we interpret a set length of line as longer when it seems to project
away from us and shorter when it seems to project toward us.

The **front-horizontal foreshortening theory** suggests that we interpret
vertical lines as horizontal lines extending into the distance. In the horizontal–
vertical illusion, we interpret the vertical line as extending away from us, and
we know that a line of set length that is farther away from us must be longer.

These two theories share some common characteristics. Both assume that
the way we see the world is developed over time through our experiences.
What we see is a combination of the way the object reflects light to our eyes
and our learning about how to see things in general. Although learning helps
us see well most of the time, it is the very thing that causes us to misjudge optical illusions. The second idea these theories share is that we live in a three-
dimensional world that is projected onto our eyes in two dimensions. Our eyes
are nearly flat, and light striking the eye in two places right next to each other
may be coming from very different distances. Thus, we need to interpret distance and depth from cues other than where the light falls on the eye.

A number of cross-cultural studies challenge our traditional notions about
optical illusions, as would be expected if experience contributes to our perceptions. As early as 1905, W. H. R. Rivers compared the responses to the Mueller–
Lyer and horizontal–vertical illusions using groups in England, rural India, and
New Guinea. He found that the English people saw the lines in the Mueller–
Lyer illusion as being more different in length than did the two other groups.
He also found that the Indians and New Guineans were more fooled by the
horizontal–vertical illusion than were the English. These results surprised Rivers and many other people from Europe and the United States. They believed
that the people of India and New Guinea were more primitive and would therefore be more readily fooled by the illusions than the more educated and "civi-
lized" people of England. The results showed that the effect of the illusion
differed by culture, but that something besides education was involved. The

researchers concluded that culture must have some effect on the way the world is "seen." How this difference in perception comes about has been a source of curiosity ever since.

Both the carpentered world theory and the front-horizontal foreshortening theory can be used to explain Rivers's results. Whereas the English people in Rivers's study were used to seeing rectangular shapes, people in India and New Guinea were more accustomed to rounded and irregular environments. In the Mueller–Lyer illusion, therefore, English people would tend to see the figures as squared corners projecting toward or away from them, but Indians and New Guineans would have less tendency to make the same perceptual mistake. The front-horizontal foreshortening theory can also account for the cultural differences obtained in Rivers's study. With fewer buildings to block long-distance vistas in India or New Guinea, the Indians and New Guineans had learned to rely more on depth cues than did the English. As a result, they were more likely to see the horizontal–vertical figure as three-dimensional, and therefore to misjudge the line lengths.

A third theory has been offered to explain cultural differences in visual perception. The **symbolizing three dimensions in two** theory suggests that people in Western cultures focus more on things on paper than do people in other cultures—and in particular, spend more time learning to interpret pictures. Thus, people in New Guinea and India are less likely to be fooled by the Mueller–Lyer illusion because it is more "foreign" to them. They are more fooled by the horizontal–vertical illusion, however, because it is more representative of their lifestyle (although in this example it is unclear whether the differentiation between the cultures is Western versus non-Western or industrialized versus nonindustrialized).

To ensure that Rivers's findings held for cultures in general, Segall and colleagues (1963, 1966) compared people from three industrialized groups to people from 14 nonindustrialized groups on the Mueller–Lyer and the horizontal–vertical illusions. They found that the effect of the Mueller–Lyer illusion was stronger for the industrialized groups, whereas the effect of the vertical–horizontal illusion was stronger for the nonindustrialized groups. Rivers's findings were supported.

Segall and colleagues (1963, 1966), however, also found some evidence that did not fit with any of the three theories—namely, that the effects of the illusions declined and nearly disappeared with older subjects. Based on the theories, we might expect the effects of the illusions to increase with age because older people have had more time to learn about their environments than younger people.

Wagner (1977) examined this problem using different versions of the Ponzo illusion and comparing the performance of people in both rural and urban environments, some of whom had continued their education and some of whom had not. One version of the Ponzo illusion looked like Figure 6.3; another showed the same configuration of lines embedded in a complete picture. Wagner found that with the simple line drawing, the effect of the illusion declined with age for all groups. With the illusion embedded in a picture, however, he found that the effect of the illusion increased with age, but only for urban people and people who continued their schooling. This study provides more direct evidence of the effects of urban environments and schooling on the Mueller–Lyer illusion.

There is also a physical theory that must be considered. Pollack and Silvar (1967) showed that the effects of the Mueller–Lyer illusion are related to the ability to detect contours, and this ability declines with age. They also noted that as people age and are more exposed to sunlight, less light enters the eye, and this may affect people's ability to perceive the lines in the illusion. In addition, they showed that retinal pigmentation is related to contour-detecting ability. Non-European people have more retinal pigmentation, and so are less able to detect contours. Thus, Pollack and Silvar (1967) suggested that the cultural differences could be explained by racial differences in retinal pigmentation (although how the researchers conceptually defined and actually measured race in their study may be problematic, given the ambiguity of that concept).

To test whether the racial or the environmental learning theory was more correct, Stewart (1973) noted that both race and environment need to be compared without being mixed together, as was done in the study by Segall and his colleagues. Stewart first tested the effects of the Mueller–Lyer illusion on both black and white children living in one American town (Evanston, Illinois). She found no differences between the two racial groups. She then compared groups of elementary school children in Zambia in environments that ranged from very urban and carpentered to very rural and uncarpentered. She found that the effects of the illusion depended on the degree to which the children lived in a carpentered environment. She also found that the effect declined with age, suggesting that both learning and physiology played roles in the observed cultural differences.

Hudson (1960) also conducted an interesting study that highlighted cultural differences in perception. He had an artist draw pictures, similar to those in the Thematic Apperception Test (TAT), that psychologists thought would evoke deep emotions in Bantu tribe members. They were surprised to find that the Bantu often saw the pictures in a very different way than anticipated; in particular, they often did not use relative size as a cue to depth. In Figure 6.4, for example, most Americans would see the hunter preparing to throw his spear at the gazelle in the foreground, while an elephant stands on a hill in the background. Many of the Bantu, however, thought the hunter in a similar picture was preparing to stab the baby elephant. In another picture, an orator, who we would see as waving his arms dramatically with a factory in the background, was seen as warming his hands over the tiny chimneys of the factory. Hudson (1960) found that these differences in depth perception were related to both education and exposure to European cultures. Bantu people who had been educated in European schools, or who had more experience with European culture, saw things as Europeans did. Bantu people who had no education and little exposure to Western culture saw the pictures differently.

One might suppose that the cultural differences found in fundamental psychological processes of perception would have considerable implications for

Figure 6.4 Hudson's (1960) picture of depth perception

What is the hunter's target? Americans and Europeans would say it is the gazelle in the foreground. The Bantu in Hudson's (1960) research, however, said it was the elephant.

conflicts that may arise in intercultural interactions. If people from different cultures have learned different ways of perceiving and interpreting the world, what happens when they interact across cultures? Those learned patterns that each culture takes for granted may no longer be valid.

At the same time, however, one has to question the generalizability of these findings beyond the sorts of the tasks used in the studies. For example, in most research on visual perception and optical illusions, the stimuli are presented in two dimensions—either on a piece of paper or projected on a screen. Cultural differences in depth perception may certainly exist using these types of stimuli (as shown in the studies described here, as well as in drawing and other artwork). But to what extent do such effects actually exist in the three-dimensional world? Would Bantu tribespeople see the hunter ready to stab the elephant, and not the gazelle, if the same scene were portrayed out in the open space of their actual environment?

Motivation may be a factor as well. That is, people of different cultures may be differently motivated to perceive certain types of objects, or to perceive them in certain ways. In one study that demonstrated this effect (Broota & Ganguili, 1975), Hindi, Muslim, and American children in India perceived faces associated with either a reward or a punishment in a pretraining session. In the testing session, the participants viewed these and other faces, and judged their characteristics. Significant differences existed between the groups, with the Hindi and Muslim children perceiving more of the faces associated with punishment than reward, while the American children perceived more faces associated with reward rather than punishment.

Future research will need to address the question of the generalizability of previous findings to real-life scenarios, especially controlling for the motivational aspects of such perceptual processes. The literature to date is unclear on these practical issues (despite being quite convincingly clear on the cultural effects in the typical optical illusion paradigm), because there is little if any research that compares perceptual processes in real-life situations and on two-dimensional optical illusions across cultures. One way to address this issue would be to test for differences in perception using both types of stimuli, and to see whether the results using one type of test replicate the results using the other; such a study would also have to control for motivational level and prior experience with such stimuli. Hopefully, future research can address such issues, not only cross-culturally, but within cultures as well.

Culture and Cognition

Just as culture influences the way we receive information about the world around us, culture also influences the way we process that information. Psychologists use the term **cognition** to denote all the mental processes we use to transform sensory input into knowledge. These processes include perception, rational thinking and reasoning, language, memory, problem solving, decision making, and the like. In this section, I will review cross-cultural research in six areas of cognition: categorization and concept formation, memory, face recognition, problem solving, decision making, and creativity.

Culture, Categorization, and Concept Formation

One basic mental process is the manner in which people group things together into categories. People **categorize** on the basis of similarities and attach labels (words) to groups of objects perceived to have something in common. In so doing, people create categories of objects that share certain characteristics. People often decide whether something belongs in a certain group by comparing it to the most common or representative member of that category. For instance, a beanbag chair, a straight-backed dining room chair, and a seat in a theater differ in appearance from one another, but all belong to the basic category *chair.* All these things can be grouped together under the label *chair,* because all share a common function. When we say "That thing is a chair," we mean that the item can and should be used as something for people to sit on (Rosch, 1978).

Some categories appear to be universal across cultures. Facial expressions that signal basic emotions—happiness, sadness, anger, fear, surprise, and disgust—are placed in the same categories across cultures (see Chapter 11). Likewise, there is widespread agreement across cultures about which colors are primary and which are secondary. The way people select and remember colors appears to be largely independent of both culture and language. Regardless of whether people speak a language that has dozens of words for colors or one that distinguishes colors only in terms of whether they are bright or dark, individuals universally group colors around the same primary hues. They also remember primary colors with greater ease when asked to compare and recall colors in an experimental setting. For example, an individual from a culture that has only one word for red/yellow/white will select the same kind of red as the best example of this category as graduate students at Harvard will. Also, both groups of people will remember this particular shade of red more easily than they will a shade like lilac or orange pink, despite having a very different set of names for colors (see Chapter 12 for a fuller discussion of color perception and the categorization of colors).

Culture and the process of categorization share an important and interesting relationship in other ways as well. In Chapter 4, for example, we discussed the process of stereotyping, which many people contend is a special form of categorization involving people. Culture plays a role in the process of stereotyping through the use of cultural filters, which color people's interpretations of the world around them. Culture also plays a role in the maintenance and reinforcement of stereotypes. As you will see in the next chapter, some people believe that culture itself is represented in categories during the development of culture from childhood.

People across cultures tend to categorize shapes in terms of the best examples of basic forms (perfect circles, equilateral triangles, and squares) rather than forming categories for irregular geometrical shapes. These cross-cultural parallels suggest that physiological factors influence the way humans categorize certain basic stimuli. That is, humans seem to be predisposed to prefer certain shapes, colors, and facial expressions.

Research has also shown how cultures differ in categorization. For example, even though a particular category (for example, facial expressions or chairs) may be universal to all cultures, its exact prototype may differ across cultures. Because all people of the world have the same facial morphology (Oster & Ekman, 1979), facial prototypes of emotional expressions will not necessarily differ. However, because the materials used to construct furniture differ across cultures, the prototype of a chair is more likely to differ.

One common way to study cultural differences in categorization involves the use of sorting tasks. When presented with pictures that could be grouped either in terms of function, shape, or color, young children in Western cultures tend to group by color. As they grow older, they group by shape, and then by function (see Bruner, Oliver, & Greenfield, 1966). Western adults thus tend to put all the tools in one group and all the animals in another, rather than grouping all the red things or all the round things together. It had been assumed that this trend was a function of basic human maturation. But given similar sorting tasks, adult Africans showed a strong tendency to group objects by color rather than function (Greenfield, Reich, & Oliver, 1966; Suchman, 1966), suggesting that something besides simple maturation must be responsible for the category shifts.

These differences may be due to culture or education. Evans and Segall (1969) attempted to separate the effects of maturation from those of schooling by comparing children and adults in Uganda. Some of the subjects had received formal schooling; others had not. The researchers gave sorting tasks to all their subjects and found a preference for color grouping most common among people with little or no formal schooling. However, it is still not clear whether cultural differences in sorting tasks and categorization are best attributed to differences in cultural heritage or to differences in formal schooling. Future research on this topic is needed to sort these influences out and determine how culture and educational system jointly influence this cognitive process. Such research will also need to deal conceptually and empirically with the question of how culture, itself represented in categories, relates to the process, function, and development of other mental categories.

Culture and Memory

Another basic intellectual task we all share is remembering things. We have all agonized over the task of memorizing for tests and experienced the difficulty of memorizing lists of dates or names or scientific terms. Whenever we can, we use memory aids, such as shopping lists and calendars, to help us remember things we are likely to forget.

Many of us have heard the claim that individuals from nonliterate societies develop better memory skills because they don't have the ability to write things down to remember them (Bartlett, 1932). Is it true that our memories are not as good when we habitually use lists as aids in remembering? Ross and Millson (1970) suspected that reliance on an oral tradition might make people better at remembering. They compared the memories of American and Ghanian college students in remembering stories that were read aloud. They found that, generally, the Ghanian students were better than the Americans at remembering the stories. Thus, it seemed that cultures with an oral tradition were better at remembering things. But Cole and his colleagues (Cole, Gay, Glick, & Sharp, 1971) found that nonliterate African subjects did not perform better when they were tested with lists of words instead of with stories. These findings suggest that cultural differences in memory as a function of oral tradition may be limited to meaningful material.

One of the best-known aspects of memory, established by research in the United States, is the **serial position effect**. This effect suggests that we remember things better if they are either the first (primacy effect) or last (recency effect) item in a list of things to remember. Interestingly, Cole and Scribner (1974) found no relation between serial position and the likelihood of being remembered in studying the memory of Kpelle tribespeople in Liberia.

Wagner (1980) hypothesized that the primacy effect depends on rehearsal—the silent repetition of things you are trying to remember—and that this memory strategy is related to schooling. Wagner compared groups of Moroccan children who had and had not gone to school and found that the primacy effect was much stronger in the children who had been to school. Wagner suggested that the process of memory has two parts: a "hardware" part, the basic limitation of memory, which does not change across cultures; and a "software" or programming part that has to do with how we go about trying to remember, which is learned. It is the software part that varies across cultures.

The ability to remember unconnected information appears to be influenced not so much by culture but by whether people have attended school. In a class-room setting, children are expected to memorize letters, multiplication tables, and other basic facts. Subjects who have been to school, therefore, have had more practice in memorizing than unschooled individuals. They are also able to apply these skills in test situations that resemble their school experience. A study by Scribner (1974) with educated and uneducated Africans supported this idea. Educated Africans were able to recall lists of words to a degree similar to that of American subjects, whereas uneducated Africans remembered fewer words. It is not clear whether culture or schooling or both contribute to the observed differences.

Memory has interesting implications for a wide range of psychological phenomena, including the production of stereotypes. In one study (Bigler & Liben, 1993), for example, European American children were asked to recall stories about European or African Americans that were either consistent or inconsistent with racial stereotypes. Negative traits were associated with either the European or African American child in the stories. The results indicated that children with better memory for counter-stereotypic stories had lower degrees of racial stereotyping and greater ability to classify people along multiple dimensions. Memory, therefore, may affect stereotypes and the ways by which we understand people.

Despite cultural differences in memory ability (that may be mediated by exposure to formal educational systems), there may be some constants about memory across cultures as well, particularly in the relationship between memory and aging. Studies have shown that memory abilities tend to decrease as people get older (or, at least people become more selective about what they remember!). One study showed that such memory decreases with age were consistent across cultures. In this study (Crook, Youngjohn, Larrabee, & Salama, 1992), Belgian and American participants ranging in age from 14 to 88 years, were matched on gender and age and asked to perform computer-simulated everyday memory tasks. They found that age-related memory decline was consistent in the two groups.

The relationship between memory and oral traditions, and the possible influence of culture versus formal educational experiences on those traditions, raises some interesting questions for our understanding of the effects of culture on memory. Oral traditions are not necessarily limited to cultures with no formal educational systems; they are evident in epics, ballads, and rhymes in many cultures, including our own. Oral traditions can thus tell us something about the workings of memory in any culture (Rubin, 1995). To add to the complexity of these issues, some studies in the anthropology of language have indicated that linguistic structures in written language depend on the practice of orality in the development of writing (for example, Patel, 1996). Future research in this area, therefore, needs to control not only for the effects of education, but also for the cultural meanings of orality, written language, and the specific content of the thing being remembered. At this point, we know that culture influences memory, but we don't know what about culture influences what about memory for what kinds of events, and why.

Culture and Face Recognition

One area of research related to the issue of culture and memory that has received considerable attention in the past two decades is face recognition. Early research in this field showed the existence of a same-race bias in the ability to recognize faces. Malpass and Kravitz (1969), for example, showed photographs of either African American or European American individuals to observers in either a predominantly African American or European American university. The results indicated that observers recognized individuals of their own race better than they did people of the other race. These results have been replicated a number of times (for example, Malpass, 1974), and supported in meta-analyses examining findings across multiple samples and studies (for example, Bothwell, Brigham, & Malpass, 1989). Recent research has documented this effect for Asian faces as well, comparing European and Asian American judgments of European and Asian faces (O'Toole, Deffenbacher, Valentin, & Abdi, 1994). Other recent studies have also demonstrated a same-race bias in discriminating between male and female faces (O'Toole, Peterson, & Deffenbacher, 1996).

Over the years, a number of people have suggested some reasons as to why this bias in face recognition may occur. Brigham and Malpass (1985), for example, suggest that attitude toward people of same and other races, social orientation, task difficulty, and experience all contribute to this differential recognition ability. Brigham and Malpass (1985) also suggest that the explanation provided by intergroup contact theories—that differential recognition stems from limited experience with members of other groups—has received only weak support in the research literature. Devine and Malpass (1985) showed that orienting strategies can affect differential face recognition. When observers in their study were told that they were participating in a reaction time experiment and would later be asked to make differential judgments about the people they observed, no difference in recognition rates occurred. A study by Levy, Lysne, and Underwood (1995) also established conditions in which same-sex, same-age, and same-race information was not associated with better memory recall. These researchers suggested that different self-schemas held by the observers accounted for the differences. Finally, there is some research that suggests that same-race and other-race faces may actually be perceived and classified differently, with race features being coded differently in same-race and other-race perceptions (Levin, 1996).

Regardless of the reason for this effect, these findings have important real-life implications, especially in the area of eyewitness testimony (for example, see Brigham & Malpass, 1985; Malpass, 1981). They suggest, for example, that cross-race face recognition of alleged criminals may be subject to a higher probability of error. These findings also have important implications for intergroup relations and stereotyping. For these reasons, future research should continue to examine the limitations of these findings, broadening its search for the parameters under which they do or do not hold. Future studies also need to examine more closely exactly what it is about culture—experience, motivation, meaningfulness, and the like—rather than race per se that influences the face recognition process, and why.

Culture and Problem Solving

Problem solving refers to the process by which we attempt to discover ways of achieving goals that do not seem readily attainable. Psychologists have tried to isolate the process of problem solving by asking people from different cultures to solve unfamiliar problems in artificial settings. One such experiment (Cole et al., 1971) presented American and Liberian subjects with an apparatus containing various buttons, panels, and slots. After basic instruction in how to work the apparatus, subjects were to figure out how to open the device and obtain a prize. The solution involved combining two different procedures, first pressing the correct button to release a marble, and then inserting the marble into the appropriate slot to open a panel. American subjects under the age of 10 were generally unable to obtain the prize, but older American subjects combined the two steps with ease. However, Liberian subjects of all ages and educational backgrounds experienced great difficulty solving the problem; less than a third of the adults were successful. One might conclude from this experiment that Americans are better at advanced problem solving than Liberians and that the Liberian culture produces adults who lack a capacity for logical reasoning.

Despite its apparent objectivity, however, this experiment may have been biased in favor of the Americans. That is, the Americans may have benefited from the hidden advantage of living in a technological society. Americans are accustomed to mechanical devices; buttons, levers, dials, and slots on machines are common in our daily environment. In some non-Western cultures, people seldom operate machines, and the unfamiliarity of the apparatus may have influenced the outcome by intimidating or bewildering the Liberian subjects. (Remember the first time you ever worked on a computer?)

Cole and his colleagues repeated their experiment with materials familiar to people in Liberia, using a locked box and keys instead of the mechanical contraption. In the new version of the two-step problem, the Liberian subjects had to remember which key opened the lock on the box and which matchbox container housed the correct key. Under these conditions, the great majority of Liberians solved the problem easily.

The success of the Liberians in solving a two-step problem with a familiar set of materials brings us back to the question of whether the experiment tested their ability to think logically or tested their previous knowledge and experience with locks and keys. In an attempt to clarify this issue, the researchers designed a third experiment, combining elements from both the first and second tests. Liberian and American subjects were again presented with a locked box, but the key that opened the box had to be obtained from the apparatus used in the first experiment. To the surprise of the researchers, the third test produced results similar to the first experiment. While Americans solved the problem with ease, most Liberians were not able to retrieve the key to open the box.

Cole and his colleagues concluded that the Liberians' ability to reason logically to solve problems depended on context. When presented with problems using materials and concepts already familiar to them, Liberians drew logical conclusions effortlessly. When the test situation was alien to them, however, they had difficulty knowing where to begin. In some cases, the problem went beyond confusion; uneducated Liberians appeared visibly frightened by the tests involving the strange apparatus and were reluctant to manipulate it. Although adult Americans did very well in these experiments in comparison to the Liberians, how might average Americans react if placed in a similar experimental situation that required the Americans to use wholly unfamiliar concepts and technology—for example, tracking animals by means of footprints and smells?

Another type of problem that has been studied cross-culturally involves syllogisms (for example: All children like candy. Mary is a child. Does Mary like candy?). In wide-ranging studies of tribal and nomadic peoples in East and Central Asia, Luria (1976) documented sharp differences in the way people approached these problems. As with other cultural differences in cognition and thought, the ability to provide the correct answer to verbal problems was found to be closely associated with school attendance. Individuals from traditional societies who were illiterate were generally unable to provide answers to syllogisms containing unfamiliar information. Individuals from the same culture and even from the same village who had received a single year of schooling could respond correctly.

Various explanations have been proposed to account for the inability of uneducated people to complete word problems. Luria (1976) concluded that illiterate people actually think differently from those who are educated. According to this hypothesis, logical reasoning is essentially artificial; it is a skill that must be learned in a Westernized school setting. Some studies lend support to this interpretation. Tulviste (1978) asked schoolchildren in Estonia ages 8 to 15 to solve verbal problems and explain their answers. Although the children were able to solve most of the problems correctly, they explained their answers by citing the logical premises of the problem only in areas where they did not have firsthand knowledge. Elsewhere, their answers were justified with appeals to common sense or statements about their personal observations.

Scribner (1979) questioned whether illiterate subjects are truly incapable of thinking logically and looked more closely into the reasons uneducated people fail to give correct responses to verbal problems. When uneducated peasants were asked to explain illogical answers to syllogism problems, they consistently cited evidence that was known to them personally or stated that they didn't know anything about the subject, ignoring the premises given to them. For example, in response to the word problem "All children like candy; Mary is a child; does Mary like candy?" subjects might shrug their shoulders and comment, "How would I know whether Mary likes candy? I don't even know the child!" or "Maybe she doesn't like candy; I've known children who didn't." These individuals appear to be unable or unwilling to apply concepts of scientific thinking to verbal problems. But this is not because they lack the capacity to reason logically; rather, they do not understand the hypothetical nature of verbal problems or view them with the same degree of importance. People who have been to school have had the experience of answering questions posed by an authority figure who already knows the correct answers. Uneducated people, however, have difficulty understanding the notion that questions need not be requests for information.

In summary, therefore, cross-cultural research on problem solving has documented a number of ways in which people of different cultures solve problems differently. Although many studies have shown that some people of some cultures are at a disadvantage in solving problems, many of these findings may be accounted for by such variables as experience with, meaningfulness of, and relevance of the problem to the participants' lives. It seems to me that all cultures foster the skills necessary for their members to solve problems that are appropriate and relevant in their lives within their cultural milieus. On this level, therefore, the process and goals of problem solving would be cross-cultural in nature. People's specific processes and abilities, however, would naturally differ across cultures because of differences in relevance, meaning, and experience with problems in different cultural milieus. This area of research may benefit from a combined effort of ethnographic and qualitative study, as well as traditional psychological research based in quantitative methods, to examine both similarities and differences in these abilities.

Culture and Decision Making

We make many decisions in our everyday lives. Research in the United States on decision-making processes has shown that we generally use certain strategies when we make decisions. We seek information to confirm a solution, make judgments about the representativeness of the event to a prototype, make judgments based on what comes to mind first, compare the information we have to a standard, and judge positive and negative outcomes of an event (Kahneman & Tversky, 1973; Tversky & Kahneman, 1981). Many people exhibit a *confirmation bias*—a tendency to commit to one type of judgment without adequately considering or testing other hypotheses.

Cross-cultural research on decision making suggests that people of many different cultural groups may use the same types of strategies. What may differ across cultures, however, is the relative weighting or importance of these various processes, and their precise manifestations. Americans, for example, may favor considering many possibilities, testing each as a hypothesis, and then choosing the best solution based on the available information. Tighter (more homogeneous) cultures or cultures high in uncertainty avoidance (those with many rituals to avoid anxiety about uncertainty) may have a greater tendency to make judgments based on representativeness.

Besides favoring certain types of strategies over others, people of different cultures manifest their use in different ways. For example, people of individualistic cultures are more likely to seek further information about an event themselves, whereas people of collectivistic cultures have a much greater tendency to involve others in their decision-making processes, asking opinions and advice from friends, families, and loved ones. People of collectivistic cultures are also more apt to adopt the advice of others, especially those in authority positions within that culture (such as parents or husband).

Recent research on decision making illustrates some of these concepts. Keltikangas-Jaervinen and Terav (1996), for example, showed cultural differences in social decision-making strategies between Finnish and Estonian adolescents. They interpreted their findings as indicative of individualistic versus collectivistic differences, and concluded that personal responsibility (a typically individualistic trait) may not develop if collective identity is expected to be present before personal identity has a chance to form. Cultural differences have also been documented in relation to such topics as applying to college (Valadez, 1998), sex (Flores, Eyre, & Millstein, 1998), career choice (Martin & Farris, 1994), and organizational management (Walters, 1994).

However, cross-cultural research has been slow to map out exactly how different cultural tendencies may be related to what kinds of decision-making strategies, and how these strategies may differ according to context. Such a line of research would require examining multiple decision-making processes in the same individuals across multiple contexts, and comparing individuals from different cultural milieus. Future studies will need to tackle this large but important task.

Culture and Creativity

Another aspect of cognition that has received attention in the literature is creativity. Research on creativity in the United States suggests that it depends on divergent thinking, rather than the convergent thinking that is typically assessed in measures of intelligence. Creative individuals have been shown to have a high capacity for hard work, a willingness to take risks, and a high tolerance for ambiguity and disorder (Sternberg & Lubart, 1995).

These same characteristics appear to be true of creative individuals in other cultures as well. For example, Khaleefa, Erdos, and Ashria (1996) highlighted these characteristics in their study of creativity in a conformist culture (Sudanese); Simonton (1996) documented them in his study of creative individuals in Japanese history; and Satoh (1996) described their implementation in kindergarten programs in Japan to foster the development of creativity in children in that culture. All of these examples are consistent with Sternberg and Lubart's (1995) study of the processes that creative individuals go through, particularly in overcoming obstacles provided to them by conformist-centered organizations.

There are, however, some important differences in the specific ways in which creativity can be fostered in different cultures. Shane, Venkataraman, and MacMillan (1995), for example, studied innovative strategies among a sample of 1,228 individuals from 30 countries who were employees of four different work organizations. The authors characterized the countries in terms of Hofstede's dimensions of individualism, power distance, and uncertainty avoidance (see Chapter 2 for a review). They found that countries high on uncertainty avoidance prefer creative individuals to work through organizational norms, rules, and procedures. Countries higher on power distance preferred creative individuals to gain support from those in authority before action is taken, or to build a broad base of support among members for new ideas. Collectivistic countries preferred creative people to seek cross-functional support for their efforts.

Thus, while creative individuals may share in some common core characteristics across cultures, they need to adapt their abilities to the specific cultural milieu within which they exist, particularly in the implementation and adoption of their creative ideas. Creativity requires people to "get outside of their own box" or framework; another area of cultural difference would be the degree to which this ability is fostered. Future research in this area will need to examine more formally the cross-cultural generalizability of the characteristics of creative individuals and thought processes, as well as the ways in which such processes can be engaged in different cultural milieus and the obstacles that these milieus may present. Future studies, and their authors, will need to be creative to achieve these goals!

Culture and Cognition: A Summary

The research reviewed in this section highlights some interesting and important cultural differences in the ways in which people think. That research has shown differences in categorization, memory, face recognition, problem solving, decision making, and creativity. At the same time, however, there are important similarities across people of different cultures in each of these areas. In general, the processes and goals underlying many of these cognitive abilities may be similar across cultures, but the specific ways in which they are manifested and acted upon appear to differ substantially. Research has generally been preoccupied with the discovery of differences, and has been slow to examine the simultaneous similar and different aspects of these cognitive abilities. Future research is also likely to uncover both similarities and differences in the same individuals across time.

Cross-cultural studies have been conducted in other cognitive areas of psychology as well, such as future-thinking and fantasies (Oettingen, 1997) and cognitive styles (Tullett, 1997). Another important area of cognitive skills that has received considerable attention in the cross-cultural literature is language and language processing (see Chapter 12 and Altarriba, 1993, for reviews). This ever-growing literature has important practical ramifications for all of us, especially those of us in the educational system, and those of you contemplating becoming educators. How do people of different cultures learn? What are the similarities and differences across people and across cultures in the development of cognitive skills and abilities? How do context, culture, and social institutions interact to affect these skills and abilities?

These are just a few of the questions we face today because of an increasing awareness of culture (see also Jacob, 1997). Hopefully, cross-cultural research in this area will lead us to develop new ways of understanding these complex processes, and engaging with them.

Culture and Consciousness

A topic of long-standing interest in culture and psychology is the relationship between culture and consciousness. In contemporary psychology, we generally define *consciousness* as a state of sensations, thoughts, and feelings. The content of this state, of course, may change from moment to moment, as exemplified in the difference between our waking and sleeping states.

People interested in the relationship between culture and consciousness have come at this problem from a variety of angles. Some authors, for example, have examined the content of dreams across cultures, noting that dream content may have different interpretations and meanings in different cultural contexts (for example, Tedlock, 1987). Others have examined psychopathologies and abnormal behaviors across cultures, including behaviors that appear to be dissociative from reality that are pathological in one culture and not so in another (for example, see the work by Bletzer, 1991). Much work has been done on time perspectives and orientations, considerable cultural variations have been found. Still another line of inquiry in this area involves the perception of pain (for example, Morinis, 1985).

Some contemporary authors have suggested that consciousness itself is a cultural construction (for example, Lutz, 1992). That is, our states of feeling, perceiving, and sensing the world around us are as much a social and cultural construction as anything else. This logic suggests that, just as there are differences in cultures across societies, there are necessarily differences in our states of consciousness as well. Another extension of this notion is that individual consciousness must differ from one person to another, because of the differences inherent in personal experiences and development. The same viewpoint would suggest that there are also similarities in consciousness across individuals, to the degree that there are similarities in experience and development. If such similarities of learning experiences exist on the level of culture, the same viewpoint would suggest the existence of cross-cultural similarities in consciousness as well.

This section examines some of the cross-cultural and anthropological literature on the relationship between culture and consciousness through the study of dreams, time, and pain perception.

Culture and Dreams

Psychologists who study and use dreams usually make a distinction between two aspects of them—latent and manifest content. Manifest content refers to the actual content of the dream as seen and experienced by the dreamer. The latent content refers to the psychological themes that are thought to underlie or be represented in the manifest content.

Not surprisingly, cross-cultural research on dreams has found considerable cultural differences in the manifest content of dreams. Punamaeki and Joustie (1998), for example, examined how culture, violence, and personal factors affected dream content among Palestinian children living in a violent environment (Gaza), Palestinian children living in a peaceful area, and Finnish children living in a peaceful area. Participants recorded the dreams they recalled every morning for seven days, and researchers coded their manifest contents. The results indicated that the dreams of the Palestinian children from Gaza incorporated more external scenes of anxiety, whereas the Finnish children's dreams had more "inner" anxiety scenes. Cultural differences in manifest dream content were also reported by Levine (1991) in her study of Irish, Israeli, and Bedouin children, and by Kane (1994) in her study of Anglo-, Mexican-, and African-American women.

The results of Punamaeki and Joustie's (1998) study, however, indicated that culture is not the only factor that influences dream content. That is, children living in the dangerous areas of Gaza had intensive and vivid dreams including themes related to persecution and aggression. These themes, of course, are present in these children's everyday lives, and affected the dreams considerably as well.

Some interesting research has also highlighted important differences in the role of dreams in different cultures. Tedlock (1992), for example, reported that dream sharing and interpretation was a common practice among Mayan Indians in Central America, regardless of the role or position of the person in the culture, and was important in the teaching of cultural folk wisdom. Thus dreams were an important part of the cultural system, involving an organized, conventional set of signs. Likewise, Desjarlais (1991) examined dream usage among the Yolmo Sherpa of Nepal. Here, too, dreams constituted a local system of knowledge that helped in the assessment and communication of personal and social distress and conflict, and hence an important vehicle for social understanding.

Clearly, dream content and usage differ in some important and interesting ways in different cultures. Because American culture does not place much emphasis on the importance of dreams as a symbol of individual and social concerns, American scientists have given relatively little consideration to the study of dreams as a way of understanding culture. Future studies will hopefully address this gap in our knowledge, and perhaps in our ways of understanding consciousness.

Culture and Time

People of different cultures experience time differently, even though time should be technically and objectively the same for everyone. Differences in time orientation and perspective are often a source of confusion and irritation for visitors to a new culture. Many visitors from cultures where time is respected and punctuality is cherished have difficulty adjusting to U.S. public transportation systems, which may not always be on time as scheduled! Visitors from other cultures, however, where time is not so much of the essence and queuing is commonplace, seem less affected by such deviations from schedule, viewing them as trivial and to be expected.

Time orientation can also be a source of pride for the people of a culture. Witness, for example, the clockwork precision of many of the rail systems of Europe and Japan. When I visited Moscow in the early 1990s, I was impressed by the efficiency of the Moscow subway system. My host observed that, given the upheaval that was occurring in the culture and society of the time, "the Moscow Metro is the only thing with any order that we can rely on anymore." In the early days of Perestroika, such reliance must have been a welcome relief for many.

Hall (1973) was one of the first to suggest that cultures differ in their time perspective and orientation. He analyzed differences among people of different cultures in their use of time, and how these differences manifested themselves in actual behavioral practices within such contexts as business. As you can imagine, cultural differences in the use and view of time can be especially agonizing in intercultural negotiation situations (see Chapter 17).

Since that early work, a number of studies have documented cultural differences in time orientation and perspective. Manrai and Manrai (1995), for example, classified individuals from cultures of Western Europe as low-context and individuals from Asia, Japan, the Middle East, and South America as high-context. They found that perceptions of work time were higher in the high-context cultures, whereas perceptions of leisure time was higher in low-context cultures. Levine (1988) studied perceptions of pace of life in Brazil, the United States, Taiwan, Japan, Indonesia, Italy, and England, and found not only that these cultures differed in their perceptions of pace of life, but also that these perceptions were related to well-being. Meade (1971) studied time perspective differences between students in the United States and India through the stories they generated on a semi-projective task, and found that Americans preferred future time orientations in their stories while Indians preferred past orientations.

These types of cultural differences in time orientation and perspective have important implications for real-life situations, such as in business (negotiation), working in groups in school or at work, or just in everyday life (riding the bus or train, getting help at a store). Even though we may take such matters for granted within the cultural milieu in which we live, these differences can be a source of confusion, irritation, and conflict for many who travel across cultural boundaries. Future research will need to explore more fully the nature of the relationship between culture and time, identifying what it is about culture that affects the perception of time. With such knowledge, we can better anticipate conflicts before they arise, and deal with them when they do occur.

Culture and the Perception of Pain

Cross-cultural psychologists and anthropologists alike have long been interested in the relationship between culture and pain, mainly because of anecdotal reports and observations of considerable differences in pain management and tolerance in different cultures. More than 30 years ago, scientists began to formally recognize the influence of culture and attitudinal factors on the response to pain (Wolff & Langley,1968). Today, we know that culture influences the experience and perception of pain in several ways, including (1) the cultural construction of pain sensation, (2) the semiotics of pain expression, and (3) the structure of pain's causes and cures (Pugh, 1991). There is also a growing literature documenting the important implications and ramifications of cultural differences in the perception and management of pain, such as in doctor–patient interactions (Streltzer, 1997).

One hypothesis concerning cultural differences in pain experience has to do with the effect of language on perception and cognition. The Sapir-Whorf hypothesis (discussed in Chapter 12) suggests that the structure of language, which is highly dependent on culture, affects our perceptions and cognitions of the world around us—including our pain experiences. Because the structure, content, and process of language differ across cultures, so does the experience of pain (Fabrega, 1989).

Another related topic is that of cultural display rules (discussed in Chapter 11 on culture and emotion). Just as people of different cultures may have different rules for the appropriate expression of emotion, they may have similar rules governing the expression, perception, and feeling of pain. And just as the strength of people's emotional expressions are correlated with the intensity of their emotional experiences, so the rules governing the expression of pain will ultimately affect people's subjective experiences of pain.

The tolerance of pain may also be rooted in cultural values. Sargent (1984), for example, interviewed females of reproductive age and 18 indigenous midwives in the Bariba culture of Benin, West Africa. In this culture, stoicism in the face of pain was idealized, and the "appropriate" response to pain was considered intrinsic to Bariban identity. Features such as the tolerance of pain through circumcision or clitoridectomy signaled courage and honor, and were considered crucial values within the culture.

Although we know that there are considerable cross-cultural differences in the perception of pain, research has not yet examined systematically exactly what aspects of culture produce those differences, and why. Future studies need to take up this important topic, which is of considerable practical importance to real-life events. Cultural differences in pain management affect how many professionals in the health services physicians, nurses, dentists, psychotherapists, counselors, and others—interact with clients and patients. Even outside of the clinical setting, these issues are becoming more real and important for a growing number of people who deal with intercultural issues in their daily lives at home and work. Future research needs to address these issues and their potential consequences.

Culture and Intelligence

Traditional Definitions of Intelligence in Mainstream American Psychology

The English word *intelligence* is derived from the Latin word *intelligentia*, coined 2000 years ago by the Roman orator Cicero. In the United States, we use the term *intelligence* to refer to a number of different abilities, skills, talents, and knowledge, generally mental or cognitive in nature. Thus, we traditionally consider a number of processes to represent intelligence, such as memory (how well and how much we can remember for how long), vocabulary (how many words we know and can use properly), comprehension (how well we can understand a passage or a set of ideas or statements), mathematical abilities (addition, subtraction, and so forth), and logical reasoning (how well we can understand underlying logic or sequence among events, things, or objects).

A number of theories have dominated our understanding of intelligence in psychology. Piaget's theory (described in Chapter 7) views intelligence as a reflection of cognitive development through a series of stages, with the highest stage corresponding to abstract reasoning and principles. Spearman (1927) and Thurstone (1938) developed what are known as factor theories of intelligence. These theories view intelligence as a general concept comprised of many subcomponents, or factors, including verbal or spatial comprehension, word fluency, perceptual speed, and others. Guilford (1985) built on factor theories to describe intelligence using three dimensions—operation, content, and product—each of which has separate components. Through various combinations of these three dimensions, Guilford suggests that intelligence is actually composed of more than 150 separate factors.

Spearman (1927) also proposed, along with the multiple factors of intelligence, a "general" intelligence representing overall mental ability. This factor, called *g*, is typically measured through a process of combining and summarizing the various component scores of a multiple-factor intelligence test. Although *g* may be a theoretically useful construct, its measurement and meaning have come under considerable scrutiny in the past several decades.

In short, intelligence in contemporary American psychology has generally been considered a conglomeration of numerous intellectual abilities centering around verbal and analytic tasks. Aside from pure knowledge, the ability to reason logically and deductively about hypothetical and abstract issues and events is generally considered a part of intelligence. This definition of intelligence has dominated its measurement and, consequently, the research in this area.

Cross-Cultural Research on Intelligence

Modern intelligence tests were first developed in the early 1900s for the purpose of identifying mentally retarded children. Intelligence tests provided a way to distinguish children in need of special education from those whose schoolwork suffered for other reasons. In the years that followed, intelligence tests came into widespread use in public schools and other government programs.

But not everyone benefited from the new tests of intelligence. Because such tests relied at least in part on verbal performance and cultural knowledge, immigrants who spoke English poorly and came from different cultural backgrounds were at a disadvantage. For example, when tests of intelligence were administered to immigrants at Ellis Island beginning in 1913, more than three-quarters of the Italian, Hungarian, and Jewish immigrants tested as mentally defective. Such low scores for certain immigrant groups provoked a storm of controversy. Some people defended the scientific nature of the new tests, charging that southern European immigrants were not fit to enter the country. Others responded that intelligence tests were biased and did not accurately measure the mental ability of people from different cultures. Thus, less than a decade after the invention of intelligence tests, using them with people from different cultures became a matter of political controversy.

At the end of the century, this controversy has again resurfaced. The debate surrounding the interpretation of test scores of groups who do not belong to the dominant culture continues today, although the groups of people scoring low on standard tests have changed. The average scores of some minority groups in the United States are 12 to 15 percentage points lower than the average for European Americans. This does not mean that all the individuals in these groups test poorly—high-scoring individuals can also be found in minority subcultures—it simply means that larger percentages of the minority populations score low. In a controversy that has come to be known as the "nature versus nurture" debate, people have differed sharply in their interpretations of these scores. This debate is very important in psychology in general, and in cross-cultural psychology in particular.

Is IQ biologically predetermined?   The nature side of the debate argues that differences in IQ scores between different societies and ethnic groups are mainly heredity or innate. Arthur Jensen (1969, 1980, 1981) is one of the best-known proponents of this position. He conducted many different studies on this topic, mostly examining differences between African and European Americans (for example, Jensen, 1968, 1969, 1971, 1973, 1977, 1980, 1981, 1983, 1984), and found that African Americans typically scored lower on IQ tests than European Americans. Jensen takes the position that about 80% of a person's intelligence is inherited and suggests that the gap between the scores of whites and ethnic minorities in the United States is due to biological differences. Based on the results of his studies, Jensen has argued that special educational programs for the underprivileged are a waste of money, time, and effort because inborn intellectual deficiencies of ethnic minorities are mostly responsible for their poorer performance on IQ tests. To support his claim, Jensen has also provided a substantial database examining the effectiveness of educational and remedial programs to bolster the intellectual capacity and abilities of ethnic minorities. When extraneous factors are controlled, he concludes, those programs have had little or no effect on improving intelligence in ethnic minority groups.

Studies of twins have also provided some evidence for the nature hypothesis. The most important of these studies compared identical twins who grew up in separate homes to fraternal twins raised together (Bouchard & McGue, 1981). If test scores are determined by heredity, identical twins raised apart should have very similar scores. But if environment is primary, the scores of the fraternal twins raised together should be more similar. These twin studies revealed that the scores of identical twins raised in different environments were significantly more alike than those of fraternal twins raised together. However, the scores of identical twins raised apart varied more than those of identical twins raised together.

Jensen himself earlier reviewed a number of twin studies (Jensen, 1970), and concluded that the correlation between twins on IQ was .824, which he interpreted as constituting an upper limit on the heritability of IQ. Environmental factors, however, were normally distributed, and IQ was not correlated with those factors. Jensen concluded that environmental factors could not have been systematically related to the intelligence levels of twin pairs.

Results from the twin studies have been used by both proponents and opponents of Jensen's views. While proponents interpret the results to support the claim that much of intelligence is genetic, opponents offer considerably lower estimates of the genetic component. There is widespread agreement, however, that at least 40% of intelligence can be attributed to heredity (Henderson, 1982; Jencks et al., 1972).

Much of Jensen's research of the past two decades has involved studies that followed up his original thesis, in an attempt to uncover the biological bases underlying the ethnic and racial differences in IQ. For example, in some of his earlier research in this area, he documented differences in reaction and inspection times of different ethnic and racial groups of participants to a variety of cognitive tasks (for example, Jensen & Munro, 1979; Jensen & Reed, 1990; Jensen & Whang, 1993; Krantzler & Jensen, 1989). In subsequent research, he has examined the brain correlates of such reaction time measures and IQ, demonstrating a link between brain activity and processes on the one hand and reaction time and IQ on the other (for example, Reed & Jensen, 1992, 1993a, 1993b). Some of his latest research has also documented a relationship among brain size, reaction times, and IQ (for example, Jensen & Johnson, 1994; Reed & Jensen, 1993).

The considerable amount of research generated by Jensen, his colleagues, and others in this area provides a substantial base of data suggesting that at least a large portion of intellectual capacity, as measured by typical IQ tests, is associated with biological characteristics, many of which are genetically heritable. These biological characteristics appear to be related to brain size and function, which in turn appear to be related to racial or ethnic differences.

Is IQ culturally or environmentally determined? As you can imagine, such findings have stirred up considerable controversy. The findings originally reported by Jensen have been countered numerous times in the literature by proponents of the nurture side of the debate, who argue that culture and environment fully account for the difference in IQ scores between whites and minorities in the United States. Those who hold this position claim that minorities score lower because most subcultures in this country are economically deprived (Blau, 1981; Wolf, 1965). Advocates of this position have turned to studies showing that IQ scores are strongly related to social class. The average IQ score of poor whites, for instance, is 10 or 20 percentage points lower than the average score of the middle class. The effect of environment over race can be seen most clearly in studies showing that poor whites tested in Southern states scored lower than blacks who lived in Northern states. It is also possible that between-group differences in intelligence scores are the result of (1) different beliefs about what intelligence is or (2) culturally inappropriate measures of intelligence. What we do know is that intelligence tests are a good predictor of the verbal skills necessary for success in a culture associated with the formalized educational systems of modern industrial societies and increasingly adopted as a model throughout the world. However, such tests may not measure motivation, creativity, talent, or social skills, all of which are important factors in achievement.

A number of other authors and findings support this side of the debate. Scarr and Weinberg (1976), for example, showed that black and interracial children adopted by white families scored above the IQ and school achievement means for whites. Such a finding argues against biological predetermination and in favor of cultural and environmental factors. Greenfield (1997) has argued that intelligence tests can be understood in terms of symbolic culture, and therefore have little translatability (reliability or validity) when used with people of different cultural backgrounds—whether ethnic minorities within one country, or across countries. Such arguments have been proffered for decades now, and have led to the development of a number of "culture-free" or "culture-fair" tests of intelligence, such as the Cattell Culture Fair Intelligence Test.

Collectively speaking, there appears to be an equally large and strong literature base suggesting that IQ is at least malleable to cultural and environmental factors, and that previous findings indicating racial or ethnic differences in IQ are equivocal because of problems of validity in the tests used to measure intelligence in different cultural groups.

Reconciling the two positions.   The topic of intelligence is one that is emotionally charged for many people, scientists and laypersons alike. It has important practical ramifications as well, including the development of appropriate and effective educational programs, and selection of individuals for employment or admission to organizations. These issues have been so emotionally and politically charged, in fact, that many people have suggested that doing research on intelligence is unethical. Such sentiments have undoubtedly persuaded many researchers and other psychologists to stay away from discussions of this topic, let alone conduct research on it.

I prefer to take a more empirical and objective stance on the theoretical and empirical questions these issues raise. There are, in fact, problems on both sides of the issue. On the nature side, the use of race or ethnicity as a classifying variable is problematic because of the ambiguity of these concepts, which may not actually refer to anything meaningful about biology or psychology. As discussed in Chapter 2, these concepts are basically a social construction—categories that we create in our minds to help us classify people in the world around us. In actuality, whether there are truly distinct races of people is still an unanswered question; if anything, the literature suggests that those distinctions really do not exist. While observable differences in "traditionally" racial characteristics such as skin color, face morphology, and the like surely exist, evidence is not conclusive that they are correlated with distinctive biological differences among reliable racial categories.

Given the problems with the concept of race, therefore, we need to recast the findings provided by Jensen and his colleagues concerning the relationship between race or ethnicity and IQ. The findings may indeed exist (data do not generally lie), and they may indeed be related to biological characteristics that have been examined until now, such as brain function, activity, and size. But should these findings be interpreted as indicative of a terminal, unchangeable biological condition? The potential surely exists that biology itself is influenced by cultural and environmental factors, not only over the long term through evolution, but also in the short term as a result of recent social history and even individual experience within the lifetime. Future research is needed to explore how these environmental and cultural factors may indeed affect brain structure and functioning, and how these components, in turn, are related to intellectual processes.

Some arguments on the nurture side of the controversy also have problems. If intelligence really is a cultural construct, then it would be impossible to construct a test that is indeed "culture-fair" or "culture-free," because any such test would, by definition, have to include specific items that are generated within a specific cultural milieu. Even culture-free tests and items would have the underlying bias of culture—a "culture of no culture." In fact, some studies have shown that such tests do suffer from the very biases they were designed to address. Nenty (1986), for example, administering the Cattell Culture Fair Intelligence Test to Americans, Indians, and Nigerians in order to test the validity of the scale, found that 27 of the 46 items administered were culturally biased, thus rendering scores for the three cultures incomparable to one another.

Proponents of the nurture side of the controversy raise many interesting and important issues concerning other possible influences of cultural and racial differences on intelligence, including motivational levels of the participants, experience with similar tests, and difficulty of the items. Such potential confounds raise issues and questions that can only be addressed empirically through research, not through argument and rationalizations. In fact, many of these issues were raised and addressed in Herrnstein and Murray's (1994) recent book, *The Bell Curve*. Although this book stirred up its own share of controversy and debate, it did review a number of studies that examined the potential influence of many of the possible confounding effects that critics of the Jensen studies have suggested. Rhetoric aside, the evidence should be examined objectively in its own right.

For example, Herrnstein and Murray reviewed studies that examined whether the intelligence tests used in previous research had different external validities for different groups—that is, whether those tests predicted performance for African Americans in the real world (jobs, schooling) in the same way that they did for European Americans. Their review of hundreds of studies found no evidence of differential external validity, ruling out this potential cause of differences. They also reviewed studies that examined evidence of bias in internal validity by comparing the difficulty of specific items for different groups. They reported that black/white differences were actually found on culturally neutral items, not culturally biased items, thus ruling out this potential cause of the differences. They examined studies investigating differences in students' motivation to try to do well on the intelligence tests, and found that lack of motivation could not explain the differences in scores. They also examined whether blacks and whites differed in the amount of coaching they received on similar tests, the amount of experience and exposure to such tests, English language fluency, and the racial congruence of the test administrators. They found no effect for any of these variables on the black/white differences, and thus ruled these potential effects out as well. They examined the potential effect of SES, and found that this variable did account for some of the differences between blacks and whites, but not all; in fact, black/white differences in intelligence actually increased with higher SES. Comparisons were also made with studies involving black participants in Africa, the rationale being that these individuals would not have been subjected to the same social legacies as blacks in America. The results across studies, however, showed that the same differences occurred.

The contribution of this work, as I see it, is its attempt to address the issues raised by many previous authors empirically, rather than through argument or rhetoric. And I believe that evidence should be examined objectively for whatever it may be worth. Because these are such highly politically and emotionally charged issues, it is easy to get wrapped up in the arguments of the debate, and relatively more difficult to extract oneself from the argument to lay out the questions that are raised by the arguments. These questions, in turn, form the bases of hypotheses that should be answered by research, not rhetoric or sweeping interpretations and generalizations that become ends in themselves. Herrnstein and Murray (1994) themselves sum up these sentiments in the conclusion of their literature review:

> We cannot think of a legitimate argument why any encounter between individual whites and blacks need be affected by the knowledge that an aggregate ethnic difference in measured intelligence is genetic instead of environmental. . . . In sum: If tomorrow you knew beyond a shadow of a doubt that all the cognitive differences between races were 100 percent genetic in origin, nothing of any significance should change. The knowledge would give you no reason to treat individuals differently than if ethnic differences were 100 percent environmental. By the same token, knowing that the differences are 100 percent environmental in origin would not suggest a single program or policy that is not being tried. It would justify no optimism about the time it will take to narrow the

existing gaps. It would not even justify confidence that genetically based differences will not be upon us within a few generations. The impulse to think that environmental sources of differences are less threatening than genetic ones is natural but illusory. (pp. 313–315)

Gaining some perspective on the research. Sometimes we get so wrapped up in the literature concerning black/white differences in intelligence that we ignore the considerable literature on differences among other cultural groups. Studies have measured intelligence and its correlates in a wide variety of cultural groups, and compared them with one another. These groups have included Asian Americans (Herrnstein & Murray, 1994), Iranian children (Shahim, 1992), Bulgarians (Lynn, Paspalanova, Stetinsky, & Tzenova, 1998), Chinese and Germans (Willmann, Feldt, & Amelang, 1997), Filipinos (Church & Katigbak, 1988), Chinese and Australians (Keats & Fang, 1987), Indians and Nigerians (Nenty, 1986), New Zealanders (Petrie, Dibble, Long-Taylor, & Ruthe, 1986), Hindi Indians (Ajwani, 1982), Nigerian high-schoolers (Nenty & Dinero, 1981), Mexican Americans (Hays & Smith, 1980), Peruvians (Weiss, 1980), Costa Ricans (Fletcher, Todd, & Satz, 1975), Fijians (Chandra, 1975), Israelis (Miron, 1975), Irish (Hart, 1971), Metis and Eskimo schoolchildren (Rattan & MacArthur, 1968), Native Alaskans (Hanna, House, & Salisbury, 1968), Congolese (Claeys, 1967), aborigines in central Australia (David & Bochner, 1967), secondary school pupils in Tanzania (Klingelhofer, 1967), and Guatemalan children (Johnson, Johnson, & Price-Williams, 1967).

While most of this research has been concerned with documenting differences, I personally don't believe in the utility of testing for differences per se. Although it may have been important at one time to document such differences, I believe the field has evolved to the point where cross-cultural research of the future must try to specify what it is about culture that produces differences in what kinds of measurements of intelligence, and why. What learning processes, environmental factors, and developmental constituents influence the development of intelligence in different cultures? Is the contribution of these factors different for different methods of measuring intelligence? What is the contribution of biological endowment and genetic heredity to these correlations? These are the types of difficult questions that face the field. On the one hand, the breadth and scope of the research in this area around the world helps us keep a more healthy perspective on ethnic differences in intelligence within the United States. On the other hand, it highlights the important questions that still need to be asked and answered by future research.

Cultural Differences in the Meaning and Concept of Intelligence

The concept of intelligence in other cultures. One of the positive outcomes from so much research on the relationship between culture and intelligence is an expanded view of what intelligence may be, and how it may be conceptually related to culture. This issue is intricately intertwined with cross-cultural research on intelligence because one of the possible confounding factors in previous studies that documented cultural differences has been cultural differences in the very concept and meaning of intelligence.

Researchers in this area have discovered that many languages have no word that corresponds to our idea of intelligence. The closest Mandarin equivalent, for instance, is a Chinese character that means "good brain and talented." Chinese people often associate this concept with traits such as imitation, effort, and social responsibility (Keats, 1982). Such traits do not constitute important elements of the concept of intelligence for most Americans.

African cultures provide a number of examples. The Baganda of East Africa use the word *obugezi* to refer to a combination of mental and social skills that make a person steady, cautious, and friendly (Wober, 1974). The Djerma-Songhai in West Africa use the term *akkal*, which has an even broader meaning—a combination of intelligence, know-how, and social skills (Bissilat, Laya, Pierre, & Pidoux, 1967). Still another society, the Baoule, uses the term *n'glouele*, which describes children who are not only mentally alert but also willing to volunteer their services without being asked (Dasen et al., 1985).

Because of the enormous differences in the ways cultures define intelligence, it is difficult to make valid comparisons from one society to another. That is, different cultures value different traits (their definition of "intelligence") and have divergent views concerning which traits are useful in predicting future important behaviors (also culturally defined). People in different cultures not only disagree about what constitutes intelligence but also about the proper way to demonstrate those abilities. In mainstream North American society, individuals are typically rewarded for displaying knowledge and skills. This same behavior may be considered improper, arrogant, or rude in societies that stress personal relationships, cooperation, and modesty.

These differences are important to cross-cultural studies of intelligence because successful performance on a task of intelligence may require behavior that is considered immodest and arrogant in Culture A (and therefore only reluctantly displayed by members of Culture A) but desirable in Culture B (and therefore readily displayed by members of Culture B). Clearly, such different attitudes toward the same behavior could lead researchers to draw inaccurate conclusions about differences in intelligence between Culture A and Culture B.

Another reason it is difficult to compare intelligence cross-culturally is that tests of intelligence often rely on knowledge that is specific to a particular culture; investigators based in that culture may not even know what to test for in a different culture. For example, one U.S. intelligence test contains the following question: "How does a violin resemble a piano?" Clearly, this question assumes prior knowledge about violins and pianos—quite a reasonable expectation for middle-class Americans, but not for people from cultures that use different musical instruments.

Recent developments in theories about intelligence. Our expanding knowledge about cultural differences in the concept of intelligence has had important ramifications for our theoretical understanding of intelligence in mainstream American psychology as well. Although traditional thinking and reasoning abilities have dominated views of intelligence in the past, in recent years psychologists have begun to turn their attention to other possible aspects of intelligence. Until very recently, for example, creativity was not considered a part of intelligence; now, however, psychologists are increasingly considering this important human ability as a type of intelligence. Other aspects of intelligence are also coming to the forefront. Gardner and Hatch (1989) have suggested that there are really seven different types of intelligence: logical mathematical, linguistic, musical, spatial, bodily kinesthetic, interpersonal, and intrapersonal. According to this scheme, not only do the core components of each of these seven types of intelligence differ but so do some sample end-states (such as mathematician versus dancer).

Sternberg (1986) has proposed a theory of intelligence based on three separate "subtheories": contextual, experiential, and componential intelligence. *Contextual intelligence* refers to an individual's ability to adapt to the environment, solving problems in specific situations. *Experiential intelligence* refers to the ability to formulate new ideas and combine unrelated facts. *Componential intelligence* refers to the ability to think abstractly, process information, and determine what needs to be done. Sternberg's theory focuses more on the processes that underlie thought than on specific thought outcomes. Because this definition of intelligence focuses on process rather than outcome, it has the potential for application across cultures.

Perhaps the field is coming to realize that intelligence in its broadest sense may be more aptly defined as "the skills and abilities necessary to effectively accomplish cultural goals." If your culture's goals, for example, involve successfully pursuing a professional occupation with a good salary in order to support yourself and your family, that culture will foster a view of intelligence that incorporates cognitive and emotional skills and abilities that allow for pursuing such an occupation. Those skills and abilities may include deductive reasoning, logical thought, verbal and mathematical skills—the sorts of skills that are fostered in contemporary American culture. If your culture's goals, however, focus more on the development and maintenance of successful interpersonal relationships, working with nature, or hunting and gathering, intelligence will more aptly be viewed as the skills and abilities related to such activities. On one level, therefore, people of all cultures share a similar view of intelligence, in that intelligence is a catchall concept that summarizes the skills and abilities necessary to live effectively in one's culture. At the same time, however, cultural differences naturally exist because of differences in how cultures define goals and the skills and abilities needed to achieve those goals. Future research will need to delve into these dual processes, searching for commonalities as well as differences across cultures and exploring what contextual variables affect intelligence-related behaviors, and why.

Culture, Intelligence, and Selection Issues

In the meantime, however, we are left with current ways of understanding and measuring intelligence, and the issues they raise when such tests are used for selection decisions for employment or admission to schools. Before leaving this section on intelligence, I would like to discuss briefly the important ramifications that potential cultural, racial, and ethnic differences have on such selection issues. When intelligence tests are used to predict performance (for example, in a job or at school), the validity of the criterion used to judge the outcome of the test becomes a practical issue. A test may be perceived as culturally "biased," yet still be the best predictor of performance at a certain task. Altering the test to reduce the cultural bias may actually weaken the ability of the test to predict performance. If people are admitted based on faulty data, their overall performance may not be as high as it could have been with the use of the better predictor, even though it is the more culturally biased test. If you were in an organization (or business) that needed to base selection on test scores, what would you do? This difficult issue has faced not only many business organizations, but many schools and universities around the country.

One response by some agencies to gender, race, and ethnic group differences in mean scores on tests for employment has been to convert applicants' scores to percentile scores adjusted for their racial, ethnic, or gender group. This procedure, known as *within-group norming,* was widely used by government, educational, and private organizations through the 1980s. The underlying rationale was that such norming would equalize differences among groups that may have resulted from prior social inequalities, cultural bias in the tests, or other such factors (Sackett & Wilk, 1994).

These procedures, however, have not been without their own set of philosophical and legal controversies. On the one hand, the use of existing tests of intelligence and personnel selection leads to disparate impact—racial imbalance—as long as racial or ethnic differences in test ability exist. Such disparate impact is generally considered evidence of unlawful discrimination (Gottfredson, 1994). On the other hand, employers can only avoid disparate impact if they engage in unlawful disparate treatment through racial preferences. As public attention was drawn to these difficult issues, it led to the Civil Rights Act of 1991, which prohibited within-group norming. The latest approach to this problem has been through a process known as *banding*—the grouping of individuals' test scores within ranges of scores. For example, all scores between 90 and 100 would be in Band 1, 80 and 89 in Band 2, 70 and 79 in Band 3, and so on. People whose scores fall in Band 1 would be selected before those in Band 2, and likewise down the line. All people within Band 1 would be treated as equals, individual differences within the band would be ignored.

Banding has many different manifestations, and entails numerous issues, including determination of bandwidth and movement of the band after selections are made. Like any procedure, it has both advantages and disadvantages. Future research will need to examine the pros and cons of this and other procedures in assessing the validity of tests of aptitude and intelligence for employment or admission to schools. In these studies, the biases and moral assumptions that inevitably underlie research procedures need to be made more explicit than they are now. The final issue, indeed, may not be the outcome of such research, but whether there is full disclosure of the moral decisions made by the researchers in the course of their research.

Conclusion

In this chapter, we have examined how culture influences the basic psychological processes of perception, cognition, consciousness, and intelligence. We also speculated about the possible impact of culture on the biological bases of behavior. These influences have profound implications for our understanding of the impact of culture on people and behavior. I remember fondly when I was first introduced to the material concerning cultural influences on visual perception and optical illusions. I had never thought that culture, and experience in general, could have the effect that it does on what I thought must be innate, basic properties. When I learned of cultural differences in optical illusions, it gave me a new perspective on the nature and pervasiveness of culture.

The issues discussed in this chapter serve as the basis for understanding findings from many cross-cultural studies to be discussed in subsequent chapters. Perception, cognition, and consciousness lie at the core of many psychological constructs, and cultural differences in these processes demonstrate the various levels of psychology that culture influences. As consciousness reflects our subjective experience of the world, we take for granted that our consciousness is shared by others; research in this area, however, has shown that there may be large cultural, as well as individual, differences in consciousness. And though we all share similar characteristics in our biological composition, there may also be important differences in that biology and physiology that underlie our psychological makeups.

These differences have important ramifications for intercultural interactions and applied settings. If people from different cultural backgrounds can view such things as optical illusions differently, it is no wonder they perceive so much of the rest of the world differently as well. When this information is coupled with information concerning other basic psychological processes such as attribution, emotion, and personality, the effect of culture on individual psychology is amazing.

Likewise, cultural differences and similarities in definitions and processes of intelligence have considerable relevance to various applied settings. Many current curriculum transformation movements in the United States, for example, are based on a particular view and definition of intelligence and cognitive development. It is not uncommon to hear allegations of cultural bias in these types of educational reforms. Indeed, if broad, sweeping educational changes are implemented in the United States without recognition and awareness of deeply embedded cultural differences in the nature and definition of intelligence, we may actually be broadening the gaps that already exist between groups and increasing, rather than decreasing, intergroup conflict in the name of "education."

Awareness of cultural differences in intelligence raises difficult questions concerning testing and the use of test scores. Should bias in testing be eliminated at the expense of the predictive validity of the test? Many educational institutions and business organizations today face this difficult question, which is compounded by legal ramifications and the constant threat of litigation. Perhaps we need to give consideration to yet another aspect of intelligence—that is, our attitudes regarding intelligence. A cross-cultural understanding of differences in the definitions and processes of intelligence should help to deepen our appreciation and respect for cultures different from our own, and help us to find similarities as well as differences among people.

Glossary

blind spot A spot in our visual field where the optic nerve goes through the layer of receptor cells on its way back toward the brain, creating a lack of sensory receptors in the eye at that location.

carpentered world theory A theory of perception that suggests that people (at least most Americans) are used to seeing things that are rectangular in shape, and thus, unconsciously expect things to have square corners.

categorize To classify objects on the basis of perceived similarities and attach labels (words) to those classifications.

cognition The way we process information in our minds, transforming sensory input into knowledge.

front-horizontal foreshortening theory A theory of perception that suggests that we interpret vertical lines as horizontal lines extending into the distance. Because we interpret the vertical line in the horizontal–vertical illusion as extending away from us, we see it as larger.

optical illusions Perceptions that involve an apparent discrepancy between how an object looks and what it actually is.

perception The process of gathering information about the world through our senses.

serial position effect The finding that people tend to remember something better if it is either the first or last item in a list.

symbolizing three dimensions in two A theory of perception that suggests that people in Western cultures focus more on things on paper than do people in other cultures, and in particular spend more time learning to interpret pictures.

Culture and Development

When the study of culture and psychology uncovers cultural differences, a natural question is, How did these differences arise in the first place? What happens during development that makes people of different cultures different? What are the relative influences of parents, families, extended families, schools, and other social institutions? Are people born with inherent, biological predispositions to behavioral and cultural differences, or are such differences due entirely to environment and upbringing? What psychological differences are there in childhood and development when people are raised in different cultures?

This chapter examines two main questions. First, how does the process of enculturation work? That is, how do people come to acquire their cultures? Research in this area has focused on temperament, attachment, parenting styles, and the educational system. Second, what kind of psychological differences appear to exist across cultures during childhood and throughout development? This question involves aspects of cognitive, moral, and socioemotional development.

Enculturation and Socialization

Childhood in any society is a period of considerable change and flux, subject to more cultural and environmental influences than any other in the life span. One aspect of childhood that is probably constant across cultures is that people emerge from this period with a wish to become happy, productive adults. Cultures differ, however, in exactly what they mean by "happy" and "productive."

Despite similarities in the overall goals of development, therefore, cultures exhibit a tremendous degree of variability in its content.

Each culture has some understanding of the adult competencies needed for adequate functioning (Ogbu, 1981), but these competencies differ by culture and environment. Children are socialized in ecologies that promote their specific competencies (Harrison, Wilson, Pine, Chan, & Buriel, 1990). For example, children who need a formal education to succeed in their culture are likely to be exposed to these values early in childhood. They may receive books and instruction at a young age. Children in another culture may have to do spinning and weaving as part of their adult livelihood. These children are likely to receive early exposure to those crafts. We are all truly integrated in our own societies and cultures. By the time we are adults we have learned many cultural rules of behavior, and we have practiced those rules so much that they are second nature to us. Much of our behavior as adults is influenced by these learned patterns and rules, and we are so well practiced at them that we engage in these behaviors automatically and unconsciously, without giving them much thought.

Still, at some time in our lives, we must have learned those rules and patterns of behavior. Culture, in its truest and broadest sense, involves so many different aspects of life that it is impossible to simply sit somewhere and read a book and learn about, let alone thoroughly master, a culture. Culture must be learned through a prolonged process, over a considerable period of time, with much practice. This learning involves all aspects of the learning processes that psychologists have identified over the years, including classical conditioning operant conditioning, and social learning. In learning about culture, we make mistakes along the way, but people or groups or institutions are always around to help us, and in some cases force us, to correct those mistakes.

Socialization is the process by which we learn and internalize the rules and patterns of behavior that are affected by culture. This process, which occurs over a long period of time, involves learning and mastering societal and cultural norms, attitudes, values, and belief systems. The process of socialization starts early, probably from the very first day of life. Some people believe that the biological temperaments and predispositions we bring with us into the world at birth are actually part of the socialization process. While this is an interesting and intriguing idea, most of what we know about the socialization process and the effects of socialization concern life after birth.

Closely related to the process of socialization is the process called **enculturation**. This is the process by which youngsters learn and adopt the ways and manners of their culture. There is very little difference, in fact, between the two terms. Socialization generally refers more to the actual process and mechanisms by which people learn the rules of society and culture—what is said to whom and in which contexts. Enculturation generally refers to the products of the socialization process—the subjective, underlying, psychological aspects of culture that become internalized through development. The similarities and differences between the terms *enculturation* and *socialization* are thus related to the similarity and difference between the terms *culture* and *society*.

A close relative of enculturation is a term we hear often today—**accultura-tion**. This term refers to the process of adapting to (and in many cases adopting) a different culture from the one in which a person was enculturated. The term is generally used in connection with immigration—moving from one country to another and learning to live in that "foreign" culture.

Socialization (or enculturation) **agents** are the people, institutions, and organizations that exist to help ensure that socialization occurs. The first and most important of these agents is parents. They help instill cultural mores and values in their children, reinforcing those mores and values when they are learned and practiced well and correcting mistakes in that learning.

Parents, however, are not the only socialization agents. Siblings, extended families, friends, and peers are important socialization and enculturation agents for many people. Organizations such as school, church, and social groups such as the Boy or Girl Scouts also become important agents of these processes. In fact, as you learn more about the socialization process, you will find that culture is enforced and reinforced by so many people and institutions that it is no wonder we all emerge from the process as masters of our own cultures.

In this section, I will examine research that has been conducted on the developmental processes thought to contribute to the process of enculturation. Fortunately, there is a wealth of studies on cultural differences in developmental processes that should inform us about how cultures "do" socialization differently. A considerable amount of research has also been conducted on schooling and education in different cultures, which should tell us something about how culture is transmitted through a major institution in many people's lives. In recent years, researchers have tried to examine the process of enculturation itself, looking at how people's interactions with the various socialization agents help to produce cultures, and how we develop cultural and ethnic identities. I begin this review by examining the possibility that children of different cultures are born with different biological predispositions to learn certain cultural practices—that is, the issue of temperament.

Culture and Temperament

Traditional knowledge. Any parent can tell you that no two babies are alike. It is not simply that they look different but that they differ from the very beginning in **temperament**. Each baby has its own way of being in the world—easygoing or fussy, active or quiet. These qualities of responsiveness to the environment exist from birth and evoke different reactions from people in the baby's world. Temperament is generally considered to be a biologically based style of interacting with the world that exists from birth.

In mainstream psychology, Thomas and Chess (1977) have described three major categories of temperament: easy, difficult, and slow-to-warm-up. **Easy temperament** is defined by a very regular, adaptable, mildly intense style of behavior that is positive and responsive. **Difficult temperament** is an intense, irregular, withdrawing style generally marked by negative moods. **Slow-to-warm-up** infants need time to make transitions in activity and experiences.

Though they may withdraw initially or respond negatively, given time and support they will adapt and react positively.

The interaction of a child's temperament with that of the parents, known as **goodness of fit**, seems to be a key to the development of personality. Parental reactions to a child's temperament can promote stability or instability in the child's temperamental responses to the environment. The parents' responses to the child's temperament will also affect subsequent attachment.

Cross-cultural studies on temperament.   Several studies have examined whether children of non-American cultures have general styles of temperament that differ from those described for American infants. The implications of differences in temperament, if they exist, are large. If children of other cultures have different temperaments at birth, they will respond to the environment differently. Moreover, they will evoke responses from the environment and caregivers that are different from what Americans would expect. These two fundamental differences—in temperament and environmental response—should produce a fundamental difference in the learning and social experiences of those children, and consequently in their worldview and culture as they grow older.

Indeed, Freedman (1974) found that Chinese American babies were calmer and more placid than European American babies or African American babies. When a cloth was placed on their faces covering their noses, the Chinese American babies lay quietly and breathed through their mouths. The other babies turned their heads or tried to pull the cloth off with their hands. Freedman found similar differences with Japanese American and Navajo babies when compared to European Americans. Likewise, Chisholm (1983) extensively studied Navajo infants and found that they were much calmer than European American infants.

Chisholm (1983) argues that there is a well-established connection between the condition of the mother during pregnancy (especially high blood pressure levels) and the irritability of the infant. This connection between maternal blood pressure and infant irritability has been found in Malaysian, Chinese, Aboriginal and white Australian infants, as well as in Navajo infants (Garcia Coll, 1990). Garcia Coll, Sepkoski, and Lester (1981) found that differences in the health of Puerto Rican mothers during pregnancy were related to differences in their infants' temperaments when compared to European American or African American infants. The Puerto Rican babies were alert and did not cry easily. The African American babies scored higher on motor abilities—behaviors involving muscle movement and coordination.

An important cultural factor to consider is the interaction between parents' responses and infant temperament. This interaction is certainly one of the keys to understanding the development of culture and socialization processes. The quiet temperament and placidity that are notable in infants from Asian and Native American backgrounds are probably further stabilized in later infancy and childhood by the response of the mothers. Navajo and Hopi babies spend long periods of time tightly wrapped in cradle boards; Chinese parents value the harmony that is maintained through emotional restraint (Bond & Wang,

1983). Thus, differences in infant temperament may make it easier for parents of different cultures to engage in parenting styles and behaviors that teach and reinforce their particular cultural practices. Temperament, therefore, may serve as a baseline biological predisposition of the infant that allows this type of learning to occur.

Why does temperament differ across cultures? It is possible that differences in temperament reflect differences in genetics and in reproductive histories. Thus, environmental and cultural pressures over generations may have helped to produce minor biological differences in infants through a functionally adaptive process. In addition, the cultural experiences of the mother during pregnancy, including diet and other culture-related practices, may contribute to a prenatal environment that modifies an infant's biological composition to correspond to those cultural practices. To my knowledge, research is not yet clear on the exact nature of this relationship.

One problem inherent in conducting and interpreting research on differences in temperament is the difficulty in defining race and racial differences (see Chapter 2). Nevertheless, these differences that are evident from birth contribute to the personality differences we observe in adults of different cultures. Therefore, it is important to understand the magnitude of their contributions as building blocks in the development of adult members of the cultures of the world. Future research in this area should focus on the cultural practices and actual behaviors of people of different cultural groups, and examine the relationship between those and infant temperament.

Culture and Attachment

Traditional knowledge. **Attachment** refers to the special bond that develops between the infant and its primary caregiver. Many psychologists believe that the quality of attachment has lifelong effects on our relationships with loved ones. Attachment provides the child with emotional security. Once attached, babies are distressed by separation from their mothers (separation distress or anxiety). The studies on attachment in rhesus monkeys by the Harlows (Harlow & Harlow, 1969) highlighted the importance of contact and physical comfort in the development of attachment. Bowlby (1969) concluded that infants must have a preprogrammed, biological basis for becoming attached to their caregivers. This innate behavioral repertoire includes smiling and cooing to elicit physical attachment–producing behaviors on the part of the mothers.

Ainsworth, Blehar, Waters, and Wall (1978) have described three different styles of attachment: secure, avoidant, and ambivalent. Mothers of **securely attached** babies are described as warm and responsive. Mothers of **avoidant** children, who shun their mothers, are suspected of being intrusive and overstimulating. **Ambivalent** children are uncertain in their response to their mothers, going back and forth between seeking and shunning her attention. These mothers have been characterized as insensitive and less involved.

Attachment underpins the concept of trust. Erikson (1963) described the formation of basic trust as the important first step in the lifelong process of psychosocial development. Poor attachment is a component of mistrust—the unsuccessful resolution of the needs of the infancy stage. Basic trust is presumed to affect our later relationships and the subsequent stages of development. Erikson described the other stages of childhood as involving the tasks of establishing autonomy, initiative, and competency. All of these parts of the developing self are influenced by how mothers and important others in the child's life respond to him or her.

Cross-cultural studies of attachment.   In the United States, secure attachment is assumed to be the ideal. The very term that Ainsworth and colleagues chose to describe this type of attachment, and the negative terms used to describe others, reflects this underlying bias. Cultures differ, however, in their notion of "ideal" attachment. For example, German mothers value and promote early independence and regard avoidant attachment as the ideal. German parents see the "securely" attached child as "spoiled" (Grossmann, Grossmann, Spangler, Suess, & Unzner, 1985). Of Israeli children who are raised on a kibbutz (collective farm), half display anxious ambivalent attachments, and only a third appear to be securely attached (Sagi, Lamb, Lewkowicz, Shoham, Dvir, & Estes, 1985). Children raised in traditional Japanese families are also characterized by a high rate of anxious ambivalent attachment, with practically no avoidant types (Miyake, Chen, & Campos, 1985). These traditional mothers seldom leave their children (such as with babysitters) and foster a strong sense of dependence in their children (which in itself is curious, because studies of U.S. culture have shown that ambivalent infants are generally associated with mothers who are less involved). This dependence supports the traditional cultural ideal of family loyalty. In nontraditional Japanese families, where the mother may have a career, attachment patterns are similar to those in the United States (Durrett, Otaki, & Richards, 1984).

Some cross-cultural studies also challenge the notion that closeness to the mother is necessary for secure and healthy attachment. Indeed, this notion is prevalent in traditional theories of attachment based on research in the United States. Studies involving an African tribe of forest-dwelling foragers known as the Efe (erroneously referred to by most people as pygmies, a name they do not like) show a very different pattern from the one psychologists have come to accept as necessary to healthy attachment (Tronick, Morelli, & Ivey, 1992). Efe infants spend most of their time away from their mothers and are cared for by a variety of people. They are always within earshot and sight of about ten people. They have close emotional ties to many people other than their mothers and spend very little time with their fathers. The researchers found these children to be emotionally healthy despite having multiple caregivers.

Although this study demonstrated that closeness or proximity to their mothers is not necessary for healthy attachment among the Efe, this is not necessarily the case for children of other cultures. And the situation is certainly not comparable to that of North American children who attend day-care centers. The Efe have large extended families, and these families are permanent parts of the growing Efe children's lives. In North American day care, by contrast, staff turnover is typically high and relationships with children are not long-term. What the Efe may be revealing is that multiple caregivers who remain stable in a child's life are a healthy alternative to our traditional ideas.

Studies by Miyake (1993) and his colleagues on infant attachment patterns in Japan summarize and highlight many of these points. In numerous studies on this topic, Miyake (1993) has reported finding no avoidantly attached children. In contrast to the United States, where most attachments are characterized as secure, attachments in Japan are overwhelmingly characterized as ambivalent, indicating a strong desire to prevent separation (and thus to foster dependence between mother and infant). Some of their other studies, moreover, have demonstrated the close relationship between temperament and attachment. These researchers measured irritability in response to interruption of sucking—a common measure of temperament—during the 2nd and 5th days of life. They then classified the neonate's cries as either smooth (fast rise time, brief duration, quick quieting) or effortful (prone to interruption, raucous in quality, and with facial and vocal expressions disorganized). They found that the nature of these cries in the 2nd and 5th days of life predicted attachment one year later, with smooth criers being associated with secure attachments, and effortful criers being associated with ambivalent attachment (the Japanese mode).

There is still much to be done to understand the attachment patterns in other cultures, and the relationship among cultural milieu, infant temperament, and attachment styles. The studies that do exist, however, do not support the assumption that the patterns typical of European American culture are best or most descriptive for all. Notions about the quality of attachment and the processes by which it occurs are qualitative judgments made from the perspective of each culture. Each culture has different but not necessarily better values than others.

Culture, Child Rearing, Parenting, and Families

Traditional knowledge. Clearly, our parents play an important if not the most important role in our development. Parenting styles differ dramatically. Baumrind (1971) has identified three major patterns of parenting. The **authoritarian parent** expects unquestioned obedience and views the child as needing to be controlled. **Permissive parents** allow children to regulate their own lives and provide few firm guidelines. The **authoritative parent** is firm, fair, and reasonable. This style is seen as promoting psychologically healthy, competent, independent children who are cooperative and at ease in social situations. Other researchers (Maccoby & Martin, 1983) have identified a fourth type of parenting style called uninvolved. **Uninvolved parents** are often too absorbed in their own lives to respond appropriately to their children and may seem indifferent to them.

Relationships with people other than our parents also influence our development. As children move out of early childhood, friendships change. These changes are due largely to cognitive development. The new ability to think about themselves and others and to understand their world allows children to develop peer relations that have more depth and meaning.

Cross-cultural research on parenting styles.   Over the past two or three decades, a considerable amount of cross-cultural research has examined differences in parenting styles across cultures and investigated the degree to which these parenting differences contribute to cultural differences on a variety of psychological constructs. Much of this research has centered on differences between American and Japanese parenting styles, mainly because Japanese culture seems to be very different from that of the United States yet is relatively accessible to American researchers. Studies of European cultures and Indian culture have been conducted as well, and also provide valuable information on this topic.

One interesting study investigated the strategies that Japanese and American mothers use to gain compliance from young children. In this study (Conroy, Hess, Azuma, & Kashiwagi, 1980), American and Japanese mothers and their firstborn infants were interviewed about six hypothetical situations, each representing an action on the part of the child that the mother was likely to encounter in their daily interactions and that was likely to evoke an adult intervention. On the basis of the responses, the mothers' control strategies were then coded into categories such as appeals to authority, rules, feelings, consequences, or modeling. The results indicated that the Japanese mothers were more likely to engage in feeling-oriented appeals, and demonstrated greater flexibility than the American mothers, who relied more extensively on their authority as mothers. The authors concluded that the findings reflected broad cultural differences in patterns of enculturation and socialization, with the focus in Japan on personal and interpersonal ties, in contrast to the American focus on direct instrumental processes with greater reliance on rewards and punishments.

Differences in child-rearing practices have also been found for other cultural groups. Kelley and Tseng (1992), for example, compared European American and Chinese American mothers. They found that the European American mothers scored higher on sensitivity, consistency, nonrestrictiveness, nurturance, and rule setting, whereas the Chinese American mothers scored higher on physical punishment and yelling. The authors related these results to the need for Chinese Americans to maintain their ties to their culture of origin. Devereux, Bronfenbrenner, and Suci (1962) reported that Germans engaged in more parenting behaviors related to affection, companionship, and direct punishment and control than did American parents.

Of the many different child-rearing behaviors people of different cultures engage in, one of the most representative of cultural differences concerns sleeping arrangements. One of the single greatest concerns of urban-dwelling Western parents, especially Americans, is getting their baby to sleep through the night, and to do so in a room separate from the parents'. Americans shun co-sleeping arrangements, with the underlying assumption that sleeping alone will help develop independence. Some assistance is offered to the child by way of "security objects" such as a special blanket or toy.

Many other cultures do not share this value. In rural areas of Europe, for example, infants sleep with their mothers for most, if not all, of their first year.

This is true for many other cultures in the world, and comfort objects or bedtime rituals are not common in other cultures. Mayan mothers allow their children to sleep with them for several years because of a commitment to forming a very close bond with their children. When a new baby comes along, older children move to a bed in the same room or share a bed with another member of the family (Morelli, Oppenheim, Rogoff, & Goldsmith, 1992). In traditional Japanese families, the child sleeps with the mother, either with the father on the other side or in a separate room. Again, these practices foster behaviors and values that are consonant with the developmental goals of the culture.

Cross-cultural research has also shown considerable differences in gender role differentiation between parents. Best, House, Barnard, and Spicker (1994), for instance, examined gender differences in parent–child interactions in France, Germany, and Italy. They found that French and Italian fathers engaged in more play than mothers, but the opposite was true in Germany. Devereux, Bronfenbrenner, and Suci (1962) found that the relative prominence of the mother is much more marked in American families than in German ones; that is, their American sample showed greater gender role differentiation than did their German sample. Bronstein (1984), studying parent–child dyads in Mexican families, found that fathers were more playful and companionable than mothers, whereas mothers were more nurturant in providing for immediate physical needs.

Many of these cultural differences in parenting styles may be related to expectations that parents have about child rearing and culture. Joshi and MacLean (1997), for example, investigated maternal expectations of child development in India, Japan, and England. In this study, mothers were asked to indicate the age at which they expected a child to achieve each of 45 developmental tasks. Japanese mothers had higher expectations than British mothers in the domains of education, self-care, and environmental independence. Indian mothers had lower expectations than the Japanese and British in all domains except environmental independence. Another study (Kuthar & Uinlan, 1993) found that images about parental style in India and the United States were related to perceptions of care, ego resilience, and depressive tendencies.

Cross-cultural research has not only demonstrated cultural differences in parenting styles; it has documented numerous cultural similarities as well. Kelley and Tseng (1992), for example, found that both European American and Chinese American mothers place more emphasis on manners, school-related skills, and emotional adjustment when their children are 6–8 years of age than when they are 3–5. Solie-Camara and Fox (1995), using a 100-item rating scale called the Parent Behavior Checklist, found that Mexican and American mothers did not differ in their developmental expectations or in their parenting practices. Papps, Walker, Trimboli, and Timboli (1995) found that mothers from Anglo-American, Greek, Lebanese, and Vietnamese ethnic groups all indicated that power assertion was their most frequently used disciplinary technique. And Keller, Chasiotis, and Runde (1992) reported cultural similarities among American, German, and Greek parents in the latencies of verbal and vocal behaviors toward children.

Thus, research evidence suggests both differences and similarities across cultures in parenting styles and child rearing. All of the studies have shown that parenting styles tend to be congruent with developmental goals dictated by culture; that is, cultural differences in specific values, beliefs, attitudes, and behaviors necessary for survival are associated with different developmental goals so that developing members of a society can carry on culture-relevant work related to survival. It seems that all people are similar in that their developmental processes are designed to meet cultural goals; people differ, however, in the specific nature of those goals.

Cultural differences in parenting styles reflect other social factors as well. Two of the most important are economics and extended families.

Diversity in parenting as a function of economics.

Parenting and child rearing often occur in very different economic conditions in different countries and cultures, and even within the United States. These diverse conditions produce socialization processes that vary widely from culture to culture. Child-rearing practices may differ not only because of difference in beliefs but also because of marked differences in standards of living. Applying U.S. standards to evaluate parenting in other countries and cultures can lead to harsh conclusions. Consider the case of a slum-dwelling Brazilian mother who leaves her three children under the age of 5 locked in a bare, dark room for the day while she is out trying to meet their basic needs for food and clothing. We cannot judge the practices of others by the standards of the affluent and well-fed.

One recent study highlighted these issues. In this study, the reasons why mothers work and the number of hours they work were examined for mothers of firstborn children in the United States and Argentina (Pascual, Haynes, Galperin, & Bornstein, 1995). In both countries, both length of marriage and whether a woman worked during pregnancy predicted whether she worked after giving birth. In the United States, however, better-educated women with higher-status occupations worked longer hours, whereas in Argentina, better-educated women with higher-status occupations worked shorter hours. Thus, different cultural and economic conditions mediated the women's decisions to work in these two countries.

It is common folklore that picking up a baby and bringing it to the shoulder reduces bouts of crying and that babies who are ignored and allowed to cry for fear of spoiling them actually cry more. However, in remote rural river regions of China, few-week-old infants are left for long periods of time while their mothers work in the fields. These babies are placed in large sacks of sand that support them upright and act as an absorbent diaper. These babies quickly cease to cry because they learn early that it will not bring about any response at all.

If a society has a high rate of infant mortality, parenting efforts may concentrate on meeting basic physical needs. Parents may have little choice but to disregard other developmental demands. Sometimes the response to harsh and stressful conditions is parenting behavior that we might consider positive. In the Sudan, for example, the mother traditionally spends the first 40 days after delivery entirely with her baby. She rests while her relatives tend to her, and she focuses all her energy on her baby (Cederblad, 1988).

Levine (1977) has theorized that the caregiving environment reflects a set of goals that are ordered in importance. First is physical health and survival. Next is the promotion of behaviors that will lead to self-sufficiency. Last are behaviors that promote other cultural values, such as morality and prestige. Many families in the United States are fortunate in that they can turn their attention to meeting the second two goals. In many countries, the primary goal of survival is all-important and often overrides the other goals in the amount of parental effort exerted. Indeed, this is true in many areas of the United States as well.

Extended families.   The structure of the family also has a large impact on child rearing and caregiving. In many non–European American cultures, extended families are prevalent. In the United States in 1984, for example, 31 % of African American children lived in extended families, while only 19.8 % of children of other races lived in such families (U.S. Bureau of the Census, 1985). Extended families are a vital and important feature of child rearing, even when resources are not limited. Many cultures view extended-family child rearing as an integral and important part of their cultures. It can provide a buffer to stresses of everyday living. It is also an important means of transmitting cultural heritage from generation to generation.

Extended families can support and facilitate child rearing in ways that are completely different from the European American nuclear family. Research on parenting style (authoritarian, permissive, authoritative, or neglectful) tends to assume a nuclear family structure. In the United States, ethnic minority families have been characterized as extended and generally more conservative than European American families. For example, Japanese American families have been characterized as extended, with strict age and sex roles, and emphasizing children's obedience to authority figures (Trankina, 1983; Yamamoto & Kubota, 1983).

In an extended family situation, even though mothers are still seen as the primary caregiver, children experience frequent interaction with fathers, grandparents, godparents, siblings, and cousins. Hispanic and Filipino families see godparents as important models for children, and as sources of support for the parents. Sharing households with relatives, characteristic of extended families, is seen as a good way of maximizing the family's resources for successful child rearing.

One need not look outside the United States to recognize the importance of extended families. One major difference, however, is that participation in child rearing via extended families in the United States is often seen as a consequence of poor economics rather than a desirable state of affairs. Limited resources are a reality, with 11.2 million children in the United States living below the poverty level in 1990. Many are born to single mothers, and here the extended family plays an important role in the child-rearing process. Grandmothers are more actively involved with their grandchildren when they live with their single adult daughters. These children experience a greater variety of main caregivers and have different social interactions than their middle-class European American counterparts. Compounding this picture is the reality that ethnicity also confounds social class.

Teenage parenting also forces us to think differently about traditional notions of parenting. The presence of the maternal grandmother in these families has been found to cancel out some of the negative results associated with teen mothering (Garcia Coll, 1990). The grandmother often serves as a valuable source of information about child development. She also tends to be more responsive and less punitive with the child than the teen mother is. The grandmother in these three-generation households plays a very important role as teacher and role model to her daughter and can provide favorable, positive social interaction for her grandchild.

Extended families differ in their composition from one culture to another but have in common a sharing of resources, emotional support, and caregiving. The experiences of a child growing up in these situations can be quite different from those of a child in a European American nuclear family. In addition, we need to be aware that the traditional two-parent household is changing for many European Americans as well. Future studies will undoubtedly change the way we view parenting in this culture as well.

Temperament, Attachment, and Child Rearing: A Summary

The information presented so far speaks to just a few of the many ways in which enculturation occurs around the world. Children may be born with differences in biological predispositions or temperament that may make it easier for them to engage in the cultural learning that occurs throughout socialization and enculturation. Differences in attachment, parenting styles, and child rearing provide learning platforms for children that allow them to achieve developmental goals fostered by their particular cultures. Each culture's way of raising children—through parenting, preferred attachment styles, sleeping arrangements, and other concrete mechanisms—represents that culture's way of ensuring that its values and norms are transmitted to those children. In all cultures, these practices are ritualized so that this transmission of information can occur in generation after generation. Learning cultural values is as much a part of the process of socialization as it is an outcome of socialization.

What does contemporary cross-cultural research say about how all this occurs? According to Bornstein (1989), some early cross-cultural work in development (for example, Caudill & Frost, 1973; Caudill & Weinstein, 1969) focused primarily on the role of culture in "driving" parenting behaviors that resulted in changes in the infant and young child. This model suggests that culture unidirectionally provides the structure and environment for parents, particularly mothers, to affect their children in culturally appropriate ways:

$$culture \rightarrow mother \rightarrow infant$$

Others (for example, Shand, Kosawa, & Ellis, 1988) have focused on biology, proposing a developmental model that starts with the effects of genes, biology, and heredity on infant temperament, which then affects the mother's behaviors, which in turn produce cultural differences:

$$genes \rightarrow infant \rightarrow mother \rightarrow culture$$

The available cross-cultural research provides support for both models of understanding. The work on parenting styles, for instance, supports the first model, while the work on temperament and attachment supports the second. Most recent work in this area (for example, Holloway & Minami, 1996) suggests a rapprochement between the two, conceptualizing both parents and children as interactive partners in the joint creation of cultural meanings. This view suggests that children's active processing of information results in the reproduction of culture, and the production of new elements of culture. The interaction of language between parent and child provides the platform on which divergent points of view construct new realities. These recent theories also attempt to discover cultural meanings held in common between parents and children, rather than assuming a common understanding "imposed" by an outside culture.

Future research in this area will hopefully bridge the gaps among all of these various components, assessing the interplay of temperament, attachment, parenting styles, and psychological culture in the milieu. Ideally, longitudinal studies will enable researchers to examine the interactions among these various components of the enculturation process in the same individuals across time.

As mentioned earlier, however, parents and families are not the only enculturation agents in complex societies. The single most important formalized mechanism of instruction in many societies and cultures today is the educational system.

Culture and Education

Most of us think of a country's educational system solely as an institution that teaches thinking skills and knowledge. But a society's educational system is probably the most important institution socializing its children and teaching and reinforcing its cultural values. Much of the cross-national and cross-cultural research in this area has focused on cross-national differences in math achievement.

Cross-national differences in math achievement.   Mathematics learning occupies a special place in our understanding of culture, socialization, and the educational system. Of course, learning math skills is crucial to the ultimate development of science in any society, which is probably why it has received so much research attention, as well as funding from government and private sources. Still, math and culture have a very special relationship because, as Stigler and Baranes (1988) put it, math skills "are not logically constructed on the basis of abstract cognitive structures, but rather are forged out of a combination of previously acquired (or inherited) knowledge and skills, and new cultural input" (p. 258). Culture is not only a stimulator of math but is itself represented in math, and how a society teaches and learns it.

Cross-national research on math learning in schools has traditionally compared the math abilities of students around the world. An early study conducted by the International Association for the Evaluation of Education Achievement (IEA) (Husen, 1967), for example, measured math achievement scores in 12 different countries at the 8th and 12th grades. The overall performance for the American 8th graders was ranked 11th, and their mean scores were below the international mean in every area of math assessed. The performance of the American 12th graders was even worse. A later IEA study comparing 17 countries found that the performance of American students relative to the rest of the world had declined even further. According to Geary (1996), the top 5% of American elite math students (those enrolled in college-prep math courses) had average scores in relation to the international standard in algebra and calculus, and only slightly above average scores in geometry. American students who score at the 95th percentile in the United States would score at the 30th percentile in Japan and the 50th percentile in England.

These findings have been corroborated by other research involving primary school children (for example, Stevenson, Chen, & Lee, 1993). Even in first grade, the superiority of the Japanese and Chinese in math performance is already striking, reaching "dynamic" proportions by fifth grade (Stevenson, Lee, & Stigler, 1986; Stigler & Baranes, 1988, p. 291). The relatively poor performance of American children has also been documented in comparisons with Korean children (Song & Ginsburg, 1987). Moreover, the differences were observed not only in computational tests but in all math tests produced and administered by the researchers.

Of course, such findings have been alarming to educators at all levels in the United States for many years. The relatively poor performance of American youth in these skills is not only an important social concern; it is also of major concern for the future health of the U.S. economy, as more and more potentially unskilled or underskilled employees enter the workforce (Geary, 1996). Math abilities—and, more important, the logical reasoning skills underlying math and the mental discipline associated with math—are essential in many walks of life. The relatively poor performance of American students, therefore, does not bode well for the future.

In searching for the possible causes of these differences, Geary (1996) has suggested a distinction between primary and secondary math abilities. Primary math abilities refer to natural abilities that are shaped by evolutionary processes that all people presumably share (for example, language, counting). Secondary abilities refer to unnatural abilities that are based in large part on primary systems. Whereas the motivation to acquire primary abilities is likely to be inherent, the motivation to acquire secondary abilities may be more strongly influenced by culture.

Possible biological causes of cross-national differences in math abilities.
If biological factors were responsible for cross-national differences in math

ability, then cross-national differences in primary math abilities should exist. Although the research is not definitive, indirect evidence indicates no cross-national differences in primary math abilities. Those cross-national differences that have been found appear to be related to secondary, not primary, math achievements (Geary, 1996). Some people may suggest that research presented in the previous chapter on possible racial differences in IQ or head (brain) size may also be related to differences in math achievement and thus imply biological causes for those differences. Those IQ differences, however, tend to be small, and not robust enough to account for the rather large differences in math abilities. Moreover, comparisons of mean IQ scores of American, Japanese, and Chinese children (for example, Stevenson et al., 1985) have found no differences; thus, IQ cannot possibly account for cross-national differences among these children. As noted throughout this book, moreover, interpretation of biological differences based on classifications of race are always problematic.

Social and cultural factors that influence math achievement.   That cross-national differences in math achievement are related to secondary rather than primary math abilities implies that social and cultural factors play a major role in producing those differences. A number of possible contributing factors have been examined in the literature, including differences in language, school systems, parental and familial values, teaching styles and teacher–student relationships, and attitudes and appraisals of students. Work in each of these areas supports the contribution of each factor to cross-national differences in math achievement, and collectively constitutes a wealth of evidence concerning the relationship between culture and education.

Language.   Research by Stigler, Lee, and Stevenson (1986) has shown that cross-national differences among Chinese, Japanese, and American children in counting and memory exercises may be largely a function of differences in the Chinese, Japanese, and English languages related to counting and numbers. The Japanese language, for example, has unique verbal labels only for numbers one through ten. Number eleven is then 10-1, twelve is 10-2, and so on; twenty is 2-10, twenty-one is 2-10-1, and so forth. English, however, has unique labels for numbers 1 through 19 as well as all the decade numbers (20, 30, 40, and so forth). Research has shown that East Asian students make fewer errors than Americans in counting, and understand some basic math concepts related to counting and numbers better (Miura, Okamoto, Kim, Steere, & Fayol, 1993). These differences may account for some, but not all, of the cross-national differences in math abilities.

School systems.   Research has shown that the educational system in which children take part plays an important role in producing cross-national differences in math abilities, while at the same time imparting cultural values. First of all, the content of what is taught in the schools reflects a priori choices by that culture or society regarding what it believes is important to learn. Different cultures believe different topics to be important for later future success in that society. By teaching a certain type of content, the educational system reinforces a particular view of cognition and intelligence.

Another important factor to consider is the environmental setting in which education occurs. Many industrialized societies have a formal educational system, with identifiable areas and structures (schools) and identifiable education agents (teachers) to "do" education. In other cultures, formalized education may take place in small groups led by elders of the community. In yet other cultures, formalized education may be a family task (for example, the mother tutoring her own children in cognitive and other skills necessary for members of their community). Regardless of the environmental setting, the vehicle by which education occurs reinforces certain types of cultural values in its recipients.

The organization, planning, and implementation of lesson plans is another important cultural socializer. Some cultures encourage a didactic model of teaching, in which an expert teacher simply gives information to students, who are expected to listen and learn. Other cultures view teachers as leaders through a lesson plan, providing the overall structure and framework by which students discover principles and concepts. Some cultures view imparting of praise as an important process. Other cultures focus on mistakes made by students in the learning process. Some cultures have special classes and mechanisms to deal with many different types of students—for example, students with learning disabilities, physical handicaps, and special gifts or talents. Other cultures tend to downplay such differences among their students, treating them all as equals.

Once in school, children spend the majority of their waking hours away from their parents. The socialization process that began in the primary relationship with the parents continues with peers in play situations and in school. School institutionalizes cultural values and attitudes and is a significant contributor not only to the intellectual development of the child but, just as important, to the child's social and emotional development.

To highlight the role of the educational system as an enculturation agent, one need only recognize that not all cultures of the world rely solely on an institutionalized school setting to teach math. For example, important math skills are taught to Micronesian islanders in the Puluwat culture through navigation, to coastal Ghanaians by marketing fish, and even to bookies in Brazil (Acioly & Schliemann, 1986; Gladwin, 1970; Gladwin & Gladwin, 1971). Important math skills are imparted through nonschool activities not only in more "exotic" cultures, but also through activities such as dieting and athletic training in the United States (Stigler & Baranes, 1988).

Regardless of the way education occurs, the choices a society and culture make concerning its structure, organization, planning, and implementation all encourage and reinforce a certain view of culture. We are not always cognizant of our own cultural view because we are in the middle of it. To see our own biases and choices, we need to observe education in other cultures and compare what is done elsewhere to what we do. Through such comparisons the differences and the similarities often become quite clear.

Parental and familial values.   Research has shown that a number of important differences in cultural values and belief systems among Americans, Japanese, and Chinese have an impact on education. For example, Japanese and Chinese parents and teachers are more likely to consider all children as equal, with no differences between them. American parents and teachers are more likely to recognize differences and find reasons to treat their children as special. This difference is clearly rooted in a cultural tension between individualism and collectivism among the three cultures.

American parents and teachers are more likely to consider innate ability more important than effort; for the Japanese and Chinese, however, effort is far more important than ability. This difference is also rooted in cultural differences among the three countries and has enormous implications for education. American parents tend to be more easily satisfied at lower levels of competence than either the Japanese or the Chinese. Also, when problems arise, Americans are more likely to attribute the cause of the problem to something they cannot do anything about (such as ability). These cultural differences in attribution of causality are directly related to cultural differences in self-construals, discussed in Chapter 3.

Believing that ability is more important than effort has yet another side to it—a belief that each child is *limited* in his or her abilities. Once this belief becomes a cultural institution, it dictates how the educational system should respond. The resulting emphasis in the case of the American system is to seek unique, innate differences among the students, to generate separate special classes for these unique groups of students, and generally to individualize the process of education. As a result, more time is spent on individualized instruction and less on whole-group instruction.

Research has documented other interesting effects of parental and familial values related to achievement and academic success. Chao (1996), for example, found that Chinese mothers of preschoolers conveyed a high value on education, the high investment and sacrifice they themselves need to make in order for their children to succeed, their desires for direct intervention approaches to their children's schooling, and a belief that they play a major role in their children's success. American mothers of preschoolers in her study, however, conveyed a negation of the importance of academic skills, a desire for a less directive approach in instruction, and concerns for building their children's self-esteem. Kush (1996) found that although European Americans and Mexican Americans differed in level of academic achievement, these differences disappeared when parental education was statistically controlled in the analysis. These findings suggest the importance of parental education in predicting and contributing toward cultural differences in academic achievement. Finally, Yao (1985) compared family characteristics of European American and Asian American high achievers. This study found that the family life of the European Americans was less structured, and provided fewer formal educational experiences for children on weekends and after school. Asian families, however, structured their children's lives more, and actively sought more after-school and extracurricular programs to complement school learning.

These, and other, differences discussed in this section implicate the important role of parental attitudes and family characteristics in the contribution of cross-national and cross-cultural differences in math and academic achievement. Related differences also exist in the students in these families.

Attitudes and appraisals of students. A number of studies have examined cultural differences between Asian or Asian American children and European Americans. Pang (1991), for example, studied the relationships among test anxiety, self-concept, and student perceptions of parental support in Asian American and European American middle school students, and found that Asian American students exhibited a stronger desire to please parents, greater parental pressure, but also higher levels of parental support, than did the European American students. Yan and Gaier (1994) looked at causal attributions for college success and failure in Asian and American college undergraduate and graduate students, and found that American students attributed academic achievement more often to ability than did Asian subjects. American students also believed that effort was more important for success than lack of effort was for failure, whereas Asian students considered effort equally important for success or failure. These results are consonant with similar tendencies in parental attitudes described earlier, and with attributional biases discussed elsewhere in this book. Similar findings were obtained with fourth graders in Japan, China, and the United States (Tuss, Zimmer, & Ho, 1995).

Cross-national differences have been found in other samples as well. Little, Oettingen, Stetsenko, and Baltes (1995), for example, compared American, German, and Russian beliefs about school performance. They found that American children had the highest levels of personal agency and control expectancy, but the lowest belief–performance correlations. That is, Americans believed they had the most control over their academic outcomes, but this degree of perceived control was unrelated to their actual performance. Birenbaum and Kraemer (1995) also demonstrated differences in causal attributions in relation to academic success and failure in Arab and Jewish high school students. Together, these findings suggest that students around the world approach their academic work with quite different worldviews, attitudes, and attributional styles; that these differences are related to parental differences found in other research; that they may account for cross-national differences in academic achievement; and that they are intimately related to culture.

Teaching styles and teacher–student relationships. Stigler and his colleagues have examined classrooms to find possible roots of the cross-national differences in math achievement reported earlier (for example, Stigler & Perry, 1988). Several major differences in the use of classroom time appear to underlie math performance differences. The Japanese and Chinese spend more days per year in school, more hours per day in school, a greater proportion of time in school devoted to purely academic subjects, and a greater proportion of time devoted to math. In addition, Japanese and Chinese teachers spend a greater proportion of time working with the whole class than do American teachers.

This difference is even more dramatic because average class size is smaller in the United States than in Japan or China. As a result, American students spend less time working under the supervision and guidance of a teacher.

During class, it was observed, American teachers tend to use praise to reward correct responses. Teachers in Japan, however, tend to focus on incorrect answers, using them as examples to lead into discussion of the computational process and math concepts. Teachers in Taiwan tend to use a process more congruent with the Japanese approach. These teaching differences speak to the cultural emphasis in the United States on rewarding uniqueness and individualism and the emphasis in Japan and China on finding ways to engage in group process and sharing responsibility for mistakes with members of the group. Praise, while nice, often precludes such discussion.

Of course, differences exist in other cultures as well. McCargar (1993), for example, documented differences among ten cultural groups of students on 8 scales of student role expectations and 11 scales of teacher role expectations. Taken together, these studies highlight important differences that are present every day in the classroom in terms of teaching style, expectations, and actual behaviors that may account for cross-national differences in academic achievement.

Summary. We know that cross-national differences in academic achievement are not necessarily accounted for by biological differences between people of different cultures. And although differences in languages, especially related to counting systems, may be a factor, they cannot account for the size of the differences. Instead, research indicates that cross-national differences in academic achievement are the result of many social and cultural factors, some of which are institutionalized in educational systems, others found in parents and parental values, others in children's cognitive and attributional styles, and yet others in specific classroom practices. No research suggests that any single factor can fully account for cross-national differences in achievement; instead, it is a combination of these and other factors that lead to differences.

Nor are cross-national differences in academic performance, and the other cross-cultural differences that underlie them, solely products of culture. The performance of students of any culture, in any subject area, is the result of a complex interplay of economics, geography, resources, cultural values and beliefs, abilities, experiences, language, and family dynamics.

Research on differences in academic performance also highlights the role of the educational system as an important enculturation agent in any society. That is, not only do all of the differences discussed here contribute to cross-national differences in academic achievement; they also contribute to differences in culture itself. Parents' and children's attitudes, educational practices and curricula, teacher behaviors, and all other associated factors are important transmitters of culture. They impart important cultural knowledge to the students as members of a culture or society, and thus play a major role in the socialization and enculturation of the child members of many societies of the world. Differences in these institutions not only reflect but reinforce cultural differences in values, beliefs, attitudes, norms, and behaviors and help transmit this important cultural information from one generation to the next. The school-age period of life is indeed a critical time in any culture, when culture is strongly reinforced in children by society as a whole. This process is pervasive.

Putting It All Together: The Development of Culture and Cultural Identity

This section has examined a multitude of factors that may influence how people become enculturated—temperament and biological dispositions, attachment and parenting styles, child-rearing practices, and the educational system. Just how is it that all these processes are assembled in people's minds as enculturation occurs? Research that directly addresses this question is sorely lacking. Much of what we do know comes from theoretical and conceptual research in anthropology and cross-cultural psychology that attempts to aggregate the various pieces of evidence into a coherent whole.

Tomasello (1993), for example, has suggested that cultural learning manifests itself in three different ways in human development: imitation, instruction, and collaboration. These processes, in turn, are supposedly related to the development of social and cognitive concepts and processes that are necessary for enculturation to occur. Imitation relies on a concept of intentional agent, and requires perspective taking. Instructional learning requires mental agents and involves interactive and coordinated perspective taking. Collaborative learning relies on the ability to reflect, and involves integrated perspective taking. Correlations between these aspects of social cognition and cultural learning in normal and autistic children, and in wild and enculturated chimpanzees, offer further support for these mechanisms. (The importance of imitation in cultural learning has drawn some criticism, however; see Heyes, 1993.)

Some authors have suggested that culture can best be characterized as the conglomeration of situated context-related learning. Jacobson (1996), for instance, suggests that contexts are inseparable from cognitive processes. As culture-appropriate learning occurs in multiple and different contexts, such culture-specific learning is joined together across contexts into a cohesive whole, either on the level of understanding, appreciation, or behavior. Likewise, Shore (1991) defines cultural cognition as the product of an organization of cultural texts and models, and the subjective processes of meaning construction through which we become aware of cultural symbols through subjective experience. Different cognitive processes and sensory experiences help to link schemas across contexts and provide cultural meaning which is constructed through that experience.

Super and Harkness (1986, 1994) suggest that enculturation occurs within what they term a *developmental niche*. This niche forms the structural and subjective framework within which children come to learn the cultural values and mores important to their society. According to these authors, this niche includes three major components: the physical and social setting, the customs of child care and child rearing, and the psychology of the caregivers. The developing child is influenced by all three components, or more precisely by their interaction, all of which occurs within a larger environmental and human ecology. In this niche, developing children are able to receive the influences of the various socialization agents and institutions around them, ensuring their enculturation, while at the same time the child also brings his or her temperamental disposition to the interaction.

The issue of enculturation is related to that of ethnic identity development, a topic that has received considerable attention in recent years. The concept of identity differs from that of enculturation in that identity typically refers to an awareness of one's culture or ethnicity. Certainly, people can become enculturated without having conscious awareness of that cultural learning. In fact, research has tended to show that the development of ethnic identity occurs in stages. In studying ethnic identity development in Mexican Americans, for example, Bernal (1993) has found that very young children (around 4 years of age) tend to have very limited knowledge of their ethnic identity. As they get older, however, their understanding of their heritage grows broader and more complex. Phinney and Chavira (1992) have shown that ethnic identity continues to grow through adolescence and young adulthood, and is related to self-esteem.

Thus, available studies suggest that culture may be learned through situated cognitive schemas and structures related to specific contexts, and that cultural meaning is constructed across these contexts as individuals develop social cognitive abilities that allow for such construction to occur. Awareness of the meanings associated with these cultural constructions leads to the development of cultural or ethnic identity, which appears to develop later than gender or racial identity. Future research will need to test these ideas directly and explore the degree to which these processes are similar or different in people of different cultures around the world.

Culture and Psychological Processes in Development

The first half of this chapter has explored the nature of enculturation—how people acquire the contents of their culture. The second half examines cultural similarities and differences in a variety of developmental processes, including cognitive, socioemotional, and moral development. These topics are of great interest to developmental psychologists, both mainstream and cross-cultural, and speak to the pervasive influence of culture on developmental processes.

Cognitive Development

Piaget's theory. **Cognitive development** is a specialty in psychology that studies how thinking skills develop over time. Theories of cognitive development have traditionally focused on the period from infancy to adulthood. The theory that has dominated this field during the latter half of the 20th century is Piaget's stage theory of cognitive development. Piaget based his theories on observations of Swiss children. He found that these children tended to solve problems quite differently at different ages. To explain these differences, Piaget (1952) proposed that children progress through four stages as they grow from infancy into adolescence.

1. *Sensorimotor stage.* This stage typically lasts from birth to about 2 years of age. Anxiety in the presence of strangers—stranger anxiety—is common during this period. The most important achievement of this stage is the acquisition of object permanency—that is, knowing that objects exist even when they cannot be seen. Early in this stage, children appear to assume that when a toy or other object is hidden (for example, when a ball rolls under a sofa), it ceases to exist. Later in this stage, children will search under the sofa for the lost ball, demonstrating that they have come to understand that objects exist continuously. Other cognitive developments typical of this stage, including deferred imitation, language acquisition, and mental imagery, have important implications for later cognitive development and enculturation. Imitation and imagery are important cognitive components of observational learning, and language skills are necessary to ensure proper communication of verbal socialization processes.

2. *Preoperational stage.* This stage lasts from about 2 to 6 or 7 years of age. Piaget defines this stage in terms of five characteristics: conservation, centration, irreversibility, egocentrism, and animism. **Conservation** is the awareness (or in this stage, the lack of such awareness) that physical quantities remain the same even when they change shape or appearance. **Centration** is the tendency to focus on a single aspect of a problem. **Irreversibility** is the inability to imagine "undoing" a process. **Egocentrism** is the inability to step into another's shoes and understand the other person's point of view. **Animism** is the belief that all things, including inanimate objects, are alive. For example, children in the preoperational stage may regard a book lying on its side as "tired" or "needing a rest," or they may think that the moon is following them.

3. *Concrete operations stage.* This stage lasts from about 6 or 7 years until about 11 years of age. During this stage, children acquire new thinking skills to work with actual objects and events. They are able to imagine undoing an action, and they can focus on more than one feature of a problem. Children also begin to understand that there are different points of view from their own. This new awareness helps children master the principle of conservation. A child in the concrete operations stage will understand that six apples are always six apples, regardless of how they are grouped or spaced, and that the amount of clay does not change as a lump is molded into different shapes. This ability is not present in the preoperational stage. However, instead of thinking a problem through, children in this stage tend to rely on trial-and-error strategies.

4. *Formal operations stage.* This stage extends from around 11 years of age through adulthood. During this stage, individuals develop the ability to think logically about abstract concepts, such as peace, freedom, and justice. Indi-

viduals also become more systematic and thoughtful in their approach to problem solving.

The transition from one stage to another is often gradual, as children develop new abilities alongside earlier ways of thinking. Thus, the behavior of some children may represent a "blend" of two stages when they are in a period of transition from one to the other.

Piaget hypothesized that two primary mechanisms are responsible for movement from one stage to the next: assimilation and accommodation. **Assimilation** is the process of fitting new ideas into a preexisting understanding of the world. **Accommodation** refers to the process of changing one's understanding of the world to accommodate ideas that conflict with existing concepts.

Piaget's theory in cross-cultural perspective.   Cross-cultural research on Piaget's theory has focused on four central questions. The findings to date show an interesting blend of cultural similarities and differences in various aspects of cognitive development that parallel Piaget's stages.

Do Piaget's stages occur in the same order in different cultures? Studies that have addressed this question have convincingly demonstrated that Piaget's stages occur in the same fixed order in other cultures. For instance, a large cross-cultural survey that tested children in Great Britain, Australia, Greece, and Pakistan (Shayer, Demetriou, & Perez, 1988) found that schoolchildren in these different societies performed Piagetian tasks within the same stage of concrete operations. We do not find cultures in which 4-year-olds typically lack an awareness of object permanency or 5-year-olds understand the principle of conservation. Thus, we know that children from very different cultures do indeed learn groups of Piagetian tasks in a similar order.

Are the ages that Piaget associated with each stage of development the same in all cultures? Studies have found surprising cultural variations in the ages at which children in different societies typically reach the third and fourth Piagetian stages. In some cases, the difference may be as much as 5 or 6 years. However, it has often been overlooked that children may have the potential to solve tasks sooner than their answers would indicate. For example, a child in the concrete operations stage will typically give the first answer that comes to mind during a test. If the child comes from a culture in which he or she has had practice performing the task in question, this answer is likely to be correct. However, a child who has never thought about the concept before may well utter the wrong answer and only later realize the mistake. When researchers checked for this possibility by repeating tests a second time at the end of testing sessions, they found that many children corrected their previous answers on the second attempt (Dasen, 1982; Dasen, Lavallee, & Retschitzki, 1979; Dasen, Ngini, & Lavallee, 1979). Thus, it is important to remember that performance on a task may not reveal actual cognitive competence or ability.

Are there cultural variations within, rather than between, Piaget's stages? There is considerable cultural variation in the order in which children acquire specific skills within Piaget's stages. In a comparative study of tribal children (the Inuit of Canada, the Baoul of Africa, and the Aranda of Australia), half of all Inuit children tested solved a spatial task at the age of 7 years, half of the Aranda solved it at 9 years, and the Baoul did not reach the halfway point until the age of 12 (Dasen, 1975). On a test of the conservation of liquids, however, the order changed dramatically: half of the Baoul children solved the problem when they were 8 years old, the Inuit at 9 years, and the Aranda at 12 years. Why did the ages at which these children could perform the same task vary so much? The Inuit and Aranda children live in nomadic societies, where children need to learn spatial skills early because their families are constantly moving. The Baoul children live in a settled society, where they seldom travel but often fetch water and store grain. The skills these children used in their everyday lives seem to have affected the order in which they were able to solve Piagetian tasks within the concrete operations stage.

Do non-Western cultures regard scientific reasoning as the ultimate developmental end point? Piaget's theory assumes that the scientific reasoning associated with formal operations is the universal end point of cognitive development—that the thinking most valued in Swiss and other Western societies (formal operations) is the yardstick by which all cultures should be judged. Because Piaget considered scientific reasoning to be the ultimate human achievement, his stage theory is designed to trace the steps by which people arrive at scientific thinking. This perspective has been widely accepted within North American psychology, and generally by the North American public, at least until very recently.

Cross-cultural research indicates that this perspective is by no means universally shared. Different societies value and reward different skills and behaviors. For example, until recently the most respected scholars in traditional Islamic societies were religious leaders and poets. Although the Islamic educational system included science and mathematics, its primary goal was not to train people in the scientific method but to transmit faith, general knowledge, and a deep appreciation for poetry and literature. People from such cultures could be expected to be at a disadvantage when confronted with advanced Piagetian tasks, which are drawn almost exclusively from Western physics, chemistry, and mathematics.

Many cultures around the world do not share the conviction that abstract, hypothetical thought processes are the ultimate or desired end point in the cognitive development process. Many cultures, for example, consider cognitive development to be more relational—involving the thinking skills and processes needed to engage successfully in interpersonal contexts. What North Americans refer to as "common sense," rather than cognitive development per se, is considered a much more desired outcome in many cultures. This value structure is especially apparent in more collectivistic and group-oriented cultures, in which high-level, individualistic, abstract thinking is often frowned upon.

Piaget's theory: summary and discussion.   Cross-cultural studies of Piaget's stage of formal operations have found that in some cultures, very few people are able to complete fourth-stage Piagetian tasks. Does this mean that entire cultures are suspended at a lower stage of cognitive development? To answer this question, we must first ask whether Piagetian tasks are a culturally appropriate way of measuring an advanced stage of cognitive development. In fact, those tasks may not be meaningful in other cultures. Besides the issue of cultural appropriateness, there is also the issue of what is being tested. Tests of formal operations may tell us whether people can solve a narrow range of scientific problems, but they do not tell us whether people in different cultures develop advanced cognitive skills in areas other than those selected by Piaget. We can say with certainty, however, that people who have not attended high school or college in a Westernized school system perform very poorly on tests of formal operations (Laurendeau-Bendavid, 1977; Shea, 1985). These findings again raise the question of the degree to which Piagetian tasks depend on previous knowledge and cultural values rather than cognitive skills.

It is also important to remember the wide range of differences in cognitive development within a given culture. These within-culture differences make it extremely difficult to draw valid conclusions or inferences about differences in cognitive development between cultures. For example, not only do members of non-Western cultures have difficulty with tests of formal operations, but many adults in North American society also have such difficulties. Scientific reasoning does not appear to be as common in Western societies as Piaget thought, and it is frequently limited to special activities. Individuals who apply scientific logic to a problem on the job may reason quite differently in other situations.

Because large numbers of people are unable to complete Piagetian tasks of formal operations, it has not been possible to demonstrate the universality of the fourth stage of Piaget's theory of cognitive development. It is possible that most adults do possess the ability to complete Piagetian tasks but lack either the motivation or knowledge of how to demonstrate such ability. To demonstrate success on a task purporting to measure some aspect of cognitive ability or intelligence, it is crucial that the test-taker and the test-maker agree on what is being assessed. Cultural differences in the desired end point of cognitive development, as well as in definitions of intelligence (see Chapter 6), contribute to this dilemma.

Other theories of cognitive development.   Although Piaget's theory is the most influential theory in the United States, it is only one of many stage theories that have been proposed by Western social scientists. The 18th-century German philosopher Hegel, for example, ranked all societies on an evolutionary scale based on a classification of religious beliefs, with Christianity at the top. Stage theories multiplied in the 19th century after Darwin's theory of evolution became well known. Several writers (for example, Morgan, 1877; Spencer, 1876; Tylor, 1865) proposed that humanity had progressed from savagery to civilization in a series of stages.

One of the most influential stage theories of the early 20th century was proposed by the French philosopher Levy-Bruhl (1910, 1922, 1949). In common with earlier scholars, Levy-Bruhl drew most of his conclusions from material related to the mystical and religious beliefs of non-Western peoples. Levy-Bruhl put forth the **great divide theory,** separating the thought of Westerners from that of people who lived in primitive societies. He described non-Western peoples as having a distinct way of thinking, which he attributed to the effects of culture. According to Levy-Bruhl, non-Westerners were not bothered by logical contradictions, and they lacked a clear sense of individual identity. More recently, some scientists (Goody, 1968, 1977; Hippler, 1980; Luria, 1976) have put forward new great divide theories. Although these researchers have various names for the two groups, their division of humanity breaks down along similar lines. In all of these theories, the cultural development or thought of non-Westerners is usually judged as deficient or inferior to that of Europeans.

Several points need to be made about these theories. First, it is probably more than coincidence that stage theories produced by Westerners judge people from other cultures (and minorities within their own countries) in terms of how closely they resemble Westerners, thereby placing themselves at a relatively superior level of development. The popularity of stage theories in the 19th century, for example, coincided with the colonial imperialism of the period. Stage theories provided justification for imposing European rule around the world, based on the demonstrated superiority of European civilization.

Other problems also existed. Stage theorists persisted in evaluating the rationality of non-Westerners in terms of their magical and religious beliefs, while the rationality of Western beliefs was usually not questioned. Levy-Bruhl's theory has been fiercely attacked over the years by field anthropologists who have objected to both his methodology and his conclusions. Levy-Bruhl based his work on stories told by missionaries and travelers, many of whom could barely speak native languages.

But Westerners are not the only ones who have ethnocentric assumptions. Cross-cultural studies have shown that people from many cultures prefer their own groups and rate them more positively than they rate outsiders. For example, a study that compared what people in 30 different East African societies thought of themselves and others demonstrated that members of each society rated themselves highly and judged outsiders to be "advanced" when they were culturally similar to their own group (Brewer & Campbell, 1976).

This brings us back to Piaget's theory, which has several strong points. Piaget's theory is considerably more sophisticated than earlier theories. By devising tasks to measure concepts in an experimental setting, Piaget established a new standard by which to gauge cognitive development, one that appears to be less vulnerable to ethnocentric bias. Piaget's tests can be, and have been, administered cross-culturally, with clear-cut results that do not rest on the subjective beliefs of the researcher (although the choice of research instruments and the interpretation of data are still subject to researcher bias). Still, cognitive development is complicated, and it is unlikely that such tasks can capture all of its complexity.

Moral Reasoning

Another area of development crucial to our becoming functional adults in society and culture concerns moral judgments and reasoning. As they grow, children develop increasingly complex ways of understanding their world. These cognitive changes also bring about changes in their understanding of moral judgments. Why something is good or bad changes from the young child's interpretation of reward and punishment conditions to principles of right and wrong.

Morality and culture share a very close relationship. Moral principles and ethics provide guidelines for people's behaviors with regard to what is appropriate and what is not. These guidelines are products of a specific culture and society, handed down from one generation to the next. Morality is thus heavily influenced by the underlying, subjective, and implicit culture in which it is embedded. Morality also serves as the basis of laws, which are formalized guidelines for appropriate and inappropriate behavior. In this way, culture also affects the laws of a society. For these and other reasons, morality occupies a special place in our understanding of culture and cultural differences.

Our knowledge of the development of moral reasoning skills, at least in the United States, has been heavily influenced by the work of a psychologist named Lawrence Kohlberg. His model of moral reasoning and judgment is based in large part on Piaget's model of cognitive development.

Kohlberg's theory of morality.   Kohlberg's theory of moral development (1976, 1984) proposes three general stages of development of moral reasoning skills. (Kohlberg further divided each of these three general stages into two stages, for a total of six substages of moral development.)

1. **Preconventional morality** involves compliance with rules to avoid punishment and gain rewards. A person operating at this level of morality would condemn stealing as bad because the thief might get caught and be thrown in jail or otherwise punished. The focus of the justification is on the punishment (or reward) associated with the action.
2. **Conventional morality** involves conformity to rules that are defined by others' approval or society's rules. A person operating at this level of morality would judge stealing as wrong because it is against the law and others in society generally disapprove of it.
3. **Postconventional morality** involves moral reasoning on the basis of individual principles and conscience. A person operating at this level of morality would judge stealing within the context either of societal or community needs or of his or her own personal moral beliefs and values, which supercede perceived societal and community needs.

Gilligan and her colleagues (Gilligan, 1982) have challenged Kohlberg's theory by suggesting that its stages are biased toward the particular way in which males as opposed to females view relationships. She argues that male moral reasoning is based on abstract justice, whereas female moral reasoning is based on obligations and responsibilities. Despite the fervor of the debate, however, reviews of the research seem to indicate few gender differences in moral reasoning (Walker, 1984). Cross-cultural research may shed more light on this issue.

Cross-cultural studies of moral reasoning.   The universality or cultural specificity of moral principles and reasoning has been an area of interest for anthropologists and psychologists alike. A number of anthropological ethnographies have examined the moral principles and domains of different cultures (see review by Shweder, Mahapatra, & Miller, 1987). Many of these works have complemented and challenged traditional American views of morality, and for good reason. Culture, morality, ethics, and law share a close relationship.

The findings from a number of cross-cultural studies suggest that many aspects of Kohlberg's theory of morality are universal. Snarey (1985), for example, reviewed 45 studies involving participants in 27 countries and concluded that Kohlberg's first two stages could be regarded as universal. Others reached similiar conclusions, including Ma (1988), in a study involving Hong Kong and mainland Chinese as well as British participants; Ma and Cheung (1996), in a study involving Hong Kong, mainland Chinese, British, and Americans; and Hau and Lew (1989), in a study of Hong Kong Chinese participants.

However, a number of cross-cultural studies on moral reasoning raise questions about the universal generalizability of Kohlberg's higher stages. One of the underlying assumptions of Kohlberg's theory is that moral reasoning on the basis of individual principles and conscience, regardless of societal laws or cultural customs, represents the highest level of moral reasoning. This assumption is grounded in the cultural milieu in which Kohlberg developed his theory, which had its roots in studies involving American males in the midwestern United States in the 1950s and 1960s. Although democratic notions of individualism and unique, personal conscience may have been appropriate to describe his samples at that time and place, it is not clear whether those same notions represent universal moral principles applicable to all people of all cultures.

In fact, some researchers have criticized Kohlberg's theory for harboring such cultural biases (Bronstein & Paludi, 1988). Miller and Bersoff (1992) compared the responses to a moral judgment task by respondents in India and the United States. The Indian subjects, both children and adults, considered not helping someone a moral transgression more than did the American subjects, regardless of the life-threatening nature of the situation or whether the person in need was related. These researchers interpreted the cultural differences as having to do with values of affiliation and justice, suggesting that Indians are taught a broader sense of social responsibility—individual responsibility to help a needy person. The issue of interpersonal responsiveness Miller and Bersoff (1992) raised is related to Gilligan's (1982) claims of gender bias in U.S. studies. It is entirely possible that Gilligan's findings were influenced by cultural as well as gender differences.

Snarey's (1985) review, mentioned earlier, also concluded that moral reasoning at the higher stages is much more culture-specific than Kohlberg originally suggested. Other reviews of the cross-cultural literature by Bergling (1981) and Edwards (1981) reached similar conclusions. Kohlberg's theory, as well as the methodology for scoring moral stages according to verbal reasoning, may not recognize higher levels of morality as defined in other cultures. Should different cultures define those higher levels of morality along totally different dimensions, those differences would imply profound differences in people's judgments of moral and ethical appropriateness. Fundamental differences in the bases underlying morality and ethics across cultures are not at all impossible, given that they feed and are fed by subjective culture. Above all, those fundamental differences in morality as a function of culture form the basis for the possibility of major intercultural conflicts.

One recent study exemplifies how the examination of morality at different levels of abstraction—from internalized ideals to actual behaviors—may be important to understanding cultural similarities and differences in moral judgment. In this study (Carlo, Koller, Eisenberg, DaSilva, & Frohlich, 1996), researchers examined prosocial moral reasoning in Brazilian and American adolescents. In addition, they assessed actual prosocial behaviors through peer ratings. In both cultures, age and gender differences in prosocial moral reasoning were the same, as was the relationship between prosocial moral reasoning and prosocial behaviors. There were, however, cultural differences in internalized moral reasoning, with American adolescents scoring higher than Brazilian adolescents. These findings suggest that cultural similarities and differences in moral reasoning and behavior may be explained by taking into account different levels of morality than are being examined. Future cross-cultural studies will need to incorporate such a multilevel view of morality to investigate similarities and differences in the same groups of participants across a broad range of morality-related psychological phenomena.

Socioemotional Development

In socialization, cognitive and moral development are two parts of the total picture of the developing person. A third major piece of the puzzle is social and emotional development. Indeed, this aspect of our lives is as important to us as the development of our thinking skills.

Erikson's theory of socioemotional development. One of the dominant theories of socioemotional development was proposed by the noted scholar Erik Erikson (1950). Erikson's theory of socioemotional development is really a theory of socialization across the life span. Erikson views development as a continuing and ongoing process from birth until old age. He posits eight general stages of a person's life, each characterized by the conflict or tension that the person must resolve in his or her own way.

1. *Basic trust versus mistrust* (infancy). In infancy, the major tension is one of trust versus mistrust. This tension is resolved in each person to different degrees as a function of how the infant interacts with his or her caretaker and

others in the environment. Human infants are perhaps the most dependent of all newborn animals and must trust others to provide for their needs. It is in this interaction between the infant and the caretakers who meet the infant's needs that the infant will develop a sense of trust or mistrust.

2. *Autonomy versus shame and doubt* (toddler). As infants develop motor skills and muscular coordination, they begin to operate in the world as autonomous beings. Mobility brings with it a sense of independence, competence, and mastery (ask anyone who has just received a driver's license!). How caretakers and the environment around the developing toddler deal with these newfound skills forms the basis for resolving the conflict that is associated with the development of these skills.

3. *Initiative versus guilt* (preschool). At this stage of development, youngsters begin to coordinate their continuously developing motor skills with planned goals to produce purposeful actions. How the environment around these youngsters meets the new challenges they present is central to the conflict underlying this stage. Will efforts at initiation be reinforced? Or will they be thwarted by caretakers or others? The answers to these questions form the basis on which youngsters resolve the core issue of this stage.

4. *Industry versus inferiority* (young childhood, 6–12). In many societies and cultures, this age range corresponds to the time when formalized instruction begins, often representing the elementary school years. According to Erikson, it is in this period of life that youngsters find themselves addressing concerns about work ethic and discipline—concepts related to a sense of industry. To the extent that a sense of industry is not developed, this period of life can impact a sense of inferiority.

5. *Identity versus role confusion* (adolescence). Puberty brings with it biological and physiological changes in adolescents as well as profound sociopsychological questions. This period of life is marked by the central question of who we are, in terms of an individual identity, place, and role in life. Puberty forces all of us to ask and answer this question. To the degree to which we address this question, we can develop a sure sense of identity. Otherwise, we may be confused about our roles.

6. *Intimacy versus self-absorption* (young adulthood). Intimacy refers to the degree to which individuals can develop close and intimate relationships with others. The opposite of intimacy is self-absorption, the inability to develop such relationships. Erikson's suggestion of the importance of this stage of life highlights the social nature of his theory, and his understanding of people as social creatures.

7. *Generativity versus stagnation* (middle age). As adults, we face challenges in later years regarding our productiveness in life. The degree to which we feel we have been useful to society in some way, or productive in our work or relationships, marks the degree of generativity of our lives. An important aspect of generativity is the notion that something we have done is meaningful to the

next generation. An unsuccessful resolution of this conflict brings with it feelings of stagnation and a questioning of the purpose and utility of life.

8. *Integrity versus despair* (old age). The final stage of life is marked by reflection over and across the life span. As we examine and reflect on our lives, we question how we entered each stage of life and how we resolved each question and conflict. To the extent that we can look back on our lives and be proud of how we entered and resolved each conflict, we develop a sense of integrity about our lives and about ourselves. The opposite, however, is marked by despair and disgust.

Erikson's theory in the context of enculturation.   Although Erikson developed his theory while working in the United States, the research on which it was based included studies of individuals from many different cultures—European, American, and Native American. Erikson himself was born and raised not in the United States but in Europe, giving him at least some degree of multicultural experience and perspective. This perspective enabled him to develop a theory of socialization and socioemotional development that he himself intended to be cross-cultural in nature. In general, cross-cultural and anthropological research has supported Erikson's theory (Ferrante, 1992).

A number of important points about this theory are helpful to our understanding of enculturation processes. First, the conflicts characterizing each stage do not produce either/or resolutions. Instead, they should be seen as labels on a continuum on which each individual marks him- or herself. Differences between people are understood as differences in degree, not as absolute differences in dichotomous resolutions to these conflicts.

Second, "successful" resolutions at one stage depend in part on successful resolutions at a prior stage. There is linkage in this work that connects life span issues together. Viewed in this way, enculturation can be considered a package of phenomena linked together by a series of resolutions across the life span.

Third, cultures may differ in how they define what a "successful" resolution is. For example, whereas the individualistic American culture may view a sense of autonomy in Stage 2 as a preferred outcome, other cultures may prefer children to be less autonomous and more dependent on others. What is important in terms of Erikson's theory is not that it posits a preferred resolution at each stage but that it posits the conflict individuals must go through. Different cultures may provide different tendencies for these conflict resolutions.

Fourth, the labels that Erikson originally used to describe the conflicts underlying each stage may be less appropriate cross-culturally. "Shame and doubt," definitely carry negative connotations in English. As an alternative to "autonomy," however, they may be preferred outcomes in another culture, which may choose to label that outcome differently. People of collectivistic cultures that discourage individual autonomy and foster a sense of dependence on others may consider the alternative to autonomy to be "dependence" or "merging relations." Interestingly, shame is often used in these cultures as a social sanction against too much autonomy.

Finally, Erikson (1950) makes it clear that although progression through these stages is somewhat ordered they need not be fixed in any sense. The conflicts described may, in fact, exist throughout the life span but have particular relevance at certain periods. This view of socioemotional development gives Erikson's theory a particularly useful flexibility in understanding socialization across cultures.

Erikson's theory provides a framework that can be used to understand the socioemotional context of development and the enculturation process and should be considered a companion to the cognitive and moral contexts of development discussed earlier. By highlighting the emotional conflicts that children and adults must negotiate, this theoretical framework helps us realize that the processes of socialization and enculturation are filled with emotional conflicts that add important affective meaning to development.

Other Developmental Processes

Cross-cultural research on psychological processes in development continues to be one of the most popular and thoroughly studied areas of the field, for good reason. This research offers important insights into the question of just how the differences observed in adults in many other studies over the years have come to be. In seeking to explain how and why cultural differences occur among adults, psychologists, mainstream and otherwise, have turned to developmental research to explicate the causes and contexts of the ontogenesis of cultural differences.

The past decade has witnessed a renewed interest in cross-cultural developmental research, no doubt due in large part to the increased interest in culture in all areas of psychology. This research has spanned many processes related to development, including future-oriented goals and commitments (Nurmi, Poole, & Seginer, 1995), appraisal processes (DiMartino, 1994; Dalal, Sharma, & Bisht, 1983), social expectations (Rotherram-Borus & Petrie, 1996), affective relationships in adolescence (Takahashi, 1990; Takahashi & Majima, 1994), task persistence (Blinco, 1992), preschoolers' responses to conflict and distress (Zahn-Waxler, Friedman, Cole, Mizuta, & Hiruma, 1996), coping (Olah, 1995; Seiffge-Krenke & Shulman, 1990), and social interaction (Farver & Howes, 1988). Other studies examining other developmental topics no doubt exist as well. Collectively, these studies highlight both similarities and differences in development across cultures, and pave the way for exciting new research in these areas in the future.

▨ Conclusion

In the first half of this chapter, we saw how the fields of developmental psychology, education, sociology, and anthropology have all contributed to the vast knowledge we have concerning the process known as socialization or enculturation—not only in the formative infant and childhood years but in adolescence, young adulthood, and throughout the life span. In the second half of the chapter, we saw how culture produces similarities as well as differences in various areas of development, including cognitive, moral reasoning, and socio-emotional development.

The developmental research presented in this chapter provides a comprehensive view of how enculturation occurs, and how culture influences a number of developmental psychological processes. Still, there is much more work to be done. Future studies need to examine directly the nature of the enculturation process, investigating the influence of multiple sources of enculturation on the development of culture itself. It may be that our definition and understanding of culture, and thus our measurement of it in developmental research, are different at different stages of development. Culture, for example, may be represented solely as schemas or reinforced action patterns beneath the level of identity and verbal awareness in the young child. Future research will need to explore how culture is manifested in these and other ways, and how developmental practices related to attachment, child rearing, and the like, influence these definitions of culture.

At the same time, there is also much work still to do in examining cultural influences in developmental processes. In particular, while much cross-cultural developmental work has focused on infants and children, mainstream psychology has come to recognize the importance of developmental processes throughout the life span, including adolescence and young, middle, and older adulthood. Future cross-cultural research will need to explore the similarities and differences across cultures in lifelong development, investigating the potential universality or cultural relativity of theories such as Erikson's and others in a long-term, cross-cultural perspective. Such research promises to have a major impact on the field for years to come.

The developmental differences discussed in this chapter all speak to how a sense of culture develops in each of us. As cultures exert their influence in their own special and unique ways, they produce specific tendencies, trends, and differences in their members when compared to others. When we are in the middle of a culture, as we all are, we cannot see those differences or how culture itself develops in us. Only when we look outside ourselves and examine the developmental and socialization processes of other cultures are we able to see what we are ourselves. Only then can we come to appreciate that those differences and similarities are our culture, or at least the manifestations of our culture. Thus, while cultures produce differences in development that we observe in our research, these differences simultaneously contribute to the development of culture.

 # Glossary

accommodation The process of changing one's understanding of the world to accommodate ideas that conflict with existing concepts.

acculturation The process of adapting to, and in many cases adopting, a different culture from the one in which a person was enculturated.

ambivalent attachment   A style of attachment in which children are uncertain in their response to their mothers, going back and forth between seeking and shunning her attention. These mothers have been characterized as insensitive and less involved.

animism   The belief that all things, including inanimate objects, are alive.

assimilation   The process of fitting new ideas into a preexisting understanding of the world.

attachment   The special bond that develops between the infant and its primary caregiver. The quality of attachment has lifelong effects on our relationships with loved ones.

authoritarian parent   A style of parenting in which the parent expects unquestioned obedience and views the child as needing to be controlled.

authoritative parent   A style of parenting that is viewed as firm, fair, and reasonable. This style is seen as promoting psychologically healthy, competent, independent children who are cooperative and at ease in social situations.

avoidant attachment   A style of attachment in which children shun their mothers, who are suspected of being intrusive and overstimulating.

centration   The tendency to focus on a single aspect of a problem.

cognitive development   A specialty in psychology that studies how thinking skills develop over time. The major theory of cognitive development is that of Piaget.

conservation   An awareness that physical quantities remain the same even when they change shape or appearance.

conventional morality   The second stage of Kohlberg's theory of moral development, emphasizing conformity to rules that are defined by others' approval or society's rules.

difficult temperament   A type of temperament that is characterized by an intense, irregular, withdrawing style that is generally marked by negative moods.

easy temperament   A type of temperament that is defined by a very regular, adaptable, mildly intense style of behavior that is positive and responsive.

egocentrism   The inability to step into another's shoes and understand the other person's point of view.

enculturation   The process by which individuals learn and adopt the ways and manners of their culture.

goodness of fit   The interaction of a child's temperament with that of the parents, considered a key to the development of personality.

great divide theories   Theories of cognitive development that suggest that the thought of Westerners is superior to that of people who live in primitive societies.

irreversibility   The inability to imagine "undoing" a process.

permissive parents   A style of parenting in which parents allow children to regulate their own lives and provide few firm guidelines.

postconventional morality   The third stage of Kohlberg's theory of moral development, emphasizing moral reasoning on the basis of individual principles and conscience.

preconventional morality   The first stage of Kohlberg's theory of moral development, emphasizing compliance with rules to avoid punishment and gain rewards.

secure attachment   A style of attachment in which babies are described as warm and responsive.

slow-to-warm-up   A type of temperament in which infants need time to make transitions in activity and experiences. Though they may withdraw initially or respond negatively, given time and support they will adapt and react positively.

socialization   The process by which we learn and internalize the rules and patterns of behavior that are affected by culture. This process, which occurs over a long period of time, involves learning and mastering societal and cultural norms, attitudes, values, and belief systems.

socialization agents   The people, institutions, and organizations that exist to help ensure that socialization occurs.

temperament Qualities of responsiveness to the environment that exist from birth and evoke different reactions from people in the baby's world. Temperament is generally considered to be a biologically based style of interacting with the world.

uninvolved parents A style of parenting in which parents are often too absorbed in their own lives to respond appropriately to their children and often seem indifferent to them.

Culture and Gender

As with so many other aspects of our lives, culture influences the behaviors associated with being male or female. In the past 20 or 30 years, we have witnessed many changes in the behaviors Americans consider appropriate for males and females. Certainly, American culture is one of the most dynamic in the exploration of sex and gender differences (or similarities). This dynamism has led to a great deal of confusion and conflict, but it has also produced excitement about the changing nature of human relations and culture itself.

In this chapter, we will examine how culture influences behavior related to sex and gender. First, we will discuss some similarities between gender and culture concerns within mainstream psychology. Second, we will discuss some terminology and definitions concerning sex and gender that will help us understand what we are talking about and how to focus on cultural influences. Then, we will discuss cross-cultural research on gender differences, including gender stereotypes, sex roles and self-concepts, Hofstede's research, and other psychological constructs. We will discuss some theoretical notions of how psychologists believe gender differences come to exist, and why cultures seem to differ in these differences. We will also discuss ethnicity and gender-related issues in the United States. Throughout this discussion, we will see that the issues surrounding gender and gender differences, both pancultural and culture-specific, are complex as well as interesting.

The Relationship of Gender and Culture to Mainstream Psychology

Before turning to the cross-cultural literature on gender differences, it is interesting to note some parallels between the impact of gender and culture on mainstream psychology. Beginning 20 or 30 years ago, what is commonly known as the women's movement in the United States led American academic communities to evaluate the treatment and presentation of women in textbooks and research. They found that most research was conducted using men as subjects, and that most information presented about "people" in academic textbooks and university courses was based on information gathered from men. This gender bias also affected what scholars considered important to study, the relative status of different studies and topics, and the probability and outlet for publication. Psychologists became increasingly aware of the possibility that men and women may differ psychologically, calling into question previous research findings and the theories based on them. Scholars, researchers, teachers, and students alike began to question whether knowledge based primarily on men was accurate for people in general.

One consequence of this growing awareness among researchers and scholars was a conscious effort to include women as research participants, to ensure that research findings would be applicable to women as well as men. At the same time, an increasing number of women became researchers and scholars, bringing different perspectives to the field, its theories, and its findings. Today, psychology enjoys more balanced contributions by both men and women, at least in the United States, and this combination of different perspectives and concerns makes for a dynamism that is rich, interesting, and important for the field.

As a result, we have come a long way toward improving our knowledge about both men and women in the social sciences. Although questioning the imbalance of research on men and women was difficult, many behavioral and social scientists have responded well to this inequity in our knowledge and practice. Today, studies of gender differences are commonplace in social science research, and textbooks routinely incorporate sex and gender differences when imparting knowledge about people (although the degree to which such material is presented and incorporated is still questioned and debated).

We have witnessed the same type of questioning with regard to cultural norms for women and men. Just as knowledge about women and women's concerns was missing from research and scholarship 30 years ago, so too was knowledge about cultural similarities and differences and cultural diversity. Much of this gap still exists today. Many of the same questions are still being raised concerning whether what we are learning in classes and in our laboratories is indeed true for people of all cultures and ethnicities. The answer so far has been "not necessarily." To address this gap, many researchers have made a conscious effort to study behaviors across cultures to learn what is similar across cultures and what is different. Academic institutions have also made a conscious effort to recruit and train people of diverse cultural backgrounds, so that they too can contribute to the research, teaching, and scholarship in psychology.

I interpret these changes as evidence of a continuing evolution in the field, similar to what has happened in relation to gender. That is, psychology is constantly changing and evolving, as the nature of the people it is supposed to be describing continues to change. As the United States and the entire world become increasingly diverse, the need for mainstream psychology to incorporate, explain, and describe that diversity increases. The field has become aware of this need only in the past decade or so (although cross-cultural psychology and cross-cultural research have a much longer history). Theories, research, and teaching are becoming more culturally sensitive, and this increasing awareness is bound to bring with it another evolution in the face and content of psychology. For this reason, it is an exciting time in both mainstream and cross-cultural psychology, as the gap between them narrows.

Some Definitions

Before examining cultural influences with regard to sex and gender, we first need to make clear what we mean by those terms. Social scientists have offered a variety of ideas to define and differentiate between *sex* and *gender* (for example, Prince, 1985).

The term **sex** generally refers to the biological and physiological differences between men and women, the most obvious being the anatomical differences in their reproductive systems. Other biological differences between the sexes include physiological, hormonal, and biochemical differences.

The term **sex roles** is used to describe the behaviors and patterns of activities men and women may engage in that are directly related to their biological differences and the process of reproduction. An example of a sex role for females is breastfeeding, a behavior that only women can engage in (Brislin, 1993). The term **sexual identity** is used to describe the degree of awareness and recognition of sex and sex roles an individual may have. Male sexual identity includes "his awareness that he has the potential to impregnate women and knows the necessary behaviors. Female sexual identity includes the woman's awareness of her reproductive potential and her knowledge about behaviors that lead to pregnancy" (p. 287).

In contrast, **gender** refers to the behaviors or patterns of activities that a society or culture deems appropriate for men and women. These behavior patterns may or may not be related to sex and sex roles, although they often are. For example, traditional gender roles that we all know about or have heard of suggest that males are aggressive and unemotional (with the exception of anger) and that the male should leave the home every day to make a living and be the principal wage earner. Traditional gender roles for females suggest that women are nurturant, caring, and highly emotional and that they should stay at home and take care of the home and children. **Gender role** refers to the degree to which a person adopts the gender-specific behaviors ascribed by his or her culture. **Gender identity** refers to the degree to which a person has awareness or recognition that he or she adopts a particular gender role. Finally, **gender stereotypes** refer to the psychological or behavioral characteristics typically associated with men and women.

Not everyone can be pigeonholed into stereotypes according to sex or gender roles, as there are considerable individual differences across people with regard to these roles. In addition, gender role stereotypes interact with other forms of group membership. African American women, for example, are generally not perceived in terms of the traditional gender roles just described (Binion, 1990), nor are women who are disabled or who have a different sexual orientation.

Separating the biological and physiological facts of sex from the behavioral aspects of gender is the first step in understanding differences between males and females. Indeed, it should become clear from this differentiation that we are mostly concerned with gender differences, not sex differences. Culture, as a macro construct, is likely to influence our perception of gender differences.

Cross-Cultural Research on Gender

Cross-cultural research on gender differences has spanned a considerable number of psychological themes and constructs that help us piece together how gender differences exist in different cultures, and help us speculate about the reasons for those differences. For the purposes of the presentation here, I have categorized the research into four areas: gender stereotypes, gender roles and self-concept, Hofstede's study, and psychological gender differences, which include perceptual/spatial/cognitive differences, conformity and obedience, aggression, and other psychological constructs. These classifications are, of course, entirely arbitrary; they are my attempt to provide some structure to the broad array of cross-cultural studies on gender differences. In addition, this review is not comprehensive, but only representative of the vast amount of research that exists on many different psychological topics examining gender differences across culture.

Culture and Gender Stereotypes

The Williams and Best studies. The number of roles available to males and females is limitless. Some cultures foster a certain gender distinction; other cultures foster other distinctions. We are all familiar with traditional gender role differentiations—the notion that males should be independent, self-reliant, strong, and emotionally detached, while women should be dependent, reliant, weak, nurturant, and emotional. To what degree is this an American or Western cultural phenomenon?

The best-known study of gender stereotypes across cultures is one conducted by Williams and Best (1982). These researchers sampled people in 30 countries, 52–120 respondents per country, for a total of almost 3,000 individuals. The study used a questionnaire known as the Adjective Check List (ACL). The ACL is a list of 300 adjectives. Respondents in each country were asked to decide whether each adjective was more descriptive of a male or of a female. Whether the subjects agreed with the assignment of an adjective to males or females was irrelevant; instead, they were asked merely to report the characteristics generally associated with males and females in their culture.

The researchers tallied the data from all individuals. Looking at responses within each culture, Williams and Best (1982) established the criterion that if more than two-thirds of a sample from a country agreed on a particular term for either males or females, there was a consensus within that culture on that general characteristic. Then, looking at responses across the cultures, the researchers decided that if two-thirds of the cultures reached a consensus on the characteristic, there was a cross-cultural consensus on that characteristic to describe males and females. The results indicated a high degree of pancultural agreement across all the countries studied in the characteristics associated with men and women. Table 8.1 lists the 100 items of the pancultural adjective checklist that Williams and Best (1994) reported for men and women.

The degree of consensus these adjectives received in describing males and females is amazing. In fact, Berry and colleagues (1992) suggested that "this degree of consensus is so large that it may be appropriate to suggest that the researchers have found a psychological universal when it comes to gender stereotypes" (p. 60)—while at the same time cautioning against such sweeping generalizations. But the possibility of a universally accepted gender stereotype has interesting ramifications for possible evolutionary similarities across cultures in division of labor between males and females and the psychological characteristics that result from that universal division of labor.

Williams and Best (1982) conducted a second type of analysis on their data in order to summarize their major findings. They scored the adjectives in each country in terms of favorability, strength, and activity to examine how the adjectives were distributed according to affective or emotional meaning. They found surprising congruence in these analyses: The characteristics associated with men were stronger and more active than those associated with women across all countries. On favorability, however, cultural differences emerged: Some countries (such as Japan and South Africa) rated the male characteristics as more favorable than the female, whereas other countries (for example, Italy and Peru) rated female characteristics as more favorable.

How are we to interpret these results? It could be that a division of labor for males and females according to reproductive processes produced differences in behaviors that, in turn, produced differences in psychological characteristics. It

Table 8.1 The 100 Items of the Pancultural Adjective Checklist

Male-Associated		Female-Associated	
Active	Loud	Affected	Modest
Adventurous	Obnoxious	Affectionate	Nervous
Aggressive	Opinionated	Appreciative	Patient
Arrogant	Opportunistic	Cautious	Pleasant
Autocratic	Pleasure-seeking	Changeable	Prudish
Bossy	Precise	Charming	Self-pitying
Capable	Progressive	Complaining	Sensitive
Conceited	Rational	Confused	Sexy
Confident	Realistic	Curious	Shy
Courageous	Reckless	Dependent	Softhearted
Cruel	Resourceful	Dreamy	Sophisticated
Cynical	Rigid	Emotional	Submissive
Determined	Robust	Excitable	Suggestible
Disorderly	Serious	Fault-finding	Superstitious
Enterprising	Sharp-witted	Fearful	Talkative
Greedy	Show-off	Fickle	Timid
Hardheaded	Steady	Foolish	Touchy
Humorous	Stern	Forgiving	Unambitious
Indifferent	Stingy	Frivolous	Understanding
Individualistic	Stolid	Fussy	Unintelligent
Initiative	Tough	Gentle	Unstable
Interests wide	Unfriendly	Imaginative	Warm
Inventive	Unscrupulous	Kind	Weak
Lazy	Witty	Mild	Worrying

Source: "Cross-Cultural Views of Women and Men," by J. E. Williams and D. L. Best. In W. J. Lonner & R. Malpass (Eds.), *Psychology and Culture,* p. 193. Copyright © 1994 Allyn & Bacon. Reprinted by permission.

may be that these psychological characteristics had some evolutionary and adaptive advantages for males and females to fulfill their roles as prescribed by the division of labor. It could be that men and women in all cultures became locked into these set ways, accounting for universal consensus on these descriptors. It could be that men and women become locked into a particular mindset about cultural differences because of perceived social inequality or social forces and indirect communication via mass media and the like. Or these findings could all be a function of the way the research was conducted, using university students as participants, which would tend to make the entire sample more homogeneous than if people were sampled randomly from each culture.

Although it is impossible to disentangle these factors, it is important to note that Williams and Best themselves collected and analyzed data concerning gender stereotypes from young children and found a considerable degree of agreement between the findings for children and those for university students (Williams & Best, 1990). These results argue against (but do not entirely eliminate) the notion that the original findings were due to homogeneity among university students.

Williams and his colleagues have since extended their earlier work on gender stereotypes in important ways. Williams, Satterwhite, and Best (in press), for example, took the ACL data from 25 countries in their previous work, and rescored the ACL in terms of five personality dimensions known as the Big Five, or Five Factor Model of Personality. As you will see in Chapter 15, these terms refer to the five personality traits or dimensions that are considered universal or consistent around the world: They found that, overall, males had significantly higher scores than females on all traits except agreeableness; females, however, had significantly higher scores than males on this personality dimension.

In a subsequent follow-up study, Williams, Satterwhite, Best, and Inman (in press) took their ACL data from 27 countries and rescored these data according to the five-factor model of personality. They then examined male–female differences on the personality traits separately in each country. They found that the results they had obtained earlier were generally supported in all of the countries. In addition, they correlated the male–female differences with culture scores from two large value surveys (Hofstede, 1980, and Schwartz, 1994), some demographic variables, and gender ideology scores from a previous study (Williams & Best, 1990). They found that gender stereotype differentiation tended to be higher in countries that were conservative and hierarchical, with a lower level of socioeconomic development, a relatively low degree of Christian affiliation, and a relatively low proportion of women attending university. Countries that valued harmony and egalitarianism, had less traditional sex role orientations, and viewed male stereotypes as less favorable than female stereotypes were associated with less gender stereotype differentiation on the five factors.

In summary, this set of studies informs us that gender stereotypes around the world are rather stable, and are related to interesting and important psychological characteristics. Men are generally viewed as active, strong, critical, adultlike, with psychological needs such as dominance, autonomy, aggression, exhibition, achievement, and endurance. Men are also associated more with the personality traits of conscientiousness, extroversion, neuroticism, and openness. Women are generally viewed as passive, weak, nurturing, adaptive, with psychological needs such as abasement, deference, succorance, nurturance, affiliation, and heterosexuality. They are also associated with higher scores on the personality trait of agreeableness. As described earlier, the degree of stability of these findings across a wide range of countries and cultures provides a strong base of evidence for some pancultural universality in psychological attribution.

Other studies. A number of other studies have also investigated gender and sex role stereotypes in different countries and cultures. Rao and Rao (1985), for example, examined sex role stereotypes in the United States and India; they found that Indians endorsed much more traditional stereotypes concerning mother, wife, and father roles than did the Americans. Trommsdorff and Iwawaki (1989) examined gender role differences between German and Japanese adolescents. They found that Japanese mothers were seen as more controlling than fathers, while German mothers were viewed as less controlling. The Japanese also had more traditional gender role orientations than did the Germans. In general, the results from these two studies support the overall findings of Williams and Best.

Other studies have tried to shed light on how gender role stereotypes develop. Albert and Porter (1986), for example, reported that gender stereotypes increase with age, and that children are more likely to sex-type same-sex figures. Munroe, Shimmin, and Munroe (1984) found that children's understanding of gender and sex role preferences appear to be related to cognitive development. Still, many questions remain unanswered in this important area of psychology. How congruent are people's behaviors with their stereotypes, and does this congruence differ across cultures and countries? Are stereotypes related to important psychological constructs or behaviors that affect everyday lives? How do we come to develop such stereotypes—what are the factors that produce them, and their boundaries? These and other questions provide the basis for important future research.

Culture, Gender Role Ideology, and Self-Concept

Another important topic that has been studied across cultures is **gender role ideology**—judgments about what males and females ought to be like or ought to do. To examine gender role ideologies, Williams and Best (1990) asked subjects in 14 countries to complete the ACL in relation to what they believe they are, and what they would like to be. The subjects also completed a sex role ideology scale that generated scores between two polar opposites, labeled "traditional" and "egalitarian." The traditional scores tended to describe gender roles that were consistent with the traditional or universal norms found in their earlier research; egalitarian scores reflected a tendency toward less differentiation between males and females on the various psychological characteristics.

The most egalitarian scores were found in the Netherlands, Germany, and Finland; the most traditional ideologies were found in Nigeria, Pakistan, and India. Women tended to have more egalitarian views than men. Gender differences within each country, however, were relatively small compared to cross-country differences, which were considerable. In particular, countries with relatively high socioeconomic development, a high proportion of Protestant Christians, a low proportion of Muslims, a high percentage of women employed outside the home, a high proportion of women enrolled in universities, and a greater degree of individualism were associated with more egalitarian scores. These findings make sense, as greater affluence and individualistic tendencies tend to produce a culture that allows women increased access to jobs and education, thus blending traditional gender roles.

In addition to studying gender stereotypes and ideologies, Williams and Best (1990) also examined gender differences in self-concept. The same students in the same 14 countries rated each of the 300 adjectives of the ACL according to whether it was descriptive of themselves or their ideal self. Responses were scored according to masculinity/femininity as well as in terms of favorability, strength, and activity. When scored according to masculinity/femininity, both self and ideal-self ratings for men were more masculine than were women's ratings, and vice versa, across all countries. However, both men and women in all countries rated the ideal self as more masculine than the actual self. In effect, they were saying that they wanted to have more of the traits traditionally associated with males.

When scored according to the three emotional dimensions, male self-concepts tended to be rated stronger than female self-concepts. In some countries, the ratings on the three dimensions were relatively similar between men and women, whereas in other countries the ratings were quite divergent. The degree of differentiation among the ratings may be related to other variables, Williams and Best (1990) suggest, including socioeconomic status, religion, and proportion of women employed outside the home.

Again, these findings provide interesting information about the nature of gender differences, and the stability of those differences across cultures. Taken together with the research on gender stereotypes, they reinforce the idea of a set of universal psychological constructs. To the extent that such gender-related universals exist, they raise important questions about the interaction among culture, personality, and biology, and the degree to which biological sex differences produce psychological needs and demands in all people across all cultures. Future research will need to examine this relationship in more detail, documenting how different cultures may address the same biological needs differently depending on the resources available to address them, yet produce similarities in the psychological constructs associated with those demands.

Hofstede's Study

In Chapters 2 and 17, I discuss research by Hofstede, who studied work-related attitudes across 50 countries. Because his research is relevant to the issue of culture and gender, I will briefly review his study here. Hofstede (1980) conducted a large-scale survey of work-related values in a major multinational corporation. Based on the data obtained, he generated four dimensions of differentiation among the cultures in his sample. One of these dimensions was called "masculinity" (MA). This dimension refers to the degree to which a culture will foster, encourage, or maintain differences between males and females. Cultures scoring high on MA tended to endorse items and values thought to be associated with masculinity and male gender roles in the workplace. Japan, Austria, Venezuela, and Italy had the highest MA scores. Cultures scoring low on MA minimized differences between the sexes and genders. Denmark, the Netherlands, Norway, and Sweden had the lowest scores.

Although Hofstede's study focused entirely on work-related values, his findings highlight a major point of this chapter—that cultures will arrive at different ways of dealing with differences between men and women. The behaviors men and women engage in produce different psychological outcomes that have direct ramifications for actual life behaviors (such as work-related behaviors). Cultures vary in how they act on these gender differences, with some cultures fostering and encouraging great differences between the genders and other cultures minimizing those differences. It is precisely these cultural differences in gender roles that Hofstede's data on MA speak to.

Psychological Gender Differences across Cultures

Culture, biology, gender roles, and gender role ideology all interact to produce differences between the genders on a variety of psychological and behavioral outcomes. That is, the division of labor and actual behaviors males and females engage in as a result of their biological and physiological differences help to produce a different psychology or mindset as well. These psychological differences between genders can be considered a product of the differences between males and females because of the division of labor and behaviors surrounding reproduction.

Just as there will be psychological differences between males and females in any one culture, psychological differences can also be found across cultures. And the degree, direction, or exact nature of those gender differences may differ across cultures. That is, while one culture may foster a certain type of gender difference, another culture may not foster that difference to the same degree. A third culture may foster that difference even more than the first two cultures. Psychological gender differences across cultures are not simply products of biology and culture; they are also important reinforcers of culture, feeding back onto the culture, behaviors, gender roles, and gender role ideologies. In this cyclical fashion, the psychological products of gender differentiation also become a crucial aspect of the culture–behavior–psychology linkage that exists among a people and their rituals, traditions, and behaviors.

The cross-cultural literature on psychological differences between the genders highlights three general areas of difference: perceptual/spatial/cognitive abilities, conformity and obedience, and aggressiveness (Berry et al., 1992). Studies in each of these areas show that while there are general differences between genders, the degree of those differences is indeed different across cultures.

Perceptual/spatial/cognitive differences. At least in American society, it is common folklore that males are better at mathematical and spatial reasoning tasks, whereas females are better at verbal comprehension tasks. An analysis of the scores for males and females on standardized tests in elementary school, college entrance examinations, or graduate school entrance examinations shows some degree of support for these notions, although the difference between males and females seems to have narrowed in recent years. In their review of the literature, Maccoby and Jacklin (1974) also concluded that males tend to do better on spatial tasks and other tasks having a spatial component. Years ago, however, Berry (1966) pointed out that such differences do not appear to exist among males and females of the Inuit culture in Canada. Berry suggested that the gender difference did not exist because "spatial abilities are highly adaptive for both males and females in Inuit society, and both boys and girls have ample training and experience that promote the acquisition of spatial ability" (Berry et al., 1992, p. 65).

Following up on the possibility of cultural differences on this gender difference, Berry (1976) and his colleagues conducted a study in which a block design task was given to males and females in 17 different cultures. A stimulus card depicting a geometric representation of a set of blocks was presented, and the task was to manipulate an actual set of blocks to emulate the design provided. The results were interesting and provocative. While there were indeed a number of cultures in which males did better than females on the task, there also were a considerable number of cultures in which females did better than males. In interpreting these data, Berry et al. (1992) suggested that male superiority on the task tended to be found in cultures that were tight (that is, relatively homogeneous), sedentary, and agriculturally based, but that female superiority was found in cultures that were loose, nomadic, and based on hunting and gathering. In these latter cultures, the roles ascribed to males and females are relatively flexible, with more members performing a variety of tasks related to the survival of the group. Future research, of course, needs to follow up these interpretations as hypotheses, and investigate the exact nature of and reasons for these differences.

A similar finding was reported in a meta-analysis of the research literature by Born, Bleichrodt, and Van der Flier (1987). They reported that although no gender differences in overall intelligence were found, gender differences on various subtests of intelligence did occur. Although their findings leave open the question of the exact role of culture in creating or maintaining the gender difference, they do show that the differences in the cognitive test scores between males and females are variable across cultures. In another study (Pontius, 1997), the male advantage in spatial abilities was not found on two spatial tasks in eastern Ecuador, a culture that emphasizes women's traditional tasks, such as sewing and needlework, that require spatial representation.

Thus, some cultures foster male superiority in these types of tasks, but others foster female superiority, and still others foster no differences. Although some suggestions have been made as to the nature and causes of these various gender differences, research has yet to pinpoint exactly what factors influence which types of differences, and why. Future research will need to explore these and other issues regarding perceptual/spatial/analytic abilities. With the increasing plurality of the world, this research will also need to be sensitive to the particular time period in which the research is conducted, as differences may be decreasing in many societies and cultures today.

Conformity and obedience.   One of the most common gender role stereotypes is that females are more conforming and obedient than males. This stereotype is no doubt related to the traditional gender roles females and males have occupied, with males traditionally being "head of the household," making primary decisions over big-ticket items that involve the family. In this traditional social arrangement, females were not to be concerned with authority and decision-making power; rather, the female role focused on caring for the children and managing the household affairs. In short, females were expected to conform to decisions imposed upon them by males or by society in general.

The degree to which this difference is enacted varies considerably from culture to culture. In Berry's (1976) study, the researchers also obtained an index of the degree to which each person conformed in the 17 cultures included in the sample. Across the 17 cultures, clear variations emerged; as with gender differences in spatial reasoning, these variations appeared to be related to the cultural concept of tightness. Cultures that were tighter appeared to foster a greater gender difference on conformity, with females more conformist than males; tight cultures may require a greater degree of conformity to traditional gender roles on the part of both males and females. In contrast, cultures that were looser fostered less gender difference on conformity, and in some of these cultures, males were found to be more conforming than females. Thus, while traditional gender stereotypes of females as more conforming than males appears to have some validity, considerable cross-cultural difference exists in the degree, and in some cases the direction, of this difference.

Future research needs to test these ideas further, examining the links between cultural variables such as tightness and psychological constructs such as conformity, and the degree to which gender differences on such constructs are fostered. Future research will also need to examine the degree to which gender differences on conformity are related to differences on perceptual, analytic, or spatial skills, or on other psychological traits and constructs such as aggressiveness.

Aggressiveness.   Another common gender stereotype is that males are more aggressive than females. Indeed, there is support for this stereotype in all cultures for which documentation exists (Block, 1983; Brislin, 1993). Males account for a disproportionate amount of violent crime in both industrialized and nonindustrialized societies. The focus in research on this topic has been adolescent males. Several researchers have searched for the biological correlates of aggression. In particular, some researchers have questioned whether increased levels of the hormone testosterone during male adolescence may account for or contribute to increased aggression in males. Increased testosterone levels have been associated with dominance hierarchies in some nonhuman primates, but the human analog is less clear. On the basis of the evidence available, it appears that hormones may contribute to some degree to aggressiveness, but culture and the environment can certainly act to encourage or discourage its emergence (Berry et al., 1992).

A study by Barry, Josephson, Lauer, and Marshall (1976) examined the degree to which cultures foster aggressive tendencies in the socialization of children. These researchers found a sex-related difference in the average amount of teaching about aggressiveness across 150 different cultures. Inspection of their data, however, reveals that this average difference was produced by a disproportionate number of high-scoring cultures in which teaching aggression actually occurs. In fact, a large majority of societies did not show a sex-related difference in teaching aggression.

Such interpretations have been bolstered by anthropological studies of some cultures known for their aggressive tendencies. Among these is the Yanomami culture of Venezuela and Brazil (for example, Sponsel, 1998), often referred to in anthropological circles as the "fierce people." Yet, even with regard to these supposedly aggressive groups, more recent research and discussion have begun to call into question the potential bias in anthropological and comparative methods that may see only part of the culture (Sponsel, 1998). Such concerns affect cross-cultural research as well, bringing into question the specific definitions and measurements of aggressiveness and their degree of sensitivity to a variety of contexts.

Neither biology nor sex differences in teaching aggressive acts can account for gender differences in aggression observed across cultures. Some researchers (Berry et al., 1992; Segall, Dasen, Berry, & Poortinga, 1990) offer yet another possible explanation for gender differences in aggression across cultures. They suggest that male aggression may be a compensatory mechanism to offset the conflict produced by a young male's identification with a female care provider and his initiation into adulthood as a male. In this model, aggressiveness is viewed as "gender marking" behavior.

Regardless of the precise mechanisms that produce gender differences in aggression, it is clear that although the gender stereotype of aggressiveness may be generally true, considerable differences do exist across cultures. What is true for one culture may not be true for another. Future research needs to examine the exact mechanisms accounting for these differences, taking into account the complex interplay among biology, culture, and psychology. This research will need to be sensitive to the context specificity of aggressive acts, and the influence of the research methodology and data collection itself on the reporting or acting out of aggression.

Other psychological constructs.   Over the years, many other studies have documented culture and gender differences on a wide variety of psychological constructs. In the past five to ten years alone, research examining gender and cultural differences has addressed topics including gender identity (Harris, 1996), career plans (Morinaga, Frieze, & Ferlingoj, 1993), self-presentations (Reid & Trotter, 1993), dress (Reece, 1996), suicidal behavior (Wassenaar, van der Veen, & Pillay, 1998), dream content (Punamaeki & Joustie, 1998), personal relationships (Burleson, 1997), cognitive and coping styles related to sports (Anshel, Williams, & Hodge, 1997; Williams, Anshel, & Quek, 1997), self-esteem (Watkins, Akande, Cheng, & Regmi, 1996), conflict resolution (Itoi, Ohbuchi, & Fukuno, 1996), response styles (Watkins & Cheung, 1995), nonverbal behaviors (Remland, Jones, & Brinkman, 1995), and personal entitlements (Wainryb &Turiel, 1994). Cross-cultural work over the past few decades has uncovered culture and gender differences across other constructs as well.

There is little doubt, therefore, that gender differences exist on a wide variety of psychological constructs, and that cultures differ in the exact degree and nature of those gender differences. Some research has examined how such culture and gender differences come to manifest themselves. Dasgupta (1998), for example, examined the relationship between ethnic identity and two scales related to women and dating among Asian Indian immigrants in the United States, and found a strong similarity between parents and children on many target attitudes. This finding provides evidence for the important role parents play as enculturation agents in maintaining traditional cultural values, including gender differences.

How Does Culture Influence Gender?

How can we understand the influence of culture on gender? In terms of the definitions presented earlier, a newborn has sex but no gender. Gender is a construct that develops in children as they are socialized in their environments. As children grow older, they learn specific behaviors and patterns of activities appropriate and inappropriate for their sex, and they either adopt or reject those gender roles.

Ensuring that reproduction occurs fulfills men's and women's sex roles. But what happens before and after that depends on a host of variables. One of these variables is culture. The biological fact and necessity of reproduction, along with other biological and physiological differences between men and women, lead to behavioral differences between men and women. In earlier days, these behavioral differences were no doubt reinforced by a necessary division of labor. Someone had to look after children while someone else had to find food for the family; no one person could have done it all. Thus, the existence of reproductive differences led to a division of labor advantageous to the family as a unit. These differences, in turn, produced differences in a variety of psychological traits and characteristics, such as aggressiveness, nurturance, and achievement.

Berry and his colleagues (1992) have suggested that the model presented in Figure 2.3 in Chapter 2 describes how cultural practices can affect gender differences in psychological characteristics, and I think it is an excellent springboard for understanding the effects of culture on gender. However, it is important to remember that the factors involved in understanding culture and gender that are outlined in Figure 2.3 are not static or unidimensional. Indeed, the entire system is dynamic and interrelated and feeds back on and reinforces itself. As a result, this system is not a linear unit with influences going in a single direction; it acquires a life of its own. And the life of this system is reinforced by the glue we know as culture.

As different societies live in different environments, survival requires that they balance a number of factors, including natural resources, affluence, and population density. These external factors help to frame and mold specific behaviors that may affect the division of labor between men and women originally necessitated by biological differences. These differential behaviors that occur because of differences in external, environmental factors lead to patterns of behaviors across time that are associated with men and women. This pattern of behaviors across time, of course, is culture. In turn, it feeds back reciprocally onto the pattern of behaviors, reinforcing behaviors, beliefs, attitudes, and values. Thus, as different cultures must deal with different external factors, it is only natural that gender differences vary by culture. One culture may foster considerable equality between women and men and relatively few differences in their cultural practices and psychological characteristics. Another culture may foster considerable differences between the sexes, their cultural practices related to reproduction, and psychological characteristics associated with sex roles. Some cultures may foster differences between the sexes in one direction (for example, males as primary decision makers, females compliant and obedient); another culture may foster differences in the opposite direction. This type of explanatory model may account for the range of differences obtained in previous cross-cultural research on psychological constructs.

Yet the evidence also suggests that stereotypes and attitudes concerning gender differences are relatively constant across cultures, despite actual differences in psychological behaviors brought about by real differences in demands placed on cultures and societies by their environment. Some researchers, in fact, go as far as to say that the persistence of gender stereotypes across culture cannot be attributed to sociocultural factors, and can only be explained by sociobiological models (Lueptow, Garovich, & Lueptow, 1995).

Future research will need to tackle the important questions posed by this theoretical understanding of cultural and gender differences, elucidating on the mechanisms and factors that help produce and maintain those differences in individual cultures, and then across cultures. In addition, future research will need to explore the relationship between differences in actual behaviors and psychological constructs and gender-related stereotypes, investigating whether these are two different psychological systems of the mind, or whether they are linked in ways that are not yet apparent. Indeed, research to date is rather silent on the mechanisms that produce gender and cultural differences, and the interrelationship among different psychological processes. The important point to remember is that different cultures may arrive at different outcomes through the same process. Men and women will have gender-specific roles in any society or culture. All cultures encourage particular behavioral differences between the genders and help to define the roles, duties, and responsibilities appropriate for males and females.

Ethnicity and Gender in the United States

Among the most pressing issues and concerns facing the United States today are gender differences across different ethnicities and the continuing struggle for gender equity across all cultural and ethnic groups. Just as people in different cultures in faraway lands may have different gender roles and expectations, people of different ethnic backgrounds in the United States can have different gender role expectations as well. Many of these gender differences across ethnic lines are rooted in the cultures people of these ethnicities brought with them when they originally came to the United States. But gender differences in the United States today definitely reflect an "American" influence, making gender issues unique in American culture.

There is really very little research on gender differences between African American males and females. The research that exists typically compares African American males and females to European American males and females. African American males are more likely than European American males to live below the poverty line, die at an early age, make less money, be in jail, and be executed for a crime. With regard to psychological processes, African American males are especially adept at body language, nonverbal encoding and decoding, and improvised problem solving (Allen & Santrock, 1993).

Research on the concerns of African American females has painted a changing picture over the past 20 years (Hall, Evans, & Selice, 1989). Early research focused almost exclusively on generally negative characteristics and situations. Of late, however, an increasing amount of research has focused on many other psychological aspects of African American females, including self-esteem or achievement. For example, the number of Ph.D.'s awarded to African American women increased by 16% between 1977 and 1986 (Allen & Santrock, 1993), indicating some improvement in the accessibility of advanced graduate degrees for African American women and increased motivation to achieve those degrees.

Some research has suggested that the gender identities of African Americans are more androgynous than those of European Americans. *Androgyny* refers to a gender identity that involves endorsement of both male and female characteristics. Harris (1996), for example, administered the Bem Sex Role Inventory, a widely used scale to measure gender identity, to African and European American males and females, and found that both African American males and females were more androgynous than European American males and females. In addition, he found that African American males and females have an equal propensity to endorse typically masculine traits, whereas European American males regard more masculine traits as self-descriptive than European American females do.

Many Asian American families have carried on traditional gender roles associated with males and females from their original culture. Asian females are often expected to bear the brunt of domestic duties, to raise children, and to be a "good" daughter-in-law. Asian American males are often raised to remain aloof, unemotional, and authoritative, especially concerning familial issues (Sue, 1989). Some studies, however, have suggested a loosening of these rigid, traditional gender roles for Asian American males and females. Although Asian American males may still appear as figurative head of the family in public, in reality much decision-making power within the family in private is held by the Asian American female head of the household (Huang & Ying, 1989).

As with Asian American gender roles, the traditional role of the Mexican American female was to provide for the children and take care of the home (Comas-Diaz, 1992). Likewise, Mexican American males were traditionally expected to fill the role of provider for the family. These differences are related to the concept of **machismo**, which incorporates many traditional expectations of the male gender role, such as being unemotional, strong, authoritative, aggressive, and masculine (see Table 8.1, p. 214). However, recent research has shown that these gender differences for Mexican American males and females are also on the decrease. Mexican American women are increasingly sharing in decision making in the family, as well as taking on a more direct role as provider through work outside the home (Espin, 1993). Although adolescent Mexican American males are generally still given more freedom outside the home than are females, gender differences may be decreasing in the contemporary Mexican American family.

Gender role differentiation for Native Americans seems to depend heavily on the patriarchal or matriarchal nature of the tribal culture of origin. In patriarchal tribes, women assume primary responsibility for the welfare of the children and extended family members. But males of the Mescalero Apache tribe often take responsibility for children when they are with their families (Ryan, 1980). As with other ethnic groups, the passage of time, increased interaction with people of other cultures and with mainstream American culture, and the movement toward urban areas seems to have effected changes in these traditional values and expectations for Native American males and females.

Certainly, the picture I have painted for these ethnic groups is not universally true or salient for all males and females within them. Instead, they serve as generalized descriptions of the gender roles males and females of these ethnic groups may have been socialized into in the past. While many of these cultural tendencies are rooted in the original cultures these peoples came from, their intermixing and interaction in contemporary American society and culture makes for an interesting blend of traditional values with contemporary equity. This balance, of course, produces tension, and how well we can all negotiate this tension between ethnic and American cultures, with regard to gender and other psychological constructs, may be indicative of our effectiveness in this society.

Conclusion

Sex refers to the biological and physiological differences between males and females. Sex roles refers to behaviors expected of males and females in relation to their biological differences and reproduction. Gender refers to the psychological and behavioral traits and characteristics cultures carve out using sex differences as a base. Gender roles refer to the degree to which a person adopts the gender-specific behaviors ascribed by his or her culture. It is gender and its permutations—roles, identities, stereotypes, and the like—that shares an important link with culture.

Gender roles are different for males and females in all cultures. Some stereotypic notions about gender differences seem to be universal across cultures, such as aggressiveness, strength, and lack of emotionality for males, and weakness, submissiveness, and emotionality for females. Other research, however, has shown that the degree, and in some case the direction, of these differences varies across cultures. That is, not every culture will necessarily harbor the same gender differences in the same way as other cultures. Further research is needed to gain a better understanding of culture-constant and culture-specific aspects of gender differences.

Examining gender differences in the United States is especially challenging because of the cultural and ethnic diversity within this single country and the influence of interactions with mainstream American culture. While each ethnic group has its own cultural preferences for gender differentiation, some blending of the old with the new, the traditional with the modern, appears to be taking place. Without evidence to the contrary, it is probably best to consider this blending as an addition of different cultural repertoires concerning gender differences rather than a subtraction from the old ways.

As we meet people from different cultural backgrounds, we may encounter gender roles that are different from our own. Oftentimes, we feel strongly and negatively about these differences. Yet despite our own personal outlook, we must exercise considerable care and caution in imposing our preferences on others. In most cases, people of other cultures feel just as strongly about their own way of living. Many people of many other cultures, particularly women, still harbor many of the traditional values of their ancestral culture, and I have seen conflicts arise because Americans—men and women alike—look down upon these traditional ways, criticize them, and attempt to force change. Many women in many cultures want to marry early, stay home, and take care of the family; many men want to adopt the traditional male roles as well. These tendencies are alive in many different people within the most egalitarian cultures and societies, including the United States. We need to respect these differences, rather than attempt to change them because they are not consonant with our own individual or cultural preferences. Still, this is a delicate balancing act for all of us, because there is a fine line between cultural relativity (a desired state of comprehension) and the unacceptable justification of oppression.

 # Glossary

gender The behaviors or patterns of activities a society or culture deems appropriate for men and women. These behavioral patterns may or may not be related to sex and sex roles, although they often are.

gender identity The degree to which a person has awareness of or recognition that he or she has adopted a particular gender role.

gender role The degree to which a person adopts the gender-specific behaviors ascribed by his or her culture.

gender role ideology Judgments about what gender roles in a particular culture ought to be.

gender stereotype The psychological or behavioral characteristics typically associated with men and women.

machismo A concept related to Mexican American gender role differentiation that is characterized by many traditional expectations of the male gender role, such as being unemotional, strong, authoritative, aggressive, and masculine.

sex The biological and physiological differences between men and women, the most obvious being the anatomical differences in their reproductive systems.

sex roles The behaviors and patterns of activities men and women may engage in that are directly related to their biological differences and the process of reproduction.

sexual identity The degree of awareness and recognition by an individual of his or her sex and sex roles.

9

Culture and Physical Health

One major role of education is to improve the lives of the people we touch. Whether through research, service, or provision of primary or secondary health care, we look forward to the day when we can adequately diagnose and treat medical diseases, prevent abnormal behavior, and foster positive states of being in balance with others and the environment. This is not an easy task; a multitude of forces influences our health and our ability to prevent and treat illness.

As we strive to meet this challenge, the important role of culture in contributing to the etiology, maintenance, and treatment of disease has become increasingly clear. Although our goals of prevention and treatment of disease and maintenance of health may be the same across cultures, cultures vary in their definitions of what is considered "healthy" or "mature" (Tseng & McDermott, 1981). Cultural differences also exist in perceptions of problems and in preferred strategies for coping with them (Terrell, 1992). Our job is made more difficult because cultural beliefs and practices influence treatment, and they shape both the therapist's and the client's definitions and understandings of the problem (Berry et al., 1992). Traditional approaches to treatment of abnormal behavior may prove insensitive or inappropriate when applied across cultures.

This chapter explores how cultural factors influence physical health and disease processes, and attempts to treat them; the next chapter will deal with cultural influences on mental health and psychological interventions. We begin with an examination of cultural differences in the definition of health, and then explore cultural differences in conceptions of the body. We will then review the considerable amount of research concerning the relationship between

29

229

culture and heart disease, other physical disease processes, eating disorders, and suicide. We will also explore the way cultural differences influence help-seeking, treatment compliance, and issues of responsibility, trust, and self-control over personal health and disease processes. I will summarize the research in the form of a model, then use this information to consider ways of developing culturally relevant, sensitive, and effective treatment programs.

Cultural Differences in the Definition of Health

Before we look at how culture influences health and disease processes, we need to examine exactly what we mean by *health*. In the United States, our views of health have been heavily influenced by what many call the **medical model** of health and disease. This model views disease as resulting from a specific, identifiable cause originating inside the body. These causes, whether viral, bacterial, or otherwise, are referred to as **pathogens** and are seen as the root of all physical and medical diseases. Cardiovascular disease, for example, has been linked to specific pathogens such as clotting from lipids and cholesterol.

The medical model of disease has influenced psychology's view of abnormal behavior and psychopathology. Traditional psychological approaches view the origin of abnormal behaviors as residing within the person. Such abnormalities may result from lack of gratification or overgratification of basic, instinctual processes (such as suggested by Freudian psychoanalytic theory) or from learned responses (as suggested by classical or operant conditioning).

The traditional medical model of health in both medicine and psychology has had a profound influence on treatment approaches. If specific medical or psychobehavioral pathogens exist within a person's body, those pathogens must be dealt with when treating disease. Medical treatment and traditional psychological approaches focus on making an intervention within a person. In the traditional medical model, health is characterized as *the lack of disease*. If a person remains free of disease, the person is considered healthy.

Views of health from other cultures suggest different definitions of health. People of ancient China and Greece, for example, viewed health not only as the absence of negative states but also as the presence of positive ones. Balance between self and nature and across the individual's various roles in life is viewed as an integral part of health in many Asian cultures. This balance can produce a positive state—a synergy of the forces of self, nature, and others—that many call *health*. Alternative views of health that incorporate the presence of positive as well as the absence of negative states are important in many cultures today.

Incorporating balance as a positive aspect of health is not foreign in the United States today. In the past decade or two, we have seen a rising frustration with defining health solely as the absence of disease. Americans have become much more aware of how lifestyle factors can contribute not only to the absence of negative states but also to the presence of positive ones. In particular, the concept of **hardiness** has been used in recent years in contemporary psychology to denote not only a lack of disease but the presence of positive health states. Biobehavioral medicine and health psychology, nonexistent even a few years ago, represent responses by the health care and academic professions to a growing interest in definitions of health different from those afforded by the traditional medical model. We now know that many of the leading causes of death are directly and indirectly attributable to lifestyle choices and unhealthy behaviors (Feist & Brannon, 1988), many of which will be explored in the remainder of this chapter. These findings contribute to our growing knowledge of the impact of behavior on health. And because behavior is heavily influenced by culture, an increased awareness of the links among health, lifestyle, and behavior can help us understand the sociocultural influences on health and disease.

Culture and Conceptions of the Body

Cultures differ in how they view the human body. These different conceptions of the human body influence how people of different cultures approach health and disease, treatment, and perhaps even the types of diseases that affect them.

MacLachlan (1997) has suggested that cultures have different metaphors for how they conceptualize the human body. The most widely held view, according to MacLachlan (1997), involves the notion of balance and imbalance in the body: The various systems of the body produce harmony or health when in balance, illness and disease when in imbalance. A theory first developed by Hippocrates, which heavily influences views of the human body and disease in most industrialized countries and cultures today, suggests that the body is comprised of four humors: blood, phlegm, yellow bile, and black bile. Too much or too little of any of these throws the body out of balance, resulting in disease. Derivatives of these terms—such as sanguine, phlegmatic, and choleric—are widely used in health and medical circles today.

MacLachlan (1997) points out that common theories of disease in many Latin American cultures involve a balance between hot and cold. These terms do not refer to temperature, but to the intrinsic power of different substances in the body. Some illnesses or states are hot, others cold. A person who is in a hot condition is given cold foods to counteract the situation, and vice versa. The Chinese concept of yin and yang shares similarities to this concept.

Social and cultural factors play a major role in the perception of one's own and others' body shapes, and these perceptions influence the relationship between culture and health. For example, a number of studies have found an inverse relationship between social class and low body weight in many American and European cultures; that is, individuals of higher social class generally have lower body weights than individuals of lower social class (reviewed in Furnham & Alibhai, 1983). The inverse, however, is true in many other cultures. And it has also been shown that the longer immigrants have lived in traditionally Western cultures, the less obese they tend to be. Furnham and Alibhai (1983) examined how Kenyan Asian, British, and Kenyan British females perceived female body shapes. In their study, participants were shown drawings of women ranging from extremely anorexic to extremely obese, and were asked to rate each on a series of bipolar adjectives. The results indicated that the Kenyan Asians rated larger figures more favorably and smaller figures less favorably than did the British, as predicted. The Kenyan British were similar to the British group in their perceptions.

A later study by Furnham and Baguma (1994) also confirmed the role of culture in the perception of body shape. In this study, British and Ugandan students rated 24 drawings of male and female figures on 12 bipolar scales. Again, the figures ranged from extremely anorexic to extremely obese. The results showed cultural differences on the extreme pictures, with Ugandans rating the obese female and anorexic male figures as more attractive than British observers. Again, these findings point to the important role of culture and cultural stereotypes in the perception and evaluation of body shapes, which in turn has implications for health and disease processes. Other studies (for example, Henriques, Calhoun, & Cann, 1996) have documented similar differences among ethnic groups in the United States. Future research will need to establish the links between these types of perceptions and actual health-related behaviors, in order to document the degree to which these perceptions influence health and disease processes.

Sociocultural Influences on Physical Health and Medical Disease Processes

Psychosocial Determinants of Health and Disease

In the past few years, psychology as a whole has becoming increasingly aware of the important role that culture may play in the maintenance of health and the production of disease processes. This awareness can be seen on many levels, from more journal articles published on these topics to the establishment of new journals devoted to this area of research. This increased awareness is related to a growing concern with psychosocial determinants of health and illness in general.

Scholars have long been interested in the close relationship between mental and physical health. Research linking Type A personality patterns and cardiovascular disease is a good example of this area of study. As most people are aware, research originally conducted more than two decades ago showed that individuals who were pressed for time, always in a rush, agitated and irritable, and always on the go—characterized as Type A personality syndrome—appeared to be at greater risk for developing cardiovascular disease and heart attacks than non–Type A personalities. This linkage was important not only in informing us about the etiology and possible prevention of cardiovascular disease; it also opened the door to examining the close relationship between psychology and physiology—the field we now know as *health psychology*.

Over the past two decades, a number of important and interesting studies have continued to document the linkage between psychosocial factors and health/disease states. Steptoe and his colleagues (1991; Steptoe & Wardle, 1994) have reviewed many of the previous studies, highlighting the links between unemployment and mortality, cardiovascular disease, and cancer; goal frustration and negative life events and gastrointestinal disorders; stress and myocardial ischemias and the common cold; bereavement and lymphocyte functions; pessimistic explanatory styles and physical illnesses; and hardiness and physical illnesses, among others. Indeed, the field has come a long way beyond Type A personality patterns and cardiovascular disease in demonstrating the close relationship between psychosocial factors and health/disease outcomes.

More recently, Adler and her colleagues (1994) have reported that socioeconomic status (SES) is consistently associated with health outcomes, with people of higher SES enjoying better health than do people of lower SES. This relationship has been found not only for mortality rates, but for almost every disease and condition studied. Research, however, has not been able to identify the exact mechanisms that mediate the linkage between SES and health. Adler and colleagues (1994) suggest that health-related behaviors such as smoking, physical activity, and alcohol use may mediate that relationship, as these variables appear to be related to SES. In addition, psychological characteristics such as depression, hostility, stress, and social ordering—one's relative position in the SES hierarchy—may also mediate the relationship between SES and health, because each of these variables appears to be related to SES.

Thus, research of the past two decades has demonstrated convincingly that psychosocial factors play an important role in maintaining and promoting health, and in the etiology and treatment of disease. Still, many avenues remain open for future research, including establishing direct links between particular psychosocial factors and specific disease outcomes, and identifying the specific mechanisms that mediate those relationships. Hopefully, research of the next two decades will be as fruitful as that of the past two decades in providing much-needed knowledge about these processes.

Beyond looking at psychosocial factors, many scholars and health care practitioners alike have long been interested in the contribution of sociocultural factors to health. In the past decade, a number of important studies have shown how culture may play a major role in the development and treatment of illness. These studies, to be reviewed in this chapter, destroy the common notion that physical illness has nothing to do with sociocultural or psychological factors, and vice versa. Indeed, they contribute to our combined knowledge of psychological factors on physical disease processes. Changes in lifestyle (for example, diet, smoking, exercise, and alcohol consumption) can be seen as our response to this increasing recognition of the complex interrelationship among culture, psychology, and medical processes.

Social Isolation and Mortality

Some of the earliest research on sociocultural factors in health and disease processes examined the relationship between social isolation or social support and death. Earlier research had highlighted the potential negative effects of social isolation and social disadvantage on health and disease (Feist & Brannon, 1988). One of the best-known studies in this area is the Alameda County study (Berkman & Syme, 1979), named after the county in California where the data were collected and the study conducted. Researchers interviewed almost 7,000 individuals to discover their degree of social contact; the final data set included approximately 4,725 people, as some people were dropped from the study. Following the initial assessment interview, deaths were monitored over a nine-year period. The results were clear for both men and women: Individuals with the fewest social ties suffered the highest mortality rate, and people with the most social ties had the lowest rate. These findings were valid even when other factors were statistically or methodologically controlled, including the level of physical health reported at the time of the initial questionnaire, the year of death, socioeconomic status, and a number of health-related behaviors (such as smoking and alcohol consumption). This study was one of the first to demonstrate clearly the enormous role that sociocultural factors may play in the maintenance of physical health and illness, and raised the awareness of scientists and theorists alike concerning the possible role of social factors in health/disease processes.

Individualism and Cardiovascular Disease

For many years now, researchers have examined how social and psychological factors influence the development and treatment of cardiovascular disease. Several factors have contributed to this focus on cardiovascular disease. One is the previous work identifying a number of psychological and behavioral factors that appear to influence cardiovascular disease—notably, the Type A personality profile (see Friedman & Rosenman, 1974). Another is the relatively high incidence of cardiovascular disease in the United States, making it a major health concern for many Americans.

Although there has not been a lot of research on the role of social and cultural (as opposed to personality) factors, some studies indicate that they also contribute to cardiovascular disease. Marmot and Syme (1976), for example, studied Japanese Americans, classifying 3,809 subjects into groups according to how "traditionally Japanese" they were (spoke Japanese at home, retained traditional Japanese values and behaviors, and the like). They found that those who were the "most" Japanese had the lowest incidence of coronary heart disease—comparable to the incidence in Japan. The group that was the "least" Japanese had a three to five times higher incidence. Moreover, the differences between the groups could not be accounted for by other coronary risk factors. These findings point to the contribution of social and cultural lifestyles to the development of heart disease.

Triandis and his colleagues (1988) took this finding one step further, using the individualism–collectivism (IC) cultural dimension and examining its relationship to heart disease across eight different cultural groups. European Americans, the most individualistic of the eight groups, had the highest rate of heart attacks; Trappist monks, who were the least individualistic, had the lowest rate. Of course, this study is not conclusive, as many other variables confound comparisons between Americans and Trappist monks (such as industrialization, class, and lifestyle). Nevertheless, these findings again highlight the potential contribution of sociocultural factors to the development of heart disease. Triandis and his colleagues (1988) suggested that social support or isolation was the most important factor that explained this relationship, a position congruent with the earlier research on social isolation. That is, people who live in more collectivistic cultures have stronger and deeper social ties with others than do people in individualistic cultures. These social relationships, in turn, are considered a "buffer" against the stress and strain of living, reducing the risk of cardiovascular disease. People who live in individualistic cultures do not have the same types or degrees of social relationships; therefore, they have less of a buffer against stress and are more susceptible to heart disease.

Other Dimensions of Culture and Other Diseases

The study by Triandis and his colleagues (1988) was especially important because it was the first to examine the relationship between cultural differences and the incidence of a particular disease state (heart disease). Research has also been done on other disease states and health-related behaviors, such as cancer, smoking, stress, and pain (see Feist & Brannon, 1988). Collectively, these studies suggest the important role of sociocultural factors—most notably, social support—in contributing to health and disease.

Still, these studies are limited in that they have focused on only one aspect of culture—individualism versus collectivism—with its mediating variable of social support. As discussed in Chapter 2 and elsewhere, however, culture encompasses many other important dimensions, including power distance, uncertainty avoidance, masculinity, tightness, and contextualization. Another limitation of the previous research is that it has looked almost exclusively at mortality rates or cardiovascular disease. Other dimensions of culture, however, may be associated with the incidence of other disease processes. If members of individualistic cultures are indeed at higher risk for heart disease, for example, perhaps they are at *lower* risk for other disease processes. Conversely, if collectivistic cultures are at lower risk for heart disease, they may be at higher risk for other diseases.

Matsumoto and Fletcher (1994) investigated this possibility by examining the relationship among multiple dimensions of culture and multiple disease processes, opening the door to this line of study. These researchers obtained the mortality rates of six different medical diseases: infections and parasitic diseases, malignant neoplasms, diseases of the circulatory system, heart diseases, cerebrovascular diseases, and respiratory system diseases. These epidemiological data, taken from the *World Health Statistics Quarterly* (World Health Organization, 1991), were compiled across 28 different countries widely distributed around the globe, spanning five continents, and representing many different ethnic, cultural, and socioeconomic backgrounds. In addition, incidence rates for each of the diseases were available at five age points for each country: at birth and at ages 1, 15, 45, and 65.

To get cultural data for each country, Matsumoto and Fletcher (1994) used cultural index scores previously obtained by Hofstede (1980, 1983). Hofstede analyzed questionnaire data about cultural values and practices from large samples in each of these countries and classified their responses according to four cultural tendencies: individualism versus collectivism (IC), power distance (PD), uncertainty avoidance (UA), and masculinity (MA). Matsumoto and Fletcher then correlated these cultural index scores with the epidemiological data.

The results were quite fascinating and pointed to the importance of culture in the development of these disease processes. For example, PD was significantly correlated with rates for infections and parasitic diseases across the five age points. That is, cultures scoring higher on PD (Philippines, Mexico) also had higher rates of infections and parasitic diseases. IC was also significantly correlated with infections and parasitic diseases; individualistic cultures (United States, Australia) had lower rates of these diseases, and collectivistic cultures had higher rates. PD and IC also predicted the incidence of malignant neoplasms, but in the opposite direction. Cultures scoring higher on PD had lower rates of malignant neoplasms. And individualistic cultures had higher rates of malignant neoplasms, while collectivistic cultures had lower rates of these diseases.

PD was also predictive of circulatory diseases. Cultures scoring higher on PD had lower rates of these types of diseases. IC and UA were also predictive of these diseases. PD, IC, and UA were all predictive of heart diseases across all five age points. Cultures scoring higher on PD were associated with lower incidences of heart disease. Cultures scoring higher on UA and IC, however, had higher incidences of heart disease than cultures scoring lower on these dimensions. The findings for IC and heart disease are similar to those of Marmot and Syme (1976) and Triandis and his colleagues (1988), described earlier.

UA, IC, and MA all predicted cerebrovascular diseases. Cultures scoring higher on UA or IC had lower rates of these types of diseases than did cultures scoring lower on this dimension. MA was positively correlated with cerebrovascular diseases, suggesting that cultures that fostered greater gender differences had higher incidences of these types of diseases than cultures that minimized gender differences. Finally, UA was negatively correlated with respiratory diseases. Cultures that were low on UA had higher rates of these diseases, while cultures that were high on UA had lower rates.

The countries in this study differ economically as well as culturally, and it may well be that these economic differences—particularly with regard to the availability of treatment, diet, and sanitation—also contribute to disease. To deal with this possibility, Matsumoto and Fletcher (1994) recomputed their correlations controlling for per capita gross domestic product (GDP) of each country. Even when the effects of per capita GDP were accounted for, the predictions for infections and parasitic diseases, circulatory diseases, and heart diseases all survived. The predictions for UA and cerebrovascular and respiratory diseases, and MA and cerebrovascular diseases, also survived. Thus, these cultural dimensions predicted disease above and beyond what is accounted for by economic differences among the countries. Only the prediction for malignant neoplasms was not supported, indicating that economic differences among the countries cannot be disentangled from cultural differences in predicting the incidence of neoplasms.

A study by Bond (1991) also looked at the influence of dimensions other than IC on health and disease processes other than heart disease. Bond (1991) surveyed the relationship between cultural values and the incidence of disease processes in 23 countries. The cultural values he measured were social integration, cultural inwardness, reputation, and morality. Social integration refers to the degree to which a culture fosters the coming together of people in an environment that nurtures social relationships. This dimension was statistically correlated with an increased incidence of cerebrovascular disease, ulcers of the stomach and duodenum, and neoplasms of the stomach, colon, rectum, rectosignoid junction, and anus. Reputation was significantly correlated with acute myocardial infarction, other ischemic heart disease, neopaslsms of the colon, rectum, rectosignoid junction, and anus, and neoplasms of the trachea, bronchi, and lungs. Morality was significantly associated with cirrhosis of the liver.

How and why does culture affect medical disease processes? Triandis and colleagues (1988) suggested that culture—specifically, social support—plays an important role in mediating stress, which affects health. The findings of Matsumoto and Fletcher (1994) and Bond (1991), however, suggest a much more complex picture. Although collectivistic cultures were associated with lower rates of cardiovascular diseases, replicating the previous findings, they were also associated with death from infectious and parasitic diseases, and cerebrovascular diseases. Thus, while social support may be a buffer against life stress in the prevention of heart attacks, these data suggest that there is something else to collectivism that actually increases susceptibility to other disease processes. To be sure, these other factors may not be cultural per se. Collectivism, for example, is generally correlated with geographic location; countries nearer the equator tend to be more collectivistic. Countries nearer the equator also have hotter climates, which foster the spread of organisms responsible for infections and parasitic diseases. The relationship between collectivism and death from these types of disease processes, therefore, may be related to geography rather than culture.

Still, these findings do suggest that individualism is not necessarily bad, and collectivism is not necessarily good, as earlier findings had suggested. The latest findings suggest instead that different societies and countries develop different cultural ways of dealing with the problem of living. Each way is associated with its own specific and different set of stressors, each of which may take its toll on the human body. Because different cultural ways of living take different tolls on the body, they are associated with different risk factors and rates for different disease processes. This view may be a more holistic account of how culture may influence health and disease processes.

Future research will need to investigate further the specific mechanisms that mediate these relationships. Some studies, for example, will need to examine more closely the relationship among culture, geography, and other noncultural factors in connection with disease incidence rates. Other studies will need to examine directly the relationship between culture and specific behavioral and psychological processes, to elucidate the possible mechanisms of health and disease. Matsumoto and Fletcher (1994), for example, suggested that culture influences human emotion and human physiology, particularly with respect to autonomic nervous system activity and the immune system. For example, the link between PD and circulatory and heart diseases may be explained by noting that cultures low on PD tend to minimize status differences among their members. As status and power differences diminish, people are freer to feel and express negative emotions such as anger or hostility to ingroup others. Containing negative emotions, as must be done in high-PD cultures, may have dramatic consequences for the cardiovascular system, resulting in a relatively higher incidence of circulatory and heart diseases in those cultures. A study by Ekman, Levenson, and Friesen (1983), documenting substantial increases in heart rate associated with angry expressions, lends further credence to this hypothesis. Hopefully, future research will be able to address these and other possibilities.

Cultural Discrepancies and Physical Health

Although the studies described so far suggest that culture influences physical health, more recent research suggests that culture per se is not the only culturally relevant variable. Indeed, the *discrepancy* between one's personal cultural values and those of society may play a large role in producing stress, which in turn leads to negative health outcomes. Matsumoto and colleagues (1997) tested this idea by asking university undergraduates to report what their personal cultural values were, as well as their perceptions of society's values and ideal values. Participants in this study also completed a scale assessing strategies for coping with stress; anxiety, depression, and other mood measures; and scales assessing physical health and psychological well-being. Discrepancy scores in cultural values were computed by taking the differences between self and society, and self and ideal, ratings. These discrepancy scores were then correlated with the scores on the eight coping strategies assessed. The results indicated that discrepancies between self and society's cultural values were significantly correlated with all eight coping strategies, indicating that greater cultural discrepancies were associated with greater needs for coping. These coping strategies were significantly correlated with depression and anxiety, which in turn were significantly correlated with scores on the physical health symptoms checklist scales. In particular, higher scores on anxiety were strongly correlated with greater health problems. The results of this study, therefore, suggest that greater discrepancy between self and societal cultural values may lead to greater psychological stress, which necessitates greater degrees of coping, which affects emotion and mood, which causes greater degrees of anxiety and depression, which then lead to more physical health problems.

Of course, this single study is not conclusive; future research will need to replicate these findings, and elaborate on them. They do suggest, however, the potential role of cultural discrepancies in mediating health outcomes, and open the door for new and exciting research in this area of psychology.

Culture and Eating Disorders

One health-related topic that has received considerable attention concerns eating disorders and obesity. As mentioned previously, a number of studies have reported a negative correlation between body weight and income in the United States: As people get wealthier, they tend to become thinner. In many other countries, the relationship is exactly the opposite: As people get wealthier, they tend to become larger, and size is associated with wealth and abundance. A number of studies, in fact, have found considerable cultural differences in perceptions of and stereotypes about thinness and obesity. Cogan, Bhalla, Sefa-Dedeh, and Rothblum (1996), for example, asked university students in Ghana and the United States to complete questionnaires about their weight, frequency of dieting, social activities, perceptions of ideal bodies, disordered eating, and stereotypes of thin and heavy people. They found that the Ghanaians were more likely to rate larger body sizes as ideals in their society. Americans, especially females were more likely to have dieted. American females also scored higher on dietary restraint, disordered eating behavior, and experiencing weight as a social interference.

Crandall and Martinez (1996) reported similar findings. These researchers compared attitudes about weight and fatness in American and Mexican students, by asking students to complete an anti-fat attitude scale and a scale on political ideologies and beliefs. The results indicated that Mexican students were less concerned about their own weight, and more accepting of fat people, than were the American students. Additionally, anti-fat attitudes in the United States appeared to be part of a social ideology that holds individuals responsible for their life outcomes. Attributions of controllability and responsibility were less important in predicting anti-fat attitudes in Mexico, where antipathy toward fat people did not appear related to any ideological framework.

Not only are such cultural differences in attitudes apparent across cultures outside the United States; a number of studies have recently documented similar findings across different cultural groups within the United States as well. Akan and Grilo (1995), for example, reported similar findings in comparing African, Asian, and European Americans. Harris and Koehler (1992) reported similar findings in comparing Anglo and Hispanic Americans in the southwest United States. Abrams, Allen, and Gray (1993) reported similar findings comparing black and white female college students. And Hamilton, Brooks-Gunn, and Warren (1985) reported similar findings comparing black and white professional female ballet dancers.

Cultural differences in attitudes about fatness and thinness appear to be related to cultural differences in attitudes toward eating behaviors. In Akan and Grilo's (1995) study, for instance, European Americans reported greater levels of disordered eating and dieting behaviors, and greater body dissatisfaction, than did Asian and African Americans. Low self-esteem and high public self-consciousness were associated with greater levels of problematic eating behaviors, attitudes, and body dissatisfaction. In Abrams, Allen, and Gray's (1993) study, white females demonstrated significantly greater disordered eating attitudes and behaviors than black females. Disordered eating behaviors, in turn, were related to depression, anxiety, and low self-esteem. In Hamilton, Brooks-Gunn, and Warren's (1985) study, none of the black dancers reported anorexia or bulimia, while 15% and 19% of the white dancers did, respectively. Self-reported anorectics had higher disordered eating attitudes, exhibited more psychopathology, and had a poorer body images than nonanorectics. The bulimics valued their career less, dieted more, and exercised less frequently than non-bulimics.

Collectively, these studies demonstrate convincingly that attitudes toward body size and shape, and eating, are heavily influenced by culture. Cultural values, attitudes, beliefs, and opinions about wealth, abundance, beauty and attractiveness, power, and other such psychological characteristics likely play a major role in determining attitudes toward eating, thinness, and obesity. These latter attitudes, in turn, most likely directly affect health-related behaviors such as eating, diet, and exercise. The research also suggests that these tendencies may be especially prevalent in the United States, especially among European American females. Crandall and Martinez's (1996) study suggests that this tendency in the United States may be related to specific ideologies about people, power, and responsibility. However, such tendencies are not solely an American phenomenon. Cross-cultural research has pointed to similarities between Americans and members of other cultures in their attitudes toward eating and preoccupation with thinness—for example, the Japanese (Mukai & McCloskey, 1996).

Future research will need to tackle the difficult question of exactly what it is about culture that influences attitudes about eating and stereotypes about thinness and obesity, and where cultures draw the line between healthy patterns and disordered eating behaviors that have direct, negative impacts on health. Future research will also need to tie specific eating behaviors to specific health and disease outcomes, and attempt to link culture with these relationships.

Culture and Suicide

No other behavior has health consequences as final as suicide—the taking of one's own biological life. Psychologists, sociologists, and anthropologists have long been fascinated by suicide, and have studied this behavior across many cultures. The research to date suggests many interesting cross-cultural differences in the nature of suicidal behavior, all of which point to the different ways in which people of different cultures view not only death, but life itself.

One of the most glorified and curious cultures with regard to suicidal behavior is that of Japan. Tales of Japanese pilots who deliberately crashed their planes into enemy targets during World War II stunned and mystified many people of other cultures. These individuals clearly placed the welfare, spirit, and honor of their country above the value of their own lives. To be sure, such acts of self-sacrifice were not limited to the Japanese, as men and women on both sides of war reach into themselves in ways many of us cannot understand to sacrifice their lives for the sake of others. But the Japanese case seems to highlight the mysterious and glorified nature of some acts of suicide in that culture.

Among the most glorified acts of suicide in Japan (called *seppuku* or *hara-kiri*—the slitting of one's belly) were those of the masterless samurai swordsmen who served as the basis for the story known as *Chuushingura*. In this factual story, a lord of one clan of samurai was humiliated and lost face because of the acts of another lord. In disgrace, the humiliated lord committed *seppuku* to save the honor of himself, his family, and his clan. His now masterless samurai—known as *ronin*—plotted to avenge their master's death by killing the lord who had humiliated him in the first place. Forty-seven of them plotted their revenge, and carried out their plans by killing the lord. Afterward, they turned themselves into authorities, admitting to the plot of revenge and explaining the details and reasons for their actions. It was then decided that the only way to resolve the entire situation was to order the 47 *ronin* to commit *seppuku* themselves—which they did. In doing so, they laid down their lives, voluntarily and through this ritualistic method, to preserve the honor and dignity of their clan and families. Although these events occurred in the late 19th century, similar acts continue in Japan today. Some Japanese businessmen have committed suicide as a way of taking responsibility for the downturns in their companies resulting from the economic crisis in Japan and much of Asia at the time of this writing.

Japan is by no means the only culture in which suicide has been examined psychologically and cross-culturally. Many studies seem to point to profound cultural changes as a determinant of suicidal behavior. Leenaars, Anawak, and Taparti (1998), for example, suggest this factor as an important influence on suicide rates among Canadian Inuits, primarily among younger individuals. Sociocultural change has long been identified as a predictor of suicide among Native American Indians, whose suicide rates are higher than those of other Americans (for example, Echohawk, 1997; Bechtold, 1988; May & Dizmang, 1974; Resnik & Dizmang, 1971). Stresses associated with social and cultural changes have also been implicated in the suicide rates of many other cultural groups, including Native Hawaiians (Takeuchi et al., 1987), Greeks (Beratis, 1986), English (Robertson & Cochrane, 1976), Eskimos (Parkin, 1974), and many other groups.

Some researchers have attempted to identify other factors common to different cultures that may predict suicidal behavior. Literacy does not appear to affect suicide rates; one study comparing 54 cultural groups found no differences between literate and non-literate cultures in those rates (Palmer, 1971). In another study, Boor (1976) compared suicide rates in ten countries—New Zealand, Israel, the United States, Canada, Italy, Australia, West Germany, France, Japan, and Sweden—and correlated those rates with mean scores on an internal–external control scale. The results indicated that cultures that foster high perceptions of external control are associated with higher suicide rates. Although this study was conducted more than 20 years ago, its findings are congruent with more contemporary analyses suggesting that suicide may be a product of the collectivity of ideas within a culture in relation to death and life (Kral, 1998). Another factor that may be closely related to culture and suicide is religious beliefs.

Cross-cultural research over the past few decades has thus given us important glimpses into this difficult yet fascinating topic. Still, many questions remain unanswered. What is it about culture that produces differences in suicidal behaviors, and why? Why are there still considerable individual differences in attitudes toward suicide even in cultures where it is relatively more acceptable? Despite the glorified stories concerning suicide in Japan, for instance, there is still a relatively strong stigma against it and intense prejudice toward the mental disorders related to it, resulting in reluctance to seek help (Takahashi, 1997). When may suicide be an acceptable behavior in *any* culture? Given recent and ongoing advances in medical technology, such questions that run the borders of medicine, culture, and ethics are bound to increase in prominence. In the past few years, physician-assisted suicide has emerged as an issue in the United States. Future research within and between cultures may help to elucidate some of the important decision points as we approach these questions.

Summary

In this section, we have discussed a considerable amount of research concerning the influence of psychological, social, and cultural factors on health. We know that these factors can influence rates of mortality, heart disease, and several other disease processes. We also know that cultural discrepancies may be related to health, with greater discrepancies leading to greater stress and consequently more anxiety and greater health problems. We have seen how culture influences attitudes about body shape, eating, and eating disorders. And we have discussed how culture may play a role in suicidal behaviors.

Clearly, research in this area is still in its infancy. But future studies will begin to bridge the gap between culture as a macroconcept and specific medical disease processes in the body. Whatever the exact mechanisms, the contribution of culture to physical health and disease is clearer now than ever before. Future research will expand our understanding of how and why this relationship exists.

Cultural Influences on Attitudes and Beliefs Related to Health and Disease

Culture can influence health in many ways. Culture affects attitudes about health care and treatment, attributions about the causes of health and disease processes, the availability of health care and health care delivery systems, help-seeking behaviors, and many other aspects of disease and health care. We are only now becoming aware of the importance of sociocultural differences when developing treatment and intervention programs for medical and psychological problems.

In a recent study, Matsumoto and his colleagues (1994) recruited Japanese and Japanese American women over the age of 55 living in the San Francisco Bay Area to participate in a study of attitudes and values related to osteoporosis and its treatment. Osteoporosis is a medical disorder in which a decrease in bone density leads to a gradual weakening of the bones. It can be a particularly devastating disease for older women of European or Asian descent. The research included a complete medical history, an assessment of risk factors particular to osteoporosis, an attitudes survey about the disease, and a health care issues assessment. In addition, a subsample of the women were assessed for their bone mineral density (BMD) levels.

Among the most interesting results of this study were the cultural differences found in the attitudes survey and the health care issues assessment. The entire sample of women was divided into two groups: those born and raised in the United States who spoke English as their primary language, and those born and raised in Japan who spoke Japanese as their primary language. When asked about the types of problems they would have if they were diagnosed with osteoporosis, more Japanese than American women reported problems with finances and with finding help. The major concern for American women was "other" problems, including mobility. This finding is especially interesting because mobility is such a central element of individualism, which is more characteristic of the United States than Japan. When asked what kinds of problems they would have if they had to take care of someone with osteoporosis, more Japanese women mentioned not enough time. American women again mentioned "other" problems involving their physical abilities.

The researchers also asked about the types of support services the women would want to have available if they were diagnosed with osteoporosis. More Japanese women reported that they wanted institutions, temporary homes, rehabilitation centers, nursing homes, information services, social service organizations, and organizations to find help. More American women reported wanting "other" services such as medical care.

More American women knew what osteoporosis is. More Japanese women, however, reported that it was of major concern to them and that they would view it very negatively if diagnosed. Also, more American than Japanese women reported that people other than friends or family would care for them if diagnosed. If diagnosed with osteoporosis, Japanese women were more likely to attribute the cause of the illness to fate, chance, or luck; American women were more likely to attribute the illness to diet. Interestingly, there were no differences between the groups in degree of personal responsibility or control, nor in the number of women who specifically asked for osteoporosis examinations, nor in their feelings about estrogen therapy.

A final striking finding was that more Japanese women reported that they would comply with invasive treatment, even though fewer Japanese women had positive feelings about their physicians or reported that they trusted their physicians. This finding is related to the Japanese culture's emphasis on compliance with authority; it suggests that the relationship between interpersonal trust and compliance with authority figures in the Japanese culture is not the same as it is in the United States.

Many other studies also suggest the importance of culture in molding attitudes, beliefs, and values about illness and treatment. Domino and Lin (1993), for example, asked students in Taiwan and the United States to rate various metaphors related to cancer. The metaphors were then scored according to four different scales. The results indicated that the Taiwanese students had significantly higher scores than the Americans on both terminal pessimism and future optimism; that is, they appeared to be both more pessimistic and more optimistic than their American counterparts.

Cook (1994) also reported differences in beliefs about chronic illness and the role of social networks among Chinese, Indian, and Angloceltic Canadians. In his study, Cook (1994) asked participants from all three cultural groups to respond to three scales designed to assess psychosocial, phenomenological, and social networking issues related to treatment options, illness, and social support. Data analyses indicated significant differences among the three cultural groups on ratings concerning the phenomenological causes of illness, the psychosocial and phenomenological results of illness, the psychosocial and phenomenological treatment aspects, and in social networks.

Other studies conducted in the past decade also suggest the importance of cultural influences on disease processes. Edman and Kameoka (1997), for example, documented cultural differences between Filipinos and Americans in illness schemas and attributions. Poole and Ting (1995) documented differences between Euro-Canadian and Indo-Canadian patients' attitudes toward maternity care. Mathews, Lannin, and Mitchell (1994) conducted interviews with black women with advanced breast disease, and commented on the importance of multiple sources of knowledge in coming to terms with the diagnosis of breast cancer in this group of women. Jilek-Aall, Kilek, Kaaya, Mkombachepa, and Hillary (1997) conducted a study on epilepsy in two isolated tribes in Africa; they reported significant differences in attitudes toward epilepsy, which influenced treatment approaches. Guinn (1998) reported data on Mexican American adolescents documenting the importance of psychological variables such as locus of control in influencing beliefs about health. Muela, Ribera, and Tanner (1998) reported on the influence of witchcraft on help-seeking behaviors of Tanzanians in regard to malaria. They found that such beliefs had consequences for noncompliance with treatment, and for delay in seeking diagnosis or treatment.

Taken collectively, a growing literature in the field is showing an increased awareness of cultural influences on a host of psychological variables that ultimately have implications for health and disease. These findings suggest that health care providers need to deal not only with a patient's disease but also, and perhaps more important, with the psychological correlates of the disease. These may include such variables as attributions and beliefs about the causation of disease; attitudes about health, illness, and treatment; preferences with regard to social support and networks; psychosocial needs with regard to autonomy versus reliance on others; and treatment compliance. Also, we cannot forget cultural differences in attitudes about body shapes and in definitions of health and disease, discussed earlier in this chapter. Contemporary health practitioners and the institutions in which they work—clinics, hospitals, laboratories—have become increasingly sensitized to these issues, and are now struggling with the best ways to understand and incorporate them for maximum effectiveness.

A Model of Cultural Influences on Physical Health

So far in this chapter we have reviewed a considerable amount of literature concerning the influence of culture on health and disease processes. This research has begun to affect the ways in which we deliver treatment and other services to people of varying cultural backgrounds, and the type of health care systems we create. It has also made scholars in the field more sensitive to the need to incorporate culture as a major variable in their studies and theories.

So, just how does culture influence physical health and disease processes? Figure 9.1 summarizes what we know so far. We know from other research, not reviewed in this chapter, that culture affects rates of alcohol consumption, tobacco use, and exercise and activity levels. Each of these variables, in turn, has implications for health and disease. The research concerning the relationship between cultural dimensions and the incidence of various diseases also implicates lifestyles and behaviors as possible mediators. In particular, research seems to suggest that stress and emotion, and the ways we cope with them, are important determinants of health and well-being.

We have also discussed the contribution to health and disease of other psychological factors, most notably attitudes and beliefs about disease processes, causations, treatment, and help seeking. Finally, although this chapter has focused on the role of sociocultural factors in health and disease, we cannot ignore the contributory roles of the environment and available health care systems in promoting health and well-being.

This figure is meant to provide a general overview of the role that culture and other social factors may play in the area of physical health. All of these factors will need to be fleshed out in greater detail, then tied together into a comprehensive and systematic whole to further our understanding of health and disease processes. Future research will also need to operationalize health according to dimensions other than mortality rates or incidence rates of various diseases. Incorporating cultural, environmental, social, and psychological factors in determining multiple definitions of health is an enormous job for the future, but it is one that we must work toward if we are to get a clearer and more complete picture of the relative contribution of all these factors.

Figure 9.1 A psychological model of cultural influences on physical health

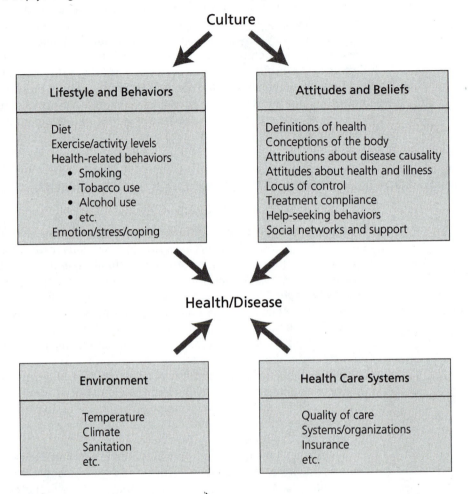

Cultural Differences in Dealing with Illness

In this final section of the chapter, we turn to the question of how health care professionals can provide appropriate and sensitive treatment and other health care services to a diverse population. We begin with a review of differences in health care and medical delivery systems around the world, and then look at some research on the development of culturally sensitive treatment approaches.

Differences in Health Care and Medical Delivery Systems

Different countries and cultures have developed their own unique ways of dealing with health care. A country's health care delivery system is a product of many factors, including social and economic development, technological advances and availability, and the influence of neighboring and collaborating countries. Also affecting health care delivery services are a number of social trends, including urbanization, industrialization, governmental structure, international trade laws and practices, demographic changes, demands for privatization, and public expenditures.

National health systems can be divided into four major types: entrepreneurial, welfare-oriented, comprehensive, and socialist (Roemer, 1993). Within each of these general categories, individual countries vary tremendously in terms of their economic level. For instance, the United States is an example of a country with a relatively high economic level that uses an entrepreneurial system of health care, characterized by a substantial private industry covering individuals as well as groups. The Philippines and Ghana also use an entrepreneurial system of health care, but have moderate and low economic levels, respectively. France, Brazil, and Burma are examples of high-, moderate-, and low-income countries with welfare-oriented health systems. Likewise, Sweden, Costa Rica, and Sri Lanka have comprehensive health care, and the former Soviet Union, Cuba, and China have socialist health systems.

A quick review of the countries listed here suggests that cultural differences are related to the type of national health system a country is likely to adopt. It makes sense that an entrepreneurial system is used in the United States, for example, because of the highly individualistic nature of American culture. Likewise, it makes sense that socialist systems of health care are used in China and Cuba, given their collectivistic, communal nature. However, cultural influences cannot be separated from the other factors that contribute to national health care systems. In the complex interactions among culture, economy, technology, and government, social aspects of culture are inseparable from social institutions.

The Development of Culturally Sensitive Treatment Approaches

In the past decade, a number of important studies have examined the issue of culturally sensitive treatment approaches for people of diverse cultural backgrounds. In the past, at least in the United States, health professionals and medical communities tended to approach health and the treatment of physical diseases in all people similarly, with the underlying assumption that people's bodies are all the same. As the American population has diversified, however, and as research continues to uncover more ways in which people of different cultural backgrounds differ from one another, the health professions are slowly becoming aware of the need to develop culturally sensitive and appropriate treatment approaches.

The need for such approaches is borne out in the literature. Ponchilla (1993), for example, reports that cultural beliefs among Native Americans, Mexican Americans, and Pacific Islanders affect the success of health-related services to native peoples who are suffering vision loss as a result of diabetes. These cultural beliefs include the circle of life, identification with persons with disabilities, the value of silence, and even the healing power of blindness itself. Ponchilla also suggests that the increase in the incidence of diabetes among these cultural groups is due to their adoption of Western diets and lifestyles.

Other findings also suggest the influence of culture on treatment success. Wing, Crow, and Thompson (1995) examined barriers to seeking treatment for alcoholism among Muscogee Indians, and found that this group traditionally perceives alcoholism to be caused by a lack of spirituality. Admission of alcohol abuse thus causes embarrassment and shame, and the practice of humility in Western-oriented alcoholism programs hinders treatment. Talamantes, Lawler, and Espino (1995) examined issues related to caregiving and the use of hospice services by Hispanic American elderly, who are less likely to use such long-term care services. They found that factors affecting level of use included alienation; language barriers; availability of culture-sensitive services; beliefs regarding illness, suffering, coping, and death; socioeconomic and demographic factors; acculturation; and the availability of informal care, most notably via extended family and community support. Delgado (1995) also pointed out the importance of such natural support systems among the Hispanic cultures in the treatment of alcoholism.

Studies of other cultural groups also highlight the importance of families and communities in the treatment of health-related problems. Nemoto and colleagues (1998), for example, examined cultural factors such as family support in the treatment and prevention of drug abuse in Filipino and Chinese individuals. More specifically, they examined factors that prevent drug abuse and the escalation of drug use in these groups, including family support, cultural competence, religious beliefs, and life satisfaction. One of the interesting findings of this study was that some drug users received financial support from family members who knew the recipients' drug habits. Family members tried not to talk about the problems in the family, yet continued to provide financial support to the user. The authors concluded that culturally sensitive and appropriate treatment needs to involve the immediate family and extended family members if the treatment is to be effective. These and other findings suggest that health problems arise as much from a collective system of individuals and social agents as from a single individual. This collective system, therefore, must be engaged if treatment is to be relevant and effective.

It is extremely difficult to grasp the complexity that culture brings to the development of successful and effective treatment approaches. Besides family issues, a host of variables may include religion and spirituality, social support networks, beliefs and attitudes about causes and treatments, socioeconomic factors, language barriers, shame, face, and many others. While some culturally relevant programs have been shown to be successful (for example, Uziel-Miller, Lyons, Kissiel, & Love, 1998; Damond, Breuer, & Pharr, 1993), others have not (for example, Rossiter, 1994). Thus, it is not clear what the exact ingredients for successful treatment interventions are, and whether these ingredients differ depending on the cultural group or individual that is seeking help. Basic educational programs about health and disease prevention that tap cultural groups in relevant ways may be a relatively easy way to access many individuals. One such program (Hiatt et al., 1996) investigated knowledge, practices, and attitudes of 4,228 women from five ethnic groups in the San Francisco Bay Area with regard to barriers to utilizing breast and cervical cancer screening tests. Latina, white, and black women had screening levels that were higher than national averages; Chinese and Vietnamese women, however, did not. The data underscored the importance of basic educational programs that may help make it easier for more women to obtain such screening at earlier ages, thus increasing the potential for effective treatment if and when problems are found.

Clearly, the field is still struggling to discover what the most important culturally relevant variables are and whether these variables are similar or different across cultural groups. My guess would be that there are some culture-constant needs that need to be addressed, but that these needs are manifested in different ways in different attitudes, values, beliefs, social support, extended families, and the like. Future research has a large job in evaluating the host of potentially important variables to distill a set of guidelines that can be useful for health care professionals in their attempts to improve people's lives.

⊠ Conclusion

Many factors contribute to health and disease processes. Besides effects of the environment, diet, direct health-related behaviors (smoking, alcohol consumption), and health care availability, culture is also a major factor. Understanding the role that culture plays in the development of disease, whether medical or psychological, will take us a long way toward developing ways of preventing disease in the future. As research uncovers the possible negative consequences of cultural tendencies, we can also look to an understanding of cultural influences to help us treat people of different cultures better than we have in the past.

In this chapter, we have examined how cross-cultural research has attempted to explore the influence of culture on physical health. We have seen how different cultures have different definitions of health and disease, and different conceptions of the body. We have reviewed a considerable amount of research that shows how culture appears to be related to a number of different disease processes around the world. This literature complements the already large literature that highlights the importance of other psychosocial determinants of health and disease, such as personality, and socioeconomic status. We have also seen how individual cultural discrepancies may be related to health, and how culture influences specific behaviors such as eating and suicide. We have explored the nature of culturally relevant and sensitive treatment approaches, including the importance of family and community in some cultural groups.

Still, much remains to be learned, and many questions remain unanswered. What is the relative contribution of cultural variables to the development of disease or the maintenance of health, in relation to other determinants such as psychological, social, demographic, economic, and environmental factors? What is it about culture that influences health and disease, and why? What are the basic ingredients of a culturally relevant and effective treatment approach, and to what degree are these ingredients constant across cultures and individuals?

Recognition of the role of culture in influencing the definition and expression of health suggests that we must modify our methods of assessing and treating disease. Developing adequate assessment strategies requires that culturally based definitions of health and disease be taken into account. Awareness of culture-specific systems of healing is also necessary to develop effective methods of both assessment and treatment. Culturally sensitive assessment and treatment methods are vital to improving our ability to meet the health needs of culturally diverse populations, both in the United States and globally.

Glossary

hardiness A positive state of health that goes beyond the absence of disease.

medical model A model of health that views disease as resulting from a specific, identifiable cause originating inside the body.

pathogen In the medical model, a cause of disease, whether viral, bacterial, or otherwise; the root of all physical and medical diseases.

10

Culture and Mental Health

One important goal of psychology is to use the knowledge gained through research to help people suffering from psychological disorders to rid themselves of symptomatology and lead more effective, productive, and happy lives. Several themes have guided research and practice in this area of psychology. First and foremost are questions concerning definitions of abnormality—what is abnormal behavior? A second set of questions relates to the expression of abnormal behavior and our ability to detect it and classify it when it is expressed (assessment). A third question concerns how we should treat abnormal behavior when it is detected.

Culture adds an important dimension to these basic questions. Incorporating culture into our psychological theories and concepts raises a number of important issues with regard to abnormal behaviors (Marsella, 1979). These include:

- Do definitions of normality and abnormality vary across cultures, or are there universal standards of abnormality?
- Do cultures vary in rates of abnormal behavior?
- Is abnormal behavior expressed in the same way across cultures, or can we identify culturally distinct patterns of abnormal behavior?
- Can the field develop cross-culturally reliable and valid ways of measuring, classifying, and diagnosing abnormal behaviors?
- How do psychotherapeutic approaches need to be modified in order to deal effectively with cultural influences on abnormality?

The answers to these questions have important implications for how we identify abnormal behavior and intervene to effect change.

This chapter is devoted to the considerable amount of research and writing that seeks to address these questions and concerns. First, we will discuss the role of culture in defining abnormality, review studies of the prevalence and course of schizophrenia and depression across cultures, and describe a number of culture-specific psychological disorders. As you will see, culture plays a major role in shaping people's experience of psychological disorder. Second, we will discuss the role of culture in the assessment of abnormal behaviors, examine the classification schemes currently in use, and explore some issues surrounding the actual measurement of abnormality. Third, we will discuss the impact of culture on psychotherapy and other treatment approaches.

Defining Abnormality

Some Core Issues

Psychologists and other social scientists have long been interested in the influence of culture on psychopathology, or abnormal behaviors. Historically, the literature has been somewhat divided between two points of view (for a more detailed review, see Draguns, 1997). One view suggests that culture and psychopathology are inextricably intertwined, and that abnormal behaviors can only be understood within the cultural framework within which they occur. This perspective is known as **cultural relativism**. The contrasting view suggests that although culture plays a role in determining the exact behavioral and contextual manifestations of abnormal behavior, there are cross-cultural similarities, even universalities, in the underlying psychological mechanisms and subjective experiences of many of the psychological disorders.

Consider, for example, the following scenario:

> A woman is in the midst of a group of people but seems totally unaware of her surroundings. She is talking loudly to no one in particular, often using words and sounds the people around her find unintelligible. When questioned later about her behavior, she reports that she had been possessed by the spirit of an animal and was talking with a man who had recently died.

Is this woman's behavior abnormal? In defining abnormal behavior, American psychologists often use a statistical approach or apply criteria of impairment or inefficiency, deviance, or subjective distress. Using a statistical approach, for example, we could define the woman's behavior as abnormal because its occurrence is rare or infrequent. Being out of touch with your surroundings, having delusions (mistaken beliefs) that you are an animal, and talking with the dead are not common experiences. One problem with this approach to abnormality, however, is that not all rare behavior is disordered. Nor is all disordered behavior rare! Composing a concerto and speaking four languages are uncommon behaviors, yet we generally view them as highly desirable. Conversely, drinking to the point of drunkenness occurs quite frequently in the United States (and in many other countries of the world). Nevertheless, drunkenness is widely recognized as a sign of a possible substance abuse disorder.

Another traditional approach to defining abnormality focuses on whether an individual's behavior is associated with impairment or inefficiency when carrying out customary roles. It is hard to imagine the woman described here carrying out normal day-to-day functions, such as caring for herself and working, while she believes herself to be an animal. In many instances, psychological disorders do involve serious impairments or a reduction in an individual's overall functioning. However, this is not always the case. Some people suffering from bipolar disorder (manic-depression), for example, report enhanced productivity during manic episodes.

If we examine the woman's behavior in terms of deviance, we might also conclude that it is abnormal, because it seems to go against social norms. But not all behavior that is socially deviant can be considered abnormal or psychologically disordered. For example, many people continue to believe that homosexuality is deviant, although it is no longer classified as a mental disorder (American Psychiatric Association, 1987). Although some Americans may view homosexuality as abnormal, in other cultures and at various periods in history homosexuality has been widely practiced. Using societal norms as a criterion for abnormality is difficult not only because norms change over time but because they are subjective. What one member of a society or culture considers deviant, another may accept as normal.

Reliance on reports of subjective distress to define abnormal behavior is also problematic. Whether a person experiences distress as a consequence of abnormal behavior may depend on how others treat him or her. For example, if the woman I described is ridiculed, shunned, and viewed as "sick" because of her behavior, she may well experience distress. Conversely, if she is seen as having special powers and is part of an accepting circle, she may not be distressed at all.

Each of these more or less traditional ways of defining abnormality has advantages as well as disadvantages. These issues become even more complex when culture is considered. Definitions of abnormality may vary both within and across cultures.

As an alternative to these traditional approaches, many cross-cultural scholars argue that we can understand and identify abnormal behavior only if we take the cultural context into account. This viewpoint suggests that we must apply the principle of cultural relativism to abnormality. For example, the woman's behavior might appear disordered if it occurred on a street corner in a large city in the United States. It could, however, appear appropriate and understandable if it occurred in a shamanistic ceremony in which she was serving as healer. Cultures that believe in supernatural interventions are able to clearly distinguish when trance states and talking with spirits are an acceptable part of a healer's behavioral repertoire and when the same behaviors would be considered a sign of disorder (Murphy, 1976). Examples of such cultures include the Yoruba in Africa and some Eskimo tribes in Alaska.

Some behaviors, particularly those associated with psychosis (for example, delusions, hallucinations), are universally recognized as abnormal (Murphy, 1976). However, some investigators (for example, Kleinman, 1988; Marsella, 1979, 1980) argue that abnormality and normality are culturally determined concepts. These investigators point to the fact that cultures differ in their beliefs and attitudes about abnormal behavior.

Reliance on reports of subjective distress to define abnormal behavior is also problematic when considering abnormality across cultures. There is some indication that cultural groups vary in the degree of distress they report experiencing in association with psychological disorders. Kleinman (1988) describes research indicating that depressed Chinese and African samples report less guilt and shame than do depressed European American and European samples. The Chinese and African samples, however, report more somatic complaints. These findings may reflect a cultural response bias (see Chapter 5). Some cultural groups may have values that prohibit reporting or focusing on subjective distress, in contrast to Western notions of the importance of self-disclosure.

Whether to accept universal or culturally relative definitions of abnormality is a source of continuing controversy in psychology. Examination of the cross-cultural literature may help provide clues on how to understand the role of culture in contributing to abnormality.

Cross-Cultural Research on Abnormal Behaviors

Cross-cultural research over the years has provided a wealth of evidence suggesting that abnormal behaviors and psychopathology have both universal and culture-specific aspects. In this section, we will look at schizophrenia, depression, somatization, and a number of apparently culture-specific disorders.

Schizophrenia.   Schizophrenia is part of a "group of psychotic disorders characterized by gross distortions of reality; withdrawal from social interaction; and disorganization of perception, thought, and emotion" (Carson, Butcher, & Coleman, 1988, p. 322). Some theories concerning the etiology (causes) of schizophrenia give primacy to biological factors (for example, excess dopamine or other biochemical imbalances). Other theories emphasize family dynamics (for example, expression of hostility to ill person). The diathesis–stress model of schizophrenia suggests that individuals with a biological predisposition to the disorder (diathesis) may develop the disorder following exposure to environmental stressors.

The World Health Organization (WHO, 1973, 1979, 1981) sponsored the International Pilot Study of Schizophrenia (IPSS) to compare the prevalence and course of the disorder in several countries: Colombia, Czechoslovakia, Denmark, England, India, Nigeria, the Soviet Union, Taiwan, and the United

States. Following rigorous training in using the research assessment tool, psychiatrists in each of the countries achieved good reliability in diagnosing schizophrenia in patients included in the study. As a result, WHO investigators were able to identify a set of symptoms present across all cultures in the schizophrenic samples. These symptoms include lack of insight, auditory and verbal hallucinations, and ideas of reference (assuming one is the center of attention) (Leff, 1977). The WHO studies are widely cited to bolster arguments for the universality of schizophrenia.

But some important cross-cultural differences emerged as well. In a finding that took the investigators by surprise, the course of the illness was shown to be easier for patients in developing countries compared to those in highly industrialized countries. Patients in Colombia, India, and Nigeria recovered at faster rates than did those in England, the Soviet Union, or the United States. These differences were attributed to cultural factors such as the presence of extended kin networks and the tendency to return to work in developing countries.

The researchers also noted differences in symptom expression across cultures. Patients in the United States were less likely to demonstrate lack of insight and auditory hallucinations than were Danish or Nigerian patients. These findings may be related to cultural differences in values associated with insight and self-awareness, which are highly regarded in the United States but less well regarded in the other countries. Also, cultures may differ in their tolerance for particular symptoms; the Nigerian culture as a whole is more accepting of the presence of voices. Nigerian and Danish patients, however, were more likely to demonstrate catatonia (extreme withdrawal or agitation).

Kleinman (1988) and Leff (1981) have discussed some of the methodological problems that plagued the WHO studies—among them, an assessment tool that failed to tap culturally unique experiences and expressions of disorder. Kleinman also noted that the samples were made artificially homogeneous because of the selection criteria. He argued that the findings of cross-cultural differences might have been greater still had not the heterogeneity of the sample been reduced.

Other cross-cultural comparisons of schizophrenia (Leff, 1977; Murphy, 1982) have found evidence of cultural variations in rates and symptomatology. Murphy (1982) found that rates of admissions for schizophrenia are four times higher in Ireland than in England and Wales, suggesting that some features of Irish culture (for example, sharp wit, ambivalence toward individuality) may affect the incidence of schizophrenia. In an early study of New York psychiatric cases, Opler and Singer (1959) found that Irish American schizophrenic patients were more likely to experience paranoid delusions than were Italian American patients. The authors cited cultural differences in parenting to account for the difference. A study of Japanese schizophrenics (Sue & Morishima, 1982) indicated that they are more likely than their European American counterparts to be withdrawn and passive, conforming to cultural values.

Recent studies of schizophrenics have tested the theory that expressed emotion—family communication characterized by hostility and overinvolvement—increases the risk of relapse. The expressed emotion construct is important because it suggests that family and social interactions influence the course of schizophrenia. These interactions are in turn influenced by cultural values. Research indicates that expressed emotion predicts relapse in Western samples (Mintz, Mintz, & Goldstein, 1987). Kleinman (1988), however, notes the difficulties in using this construct in other cultures, particularly those that emphasize nonverbal communication. Karno and associates (1987) reported that expressed emotion also predicts relapse in Mexican Americans, but Kleinman (1988) questions whether measures of expressed emotion developed in one cultural context have validity in another.

Reports of cultural differences in diagnosis have also raised questions about the validity of assessment techniques used in cross-cultural comparisons of schizophrenia and other disorders (Kleinman, 1988; Leff, 1977). In a reanalysis of some of the early WHO data, Leff (1977) found that U.S. psychiatrists were more likely to give diagnoses of schizophrenia than were psychiatrists in England, and less likely to give diagnoses of depression. Abebimpe (1981) and Thomas and Sillen (1972) have documented that African Americans are more likely than European Americans to receive diagnoses of schizophrenia rather than depression, even when the symptom picture is the same. Racial bias seems to account for some of the differential pattern (Thomas & Sillen, 1972), and cultural differences in expression of symptomatology may also be important.

In summary, the WHO studies provide ample evidence of a universal set of core symptoms that may be related to schizophrenia. Other studies, however, help to temper this interpretation by documenting specific cultural differences in the exact manifestations, experience, and diagnosis of schizophrenia in different cultural contexts.

Depression. All of us have experienced moods of depression, sadness, or the blues in our lives. We may have these feelings in response to a death in the family, the breakup of a relationship, falling short of a goal, and other stresses or disappointments. The presence of a depressive disorder, however, involves symptoms of "intense sadness, feelings of futility and worthlessness, and withdrawal from others" (Sue, Sue, & Sue, 1990, p. 325). Depression is often characterized by physical changes (such as sleep and appetite disturbances) as well as emotional and behavioral changes (Berry et al., 1992). Along with schizophrenia, depression is one of the most common psychological disorders in the United States. In a large-scale study, Myers and associates (1984) found that 3% and 7% of the adult male and female population, respectively, had experienced a depressive disorder in the previous six-month period. Lifetime prevalence rates for depression may be as high as 26% for women and 12% for men (Sue et al., 1990). There is also some evidence to suggest that the incidence of depression has risen over the past few decades (Robins et al., 1984).

A study by WHO (1983) investigated the symptoms of depression in four countries—Canada, Switzerland, Iran, and Japan—and found that the great majority of cases reported cross-culturally constant symptoms, including direct expressions of depression. Based on these findings, Marsella (1980; Marsella et al., 1985) suggested that vegetative symptoms such as loss of enjoyment, appetite, or sleep are cross-culturally constant ways in which people experience depression. Other studies (for example, comparing Hungarians with Americans and Canadians, Keitner, 1991; with Iranians, Haghighatgou & Peterson, 1995; and with children in six countries, Yamamoto, Soliman, Parsons, & Davies, 1987) have tended to support this viewpoint.

Other cross-cultural studies of depression, however, document wide variations in expression of symptomatology of this disorder. Some cultural groups (for example, Nigerians) are less likely to report extreme feelings of worthlessness. Others (for example, Chinese) are more likely to report somatic complaints (Kleinman, 1988). As with schizophrenia, rates of depression also vary from culture to culture (Marsella, 1980).

Leff (1977) argues that cultures vary in terms of their differentiation and communication of emotional terminology and, hence, in how they experience and express depression. Some cultures have few words to convey emotions such as sadness or anger (see Chapter 11). Also, cultures locate feeling states in different parts of the body. This may explain why some cultural groups emphasize somatic complaints in the expression of depression. Kleinman (1978) takes the position that depressive *disease* reflects a biologically based disorder, whereas depressive *illness* refers to the personal and social experience of depression. In arguing for a culturally relative definition of depression, Kleinman (1988) writes that

> depression experienced entirely as low back pain and depression experienced entirely as guilt-ridden existential despair are such substantially different forms of illness behavior with distinctive symptoms, patterns of help seeking, and treatment responses that although the disease in each instance may be the same, the illness, not the disease, becomes the determinative factor. And one might well ask, is the disease even the same? (p. 25)

Although Kleinman accepts the idea that depressive disease is universal, he argues that the expression and course of the illness are culturally determined.

Marsella (1979, 1980) also argues for a culturally relative view of depression, saying that depression takes a primarily affective form in cultures with strong objective orientations (that is, individualistic cultures). In these cultures, feelings of loneliness and isolation dominate the symptom picture. In subjective cultures (those having a more communal structure), somatic symptoms such as headaches are dominant. Marsella (1979) has also proposed that depressive symptom patterns differ across cultures because of cultural variations in sources of stress as well as in resources for coping with the stress.

Thus, as with the cross-cultural work on schizophrenia, the literature on depression points to both universal and culture-specific ways in which the disorder may occur and be experienced across cultures.

Somatization. Many cross-cultural psychologists, psychotherapists, and counselors are sensitive to the issue of **somatization**—essentially, bodily complaints as expressions of psychological distress. Some studies have suggested that members of certain cultural groups, such as Hispanics (Koss, 1990), Japanese (Radford, 1989), and Chinese (Kleinman, 1982) tend to somaticize more than Europeans or Americans. In fact, it has been commonly thought that such somatic complaints (for example, low back pain or intestinal problems) are just a code or camouflage for psychological symptoms.

Recent cross-cultural studies, however, challenge this viewpoint. Kirmayer (1984), for example, reviewed the available evidence and concluded that there was not much support for the notion that the degree and amount of somatization vary across cultures. Moreover, although Kleinman (1982) concluded that Chinese diagnoses of neurasthenia were really cases of depression, this view was not shared by the mainland Chinese psychiatrists (reported in Draguns, 1997). Isaac, Janca, and Orley (1996) have also reported that somatic expression of psychological distress is a universal phenomenon and that the presence of large numbers of somatic symptoms is strongly related to the overt expression of psychological distress in European and American cultures, too. Finally, Cheng, Leong, and Geist (1993) have shown that although Asian American students more often present academic and career issues when seeking counseling, these issues are actually associated with greater personal and emotional problems than European American students.

Thus, the available research tends to suggest that, although previously considered a culture-specific phenomenon, somatization may be a universal phenomenon with culture-specific meanings and expression modes.

Culture-bound syndromes.   The approach used in cross-cultural studies of depression and schizophrenia can be characterized as etic; that is, it assumes universally accepted definitions of abnormality and methodology (review Chapter 2 for definitions of *etic* and *emic*). In contrast to this etic approach are various ethnographic reports of **culture-bound syndromes**—forms of abnormal behavior observed only in certain sociocultural milieus. Findings concerning differential rates and courses of a disorder across cultures, and of culturally distinct forms of the disorder, suggest the importance of culture in shaping the expression of abnormal behavior. In fact, ethnographic reports of culture-bound syndromes provide perhaps the strongest support for cultural relativism in understanding and dealing with abnormality.

Using primarily emic (culture-specific) approaches involving ethnographic examinations of behavior within a specific cultural context, anthropologists and psychiatrists have identified several apparently unique forms of psychological disorder. Some similarities between symptoms of these culture-specific disorders and those recognized across cultures have been observed. The particular pattern of symptoms, however, typically does not fit the diagnostic criteria of psychological disorders recognized in Western classification schemes. Consider, for example, the following disorders that have been documented by various writers.

Amok, the most widely observed culture-bound syndrome, has been identified in several countries in Asia (Malaysia, Philippines, Thailand). The disorder is characterized by sudden rage and homicidal aggression. It is thought to be brought on by stress, sleep deprivation, and alcohol consumption (Carson et al., 1988), and has been observed primarily in males. Several stages of the disorder have been identified, ranging from extreme withdrawal prior to the assaultive behavior to exhaustion and amnesia for the rage. The term *running amok* derives from observations of the disorder.

Witiko (also known as *windigo*) is a disorder that has been identified in Algonquin Indians in Canada. It involves the belief that the individual has been possessed by the witiko spirit—a man-eating monster. Cannibalistic behavior may result, along with suicidal ideation to avoid acting on the cannibalistic urges (Carson et al., 1988).

Anorexia nervosa is a disorder identified in the West but not at first observed in Third World countries (Swartz, 1985). The disorder is characterized by a distorted body image, fear of becoming fat, and a serious loss of weight associated with food restraining or purging. Several factors have been cited as possible causes of this disorder, including a cultural emphasis on thinness as an ideal for women, constricted sex roles, and an individual's fear of being out of control or of taking on adult responsibilities. Recent research, however, has suggested that it is not limited to Europe and North America, but may now be found in many urbanized parts of the world (for example, Hoek, van Harten, van Hoeken, & Susser, 1998; Lee, 1995).

Zar is an altered state of consciousness, observed among Ethiopian immigrants to Israel (Grisaru, Budowski, & Witztum, 1997). The belief in possession by Zar spirits is a very common belief in Africa, and is expressed by involuntary movements, mutism, and incomprehensible language.

Whakama is a New Zealand Maori construct that includes shame, self-abasement, feelings of inferiority, inadequacy, self-doubt, shyness, excessive modesty, and withdrawal (Sachdev, 1990). It does not have an exact equivalent in European or American societies.

"Sinking heart" is a condition of distress in the Punjabi culture (Krause, 1989). It is experienced as physical sensations in the heart or chest, and is thought to be caused by excessive heat, exhaustion, worry, or social failure. It has some characteristics of depression but also resembles a cardiovascular disorder.

Avanga is actually a constellation of other, more specific forms of disorder, all of which include a vivid, imaginary companionship with a single external spirit. Originating in Tongan culture, its incidence is on the rise as people move toward cities and urbanization (Puloka, 1997).

Other culture-bound syndromes, cited in literature reviews by Kiev (1972) and Yap (1974), include *latah* (characterized by hysteria and echolalia, observed primarily in women in Malaysia), *koro* (impotence resulting from fear that the penis is retracting, observed in Southeast Asian men), and *susto* (characterized by depression and apathy thought to reflect "soul loss," observed in Indians of the Andean highlands). Other writers have also suggested that some conditions found in American society, such as premenstrual syndrome and adolescence, are culture-bound syndromes (for example, Hill & Fortenberry, 1992; Johne, 1987). Many other such culture-bound syndromes have been documented around the world.

Yap (1974) has attempted to organize information concerning culture-bound syndromes into a classification scheme that parallels Western diagnostic schemes. In this scheme, for example, *latah* and *susto* are viewed as unique cultural expressions of universal primary fear reactions, and *amok* is seen as a unique cultural expression of a universal rage reaction. Yap recognizes that his attempt to subsume culture-bound syndromes into a universal classification scheme may be premature, particularly since Western clinical tools and methods of research may make it difficult to assess culturally diverse expressions of abnormal behavior.

Pfeiffer (1982) has identified four dimensions for understanding culture-bound syndromes. First, he cites culture-specific areas of stress, including family and societal structure and ecological conditions. For example, *koro* might be best understood as resulting from the unique emphasis on potency in certain cultures that emphasize paternal authority. Then, culture-specific shaping of conduct and interpretations of conduct may mean that certain cultures implicitly approve patterns of exceptional behavior. An example is *amok,* in which aggression against others "broadly follows the patterns of societal expectations" (p. 206). Finally, Pfeiffer argues that how a culture interprets exceptional behavior will be linked to culture-specific interventions. For example, interventions to heal the soul loss associated with *susto* will involve sacrifices carried out by a native healer to appease the earth so that it will return the soul.

Some scholars (for example, Kleinman, 1988; Marsella, 1979; Pfeiffer, 1982) argue that current Western classification schemes cannot be used to understand culture-bound syndromes because they are experienced from a qualitatively different point of view. They argue that culture shapes the experience of psychological disorder, both in determining the expression of symptoms of universal disorders and in contributing to the emergence of culture-specific disorders. Recognizing the role of culture in shaping abnormal behavior requires that we reexamine the way we assess and treat individuals with psychological disorders.

Summary

The material reviewed in this section suggests that there are universal aspects of symptomatology and disease expression for at least some of the major psychopathologies such as depression and schizophrenia. At the same time, however, it also suggests that psychopathologies are heavily influenced by culture, especially in terms of the specific behavioral and contextual manifestations of the abnormal behavior, and the meaning of the behavior to the lifestyles and lives of individuals. The existence of culture-bound syndromes—disorders that appear to occur only in specific cultural milieus—reinforces the position of the cultural relativists.

We began this section by positing two viewpoints about the relationship between culture and abnormal behavior: the universalist position and the cultural-relativist position. The research reviewed here provides ample evidence for both positions, indicating that psychopathology across cultures contains both universal and culturally specific components. Other writers who have reviewed the field in far more depth—including Al-Issa (1995), Draguns (1997), Pfeiffer (1994), and Tanaka-Matsumi and Draguns (1997) have reached the same conclusion—Draguns (1997), for example, concludes that "neither [position] should be disregarded or exaggerated and both should be sensitively and realistically blended in providing service across cultural lines" (p. 230).

Culture and the Assessment of Abnormal Behavior

Assessment of abnormal behavior involves identifying and describing an individual's symptoms "within the context of his or her overall level of functioning and environment" (Carson et al., 1988, p. 531). The tools and methods of assessment should be sensitive to cultural and other environmental influences on behavior and functioning. Although the field has made considerable progress over the years, the literature on standard assessment techniques indicates that there may be problems of bias or insensitivity when psychological tests and methods developed in one cultural context are used to assess behavior in a different context.

Culture and Psychiatric Diagnoses

In assessing abnormal behavior, psychologists seek to classify abnormal behaviors into categories—diagnoses—that are both reliable and valid. Reliability, as you will recall, has to do with the degree to which the same diagnoses would be made consistently over time and by different clinicians; validity refers to the degree to which the diagnosis accurately portrays the clinical disorder it is supposed to describe.

Because culture exerts some degree of influence on the creation, maintenance, and definition of abnormal behaviors, cross-cultural issues arise concerning the reliability and validity of diagnoses, and even of the diagnostic categories used. If all abnormal behaviors were entirely etic in their expression and presentation—that is, entirely the same across cultures—then creating reliable and valid diagnostic categories would not be a problem. But just as individuals differ in their presentation of abnormality, cultures also vary; indeed, some culture-bound syndromes appear to be limited to only one or a few cultures. Thus, developing diagnostic systems and classifications that can be reliably and validly used across cultures around the world, or across different cultural groups within a single country, becomes a challenge.

One of the most widely used systems of classification is the American Psychiatric Association's *Diagnostic and Statistical Manual of Mental Disorders*

(DSM). The DSM, originally published in 1952, has undergone several major revisions and is now in its fourth edition (DSM-IV). Much of the change from DSM-III to DSM-IV represents the field's response to heavy criticism by cross-cultural psychiatrists.

> A large number of disorders described in the manual were different or simply did not exist in societies and cultures beyond the Western world. It was repeatedly noted that, after all, 80% of the world population does not belong to the Western cultural sphere, and that the manual could lose credibility, its international popularity notwithstanding.
>
> . . .
>
> Diagnosis does not mean to drive an individual into a particular slot; ethnicity, diversity, and pluralism should be duly recognized as politically important. . . . For culture to be built into the DSM-IV, diagnosticians always should be reminded that their task is essentially cultural: The patient and the clinician each brings his or her own culture, and the clinician–patient encounter realizes culture. (Alarcon, 1995, pp. 452, 455)

Diagnosis according to DSM-IV (APA, 1994) is made along five different axes or dimensions, each of which is acknowledged to be influenced by culture. For example, Axis I involves a description of the clinical expression of symptoms, which is heavily influenced by culture. Axis IV concerns psychosocial stressors, which inevitably reflect culturally determined circumstances of the individuals and the groups to which the individual belongs. Thus, the DSM-IV has taken considerable steps to incorporate the role of culture in the expression and reliable classification of psychological disorders. Challenges to the DSM-IV remain, however, especially concerning its difficulty in classifying culture-bound syndromes.

Another well-known and often-used classification system is the International Classification of Diseases, Tenth Edition (ICD-10). Its section on mental health includes 100 major diagnostic categories encompassing 329 individual clinical classifications. It is intended to be descriptive and atheoretical. Unfortunately, reviews of ICD-10 (for example, Alarcon, 1995) have suggested that it fails to recognize the importance of culture in influencing the expression and presentation of disorder.

Having a reliable and valid classification system of diagnoses would be a major plus for all health professionals and the people they seek to help. The DSM-IV seems to have made major strides toward creating such a system. Still, work in this area is continually evolving, and we are sure to see future changes in this and other classification systems. Hopefully, those changes will be informed by meaningful and relevant cross-cultural research.

Cross-Cultural Assessment of Abnormal Behavior

Not only is it important to have a reliable and valid system of classification of abnormal behaviors; it is also important to have a set of tools that can reliably and validly measure behaviors, feelings, and other psychological parameters related to mental illness. Those tools may include questionnaires, interview protocols, or standardized tasks that require some sort of behavior on the part of the test taker.

Needless to say, many of the issues that concern the valid and reliable measurement of *any* psychological variable cross-culturally for research purposes are also relevant to discussions of measurement tools for abnormality. Draguns (1997) recently reviewed a number of issues in this area, including stimulus equivalence, sample characteristics, comparability of constructs, structured self-reports, personal interviews, experimental apparatuses, and the impact of the examiner. These issues, and others, make valid and reliable measurement of pathology across cultures very difficult and complex.

Unfortunately, a critical examination of how the tools in use fare across cultures provides a stark glimpse of reality. Traditional tools of clinical assessment in psychology are generally based on a standard definition of abnormality and use a standard set of classification criteria for evaluating problematic behavior. Therefore, the tools may have little meaning in cultures with varying definitions, however well translated into the native language; and they may mask or fail to capture culturally specific expressions of disorder (Marsella, 1979). The assessment problems encountered in studying schizophrenia and depression across cultures illustrate the limitations of traditional assessment methods.

The Present State Examination (PSE), for example, was used to diagnose schizophrenia in the WHO studies described earlier. Leff (1986) commented on the ethnocentric bias of procedures such as the PSE and the Cornell Medical Index. In a psychiatric survey of the Yoruba in Nigeria, investigators had to supplement the PSE to include culture-specific complaints such as feeling "an expanded head and goose flesh."

Standard diagnostic instruments to measure depressive disorder may also miss important cultural expressions of the disorder in Africans (Beiser, 1985) and Native Americans (Manson, Shore, & Bloom, 1985). In an extensive study of depression among Native Americans (Manson & Shore, 1981; Manson et al., 1985), the American Indian Depression Schedule (AIDS) was developed to assess and diagnose depressive illness. The investigators found that depression among the Hopi includes symptoms not measured by standard measures of depression such as the Diagnostic Interview Schedule (DIS) and the Schedule for Affective Disorders and Schizophrenia (SADS). These measures, based on diagnostic criteria found in the DSM-III (APA, 1987), failed to capture the short but acute dysphoric moods sometimes reported by the Hopi (Manson et al., 1985).

Several researchers (Higginbotham, 1979; Lonner & Ibrahim, 1989; Marsella, 1979) have offered guidelines for developing measures to use in cross-cultural assessment of abnormal behavior. They suggest that sensitive assessment methods examine sociocultural norms of healthy adjustment as well as culturally based definitions of abnormality. Higginbotham (1979) also suggests the importance of examining culturally sanctioned systems of healing and their influence on abnormal behavior. There is evidence that people whose problems match cultural categories of abnormality are more likely to seek folk healers (Leff, 1986). Failure to examine **indigenous healing systems** thus overlooks some expressions of disorder. Assessment of culturally sanctioned systems of cure should also enhance planning for treatment strategies, one of the primary goals of traditional assessment (Carson et al., 1988).

Finally, one interesting topic that has turned up in the literature recently concerns language issues in psychological testing. In more and more cases today, test takers (such as patients or clients) have a first language and culture that differ from the diagnostician's or clinician's. Some writers (for example, Oquendo, 1996) have suggested that evaluation of such bilingual patients should really be done in both languages, preferably by a bilingual clinician or with the help of an interpreter trained in mental health issues. The reason, as will be discussed further in Chapter 12, is that cultural nuances may be encoded in language in ways that are not readily conveyed in translation. That is, translations of key psychological phrases and constructs from one language to another may give the closest semantic equivalent, but may not have exactly the same nuances, contextualized meanings, and associations. Also, Oquendo (1996) suggests that patients may use their second language as a form of resistance to avoid intense emotions. Administration of tests and therapy bilingually may help to bridge this gap.

Summary

Psychiatric diagnoses, classification schemes, and measurement of abnormality are complex and difficult issues. To the extent that there are both etic and emic aspects of psychopathology, classification systems and assessment methods need to contain both etic and emic elements. Where to draw the lines, and how to measure psychological traits and characteristics within this fluid, dynamic, and ever-changing system, is the challenge that faces this area of psychology today. Although the field has made vast improvements in this area in the past few years, future research will need to elaborate even further on these issues so that classification and measurement can be made more precise, meaningful, and relevant.

Culture and the Treatment of Abnormal Behavior

Culture and Psychotherapy

As you know, one of the primary goals of psychology is to use the knowledge generated by research to help people improve their lives. Among the many ways in which practicing or applied psychologists pursue this goal is through psychological interventions with people who have abnormal behavior disorders, and whose lives are dysfunctional because of those disorders. The primary vehicle for delivering such intervention is psychotherapy.

Contemporary psychotherapeutic approaches have their roots in hypnosis and psychoanalysis developed by Freud. Over the course of the past century, however, traditional psychoanalytic psychotherapy has been transformed, modified, and evolved into many different forms and types of psychotherapeutic approaches. These approaches may differ in their theoretical perspective, activity/passivity of the therapist, guidance, focus of treatment on actual behaviors or underlying psychology, and a host of other factors. They are all similar, however, in their goal of improving the patient/client's life, their one-on-one approach, and the use of psychological principles to effect behavioral change.

In a diverse world, many psychologists have come to see these "traditional" psychotherapeutic approaches as effective for some people, but less so for others, particularly those of non-European descent. Some authors (e.g., Wohl, 1989) have proposed that psychotherapy itself is inescapably bound to a particular cultural framework (see also Alarcon & Leetz, 1998). This notion may make sense, for several reasons. First, as we have seen, expressions of abnormality, and their underlying psychological causes, are at least partly bound to culture. Second, the ability of the therapist or clinician to assess and deal with such behaviors is intimately related to his or her knowledge, understanding, and appreciation of the cultural context within which the behaviors occur. Third, if the goal of psychotherapy is to help people to become more functional within their society, then functionality itself is culturally determined; that is, different cultures and societies would necessitate different outcomes.

In examining the roots and history of the development of psychotherapy, some writers have suggested that psychoanalysis—the basis for contemporary psychotherapy—was developed specifically within a Jewish cultural framework, and that it shares features with Jewish mysticism (Langman, 1997). In fact, the development of other psychotherapeutic approaches, such as behavioral or humanistic approaches, could be considered a "culturalization" of traditional psychoanalysis to American culture and society. Viewed in this fashion, psychotherapy can be considered a cultural product, reflecting and reproducing a cultural context. Because cultural context is in part composed of moral traditions embedded in political structures, psychotherapy is itself unavoidably a moral practice with political consequences embedded within a cultural framework. In this sense, there can be no value-free psychotherapy, because all psychotherapy is bound to a particular cultural framework, and cultures are inextricably tied to moral values and systems.

Treatment of Abnormal Behavior across Diverse Cultures in the United States

It is within this analysis of the close relationship between culture and psychotherapy that a steadily growing literature has suggested that culturally diverse clients may be underserved or inappropriately served by traditional treatment methods. In a pioneering study of ethnic differences in response to standard mental health services in the Seattle area, Sue (1977) found lower rates of utilization of services by Asian Americans and Native Americans than by European Americans and African Americans. More dramatically, he found that relative to European Americans, all other groups had higher dropout rates and poorer treatment outcomes. A later study in the Los Angeles area produced similar findings (Sue, 1991). Sue (1977; Sue & Zane, 1987) concluded that low utilization and high attrition rates were due to the cultural insensitivity of standard treatment methods.

One of the pioneers of research in this area is Stanley Sue, who directs the National Research Center for Asian American Mental Health. Sue suggests that some of the reasons why Asian Americans underutilize mental health services include shame, active avoidance of morbid thoughts, attributions of causes of mental illness to biological factors, willpower, and fear of a system not set up to deal with cultural differences well. Likewise, Tolman and Reedy (1998) suggest that reduced utilization of services by Native Americans may be the result of cultural beliefs that sickness comes from disharmony with oneself, one's community, and nature. Other cultural groups in the United States that underutilize mental health services no doubt have their own sets of culture-specific reasons that prevent them from utilizing available resources.

These types of problems—especially different ethnic and cultural groups' perceptions of the effectiveness of counseling and psychotherapy—are not easy to deal with. In one recent study (Lee & Mixson, 1995), for example, Asian and Caucasian clients at a university counseling center were asked to rate counseling helpfulness, counselor characteristics, and other aspects of their counseling experiences. The Asians tended to rate counseling as less helpful for personal and emotional concerns and to rate their counselors as less competent than did the Caucasians. To the extent that such perceptions are generalizable to larger populations of ethnically and culturally diverse peoples, they do not bode well for the ability of some contemporary mental health services to deal effectively with the emotional concerns of a wide variety of people.

To fashion more culturally sensitive services, Sue and others (Comas-Diaz & Jacobsen, 1991; Higginbotham, 1979; Sue & Zane, 1987; Tseng & McDermott, 1981) suggest that treatment methods should be modified to improve their fit with the worldviews and experiences of culturally diverse clients. For example, psychoanalytic approaches are derived from a worldview that assumes that unconscious conflicts (probably sexual) give rise to abnormal behavior. This worldview may reflect the experience of the well-to-do Austrian women Freud treated and based many of his theoretical assumptions on. However, a therapeutic approach based on such a worldview may prove inappropriate for cultures that attribute abnormality either to natural factors (for example, physical problems or being out of harmony with the environment) or supernatural causes (for example, spirit possession). Cultural systems of cure and healing may be effective precisely because they operate within a particular culture's worldview (Tseng & McDermott, 1981). For example, a spiritual ceremony performed by a native shaman (priest or healer) may prove to be a more effective treatment of the culture-bound syndrome *susto* than the cognitive behavioral approach typically used in the United States.

A large body of research on preferences for therapeutic approaches in ethnically different populations in the United States indicates that non–European American clients tend to prefer action-oriented therapy to nondirective approaches such as psychoanalytic or humanistic therapy (Sue & Zane, 1987). There is also some indication that culturally diverse clients prefer to see therapists who are similar in terms of cultural background and gender. But more recent research indicates that similarity of worldviews and attitudes to treatment between client and therapist may be more important than ethnic similarity (Atkinson, Ponce, & Martinez, 1984). Acculturation status may also determine client responses to treatment (Atkinson, Casa, & Abreu, 1992). Culture-sensitive counselors have been rated as being more credible and competent to conduct treatment across cultures by African Americans (Atkinson, Furlong, & Poston, 1986), Asian Americans (Gim, Atkinson, & Kim, 1991), and Mexican Americans (Atkinson et al., 1992).

Not only do client views of the therapist differ depending on the match between therapist and client; therapist views of the client also differ. In one study (Russell, Fujino, Sue, Cheung, & Snowden, 1996), for example, the records of thousands of African, Asian, Mexican, and European American outpatient clients in the Los Angeles County mental health system were examined for ethnic match with their therapist. Results indicated that ethnically matched therapists tended to judge clients to have higher mental functioning than did mismatched therapists. This finding held even after controlling for variables such as age, gender, marital status, and referral source. Thus, how the therapist perceived the client differed according to whether the therapist was of the client's ethnic group or not.

Several authors (for example, Higginbotham, 1979; Sue, Akutsu, & Higashi, 1985; Sue & Zane, 1987; Tseng & McDermott, 1981) have outlined the competencies and knowledge base necessary for therapists to conduct sensitive and effective treatment across cultures. Sue and associates (1985) suggest that the culturally sensitive therapist will have acquired (1) knowledge of diverse cultures and lifestyles, (2) skill and comfort in using innovative treatment methods, and (3) actual experience working with culturally diverse clients. It is also critically important that the therapist be aware of his or her own cultural background and its influences on definitions and perceptions of abnormal behavior. Furthermore, the therapist must be aware of how cultural beliefs and experiences influence the course of treatment. Comas-Diaz and Jacobsen (1991) have outlined several ways in which ethnocultural factors may shape therapy, including the elicitation of strong transference reactions on the part of the client (unconscious projections onto the therapist) and barriers to empathy on the part of the therapist (understanding of another's experience).

Treatment of Abnormal Behavior in Other Cultures

A focus in recent discussions of cross-cultural treatment of abnormal behavior has been culture-specific interventions. Several culture-specific forms of treatment have been identified in the literature, including *naikan* and *morita* therapy in Japan, and *espiritismo* practiced among some Puerto Ricans. These approaches are generally very "foreign" to many Americans. *Naikan* therapy, for example, involves a "process of continuous meditation based upon highly structured instruction in self-observation and self-reflection" (Murase, 1986, p. 389). Patients are usually placed in a small sitting area and practice their meditations from early in the morning (5:30 A.M. or so) until the evening (9:00 P.M. or so). Interviewers come every 90 minutes to discuss progress, usually for about 5 minutes. Patients are instructed to examine themselves severely, much as a prosecutor would examine an accused prisoner.

Psychological interventions in other cultures, however, are not limited to culture-specific interventions. In fact, there is a considerable movement in many other countries and cultures to merge aspects of traditional psychotherapy with culture-specific methods and beliefs to produce unique systems of healing in other cultures. Writers have pointed to a variety of ways in which traditional methods of psychotherapy need to blend with and accommodate culture-specific issues, such as the discouragement of egoistic and individualistic strivings, and the doctrine of karma and reincarnation in India (Hoch, 1990); issues of deculturation, outmigration, alienation, distrust, and despair among Native American Indian and Alaska Native cultures (Rodenhauser, 1994); issues of guardianship, social network, and social support in Shanghai (Zhang, Yan, & Phillips, 1994); and the interaction of spiritual, emotional/mental, physical, and family health in Maori New Zealand (Durie, 1997).

Prince (1980) argues that what is common to treatment across cultures is the mobilization of healing forces within the client. If, for example, Native Americans believe that illness results from disharmony among self, community, and nature, treatment should revolve around resolving the disharmony and restoring a state of balance and integration (Tolman & Reedy, 1998). Several others (for example, Torrey, 1972; Tseng & McDermott, 1981) have also attempted to determine universal features of culture-specific systems of treatment. Viewed in this fashion, culture-specific systems of treatment share the common characteristic of mobilizing healing forces within the client, but cultures (and psychotherapeutic approaches) differ in the exact ways in which the mobilization of healing forces occurs. While selecting an approach may be as much an art as it is a science, cross-cultural research in the future should play an important role in evaluating the effectiveness of different approaches to mobilizing those healing forces within the client, and hence the overall effectiveness and outcomes of treatment.

Culture and Clinical Training

Because of all the issues discussed in this chapter, and throughout the book, all accredited programs of clinical training in the United States have, for some time now, been mandated to incorporate culture and diversity in their training programs. Clinical psychologists who will be in the field actually applying psychological knowledge and principles to people who seek help need to have a base for understanding the role of culture in the expression and presentation of mental illness, the difficulties and complexities involved in psychological assessment, and the issues regarding culturally sensitive yet effective treatment. Beyond these factors, however, contemporary clinicians and therapists receive training in the broad base of culture's influence on all aspects of psychology, from perception and sensation through development to social behavior and personality. It is only within this broad base of training that contemporary psychologists can gain the perspective necessary to work effectively with their clients and patients to help them improve their lives.

Issues regarding culture and diversity also arise in areas outside of traditional one-on-one psychotherapy—for example, the role of culture in the development and treatment of children (Tharp, 1991) and ethnic and cultural diversity in group therapy (Brook, Gordon, & Meadow, 1998). Finally, the increasing number of bilingual/bicultural individuals seeking help raises its own set of special issues, including the language and cultural framework within which psychotherapy and healing will occur. A number of writers have suggested that language proficiency, level of acculturation, and the degree to which cultural expressions represent symptomatology should be considered in the development of an effective treatment plan (for example, Altarriba & Santiago-Rivera, 1994; Ben-David, 1996; Santiago-Rivera & Azara, 1995). The need for multiple language and cultural fluency adds to the growing list of requirements for culturally competent therapists.

These issues are not only relevant to people of different ethnicities, races, or nationality. Given that psychotherapy is inescapably bound to a particular cultural framework, perhaps *all* psychotherapy can be seen as essentially cross-cultural, in that no two people have internalized identical constructions of their cultural worlds (Wohl, 1989); this view is consistent with the emphasis in this book on culture as a psychological phenomenon. Perhaps sound principles and concepts of psychotherapy can be applied cross-culturally as long as cultural differences are taken into account; this notion is consistent with the view that cross-cultural research methods are nothing more than good traditional research methods applied cross-culturally. Although some issues (such as language) are specific to applying research methods or therapeutic approaches across cultural lines, the coming together of traditional and cross-cultural approaches could provide the basis for a fundamental revision in the training of psychotherapists and clinicians in the future.

✕ Conclusion

In this chapter, we have discussed the important role culture plays in defining abnormality, influencing its expression and presentation in individuals, affecting our ability to reliably and validly assess and diagnosis it, and helping or hindering our ability to help people with mental disorders improve their lives. The material in this chapter is not only relevant on its own, but is informed by material in the entire book showing the pervasive influence of culture in all aspects of our psychological composition. It is only within this larger perspective of the influence of culture that we can begin to truly grasp and appreciate the difficulties and complexities of diagnosing and treating abnormal behavior in a diverse world.

The difficulties presented, however, should be viewed as challenges, not obstacles. Through the study of culture, psychopathology, assessment, and psychotherapy, we are afforded the chance to expand our theoretical and conceptual horizons regarding abnormality and treatment, and to help our treatment systems evolve into bigger and better systems effectively serving larger and larger groups of people. We are currently engaged in the search for principles and knowledge that will help us achieve those goals.

Continued cross-cultural research on clinical issues—defining and assessing abnormality, designing treatment approaches that effectively mobilize healing forces within clients—is a must. But research on these major issues of definition, assessment, and treatment should proceed cautiously and systematically. Future research should continue to search for emic as well as etic factors relevant to all forms of disorder, and for psychometrically valid and reliable ways of measuring those factors. Future research will also need to explore the efficacy of different treatment approaches that address both etic and emic concerns, blending approaches that represent combinations of traditional and culture-specific modalities in an overall, comprehensive fashion.

 Glossary

cultural relativism A viewpoint that suggests that the unique aspects of a particular culture need to be considered when understanding and identifying behavior.

culture-bound syndromes Forms of abnormal behavior observed only in certain sociocultural milieus.

indigenous healing systems Systems of cure, such as folk healers, particular to a certain culture.

somatization Bodily complaints as expressions of psychological distress.

Culture and Emotion

The Importance of Emotion in Our Lives

It is difficult to imagine life without emotion, devoid of feeling. We treasure our feelings—the joy we feel at a ball game, the pleasure of the touch of a loved one, the fun we have with our friends on a night out, seeing a movie, or visiting a nightclub. Even our negative or unpleasant feelings are important: the sadness when we are apart from our loved ones, the death of a family member, the anger we feel when violated, the fear that overcomes us in a scary unknown situation, and the guilt or shame we feel toward others when our sins are made public. Emotions color our life experiences. They inform us of who we are, what our relationships with others are like, and how to behave. Emotions give meaning to events. Without emotions, those events would be mere facts of our lives.

Emotions separate us from computers and other machines. Technological advances have brought machines that are increasingly capable of recreating many of our complex thought processes. Computers now handle much of our work more efficiently than humans can. But no matter how much a computer can accomplish, no technology can make a computer *feel* as we feel. (Not yet, anyway!)

Feelings and emotions may be the most important aspect of our lives. All people of all cultures have them, and all must learn to deal with them, to attribute some degree of value and worth to them. Life around us may appear to be focused on developing technological capabilities for artificial intelligence and critical thinking and reasoning skills. But our emotions hold the key to make it all happen.

The world of emotion underscores the great diversity among people. How we package emotion, what we call it, how much importance we give it, how we express and perceive it, and how we feel it—these are questions that all people and all cultures answer differently. These differences among individuals and among cultures contribute substantially to the great diversity that we see and, more important, feel among people of different lands and nations.

This chapter explores the nature of those differences—as well as similarities—in human emotion across cultures. We begin by exploring how some emotions may be universal in their expression, regardless of culture, whereas others may differ in their expression across cultures. We then discuss both pancultural and culture-specific aspects of emotion perception, the experience of emotion, emotion antecedents (the events that elicit emotion), the process of appraising or evaluating emotions, and finally, the concept and language of emotion. We will find that at least a small set of emotions share a universal base across all human cultures, and that they provide a base of similarity in all aspects of emotion—expression, perception, experience, antecedents, appraisal, and concept. Building on this common base, culture exerts its influence in molding our emotional worlds, resulting in cultural differences as well as similarities. The integration of both universality and cultural differences is the challenge that faces cross-cultural work on human emotion.

Culture and Emotion Expression

Our examination of the influence of culture on human emotion begins with the topic of emotional expression for several reasons. First, cross-cultural work on emotional expressions, especially facial expressions, lay much of the groundwork for contemporary research on emotion, both cross-cultural and mainstream. Thus, the cross-cultural study of facial expressions of emotion has an important historical significance to this area of psychology. Second, cross-cultural research on facial expressions of emotion has demonstrated convincingly that there is a small set of facial expressions that appear to be universal across all human cultures. Other studies have suggested their biological innateness. Therefore, it is important to have a firm grasp of the biological substrates of emotion that may exist for all humans regardless of culture, and before considering cultural influences on emotional processes above and beyond what may be inborn. Thus, we begin by looking at the universality of facial expressions of emotion.

The Universality of Facial Expressions of Emotion

Although philosophers have argued and discussed the possible universal basis of facial expressions of emotion for centuries (see Russell, 1995, for a review), much of the impetus for contemporary cross-cultural research on facial expressions of emotion stems from the writing of Charles Darwin. Many people are familiar with Darwin's theory of evolution, outlined in his work *On the Origin of Species* (1859). Darwin suggested that humans had evolved from other, more primitive animals, such as apes and chimpanzees, and that our behaviors exist today because they were selected through a process of evolutionary adaptation. In a subsequent volume, *The Expression of Emotion in Man and Animals* (1872; see also the new 1998 edition), Darwin suggested that facial expressions of emotion, like other behaviors, are biologically innate and evolutionarily adaptive. Humans, Darwin argued, express emotions in their faces in exactly the same ways around the world, regardless of race or culture. Moreover, those facial expressions can also be seen across species, such as in gorillas. According to Darwin, facial expressions of emotion have both communicative and adaptive value, and ensure the survival of the species by providing both intrapsychic information to the individual about well-being and person–environment relationships and social information for others in the community.

During the early to mid-1900s, several studies were conducted to test Darwin's ideas concerning the universality of emotional expressions (for example, Triandis & Lambert, 1958; Vinacke, 1949; Vinacke & Fong, 1955). Unfortunately, many of them had methodological problems that made drawing conclusions based on them difficult (see Ekman, Friesen, & Ellsworth, 1972, for a review). At the same time, prominent anthropologists such as Margaret Mead and Ray Birdwhistell argued that facial expressions of emotion could not be universal; instead, they suggested that facial expressions of emotion had to be learned, much like a language (Ekman, Friesen, & Ellsworth, 1972). Just as different cultures had different languages, they also had different facial expressions of emotion.

It was not until the 1960s, when psychologists Paul Ekman and Wallace Friesen (Ekman, 1972) and, independently, Carroll Izard (1971) conducted the first set of methodologically sound studies, that this debate was laid to rest. Spurred on by the work of Sylvan Tomkins (1962, 1963), these researchers conducted a series of studies now called the **universality studies**. Four different types of studies were originally included in the series. Since their first publication, many of the findings have been replicated in numerous studies in many different countries and cultures by other investigators, ensuring the robustness of their work.

In the first of these studies, in conjunction with Tomkins, Ekman and Friesen selected photographs of facial expressions of emotion they thought portrayed universally recognizable emotions (Ekman, 1972). The researchers showed these photographs to observers in five different countries (the United States, Argentina, Brazil, Chile, and Japan) and asked the observers to label each expression. If the expressions were universal, the researchers reasoned, judges in all cultures would agree in what emotion was being portrayed; if the expressions were culturally specific, the judges from different cultures should disagree. The data revealed a very high level of agreement across all observers in all five cultures in the interpretation of six emotions—anger, disgust, fear, happiness, sadness, and surprise. Izard (1971) conducted a similar study in other cultures and obtained similar results.

One problem with these studies was that all of the cultures included in the research were literate, industrialized, and relatively modern. It was possible, therefore, that the observers in those cultures could have *learned* how to interpret the facial expressions in the photographs. The fact that these cultures shared mass media—television, movies, magazines, and so forth—reinforced this possibility. The research was criticized, therefore, on the basis of *shared visual input* across the cultures studied.

To address this concern, Ekman, Sorenson, and Friesen (1969) conducted similar studies in two preliterate tribes of New Guinea. Because of the nature of the participants in these studies, Ekman and his colleagues were forced to change the nature of the experiment, allowing participants to select a story that best described a facial expression instead of using emotion words. When these participants were asked to identify the emotions in the photographs, the data were amazingly similar to those obtained in literate, industrialized societies. Thus, judgments of posed expressions by preliterate cultures constituted a second source of evidence in support of universality.

Ekman and his colleagues took their research in New Guinea a step further, asking different tribe members to show on their faces what they would look like if they experienced the different emotions. Photographs of these expressions were brought back to the United States and shown to American observers, none of whom had ever seen the tribe members from New Guinea. When asked to label the emotions shown on the tribe members' faces, the data were again similar to those found in previous studies. Judgments of expressions posed by preliterate tribes thus constituted a third source of evidence for universality.

All of the research conducted so far had involved judgments of facial expressions of emotion, and were based on the researchers' assumption that people of different cultures would agree on what emotion is being portrayed in a face if the expression were universal. Still, a question remained as to whether people actually, spontaneously display those expressions on their faces when they experience emotion. To address this question, Ekman (1972) and Friesen (1972) conducted a study in the United States and Japan, asking American and Japanese subjects to view highly stressful stimuli as their facial reactions were videotaped without their awareness. Later analysis of the video records indicated that Americans and Japanese did indeed show exactly the same types of facial expressions at the same points in time, and these expressions corresponded to the same expressions that were considered universal in the judgment research. Data from spontaneous facial expressions of emotion, therefore, constituted the fourth line of evidence in the original set of universality studies. Figure 11.1 shows the original six emotional expressions—anger, disgust, fear, happiness, sadness, and surprise—that were found to be universally expressed and recognized across cultures. (The seventh expression, contempt, will be discussed in connection with more recent studies.)

Although these four sets of findings constitute the bulk of the evidence traditionally considered to comprise the universality studies, it is not the entire

Figure 11.1 The seven universal expressions of facial emotion

anger

disgust

fear

happiness

sadness

surprise

contempt

evidentiary basis of support for the universality thesis. Important studies involving nonhuman primates and congenitally blind infants (reviewed in Ekman, 1973) also support the universality contention. The studies involving nonhuman primates lend support to Darwin's original thesis concerning the

276 ■ Chapter 11

evolutionary basis of facial expressions of emotion. Research involving con-genitally blind infants shows that visual learning cannot account for the fact that humans within or across cultures share the same set of facial expressions. Collectively, these studies constitute a considerable body of evidence demon-strating quite convincingly that facial expressions of emotion are universal and biologically innate.

If these conclusions are correct, they have far-reaching implications. They suggest that all humans are born with the capacity to express the same set of emotions in the same ways. Moreover, they imply similarities in other aspects of emotion. They suggest that all humans have the capacity to experience these same emotions in basically the same ways, and that many of the same kinds of events or psychological themes evoke the same types of emotions in all people across cultures. In short, they suggest that we are all born with the capacity to experience, express, and perceive the same basic set of emotions.

Of course, we experience a range of emotion that is much broader than the set of emotions considered to be universally expressed—love, hate, jealousy, pride, and many others. The existence of basic emotions, however, suggests that these emotions blend with our experiences, personality, and sociocultural milieu to create an infinite degree of shading, blends, and coloring in our emo-tional world. Much like colors on a color wheel, the existence of basic emotions suggests that cultures shape, mold, and color our emotional lives *by using the set of basic emotions as a starting point* to create other emotions.

At the same time, the existence of basic, universal emotions does not imply that cultures cannot differ in the ways they express, perceive, or experience emotion. Indeed, much of the research that will be reviewed in this chapter in-dicates that cultures exert a considerable influence on all these facets of emo-tion. What the universality of emotion does suggest is that basic emotions pro-vide cultures with a base from which the molding and shaping can start. This perspective is important to keep in mind as we examine the research on cul-tural differences in emotion.

Cultural Differences in Facial Expressions: Display Rules

Despite the fact that facial expressions of emotion may be universal, many of us have experienced uncertainty about how to interpret the expressions of someone from a different cultural background. At the same time, we may wonder whether our own expressions are being interpreted in the way we in-tend. Although we see emotional expressions that are similar to ours in people from very diverse backgrounds, more often than not we see many dif-ferences as well. These experiences run counter to what scholars typically be-lieved about facial expressions until only a few decades ago. How is it that our everyday experiences, and the experiences of well-known scholars such as Margaret Mead, can lead us to believe that people's emotional expressions differ from one culture to another, when the findings from so many studies say otherwise?

Ekman and Friesen (1969) pondered this question many years ago and came up with the concept of **cultural display rules** to account for the discrepancy. Cultures differ, they reasoned, in the rules governing how universal emotions can be expressed. These rules center on the appropriateness of displaying each of the emotions in particular social circumstances. These rules are learned early, and they dictate how the universal emotional expressions should be modified according to social situation. By the time of adulthood, these rules are automatic, having been very well practiced.

Ekman (1972) and Friesen (1972) designed a study to document the existence of these cultural display rules and their role in producing cultural differences in emotional expressions. In the study described earlier, American and Japanese subjects were asked to view highly stressful films while their facial reactions were videotaped. That experiment actually had two conditions. In the first condition, described earlier, subjects viewed the stimuli by themselves. In a second condition, an older, higher-status experimenter came into the room and asked the subjects to watch the films again, with the experimenter observing them. Their facial reactions were again videotaped. Analysis of the videotapes showed that the Americans in general continued to show negative feelings of disgust, fear, sadness, and anger. The Japanese, however, invariably *smiled* in these instances. These findings show how universal, biologically innate emotional expressions can interact with culturally defined rules of display to produce appropriate emotional expressions. In the first condition, when display rules did not operate, the Americans and the Japanese exhibited the same expressions. In the second condition, display rules were operative, forcing the Japanese to smile in order not to offend the experimenter, despite their obvious negative feelings. These findings are especially impressive because the subjects in the second condition that produced differences were the same individuals as in the first condition that produced similarities.

Thus, facial expressions of emotion are under the dual influence of universal, biologically innate factors and culturally specific, learned display rules (see Figure 11.2). When an emotion is triggered, a message is sent to the facial affect program (Ekman, 1972), which stores the prototypic facial configuration information for each of the universal emotions. This prototypic configuration is what constitutes the universal aspect of emotional expression, and is biologically innate. At the same time, however, a message is sent to the area of the brain storing learned cultural display rules. The resulting expression represents the joint influence of both factors. When display rules do not modify an expression, the universal facial expression of emotion will be displayed. Depending on social circumstances, however, display rules may act to neutralize, amplify, deamplify, qualify, or mask the universal expression. This mechanism explains how and why people can differ in their emotional expressions despite the fact that we all share the same expression base.

Figure 11.2 The neurocultural theory of emotional expression

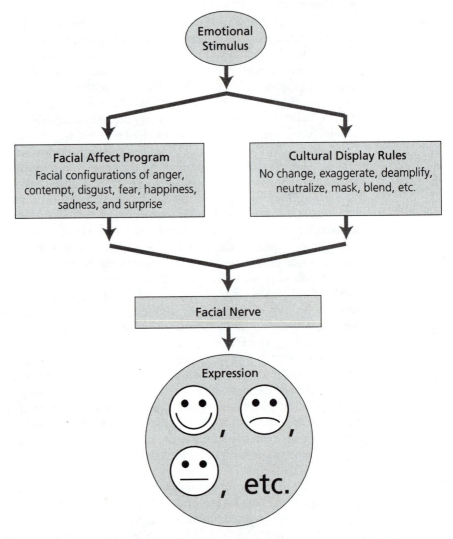

Source: Adapted from P. Ekman, "Universals and Cultural Differences in Facial Expression of Emotion," in J. Cole (ed.), *Nebraska Symposium of Motivation, 1971,* vol. 19 (Lincoln: University of Nebraska Press, 1972).

Recent Cross-Cultural Research on Emotional Expression and Display Rules

After the original publication of the universality studies, along with the concept and documentation of cultural display rules, an interesting phenomenon occurred in the field. These findings were so well received that they opened the door to research on emotion in all areas of psychology. Shortly after the publication of the universality research, scientists turned their efforts to developing methods of measuring facial expressions as a way of objectively measuring emotion without reliance on self-reports, which tend to be unreliable. With the development of such facial measurement tools as Ekman and Friesen's (1978) Facial Action Coding System (FACS), research on emotion began to flourish in many other areas of psychology, including developmental, clinical, social, personality, and physiological psychology. Emotion research caught on so well in these areas, in fact, that it was years before cross-cultural research on emotional expression was conducted again. Ironically, therefore, despite the importance of earlier cross-cultural research on emotional expressions, there is actually a large gap in research on emotional expression from the early 1970s until the late 1980s and early 1990s.

In recent years, however, a number of cross-cultural studies on emotional expression has extended our knowledge of the influence of culture on expression and display rules in interesting ways. For example, Stephan, Stephan, and de Vargas (1996) compared expressions of Americans and Costa Ricans by asking participants in both countries to rate 38 emotions in terms of how comfortable they would feel expressing them toward their family and to strangers. They also completed a self-concept scale of independence versus interdependence (see Chapter 3), and rated the emotions as to whether they were positive or negative, and independent or interdependent. The results indicated that Americans were more comfortable than Costa Ricans in expressing both independent and interdependent emotions. Costa Ricans were significantly less comfortable in expressing negative emotions.

Research has also documented the existence of cultural differences in emotional expression among ethnic groups in the United States. In one study (Matsumoto, 1993), American subjects were self-classified into one of four major ethnic categories: Caucasian, black, Asian, and Latino. These participants viewed the universal facial expressions of emotion and rated the appropriateness of displaying them in different social situations. The findings showed that Caucasians rated contempt as more appropriate than Asians, disgust as more appropriate than blacks and Latinos, fear as more appropriate than Latinos, and sadness as more appropriate than blacks and Asians. In addition, Caucasians rated the expression of emotions in public and with children as more appropriate than Latinos, with casual acquaintances as more appropriate than blacks, Asians, and Latinos, and with lower-status others as more appropriate than blacks or Latinos. Interestingly, however, in another part of the experiment, blacks reported expressing anger more often than Caucasians, Asians, and Latinos. In another study on the same vein, Aune and Aune (1995) found that Filipino Americans expressed emotions more intensely than did Japanese Americans when positive and negative emotions were aroused in a romantic relationship.

A couple of interesting recent studies also demonstrate the existence of cultural differences in stereotypes about emotional expression. In one study (Pittam, Gallois, Iwawaki, & Kroonenberg, 1995), participants in Australia and

Japan rated how they expressed eight emotions through 12 behaviors, and how they thought a person of the other country expressed them. Both groups rated Australians as more expressive than the Japanese on positive emotions. But both groups rated the other group as more expressive than themselves on negative emotions. In a much larger study, Pennebaker, Rime, and Blankenship (1996) asked more than 2,900 college students in 26 countries to rate themselves, people in the northern part of their country, and people in the southern part of their country, on emotional expressiveness. Interestingly, these researchers found that people from warmer, southern climates were perceived as more expressive than people from northern areas.

Although the studies reviewed so far point to many ways in which cultures differ in their expressivity, it is not exactly clear how expressions are controlled when display rules are enacted. Two recent studies, shed some light on these processes. In the first (McConatha, Lightner, & Deaner, 1994), males and females in the United States and England completed four scales related to emotional control: rehearsal, inhibition, aggression control, and benign control (impulsiveness). American males exhibited more rehearsal and inhibition than did British males. American females also engaged in more inhibition than did British females. British females, however, engaged in more aggression control and benign control than did American females.

In the second study, Matsumoto and his colleagues (1998) surveyed participants in four countries—the United States, Japan, Russia, and South Korea—and asked them to select what they would do if they felt one of 14 emotions in four different social situations. The seven response alternatives were as follows:

1. Express the feeling with no modification
2. Deamplify or reduce the expression
3. Amplify or exaggerate the expression
4. Mask or conceal your feelings by showing something else
5. Qualify your expression with a smile
6. Neutralize your expression
7. Something else

The results indicated that, although cultural differences did exist, participants from all cultures selected all of the alternatives, indicating that these alternatives are a fair representation of the response repertoires available to people as they modify their emotional expressions in social contexts.

Finally, research of the past decade has gone beyond documenting differences in emotional expression to develop a theoretical framework of how and why cultures produce these differences. Matsumoto (1991), for example, has used the concept of ingroups and outgroups (see Chapter 16) to suggest that cultural differences in the meaning of self–ingroup and self–outgroup relationships have particular meaning for the emotions expressed in social interactions. In general, the familiarity and intimacy of self–ingroup relations in all cultures provide the safety and comfort to express emotions freely, along with tolerance for a broad spectrum of emotional behaviors. Part of emotional socialization involves learning who are ingroup and outgroup members and the appropriate behaviors associated with them. In Matsumoto's framework, collectivistic cultures foster more positive and fewer negative emotions toward ingroups because ingroup harmony is more important to them. Positive emotions ensure maintenance of this harmony; negative emotions threaten it. Individualistic cultures, however, foster more negative emotions and fewer positive emotions toward ingroups; because harmony and cohesion are less important to these cultures, it is considered appropriate to display emotions that may threaten group cohesion. Individualistic cultures foster more positive and less negative emotions toward outgroups, because it is less important in individualistic cultures to differentiate between ingroups and outgroups; thus, they allow expression of positive feelings and suppression of negative ones toward outgroup members. Collectivistic cultures, however, foster more negative expressions toward outgroups to distinguish more clearly between ingroups and outgroups and to strengthen ingroup relations (via the collective expression of negative feelings toward outgroups). These variations in the expressions of personal emotions are summarized in Table 11.1.

Two studies have confirmed many of these hypotheses. Matsumoto and Hearn (1991; reported in Biehl, Matsumoto, & Kasri, in press), for example, examined cultural display rules in the United States, Poland, and Hungary. Participants in each of the three countries viewed each of the six universal emotions and rated how appropriate it would be to display them in three different social situations: (1) by yourself, (2) with others considered as "ingroup" members (for example, close friends, family members), and (3) with others considered "outgroup" (for example, in public, with casual acquaintances). Poles and Hungarians reported that it was less appropriate to display negative emotions in ingroups and more appropriate to display positive emotions; they also reported that it was more appropriate to display negative emotions to outgroups. Americans, in contrast, were more likely to display negative emotions to ingroup members and positive emotions to outgroup members. Compared to

Table 11.1 Expression of Personal Emotions in Self–Ingroup and Self–Outgroup Relationships in Individualistic and Collectivistic Cultures

	Type of Culture	
	Individualistic	Collectivistic
Self–ingroup relations	Okay to express negative feelings; less need to display positive feelings	Suppress expressions of negative feelings; more pressure to display positive feelings
Self–outgroup relations	Suppress negative feelings; okay to express positive feelings as would toward ingroups	Encouraged to express negative feelings; suppress display of positive feelings reserved for ingroups

Americans, Poles also reported that the display of negative emotions was less appropriate even when they were alone. Matsumoto and Hearn (1991) interpreted these results as supportive of Matsumoto's (1991) theoretical predictions. The findings from a United States–Japan comparison also supported these predictions (Matsumoto, 1990).

Thus, research of the past decade has gone well beyond the original documentation of universality of facial expressions and the existence of cultural display rules conducted by Ekman and his colleagues. The available research shows that culture exerts considerable influence over our emotional expressions via culturally learned display rules, and gives us an idea of what those rules are like. Recent research also suggests what it is about cultures that produces cultural differences in emotional expressions, and why. Given that most interactions among people are social by definition, we should expect that cultural differences via display rules are operative most, if not all, of the time.

To understand the emotional expressions of people of different cultures, then, we must understand, first, what universal bases underlie those expressions and, second, what kinds of cultural display rules are operating when we interact with them. Still, many gaps in our knowledge remain to be filled. For example, future research will need to examine how people of different cultures come to learn their various display rules, and what those display rules are. Future studies will also need to examine further how and why cultures produce differences in emotional behavior, incorporating dimensions other than individualism versus collectivism, such as power or status differentiation.

Culture and Emotion Perception

The Universality of Emotion Recognition

Many of the judgment studies documenting the universal expression of emotion also tell us that facial expressions of emotion can be universally recognized. When shown photographs of the universal facial emotions, observers in all countries and cultures studied agreed on what emotion was being portrayed in the expressions, at quite high levels across cultures (Ekman, 1972; Ekman & Friesen, 1971; Ekman, Sorenson, & Friesen, 1969; Izard, 1971). As you will remember, these studies involved posed expressions not only judged by people in both literate and preliterate cultures, but posed by people in both literate and preliterate cultures. Another study (reported in Ekman, 1972) also found universality in the judgment of spontaneous facial expressions of emotion.

Numerous studies conducted since the original universality research have replicated the original findings (for example, Boucher & Carlson, 1980; Markham & Wang, 1996; see Ekman, 1982, and Matsumoto, Wallbott, & Scherer, 1987, for reviews). For example, Ekman and colleagues (1987) asked observers in ten different cultures to view photographs depicting each of the six universal emotions. The judges not only labeled each emotion by selecting an emotion word from a predetermined list but also rated how intensely they perceived the emotion to be expressed. The judges in all ten cultures agreed on what emotion was being displayed, highlighting the universality of recognition. In addition, observers in each culture gave the strongest intensity ratings to the emotions that corresponded with the facial expressions they were judging.

The findings from these numerous studies have shown unequivocally that people of all cultures can recognize the universal facial expressions of emotion depicted in Figure 11.1. As with emotional expression, this principle was so well accepted by the field that research on the relationship between culture and emotional perception virtually stopped. Because researchers knew that people of different cultures could differ in their expressions of emotion according to cultural display rules, however, they came to realize that people of different cultures must learn different ways of perceiving emotions in others. In the past decade, numerous studies have been conducted on this topic. They suggest that, like emotional expression, the perception of emotion has both universal, pan-cultural elements and culturally specific aspects.

Evidence for More Cross-Cultural Similarities in Emotional Perception

A universal contempt expression.   Since the original university studies, a number of studies have reported the universality of a seventh facial expression of emotion, contempt. Initial evidence was collected from ten cultures, including West Sumatra (Ekman & Friesen, 1986; Ekman & Heider, 1988). These findings were later replicated by Matsumoto (1992b) in four cultures, three of which were different from Ekman and Friesen's original ten cultures. This seventh universal expression has received considerable attention and criticism (Izard & Haynes, 1988; Russell, 1994a, 1994b). Russell (1994a, 1994b), for example, suggested that the context in which the expression was shown influenced the results in favor of universality. In his study, the contempt expression was more often labeled as either disgust or sadness when shown either alone or after showing a disgust or sadness picture (Russell, 1991). Ekman, O'Sullivan, and Matsumoto (1991a, 1991b), however, reanalyzed their data to address this criticism and found no effect of context. Biehl and associates (1997) also found no effects for other possible methodological confounds. An example of the contempt expression is included in Figure 11.1.

Relative intensity ratings.   Cultures agree on the relative intensity they attribute to facial expressions. That is, when comparing two expressions, all cultures generally agree on which is more strongly expressed. When Ekman and colleagues (1987) presented paired expressions of the same emotion, they found that 92% of the time the ten cultures in their study agreed on which was more intense. Matsumoto and Ekman (1989) extended this finding by including comparisons across different poser types, including Caucasian and Japanese posers. Looking separately at each emotion, first within culture across gender and then within gender across culture, they found that Americans and

Japanese agreed on which photo was more intense in 24 out of 30 comparisons. These findings suggest that cultures judge emotions on a similar basis, despite differences in facial physiognomy, morphology, race, and sex of the posers, and culturally prescribed rules governing the expression and perception of faces.

The association between perceived expression intensity and inferences about subjective experience.   When people see a strong emotional expression, they will infer that the poser is actually feeling the emotion strongly. When they see a weaker expression, they will infer a less emotional experience. Matsumoto, Kasri, and Kooken (in press) demonstrated this effect by obtaining Japanese and American judgments of 56 expressions posed by Japanese and Caucasians. The observers judged what emotion the poser was expressing, and then the strength of both the external display and the internal, **subjective experience of emotion**. Correlations between the two intensity ratings were computed twice, first across observers separately for each expression, and second across expressions for each observer. Regardless of the computation, the correlations were high and positive for both cultures and for all expressions. Observers associated the strength of the external display with the presumed strength of the internal experience, suggesting commonality in that linkage across culture. The link between the presence or absence of an expression and the underlying experience, and the intensity of both, is a topic of considerable importance in contemporary theories of emotion. Some authors have claimed that the linkage between expression and experience is unfounded (for example, Russell, 1997; Fernandez-Dols, 1997); others have argued that expressions and experience are intimately linked (but need not always be coupled) (Rosenberg & Ekman, 1994; see also the literature on the facial feedback hypothesis, reviewed by Matsumoto, 1987; Winton, 1986). The data from Matsumoto and colleagues (1997) clearly support notions of linkage.

Second mode of response in emotion recognition.   Cultures are also similar in the second most salient emotion they perceive in some emotional expressions. Observers in Ekman et al.'s (1987) study judged not only which emotion was portrayed in the faces, but also the intensity of each of seven emotion categories. This task allowed observers to report multiple emotions, or no emotion, instead of being forced to select an emotion to describe the face. Although previous studies had shown universality in the first mode of response, cultures might have differed in which emotion is next most prevalent. Analyses, however, supported cultural agreement. For every culture in Ekman et al.'s (1987) study, the secondary emotion for the disgust expressions was contempt, and for fear expressions surprise. For anger, the second mode varied depending on the photo, with disgust, surprise, or contempt as the second response. These findings have been replicated by Matsumoto and Ekman (1989) and Biehl and colleagues (1997), suggesting pancultural agreement on the multiple meanings derived from universal faces. This agreement may exist because of overlap in the semantics of the emotion categories, in the antecedents and elicitors of emotion, or in the facial configurations themselves.

Evidence for Cross-Cultural Differences in Emotional Perception

Emotion recognition.   Although the original universality research showed that subjects recognized emotions at well over chance rates, no study has ever reported perfect cross-cultural agreement (100 % of the judges in any or all of the cultures agreeing on what emotion is portrayed in an expression). Matsumoto (1992a), for example, comparing Japanese and American judgments, found that recognition rates ranged from 64 % to 99 %, which were consistent with earlier universality studies. Americans were better at recognizing anger, disgust, fear, and sadness than the Japanese, but accuracy rates did not differ for happiness or surprise. These results were interpreted as supportive of the universality of facial expressions of emotion because the agreement was consistently high (in most cases, well above 70 %) and statistically significant.

Some new research has also shown that although people of different cultures agree reliably on the most salient emotion message conveyed in universal facial expressions, cross-cultural differences emerge in the perception of other emotions in the same expression. Yrizarry, Matsumoto, and Wilson-Cohn (in press), for example, reanalyzed American and Japanese multiple scalar judgments of seven universal expressions. When judging anger expressions, Americans and Japanese agreed that anger was the most salient emotion portrayed in the expression. However, Americans saw more disgust and contempt in those same expressions than did the Japanese, whereas the Japanese saw more sadness in the anger expressions. Although previous research (reviewed in Matsumoto et al., in press) has consistently shown that judges see multiple emotions when viewing universal faces, this was the first study to document cultural differences in multiple emotion judgments of the same expressions.

Emotion recognition and dimensions of culture.   Given at least some cultural differences in rates of emotion recognition, several researchers have been interested in identifying the causes of such differences. Russell (1994), for example, has argued for a Western/non-Western distinction, suggesting that the methodologies that have been used to test emotion recognition across cultures have been biased in favor of Western—that is, North American and European—judges (see also rebuttals by Ekman, 1994, and Izard, 1994). Biehl and associates (1997), however, comparing emotion recognition across six cultures, demonstrated that a Western/non-Western dichotomy is not statistically supported to explain cross-national variation. Instead, Biehl and associates suggest that underlying sociopsychological variables or cultural dimensions (as postulated by Hofstede 1980, 1983) influence the emotion judgment process.

As an example of the use of such dimensions to explain cultural differences in emotion recognition rates, Matsumoto (1989) selected recognition data from 15 cultures reported in four studies, and ranked each culture on Hofstede's (1980, 1983) dimensions: power distance (PD), uncertainty avoidance (UA), individualism (IN), and masculinity (MA). (See Chapter 2 for a review of these dimensions.) Matsumoto then correlated these dimensions with recognition accuracy levels. He found that individualism was positively correlated with mean intensity ratings for anger and fear, supporting the claim that Americans (individualistic culture) are better at recognizing negative emotions than Japanese (collectivistic culture). A meta-analysis by Schimmack (1996) also found differences in emotion perception as a function of culture. Individualism was a better predictor of recognition of happiness than ethnicity (operationalized as Caucasian/non-Caucasian), supporting the notion that sociocultural dimensions account for differences in the perception of emotion. Together, these studies demonstrate the promise of using such dimensions to examine cultural influences on emotion perception, releasing researchers from an unhealthy reliance on archaic distinctions such as the Western/non-Western dichotomy.

Attributions of expression intensity. People of different cultures differ in how strongly they perceive emotions in others. Ekman et al.'s (1987) study of ten cultures was the first to document this effect. Although overall recognition data supported universality, Asians gave significantly lower intensity ratings on happiness, surprise, and fear. These data suggested that the judges were acting according to culturally learned rules about how to perceive expressions, especially given the fact that all posers were Caucasian. That is, it was possible that the Asians rated the Caucasian posers less intensely out of politeness or ignorance. To examine this notion, Matsumoto and Ekman developed a stimulus set comprised of Asian and Caucasian posers (the Japanese and Caucasian Facial Expressions of Emotion set, or JACFEE), and presented it to judges in the United States and Japan (Matsumoto & Ekman, 1989). For all but one emotion, Americans rated the expressions more intensely than the Japanese, regardless of the race of the person being judged. Because the differences were not specific to the poser, Matsumoto and Ekman (1989) interpreted the differences as a function of rules that the cultures may have for interpreting the expressions of others. Differences in attribution of expression intensity have also been documented among ethnic groups within the United States (Matsumoto, 1993).

Matsumoto's (1989) study described earlier also investigated the relationship between Hofstede's dimensions of culture and emotion intensity ratings. Two important findings emerged. First, there was a negative correlation between power distance and intensity ratings of anger, fear, and sadness, suggesting that cultures that emphasize status differences rate these emotions less intensely. Perhaps these emotions threaten status relationships, and thus are downplayed in emotional perception. Second, individualism was positively correlated with intensity ratings of anger and fear, suggesting that people of individualistic cultures see more intensity in these expressions. Not only can these findings be interpreted in relation to the behavioral tendencies we would expect as a result of high individualism or power distance; they also suggest that understanding dimensions of culture may be the key to explaining cultural differences in the perception of negative emotions.

Inferences about emotional experiences underlying facial expressions of emotion. Although cultures differed in their judgments of external display, it was unclear whether cultures also differed in their inferences about underlying experience, and if so, whether these differences were similar to those with regard to external display. Matsumoto, Kasri, and Kooken (in press) tested this notion by comparing American and Japanese judgments when separate ratings were obtained for expression intensity and subjective experience. Americans rated external display more intensely than the Japanese, replicating previous findings. The Japanese, however, rated internal experience more intensely than the Americans. Within-culture analyses indicated no significant differences between the two ratings for the Japanese. Significant differences were found, however, for the Americans, who consistently rated external display more intensely than subjective experience. Although the researchers had previously suggested that American–Japanese differences occurred because the Japanese suppressed their intensity ratings, these findings indicated that in fact it was the Americans who exaggerated their external display ratings relative to subjective experience, not the Japanese who suppressed. Not only are such findings wake-up calls to experienced cross-cultural researchers; they also force us to consider how culture produces these tendencies, and why.

Attributions of personality based on smiles. The smile is a common sign of greeting, acknowledgment, or acceptance. It is also used to mask emotions, and cultures may differ in the use of smiles for this purpose. In Friesen's (1972) study, for example, when Japanese and American men watched disgusting video clips with an experimenter in the room, the Japanese men used smiles to cover up their negative expressions much more often than the American men (Ekman, 1972; Friesen, 1972). To further investigate the meaning of those differences, Matsumoto and Kudoh (1993) obtained ratings from Japanese and Americans on smiling versus nonsmiling (neutral) faces with regard to intelligence, attractiveness, and sociability. Americans rated smiling faces as more intelligent than neutral faces; the Japanese, however, did not. Americans and Japanese both found smiling faces more sociable than neutral faces, but the difference was greater for Americans. These differences suggest that cultural display rules cause Japanese and Americans to attribute different meanings to the smile, and serve as a good explanation for perceived major differences in communication styles across cultures.

Implications of Cultural Differences in Emotional Perception for Emotion Universality

Over a period of 30 years, during which a large body of evidence has been collected by many cross-cultural researchers, the universality of facial expressions of emotion has gone from a possible explanatory hypothesis to a well-established psychological principle. Recently, however, some articles have questioned the research underlying universality. These criticisms of the judgment studies described earlier have centered on their methods (Russell, 1991, 1994, 1995), interpretations (Russell, 1994), and the use of language-specific terms for facial expressions of emotion (Wierzbicka, 1995).

Probably the greatest concern raised about universality involves the methods employed in the judgment studies. Over the years, many studies conducted independently by many laboratories around the world have used many methods. In his review, Russell (1994) raised several criticisms of these methods, including (1) the nature of the stimuli—the fact that photos are often preselected and the expressions are often posed; (2) the presentation of stimuli—the fact that stimuli are previewed in some studies, are generally presented to subjects in a within-subjects design, and are generally presented in a particular order that creates a context in which subjects can make better "guesses"; and (3) the response format—the fact that forced-choice methods are the predominant type of response alternative. In one of his latest efforts, Russell (1994) reanalyzed judgment data across a number of studies, separating studies by method, and also employing a Western/non-Western distinction among the countries to demonstrate that the methods employed may have biased responses in favor of Western cultures. (We discussed the validity of this distinction earlier.)

Wierzbicka (1995) has raised a different type of concern, suggesting that the six (or seven) basic emotions as generally labeled are language-specific terms. Instead, she suggests, we should speak of universals only in terms of "conceptual primitives." For example, when a person is recognizing a smile of happiness, he or she is reading the face as "I think: something good is happening, I feel something good because of this." Her position is that although facial expressions of emotion may indeed be universal, the methods that we have used to study them, including the use of emotion terms as response alternatives in judgment tasks, are limited and bound by the culture in which those terms arise, and cannot possibly be universal.

A number of writers have addressed these concerns. Ekman (1994) and Izard (1994), for example, both point out that although Russell's (1994) article appeared to be systematic in its presentation of evidence, it actually paid selective attention to those studies that helped to support his thesis. In particular, Russell's (1994) article failed to cite those studies that controlled for the various flaws that he suggested were responsible for skewing the previous universality findings. Russell's thesis was also flawed in that he used criticisms about one of several types of evidence for universality in facial expressions of emotion to argue against the entire basis of universality. He failed to mention studies on nonhuman primates and with infants and the congenitally blind, all of which strongly indicate that certain facial expressions of emotion are innate and universal. Examples in the primate literature include a recent study by Geen (1992), in which he found that rhesus monkeys reared in isolation showed "more or less normal-appearing facial expressions" (Geen, 1992, p. 277) when they were later placed with other monkeys. Hauser (1993) found evidence that, in rhesus monkeys as in humans, emotion expression is lateralized in the right hemisphere of the brain. In a review of studies conducted with blind children, Charlesworth and Kreutzer (1973) concluded that spontaneous expressions of blind children did not differ from the expressions of sighted children who had been exposed to visual examples of expressions their entire lives.

Wierzbicka's thesis has also been criticized in the literature. Winegar (1995), for example, is somewhat critical of Wierzbicka's conceptual primitives, as they are also constrained by culture. He goes so far as to suggest that one cannot ever avoid cultural specificity in studying psychological phenomena, and that even if we could agree upon, for example, the universality of evaluation, we would not be able to avoid the effect of culture on our theory building. Another writer, VanGeert (1995), agrees with the need for a coding procedure for universal emotions similar to Wierzbicka's conceptual primitives. He believes that we need a more precise measure, one in which each universal has a "specific physical definition" (p. 265). He then presents three dimensions on which he suggests that universals can be named and organized. In his description of one dimension, he eloquently suggests a distinction between what he calls "experiential" and "technical" universals. He believes that "emotions are experiential universals, that is, all people are in principle able to entertain a set of similar subjective experiences called the universal emotions. But the only way to refer to such shared emotions is by means of a technical language" (p. 206).

I agree with the basic premise of both Russell and Wierzbicka—that researchers need to be more aware of how conscious and unconscious cultural biases may affect their methods of data collection, analysis, and interpretation with regard to this and other topics. I do not believe, however, that the arguments they have proffered in the past are very convincing, for the reasons just described. In addition, I would like to make two other points germane to this topic.

First, concerns about the effect of different methodologies in the judgment studies conducted to date are empirical questions that can be addressed by research, not solely by argument. A piecemeal approach to the problem that addresses each issue in a separate study would not be a solution, for the very reason that Russell himself suggests: the interaction of multiple methodological parameters may contribute to results. Thus, the only possible empirical solution to this debate would be to conduct a "perfectly controlled and comprehensive study" (PCCS). The PCCS would systematically vary the following factors as independent variables in a multifactorial design: (1) type of subjects—literate and preliterate, and within literate, college and noncollege students; (2) type of stimuli—posed and spontaneous, and within both, emotional and nonemotional faces; (3) previewing and nonpreviewing of stimuli; (4) within- and between-subjects designs, and in within-subjects designs, different orders versus fixed orders; (5) type of response alternatives—open-ended, fixed responses, and scalar ratings; and (6) presence or absence of context manipulations, and if present, the exact type of manipulation. Any single study or group of studies that combines bits and pieces of these crucial aspects would not address the question of methodological influences on judgment, as one would never know how different levels of one factor influenced different levels of another. Only a single PCCS would address the issue. To be sure, the

PCCS is more fantasy than reality, and we will probably never see it in the literature. But it is important to understand what the parameters of the empirical response to the issues raised by Russell would look like. In the absence of evidence from such a PCCS, and with the preponderance of evidence that does exist, I see no merit in the claims concerning methodology.

Second, universality and cultural relativity are not mutually exclusive. As in the analogous nature versus nurture argument, if we view a phenomenon from only one perspective, we cannot see the whole picture. The perception of emotion can be *both* universal and culture-specific, depending on what aspect of perception we are talking about. Elsewhere (Yrizarry et al., in press), I have suggested at least five sources of variability in emotion perception that would produce cultural differences in emotion perception, even though the expression being judged may be universal. These sources include (1) semantic overlap in the linguistic categories and mental concepts related to emotion that are used in the judgment process, (2) overlapping facial components in the expressions, (3) cognitive overlap in events and experiences related to emotion, (4) personality biases in social cognition, and (5) culture. Future research needs to tease out the separate and interactive effects of all these sources on the nature of the judgment process.

In summary, therefore, the available evidence suggests that perception can have both universal and culture-specific elements. Elsewhere (Matsumoto, 1996a), I have suggested a mechanism similar to Ekman and Friesen's neurocultural theory of expression to describe how cultural similarities and differences in emotion perception or judgment can be obtained (see Figure 11.3). This mechanism implies that judgments of emotion are affected by (1) a facial affect recognition program that is innate and universal (similar to Ekman and Friesen's facial affect program), and (2) culture-specific **decoding rules** that intensify, deintensify, mask, or qualify the perception (see Buck, 1984). Thus, when we perceive emotions in others, I believe that the expression is recognized through a process analogous to template matching with the universal facial prototypes of emotion. Before a judgment is rendered, however, that stimulus is also joined by learned rules about perceiving such expressions in others. I further believe that this mechanism is as basic to emotion communication across cultures as Ekman and Friesen's original neurocultural theory of expression. Future studies will need to elaborate more fully on the contexts and parameters of the decoding rules, and how they influence judgments of not only posed expressions in the laboratory but spontaneous expressions in real life across cultures. Future research will also need to examine judgments of partial, blended, and ambiguous expressions across cultures.

Culture and the Experience of Emotion

When people of different cultures feel an emotion, do they experience it in the same or different ways? Do they experience the same types of emotions? Do they experience some emotions more frequently, or more strongly, than others?

Figure 11.3 A neurocultural theory of emotional perception

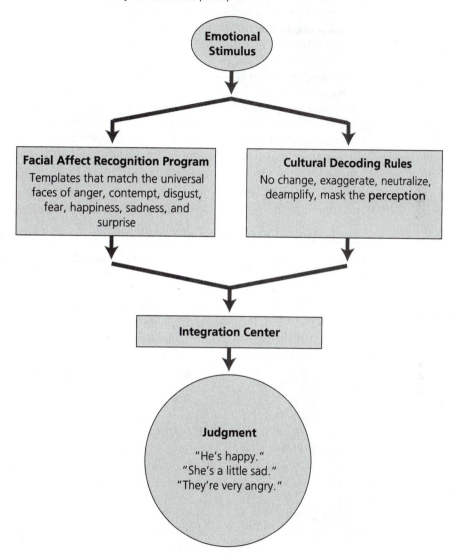

Do they have the same types of nonverbal reactions, or physiological and bodily symptoms and sensations?

These questions are important both theoretically and practically, in terms of our everyday lives. Theoretically, the work serving as the basis for the universality of emotion expression and perception suggests that all humans may also share the same experiential base of emotion—at least for those emotions that have a pancultural signal in the face. That is, however, an empirical question; it is at least hypothetically possible, though not very likely, that our emotional experiences are not necessarily associated with pancultural signals of emotion. On the practical side, knowing that we share the same experiential base of emotion is important in having empathy for other people's experiences; empathy (discussed in Chapters 14 and 18) is important for the development of intercultural sensitivity and for successful interpersonal and intercultural experiences.

In the past few years, several major research programs have examined the degree to which emotional experience is universal (common to all people of all cultures) and culturally specific (different for people of different cultures). Two major lines of research—one led by Klaus Scherer and Harald Wallbott in Europe, the other represented by a host of independent researchers—have addressed these questions. Together, they suggest that many aspects of our emotional experiences are indeed universal, whereas other aspects of our emotional lives are culture-specific.

Universality of Emotional Experiences

Scherer and his colleagues have conducted a number of studies using questionnaires designed to assess the quality and nature of emotional experiences in many different cultures. The first series of studies used basically the same questionnaire format. An initial study (Scherer, Summerfield, & Wallbott, 1983) involved about 600 participants in five European countries. In a second study (Scherer, Summerfield, & Wallbott, 1986), they collected additional data from three more European countries, raising the total to eight countries. A third study (Scherer, Matsumoto, Wallbott, & Kudoh, 1988) then compared a weighted sample of the European participants to samples from the United States and Japan, to test whether the pattern of results obtained in Europe would be the same when comparing European to non-European cultures.

The methodology was basically the same in all cultures. Participants completed a questionnaire about four basic emotions: joy/happiness, sadness/grief, fear/anxiety, and anger/rage. They began by describing a situation in which they felt that emotion—what happened, who was involved, where and when it happened, and how long it lasted. They then provided information concerning their nonverbal reactions, physiological sensations, and verbal utterances. With the exception of three scalar ratings, all responses were open-ended, and all were coded by trained coders for the purpose of data analysis.

The results from the first two studies indicated a surprising degree of similarity in the emotional experiences of the European respondents. Although their responses did vary according to culture, the effect of culture was rather small, especially in comparison to the differences among the emotions themselves. That is, the differences among the four emotions tested were much larger than the differences among the cultures. The researchers concluded that at least the emotions tested seem to share a universal experiential base across humans.

Moreover, when the European data were compared to the American and Japanese data, Scherer and his colleagues found that, although the effect of culture was slightly larger, it was still very small relative to the differences found among the emotions. Across all three studies, therefore, the researchers concluded that culture can and does influence the experience of these emotions, but this influence is considerably smaller than the basic differences among the emotions themselves. More plainly, cultures show much more similarity than difference.

The differences among the emotions that seem to be universal across cultures are summarized in Table 11.2. For example, joy and anger generally occur more frequently than sadness and fear. Joy and sadness are experienced more intensely than anger and fear, and for longer durations. Anger and fear are associated with more ergotropic arousal (muscle symptoms and perspiration) than sadness and joy, whereas sadness is associated with more trophotropic arousal (such as stomach symptoms, lump in the throat, crying). Joy and anger are also experienced with higher temperature than fear and sadness. Joy is associated with approach behavior, and joy and anger are associated with more verbal and nonverbal reactions.

The second set of studies conducted by Scherer and his colleagues, using basically the same type of questionnaire methodology, involved 2,921 participants in 37 countries on five continents (see Wallbott & Scherer, 1986, for a first report; Scherer & Wallbott, 1994, for a complete report). The original questionnaire was modified to include three more emotions—shame, guilt, and disgust—for a total of seven emotions. In addition, many of the questions were adjusted from an open-ended response format to a closed-ended format, incorporating many of the response codes from the previous studies as alternatives. Analysis of the data led to the following conclusion:

Table 11.2 Summary of the Differences among Emotions Reported in the First Set of Studies by Scherer and Colleagues

Domain	Variable	Finding
Subjective feeling	Time distance (long ago to recently)	Sadness = fear < joy = anger
	Intensity (weaker to stronger)	Anger = fear < sadness = joy
	Duration (shorter to longer)	Fear < anger < joy = sadness
	Control (weaker to stronger)	Joy < fear = sadness = anger
Physiological symptoms	Ergotropic arousal (weaker to stronger)	Sadness = joy < anger < fear
	Trophotropic arousal (weaker to stronger)	Joy < fear = anger < sadness
	Temperature (colder to warmer)	Fear < sadness < joy < anger
Behavioral reactions	Approach/withdrawal (away to toward)	Fear = sadness = anger < joy
	Nonverbal behavior (little to much)	Fear < sadness < joy = anger
	Verbal behavior (little to much)	Fear = sadness < joy = anger

Source: Based on Scherer, Summerfield, & Wallbott, 1983.

For all response domains—subjective feelings, physiological symptoms, and motor expression patterns—the seven emotions differed significantly and strongly (in terms of relative effect sizes) among each other. Geographical and socio-cultural factors, as reflected in country effect sizes, also affected emotional experience, but the effects were much smaller than those for differences among the emotions. Significant interaction effects indicate that geographical and socio-cultural factors can have differential effects on specific emotions, but that the size of these effects is relatively small. These results warrant the conclusion that there are strong and consistent differences between the reaction patterns for the seven emotions and that these are independent of the country studied. It could be argued that these universal differences in self-reports of emotional reactions are evidence for psychobiological emotional patterning. (Scherer & Wallbott, 1994, p. 317)

These findings indicate once again that the experience of these emotions is universal—that regardless of culture, people share the same basic emotional experiences. Although culture does influence the experience of these emotions, this influence is not nearly as large as the seemingly innate differences among the emotions themselves. Again, emotional experience is much more similar than different. The universal differences among emotions reported in this second, broader set of studies are summarized in Table 11.3. Another study, involving participants in four cultures—the United States, Japan, Hong Kong, and the People's Republic of China—conducted by a separate team of researchers (Mauro, Sato, & Tucker, 1992), produced similar results concerning the universality of emotional experience.

Cultural Differences in Emotional Experiences

Although cultural differences found in the studies just described were considerably smaller than differences among the emotions, they nevertheless existed. For example, in Scherer and colleagues' comparison of Europeans, Americans, and Japanese, the Japanese reported experiencing all emotions—joy, sadness, fear, and anger—more often than either the Americans or the Europeans. The Americans, in turn, reported experiencing joy and anger more often than the Europeans. Americans reported feeling their emotions for longer durations and at greater intensities than did the Europeans or the Japanese. Japanese respondents on the whole reported fewer hand and arm gestures, whole body movements, and vocal and facial reactions to the emotions than did Americans or Europeans. Americans reported the highest degree of expressivity in both facial and vocal reactions. Americans and Europeans also reported many more physiological sensations than did the Japanese. These sensations included changes in temperature (becoming flushed, hot), cardiovascular changes (heart racing, pulse changing), and gastric disturbances (stomach problems).

How and why do cultural differences in emotional experience exist? When doing such large-scale studies as those conducted by Scherer and his colleagues, it is virtually impossible to generate specific hypotheses about specific differ-

Table 11.3 Summary of Differences among Emotions Reported in the Second Set of Studies by Scherer and Wallbott

Domain	Variable	Finding
Subjective feeling	Duration (from shorter to longer)	Fear = disgust = shame ≤ anger < guilt < joy < sadness
	Intensity (from weaker to stronger)	Shame = guilt = disgust < anger = fear ≤ joy = sadness
	Control (from low to high)	Joy < anger < disgust < sadness = fear < guilt < shame
Physiological symptoms	Ergotropic arousal (from weak to strong)	Disgust = joy = guilt = sadness ≤ shame < anger < fear
	Trophotropic arousal (from weak to strong)	Joy < shame = anger – disgust ≤ guilt ≤ fear < sadness
	Temperature (from cold to warm/hot)	Fear = sadness < disgust < guilt < anger < shame < joy
Behavioral reactions	Approach/withdrawal behavior (from withdrawal to approach)	Shame = guilt = disgust = sadness < fear < anger < joy
	Nonverbal reactions (from little to much)	Guilt < disgust = shame = fear < sadness ≤ anger < joy
	Paralinguistic behavior (from little to much)	Disgust = guilt ≤ shame ≤ sadness < fear < joy < anger
	Verbal behavior (from little to much)	Fear = sadness = shame = guilt < disgust < anger = joy

Source: Adapted from Scherer & Wallbott, 1994.

ences in relation to specific countries. Instead, they have tried to account for cultural differences among the countries in their emotional experiences in two ways. In one (Wallbott & Scherer, 1995), they examined the relationship between the experience of shame and guilt and Hofstede's four dimensions of culture: individualism (IN), power distance (PD), uncertainty avoidance (UA), and masculinity (MA). They selected all countries in their second set of studies that were also included in Hofstede's multinational study of cultural values. They then classified the countries as high, medium, or low on each of the four cultural dimensions, and tested differences among these classifications in emotional experience. Their results were fascinating. Shame, for example, was experienced with relatively shorter duration, as less immoral, and more often accompanied by laughter and smiles in collectivistic cultures than in individualistic cultures. Shame in collectivistic cultures was also characterized by high felt temperature and low trophotropic arousal. The same findings were also obtained for cultures high in PD and low in UA. These findings are interesting indeed because they are contrary to what one would predict based on previous writings (for example, Piers & Singer, 1971) that have characterized collectivistic cultures as "shame cultures."

In another attempt to uncover possible bases of cultural differences in emotional experience, Wallbott and Scherer (1988) correlated their data with the gross national product (GNP) of each of the countries in their studies. They found "mostly significant negative correlations of GNP with recentness of emotional experience, duration, and intensity. These correlations indicate that the poorer the country is, the longer lasting, the more intense, and the further in the past the emotions are. Subjects from poorer countries seem to report 'more important and more severe' emotional incidents" (Wallbott & Scherer, 1988, p. 271).

A host of other researchers, led by Kitayama and Markus (1991, 1994, 1995), Wierzbicka (1994), and Shweder (1994) have taken a different approach in describing cultural influences on emotional experiences. Using a "functionalist" approach, these researchers view emotion as a set of "socially shared scripts" composed of physiological, behavioral, and subjective components. They suggest that these scripts develop as individuals are enculturated into their culture, and that they are intimately and inextricably linked to the culture in which they are produced and with which they interact. Emotion, therefore, reflects the cultural environment in which individuals develop and live, and are as integral a part of culture as morality and ethics are. Markus and Kitayama (1991; see also Chapter 2 for a review) cite evidence from a variety of sources to support this view, including studies that demonstrate a difference between cultures in the experience of socially engaged versus disengaged emotions, and in cultural patterns of feeling good and happiness.

In this view, culture shapes emotion. Because different cultures have different realities and ideals that produce different psychological needs and goals, they produce differences in habitual emotional tendencies. Their model of the "cultural construction of emotion" is summarized in Figure 11.4.

Many writers who take this functionalist approach go beyond describing the role of culture in constructing emotional experiences to challenge the universal and possibly biologically innate aspects of emotion. Basically, their argument is that precisely because of the intimate and inextricably intertwined relationship between culture and emotion, emotion could not possibly be biologically "fixed" for all people. They suggest that the universality of emotion is a misnomer, and that supportive findings derive from the experimental and theoretical biases of the researchers that have reported them.

Personally, I do not believe that the functionalist approach to emotion, based on cultural construction and socially shared scripts, is necessarily antithetical or antagonistic to the universality of emotion. For one thing, these researchers have studied different emotions. The universality position is limited to a small set of discrete emotions that have a corresponding unique facial expression. Studies conducted by the functionalists have incorporated a broad

Figure 11.4 The cultural shaping of emotion

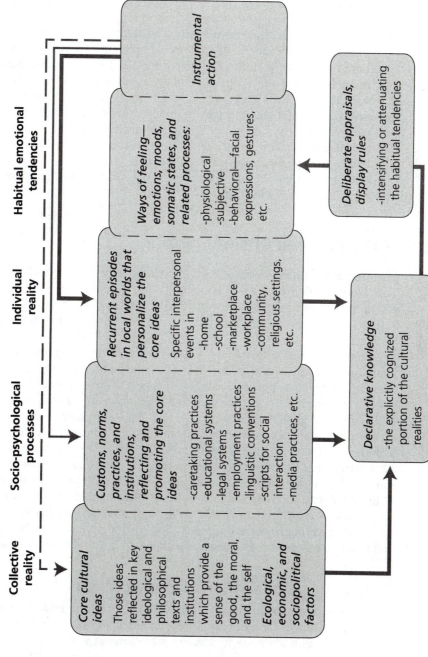

Source: Markus & Kitayama, 1994. Copyright © 1994 by the American Psychological Association. Reprinted with permission.

range of emotional experience that goes well beyond this limited set of universal emotions. Also, these researchers have studied different aspects of emotion. The universality of emotion is based on the existence of pancultural signals of emotional expression in the face. Much of the research on the cultural construction of emotion is based on the subjective experience of emotion, and the emotion lexicons in language that are used to describe and represent those experiences. It is not inconceivable that one component of emotion may be universal while the other is culturally relative. Finally, the existence of universals and innate biological substrates of emotion does not preclude the possibility that cultures can also construct much of their experience. As mentioned earlier, the universal bases of emotion may provide a standard platform upon which such construction may take place. It seems to me, therefore, that cultural construction of emotional experience can occur above and beyond the baseline that is provided by basic emotions with universal expressions. Future research in this area may be guided by such complementary viewpoints rather than driven by arbitrarily antagonistic positions.

Culture and the Antecedents of Emotion

Emotion antecedents are the events or situations that trigger or elicit an emotion. For example, losing a loved one may be an antecedent of sadness; getting an "A" in a class in which you wanted to do well may elicit happiness or joy. In the scientific literature, emotion antecedents are also known as emotion elicitors.

For many years, scholars have debated whether emotion antecedents are similar or different across cultures. On the one hand, a number of scientists have argued that emotion antecedents must be similar across cultures, at least for the universal emotions, because these emotions are panculturally similar and all humans share their experiential and expression base. The results from cross-cultural studies reviewed earlier on emotion expression, perception, and experience all tend to support such a view. On the other hand, many writers have argued that cultures must differ in their emotion antecedents; that is, the same events in different cultures can and do trigger entirely different emotions in those cultures. Sadness is not necessarily elicited in all cultures at funerals, for example, and getting an A in a class may not always elicit joy. There are many other examples of such cross-cultural differences in emotion elicitors, and research has provided considerable support for this viewpoint as well.

Cultural Similarities in Emotion Antecedents

A considerable number of studies have supported the universality of emotion antecedents. Boucher and Brandt (1981), for example, asked participants in the United States and Malaysia to describe situations in which someone caused someone else to feel anger, disgust, fear, happiness, sadness, or surprise. Their selection of the emotions to study was guided by the previous universality research. A total of 96 antecedents to the various emotions were generated. A separate group of American participants then rated the antecedents, attempting to identify which emotion each elicited. The results indicated that the Americans correctly classified the antecedents equally well regardless of whether they were originally generated by Americans or by Malaysians; that is, culture of origin did not affect the classification. Subsequently, Brandt and Boucher (1985) replicated these findings using American, Korean, and Samoan participants. Taken together, the results suggest that the antecedents shared a common base cross-culturally, supporting views of pancultural similarity in emotion antecedents.

The largest concerted effort to study emotion antecedents across cultures was the work by Scherer and his colleagues described earlier. In their studies, respondents were asked to describe a situation or event in which they experienced anger, joy, fear, sadness, disgust, shame, and guilt (four emotions in the first set of studies; all seven emotions in the second set). Again, their selection of these emotions was driven by the results of the previous universality research (some studies, not reviewed here, had shown shame and guilt to be universal). Trained coders then coded the situations described by participants into general categories such as good news and bad news, temporary and permanent separation, and success and failure in achievement situations. No culture-specific antecedent category was necessary to code the data, indicating that all categories of events generally occurred in all cultures to produce each of the seven emotions studied.

In addition, Scherer and his colleagues compared the relative frequency with which each of the antecedent events elicited emotions. Again, they found many similarities across cultures. For example, the most frequent elicitors of happiness across cultures were "relationships with friends," "temporary meetings with friends," and "achievement situations." The most frequent elicitors of anger were "relationships" and "injustice." The most frequent elicitors of sadness were "relationships" and "death." These findings also supported the view that emotion antecedents are similar across cultures.

A small number of other studies have also reported similarities across cultures in emotion antecedents. Galati and Sciaky (1995), for example, found that antecedents for anger, disgust, fear, happiness, sadness, and surprise were similar in northern and southern Italy. Buunk and Hupka (1987) reported that flirtatious behaviors were considered elicitors of jealousy in all seven cultures they studied. Levy (1973) concluded that many situations that give rise to emotions in Tahiti would give rise to the same emotions elsewhere.

Cultural Differences in Emotion Antecedents

Research has also provided considerable support for cultural differences in emotion antecedents. Scherer and associates, for example, found many cultural differences in the relative frequencies of the various antecedent events reported by their respondents (along with the cultural similarities reported earlier). Cultural events, the birth of a new family member, body-centered "basic pleasures," and achievement-related situations were more important antecedents of joy for Europeans and Americans than for the Japanese. Death of family members or close friends, physical separation from loved ones, and world news were more frequent triggers of sadness for Europeans and Americans than for the Japanese. Problems in relationships, however, produced more sadness for the Japanese than for Americans or Europeans. Strangers and achievement-related situations elicited more fear for Americans, while novel situations, traffic, and relationships were more frequent elicitors of fear for the Japanese. Finally, situations involving strangers were more frequent elicitors of anger for the Japanese than for the Americans or Europeans. Situations involving relationships brought about more anger for Americans than for Japanese. These findings make it clear that the same type of situation or event will not necessarily trigger the same emotion in people across cultures.

Several other studies have provided similar or comparable results (for example, see review by Mesquita & Frijda, 1992). Collectively, they suggest considerable differences among cultures in the antecedents to emotion.

Coexistence of Similarities and Differences in Emotion Antecedents

Given that cross-cultural research has found both similarities and differences in emotion antecedents across cultures, how can we reconcile these findings? Elsewhere (Matsumoto, 1996a), I have suggested that one useful way to interpret cross-cultural findings on emotion antecedents is to make a distinction between latent and manifest content in events and situations that produce emotions. Manifest content is the actual event or situation, such as spending time with friends, attending a funeral, or having someone cut in front of you in line. Latent content is the psychological meanings associated with the manifest content that underlie the situation or event. For example, the latent content underlying spending time with friends may be the achievement of psychological goals of warmth and intimacy with others. The latent content underlying attending a funeral may be the loss of a loved object. The latent content underlying someone cutting in front of you in line may be a perception of injustice or obstruction of a goal.

My review of the cross-cultural research suggests universality in the latent content of emotion antecedents. That is, certain psychological themes produce the same emotions for most people in most cultures. The latent content underlying sadness is inevitably loss of a loved object. The latent content underlying happiness is inevitably achievement of some goal that is important to the person. The latent content underlying anger is often injustice or goal obstruction. Similarly, a few core latent-content constructs underlie each of the universal emotions that are found consistently across cultures. These core constructs appear to allow these emotions to share some universal basis across all cultures.

At the same time, cultures differ in the exact situations, events, or occurrences that are associated with the latent content. That is, there is not always a one-to-one correspondence between latent and manifest content across cultures. Whereas death may produce sadness in one culture, for example, it may produce another emotion in another culture. In one culture, the manifest content of death may be associated with the latent content of loss of loved object, producing sadness; in another culture, the manifest content of death may be associated with a different latent content, such as achievement of a higher spiritual goal, producing a different emotion, happiness. Thus, the same manifest event, may be associated with different underlying psychological themes, which give rise to different emotions.

Also, the same latent themes may be associated with different manifest content across cultures. For example, threats to one's personal well-being may be a psychological theme underlying emotions of fear. In one culture, this theme may be associated with being out alone late at night in a large city. In another culture, this theme may be associated with traffic rather than being out late. Despite the differences in manifest content, both situations may result in fear in the respective cultures because of the similarity in latent content.

People of different cultures learn to associate culture-specific events, situations, and occurrences (manifest content) with a limited set of core psychological themes (latent content) that produce emotions. Although there is high agreement across cultures on the nature of that latent content, manifest content is more variable across cultures. This distinction explains why cross-cultural research has found both similarities and differences in emotion antecedents. This concept of latent content is also useful in connection with another emotion-related process: appraisal.

Culture and Emotion Appraisal

Cultural Similarities in Emotion Appraisal

Emotion appraisal can be loosely defined as the process by which people evaluate the events, situations, or occurrences that lead to their having emotions. This aspect of the study of human emotion has a long and complex history, yet basic questions about the nature of the appraisal process in relation to culture remain. How do people of different cultures think about or evaluate the events that trigger their emotions? Do emotions and their eliciting situations show commonalities across cultures? Or do people of different cultures think about emotion antecedents differently?

In the past decade, a number of important and interesting studies have found that many appraisal processes appear to be consistent across cultures, suggesting the possible universality of these processes in eliciting emotions. Mauro, Sato, and Tucker (1992), for example, asked participants in the United States, Hong Kong, Japan, and the People's Republic of China to complete an extensive questionnaire requiring them to describe a situation that elicited one of 16 different emotions, including the universal emotions. For each emotion, they answered a comprehensive list of questions related to a number of appraisal dimensions: pleasantness, attention, certainty, coping, control, responsibility, anticipated effort, goal/need conduciveness, legitimacy, and norm/self-compatibility. The researchers found few, if any, cultural differences on primitive dimensions of cognitive appraisal: pleasantness, attention, certainty, coping, and goal/need conduciveness. In addition, they found only a few cultural differences on two dimensions: legitimacy and norm/self-compatibility. They interpreted these findings as evidence of universality in emotion appraisal processes.

Although the selection of the appraisal dimensions included in this study was driven by theoretical considerations, Mauro and associates (1992) also tested empirically to discover the smallest number of dimensions necessary to describe the differences among the emotions. They used a statistical technique called a principal components analysis, which groups variables into a smaller number of factors, based on the interrelationships among the original set of variables in the analysis. The results of this analysis indicated that only seven dimensions were necessary to explain emotion elicitation: pleasantness, certainty, effort, attention, perceived control of others, appropriateness, and control of the circumstances. When cultural differences were tested on these dimensions, they found the same results—that there were no cultural differences on the more primitive dimensions, and only a few on the more complex ones. Again, these results suggest that these dimensions of emotion appraisal are universal, at least for the emotions included in their study.

Roseman and colleagues (1995) used a different methodology to study the appraisal processes of sadness, anger, and fear in American and Indian participants. They showed respondents a facial expression corresponding with one of these emotions and asked them to label the emotion portrayed, describe what had happened to cause the person to feel that emotion, and respond to 26 questions about their evaluations of the event. They found that, for both Americans and Indians, appraisals of powerlessness characterized incidents eliciting anger and fear, whereas appraisals of relative power differences brought forth anger. Also, in both cultures, appraisals that an event was caused by someone else elicited anger but not sadness or fear, whereas events caused by circumstances elicited sadness or fear but not anger. These findings provide further support for cultural similarities in emotion appraisal processes.

Perhaps the largest cross-cultural study on emotion appraisal processes is Scherer's, described earlier involving 3,000 participants in 37 countries. In that study, you will remember, respondents were asked to describe an event or situation in which they experienced one of seven emotions: anger, disgust, fear, happiness, sadness, shame, and guilt. Respondents then answered a series of questions designed to assess their appraisals of the events, including questions concerning novelty-expectation, intrinsic pleasantness, goal conduciveness, fairness, coping potential, norms, and self-ideals. Analyses of these data (Scherer, 1997a, 1997b) indicated that, although differences existed both among emotions and among countries, the differences according to country were much smaller than the differences according to emotion. Put another way, emotion appraisal processes were more similar than different across cultures. The appraisal processes found to be associated with the seven emotions studied were as follows:

- Happiness—high goal conduciveness and high coping potential
- Fear—sudden, novel events caused by others or by circumstances, obstructive to needs, where one feels powerless
- Anger—goal obstruction, immoral, but one has sufficient coping potential to deal with
- Sadness—low goal conduciveness and low coping potential
- Disgust—strong immorality and unfairness
- Shame and guilt—high self-attribution of responsibility for an action, high inconsistency of this action with one's internal standards

Again, these findings indicate a high degree of cross-cultural similarity in emotion appraisal processes. They support the notion that emotions are a universal phenomenon with psychobiological similarities across all humans regardless of culture, a position that is consistent with previous findings regarding the universality of many of these emotions.

Cultural Differences in Emotion Appraisal

Despite the strong evidence for cross-cultural consistency in emotion appraisal processes, each of the studies just reviewed reported a number of cultural differences as well. In all the studies, the cultural differences were relatively small compared to differences attributed to emotions regardless of culture, which is why all of the authors argued for at least some degree of universality in emotion appraisal processes. Nevertheless, the cultural differences that were obtained need to be accounted for.

For example, one early study comparing American and Japanese responses collected as part of the large-scale study by Scherer and his colleagues showed considerable cultural differences in the ways people in different cultures evaluate emotion-eliciting situations (Matsumoto, Kudoh, Scherer, & Wallbott, 1988). The effect of emotion-eliciting events on self-esteem varied by culture: Emotions had a more positive effect on self-esteem and self-confidence for Americans than they did for the Japanese. Attributions of causality of emotions also varied by culture: Americans attribute the cause of sadness-producing events to others, whereas Japanese attribute the cause of sadness to themselves. Americans are also more likely to attribute the causes of joy, fear, and shame to other people, whereas the Japanese tend to attribute the causes of these emotions to chance or fate. Japanese believe more than Americans do that no action or behavior is necessary after an emotion is elicited. For emotions such as fear, more Americans than Japanese believe they can do something to influence the situation positively. For anger and disgust, more Americans believe they are powerless and dominated by the event and its consequences. For shame and guilt, more Japanese than Americans pretended that nothing had happened and tried to think of something else.

Other cultural differences have also been reported. In Roseman et al.'s (1995) study, for example, Indians appraised sadness-, fear-, and anger-eliciting events as more consistent with their motives. They also appraised their power in those events to be less than Americans did, and the probability of those events to be lower. Mauro and associates (1992) reported differences among the four cultures in their study on dimensions of control, responsibility, and anticipated effort. They suggested that these cultural differences were related to differences on individualism versus collectivism, because differences on this dimension would be associated with differences in perceived control over events. Indeed, they found that the Americans generally had higher control scores than did respondents in the other three countries.

In both of his studies, Scherer (1997a, 1997b) reported cultural differences in emotion appraisal. In the first, Scherer (1997a) classified each of the 37 countries into one of six geopolitical regions: North/Central Europe, Mediterranean Basin, New World, Latin America, Asia, and Africa. Correlations among the appraisal dimensions across regions indicated that, although there were great similarities across regions in appraisal processes, Latin America and Africa seemed to differ slightly from the other regions. In order to get a better handle on the nature of these possible cultural differences, Scherer (1997b) further classified the countries on a number of different dimensions, according to their cultural values (using Hofstede's dimensions of individualism and masculinity), climate, and socioeconomic and demographic factors, along with geopolitical region. He found that for all emotions except happiness, participants from African countries appraised the emotion-eliciting events as higher on unfairness, external causation, and immorality than did people from other regions. Respondents from Latin America had lower scores on perceptions of immorality than did people from other regions. Analyses involving climate, cultural values, and socioeconomic and demographic factors, did not account for these differences. Still, Scherer suggested that a general factor of urbanism may account for both sets of findings (Africa and Latin America).

Collectively, these studies suggest that, although many appraisal processes appear to be universal across humans, there is room for some cultural differences, especially in appraisal dimensions that require judgments relative to cultural or social norms such as fairness and morality. It would appear, therefore, that cultural differences may occur on these more "complex" appraisal dimensions, but not on more "primitive" dimensions, as suggested by Roseman and associates (1995). There appears to be something inherent and intrinsic to all humans that allows for the elicitation of a set of universal emotional experiences, but a role for culture in complex cognitive processes that allow for finer distinctions among emotions. These findings and interpretations are entirely congruent with the findings reported throughout this chapter on the universal and culturally relative aspects of emotion. While cross-cultural research on emotion appraisals has generally involved only a small set of emotions that are considered universal, future studies can expand on these findings by including a broader range of emotions to flesh out possible greater cultural differences in appraisal processes for more culturally relative emotions.

Culture and the Concept and Language of Emotion

In the final section of the chapter, we examine how culture influences the concept of emotion itself, and the languages used to represent it around the world. Indeed, throughout this chapter, we have been discussing emotion as if it means the same thing to all people. Researchers who study emotion also fall into that same trap. And certainly, the studies documenting the universality of emotional expression, recognition, experience, antecedents, and appraisals would argue for similarity in the concept, understanding, and language of at least that small set of emotions. But what about other terms and phenomena we call "emotion"? Let's begin our examination by looking at emotions as we understand them in the United States.

Emotions in Everyday American Life

In the United States, we place a premium on feelings. We all recognize that each of us is unique and that we have our own individual feelings about the things, events, situations, and people around us. We consciously try to be aware of our feelings, to be "in touch" with them, as we say. To be in touch with our feelings and to understand the world around us emotionally is to be a mature adult in our society.

We place importance and value on feelings and emotions throughout the life span. We cherish our feelings as adults, and we actively try to recognize the feelings of our children and of other young ones around us. It is not uncommon for parents to ask their young children how they feel about their swimming lessons, their piano lessons, their teachers at school, or the broccoli on their plates. Parents often give considerable weight to the feelings of their children in making decisions that affect them. "If Johnny doesn't want to do it, we shouldn't make him do it" is a common sentiment among parents in the United States. Indeed, children's emotions are afforded almost the same status as the emotions of adults and the older generations.

Much therapeutic work in psychology centers around human emotions. The goal of individual psychotherapy systems is often to get people to become more aware of their feelings and emotions and to accept them. Much psychotherapeutic work is focused on helping individuals freely express the feelings and emotions they may have bottled up inside. In group therapy, the emphasis is on communicating feelings toward others in the group and listening to and accepting the expressions of feelings by others. This emphasis is also prevalent in work groups outside of psychotherapy. Industrial and organizational interventions are common, and much time, effort, and energy are spent establishing better lines of communication among employees and recognizing the feelings and emotions of individuals.

How American society values and structures people's feelings and emotions is directly related to the values that the American culture fosters. In the United States, rugged individualism has been a cornerstone of the dominant culture, and part of that rugged individualism means that we recognize and value the unique aspects of each and every person. Diversity of feelings and emotions is part of this package; in fact, it may be the most important part in identifying individuals because emotions themselves are highly personalized and individual. Children are valued as separate entities, and their feelings are valued. When we "fix" something through psychotherapeutic intervention, the therapist often tries to help the client discover his or her emotions and express them.

Emotions as Viewed by American Psychologists

Even the study of emotions in American science has this flavor or twist. The earliest American psychologist credited with an important theory of emotion was William James. In the second volume of his *Principles of Psychology* (1890), James suggested that emotions occur as a result of our behavioral reaction to a stimulus. For example, if we see a bear, we run away from it, and we then interpret our running and breathing and the other visceral changes in our body as an emotion we label *fear*. Another scholar, C. Lange, wrote about emotion in terms very similar to James's at about the same time (1887). This theory is called the James/Lange theory of emotion.

Various other theories about emotion have been proffered since James's. Cannon (1927), for example, argued that autonomic arousal is too slow to account for changes in emotional experience. Instead, he and Bard argued that emotional experience results from direct stimulation of brain centers in the cortex that produce the conscious experience of emotion (Bard & Mountcastle, 1948). Thus, we feel fear when we see the bear because of the stimulation of certain brain centers that trigger that reaction. In this view, our running and breathing occur as a result of that fear, not as precursors to it.

In 1962, Schachter and Singer published a very influential study on emotion, suggesting that emotional experiences depend solely on the individual's interpretation of the environment in which he or she is being aroused. According to this theory, emotions are not differentiated physiologically. Instead, what is important in the production of emotional experience is how the person interprets the events being experienced. Emotion is labeling the arousal or behavior in that situation.

Despite the apparent differences among these theories about emotion, they are similar in the way in which American culture has "guided" these scientists' approach. All suggest an important role for the subjective experience of emotion—that is, experiencing inner feelings. The James/Lange, Cannon/Bard, and Schacter/Singer theories all attempt to explain the nature of that subjective, inner state we call emotion. They all view that subjective feeling as emotion, though they offer different explanations of how it occurs. Thus, emotion is an introspective, individual, private event that has meaning to oneself as an individual. This focus on the introspective, subjective feeling of emotion helps us place primary importance on emotion in our lives, whether as children or adults, caregivers or care receivers. Being in touch with our feelings, finding ways to express them, and recognizing and accepting that others have different feelings are all ways in which American culture has molded our emotions. And these are exactly the ways American scientists have sought to understand them.

Another major source of theories and research on emotion is emotional expression, central to the universality studies described earlier. These evolutionary theories also posit a central role for subjective, introspective, inner feelings. That is, by focusing on the expression of emotion, they imply that something—emotion—is being expressed. Because emotional expressions are outward displays of inner experience, these theories assume that internal, subjective experience is an important part (perhaps the most important part) of emotion.

This view of emotion makes good, intuitive sense to many of us. But this way of understanding emotion may be specific to American culture. Do other cultures view emotion the same way? Cross-cultural studies suggest that while there is a basic consensus across cultures on what an emotion is, there are also some interesting differences.

Cultural Similarities and Differences in the Concept of Emotion

Many studies have been conducted in the fields of anthropology and psychology to address this important issue. Indeed, the sheer number of studies and the amount of information about emotion in these various social science disciplines speaks to the importance of emotion in human life and the recognition of that importance by scholars. Ethnographic approaches—the in-depth immersion and study of single cultures on their own merits that originates from anthropology—are especially useful in helping to uncover how different cultures define and understand the concept we call emotion. A few years ago, Russell (1991) reviewed much of the cross-cultural and anthropological literature on emotion concepts and pointed out many ways in which cultures do indeed differ, sometimes considerably, in their definitions and understanding of emotion. His review provides a strong basis for discussion of this topic.

The concept and definition of emotion.   First of all, Russell (1991) points out, not all cultures have a word that corresponds to our word *emotion*. Levy (1973, 1983) reports that Tahitians do not have a word for emotion; nor, according to Lutz (1980, as reported in Russell, 1991; Lutz, 1983), do the Ifaluks of Micronesia. The fact that some cultures do not even have a word that corresponds to our word *emotion* is important; clearly, in these cultures, the concept of emotion is different from ours. Perhaps it is not as important to these cultures as it is to ours. Or perhaps what we know as emotion is labeled differently, in an untranslatable way, and refers to something other than internal, subjective feelings. In this case, too, their concept of emotion would be quite different from ours.

But most cultures of the world do have a word or concept for what we call *emotion.* Brandt and Boucher (1986) examined the concepts of depression in eight different cultures, whose languages included Indonesian, Japanese, Korean, Malaysian, Spanish, and Sinhalese. Each of the languages had a word for emotion, suggesting the cross-cultural existence of this concept. But even if a culture has a word for emotion, that culture's word may have different connotations, and thus different meanings, than our English word *emotion.* For example, Matsuyama, Hama, Kawamura, and Mine (1978) analyzed emotional words from the Japanese language, which included some words that are typically considered emotions (for example, *angry, sad*). Some words were included, however, that Americans would not consider to be emotions (for example, *considerate, lucky*). Samoans do not have a word for emotion but do have a word (*lagona*) that refers to feelings and sensations (Gerber, 1975, as reported in Russell, 1991).

In summary, not all cultures of the world have a word or concept for what we label *emotion* in English, and even among those that do, it may not mean the same thing as the English word *emotion.* These studies suggest that the class of events—expressions, perceptions, feelings, situations—that we call emotion does not necessarily represent the same class of phenomena in other cultures.

Categorization or labeling of emotion.   People in different cultures also categorize or label emotions differently. Some English words, such as *anger, joy, sadness, liking,* and *loving,* have equivalents in different languages and cultures. But many English words have no equivalent in another culture, and emotion words in other languages may have no exact English equivalent.

The German language contains the word *Schadenfreude,* which refers to pleasure derived from another's misfortunes. There is no exact English translation for this word. The Japanese language contains words such as *itoshii* (longing for an absent loved one), *ijirashii* (a feeling associated with seeing someone praiseworthy overcoming an obstacle), and *amae* (dependence), which also have no exact English translation. Conversely, some African languages have a word that covers what English suggests are two emotions: anger and sadness (Leff, 1973). Likewise, Lutz (1980) suggests that the Ifaluk word *song* can be described sometimes as anger and sometimes as sadness. And some English words have no equivalents in other languages. The English words *terror, horror, dread, apprehension,* and *timidity* are all referred to by the single word *gurakadj* in Gidjingali, an Australian aboriginal language (Hiatt, 1978). This aboriginal word also refers to the English concepts of shame and fear. *Frustration* may be a word with no exact equivalent in Arabic languages (Russell, 1991).

Just because a culture does not have a word for something that we consider an emotion certainly does not mean that people of that culture do not have those feelings. The fact that there is no exact equivalent in some Arabic languages for our word *frustration* does not mean that people of these cultures never feel frustrated. Similarly, just because our English language does not have a translation equivalent for the German word *Schadenfreude* does not mean that people in the United States do not sometimes derive pleasure from someone else's misfortunes (not you or I, however!). Certainly, in the world of subjective, emotional feeling, there must be considerable overlap in the emotions we feel, regardless of whether different cultures and languages have translation equivalents for those feeling states.

The fact that translation differences exist in the exact meaning and labeling of different emotional states across languages and cultures does suggest, however, that different cultures divide their world of emotion differently. The fact that German culture, for example, contains the word *Schadenfreude* must mean that identification of that feeling state or situation has some importance in that language and culture that it does not have in American culture or the English language. The same can be said of English words that find no exact translation equivalent in other languages. The types of words that different cultures use to identify and label the emotion worlds of their members give us yet another clue about the way different cultures structure and mold the emotional experiences of their people. Not only are the concepts of emotion culture-bound, but so also are the ways each culture attempts to frame and label its emotion world.

The location of emotion. To Americans, perhaps the single most important aspect of emotion is the inner, subjective experience. In the United States, it seems most natural that our feelings take precedence over all other aspects of emotion. But the importance we place on inner feelings and the importance of **introspection** (looking inside yourself) may be culture-bound in American psychology. Other cultures can and do view emotions as originating or residing elsewhere.

Emotion words in the languages of several Oceanic peoples, such as the Samoans (Gerber, 1975), Pintupi aborigines (Myers, 1979), and Solomon Islanders (White, 1980), are statements about relationships among people or between people and events. Likewise, Riesman (1977) suggests that the African Fulani concept *semteende*, which is commonly translated as shame or embarrassment, refers more to a situation than to a feeling. That is, if the situation is appropriate to *semteende*, then someone is feeling it, regardless of what any one individual actually feels (Russell, 1991).

In the United States, we place emotion and inner feelings in the heart. Even cultures that locate emotions within the body differ in that exact location. The Japanese identify many of their emotions in the *hara*—the gut or abdomen. The Chewong of Malay group feelings and thoughts in the liver (Howell, 1981). Levy (1984) reports that Tahitians locate emotions as arising from the intestines. Lutz (1982) suggests that the closest Ifaluk word to the English word *emotion* is *niferash*, which she translates as "our insides."

That different cultures locate emotions in different places informs us that emotions are understood differently and have different meanings for different peoples. Locating emotions in the heart is convenient and important for American culture, as it speaks to the importance of feelings as something unique to oneself, that no one else can share. By identifying emotion with the heart, Americans identify it with the most important biological organ necessary for survival. The fact that other cultures identify and locate emotions outside the body, such as in social relationships with others, speaks to the importance of relationships in those cultures, in contrast to the individualism of American culture.

The meaning of emotions to people and to behavior. All the differences we have discussed in the concept and meaning of emotion point to differences in the ways different cultures attribute meanings to emotional experiences. In the United States, emotions have enormous personal meaning, perhaps because Americans typically view inner, subjective feelings as the major defining characteristic of emotion. Once emotions are defined in such a way, a major role of emotion is to inform oneself about the self. Our self-definitions—the ways we define and identify ourselves—are informed by our emotions, which are personal, private, inner experiences.

Cultures differ in the role or meaning of emotions. Many cultures, for example, consider emotions as statements of the relationship between people and their environment, be it objects in the environment or social relationships with other people. Emotions for both the Ifaluks of Micronesia (Lutz, 1982) and the Tahitians (Levy, 1984) denote statements of relationships with others and with the physical environment. The Japanese concept *amae*, a central emotion in Japanese culture, specifies an interdependent relationship between two people. Thus, the very concept, definition, understanding, and meaning of emotion can differ across cultures. Therefore, when talking to others about our feelings, we cannot simply assume that they will understand us in the way we expect, even though we are speaking of something as "basic" as human emotion. And we certainly cannot assume that we know what someone else is feeling, and what it means, just on the basis of knowing about emotions from our own limited perspective.

Views of emotion as social constructions and with social meaning have not been totally absent in American psychology (for example, Averill, 1980; Kemper, 1978), but they have received considerably less attention in mainstream academic psychology than views that center on the introspection of subjective feeling states. As Americans are increasingly exposed to cultural diversity, perhaps American social science will come to embrace thoughts, ideas, and research on emotions from a social and cultural perspective.

Summary. While there are many similarities in the concept and language of emotion around the world, across culture and language, there are many interesting differences as well. Do these differences suggest that emotions are fundamentally and inherently incomparable across cultures? Some scientists have suggested as much, most notably those who subscribe to a "functionalist" approach. Personally, I do not believe that this is an either/or question. I believe that both universal and culturally relative aspects of emotion exist in all cultures. What the studies in this section do imply, however, is the need for scientists to integrate assessments of the concept of emotion in the cultures in which they work, along with whatever other aspects of emotion they are studying. That is, scientists interested in studying emotional expression across cultures should assess concepts related to emotion in the cultures they study in addition to their behavioral expressions, in order to examine the degree to which cultural similarities or differences in expression are linked with differences and similarities in emotion concept. The same is true for all aspects or components of emotion.

⊠ Conclusion

Emotions—the most private, personal, and arguably the most important aspects of our lives—give life events meaning. They tell us what we like and what we don't, what is good and bad for us. They enrich our lives, giving color and meaning to events and the world around us. They tell us who we are and how we are faring with others. Emotion is the invisible glue that binds us with the rest of the world, whether it be events around us or people. Emotions play such a central role in our lives that it is no wonder culture, that invisible shaper of experiences, shapes and molds our emotional world. Although we may be born with certain innate abilities, such as the capacity to express and perceive emotions in our faces and to feel emotions, culture helps to shape when, where, and how we can express, perceive, and feel those emotions. Culture creates the meaning of emotions for us, whether we understand emotion as a totally personal, private, and individual experience or as an interpersonal, public, collective experience with others.

In this chapter, we have seen the universality of a small set of facial expressions of emotion that are most likely evolutionarily adaptive and biologically innate. We have seen evidence of universal recognition of this set of facial expressions around the world, as well as universal ways of experiencing them when they occur. We have also seen universality in the nature of the antecedents that elicit these emotions, and in the ways these antecedents are appraised in bringing forth emotion.

Yet we have also seen that cultures can differ in their emotional expressions through cultural display rules, and in their emotional perceptions via cultural decoding rules. People differ across cultures in the ways in which they experience emotion, and in the specific antecedent events that elicit it. Some aspects of emotion appraisal, and even the concept and language of emotion, can also differ across cultures.

The coexistence of universal and culture-specific aspects of emotion has been a source of debate for many years. I believe that these are not necessarily mutually exclusive positions; that is, universality and cultural relativity can indeed coexist. It appears that universality may be limited to a rather small set of basic emotions, which serve as a platform for interactions with learned rules, social mores, and shared social scripts, resulting in a myriad of more complex culture-specific emotions and emotional meanings. The mere fact that universality exists does not negate the potential for cultural differences. Likewise, the mere fact that cultural differences exist does not negate the potential for universality. They are two sides of the same coin, and both need to be incorporated into future theories and research on emotion, whether within or across cultures.

Indeed, the incorporation of underlying, universal, psychobiological processes into a model of cultural construction of emotion is a challenge that lies ahead of this area of research. Scientists in this area of psychology will need to take up the greater challenge of how biology interacts with culture to produce the individual and group psychologies we see around the world.

If nothing else, at least our recognition of emotions as a universal process can help bring people together, regardless of race, culture, ethnicity, or gender. As we continue our study of human feelings and emotions across cultures, perhaps it is most important to recognize how these boundaries mold our emotions. Although we all have emotions, they mean different things to different people and are experienced, expressed, and perceived in different ways. One of our first tasks in learning about emotions across cultures is to recognize and respect those differences. But an equally important task is to recognize our similarities as well.

 # Glossary

cultural display rules Culturally prescribed rules that govern how universal emotions can be expressed. These rules center on the appropriateness of displaying emotion, depending on social circumstances. Learned by people early in their lives, they dictate how the universal emotional expressions should be modified according to social situation. By adulthood, these rules are quite automatic, having been very well practiced.

decoding rules Rules that govern the interpretation and perception of emotion. These are learned, culturally based rules that shape how people of each culture view and interpret the emotional expressions of others.

emotion antecedents The events or situations that elicit an emotion.

emotion appraisal The process by which people evaluate the events, situations, or ocurrences that lead to their having emotions.

introspection The process of looking inside yourself.

subjective experience of emotion An individual's inner feelings or experiences of an emotion.

universality studies A series of studies conducted by Ekman and Friesen and Izard that demonstrated the pancultural universality of facial expressions of emotion.

12

Culture and Language

Communication is one of the most important aspects of our lives. It is a process that ties us all together, helps us get work done, have relationships, and accomplish goals. It is also important for developing, maintaining, and transmitting culture from one generation to the next, and in reinforcing cultural goals and values within generations. Thus, communication plays a special role in our understanding of culture and cultural influences on behavior.

When we think of communication, the first and perhaps most salient aspect that comes to mind is verbal language. Words and language play a major role in our communication processes, and are uniquely human. Our verbal language—whether English, French, German, Chinese, or Indonesian—is extremely important to our ability to communicate. People place great emphasis on the words we use and how we use them. Mastery of verbal language is an important part of any successful communication, and we all tend to make judgments of people based on their level of mastery of their particular language.

Of course, verbal language is not the only aspect of communication. Another large and important component is nonverbal communication, including facial expressions, tone of voice, posture, dress, distance, and the like. Nonverbal behaviors are discussed more fully in Chapter 13. Verbal and nonverbal behaviors come together in Chapter 14, focusing on the important topic of intercultural communication.

This chapter focuses on the intimate relationship between culture and language. Culture influences the structure and functional use of language, and language can be thought of as the result or manifestation of culture. Language also influences and reinforces our cultural values and worldview, thus feeding back onto them. The cyclical nature of the relationship between culture and language suggests that no culture can be fully understood without understanding its language, and vice versa. And because language influences our thinking and worldview, understanding cultural influences on language has important implications for understanding cultural differences in worldview perspectives.

In this chapter, we begin by exploring the components of language thought to be applicable to all languages of the world, along with current thinking on how we acquire languages in our development. We then discuss language differences across cultures, including differences in language lexicons as well as pragmatics. Next, we will examine an important line of reasoning in cross-cultural psychology and anthropology known as the Sapir–Whorf hypothesis. This hypothesis suggests that language helps to structure our worldview and is crucial to the culture–language relationship; we will review research that both supports and challenges its validity. Finally, we will look at the special case of bilingualism as it affects behavior and personality, and dispel some common misperceptions about bilingual individuals.

The Components of Language and Language Acquisition

Language Features

Before examining the relationship between culture and language, it is useful first to identify the basic features of language. Understanding the various components of language will enable us to consider exactly what it is about language that is influenced by, and influences, culture. It also provides a basis for reviewing research examining the relationship between culture and language, which often focuses on specific components of language. As you will see, some cross-cultural findings apply only to certain components of language; by identifying these components, we can pinpoint exactly how culture affects language.

Linguists typically try to describe language using the following five critical features, which appear to apply to all languages in all cultures:

1. The **lexicon**, or vocabulary, refers to the words contained in a language. For example, the words *tree, eat, how,* and *slowly* are each part of the English lexicon.
2. The **syntax and grammar** of a language refer to the system of rules governing word forms and how words should be strung together to form meaningful utterances. For example, English has a grammatical rule that says we add *s* to the end of many words to indicate plurality (*cat* becomes *cats*). English also has a syntactic rule that we generally place adjectives before nouns, not after (for example, small dog, not dog small).
3. **Phonology** refers to the system of rules governing how words should sound (pronunciation) in a given language. For instance, in English, we don't pronounce *new* the same as *sew.*
4. **Semantics** refers to what words mean. For example, *table* refers to a physical object that has four legs and a flat horizontal surface.

5. **Pragmatics** refers to the system of rules governing how language is used and understood in given social contexts. For example, the statement "It is cold" could be interpreted as a request to close a window or as a statement of fact about the temperature. How it's interpreted may depend on the social and environmental context.

Linguists use two other concepts to help explain the structure of language. **Phonemes** are the smallest and most basic units of *sound* in a language, and **morphemes** are the smallest and most basic units of *meaning* in a language. Phonemes thus form the base of a language hierarchy, in which language gains in complexity as sounds gain meaning, which in turn produces words, which are strung together in phrases and, finally, sentences.

Language Acquisition

To what degree are the processes of language acquisition innate or learned? The answer is not entirely clear. The evidence to date suggests that some aspects of language acquistion are learned, while others are innate. How do we learn language? A common myth in many cultures is that children learn their native language by imitating the sounds they hear in their natural environment, and by being reinforced in their attempts at producing language (Skinner, 1957). We now know that imitation is not an important strategy in learning language. In fact, children are far more sophisticated in their learning strategies than we used to believe.

In a now-famous study in the 1950s, Jean Berko (Berko, 1958; Berko-Gleason, 1989) convincingly showed that, rather than simply imitating what they hear, children generate hypotheses about language and then test these hypotheses. This hypothesis generation and testing appears to be a universal strategy by which children around the world learn their native language. Berko (1958) showed American children a picture of an imaginary creature. She told them that the picture was of a "wug" (an imaginary creature she invented for this experiment). She then showed the same children a picture of two such imaginary creatures and asked them what they saw: "Now there are two ——!" Most of the children filled in the blank by saying "wugs." Since the word *wugs* is not an English word nor one that they had ever encountered before, clearly these children could not have used imitation to produce the word *wugs*. In order to answer "wugs," they had to have prior knowledge of the rule of English grammar that we usually add *s* to nouns to indicate plurality.

Sometimes children's knowledge of grammatical rules causes them to appear to be "backsliding" in their language development. Many parents have been dismayed when their children, who previously used the correct form of the verb *to go*, begin to use an incorrect form they may never have used before. For example, after using the standard past tense form *went* in a sentence such as "I went to school," children may suddenly begin to say "I goed to school." Anxious parents may regard such apparent regression as evidence of a learning disability. More often than not, nothing could be further from the truth. The children first learned the form *went* through simple imitation without learning anything about the rules of English grammar. Later, when their linguistic understanding became more sophisticated, they learned the English grammatical rule of adding *ed* to the end of verbs to make them past tense. Using the form *goed* instead of *went* shows a higher level of linguistic development because the children are applying a grammatical rule rather than simply imitating a word they have heard. Further in the children's development, they will learn the exceptions to rules previously learned, such as the irregular past tense form *went*. The point is that knowing a grammatical rule and applying it creatively in new situations shows much greater cognitive sophistication than mere imitation, and it is a universal language-learning strategy.

People in different cultures have different beliefs about how children learn language. Cultures also differ in the way they behave toward children learning language. The Kaluli of Papua New Guinea, for example, believe that children need carefully controlled, explicit instruction in both the forms of language and conversation skills (Schieffelin, 1981, 1990; Schieffelin & Ochs, 1986). They believe children won't learn language and conversational skills unless they are explicitly taught. The Kaluli act on these beliefs and teach their children how to conduct conversations.

Samoan adults typically believe that children's early attempts at language have no meaning and, in any case, that children have nothing to say that is of any importance to adults. Because of these beliefs, Samoan adults don't engage their children in formal language training; nor do they typically engage in conversation with children. In fact, Samoan children are mostly exposed to the language of elder siblings rather than the language of adults (Ochs, 1988; Ochs & Schieffelin, 1979, 1983).

In the United States, there is a curious discrepancy between what adults believe and their actions. On the one hand, most adults believe that children need explicit instruction from caretakers to learn English properly. On the other hand, most American parents actually pay attention to what children are saying (that is, the content) rather than how they are saying it (that is, the grammar or syntax) (Chomsky, 1965, 1967, 1969).

Such differences in cultural beliefs and practices with regard to language learning are fascinating. What is even more fascinating, however, is that in all cultures, whatever their beliefs or practices, children learn their native language fluently with or without help from adults. This common outcome suggests that humans have some universal and innate ability to learn language. According to Chomsky (1967), a renowned linguist, humans possess a **language acquisition device** (LAD) that contains innate abilities concerning syntax, grammar, and pragmatics. It is this LAD that enables all normal children of all cultures to learn and use language fluently.

Although there is no direct evidence of the existence of Chomsky's LAD, there is considerable suggestive evidence. Some of this evidence comes from research on pidgin and creole speakers. Bickerton (1981), for example, at the University of Hawaii, studied a number of pidgin speakers and their development into creole speakers. Many of the linguistic features found in several unrelated creole languages were not present in any of the source languages from which the original pidgin developed. Where might such features come from? Bickerton suggested that the only plausible explanation for the use of such features by speakers of unrelated creole languages is that such features are preprogrammed or hardwired in humans as part of our LAD. While a considerable amount of suggestive evidence seems to support Chomsky's theory, there is no evidence that seems to refute it. Thus, it remains one of the best explanations we have for the fact that all normal children learn their native language fluently regardless of wide differences in the environments in which they do so.

It is clear that people of different cultures harbor different opinions and attitudes about language acquisition, but it is not clear whether the exact process of language learning differs across cultures. In the absence of evidence to the contrary, Chomsky's notion of a universal LAD that enables children to learn languages appears to be the best explanation for language acquisition. Future research may test the limits of the LAD by exploring exactly how this process occurs. Then, perhaps we can uncover some ways in which cultural differences in attitudes and opinions about language learning affect the learning process in specific cultures.

Language Differences across Cultures

Culture and Language Lexicons

Language can be thought of as both a manifestation and product of a culture. American English, its words and how we use them, is a reflection of American culture. Surely, if we examine the structure and function of American English, we will see many parallels to important aspects of American culture. The same is true for any language and culture we examine. One way to observe this relationship is by noting the association between different cultures' languages and their lexicons, or vocabulary.

Words that exist in some languages but not in others.   Many of us have heard that the Eskimo language contains more words for snow than English does. Whorf (1956) was the first to point out that the Eskimo language actually has three words for snow, while the English language uses the single word *snow* to describe all three types. Many other cultures and languages contain words that do not exist in English. In Chapter 11, for example, we encountered a number of words describing emotional states, such as the German word *Schadenfreude*, that have no English equivalent.

When we translate an English word into its literal equivalent in another language, we often think that the words mean the same. While many words do have generally the same meanings in different languages, they often have different nuances and connotations. Even common words for *breaking*, *cutting*, *eating*, and *drinking* can have entirely different connotations and nuances, and be used in different contexts, in other cultures (Suzuki, 1978). Moreover, the associations people of different cultures have with the same word may be different. When considering the relationship between words in our own language and their translated equivalents in another, we should not consider those translations as exact equivalents. If we take into account all the meanings of a word, it would be very difficult to find words in different languages that have exactly the same meaning, nuance, connotation, and associations.

Self/other referents.   In American English, we generally use one of two words, and their derivatives, to describe ourselves when talking to others: *I* and *we*. We use these words irrespective of whom we are talking to or what we are talking about. If we are talking to a university professor, we use the word *I* to refer to ourselves. If we are talking to our parents, we use the same word *I*. And we use the same word *I* when referring to ourselves with friends, family, neighbors, acquaintances, bosses, or subordinates. Likewise, we generally use a single word in English to refer to another person or group of people: *you*. In conversation with our parents, bosses, friends, lovers, strangers, children, and just about anyone, we use *you* or one of its derivatives to refer to the other person or persons.

Many languages in the world, however, have much more elaborate systems of reference that depend on the nature of the relationship between people. The Japanese language provides one of the most extreme examples. Japanese does have translation equivalents of the English words *I*, *we*, and *you*, but these words are used much less frequently in Japanese than in English. In Japanese, what you call yourself and others is totally dependent on the relationship between you and the other person. Often, the decision about what is appropriate to call yourself and another person depends on the status differential between the two people. For example, if you are of a higher status than the other person, in Japan you would refer to yourself by position or role rather than by the English equivalent of *I*. In Japan, teachers use the word *teacher* to refer to themselves when talking to students. Doctors may use the term *doctor,* and parents use the word *mother* or *father* when speaking to their children.

In the Japanese language, if you are of a lower status than the person to whom you are speaking, you refer to yourself using one of several pronoun equivalents of *I*, such as *watashi, watakushi, boku,* or *ore*. The use of these different terms for *I* depends on your sex (women cannot say *boku* or *ore*), degree of politeness, and degree of familiarity with the other person. When speaking to someone of higher status, for example, people generally use *watashi* to refer to themselves. When speaking to friends or colleagues, men usually refer to themselves as *boku* or *ore*.

Likewise, if you are speaking to someone of higher status, you generally refer to that person by role or title. When speaking to your teachers, you refer to them as *teacher,* even when addressing them directly. You would call your boss by his or her title, such as *section chief* or *president*. You would definitely not use a personal pronoun such as our English *you* in addressing a person of higher status. When speaking to a person of lower status, you would generally use a

Figure 12.1 Japanese words for self and concept

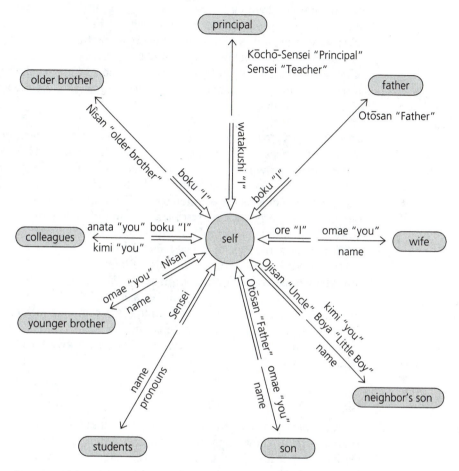

personal pronoun or the person's actual name. As with personal pronouns for *I*, the Japanese language contains several pronouns for *you*—among them, *anata*, *omae*, and *kimi*. Again, the appropriate use of each depends on the relationship; generally, *omae* and *kimi* are used when speaking to someone of lower status than you or to someone very familiar and intimate with you. Indeed, the Japanese language system of self- and other-referents is very complicated, especially when compared to American English (see Figure 12.1).

These differences between the English and Japanese languages reflect important cultural differences. In the Japanese culture, language, mannerisms, and other aspects of behavior must be modified according to the relationship and context under which the communication is occurring. The most important dimensions along which behavior and language are differentiated in Japan are status and group orientation. All aspects of behavior differ depending on whether one person is higher or lower in status than the other person in the conversation. Also, behavior and language differ depending on whether the other person is a member of your ingroup or not. Thus, the choice of appropriate self- and other-referents in the Japanese language reflects important aspects of Japanese culture.

Counting systems.   Counting systems provide yet another example of how culture influences the structure of a language. In the Japanese language, for example, different words are used to denote different things being counted. Round, cylindrical objects are counted by the suffix *hon* (*ippon, nihon, sanbon,* and so on); flat objects are counted by *mai* (*ichimai, nimai, sanmai,* and so on). Japanese has many such counters, as do many other languages. In English, however, all objects are simply counted by the number, with no such prefix or suffix to denote the type of object being counted.

In addition, the Japanese language, like many other languages, bases all numbers on the words for *one* through *ten*. Eleven is literally *ten-one* (*ju-ichi*), 12 is *ten-two* (*ju-ni*), 20 is *two-ten* (*ni-ju*). In English, however, numbers 1 through 19 are unique, and an additive system similar to Japanese numbers starts at 20. These linguistic differences are thought to contribute to differences in math achievement between the United States and Japan (see Stigler & Baranes, 1988).

Culture and Pragmatics

Culture affects not only the language lexicons, but also pragmatics—that is, the rules governing how language is used and understood in different social contexts. Kashima and Kashima (1998), for example, examined 39 languages used in 71 countries, obtaining both cultural and linguistic data from each country. The cultural scores included Hofstede's (1980, 1983) four dimensions—individualism, power distance, uncertainty avoidance, and masculinity—and 15 other culture-related dimensions. The linguistic data included an analysis of the use of first- and second-person pronouns, and whether the language permitted dropping these pronouns in conversation. The correlations between these two sets of data were analyzed in two separate ways to examine the relationship between culture and pronoun usage. Kashima and Kashima (1998) found that cultures whose languages allowed pronouns to be dropped tended to be less individualistic, which they interpreted as reflecting different cultural conceptualizations of self and others.

Gudykunst and his colleagues have also done a number of studies that demonstrate cultural variability in language use. Gudykunst and Nishida (1986), for example, asked participants in the United States and Japan to make intimacy ratings of 30 relationship terms (such as brother, employer, stranger) and, in another study, to rate communication styles in six relationships on person-alization, synchrony, and difficulty. The results indicated that the Japanese rated ingroup relationships—coworkers and university colleagues—as more in-timate than did the Americans, and that the Japanese perceived more person-alization but less synchrony across relationship terms. In a subsequent study, Gudykunst, Yoon, and Nishida (1987) tested participants from the United States, Japan, and Korea, asking them to rate the same three dimensions of communicative behavior in ingroup and outgroup relationships. They found that the Americans had the lowest personalization and synchronization scores, the Koreans the highest, and the Japanese in the middle, but only for ingroup communication. These researchers suggested that members of collectivistic cultures use a principal of equity involving greater social penetration when communicating with ingroup members than do members of individualistic cultures.

Cultural differences have also been documented in a number of other com-munication areas, such as apologies (Barnlund & Yoshioka, 1991), children's personal narratives (Minami & McCabe, 1995), self-disclosure (Chen, 1995), compliments (Barnlund & Araki, 1985), and interpersonal criticism (Barnlund & Nomura, 1983). Chen (1995), for example, asked American and Taiwanese participants to complete a measure of self-disclosure in relation to four target persons and six different conversational topics. The results indicated that Americans had a significantly higher level of self-disclosure than did the Tai-wanese Chinese across all topics and target persons. Barnlund and Yoshioka (1991) reported a qualitative pilot study and a quantitative, large-sample study to assess preferences in styles of apology in relation to 12 critical incidents. They reported that Japanese participants preferred more direct, extreme forms of apology, while Americans preferred indirect, less extreme forms. Also, Americans tended to favor explanation as a form of apology, whereas the Japa-nese preferred compensation.

Recent research has extended these findings of cultural differences by show-ing how such differences are mediated by self-construals and values held on the individual level, and by some personality dimensions. The addition of such me-diator variables is an example of research involving context variables, discussed in Chapter 5. Kim and associates (1996), for example, asked participants in Ko-rea, Japan, Hawaii, and mainland United States to rate the importance of five different conversational constraints (for example, clarity, concern for the other's feelings) in relation to six vignettes. Participants also completed a scale measuring their self-construals as either independent or interdependent (see Chapter 3). These researchers found that culture affected the self-construals, which, in turn, affected the ratings of the conversational constraints. In a similar fashion, Gudykunst and colleagues (1996) reported that self-construals and individual values mediate the use of context-dependent communication styles; Gudykunst and colleagues (1992) also reported that two variables, self-monitoring and predicted outcome value of the relationship, mediated cultural differences in communication styles in ingroup and outgroup relationships.

Summary

Collectively, the work cited in this section paints a rather complete picture of the profound influence of culture not only on language lexicons, but also on the use and function of language. Language differences reflect important differences between cultures, and they also help to reinforce culture. For example, as a result of using the complex system of self- and other-referents in the Japanese language, a person's system of thought and behavior becomes structured over time to reflect the culture. Through the use of language, an individual is transformed into an agent of the culture. Thus, the feelings, associations, connotations, and nuances of language both influence and are influenced by the culture. Over time, an individual embodies the very essence of culture via language, and in using the language, he or she reinforces that language's concepts of culture. This same relationship holds true for Japanese, American English, and all other languages and cultures (see Figure 12.2).

The reason for this reciprocal relationship is that language symbolizes culture. Culture is a group's way of structuring their world to avoid chaos and ensure survival; language is a symbol system that represents and denotes that structuring. Self- and other-referents in American English, for example, reflect important aspects of American culture. American culture in general places less

Figure 12.2 The reciprocal relation between culture and language

Culture influences thoughts, feelings, motives.

Culture influences language.

The use of language reinforces culture.

emphasis on status differences between people, or whether the other person is an ingroup member or not. American culture views each individual as a separate, unique, and independent person. Because American culture views individuals as important, not context or status, people are people, regardless of when or where they interact. Thus, Americans can use *I* to refer to themselves in almost any conversation, and *you* to refer to the other person.

These observations make it clear that people of different cultures structure the world around them differently, at least in the language they use to describe that world. Of course, two people using the same language can, and often do, use the same words with different meanings and in different ways. Language differences within a culture also contribute to possible conflicts within a culture. But the differences in language structure and use within a culture are probably less than those between cultures.

It is clear that people of different cultures "slice up" their worlds differently via their languages. But are these differences so pervasive that people actually see the same things differently? Do Americans and Eskimos actually see, think, and feel about snow differently? And are these differences related to differences in their language? Or do they see exactly the same things but just categorize them differently? Studies examining these and related questions suggest that such language differences are not just a matter of categorization, but reflect genuine differences in worldview.

Language and Worldview: The Case for Linguistic Relativity

One of the most important and long-standing debates in studies of language and behavior involves the relationship between language and thought processes. This relationship is particularly important to the cross-cultural study of language because each culture is associated with a given language as a vehicle for its expression. How does culture influence language? And how does language influence culture?

The Sapir–Whorf Hypothesis

The **Sapir–Whorf hypothesis**, also referred to as linguistic relativity, suggests that speakers of different languages think differently, and that they do so because of the differences in their languages. Because different cultures typically have different languages, the Sapir–Whorf hypothesis is especially important for understanding cultural differences (and similarities) in thought and behavior as a function of language.

Before we examine this question further, let's reflect for just a moment on exactly what this issue is about and its potential implications. If the Sapir–Whorf hypothesis is correct, it suggests that people of different cultures think differently, just by the very nature, structure, and function of their language.

Their thought processes, their associations, their ways of interpreting the world—even the same events we perceive—may be different because they speak a different language and this language has helped shape their thought patterns. This hypothesis also suggests that people who speak more than one language may actually have different thought patterns when speaking different languages.

Many studies have looked at language–cognition issues since Edward Sapir and Benjamin Whorf first proposed their hypothesis in the 1950s. While there is much evidence in support of the Sapir–Whorf hypothesis, other evidence raises questions about its validity.

Early Research Supporting the Sapir–Whorf Hypothesis

Object classification. In one of the earliest language studies, Carroll and Casagrande (1958) compared Navajo and English speakers. They examined the relationship between the system of shape classification in the Navajo language and the amount of attention children pay to shape when classifying objects. Similar to the Japanese language described earlier in this chapter, the Navajo language has the interesting grammatical feature that certain verbs of handling (for example, "to pick up," "to drop") require special linguistic forms depending on what kind of object is being handled. A total of 11 such linguistic forms describe different shapes—round spherical objects, round thin objects, long flexible things, and so forth.

Noting how much more complex this linguistic feature is in Navajo than in English, Carroll and Casagrande (1958) suggested that such linguistic features might play a role in influencing cognitive processes. In their experiment, they compared Navajo- and English-dominant children to see how often they used shape, form, or type of material to categorize objects. The Navajo-dominant children were significantly more likely to categorized by shape than were the English-dominant children. In the same study, Carroll and Casagrande (1958) also reported that the performance of low-income African American English-speaking children was similar to that of European American children. This finding is particularly important because the African American children, unlike the European Americans, were not accustomed to blocks and form-board toys.

The results of this study—along with the observations concerning the relationship between culture and language lexicons, and culture and pragmatics, reviewed earlier—provided early support for the idea that the language we speak influences the kind of thoughts we have. Language, that is, may act in a mediating role, helping to determine the ways in which children conceive of some aspects of their world. Language seems to be at least one factor that influences the way we think.

The language of color. Another source of research testing the validity of the Sapir–Whorf hypothesis has been work in the area of color perception. An early statement of this issue is Gleason's (1961): "The continuous gradation of color which exists in nature is represented in language by a series of discrete categories. . . . There is nothing inherent either in the spectrum or the human perception of it which would compel its division in this way. The specific method of division is part of the structure of English" (p. 4).

Studies of language and color perception have typically looked at how colors are categorized and how they are named in different languages. Brown and Lenneberg (1954), for example, found a positive relationship between the codability of a color and the accuracy with which a color could be remembered in a memory task. In their study, codability was defined as how well speakers of English agreed on a name for a given color, the length of the name, and the time taken to name a color. Brown and Lenneberg's results lent support to the Sapir–Whorf hypothesis.

Early Research Challenging Sapir–Whorf

Despite the positive results obtained by Brown and Lenneberg (1954), however, other early research involving color perception actually challenged the Sapir–Whorf hypothesis. Berlin and Kay (1969), for example, examined 78 languages and found that 11 basic color terms form a universal hierarchy. Some languages, such as English and German, use all 11 terms; others, such as Dani (New Guinea), use as few as two. Further, they noticed an evolutionary order in which languages encode these universal categories. For example, if a language has three color terms, those three terms describe black, white, and red. This hierarchy of color names in human language is as follows:

1. All languages contain terms for white and black.
2. If a language contains three terms, it also contains a term for red.
3. If a language contains four terms, it also contains a term for either green or yellow (but not both).
4. If a language contains five terms, it contains terms for both green and yellow.
5. If a language contains six terms, it also contains a term for blue.
6. If a language contains seven terms, it also contains a term for brown.
7. If a language contains eight or more terms, it also contains a term for purple, pink, orange, gray, or some combination of these.

To test such claims as Gleason's, Berlin and Kay (1969) undertook a study of the distribution of color terms in 20 languages. They asked international university students in the United States to list the "basic" color terms in each of their native languages. They then asked these foreign students to identify from an array of glass color chips the most typical or best examples of a basic color term the researchers specified. Berlin and Kay (1969) found a limited number of basic color terms in any language. They also found that the color chips chosen as best examples of these basic terms tended to fall in clusters they termed *focal points*. In languages that had a basic term for bluish colors, the best example of the color was found to be the same "focal blue" for speakers of all the languages. These findings suggested that people in different cultures perceive colors in much the same way despite radical differences in their languages. Many people began to doubt the validity of the Sapir–Whorf hypothesis, because it didn't seem to apply in the perceptual domain of color.

Berlin and Kay's findings were later confirmed by a series of experiments conducted by Rosch. In her experiments, Rosch (for example, 1973) set out to test just how culturally universal these focal points were. She compared two languages that differ markedly in the number of basic color terms: English, with multiple color terms, and Dani, which has only two color terms. Dani is the language spoken by a Stone Age tribe living in the highlands of Irian Jaya, Indonesian New Guinea. One color term, *mili,* was found to include both "dark" and "cold" colors (for example, black, green, and blue), while the second color term, *mola,* included both "light" and "warm" colors (for example, white, red, and yellow). Rosch also explored the relationship between language and memory. She argued that if the Whorfian position were correct, Dani's lack of a rich color lexicon would inhibit Dani speakers' ability to discriminate and remember colors. As it happened, Heider and Oliver (1972) found that Dani speakers did not confuse color categories any more than did speakers of English. Nor did Dani speakers perform differently from English speakers on memory tasks.

Interpretations concerning the validity of Sapir–Whorf on the basis of research involving color perception, however, must be tempered by the fact that the way we perceive color is determined to a significant degree by our biological makeup and, in particular, our biological visual system. This system is the same across human cultures. De Valois and his associates (De Valois, Abramov, & Jacobs, 1966; De Valois & Jacobs, 1968) studied a species of monkey with a visual system similar to that of humans. They suggested that we have cells that are only stimulated by two colors (red + green, and blue + yellow) and that, at any given moment, these cells can only be stimulated by one of these two colors. For example, our red + green cells can respond to red or to green, but not to both simultaneously. This is rather interesting because many people have noticed that while it is possible to mix red and green, it is not possible for humans to perceive such combinations in the same way we perceive a mixture of blue and green as turquoise or a mixture of red and blue as purple. Thus, "reddish green" is a perceptual as well as a semantic impossibility.

This suggests that our biology is very important in how we perceive colors, and may provide a universal basis for perceiving them, regardless of linguistic differences in their labeling. In that case, it would be surprising to find language-based differences in color perception. Thus, we cannot dismiss the Sapir–Whorf hypothesis just because language seems to have little influence on the way we perceive colors. Indeed, if we look at other areas of human behavior, we find significant evidence to support the Sapir–Whorf hypothesis.

More Recent Research Supporting Sapir–Whorf

Since the earliest research supporting and then challenging the validity of the Sapir–Whorf hypothesis, a number of other studies has been conducted, many of them confirming its validity. One area of human behavior that appears susceptible to Whorfian effects, for example, is that of causality—how we explain the reasons things happen the way they do. Niyekawa-Howard (1968) studied the relationship between Japanese grammar and Japanese perceptions of what causes events to happen. Traditionally, Japanese has an interesting passive form that includes the following meaning: Because the subject of the sentence "was caused to" take the action expressed by the main verb, he is not responsible for the act or its outcome. Of course, we can convey this information in English, but only by using cumbersome extra words and phrases. In this Japanese passive form, this meaning is conveyed in a subtle way. Niyekawa-Howard found that because of the frequency with which native speakers of Japanese are confronted with this passive form, they are more likely than English speakers to attribute responsibility to others, even when the outcome is positive.

As further evidence in support of Sapir–Whorf, Bloom (1981) reported that Chinese speakers are less likely than English speakers to give hypothetical interpretations to a hypothetical story. He interpreted these results as constituting strong evidence for the structure of language as a mediator of cognitive processes because English and Chinese differ in how they convey hypothetical meaning. In English, we use the subjunctive tense ("if I were you," not "if I am you"). Chinese has no subjunctive in the sense of a mandatory marking in each verb (the grammatical Chinese equivalent of "if I were you" would roughly be translated "be if I am you").

Yet another source of support for the Sapir–Whorf hypothesis is Kay and Kempton's (1984) finding that at least some differences in cognition depend on differences in linguistic structure. They compared the thought processes of speakers of English with those of speakers of Tarahumara, a language indigenous to the Yucatán peninsula in Mexico that does not distinguish between blue and green. They had subjects complete two nonlinguistic tasks, both of which involved choosing from a number of color chips the color that was the "most different" from the others. They found that color discrimination was better when subjects could use a naming strategy, demonstrating clearly that linguistic differences can affect the performance of a nonlinguistic task.

A number of other studies provide strong support for linguistic relativity. For example, Lucy (1992), comparing American English with the language of the Yucatec Maya in southeastern Mexico, identified distinctive patterns of thought relating to differences in the two languages. Hoosain (1986, 1991) has shown how unique aspects of the Chinese language influence the ease of processing information. Garro (1986), comparing American English and Mexican Spanish, demonstrated that language influenced memory for colors. Santa and Baker (1975) provided evidence in favor of Sapir–Whorf in their study of language effects on the quality and order of visual reproduction of figures. Lin and Schwanenflugel (1995), comparing English and Taiwanese Chinese, demonstrated that language structure was related to the structure of category knowledge in American and Chinese speakers. Collectively, these studies provide a wealth of support for the Sapir–Whorf hypothesis.

Still Other Research Challenging Sapir–Whorf

Despite the strong evidence in favor of Sapir–Whorf just reviewed, a few studies have also resulted in findings that do not support linguistic relativity. Au (1983, 1984), for example, has contested Bloom's interpretation of his data. Au (1983) reported five studies intending to replicate Bloom's (1981) study, using Chinese and English versions of stories used by Bloom. Au concluded that the use of hypothetical intepretations was probably not related to the use of the subjunctive, or to counterfactual reasoning in the Chinese (see also critique of Au's study by Bloom, 1984). Liu (1985) also failed to replicate Bloom's study.

Takano (1989) discussed both conceptual and methodological problems with Bloom's study, and suggested that the positive findings obtained by Bloom may have been an artifact of methodological flaws. He conducted three studies investigating the nature of those flaws, and concluded that differences in the amount of mathematical training, not linguistic differences, may have produced the differences Bloom originally reported.

Other studies conducted over the years also provide evidence challenging the validity of Sapir–Whorf (for example, Davies, Sowden, Jerrett, & Corbett, 1998). While my read of this literature suggests that the number and quality of these studies do not match those in support of Sapir–Whorf, they nevertheless raise important and interesting questions concerning the issue of linguistic relativity and its validity across cultures. Thus, considerable controversy remains in the scholarly literature concerning the validity of the Sapir–Whorf hypothesis, no doubt because of the importance of its implications and ramifications. In the absence of consistent evidence confirming or disconfirming Sapir–Whorf, recently a number of scholars have offered alternative models of the relationship between language and thought (for example, Gumperz & Levinson, 1996; Hadley, 1997; Lucy, 1992).

Sapir–Whorf: The Bottom Line

Perhaps the best way to make sense of this area of study comes from an analysis of the basic Sapir–Whorf hypothesis published many years earlier. Many studies of the Sapir–Whorf hypothesis read as if it were only one hypothesis; actually, there are several different Sapir–Whorf hypotheses. In 1960, Joshua Fishman published a comprehensive breakdown of the most important ways the Sapir–Whorf hypothesis has been discussed (see Table 12.1). In his description, these different approaches are ordered in increasing levels of complexity. Two factors determine the level at which a given version of the hypothesis might fall. The first factor relates to the particular aspect of language that is of interest—for example, the lexicon or the grammar. The second factor relates to the cognitive behavior of the speakers of a given language—for example, cultural themes or nonlinguistic data such as a decision-making task. Of the four levels, Level 1 is the least complex; Level 4 is the most complex. Levels 3 and 4

Table 12.1 Fishman's Sapir–Whorf Hypothesis Schema

Data of Language Characteristics	Data of Cognitive Behavior	
	Linguistic Data	Nonlinguistic Data
Lexical/Semantic	Level 1*	Level 2
Grammatical	Level 3	Level 4**

*Least sophisticated
**Most sophisticated

are actually closer to Whorf's original ideas in that they concern the grammar or syntax of language as opposed to its lexicon.

In reviewing the literature on the Sapir–Whorf hypothesis, it is extremely important to keep in mind exactly which level of the hypothesis is being tested. Carroll and Casagrande's study of object classification among Navajo and English speakers is one of the few to investigate the Sapir–Whorf hypothesis at Fishman's Level 3 or 4. In contrast, a considerable amount of research compares lexical differences and linguistic behavior (Fishman's Level 1) or nonlinguistic behavior (Fishman's Level 2). Most of this research is at Level 2, comparing lexical differences with nonlinguistic behaviors. When such comparisons have shown differences, language is assumed to have caused these differences. For example, if we describe Brown and Lenneberg's study (1954) on color memory in Fishman's terms, the language characteristics were lexical/semantic (color coding) and the nonlinguistic behavior was memory.

Viewed according to Fishman's classifications, the best-studied area is lexical differences between languages, which provides some of the weaker support for the hypothesis. This makes sense, because the lexicon seems to be only minimally related to thought processes, which may account for some skepticism about the Sapir–Whorf hypothesis. A less-studied area, however, that of syntactic and grammatical differences between languages, provides strong evidence for the claim that language influences cognition. Perhaps even stronger evidence will be found in future studies of how the pragmatic systems of different languages influence speakers' thought processes. Take the case of Javanese, for example. This Indonesian language has an elaborate system of forms of address depending on the social status, age, and sex of the person being spoken to, much like the system of self/other referents in the Japanese language described earlier. Does speaking the Javanese language influence Javanese people to be more precise in their thinking about social and status differences between people than speakers of English are? Hunt and Agnoli (1991) have suggested that exactly such a "Whorfian" process might operate among Japanese speakers as compared with speakers of English.

Language and Behavior: The Special Case of Bilingualism

Bilingualism and Its Implications for Sapir–Whorf

To this point, we have assumed monolingualism—that each person speaks only one language; in fact, most, if not all, of the research on language and culture has been limited to a comparison of monolingual populations. But what about people who are fluent in more than one language? What might the Sapir–Whorf hypothesis imply about the behavior of bilingual or multilingual populations?

One implication might be that the thoughts, feelings, and behaviors of bilingual individuals would depend on which language they are using. A Mexican American or Mexican immigrant bilingual in English and Spanish, for example, may think a certain way when speaking American English and a different way when speaking Spanish. In fact, many bilinguals report that they think, feel, and act differently depending on the language they are using at the time. Such anecdotal evidence would certainly argue in favor of linguistic relativity.

Or would it? Actually, such a phenomenon may not be strictly a "Whorfian" issue, because it does not necessarily imply that it is any aspect of the two languages (such as their lexical or grammatical systems) that causes the language-related changes in behavior. It may be simply that when we learn a language, we learn it in the context of a culture. When bilinguals learn two languages, they often do so in the context of two different cultures. Each language may simply access a different set of cultural values. Thus, bilinguals may think differently when using two languages, but the languages per se may not cause the thinking differences.

At this point, it may be advantageous to make a further distinction between "strong" and "weak" versions of the Sapir–Whorf hypothesis. A strong version would suggest that language causes differences in thinking. A weak version, however, might suggest that language is simply associated with differences in thinking, without necessarily causing them. The cause, in fact, may be found in a mediating variable, such as culture or cultural values, that is associated both with language and with differences in thinking, feeling, and acting.

Putting aside the question of whether or not language causes changes in thinking, feeling, and acting, the study of bilinguals seems a perfect complement to the research described earlier in assessing the validity of at least a weak version of the Sapir–Whorf hypothesis. Conceptually, differences in thinking or behavior in bilinguals as a function of language in use at the time of testing would certainly support at least the weak version of the Sapir–Whorf hypothesis, even though it could not be proven that different language use caused the differences in thinking. Although any correlation would not warrant inferences about causation, it would not rule them out either. It is certainly possible that language may cause differences in thinking and behavior, either directly or indirectly (via common cultural values).

Along with the potential advantages to our conceptual understanding of linguistic relativity, the study of bilinguals also offers considerable methodological advantages. When language effects on behaviors, cognitions, or emotions are tested in bilinguals, differences among individual participants in the study cannot possibly confound the results because the same individuals are in both language conditions of the study. When comparisons are made between groups of monolingual participants—for example, Chinese-speaking, Taiwanese, and English-speaking Americans—not only does language differ between the groups, but so do the individuals. If differences are found between these groups, we cannot be sure that the differences are due to language (which is the thrust of the Sapir–Whorf argument) rather than to differences between individuals. With bilinguals serving as research participants, the inherent confound of individual differences is eliminated.

One of the crucial issues in research using bilinguals is establishing the degree of equivalence between the languages being compared. For many bilinguals, one of the languages is a first, native language, whereas the second is learned later in life. And many bilinguals are more proficient or fluent in one language or the other. Such differences may preclude conclusive comparisons in research on bilinguals, because differences between languages may actually reflect differences in degree of proficiency rather than linguistic relativity. Thus, researchers who study bilinguals need to take special care in recruiting and screening participants, and in establishing equivalency in language proficiency.

Bilingualism and the United States

For much of its history and even today, the United States has remained largely monolingual. In fact, earlier in this century, many Americans thought that knowledge of more than one language should be avoided. It was commonly believed that humans have limited "room" to store language—that learning "too much" language takes "space" away from other functions such as intelligence. We now know that such notions are wrong; there is no evidence that bilinguals do worse on intellectual (or other) tasks. On the contrary, there is evidence that knowledge of more than one language may improve cognitive flexibility (for example, see Price-Williams & Ramirez, 1977).

On a global level, in fact, most people speak more than one language; monolinguals, including most Americans, are in the minority. And although English is the most widely used language in the world, Americans also constitute a minority of the world's English speakers. These linguistic facts should help Americans place themselves in a more global context with regard not only to multiple language fluency, but also to related topics such as cognitive flexibility, potential for empathy, and ethnocentrism.

Although English is still the predominant language in the United States, the country has a large (and growing) number of people who regularly use both English and another language. In many cases, this "other" language is their native tongue. Many of these people have come to the United States from somewhere else. Such bilingual immigrants pose an especially interesting issue in terms of the psychology of language, because their two languages are often associated with two different cultural systems. As noted previously, many bilinguals report that they think and feel differently depending on the linguistic context. They may even be thought of as having a different sense of self, depending on which language is being used. Changing trends in population diversity and language use in the United States, coupled with the place of monolingual Americans in a multilingual global context, underscores the importance of studying the effects of bilingualism on thinking, feeling, and acting.

Research Examining Linguistic Relativity in Bilinguals

Can we assume that bilinguals have access, through their two languages, to two culturally different modes of thought? If so, does this imply the existence of two different personalities within the same individual, each associated with one of the bilingual's two languages? Ervin (1964) compared responses from a sample of English/French bilinguals to pictures from the Thematic Apperception Test (a common test used in many cross-cultural studies). The subjects told their stories in response to the pictures once in English and then another time in French. Ervin found that subjects demonstrated more aggression, autonomy, and withdrawal in French than they did in English, and that females demonstrated a greater need for achievement in English than in French. Ervin attributed these differences to the higher value French culture places on verbal prowess and to greater sex role differences.

How might the issue of bilingualism and personality be important for immigrants to the United States? Consider, for example, a Chinese/English bilingual raised in a monolingual Chinese-speaking home who learned English naturalistically only after migrating to the United States from China at age 8. She is now a 20-year-old college student, living with her parents. She uses Chinese as the only language in the home, but English at school and with most of her peers. We might predict that when using Chinese she would be likely to behave in ways appropriate to Chinese cultural norms in the home. In English, however, she might be more likely to behave in ways that are closer to European American norms. A "Whorfian" view might account for such language-related behavioral differences in terms of the pragmatic systems of Chinese and English (as well as other linguistic differences). However, at least two other explanations have been offered for the mechanisms that underlie such language-related shifts in personality. They are known as the culture-affiliation hypothesis and the minority group–affiliation hypothesis.

The **culture-affiliation hypothesis** is simply that immigrant bilinguals will tend to affiliate themselves with the values and beliefs of the culture associated with the language in which they are currently operating. When the language is switched, so are the cultural values with which they affiliate. The **minority group–affiliation hypothesis**, in contrast, suggests that immigrant bilinguals will tend to self-identify as members of an ethnic minority group and adopt the behavioral stereotypes of the majority culture about their minority as their own when they are operating in the language associated with their minority group. To the extent that such stereotypes are accurate, the minority group–affiliation hypothesis will make the same predictions as does the culture-affiliation hypothesis; that is, when interacting in their first language, people will behave in ways more typical of their ancestral culture, which may also be consistent with majority culture stereotypes of that culture. Language context would predict differences in behavior, and also in personality.

Hull (1987) and Dinges and Hull (1992) have reported studies in which this prediction was tested. They reasoned that if any such differences were to be found, they would be most evident among a population of immigrant bilinguals. Such bilinguals are believed to have two clearly distinct cultural affiliations, accessible through the language in which much of this cultural knowledge was learned or is associated. In these studies, Chinese/English and Korean/English immigrant bilinguals were given the California Psychological Inventory (CPI), a widely used personality test. It is a particularly good test for this type of study because it has been translated into many different languages and used in cross-cultural research over many years. The immigrant bilinguals completed the CPI twice—once in their native language and once in English. The central question was, would a dual self or dual personality emerge, showing up as between-language, within-group differences in CPI scores? The answer was a resounding yes. In other words, these bilinguals presented different personalities depending on whether they were responding in their first language (Chinese or Korean) or in English (their second language). In a second study, Hull (1990a, 1990b) confirmed these earlier findings using a different measure of personality.

Some evidence also suggests that our perceptions of others are dependent on the language we speak when making those judgments. Matsumoto and Assar (1992) asked bilingual observers in India (Hindi and English) to view a set of 40 different facial expressions of emotion. The observers were asked to judge which emotion was being portrayed in the faces, and how intensely. The observers made these judgments twice, a week apart, the first time in English, and the second time in Hindi. The results showed that judgments of which emotion was being portrayed were more accurate when the judgments were made in English. But the emotions were perceived more intensely when the ratings were made in Hindi. The same people, viewing the same facial expressions, made different judgments of those expressions depending on which language they used to make those judgments.

Misperceptions about Bilinguals

The research described here demonstrates how closely language and culture are intertwined. It also demonstrates the importance of language in everyday experience. In addition, these findings help to dispel the misconception that the existence of two personalities within an individual means that the individual is suffering from a mental disorder. Such a situation is clearly a natural and healthy part of the bilingual/bicultural experience.

Other misconceptions persist, however. For example, negative impressions and stereotypes, particularly about intelligence, can occur when communicating with people in their second language because they may take more time in responding and appear to have cognitive difficulties while processing information. These difficulties, known as *foreign language processing difficulties*, arise because of nonfamiliarity or lack of fluency in speaking a language, and because of uncertainty or ambiguity about the intended meaning of messages when received in a foreign language. These difficulties are, in fact, a normal part of learning a language, and should not necessarily be used as a basis for negative inferences about intelligence or other dispositional characteristics of individuals who may be communicating in a second (or third) language.

Bilinguals may also experience difficulties in nonlinguistic thinking tasks; such difficulties are known as the *foreign language effect* (Takano & Noda, 1993). This term refers to a temporary decline in the thinking ability of people who are using a foreign language in which they are less proficient than their native language. The foreign language effect, seen in nonlinguistic thinking tasks, is a by-product of the foreign language processing difficulty seen in linguistic tasks. Takano and Noda (1993) demonstrated the existence of this effect in two studies involving Japanese/English bilinguals. In the first study, Japanese Japanese/English and American English/Japanese bilinguals performed a calculation task and responded to a question-and-answer task in either their first (native) or second (foreign) language. Performance for both groups of participants was lower when the question-and-answer task was in the foreign language. In the second study, basically the same methods were used with a different thinking task (nonverbal spatial reasoning tasks) and a different linguistic task (sentence verification), producing the same results.

Takano and Noda (1995) reported two additional studies that showed that the foreign language effect was larger when the discrepancy between the native and foreign languages was greater, and smaller when the difference between the native and foreign languages was smaller. Their first study employed the same methods as the first study in Takano and Noda (1993), using native speakers of German and Japanese, with English as a common foreign language. They found that the foreign language effect was larger for the Japanese. They explained this finding in terms of the greater difference between Japanese and English than between German and English. Their second study replicated the findings from the first, this time using native Korean and English speakers, with Japanese as the common foreign language.

Collectively, these studies indicate that interference in both linguistic (foreign language processing difficulty) and nonlinguistic (foreign language effect) tasks is a normal and expected occurrence in bilinguals. These interferences occur in the same way as interferences between any two cognitive tasks asked of the same person. Seen as normal cognitive interferences, these difficulties should not be used as a basis to form negative impressions or stereotypes of bilinguals. As discussed earlier in this book (see Chapter 4), it is easy to fall into this trap, allowing our perceptions to be driven by ethnocentrism and, in some cases, an unconscious wish to validate preexisting stereotypes. The research clearly shows, however, that such perceptions have little basis in fact.

⊠ Conclusion

Language is the principal means by which we communicate with one another and store information. Language is also the principal means by which each generation receives its cultural inheritance from the previous generation. Indeed, without language, culture as we know it would not exist at all. So it should come as no surprise that language is of particular interest to cross-cultural researchers.

Languages differ enormously from one another, and these differences are related to important differences in the customs and behaviors of the cultures in which those languages reside. As we have seen, culture is intimately related to both language lexicons and pragmatics. And despite some skepticism regarding the strength of the Sapir–Whorf hypothesis, a close examination of the cross-cultural research testing it tends to support some versions. Language also plays an important predictive role in the personalities of multilingual individuals. Finally, although the processes by which we learn language appear to be universal, cultures clearly differ in their attitudes and opinions about language acquisition. It is not yet clear how these attitudes and opinions influence language learning.

Language acquisition is an important aspect of the study of language because it helps us understand much broader issues of human behavior. By discovering which acquisition processes are universal and which are specific to single cultures, we can better address to what extent our behavior is innate (biologically determined) or learned (culturally determined).

Understanding how language is acquired is also important for practical reasons: As the world moves toward what has been called a global village (that is, greater interdependence among nations), knowledge of more than one language has become a vital tool in understanding and communicating with people of other cultures—not only internationally but also within a pluralistic, multicultural society such as the United States. No matter how important multilingualism is now, it is likely to become even more important in the future.

Understanding the relationship between culture and language is also important in understanding and becoming proficient in the process of intercultural communication. As we will see in Chapter 14, because culture and language are intimately intertwined, intercultural communication processes differ from those involved in communicating with members of one's own culture (intracultural communication). Understanding the extent and pervasiveness of this relationship is integral to gaining an appreciation of these differences. Research on foreign language processing difficulty and the foreign language effect reviewed earlier also helps in understanding and engaging in such interactions.

Recognition of the special relationship between language, culture, and behavior is especially important for students in the United States. Americans are notoriously ignorant of languages other than English, and this ignorance is often accompanied by an ethnocentric view rejecting the need to learn, understand, and appreciate other languages, customs, and cultures. Given that Americans are the most monolingual of all peoples of the world, that language is intimately tied to culture, and that multilingualism is associated with an appreciation of different cultures, it may be that Americans are actually the most ethnocentric of all people. Our ignorance of languages other than English, and the unfortunate ethnocentrism that often accompanies this ignorance, may be the root of our future downfall. For many of us who have little exposure to these issues in our everyday lives, now is the time to begin our study of language and culture for a better understanding of the partners in our global village.

Glossary

culture-affiliation hypothesis The hypothesis that immigrant bilinguals will tend to affiliate themselves with the values and beliefs of the culture associated with the language in which they are currently operating. When the language is switched, so are the cultural values with which they affiliate.

language aquisition device Proposed by Chomsky, it is the mechanism thought to account for the development of language in children.

lexicon The words contained in a language, the vocabulary.

minority group–affiliation hypothesis The hypothesis that immigrant bilinguals will tend to self-identify as members of an ethnic minority group and adopt the behavioral stereotypes of the majority culture about their minority as their own when they are operating in the language associated with their minority group.

morphemes The smallest and most basic units of meaning in a language.

phonemes The smallest and most basic units of sound in a language.

phonology The system of rules governing how words should sound (pronunciation, "accent") in a given language.

pragmatics The system of rules governing the how language is used and understood in given social contexts.

Sapir–Whorf hypothesis The proposition that speakers of different languages think differently, and that they do so because of the differences in their languages.

semantics What words mean.

syntax and grammar The system of rules governing word forms and how words should be strung together to form meaningful utterances.

13

Culture and Nonverbal Behavior

What Are Nonverbal Behaviors?

When people think about communication, they generally think about language. But language is just one part of communication—and perhaps not the most important part. In fact, we use many other vehicles of expression to communicate our thoughts, feelings, desires, and wishes to others. These other means of communication are not verbal—they do not use words or sentences—but nonverbal. Communication in its broadest sense occurs both verbally (via language) and nonverbally.

Nonverbal communication itself can be classified in two general categories: nonverbal behaviors and nonbehaviors. **Nonverbal behaviors** are all the behaviors, other than words, that occur during communication. Such nonverbal behaviors include

- Facial expressions
- Movements and gestures of the hands, arms, and legs
- Posture, lean, and body orientation
- Tone of voice and other vocal characteristics, including pitch, rate, intonation, and silence
- Interpersonal space
- Touching behaviors
- Gaze and visual attention

Nonverbal behaviors, thus, include behaviors that we typically associate with active expressitivity and others that are more subtle.

Nonbehavioral nonverbal communication involves a host of other sources of messages and signals that carry meaning in human communication, but that are not produced directly by actual behaviors. These more subtle forms of communication include the use of time, the type of clothing we wear, the type of architectural structures we live and work in, and the cosmetic changes we make to our appearance. These nonbehaviors convey messages during communication just as verbal language and nonverbal behaviors do, and are an integral part of the entire communication package.

Both behaviors and nonbehaviors fall under the general category of nonverbal communication. When you stop to think of all the different things that are actually occurring when people communicate with each other—that is, all the different channels of signals and messages that are being sent and received at any one time—it is pretty mind-boggling. People come to an interaction in a certain place that is bounded by how they have structured it physically. They come to that interaction with a certain appearance. They space themselves from one another at certain distances. They adopt certain postures when interacting. They gesture and use hand movements to illustrate what they are saying. Their faces may become animated or reserved. Their voices may become excited or suppressed. Indeed, when communication is occurring, the actual words and verbal language used are only a small part of the entire package of events and behaviors that constitute communication. In a sense, there are two languages involved when people communicate—one verbal, and the other nonverbal.

In this chapter, we focus on the relationship between culture and nonverbal behaviors, the area of nonverbal communication that has received the most attention in cross-cultural research. We will begin by reviewing how previous writers have described the various functions of nonverbal behaviors. Then, we will discuss how verbal and nonverbal behaviors combine in communication, looking at research that has examined the relative contribution of each to overall communication process and content. Next, we will examine the relationship between culture and nonverbal behaviors in communication, highlighting the rich and varied research that has been conducted on this topic. We will then discuss cross-cultural research on five specific nonverbal behavior processes: facial expressions, gaze and visual behavior, interpersonal space and proxemics, gestures, and other nonverbal behaviors. We will conclude by examining a number of recent studies that have looked at the implication of cultural differences in nonverbal behaviors in applied settings.

Classifying the Functions of Nonverbal Behaviors

We engage in a myriad of nonverbal behaviors, some having to do with communication, and some not. Each occurs for a reason, however, and usually carries some kind of inherent meaning or message that can be gleaned from the behavior. What types of information are communicated along these various channels? Several writers (for example, Efron, 1941; Ekman & Friesen, 1969) have attempted to classify the various types of nonverbal behaviors. While each classification scheme has merits and disadvantages, Ekman and Friesen's (1969) scheme may be particularly useful to us in understanding cultural influences on nonverbal behaviors.

In Ekman and Friesen's (1969) scheme, nonverbal behaviors can be classified into five major categories: illustrators, adaptors/manipulators, emblems, emotion, and regulators. **Illustrators** are nonverbal behaviors we use to highlight aspects of the words we speak. They illustrate visually what the words are trying to say symbolically. Many people, for example, use hand gestures to illustrate or highlight their speech. Gestures may be used solely to highlight characteristics of the voice, to convey how excited the person is about the message, or to describe the actual content of the message. You may notice that when violinist Itzhak Perlman strikes a high note, he raises his eyebrows. When he plays a low one, his brows lower. Perhaps the same behaviors occur when Placido Domingo or Pavaroti sings or when you raise or lower your voice.

Adaptors/manipulators are nonverbal behaviors we engage in to help our bodies adapt to the environment around us. Scratching an itch, picking our noses, biting our lips, and rubbing our eyes are all examples of adaptive behavior. While these behaviors may not be important in communication, they are important in our everyday lives (try not scratching an itch sometime), and all cultures develop rules of etiquette and manners concerning adaptors.

Emblems are nonverbal behaviors that convey a message by themselves. They do not have to occur during a conversation, although they often do. When they occur, they convey a message, just as a word, phrase, or sentence does. In the United States, for example, raising your brows, pushing your lower lip up, pulling your lip corners down, and shaking your head from side to side generally means that you question the validity of what is being said. Of course, there are simpler and more direct emblems, such as nodding the head to mean yes, shaking the head to mean no, and the good old finger. As you can probably guess, many emblems are culture-specific, and issues of cultural differences in nonverbal behaviors will be examined later in this chapter. Look at the now relatively famous picture of American servicemen taken captive in 1968 (Figure 13.1). This picture was shot by the Koreans and sent back to the United States supposedly to show that the servicemen were in good care. If you look closely, however, you will notice that several servicemen are giving the "finger." This was a clear emblematic indication to Americans viewing the photo that everything was *not* all right with them. Many also saw it as signifying defiance.

Emotion is yet another message conveyed by nonverbal behaviors. In Chapter 11, we saw how one type of nonverbal behavior, facial expression, conveys information about emotion in ways that are both universal and culture-specific. The face is the most studied channel of nonverbal behavior with respect to emotion, probably because of its ability to signal discrete, specific emotional states on a moment-to-moment basis. Other nonverbal behaviors, however, including voice and body posture, convey certain types of emotional or affective states.

Figure 13.1 These American servicemen were taken captive when North Korea seized the U.S. ship *Pueblo* in 1968. Can you find the emblem displayed by some of these men?

Finally, **regulators** are nonverbal behaviors we engage in to regulate the flow of speech during a conversation. We often use our faces to signal that we are done, or waiting, or even inviting someone else to speak. Our tone of voice also regulates speech, informing others when we are finished speaking. In many cultures, gaze and visual attention regulate speech, as do gestures inviting others to chime in.

Not only are there many different channels of nonverbal behaviors, but each channel can convey many different types of messages. It is ironic that so much information is conveyed by these nonverbal behaviors, yet we give them relatively little attention or thought when we consider issues of communication. In fact, these nonverbal behaviors are vital to successful communication, intercultural or otherwise, even though they are often unconscious and automatic.

Verbal and Nonverbal Behaviors in Communication

Communication does not occur in a vacuum; it occurs in a specific context. People have certain biases, and words are couched in a particular framework, coupled with facial expressions, gestures, postures, and other behaviors. When we interact with others, the amount of information transmitted from one person to the next is unbelievably large. We may think that the only part, or the main part, of communication is the words being spoken. Indeed, we attend to the words and the language that is used. Our formal educational experiences, from elementary school on up, center around language—words, grammar, spelling, and punctuation. We spend much of our time thinking about just the right words to use to express ourselves—our ideas, our thoughts, our opinions. We think about just the right thing to say to our boyfriends and girlfriends, business associates, acquaintances, work colleagues, or the police. We concentrate on the words and language when we speak.

But the words we use are only one part of the entire communication process. Our verbal language channel is just one of many channels activated when we communicate. All our behaviors and gestures—in short, our nonverbal behaviors—form important channels of communication as well. The only difference is that we do not think about them as much or as consciously as we think about the words we use or the language we speak. And we do not think about them as much when we listen to others speak. But even if we do not attend to them consciously, these nonverbal behaviors are very important in conveying meaning.

Nonverbal behavior can highlight or accent information. Nonverbal behaviors accent our emotional states. They convey how excited we are or whether we are angry, upset, or happy. Nonverbal behaviors convey information about the content of what we are saying. Nonverbal behaviors tell us when it is time to speak and time to listen. We can also get conflicting messages from nonverbal behaviors. The words coming out of someone's mouth may tell you one thing, but the person's nonverbal behaviors (tone of voice, gaze) may tell you something else. Someone may say "I love you" in words but communicate "not really" with nonverbal behaviors.

Many studies have reported that only a small fraction of the meaning people get in an interaction derives from the words that are spoken; most of the messages conveyed and perceived in interactions are nonverbal (for example, Mehrabian, 1981). Research demonstrating the dominance of nonverbal over verbal communication has included studies on the communication of friendly and hostile attitudes (Argyle, Alkema, & Gilmour, 1978); inferior and superior attitudes (Argyle, Salter, Nicholson, Williams, & Burgess, 1970); friendliness, approval, and consideration (Bugental, Kaswan, & Love, 1970); positivity and dominance (DePaulo, Rosenthal, Eisenstat, Rogers, & Susan, 1978; Friedman, 1978); positive, negative, and neutral evaluations (Mehrabian & Wiener, 1967); perceptions of leadership (Gitter, Black, & Fishman, 1975); honesty and deceit (Stiff, Hale, Garlick, & Rogan, 1990); and confidence (Walker, 1977).

In all these studies, the degree to which nonverbal behaviors contributed to the messages received by judges was quite large. Recently, I conducted an effect size analysis of the nonverbal dominance reported in these studies, in order to investigate exactly how large the effect is. The effect size estimate I computed was R^2, which corresponds to the degree of variability in the entire data set that is accounted for by the difference between nonverbal and verbal stimuli. Across all studies examined, the average effect size was .56 (average $r = .75$). An effect size of this magnitude is considered huge; many effect size estimates in contemporary psychology experiments are about .09 (corresponding to an r of about .30).

Moreover, the contribution of nonverbal behaviors appears to be larger when discrepant messages are transmitted. That is, when faced with ambiguous messages posed by discrepant signals in the verbal and nonverbal channels, people generally derive more meaning from nonverbal behaviors. Friedman (1978), for example, showed participants combinations of facial expressions portraying one of four emotions along with positive and negative verbal content. Judges were asked to rate the positivity in the combined stimuli. The results indicated that the nonverbal stimuli (faces) had a much stronger influence on the judgments than did the verbal stimuli. Likewise, Mehrabian and Wiener (1967) created audio stimuli that consisted of positive, neutral, and negative words spoken in a positive, neutral, or negative tone of voice. Judges heard these stimuli and made scalar positivity ratings of them. Once again, the overall findings indicated that tone influenced the ratings much more strongly than did the actual words.

Although research examining the relative contribution of verbal and nonverbal behaviors have been common in studies conducted in the United States, I know of only a few cross-cultural studies conducted on the same topic. Those few, however, also confirm the dominance of nonverbal behaviors over verbal language in influencing messages decoded during communication. Kudoh and Kaji (1988), for example, provided Japanese participants with either verbal descriptions of behaviors, stick figure drawings, or combinations of both. The verbal and nonverbal stimuli were classified as either positive or negative, depending on the participants' ratings on three semantic differential scales assessing positivity, arousal, and dominance. Combinations of the stimuli included both congruent and discrepant combinations. The findings indicated that when participants viewed discrepant stimuli, their ratings were more highly correlated with ratings for the nonverbal stimuli than for the verbal stimuli. Kudoh and Tamie (1991) replicated and extended this study by including two levels of discrepant verbal and nonverbal combinations (high and low), and by using more sophisticated multiple regression analyses to assess the independent degrees of contribution of verbal and nonverbal behaviors to the messages decoded. The results again indicated a strong dominance of nonverbal over verbal channels in the overall message perceived by the judges.

In short, communication is an intricate, complicated process with many different channels available for message transmission and many different messages being transmitted. During interaction, we all do amazing things. We take all the information we are receiving and synthesize it somehow to make sense out of it. While much conscious energy is spent understanding and interpreting the words and the language we and others use in interaction, most of how we learn to read and interpret the important nonverbal dimension is unconscious and automatic. No one ever taught us how to do this; we don't attend classes in nonverbal behavior. All of our education about nonverbal behaviors is informal, in our homes and on the streets. Yet all of us learn the rules by which members of our society and culture engage in nonverbal behaviors and interpret them. We receive nonverbal messages, process them, make sense out of it all, and put that information together with the verbal messages we receive via language. And, based on limited cross-cultural evidence, it seems that this process may be pancultural.

Cultural Influences on Nonverbal Behaviors and Their Implications for Communication

As we saw in the last chapter, culture exerts considerable influence over the verbal languages that we speak. In that domain, culture influences the language lexicons and vocabulary, and the rules by which words are put together to form meaningful phrases and sentences. Culture also influences our thoughts, feelings, and actions via language.

Just as spoken languages differ from one culture to the next, so do unspoken, nonverbal behaviors. That is, just as culture influences our verbal languages, culture also exerts considerable influence over our nonverbal languages. People of all cultures learn to use nonverbal behaviors—facial expressions, gestures, distance, gaze, and postures—as part of their communication repertoire, but people in each culture learn to use them in very specific ways. All humans are born with the capacity to form all types of sounds; culture dictates how we shape and mold those sounds into particular languages. In the same way, culture shapes and molds nonverbal behaviors into each culture's nonverbal language.

Consider, for example, American culture. When we speak to people, we look them straight in the eye. Our faces and gestures often become animated, highlighting specific, important parts of our speech. We learn to sit or stand at a certain distance when we interact, depending on whom we are interacting with and the specific context or situation in which that interaction is occurring. We learn how to signal when we are finished speaking and when we want to continue speaking. In short, we learn a very specific, American system of nonverbal behaviors to aid in our communication process, just as we have learned American English as a verbal language.

When we interact with people from our own culture, they have generally learned the same system or language of nonverbal behaviors as we have. They will most likely follow the same rules of distance, tone of voice, facial expressions, gestures, and postures. When we interact with longtime friends, for example, we know what that system is, even though we may not be able to verbalize it. We can interact with them successfully, with no ambiguity regarding the content of the message or its intent.

The same is true for our families. Family members generally "speak" the same nonverbal language. After all, it is from our families that we learned our nonverbal language. When we interact with them, we experience relatively few instances in which we are unable to read or correctly interpret the meaning of the signals we receive from all the various nonverbal channels.

The power of culture can be seen when we interact with people from our own culture who may be totally unfamiliar to us. When we meet someone for the first time, at a party—a business engagement, on the street, or in the theater—we can usually engage in some kind of conversation and successfully interpret the nonverbal messages being conveyed. The other person's nonverbal behaviors may be coy, flirtatious, or annoying—just about anything. But because we share the same nonverbal signaling and communication system, we can engage in meaningful communication because we know the "ground rules" on which the interaction is based.

The point is that we have all learned the same rules for using and interpreting nonverbal behaviors. When we see a certain action or behavior, we know how to interpret it, according to an implicit and informal set of guidelines dictated by our culture-specific nonverbal language. When the rules by which someone is engaging in nonverbal behaviors are the same as the rules by which another person is interpreting those behaviors, everything is fine. Interaction occurs smoothly and successfully, with little ambiguity about intent or message. (Whether or not you like the message or the intent is a different matter.)

Now consider a situation in which you are interacting with someone from a different culture. People from another culture bring with them their own verbal language. A person from Israel, for example, will bring the ability to speak Hebrew. A person from India will bring the ability to speak Hindi or a provincial dialect of India. But beyond the culture-specific verbal language they bring with them, they also bring a culture-specific nonverbal language. Thus, people from Israel will bring with them the Israeli- or Jewish-specific language of nonverbal behaviors; people from India will bring with them the India-specific (or Hindu- or Muslim- or Brahmin-specific) language of nonverbal behaviors. There are always two languages involved in any type of interaction—one verbal and the other nonverbal.

Some kinds of nonverbal behaviors are common to many cultures, such as greeting behaviors (for example, the eyebrow raise), whereas others differ radically (for example, touching behaviors) (Keating, 1976). In general, however, people from different cultures generate their own rules for engaging in nonverbal behaviors. These rules may be quite different from the rules you or I may be fluent in. These rules may dictate that different behaviors are enacted to get a certain point across or to accent a specific point. These rules may mean that the same behavior can actually carry quite different meanings. Developmental research has suggested that these rules are as old as verbal languages, and that children learn their cultural rules governing nonverbal behaviors as they learn the rules of vocal expression and acquire verbal language (von Raffler, 1981). If this is the case, it is no wonder that the cultural rules of nonverbal behavior are well ingrained in us by the time we are adults, and that we use them without much second thought.

Just as people from different cultures have their own rules for engaging in nonverbal behaviors, they have their own rules for interpreting the nonverbal behaviors of others. Obviously, they will have learned to associate certain behaviors with certain meanings, based on their culture and its rules.

When we interact with people from a different culture, we generally attend closely to the verbal language. But nonverbal language is also occurring, even if we don't consciously attend to it. The unconscious filters and processes through which we automatically interpret the nonverbal behaviors of others are also in active use, whether or not we are aware of them.

The problem in intercultural communication is that nonverbal language is silent, and interpretational processes are unconscious and automatic. Whether or not we attend to them, messages are being transmitted. More often than not, the nonverbal language of people of a different culture is different from what we are accustomed to. After interacting with someone from another culture, it is not uncommon to wonder whether we really "got" what was meant. Oftentimes we leave these situations feeling as though we may have missed something. These feelings arise because our unconscious system of nonverbal communication is having difficulty interpreting the nonverbal behaviors of someone from a different culture. Something just doesn't "feel" right.

Problems can occur in positive as well as negative directions. People often interpret certain types of behaviors positively when, in fact, they are not meant to be positive at all. Consider, for example, the Japanese head nodding and use of the word *hai*. The best translation of this word in English is "yes." But in Japanese, this word does not necessarily mean yes. It may mean yes, but it can also mean maybe, or even no. It is often used as a speech regulator, informing the speaker that the listener is listening. It can be a signal of deference to authority. This word and the nonverbal behaviors associated with it (head nod) most definitely do not have the same meaning in Japanese as they do in English. Yet many business and government negotiations have faltered on the interpretation of exactly this behavior, with Americans believing that the Japanese have agreed to something and that the deal is closed. The Japanese, however, may merely be signaling that they are listening. This type of cultural difference is the source of many interpersonal conflicts between spouses and lovers as well.

When we interact with people who have different nonverbal languages, we often form negative impressions of them. In the United States, for example, we learn to interact with people at a certain distance. When you interact with someone you do not know very well and this person places himself so close to you that you feel his breath when he speaks, you will probably feel quite uncomfortable and try to adjust the distance. He will follow. You will adjust again. He will follow again. You will probably want to get out of that interaction as soon as possible. You may consider the person rude or without manners. Many Arab and Middle Eastern cultures foster what Americans would consider too close interpersonal spacing during interactions, and this can be unsettling.

Or consider the opposite scenario. You are interacting with someone who stands quite far away from you, farther than you think would be normal under the circumstances. When you try to get closer, she moves farther away. You move up again; she moves back again. You probably think she has a negative impression of you and doesn't really want to interact with you.

We make these interpretations because we are trying to match observed behavior with our own rules for what those behaviors should mean. If the person you are interacting with is indeed from your own culture and operating according to the same rules, you will probably be correct in your interpretations. But what if the person is from a different culture, operating under different rules? Then your negative impressions and interpretations may be totally off base. Nonetheless, you leave feeling bad about the interaction, probably not wanting to interact again. They probably feel the same.

Nonverbal behaviors are just like a second language, albeit a silent, unspoken one. Just as cultures develop spoken, verbal languages, they also develop unspoken, nonverbal languages. Culture, along with biology, gender, and personality, is one of the most important influences on the interpretation of nonverbal behaviors; in conjunction with the social environment and other cognitive and affective mediators, it plays an important role in overall person perception (Patterson, 1995). If we are to get a handle on cultural similarities and differences in communication, we obviously need to pay more attention to cultural differences in these silent, nonverbal languages.

Cross-Cultural Research on Nonverbal Behaviors

If you were planning a trip to another country, had visitors from another country coming to stay with you, or just wanted to learn another language, what might you do? One of the things you might consider is going to your local bookstore, finding the reference or language section, and searching through the various language-learning books and dictionaries available for your language of interest. With phrase book or dictionary in hand, you would be able to look up words or phrases you wanted to say. When people spoke to you in that language, you could look up what they were saying or have them find the word or phrase and point it out to you.

Wouldn't it be great if dictionaries existed for the silent, nonverbal languages of the world as well? There could be a book or videotape reference containing all the possible nonverbal behaviors in a certain language and their translations in the American nonverbal system. If we saw some behavior or noticed a certain expression when interacting with someone from another culture, we could look it up and find out what it might mean instead of trying to interpret those behaviors according to our own, implicit, nonverbal language dictionary.

Although no such "dictionary" exists, there has been a considerable amount of research on nonverbal behaviors and how cultures differ in their use of them. This research has spanned a number of topics and types of nonverbal communication, including gaze and visual behavior, interpersonal space and proxemics, gestures, postures, nonverbal vocal cues, facial expressions, the use of time, clothing, touch, and even smell. Studies in each of these areas have produced a wealth of information about the complexity and importance of nonverbal behaviors in interpersonal communication and interaction.

In the remainder of this chapter, I will focus on five specific areas: facial expressions, gaze and visual attention, interpersonal space and proxemics, gestures, and other nonverbal behaviors. I have selected these topics for several reasons. First of all, there is a substantial base of cross-cultural research in each of these areas to inform us of how culture influences these aspects of the communication process. Also, these are primary areas of concern and interest in interpersonal interaction episodes and have the greatest relevance to our understanding and appreciation of cultural differences in communication styles. Collectively, this literature should give you a sense of just how pervasive the influence of culture is on this important aspect of communication.

Facial Expressions

Actually, we have already discussed one major channel of nonverbal behavior, facial expressions, in Chapter 11 on emotion. From that chapter, you will remember that cross-cultural research has amply demonstrated that a small set of facial expressions of emotion are universally expressed and recognized—that all people, regardless or race, culture, or gender, express anger, contempt, disgust, fear, happiness, sadness, and surprise in exactly the same ways. These facial configurations can be seen in people all around the world, and have also been documented in nonhuman primates and congenitally blind humans.

But, as we discussed in that chapter, people of all cultures also learn specific rules of expression management. These *display rules* are rules that we all learn to manage or modify our emotional expressions depending on social circumstances. The original study documenting the existence of these rules involved an American–Japanese comparison of participants' facial responses to stressful stimuli (Ekman, 1972; Friesen, 1972). When alone, the American and Japanese participants exhibited exactly the same facial expressions of emotion as those elicited on the stimulus tape. When in the presence of a higher-status experimenter in another condition of the experiment, however, there were considerable differences between the Americans and Japanese. While the Americans generally continued to show negative emotions on their faces, the Japanese for the most part masked their negative feelings by smiling. The experimenters concluded that the Japanese had learned a social rule that dictated that negative emotions are concealed in the presence of someone of higher status.

Emotion, however, is not the only function of facial expressions. Indeed, the face engages in all the functions of nonverbal behaviors, including illustrating speech (for example, raising your eyebrows when the intonation of your voice goes up and lowering them when your voice lowers); regulating conversation by signaling to your interaction partners you have finished your turn speaking; conveying emblematic information through greetings, rituals, and other behaviors that carry specific meanings; and adapting to the environment. Although the concept of display rules was originally developed in relation to emotional expression management, it is not unreasonable to suggest that we learn rules governing all other aspects of nonverbal expression management as well. Just as we learn grammatical rules governing our verbal language (add "s" to make a word plural), we learn nonverbal display rules governing our nonverbal behaviors.

While there is considerable within- and between-culture research on facial expressions of emotion and display rules, there is considerably less research on the nonemotional functions of facial expressions, particularly across cultures. This area of study is ripe for investigation to learn more about the nature and function of the rules governing nonemotional functions of the face.

Gaze and Visual Behavior

In seeking to understand possible universal and culture-specific aspects of behavior, from time to time it is useful to look at research on nonhuman primates (for example, apes, chimpanzees, gorillas). If we find that these animals engage in behaviors similar to those of humans, we may reasonably wonder if those behaviors might have evolutionary or biological bases. At the very least, these studies can help us gain a broader perspective on the nature of our behaviors and how much they are influenced by culture.

Research with nonhuman primates is especially interesting with regard to gaze and visual attention. Researchers as early as the 1960s, for example, found that mutual gazing between animals, especially staring, is a primary component of aggressive and threatening displays. This relationship between staring and aggression has been observed in male baboons, gorillas, rhesus and bonnet macaques, and old world monkeys and apes (Altman, 1962; Hall & Devore, 1965; Hinde & Rowell, 1962; Schaller, 1963, 1964; Simonds, 1965; van Hooff, 1967).

This type of research forms much of the basis of our understanding of attention structures in animal societies. An **attention structure** is an organized pattern that dictates which animals can and cannot look at others. Attention structures appear to be highly related to dominance hierarchies in animal societies. In general, comparative research on nonhuman primates has shown that animals with lower status and power in a group pay more attention to higher-status animals and adjust their behaviors accordingly.

Let's switch our attention temporarily back to humans. Have you ever played a game of staring? This game has several different names, depending on the time period and geographic area of the United States, but it involves two individuals staring at each other with a blank or neutral face. The game proceeds until one of the two people looks away, starts laughing, or generally breaks off the stare. The one who breaks off the stare is the loser.

This game exemplifies some of the dominance, status, and power themes associated with gaze that are found in the animal literature. Animal research has shown that dominance or power struggles often involve mutual glaring or staring at each other (Fehr & Exline, 1987). The power struggle between two animals will end when one of the animals backs off and breaks the gaze. Humans seem to have a taboo against these types of direct stares, as if our cultures produce rules designed to curb or control such displays of aggression or dominance.

Dominance and aggression, however, are not the only messages associated with gazing. Some writers (for example, Argyle & Cook, 1976) have suggested that gazing can also signal affiliation or nurturance. Phrases in English such as "gazing into someone's eyes" or "getting lost in one's eyes" seem to capture verbally this aspect of gaze. Fehr and Exline (1987) suggest that the affiliative aspects of gazing may have their roots in infancy, because infants gaze attentively at adults, as their source of care and protection.

It is not unreasonable to think that cultures should come up with rules concerning gazing and visual attention. Both aggression and affiliation are behavioral tendencies that are important for group stability and maintenance. Each culture derives its own set of rules concerning gazing and visual attention to ensure that its members are affiliated while at the same time curbing aggressive tendencies.

Cross-cultural research on gazing in humans has also produced some very interesting findings. Several studies have shown that people from Arabic cultures gaze much longer and more directly at their partners than Americans do (Hall, 1963; Watson & Graves, 1966). Watson (1970) studied visual attention patterns in 30 different countries and separated the countries according to whether they were a "contact" culture (that is, those that facilitated physical touch or contact during interaction) or a "noncontact" culture. Watson found that people in contact cultures engaged in more gazing than did people of noncontact cultures. People from contact cultures also exhibited more direct orientations when interacting with others, less distance, and more touching.

When a person does not look at us as much as we are used to when interacting, we tend to make negative attributions about that behavior. We may believe that the other person is not interested in us or in our conversation. We may believe that the other person does not want to be here or wants to break off the conversation. I have often heard that many Americans get frustrated and perplexed when interacting with people from some Asian cultures because the people from those cultures do not look directly at them when interacting. Americans may react negatively, wondering if the other person is angry, or not interested romantically, or lying. Conversely, Watson and Hall both mention that many people from Arabic cultures get annoyed when interacting with Americans, probably because the Americans tend to gaze less than the Arabs are used to. This is a two-way street!

Even within the United States, different groups of Americans differ in their gaze and visual behavior. A number of studies have shown that African Americans tend to gaze less directly than do European Americans when interacting with someone (Exline, Jones, & Maciorowski, 1977; LaFrance & Mayo, 1976). In studying African American and European American mixed-and same-ethnicity interactions, Fehr (1977, 1981) found that the African Americans gazed less directly, replicating the findings of other researchers. However, Fehr also found that the participants tended to prefer interacting with people who gazed about the same amount as they were accustomed to, regardless of ethnicity.

Thus, studies of nonhuman primates, across human cultures, and within American culture all indicate that gaze is an important aspect of social and interactive behavior. When we encounter people who gaze differently than we are used to, we often come away from those interactions with negative or questioning feelings about our relationship with the other person or about that person. If the other person does not gaze as much as we expect, we tend to make negative attributions about that person's interest in us or in the conversation. If the other person gazes too much, we consider the person too aggressive or domineering, much as in the staring game.

We make these attributions because we use the rules of interpretation we are accustomed to. If the person with whom we are interacting is from our own culture, our interpretations may be correct. But if the person is from another culture, operating with another set of rules, our interpretations of the person's gaze behavior may actually be wrong. The other person may be avoiding direct eye contact, for example, out of deference or appreciation for your status or power.

Interpersonal Space and Proxemics

Space is another extremely important dimension of nonverbal behavior that we often take for granted. How we use space can send important messages about power, status, and dominance. Have you ever noticed that the most powerful people in a company or organization seem to have spaces that are the most remote and difficult to access? They usually have the nicest spaces, and certainly some of the largest spaces. Even on the same floor, the people with the most power seem to have the corner spaces, with a view to the outside world and limited access from the inside. People with less power are accessible by everyone from all directions; people with more power are relatively inaccessible.

Like gaze and visual behavior, space is an important nonverbal dimension in animals of various species. Animal societies, humans included, seem to have rules about how to use space optimally, given space restrictions and other limitations placed on them for survival. Hall (1978) reports that deer, gulls, and pelicans have ordered rules about spacing in their colonies. Calhoun (1950) conducted a study with 150 rats and found that, given a certain amount of space in which to live, the rats seemed to settle "naturally" into 12 groups of approximately 12 rats each.

The rules we develop in relation to interpersonal spacing depend on the space resources available to us. These rules, in turn, have dramatic effects on the rules of social interaction, appropriateness, and politeness that we adopt to survive at a given population size and density. Finally, these rules form the basis for our cultural rules about interpersonal space. All these rules feed off space availability and population density, which in turn feed off the rules, forming a circular, self-renewing cycle.

Americans, like people from other cultures and countries, have developed rules governing the use of interpersonal space. Hall (1978) specifies four different levels of interpersonal space use depending on social relationship type. The closest type of relationship, *intimate relationships*, are characterized by interpersonal spaces of between 0 and 1.5 feet. *Personal relationships* are generally characterized by distances of 1.5 feet to 4 feet. *Social consultive relationships* are generally characterized by distances between 4 and 8 or 10 feet. Relationships that involve distances greater than 10 feet are generally considered *public relationships*.

Most cultures probably develop similar distinctions among social relationships, as suggested in Chapter 16 on social behavior. Cultures will most likely differ, however, in how much space they consider appropriate to each relationship type. Indeed, cross-cultural research on interpersonal distance and space has found considerable differences among cultures in the use of interpersonal space. Watson and Graves (1966), for example, studied pairs of male students from Arab cultures and compared their use of space with the use of space of similar pairs of American male students. They found that Arab males tended to sit closer to each other, with more direct, confrontational types of body orientations. They had greater eye contact and tended to speak in louder voices than did the Americans. Hall (1963, 1966), in fact, concluded that people from Arab cultures generally learn to interact with others at distances close enough to feel the other person's breath.

Other cross-cultural studies have shown that people of various other cultures learn to use space differently in interpersonal contexts. Forston and Larson (1968) cited anecdotal evidence that students with Latin American backgrounds tended to interact more closely than did students of European backgrounds. Noesjirwan (1977, 1978) reported that Indonesian subjects tended to sit closer than did Australian subjects. Shuter (1977) reported that Italians interacted more closely than did either Germans or Americans. Shuter (1976) also reported that people from Colombia generally interacted at closer distances than did subjects from Costa Rica.

An interesting study by Remland, Jones, and Brinkman (1991) looked at the relative influence of culture on the use of interpersonal space, compared to other factors. In this study, naturally occurring dyadic (two-person) interactions by participants from the Netherlands, France, and England were coded by trained coders. The results indicated that the Dutch participants maintained greater distances than did the French and English pairs, and the French maintained greater distances than the English. Body orientation between the pairs was more direct for the French than for either the Dutch or the English. But, interestingly, neither the sex composition of the dyad nor the sex of the individual affected the interpersonal spacing or the body orientation of the participants, as would be expected according to traditional theories and previous findings documenting gender differences in nonverbal behavior (for example, Hall, 1978). Also, age did not influence the interpersonal spacing. Culture, not age or sex, seemed to be the important determinant in defining appropriate spacing between interactants.

Differences in the rules we all have concerning the use of space in interpersonal contexts can pose major problems in intercultural communication situations. As with other nonverbal behaviors, our use of space and our interpretation of the use of space around us often happen unconsciously. We have internalized these unspoken cultural rules and act on them automatically—as do people from other cultures. But their rules may be different from ours, and we need to take these differences into account when interacting with people from other cultures.

Gestures

Say you meet someone in class whom you are attracted to. One day, you work up enough courage to go up to him or her and ask for a date. You are busy making conversation, kind of fumbling around with your words, hands, and books. Finally, you pop the question: Will he or she go out with you tonight? He or she nods. You're about ready to jump through the ceiling with excitement. But you'd better control yourself, you think to yourself, and make arrangements to see him or her later. He or she nods again. You go away calm, cool, and oh so collected. Later that evening, you show up to pick up your date, but your date is not there. Your date left word with a roommate that he or she won't be there. What happened?

Well, if your date is an American using an American gesture (head nod), then something is definitely strange. But if your date is from another culture, where nodding the head means no and shaking the head means yes, then he or she was telling you no all along! While people of most cultures seem to nod their heads when meaning yes and shake their heads when meaning no, there are some cultures (for example, some parts of Greece and Turkey) where the people do exactly the opposite (Ekman, Friesen, & Bear, 1984; Kendon, 1987).

Gestures are movements of the body, usually the hands, that are generally reflective of thought or feeling. Many gestures are culture-specific, differing in each culture. But when we use them, especially in intercultural contexts, we don't readily think about the fact that they may have a different meaning to someone else. Being unaware of these differences can definitely cause problems. At the very least, you might miss out on some dates.

Many cultures exhibit differences in the use of gestures as illustrators. Remember that illustrators are actions that highlight or accent speech or speech content. Some cultures (for example, Jewish, Italian) encourage their members to be very expressive in their gestures and mannerisms when speaking. Other cultures (for example, Japanese, Thai) encourage their members to be more reserved in using gestures as illustrators. It is amazing how accustomed we become to our cultural norms and expectations concerning gestures. In cultures that encourage gestures as illustrators (what Kendon, 1987, calls "gesticulation"), people think nothing of interacting with people who seem to flail about, using large hand movements (and hopefully some safe distance!) when talking to others. In fact, people of these cultures probably think something is wrong when they interact with people from more reserved cultures. Conversely, people from more reserved cultures may think something is strange, for even feel threatened or overwhelmed, when they interact with gesturally expressive people.

The possibility of unnecessary intercultural conflict is all too real. On the basis of cultural differences in gestures, gesticulations, and other nonverbal aspects of communication, we can come away from intercultural communication situations with negative feelings about the people we were interacting with or about the conversation topic. These feelings may generalize into detrimental stereotypes about all people of that culture.

Most cultures have quite an elaborate system of emblematic gestures. Emblems are gestures and movements that have a total meaning by themselves. The "finger," thumbs up, A-OK, head nods and shakes, and the V sign are all examples of emblems used in the United States. Shrugging your shoulders and raising both hands, palms up, is yet another emblematic gesture, signaling uncertainty or ignorance about something. We take these emblematic gestures for granted. But there are many stories of travelers from the United States getting into trouble using American gestures in other countries, where the gestures have different meanings. While traveling in some parts of Europe, for example, you don't want to use the A-OK sign. While you might mean to say "Everything's okay," in some parts of Europe it is a rude or vulgar gesture, often interpreted as an invitation for sex (Ekman et al., 1984). In some other parts of Europe, it might mean "You're nothing." Pointing your index finger toward your head and temple area in the United States signals that you are smart. In some parts of Europe and Asia, however, it means that you are stupid.

The "V for victory" sign with the index and middle fingers is another example of cultural differences in gestures. This gesture was commonly used in the United States to mean victory, and it has caught on in other countries as well. It is said that some members of the Greek and American military may have insulted former British Prime Minister Winston Churchill when they gave that sign with the palm facing backward instead of forward. Facing backward, it is a common English insult equivalent to our American saying "up yours." The original V for victory sign is signaled with the palm facing outward. But you wouldn't want to do that in Greece, because there it is an abbreviated form of an insult. The gesture evolved in Greece from a practice of throwing garbage and dirt from the streets toward criminals as they were paraded through the streets.

Japanese often signify that someone is angry by raising the index fingers of both hands, in a pointing fashion, toward the sides of their heads, pointing up. In Brazil and other South American countries, however, this signifies that one wants sex (is horny). Imagine what would happen if a Japanese person were trying to tell someone from Brazil that someone else is angry and the Brazilian interpreted the signal to mean the Japanese person is horny!

The gestures described in this section are just a few of the many different gestures used around the world, with a few of their different meanings and interpretations. Some scholars have attempted to catalog in great detail the use of gestures in various cultures. Many of these resources are in book form (for example, Ekman, Friesen, & Bear, 1984; Kendon, 1987; Morris, Collett, Marsh, & O'Shaughnessy, 1980), and there is at least one videotape on the market that demonstrates differences in the meaning and use of gestures in different cultures (Archer, 1991).

Finally, an interesting study by Poortinga, Schoots, and van de Koppel (1993) highlights both the universal and culture-specific bases for many emblematic gestures. In this study, the researchers obtained emblematic gestures from participants in three very disparate cultures—Kurdistan, China, and the Netherlands—and classified them as "referential" (meaning can be derived from the gesture itself) or "conventional" (meaning is dependent on culture-specific codes and conventions). The researchers found that with referential gestures, judges of different cultures could deduce their basic message and meaning. Conventional gestures, however, could only be interpreted by members of the cultures from which they originated. These findings demonstrate that gestures are neither entirely universal, based on a shared meaning system of action codes, nor entirely culturally relative, meaningful only for people familiar with a particular code. Instead, the findings demonstrated that some gestures may indeed be universal—shared by people of other cultures because of shared principles of psychological communication—while others are indeed specific to certain cultures. These authors have called their intermediary position—one that involves the possibility of culture-constant as well as culture-specific learning in symbols and signals—psychological universalism.

Other Nonverbal Behaviors

Although cross-cultural studies on other nonverbal behaviors are far less frequent in the literature, they do document the influence of culture on other nonverbal channels, including the semantic meanings attributed to body postures (for example, Kudoh & Matsumoto, 1985; Matsumoto & Kudoh, 1987), vocal characteristics (Matsumoto & Kishimoto, 1983), and hand and arm movements (Vrij & Winkel, 1991, 1992). Kudoh and Matsumoto (1985), for example, showed participants in the United States and Japan a series of stick figure drawings and verbal descriptions of a variety of different body postures, and asked them to rate the stimuli using a semantic differential method. Factor analyses of the ratings indicated the same psychological constructs in the American and Japanese ratings; however, the constructs differed in their degree of importance in each culture. Positive–negative evaluations were the most salient for the American judges, while interpersonal consciousness was more salient for the Japanese. These findings were replicated in a subsequent study using a different rating scale (Matsumoto & Kudoh, 1987). Both of these studies highlighted the different ways in which body postures are interpreted in the two cultures, and those methods of interpretation seem to be related to cultural concerns in the two cultures as well.

Collectively, the evidence described in this section spans a number of types of nonverbal behaviors—facial expressions, visual attention, interpersonal space, gestures, and others—and all provide ample support for the notion that culture plays a large role in molding our nonverbal behaviors. Cross-cultural research, however, has not been able to examine all aspects of nonverbal behaviors equally well, and many gaps in our knowledge remain to be filled by future cross-cultural studies.

Applied Studies Examining Cross-Cultural Differences in Nonverbal Behaviors

Over the years, evidence has gradually accumulated documenting how cultural differences in nonverbal behaviors can affect many practical situations in everyday life. Vrij and Winkel (1992), for example, examined the influence of race, beliefs, and nonverbal behaviors on impression formation in cross-cultural police–citizen interactions. Caucasian police officers participated in the experiment, in which they were told that a woman had been assaulted and raped and that the police assumed that the offender lived on the same street as the woman. Accordingly, the police began to interview all men door to door. Part of the interrogation was shown on videotape, with either a black or white interviewee (an actor for the purpose of the study). The actors portrayed having either similar or dissimilar beliefs to the police officers, and smiled according to previously collected norms associated with blacks or whites. The results indicated that black actors who portrayed dissimilar beliefs and typically black smiling patterns were assessed more negatively than others. What was also interesting was that the race of the actor by itself did not lead to negative assessments; in fact, black actors in general were assessed more positively than white actors. It was only the combination of actor race with specific attitudes and nonverbal behaviors that led to negative assessments by the police officers. These results clearly speak to the power of nonverbal behaviors in actual applied situations.

A number of other applied cross-cultural studies highlight the important role nonverbal behaviors play in our lives, along with the practical implications of cultural differences in those behaviors. For example, Masters and Sullivan (1989) examined viewer responses to three legislative candidates in France. They found that nonverbal displays of anger/threat elicited more positive responses from French viewers than Americans, suggesting important cultural differences in leadership style in the media age. Schneller (1988) demonstrated cultural differences in nonverbal behaviors among Ethiopian newcomers to Israel, and discussed their relationship to immigrant and acculturation difficulties. Galloway (1984) documented the importance of understanding cultural differences in nonverbal behaviors in teacher–student interactions, arguing that if nonverbal behavior is to have practical value to educators, it must be viewed from a multicultural perspective. Hanna (1984) investigated black–white differences in nonverbal behavior, and discussed the impact of these differences on intercultural communication between the two groups.

Studies such as these, showing the important practical ramifications of cultural differences in nonverbal behavior, lead us to ask whether formal training in nonverbal behavior interpretation can help intercultural communication processes and outcomes. If the answer is yes, then cross-cultural research can play a major role in identifying crucial variables important to the training process, thus helping to bridge the gap among people from different cultural backgrounds. While only a few studies on this topic have been published to date, their findings are indeed suggestive of the positive impact of nonverbal skills training. Collett (1971), for example, trained English subjects to engage in more visually attentive behaviors when engaging with subjects from Arabic cultures. In later ratings, Arabic subjects preferred interacting with English subjects who had received training over English subjects who had not received training—even though other English subjects could not discriminate which English people had been trained and which had not. Garratt, Baxter, and Rozelle (1981) trained police officers to engage in gaze and visually attentive behavior patterns similar to those previously found among African Americans. The police officers then used these patterns when interviewing male African American undergraduate subjects. The subjects invariably rated the trained officers more favorably than the untrained officers.

Together, these studies make it clear that cultural differences in nonverbal behaviors have important practical, real-world ramifications in all walks of our lives. With increasing interaction among diverse populations around the world and within the United States, these differences are bound to arise with growing frequency, whether at home, at work, or in social situations. Future cross-cultural research should not only continue to document the important ramifications of these differences in everyday situations, but also play a role in finding ways to bridge gaps and differences, through education about the sources of these differences and identification of variables that can lead to more successful intercultural communication and living.

Conclusion

In this chapter, we have discussed the types and functions of nonverbal behaviors, their role in the process of communication, the relative contribution of verbal and nonverbal behavior in communication, and cross-cultural research on both basic and applied issues relating to nonverbal behaviors. In reviewing the cross-cultural literature, I chose to focus on a few examples of nonverbal behaviors, including facial expressions, gaze and visual attention, interpersonal space and distance, and gestures. I chose these areas because of the wealth of cross-cultural research on these topics and because of their impact on the communication process. However, the world of nonverbal behaviors is much broader—as complex and varied as that of verbal language. The contribution of nonverbal behavior to the total communication process is no longer debated in the social sciences. And as we have seen, these behaviors can have important practical consequences.

As you will recall from the beginning of this chapter, nonverbal communication encompasses not only the sort of nonverbal behaviors discussed at length in this chapter, but also nonbehavioral forms of communication—clothing, cosmetic items, architecture, and all other nonbehavioral aspects of our lives that convey meaning and messages. These nonbehavioral aspects of nonverbal communication are also important to understanding the total impact of culture on the process of communication. Future research needs to address such issues to provide a more complete picture of the influence of culture on communication.

We know that nonverbal behaviors contribute the bulk of the messages received and interpreted in communication, and that this effect appears to be pancultural. Despite the importance of nonverbal behaviors, however, we often take them for granted. Although we receive no formal training in how to send or receive nonverbal messages and signals, by adulthood we have become so skilled at it that we do so unconsciously and automatically.

Nonverbal behaviors are just as much a language as any other. Just as verbal languages differ from culture to culture, so do nonverbal languages. Because we are aware of the differences between verbal languages, we do not hesitate to use dictionaries and other resources to help us understand different languages. But when it comes to nonverbal language, we often mistakenly assume that our systems of communicating nonverbally are all the same.

Understanding cultural differences in nonverbal behavior is the first step in the process of truly appreciating cultural differences in communication. To study intercultural communication solely in terms of verbal language means excluding an important process of communication. Some authors (for example, Cerroni-Long, 1985) even suggest that the study of nonverbal behaviors, as a microbehavioral system of symbols and signals, is instrumental to gaining a fundamental understanding of culture itself.

The research described in this chapter not only highlights basic cultural differences in the meaning and uses of nonverbal behaviors, but also documents their importance in applied situations, and suggests the possibility of developing training programs to help people understand nonverbal behaviors better in order to bridge cultural differences. Still, the real task left to those of us who study culture and cultural differences is to recognize the central role that nonverbal behaviors play in the communication process and then realize how our own cultural background influences the ways we engage and interpret the nonverbal world around us. Although these processes are usually unconscious and automatic, we can work consciously to make them more flexible and inclusive of different cultural systems.

Glossary

adaptors/manipulators   Nonverbal behaviors we engage in to help our bodies adapt to the environment around us.

attention structure   An organized pattern that dictates which animals can and cannot look at others. These structures appear to be highly related to dominance hierarchies in animal societies.

emblems   Nonverbal behaviors that convey a message by themselves.

gestures Movements of the body, usually the hands, that are generally reflective of thought or feeling.

illustrators Nonverbal behaviors used to highlight aspects of the words we speak.

nonverbal behaviors All the behaviors, other than words, that occur during communication, including facial expressions; movements and gestures of hands, arms, and legs; posture; vocal characteristics such as pitch, rate, intonation, and silence; interpersonal space; touching behaviors; and gaze and visual attention.

regulators Nonverbal behaviors we engage in to regulate the flow of speech during a conversation.

14

Intercultural Communication

As our world becomes more culturally complex and plural, the topic of intercultural communication becomes increasingly important. Our ability to communicate well across cultural barriers affects our ability to function well not only at work and school, but in our homes, with our families, and at play. As the need for intercultural communication increases, we seem to be simply thrown together and forced to fend for ourselves. Are there ways we can improve this process?

Much research has been conducted on intercultural and cross-cultural communication. In the last two chapters, we discussed how culture influences verbal language and nonverbal behaviors. In other chapters of this book, we have discussed how culture can influence our perceptions and interpretations of others. In this chapter, we put all that information together to build a model of communication. In doing so, we will compare intracultural communication with intercultural communication, and discuss the latter's unique aspects. We will also discuss how and why communication may break down, and what we can do to ensure successful communication in intercultural relationships.

We begin by defining communication and describing the components of the communication process. Then, we will examine the pervasive and profound influence of culture on both encoding and decoding processes in communication, borrowing material from other parts of the book. Next, we will compare intracultural with intercultural communication, noting that conflict and misunderstandings are inherent and inevitable in the latter. Finally, we will discuss strategies for building effective intercultural communication, focusing on emotions, conflict management, and the development of intercultural sensitivity.

Defining Communication

Many definitions of communication and intercultural communication have been offered (see reviews by Kim & Gudykunst, 1988; Samovar & Porter, 1995). Porter and Samovar (1997), for example, define communication as "that which happens whenever someone responds to the behavior or the residue of the behavior of another person" (p. 9). Samovar and Porter (1995) define communication as occurring "whenever meaning is attributed to behavior" (p. 27). In this chapter, I define communication simply as the *exchange of knowledge, ideas, thoughts, concepts, and emotions among people*.

Communication can be intentional or unintentional. Of course, communication occurs when two or more people deliberately try to convey meaning to one another. Conversations, letter writing, and even this book are forms of communication. However, communication also occurs unintentionally; that is, we convey messages and meanings to others even when we do not intend to. Communication thus refers to the fact that people attach meanings to behaviors, whether or not those meanings are intended.

In the fields of social psychology and communication, the term *interpersonal communication* usually refers to communication that occurs among people of the same cultural background; in this sense, it is synonymous with **intracultural communication**. **Intercultural communication** refers to the exchange of knowledge, ideas, thoughts, concepts, and emotions among people of different cultural backgrounds.

As we will see in this chapter, intercultural communication has its own set of special issues that make it more complex, demanding, and difficult than intracultural or interpersonal communication. In order to get a handle on exactly what these special issues are, we need to get a better idea of the basic components of the communication process.

The Components of Communication

The Two Modes of Communication

The components of the communication process can be differentiated in several ways. One way is to identify the modes by which communication can occur. People communicate using two modalities: verbal and nonverbal. These two modalities correspond to the content of the last two chapters in this book. The verbal mode involves language, with its unique set of phonemes, morphemes, and lexicon; syntax and grammar; phonology; semantics; and pragmatics. Verbal language is a meaningful system that comprises these components, symbolizes the world, and allows for the exchange of ideas, thoughts, and feelings.

The nonverbal modality includes all nonlanguage behaviors, including facial expressions, gaze and eye contact, voice and paralinguistic cues, interpersonal space, gestures, body posture, and silence. As we saw in the last chapter, nonverbal behavior is multidimensional; that is, it serves many purposes in addition to communication (remember Ekman and Friesen's classification of nonverbal behaviors as illustrators, regulators, emblems and gestures, adaptors, and emotions). Ample research, both within the United States and in other cultures, has demonstrated the relative importance of nonverbal behaviors over verbal language in the communication of messages.

Encoding and Decoding

Another way of looking at the communication process is in terms of encoding and decoding. **Encoding** refers to the process by which people select, consciously or unconsciously, a particular modality and method by which to create and send a message to someone else. Although we don't think about this process all the time as adults, as children we had to learn the rules of syntax, grammar, pragmatics, and phonology in order to encode competently. We also had to learn rules of appropriateness governing messages sent nonverbally. The person who encodes and transmits messages and meanings is often called in the research literature an *encoder* or *sender*.

Decoding refers to the process by which a person receives signals from an encoder and translates those signals into meaningful messages. Just as "proper" encoding depends on understanding and applying the rules of verbal and nonverbal behaviors, "proper" decoding depends on those rules in order for messages to be interpreted in the manner in which they were meant to be conveyed. In the scientific literature, the person who decodes messages is often called the *decoder* or the *receiver*.

Of course, communication is not a one-way street, with one person encoding and sending a message and another person decoding it. Communication is a vastly complex process of encoding and decoding in rapid succession, overlapping in time so as to occur almost simultaneously. It is this rapid give and take, back and forth, of the encoding and decoding process that makes the study of communication challenging, but also rewarding. During this process, individuals switch roles from moment to moment, from encoder to decoder and back again.

Channels, Signals, and Messages

Along with the two major modes of verbal language and nonverbal behaviors, and the two major processes of encoding and decoding, communication has a number of other components. **Signals** are the specific words and behaviors that are sent during communication—that is, the specific verbal language and nonverbal behaviors that are encoded when a message is sent. A facial expression, for example, may be a signal that is encoded with a particular message. Other signals might include specific words or phrases, body posture, or tone of voice.

Messages are the meanings that are intended or received with the signals. They are the knowledge, ideas, concepts, thoughts, or emotions that encoders intend to convey and decoders interpret. Signals are observable behaviors that do not necessarily have inherent meaning; messages are the meanings that we attribute to those behavioral signals.

Finally, **channels** refer to the specific sensory modalities by which signals are sent and messages are retrieved, such as sight or sound. The most widely used channels of communication are visual—seeing facial expressions, body postures, gestures, and the like—and auditory—hearing words, tone of voice, and so on. However, all the other senses are used in communication, including touch, smell, and taste.

The process of communication, can thus be described as one in which a sender encodes a message into a set of signals. These signals are conveyed through a variety of channels that are open and operating in the receiver. The receiver decodes the signals to interpret the message. Once a message is interpreted, the decoder then becomes the encoder, relaying back his or her own messages via the same process. The original encoder then becomes the decoder. It is this complex process of exchange, with switching roles and encoding and decoding of messages, that constitutes the process of communication.

The Role of Culture in the Communication Process

Culture has a pervasive and profound influence on verbal and nonverbal encoding and decoding processes. We have discussed many of these influences in previous chapters. Here, I would like to bring together these various pieces of information, summarizing what has been discussed previously and referring you to the relevant chapters for more detailed information. Although we discuss these influences on the communication process as if they were separate, in reality they are interrelated in a complex system in which each affects, and is affected by, the others.

Cultural Influences on Verbal Language and Nonverbal Behavior Encoding

As we saw in Chapter 12, culture has a pervasive influence on verbal language. Each language is a unique symbol system that denotes what a culture deems important in its world. You will recall that certain words may exist in some languages and not others, reflecting differences in the way cultures symbolize their worlds. Different cultures and languages often use self- and other-referents differently; for example, the English pronouns *I* and *you* may be replaced by designations of role, position, or status. Counting systems are another example of cultural influence on verbal language. Many languages have number words that specify characteristics of the objects being counted, and different languages may have different base systems for conveying number relationships.

Culture affects not only language lexicons, but also its function or pragmatics. As we saw in Chapter 12, research has shown that individualistic cultures are associated with languages that allow pronouns to be dropped from sentences. Other studies have demonstrated cultural differences in many other aspects of communication, including ingroup and outgroup communication, the use of apologies, self-disclosure, compliments, and interpersonal criticism. Collectively, these studies paint a rather complete picture of the profound influence of culture on language pragmatics.

Culture also affects the structure of thought processes via the Sapir–Whorf hypothesis. Although some studies have challenged this hypothesis over the years, it has received considerable support in relation to the influence of grammatical and syntactic aspects of language on thought. Research on bilingualism has also demonstrated the close relationship between culture and language, suggesting that bilinguals access different cultural systems in their minds when speaking their respective languages.

As we saw in Chapter 13, culture influences many of our nonverbal behaviors as well. While cross-cultural research has shown that facial expressions of anger, contempt, disgust, fear, happiness, sadness, and surprise are panculturally expressed, we also know that cultures differ in the display rules that govern how these universal expressions are used. In addition, we know that there are many cultural differences in gestures, gaze and visual attention, interpersonal space, body postures, and voice and vocal characteristics.

The research presented in Chapters 12 and 13 and summarized here describes rather completely how culture influences all aspects of how we encode messages in communication. Whether the encoding occurs verbally through language or nonverbally through facial expressions, gestures, body posture, space, or any of the other nonverbal parameters, all of the encoding processes are influenced by culture. That means that how a message is encoded into signals and exactly how signals are sent by an encoder during communication are largely culturally determined. Accurate communication, of course, depends on a decoder's being able to decipher those signals in terms of the underlying message intended. This ability, in turn, depends on the decoder's being culturally fluent in the encoding process being used.

Cultural Influences on Decoding Processes

Culture affects the decoding process in several ways. As with cultural decoding rules regarding the perception and interpretation of emotion, discussed in Chapter 11, we learn rules from early childhood on that aid us in deciphering the cultural codes inherent in speech and all other aspects of interaction. These decoding rules develop in conjunction with display or encoding rules, and are a natural part of the development of communication skills.

Culture influences the decoding process in other ways as well. By way of summary, I would like to review three of these processes that have been discussed in previous chapters.

Cultural filters, ethnocentrism, emotions, and value judgments.   In Chapter 4, we defined ethnocentrism, as the tendency to view the world through one's own cultural filters. These ethnocentric filters are one mechanism through which culture affects communication.

As we grow up, we learn cultural rules of appropriate communicative encoding with respect to both verbal and nonverbal behaviors. When we are little, these rules are constantly reinforced by parents, friends, teachers, and other enculturation agents (see, for example, Skinner, 1957, for evidence for such reinforcement during language acquisition). Many rules are also transmitted and reinforced by organizations and institutions (as in our study of language through the school system). As we get older, we need to be reminded less about these rules, and their use requires less conscious effort. The inevitable result is unique, culture-specific ways in which communication—verbal and nonverbal—occurs.

As we grow, we also learn how to perceive signals and interpret messages; that is, we learn cultural rules of appropriate decoding as well. Because we share a set of encoding and decoding rules with people of our culture, we develop a set of expectations about communication. These rules and expectations form a basis of tacit understanding that need not be spoken each time we, as adult members of the same culture, communicate with one another.

Not only do we have certain expectations about the communication process; we have also learned emotional reactions associated with those expectations. These reactions can range from acceptance and pleasure to outrage, hostility, and frustration. Our emotions, in turn, are intimately tied to value judgments, which we often make without a second thought. These judgments seem only natural because they are rooted in our upbringing; they are the only types of judgments we have learned to make. Emotions and values serve as guidelines in helping us form opinions about others and ourselves.

Thus, decoding rules, and their associated emotions and value judgments, form the basis of the "filters" that we use in seeing the world. As we become more enculturated, we add more layers to those filters. These filters are like lenses that allow us to perceive the world in a certain way. By the time we are adults, we share the same filters with others in our cultural group. They become part of our self, inseparable and invisible, and are a normal part of our psychological composition because of the way we have been enculturated.

Culture and stereotypes. As defined in Chapter 4, stereotypes are generalizations about people, particularly about their underlying psychological characteristics or personality traits. Stereotypes are inevitable products of normal psychological processes, including selective attention, appraisal, concept formation and categorization, attributions, emotion, and memory. Stereotypes are invaluable mental aids, helping us organize information about the world. As a special type of category having to do with people, they are important in helping us interact with others in our world, and are especially important in communication.

Stereotypes are easily reinforced. Stereotypes prime our expectations. We may selectively attend to events that support our stereotypes, and ignore, albeit unconsciously, events and situations that challenge them. Negative attributions may reinforce negative stereotypes. Even when we perceive events contrary to stereotype, we may convince ourselves that the stereotype is correct. Such dismissals can occur quickly, without much conscious thought or effort, and are resilient to emotion.

These psychological processes—including selective attention, attribution, and emotion—are all part of our self-concept. These processes reinforce the cultural knowledge we have learned from many years of enculturation, and thereby reinforce our sense of self. As we confirm our stereotypes, therefore, we reinforce our self-concept. Stereotypes are thus an integral part of the package of psychological processes, and are intimately tied to our emotions, values, and core self.

Culture and social cognition.   As we will see in greater detail in Chapter 16, culture influences how we interpret the actions of others—that is, our attributions regarding others. Americans, for example, tend to draw inferences about other people's internal states or dispositions that supposedly underlie or even cause their behavior. This bias is known as fundamental attribution error (Ross, 1977). Cross-cultural research has shown that this bias may not exist in other cultures. Miller (1984), for example, comparing Americans' and Hindu Indians' explanations for another person's actions, found that dispositional explanations were common for Americans but much less so for the Hindus. Instead, the Hindus provided explanations in terms of the actor's duties, social roles, and other situation-specific characteristics (see also Shweder & Bourne, 1984). Other attributional tendencies, such as self-serving bias and defensive attributions are also manifested differently in different cultures.

In summary, culture plays a large role in decoding signals during communication episodes—first because of the close relationship between cultural rules governing encoding and decoding, and second because of cultural influences in the development of ethnocentrism, stereotyping, and social cognition. Cultural decoding rules are intimately associated with emotions and value judgments, which collectively form our self-concepts. Because communication involves moment-to-moment switching from encoder to decoder and back, understanding the role of culture in this process is challenging—whether the communication is intracultural or intercultural. One way to highlight the unique circumstances under which intercultural communication occurs, however, is to compare these two types of communication.

Intracultural versus Intercultural Communication

A Note about the Difference between Cross-Cultural and Intercultural Research

In many contexts, the term *cross-cultural communication* is used synonymously with the term *intercultural communication*. In the context of communication, there is no difference between them; there is, however, an important difference between cross-cultural and intercultural *research*. *Cross-cultural* research simply refers to the comparison of two or more cultures on some variable of interest (for example, differences between cultures A and B in the expression of emotions). *Intercultural* research refers specifically to the study of the interaction between people of two cultures (for example, differences in how people of cultures A and B express emotions when they are with people of cultures B and A, respectively).

Most studies in the field of intercultural communication are cross-cultural, not intercultural. As such, they do not always generate data that are directly applicable to the intercultural episode. Many of the cross-cultural studies reviewed in Chapters 12 and 13 deal with cultural differences in communication styles, but not necessarily with how people communicate with others of a different culture. No matter how many cross-cultural studies we conduct comparing Americans and Japanese, for example, they will not inform us about how people of these two cultures communicate *when interacting with each other*.

For research to be intercultural, it must compare intercultural data with intracultural data; only those differences are attributable to intercultural communication per se. A study comparing American and Japanese intercultural communication, for instance, should examine how Americans and Japanese each interact *both* with Americans *and* with Japanese. It is only the difference between intracultural and intercultural interactions that tell us what is unique about intercultural communication.

Intracultural Communication

During intracultural communication, interactants implicitly share the same ground rules. When people communicate within the boundaries of accepted ground rules, they can focus on the content of the messages that are being exchanged. They encode and decode messages using the same cultural codes. When we communicate within the shared boundaries of culture, we make an implicit judgment that the other person is a member of our culture or is engaging in socially appropriate behavior. We may consider the individual to have been socialized "well" into our culture, and we make value judgments about the process and the person's ability to engage in that accepted process.

The intracultural communication sequence is illustrated in micromomentary detail in Figure 14.1. The two people in these panels share the same cultural background, and thus encode and decode messages using the same rules. In panel 1, person A is the encoder, while person B is the decoder. The content of the message that person A wants to convey is "packaged" into a culture-specific set of signals via verbal language and nonverbal behaviors via a cultural code. In panel 2, the culturally coded packaged signals are then transmitted through the various channels. In panel 3, the packaged signals are detected by person B, the decoder, who then interprets them via his or her own cultural decoder, which uses the same rules and codes as person A's codes. In panel 4, the package is opened and the message inside is interpreted. After this, person B would become the encoder, and person A the decoder, and the process would be reversed.

Figure 14.1 A micromomentary analysis of intracultural communication

When we communicate with others within our own culture, this process "works" because we share the same codes and rules of encoding and decoding. Thus, the coded "packages" we send when we are encoders, and those that we receive and open when we are decoders, are familiar to us because we generally share the same type of wrapping and box.

Even in intracultural situations, when we interact with people who transgress what we view as "normal" or "socially appropriate," we often have negative reactions. We have trouble interpreting the signals they are trying to send because they don't conform to the cultural rules of "packaging" that we expect of members of our culture. We react negatively because we have learned that such transgressions are not appropriate, and we may make negative dispositional attributions such as "bad," "stupid," "had a bad upbringing," or "has no common sense."

Even in intracultural communication situations, negative stereotypes can easily develop. Because our cultural filters and ethnocentrism create a set of expectations about others, communicating with people whose behaviors do not match our expectations often leads to negative attributions. Such unanticipated events require substantive processing (Forgas, 1994), which is most affected by induced emotion. If the emotion induced is negative, then it will contribute to negatively valenced attributions about others. These attributions form the core of a stereotype of such people, and reinforce the value and expectation system originally held. These processes are common even within intracultural communication episodes.

Unique Aspects of Intercultural Communication

When we examine intercultural communication in micromomentary detail (Figure 14.2), we find much the same process as with intracultural communication. This time, persons A and B are from different cultures. In panel 1, person A has a message that he or she wants to convey. This message gets packaged in person A's cultural code. In panel 2, the packaged signals are sent. In panel 3, the packaged signals are received by person B. The difference arises in panel 4, where person B has trouble opening the package because person B's cultural codes are different from person A's. As a result, the message may be unclear, distorted, or ambiguous.

Because intercultural communication occurs under these circumstances, it is associated with a host of additional psychological issues that do not normally occur in intracultural communication. Here we will discuss three issues that have gained widespread attention in the intercultural research literature: uncertainty, conflict, and context.

Intercultural communication and uncertainty.   One characteristic that sets intercultural communication apart from intracultural communication is uncertainty or ambiguity concerning the ground rules by which the interaction will occur. Because of the widespread and pervasive influence of culture on all

Figure 14.2 A micromomentary analysis of intercultural communication aspects of the communication process, we cannot be sure that the rules by which two people from different cultures operate are similar. This uncertainty is inherent in both verbal and nonverbal behaviors, in both coding and decoding modes: how to package messages into signals that will be interpreted according to one's intentions, and how to open packages according to the sender's original intentions.

Intercultural interactants often engage with each other in a verbal language that is not a native language for at least one of them, and sometimes both. Thus, there is inherent uncertainty in the meaning of the words. Cultural differences in the use of all nonverbal channels add to the uncertainty. Decoders can never be as sure as they are in intracultural situations that they are interpreting signals and messages as originally intended by encoders.

Gudykunst and his colleagues have documented how interactants work to reduce uncertainty in intercultural interactions, at least in initial encounters. Their work has been based on Berger (1979) and Berger and Calabrese (1975), who suggested that one of the primary concerns of strangers in initial encounters is to reduce uncertainty and increase predictability in themselves and others. Gudykunst and Nishida (1984) tested 100 American and 100 Japanese participants, assigning them to one of four experimental conditions: cultural similarity (intracultural communication) and attitude similarity, cultural dissimilarity (intercultural communication) and attitude similarity, cultural similarity and attitude dissimilarity, and cultural dissimilarity and attitude dissimilarity. Cultural similarity or dissimilarity was manipulated by having participants interact with a stranger from either their own culture or the other culture. Attitude similarity or dissimilarity was manipulated through a description of similar or dissimilar attitudes when introducing the stranger. For each participant, the researchers assessed intent to self-disclose, intent to interrogate, nonverbal affiliative expressions, attributional confidence, and interpersonal attraction. The results indicated that intent to interrogate, intent to self-disclose, and nonverbal affiliative expressiveness were all higher in the cultural dissimilarity condition than in the cultural similarity condition. Uncertainty reduction theory predicts that these strategies would be used more extensively in communication contexts with higher levels of uncertainty. Gudykunst, Sodetani, and Sonoda (1987) extended these findings to include members of different ethnic groups as well, demonstrating that differences in ethnicity and stage of relationship are also related to differences in communicative behaviors designed to reduce uncertainty.

In a more recent study, Gudykunst and Shapiro (1996) asked students at a large university to record their perceptions of communication episodes with other students. In one part of the study, 303 students reported on intracultural and intercultural episodes; in another part of the study, 725 students reported on intraethnic and interethnic communication episodes. Seven variables were assessed in each communication episode. The researchers found that students rated intracultural episodes higher than intercultural episodes in quality of communication and positive expectations, but rated intercultural episodes higher in anxiety, uncertainty, and social identity. Likewise, students rated intraethnic encounters as higher in quality and satisfaction, and interethnic encounters as higher in anxiety and uncertainty. These data support the notion that intercultural communication episodes are marked by a greater degree of uncertainty than intracultural encounters.

I agree with Gudykunst and his colleagues that uncertainty reduction is one of the major goals of initial intercultural encounters. (Other studies have documented the effects of uncertainty in other types of relationships across cultures as well; see Gudykunst, Yang, & Nishida, 1985.) Without uncertainty reduction, it is impossible for interactants to begin processing the content of signals and interpreting messages properly, because uncertainty renders messages inherently ambiguous. If uncertainty is reduced, interactants can then focus on the content of the signals and messages that are being exchanged. Intercultural communication is like deciphering coded language: the first step is to decipher the code (reduce uncertainty); the second is to interpret and respond to the content, once deciphered.

Intercultural communication and conflict. A second characteristic of intercultural communication is the inevitability of conflict and misunderstandings. During intercultural encounters, chances are great that people's behaviors will not conform to our expectations. We often interpret those behaviors as transgressions against our value system and morality. They produce negative emotions, which are upsetting to our self-concepts. These conflicts arise in intercultural episodes not only with people but also with other agents of a cultural system (such as public transportation, the post office, shops, businesses). These interactions are bound to accentuate differences in process, which inevitably lead to conflict or misunderstanding.

Figure 14.2 illustrates why this conflict is inevitable. Because interactants cannot send or receive signals unambiguously, as they are accustomed to in intracultural situations, the intercultural communication episode can be frustrating and patience-testing. Tempers are quick to flare in such situations, and people can easily become distraught or turned off by the extra effort such interactions require. Even if interactants are somewhat successful in unpackaging signals, the messages interpreted may be partial, ambiguous, or misunderstood. Messages may not be deciphered according to the sender's original intent, leading to miscommunication gaffes and problems later on down the line.

Of course, uncertainty contributes to this conflict. People may become impatient with or intolerant of the ambiguity, leading to anger, frustration, or resentment. Even after uncertainty is reduced, however, conflict is inevitable because of the differences in meaning of verbal language and nonverbal behaviors across cultures, and the associated emotions and values inherent in the cultural system. The result is often differences in the interpretation of underlying intent among interactants—which can sometimes occur in intracultural communication as well.

Intercultural communication and context. One of the most important cultural dimensions with regard to intercultural communication is context. Other dimensions of cultural variability, discussed in Chapter 2 and throughout this book, include individualism–collectivism, power distance, uncertainty avoidance, and masculinity–femininity. The dimension of context, first postulated by Hall (1976), is the only cultural dimension originally developed based on communication processes.

According to Hall (1976), a high-context (HC) communication or message is "one in which most of the information is either in the physical context or internalized in the person, while very little is in the coded, explicit, transmitted part of the message. A low-context (LC) communication is just the opposite; i.e., the mass of the information is vested in the explicit code" (p. 79). Hall sees context as a continuum, with high context (HC) on one end and low context (LC) on the other. Cultural groups are then situated at various points along this continuum. According to Hall (1976), American, German, Scandinavian, and Swiss cultures tend to be LC, whereas most Asian cultures tend to fall on the HC side of the continuum.

HC cultures rely less on explicit, spoken language to transmit thoughts and messages because much of the information that needs to be conveyed in a communication episode is wrapped up in the parameters of the context—the physical setting, the status relationship between the interactants, the previous history of the discussion, the future goals of the interactants, and the like. The Japanese language has a term *isshin denshin*, which translates literally as "traditional mental telepathy." This term reflects that culture's high value on implicit or tacit communication. The Korean language has a similar term, *I-sim jun-sim*, which is considered one of the highest forms of communication in Korea (Yum, 1987).

LC cultures rely much more on explicit, spoken language to transmit thoughts and messages. For this reason, they tend to place a premium on the ability to articulate one's position well verbally. Such skills are less important in HC cultures. Verbal skills are much more prized and highly valued in LC cultures (Okabe, 1983). A recent study comparing the use of silence in the United States and Japan highlights such differences between explicit and implicit communication (Hasegawa & Gudykunst, 1998).

One example of such context differences in communication is the nature of business agreements. In LC cultures such as the United States, agreements are sealed by the signing of a contract. The written contract spells out all of the terms, limitations, duties, and obligations of all parties in an explicit, straightforward manner. Businesspeople and their lawyers in the United States spend much of their time, effort, and energy in obtaining such contracts, reviewing them, and making sure they explicitly state exactly what they want them to state. In many HC cultures, however, doing business by such contracts is unheard of. The typical way of doing business may be a broad, sweeping verbal agreement between parties. Details may be relegated to the shared implicit trust that both parties will do what is "right" for the relationship and for both people. While people from LC cultures would view such an agreement as an invitation to disaster, people from HC cultures would view the American preoccupation with written contracts as equally disastrous.

A study by Gudykunst and Nishida (1986) illustrates differences in communication styles between HC and LC cultures. In this study, American and Japanese participants completed a questionnaire about their attributional confidence in communicating with people in six different types of relationships. *Attributional confidence* is defined as the degree to which one is certain of his or her interpretations of the other person's behavior. The results indicated quite clear differences between the Americans and Japanese depending on the context and relationship. Americans tended to report higher confidence with acquaintances than with classmates, and with lovers than with friends. The Japanese, however, reported exactly the opposite; they reported more confidence in their attributions with classmates rather than acquaintances, and with friends rather than lovers.

Context thus appears to be an important variable to consider in intercultural communication. Whether interactants are from low- or high-context cultures will influence the degree to which communication needs to be explicit or implicit, found in the context or found in direct verbal expressions.

Together, uncertainty, conflict, and context make intercultural communication a complex yet fascinating process that challenges even the most practiced and interculturally sensitive of people. Given these challenges, how can we develop our skills at intercultural communication and improve intercultural relationships?

Toward Effective Intercultural Communication

Stumbling Blocks to Effective Intercultural Communication

Barna (1997) has outlined six major obstacles or "stumbling blocks" to effective intercultural communication:

1. *Assumptions of similarities.* One reason why misunderstandings occur in intercultural communication episodes is that people naively assume that all people are the same, or at least similar enough to make communication easy. Certainly, all humans share a number of basic similarities in biological and social needs. Communication, however, is a uniquely human trait that is shaped by specific cultures and societies. Indeed, communication itself is a product of culture. Furthermore, people of some cultures make more assumptions of similarity than others; that is, the degree to which people assume that others are similar varies across cultures. Thus, the assumption of similarities is itself a cultural variable.

2. *Language differences.* When people are trying to communicate in a language in which they are not entirely fluent, they often think that a word, phrase, or sentence has one and only one meaning—the meaning they intend to convey. To make this assumption is to ignore all the other possible sources of signals and messages discussed in the previous two chapters, including

nonverbal expressions, tone of voice, body orientation, and many other behaviors. To the extent that people cling rigidly to single, simple interpretations of what is really a complex process, problems in communication are bound to arise.

3. *Nonverbal misinterpretations.* As we have seen, nonverbal behaviors comprise the bulk of communication messages in any culture. But it is very difficult to be totally fluent in the nonverbal language of a culture that is not one's own. Misunderstandings in relation to the interpretation of nonverbal behaviors can easily lead to conflicts or confrontations that break down the communication process.

4. *Preconceptions and stereotypes.* As discussed previously, stereotypes and preconceptions about people are natural and inevitable psychological processes that influence all of our perceptions and communications. Overreliance on stereotypes can prevent us from viewing others and their communications objectively, and from searching for cues that may help us interpret their communications in the way they were intended. Stereotypes are sustained by a host of psychological processes, including selective attention, that may influence communication in negative ways.

5. *Tendency to evaluate.* Cultural values also influence our attributions about others and the world around us. Different values may generate negative evaluations of others, which become yet another stumbling block to effective intercultural communication.

6. *High anxiety or tension.* Intercultural communication episodes are often associated with greater anxiety and stress than are more familiar intracultural communication situations. In many cases, some degree of anxiety and tension is necessary for optimal "performance," whether in intercultural communication or in other arenas of life (such as taking a test or competing in sports). Too much anxiety and stress, however, can lead to dysfunctional thought processes and behaviors. Stress and anxiety can exaggerate all of the other stumbling blocks, making it more likely that people will cling dogmatically to rigid interpretations, hold onto stereotypes despite objective evidence to the contrary, and make negative evaluations of others. Thus, too much anxiety or stress is not at all functional for intercultural communication.

Given these stumbling blocks, as presented by Barna (1997) and throughout this chapter, how can we overcome them to engage in effective intercultural communication? This question has received considerable research attention in the past decade or two, under the title of intercultural communication competence.

Intercultural Communication Competence (ICC)

Intercultural communication competence (ICC) refers to the ability to communicate effectively in intercultural contexts. In recent years, an increasing number of studies have identified various factors that appear to be related to ICC.

Table 14.1   Empirically Derived Factors of Intercultural Competence

Ability to adjust to different cultures	Frankness
Ability to deal with different societal systems	General competence as teacher (task)
Ability to deal with psychological stress	Incompetence
Ability to establish interpersonal relationships	Intellectualizing future orientation
Ability to facilitate communication	Interaction involvement
Ability to understand others	Interpersonal flexibility
Adaptiveness	Interpersonal harmony
Agency (internal locus and efficacy/optimism)	Interpersonal interest
Awareness of implications of cultural differences	Interpersonally sensitive maturity
Awareness of self and culture	Managerial ability
Cautiousness	Nonethnocentrism
Charisma	Nonverbal behaviors
Communication apprehension	Opinion leadership
Communication competence (ability to communicate)	Personal/Family adjustment
Communication efficacy	Rigidity (task persistence)
Communicative functions	Task accomplishment
Controlling responsibility	Transfer of "software"
Conversational management behaviors	Self-actualizing search for identity
Cooperation	Self-confidence/Initiative
Cultural empathy	Self-consciousness
Cultural interaction	Self-disclosure
Demand (long-term goal orientation)	Self-reliant conventionality
Dependent anxiety	Social adjustment
Differentiation	Spouse/Family communication
Empathy/Efficacy	Strength of personality
Familiarity in interpersonal relations	Verbal behaviors

Source: Spitzberg, 1997. Reprinted by permission of the author.

Models of ICC.   Table 14.1 presents a list of ICC factors from a review of the literature by Spitzberg (1997). Spitzberg (1997) has since suggested a model synthesizing and integrating these factors into three components or levels of analysis: the individual system—characteristics of individuals that facilitate intercultural communication; the episodic system—characteristics of interactants that foster competence attributions of each other; and the relational system—characteristics that enable people to generalize their ICC skills to a variety of situations and contexts.

Gudykunst (1993) offers a related but slightly different model with three main components: motivational factors, knowledge factors, and skill factors. Motivational factors include the specific needs of the interactants, attraction between the interactants, social bonds, self-conceptions, and openness to new information. Knowledge factors include expectations, shared networks, knowledge of more than one perspective, knowledge of alternative interpretations, and knowledge of similarities and differences. Skill factors include the ability to empathize, tolerate ambiguity, adapt communication, create new categories, accommodate behavior, and gather appropriate information. According to Gudykunst (1993), these three types of factors influence the amount of uncertainty in a situation and the degree of anxiety or stress interactants actually feel. Finally, these two components influence the degree to which interactants are "mindful" of the communication episode—that is, the degree to which they take conscious and deliberate steps to think through their own and others' behaviors, and to plan and interpret the interaction appropriately as it unfolds. According to this model, a high degree of mindfulness offsets uncertainty and anxiety, resulting in effective communication.

A number of other authors and studies have suggested these and other characteristics of ICC. Chen (1990), for example, suggested that ICC was related to individual characteristics in self-concept, self-disclosure, self-monitoring, social relaxation, message skills, behavioral flexibility, interaction management ability, interaction involvement, social skills, adaptation ability, and cultural awareness. Hammer, Nishida, and Wiseman (1996), studying Americans' ICC in American–Japanese intercultural situations, emphasized three dimensions of ICC: understanding Japanese situations and rule-specific behaviors, understanding Japanese culture in general, and affect toward Japanese culture. In a related study (Wiseman, Hammer, & Nishida, 1989), these researchers found that positive and negative attitudes toward the other culture, ethnocentrism, perceived social distance, and knowledge of the other culture were all predictive to various degrees of these three constructs. Finally, Martin and Hammer (1989) assessed American undergraduates' responses to hypothetical interactions with Americans, unspecified international students, Japanese students, or German students. They found that the data yielded four dimensions or sets of skills: communicative function, nonverbal, content, and conversational management.

In general, the literature suggests that knowledge and skills are necessary components of effective intercultural communication, but that they are not sufficient. Knowledge and skills must be combined with openness and flexibility in one's thinking and interpretations, and with the motivation to communicate effectively and build a successful relationship.

Research on ICC with international exchange students.

One area in which the topic of ICC has been studied quite extensively is with international exchange students. The number of international students visiting the United States has increased dramatically in the past two decades, and promises to increase even more in the future. Also, with increased immigration, the number of second- and third-generation Americans is also increasing. These students, like their parents and grandparents before them, maintain many of their ancestral culture's values and behaviors. They constitute a large proportion of the university student population that can be considered as engaged in intercultural communication on campuses today.

Research has shown that many of the factors discussed in relation to ICC are important predictors of intercultural adjustment among international exchange students. Zimmerman (1995), for example, examining the communication experiences of 101 international college students on campus and in the community, found affective and behavioral dimensions of ICC to be related to students' satisfaction with their communication skills. However, they found that the most important predictor of communication competency and adjusting to American life was talking with American students. How long the international students had lived in the United States and how long they had attended the university were not related to their perceptions of adjustment or their satisfaction with communication.

These findings make sense in terms of what we know about intercultural adjustment. Berry, Kim, and Boski (1988) have suggested four general ways in which adjustment to a new culture occurs: (1) by creating one's own little community of one's original culture; (2) by interacting solely with members of the host culture to the virtual exclusion of the original culture; (3) by neither interacting nor integrating successfully with either host or original culture; and (4) by integrating fully into the host culture while maintaining solid relationships with the original culture. To the extent that international visitors create their own little worlds with little integration into the host culture, their length of stay in the United States or how long they attend school will have little effect on ICC development.

ICC is also important in dealing with stress in international students. Redmond and Bunyi (1993) assessed ICC and level of stress in a sample of 631 international exchange students. The researchers defined ICC as communication effectiveness, adaptation, social integration, language competence, knowledge of host culture, and decentering. Results indicated that adaptation and social decentering were the best predictors of the amount of stress reported. Communication effectiveness, adaptation, and social integration were the best predictors of effectiveness in handling stress.

At least one study has documented the positive effects of integrating cultural diversity into communication courses. In this study (Carrell, 1997), 237 students enrolled in a variety of communication and culture-relevant courses were tested for empathy, a central component of ICC. Results indicated that students who completed a course on intercultural communication, as well as students enrolled in basic speech courses who received interpersonal communication instruction infused with diversity, showed significant gains in empathy as a trait, attitude, and behavior.

Collectively, these studies suggest that ICC is an important predictor of intercultural adjustment by international exchange students in the United States, and that it is an important by-product of coursework and training in related fields in the university curriculum. Most research conducted to date, however, has examined ICC as a global concept across a wide variety of international students from very disparate areas of the world. Future research needs to examine the possibility that different components of ICC are important for people of different cultures. Indeed, Redmond and Bunyi's (1993) study on stress found that students from countries that had shared heritage and culture with the United States had the least stress and were the most communicatively competent. The world, however, is getting functionally smaller every day, and we need to deal with more widespread differences than ever before. In addition, future research needs to examine ICC and intercultural adjustment of American students in other countries and cultures.

Intercultural Sensitivity

As students increase in ICC, it is only natural that they become more globally and culturally relative. Communication is one of the major building blocks of cultural relativism. But it is not the only component of intercultural competence (IC)—a person's overall ability to deal, work, live, and play with intercultural and cross-cultural differences in everyday life.

Bennett (1979, 1988) has been a leader in the development of models identifying the main components of intercultural competence. Bennett sees IC in terms of a developmental approach rather than as a conglomeration of specific behaviors, and refers to his developmental model as one of **intercultural sensitivity (IS)**. He defines IS as "the construction of reality as increasingly capable of accommodating cultural difference that constitute development" (1993, p. 4). Thus, Bennett sees IS along a developmental continuum of ethnocentrism and ethnorelativism, ranging from total denial of cultural differences to the recognition and celebration of those differences and the ability to maintain one's self at the margin of those differences, merging in and out of separate cultural realities as appropriate.

Bennett's model proposes six stages of IS. The first three describe ethnocentric stages of development; the second three describe stages of ethnorelative development.

1. *Denial*. The most primitive ethnocentric stage begins with the denial that cultural differences even exist. People at this stage may be physically or psychologically isolated from different cultural groups, or they may erect physical or social barriers to create distance and separation from such differences.

2. *Defense*. The second stage of ethnocentrism involves acknowledging that cultural differences exist, but defending oneself against them because they are perceived as threatening to the self. Many people at this stage defend against cultural differences by denigrating others and holding derogatory attitudes toward others. A related process involves evaluating one's own cultural group as superior. Interestingly, some people choose to defend against cultural differences by reversing these two processes—that is, by denigrating their own cultural group and evaluating others as superior.

3. *Minimization*. The third stage or ethnocentrism involves recognizing that cultural differences exist, but minimizing their impact or importance to one's life. One of the ways that individuals in this stage achieve minimiza-

tion is to "universalize" cultural differences when they occur ("All people are like that, so why should I do anything about it?").

4. *Acceptance*. At this first stage of ethnorelative development, cultural differences are not only recognized and acknowledged, but respected. Respect occurs at two levels: first on the level of the various behavioral manifestations of cultural differences, and second on the level of the cultural values that people of different cultures hold.

5. *Adaptation*. At the next stage of ethnorelative development, individuals accommodate to the cultural differences they have now accepted and begin to acquire new skills for relating to and communicating with people of different cultures. One of these skills is *empathy*—the ability to feel the emotions and experiences of another person from that person's point of view. As we come in contact with people of different cultures and adapt to these differences, being empathic (as opposed to sympathetic) means that not only do we understand their situation cognitively, but we can feel it as if it meant the same to us. A second skill relates to the concept of pluralism. Individuals come to embrace a philosophy of *plurality* in relation to their understanding of values, ideas, and attitudes, and they create multiple cultural contexts in their minds to contain their notions of plurality and difference. Plurality in this sense is closely related to the terms *biculturalism* and *multiculturalism*.

6. *Integration*. The final stage of ethnorelativism involves the integration of plurality, as a philosophy and a conscious understanding, into the ability to evaluate cultural differences in terms of the contexts in which they are generated. Differences are evaluated on the basis of plurality and context, rather than from a single cultural perspective. This level of integration can lead to *constructive marginality*, in which individuals can live in the margins of different cultural pluralities in their minds, going back and forth, in and out, of these different pluralities appropriately according to their social contexts.

Bennett's model of IS is unique in identifying not only the stages of development from an ethnocentric to an ethnorelative viewpoint, but also the specific skills, cognitions, and emotional processes associated with each of these stages. The model thus provides some degree of direction for growth and development of IC or IS, explicitly demonstrating the specific skills and attributes that are necessary to move along the development continuum underlying the model. This model, which grew directly out of Bennett's work on intercultural communication, has become a main staple in the field.

As with any model, Bennett's contains implicit assumptions about the nature of the development of IS and the values associated with the endpoints. One assumption is that the continuum reflects a progression from a less preferred to a more preferred mode of operation. This assumption seems applicable to many of us in today's multicultural world, and is consistent with the overall message of this book. Still, are there cultural groups for which denial, defense, or minimization may be more functional? The answer is probably yes, and the applicability of this model itself needs to occur in a contextually meaningful manner.

Another assumption is that each individual is located, at any point in time, at a single point along the continuum. But is it possible that a person may be ethnocentric in one context and ethnorelative in another? The answer to this question is also probably yes. Thus, rather than seeing the stages as absolute points along a single continuum, it may be more useful to consider them as context-relative.

Dealing with Intercultural Conflicts

As we have seen, intercultural conflicts are an inevitable part of intercultural communication and interaction. Cultural differences make it impossible for interactants to always understand each other perfectly and to communicate their intended messages well all the time. Little misunderstandings are bound to occur throughout an intercultural exchange, especially over the long term. Even when misunderstandings do not arise, we often must "swallow our pride" or ignore little things that irritate us about how someone from another culture acts, even when no offense is intended.

Being able to deal with this inevitable conflict in a productive and efficient manner is very important in building successful intercultural relationships through communication. How can we achieve this goal?

One strategy would be to become thoroughly versant in a culture, recording its cultural similarities and differences and building your own "cultural dictionary" to retrieve at any time. This is a formidable task, as there is so much about culture to learn and so little time, energy, and storage space available. This approach does have merit, however, and many people do develop such almanacs in their minds about a small number of cultures with which they have become intimately familiar through travel, business, homestay programs, and the like. In fact, many of the studies discussed earlier (for example, Kim & Gudykunst, 1988; Samovar & Porter, 1985; Wiseman, Hammer, & Nishida, 1989; Zimmerman, 1995), documenting the relationship between ICC and knowledge of and attitude toward host culture, ethnocentrism, social distance, and exposure to host culture members, would support such an approach.

But none of us can create such a dictionary of culture for all the cultures and peoples we might possibly come in contact with in our lives, and many of us do not have the opportunity to become culturally fluent in this fashion. Instead, the vast majority of us will need to rely on a *process model* of intercultural growth to engage in effective intercultural communication. In the remainder of this section, we will discuss two such models—one based on conflict management skills, and the other based on the regulation and control of emotion.

Conflict management. Ting-Toomey (1997) suggests that effective conflict management requires knowledge of and respect for cultural differences in worldviews and behaviors, as well as sensitivity to differences between high- and low-context communication patterns, and differences in cultural perceptions of time. She stresses the importance of "mindfulness" in dealing with conflict in intercultural communication (as in Gudykunst's model of ICC). According to Langer (1989; cited in Ting-Toomey, 1997), mindfulness allows people to be conscious of their own habits, mental scripts, and cultural expectations concerning communication. Mindfulness allows one to continually create new mental categories, remain open to new information, and be aware of multiple perspectives. In short, mindfulness allows one to be conscious and conscientious about the various characteristics that are associated with ethnorelativism.

Ting-Toomey (1997) offers separate suggestions for effective conflict management for people of individualistic tendencies as opposed to people with collectivitistic tendencies. People of individualistic cultural tendencies who have to deal with conflicts in a collectivistic culture should be mindful of the importance of "face" and the maintenance of face in the collectivistic culture; be proactive in dealing with low-grade conflict situations; not be pushy; be sensitive to the importance of quiet, mindful observation; practice attentive listening skills, especially in relation to the feelings of others; discard the model of dealing with problems directly; and let go of conflict situations if the other party does not want to deal with them directly. Collectivistic people who must deal with conflicts in an individualistic context should be mindful of individualistic problem-solving assumptions; focus on resolving major issues and expressing their feelings and opinions openly; engage in assertive conflict behavior; take individual responsibility for dealing with conflict; provide verbal feedback; use direct verbal messages; and commit to working out the problem directly with the other person.

In sum, according to Ting-Toomey (1997), people from both individualistic and collectivistic cultures need to be mindful of the cognitive, affective, and behavioral biases and framework within which they normally operate, and of the blinders that they often bring to communication and conflict-mediation situations. They need to be open to learning and trying new communication skills, and to create new mental categories to build more successful intercultural relationships.

Emotion regulation.   One of the messages you are probably getting from this chapter is that effective intercultural communication is not always easy! Conflict and misunderstandings are inevitable, and our normal ethnocentric and stereotypic ways of thinking often lead us to make negative value judgments about those differences, conflicts, and misunderstandings. Negative emotions are often associated with these judgments. These negative reactions make it difficult for us to engage in more constructive methods of interacting; they keep us from appreciating differences and integrating with people who are different. As conflict is inevitable in intercultural communication, it becomes extremely important to be able to control our negative emotional reactions. Those who can control their emotions will be able to engage in a more constructive intercultural process, opening the door to more successful intercultural interactions. Those who cannot will have that door closed to them. Emotions, therefore, hold the key to successful intercultural experiences.

The ability to regulate or control our emotions, in fact, is a key to personal growth. Many of us who have experience dealing with children know that, despite their often altruistic nature, when something happens to hurt or upset them, their thinking and worldview revert to a more primitive way of dealing with their world. It becomes impossible for them to engage in altruistic acts, because they are locked into a more infantile mode of operation. This concept, known as *regression*, is not limited to children and adolescents; adults regress at times as well. In such situations, people are overcome by negative feelings, which "take over" their way of being. Even the most altruistic or critically minded person may not be able to think or act constructively when overcome by such negative emotions.

When faced with cultural differences and conflict in intercultural communication, individuals who can somehow control their negative feelings—putting them on hold and not acting directly upon them or allowing them to overcome their thinking, acting, and feeling—will be able to engage in other processes that will help them broaden their appraisal and attribution of the causes of those differences. Once emotions are held in check, individuals can then engage in critical thinking about the origins of those differences, hopefully going beyond their own cultural framework to consider causes they may not have even been aware of. If this type of critical thinking can occur, individuals can be open to alternative hypotheses concerning the causes of those differences, and have the flexibility to accept or reject them.

Regulating or controlling negative emotions, therefore, is a gatekeeper ability that allows us to become more mindful of our communication and style and to engage in more constructive and open creation of new mental categories. Having the most complex mental model of effective intercultural communication will not help us one bit unless we are able to deal with the negative emotions that are bound to occur in intercultural communication episodes—to put them aside for the time being so that we can engage in more constructive thought processes that involve the creation of new mental categories via critical thinking. Regulating emotions is the key that allows us to open the door to these more advanced complex processes.

Conclusion

Communication is a rich and complex process that involves multiple messages sent via multiple signal systems. Culture has a pervasive influence on the encoding of both verbal and nonverbal signals, and the decoding of those signals. Because of this influence, conflict and misunderstanding are inevitable in intercultural communication. To overcome these obstacles, scholars have proposed a personal growth model focusing on emotion regulation and mindfulness. Individuals who can engage in these processes can enhance their intercultural sensitivity, creating new mental categories, being respectful and open to cultural differences, and empathizing with others.

Research on intercultural communication has made considerable progress in specifying the unique components of the intercultural communication process. However, much remains to be done. For example, many studies in this area are based on questionnaire surveys that use either real or imagined situations in the past, raising questions about their equivalence to real-life situations. More studies are needed that access cognitions, emotions, and behaviors in actual intercultural communication episodes as they unfold in real time.

Future research also needs to take many of the ideas discussed in this chapter (stumbling blocks, IS, ICC, conflict management, emotion regulation), turn them into meaningful and useful programs of intervention, and then generate efficacy data that demonstrate their utility in improving intercultural communication. Although such data do exist, they are more sporadic in the literature than basic research findings. Given the importance of applied intervention research in this area of psychology, they deserve a larger niche in the future.

One further development that is new to the field is the creation of psychometrically valid tests that predict the degree to which individuals will be successful at intercultural communication and intercultural adjustment. As far as I know, only two such tests are available at this time—one developed for commercial use, and the other developed for research purposes (Ratzlaff et al., 1998; Vogt et al., 1998). The latter test will be discussed in the next chapter in connection with personality and cross-cultural adjustment.

Finally, it is my hope that the information presented in this chapter has allowed you to sit back and examine what kinds of blinders and cultural scripts you have when communicating and interacting with others, and has given you an idea of how to move from an ethnocentric base of interaction to an ethnorelative one.

 Glossary

channels The specific sensory modalities by which signals are sent and messages are retrieved.

decoding The process by which a person receives signals from an encoder and translates these signals into meaningful messages.

encoding The process by which people select, consciously or unconsciously, a particular modality and method by which to create and send a message to someone else.

intercultural communication The exchange of knowledge, ideas, thoughts, concepts, and emotions among people of different cultural backgrounds.

intercultural communication competence (ICC) The ability to communicate effectively in intercultural contexts.

intercultural sensitivity (IS) A developmental continuum of ethnocentrism and ethnorelativism.

intracultural communication Communication that occurs among people of the same cultural background.

messages The meanings that encoders intend to convey and decoders interpret.

signals The specific words and behaviors that are sent during communication.

15

Culture and Personality

One of the most important and widely studied areas in cross-cultural psychology is personality. This concept is closely related to that of the self (see Chapter 3). Anthropologists, psychologists, and other social scientists have long been interested in the "national character" of people of different cultures, and the extent to which personality as we know it in North American psychology is similar or different in other cultures. Indeed, the search for the underlying bases of individual differences, which serve as the backbone of understanding personality, shares a close conceptual and empirical connection with culture in any cultural milieu.

In this chapter, we first discuss the various approaches that scholars have used to understand the relationship between culture and personality. Then, we review major cross-cultural research on personality over the past few decades, highlighting important similarities and differences in those findings. In particular, we will review research on the Five Factor Model (FFM), which suggests that five personality dimensions are universal to all humans. We discuss the measurement of personality across cultures, as well as the use of some personality scales to assess psychopathology across cultures. We also discuss indigenous approaches to personality, and some of the research that has been conducted in this area. Although culture-specific aspects of personality and universal notions of personality may seem contradictory, we will seek ways of understanding their mutual coexistence and conceptualizing and studying their duality.

Defining Personality

The first thing we need to do is define what we mean by personality. In psychology, **personality** is generally considered to be a set of relatively enduring behavioral and cognitive characteristics, traits, or predispositions that people take with them to different situations, contexts, and interactions with others, and that contribute to differences among individuals.

In North American psychology, personality is generally based on stability and consistency across contexts, situations, and interactions. This notion of personality has a long tradition in European and North American psychology. The psychoanalytic work of Freud and the neoanalytic approaches of Jung and Adler share this definition of personality. The humanistic approach of Maslow and Rogers, the trait approach of Allport, the behavioral approach of Skinner, and the cognitive approach of Rotter, Bandura, and Mischel also share this notion. Although these approaches differ in their conceptions of how personality develops, they are consistent in their basic notion of personality as stable and enduring across contexts and situations. Most scholars, even in cross-cultural psychology, adopt this or similar definitions of personality when studying it across cultures.

Cross-Cultural Approaches to the Study and Understanding of Personality

Over the course of the 20th century, several different approaches and methods have been used to elucidate the relationship between culture and personality. Some of the earliest contributions to our understanding of this relationship came from anthropologists who were interested in human psychology within their anthropological discipline. Through mostly ethnographic fieldwork, these individuals—such as Margaret Mead, Weston Labarre, and Ruth Benedict—developed ideas and theories about culture and personality that served as a basis for cross-cultural comparison of personalities and today's cultural psychology (see review in Piker, 1998). While many cultural and psychological anthropologists recognize the important contributions of biologically innate factors to personality and psychology, the main thrust of the anthropological contribution is its view of personality as culturally specific, formed by the unique forces each culture deals with in its milieu. The anthropological view of personality, therefore, attributes more importance to the learning of psychological mechanisms and personality in the environment through cultural practices than to biological and evolutionary factors.

Whereas psychological anthropology made major contributions in the first half of the 20th century, the second half was dominated by the cross-cultural psychological approach (see review by Church & Lonner, 1998). This approach generally views personality as something discrete and separate from culture, and as a dependent variable in research. Thus, two or more cultures are treated as independent variables, and they are compared on some personality traits or dimensions. In contrast to the cultural or psychological anthropological approach, the cross-cultural approach tends to see personality as an etic or universal phenomenon that is equivalently relevant and meaningful in the cultures being compared. To the extent that personality does exhibit universal aspects, how did they originate? Two separate but not mutually exclusive possibilities are (1) the existence of biologically innate and evolutionarily adaptive factors that create genetic predispositions to certain types of personality traits and (2) the possibility of culture-constant learning principles and processes (see also the discussion by MacDonald, 1998).

Cross-cultural research on personality, however, has also been concerned with the discovery of culture-specific personality traits, characteristics, and patterns. Cross-cultural psychologists describe culture-specific **indigenous personalities** as constellations of personality traits and characteristics found only in a specific culture (for more information, see reviews by Ho, 1998, and Diaz-Loving, 1998). These types of studies, though psychological in nature, are heavily influenced in approach and understanding by the anthropological view of culture and personality.

Another approach to understanding the relationship between culture and personality that has emerged in recent years is known as cultural psychology (for example, Shweder, 1979a, 1979b, 1980; Markus & Kitayama, 1998). This approach sees culture and personality not as separate entities, but as a mutually constituted system in which each creates and maintains the other.

> The cultural perspective assumes that psychological processes, in this case the nature of functioning of personality, are not just influenced by culture but are thoroughly culturally constituted. In turn, the cultural perspective assumes that personalities behaving in concert create the culture. Culture and personality are most productively analyzed together as a dynamic of mutual constitution . . . ; one cannot be reduced to the other. . . . A cultural psychological approach does not automatically assume that all behavior can be explained with the same set of categories and dimensions and first asks whether a given dimension, concept, or category is meaningful and how it is used in a given cultural context. (Markus & Kitayama, 1998, p. 66)

The cultural psychological viewpoint has been heavily influenced by the cultural anthropologists, as well as by the cross-cultural work on indigenous psychologies and personalities. It is inherently antithetical to the cross-cultural psychological search for universals and rejects the possibility of biological and genetic mechanisms underlying universality. Instead, it suggests that, just as no two cultures are alike, the personalities that comprise those cultures should be fundamentally different because of the mutual constitution of culture and personality within each cultural milieu.

The tension between the cross-cultural psychology school and the cultural psychology school, in terms of universality versus culture-specificity in personality, can be seen in the literature reviewed in this chapter. Although considerable evidence points to the universality of some aspects of personality, a considerable amount of evidence also documents the existence of indigenous personalities, as well as cultural differences in supposedly etic personality domains. How to make sense of this all is perhaps the greatest challenge facing this area of cross-cultural psychology in the near future.

Cross-Cultural Research on Personality

For many years, one of the most common and popular methods of examining the relationship between culture and personality has been cross-cultural research. In this approach, researchers take samples of individuals from two or more cultures, administer a personality scale, and compare the responses between groups. Cross-cultural differences in the personality measure are then interpreted with respect to differences in the values, behaviors, and practices observed in the cultures being compared.

This approach, while simplistic in concept, has provided a wealth of useful and interesting information about cultural similarities and differences in personality. In this section, we will review and discuss some of the major findings.

Locus of Control

One of the most widely studied personality concepts across cultures is **locus of control**. This concept was developed by Rotter (1954, 1966), who suggested that people differ in how much control they believe they have over their behavior and their relationship with their environment and with others. According to this schema, locus of control can be perceived as either internal or external to the individual. People with an internal locus of control see their behavior and relationships with others as dependent upon their own behavior. Believing that your grades are mostly dependent on how much effort you put into study is an example of internal locus of control. People with an external locus of control see their behavior and relationships with the environment and others as contingent upon forces outside of themselves and beyond their control. If you believed your grades were mostly dependent on luck, the teacher's benevolence, or the ease of the tests, you would be exemplifying an external locus of control.

Research examining locus of control has shown both similarities and differences across cultures. In general, Americans often appear to have higher internal locus of control scores, whereas non-Americans tend to have higher external locus of control scores. A number of studies have found this pattern in comparisons of Americans with Asians, especially Chinese and Japanese (for example, Hamid, 1994; see also, however, Spadone, 1992, for a nonfinding in an American–Thai comparison). Lee and Dengerink (1992) found higher internal locus of control scores among Americans than Swedes, and Munro (1979) found that Americans had higher internal locus of control scores than participants in Zambia and Zimbabwe (then Rhodesia). In a review of cross-cultural studies on locus of control, Dyal (1984) concluded that European Americans appear to be characterized by a more internal locus of control than

African Americans. Locus of control differences have also been documented in children; Paguio, Robinson, Skeen, and Deal (1987), for example, showed that American children had higher internal locus of control scores than Filipino and Brazilian children.

These findings have often been interpreted as reflecting the American culture's focus on individuality, separateness, and uniqueness, in contrast to a more balanced view of interdependence among individuals and between individuals and natural and supernatural forces found in many other cultures. People of non-American cultures may be more likely to view the causes of events and behaviors in sources that are external to themselves, such as fate, luck, supernatural forces, or relationships with others. Americans, however, prefer to take more personal responsibility for events and situations, and view themselves as having more personal control over such events.

Although such interpretations are interesting and provocative, they still leave some gaps to be filled. For example, they do not account for such phenomena as self-serving bias or defensive attributions (mentioned in Chapter 3), in which Americans tend to place the responsibility for negative events on others, not themselves. Also, some researchers have suggested that locus of control is really a multifaceted construct spanning many different domains—academic achievement, work, interpersonal relationships, and so on—and that separate assessments of each of these domains are necessary to make meaningful comparisons on this construct. Finally, Smith, Dugan, and Trompenaars (1997), in their 14-country study of locus of control and affectivity, found there were some cross-national differences in locus of control, but larger differences by gender and status across countries. Thus, the search for cross-cultural differences may obscure larger differences based on other social constructs. Future research needs to address all these concerns to further elucidate the nature of cultural influences on locus of control.

Self-Esteem

A number of studies have examined the construct of self-esteem and the related construct of self-worth. Research in the United States has repeatedly shown that European Americans have a pervasive tendency to maintain their feelings of self-esteem and self-worth. Concepts such as self-serving bias, defensive attributions, and illusory optimism have been invoked as mechanisms of self-enhancement among European Americans. These self-enhancing tendencies are not generally found in other groups, especially Asians (see review by Diener & Diener, 1995). Some researchers even suggest that Asians, particularly Japanese, are more attuned to negative rather than positive self-evaluations, in both private and public settings (Kitayama, Matsumoto, Markus, & Norasakkunkit, 1997).

Cross-cultural studies lend support to these differences in self-esteem across cultures. Wood, Hillman, and Sawilowsky (1995), for example, comparing American and Indian adolescents on self-esteem, found that Americans had significantly higher self-esteem scores than their Indian counterparts. Radford,

Mann, Ohta, and Nakane (1993), comparing self-esteem related to decision making in Australian and Japanese students, found that Australians had higher self-esteem scores than did the Japanese.

The higher self-esteem scores of Australians compared to Japanese suggests that self-esteem may be related to individualism, rather than specific to American culture. If self-esteem is related to individualism and collectivism, then perhaps individualism fosters a certain type of self-esteem—one that is often measured in psychological research—while collectivism fosters a different type of self-esteem. Tafarodi and Swann (1996) tested this "cultural trade-off" hypothesis in a study of Chinese and American college students. They hypothesized that highly collectivistic cultures promote the development of global self-esteem, which is reflected in generalized self-liking, while at the same time challenging the development of another dimension of self-esteem, reflected in generalized self-competence; individualistic cultures, they hypothesized, foster the opposite tendencies. As predicted, they found that the Chinese were lower in self-competence but higher in self-liking than the Americans. These findings support the notion that self-esteem may have multiple facets, and that different cultural milieus either support or challenge the development of different facets.

This notion also received some support in a recent study by Kitayama and Karasawa (1997). This study examined implicit rather than explicit self-esteem in a sample of Japanese individuals, by examining their preference for certain Japanese alphabetical letters and numbers over others. The results indicated that letters included in one's own name, and numbers corresponding to the month and day of one's birth, were significantly better liked than other numbers and letters. The authors interpreted these findings to suggest a dimension of self-esteem that may be fostered in a collectivistic cultural milieu, but not necessarily within an individualistic one.

These recent studies suggest the importance of delineating different aspects of self-esteem and then investigating how different cultural frameworks encourage or discourage those various aspects. This line of research raises the possibility that the need for self-esteem is a universal one across humans, but that its exact behavioral and psychological manifestations may differ depending on cultural context. Future research has a rather large job in documenting and elaborating on these ideas.

The Eysenck Personality Scales

One of the most commonly used personality scales in the cross-cultural literature is the Eysenck Personality Questionnaire (EPQ). It measures three different personality traits: toughmindedness (known in the EPQ as Psychoticism), emotionality (known in the EPQ as Neuroticism), and Extroversion. It also contains a Lying or Social Desirability Scale designed to determine the degree to which respondents may be providing false or inaccurate responses. Over the past few decades, the EPQ has been standardized and used in cross-cultural research in a number of different countries, including Nigeria, Japan, Greece, Yugoslavia, Brazil, France, and others (see review in Eysenck & Chan, 1982).

A junior version, developed for use with children, has been used in Spain, New Zealand, Hungary, Japan, and other countries.

The numerous cross-cultural studies involving the EPQ have produced a number of interesting cross-cultural findings. Eysenck and Chan (1982), for example, administered the adult and junior versions of the EPQ to adults and children in Hong Kong and England. They found that adults in Hong Kong scored higher on Psychoticism and Social Desirability and lower on Extroversion than did British adults. Children in Hong Kong scored higher on Social Desirability and lower on Extroversion and Neuroticism than British children. Eysenck and colleagues have found various other differences in comparisons of Romanian and English adults (Eysenck, Baban, Derevenco, & Pitariu, 1989), Danish and English children (Nyborg, Eysenck, & Kroll, 1982), Iranian and English children (Eysenck, Makaremi, & Barrett, 1994), and Egyptian and English children (Eysenck & Abdel-Khalek, 1989).

The goal of most of the published studies involving the EPQ has been validation of the measure for use in cross-cultural research in the countries and cultures in which the tests have been administered. These studies have provided the field with a measure that apparently "works" in a variety of cross-cultural contexts, measuring aspects of personality that are generally considered universal to all humans. However, these studies lack a consistent interpretation of the nature and causes of cultural differences when they occur. While providing a wealth of findings documenting cross-cultural differences, they tell us little about what cultural factors contribute to these differences. Are cross-cultural differences related to stable dimensions of cultural variation, such as individualism versus collectivism, or status/power differentiation? We don't know. A major goal of future research in this area, therefore, should be the generation and testing of viable hypotheses concerning the reasons and processes behind these differences and similarities.

Other Miscellaneous Studies

A number of other studies provide interesting glimpses into the nature of cultural influences on other aspects of personality. Several studies, for example, have reported cultural differences in the personality construct known as self-monitoring. This construct has been described as "self-observation and self-control guided by situational cues to social appropriateness" (Snyder, 1974, p. 526). People of individualistic cultures tend to have higher scores on self-monitoring than do people of collectivistic cultures (for example, Gudykunst, Gao, Nishida, Bond, et al., 1989; Gudykunst, Yang, & Nishida, 1987).

In another interesting study, Yamaguchi, Kuhlman, and Sugimori (1995) examined the personality correlates of allocentric (collectivistic) tendencies in individualistic and collectivistic cultures. These researchers administered a collectivism scale to participants in the United States, Korea, and Japan, and measured individual differences in the degree to which the participants exhibited allocentrism—that is, personally held collectivistic values (see Chapters 2 and 3). They also measured affiliative tendency, sensitivity to rejection, and need for uniqueness. The results indicated that individuals who scored higher on allocentrism also scored higher on affiliation and sensitivity to rejection, but lower on need for uniqueness; these relationships held in all three countries. The researchers explained their findings by suggesting that allocentric individuals are more concerned with rewards and punishments from ingroup members, and thus have less need to be unique, compared to those with greater idiocentric tendencies.

Cross-cultural differences have also been reported in studies on authoritarianism and rigidity involving Iranian respondents (Mehryar, 1970), on Cattell's 16 Personality Factors (PF) with Amish respondents (Wittmer, 1971), on the Maudsley Personality Inventory and the Manifest Anxiety Scale with Hindu Indians (De & Singh, 1972), on value systems among Australians and Chinese (Feather, 1986), on cognitive styles and field dependence in Mexican, African, and European American children (Figueroa, 1980), and on authoritarianism in German and American adolescents (Lederer, 1982).

Summary and Evaluation

While the bulk of the research documents cross-cultural differences in the various domains of personality that have been tested, the very fact that these personality dimensions have been measured across cultures could be taken as some kind of evidence for their universality. That is, the cultures studied are similar in that they share the same personality dimensions, even though they differ in where they fall along these dimensions.

To be sure, the mere fact that personality scales have been translated and used in cross-cultural research is not sufficient evidence that the personality domains they measure are indeed equivalent in those cultures. In fact, when this type of research is conducted, one of the researchers' primary concerns is whether the personality scales used in the study can validly and reliably measure meaningful dimensions of personality in all the cultures studied. As discussed in Chapter 5, the equivalence of a measure in terms of its meaning to all cultures concerned, as well as its psychometric validity and reliability, is of prime concern in cross-cultural research, if the results are to be considered valid, meaningful, and useful.

Indeed, a common practice in many of the earlier cross-cultural studies on personality was to take a personality scale that had been developed in one country or culture—most often the United States—and simply translate it and use it in another culture. In effect, the researchers simply assumed that the personality dimension measured by that scale was equivalent between the two cultures, and that the method of measuring that dimension was psychometrically valid and reliable. Thus, many studies imposed an assumed etic construct upon the cultures studied (Church & Lonner, 1998). Realistically, however, one cannot safely conclude that the personality dimensions represented by an imposed etic are equivalently and meaningfully represented in all cultures included in a study.

Many of the more recent studies in this area, however, have been sensitive to this issue, and researchers have taken steps to assure some degree of psychometric equivalence across cultures in their measures of personality. In their study of the EPQ in Hong Kong and England, for example, Eysenck and Chan (1982) included only those items that were common to scoring keys derived separately in both cultures, thus ensuring some comparability in the scale scores used in their comparison. Likewise, Tafarodi and Swann (1996) tested the cross-cultural equivalence in their measure of self-esteem by conducting a confirmatory factor analysis on the items measured in their scales in both cultures before testing for differences. In testing for cultural differences in locus of control, Hamid (1994) back-translated his measures, administered both original and translated measures to bilinguals, and assessed the parallel forms correlation of the two questionnaires before using them in the main study. Munro (1979) established equivalence in the factor structures of his locus of control questionnaires before testing for cultural differences between blacks and whites in Africa, and Smith, Dugans, and Trompenaars (1997) conducted a pancultural factor analysis on their locus of control measure before testing for differences. This procedure allowed them to derive scale scores after eliminating individual and cultural differences in the ratings of the individual items included in the scale.

Support for the notion that cross-cultural comparisons of personality are meaningful comes from other sources as well. First, the findings derived from many of these studies "make sense"; that is, they are interpretable to a large degree and match predictions based on what we might reasonably expect based on our knowledge of culture and its probable influence on personality. Findings that were uninterpretable based upon available knowledge of the cultures tested would raise questions about the psychometric validity of the scales being used. That many studies provide interpretable findings, however, suggests that the scales do measure something that is meaningful.

Another source of support comes from the data analyses used to compare cultures. While significant differences in mean values reflect between-culture differences in averages, they do not necessarily reflect the degree of overlap among individuals within the samples comprising the various cultures in the comparison. In most cases, the degree of individual variation is many times larger than the degree of difference between cultures. Analysis of such effects would surely lead one to suspect a considerable degree of individual similarity in the personality constructs being measured.

A final source of support for the notion that many of the personality scales used in previous cross-cultural studies are valid comes from recent studies investigating the possible link between genetics and personality. Indeed, an increasing number of studies in recent years have begun to show that personality has some direct relationship to genes (for example, Eley, 1997; Riemann, Angleitner, & Strelau, 1997; Saudino, 1997). To the extent that genetic and biological factors contribute to personality, they provide the basis on which stability in personality can be conceptualized, measured, and studied not only across individuals within a culture, but across cultures as well. Should such stability exist, and if this stability is related to biological factors that are in turn related to evolutionary factors and adaptive functions, it supports the argument that some aspects of personality may indeed be universal. This argument does not preclude the possibility of cultural specificity in some aspects of personality, in the manifestations of personality, or even in the emergence and existence of indigenous personalities; it merely suggests that some aspects of personality may be universal to all humans.

Culture and the Five Factor Model of Personality

The Five Factor Model (FFM) of personality is a conceptual model built around five distinct and basic personality dimensions that appear to be universal for all humans. The five dimensions are Extroversion, Neuroticism, Agreeableness, Conscientiousness, and Openness.

The FFM was conceived after a number of writers noticed the similarities in the personality dimensions that had emerged across many studies, both within and between cultures. Most notably, support for the FFM arose out of factor analyses of trait adjectives from the English lexicon that were descriptive of self and others (Juni, 1996). The factors that emerged from these types of analyses were similar to dimensions found in the analysis of questionnaire scales operationalizing personality. Further inquiry across cultures, using both factor analysis of descriptive trait adjectives in different languages and personality dimensions measured by different personality questionnaires, lent further support to the FFM. Eysenck's (1983) many studies using the EPQ, for example, provided much support for Extroversion and Neuroticism as stable, universal personality scales. In early studies of the FFM, those factors were reported in German (Amelang & Borkenau, 1982), Dutch (De Raad, Hendriks, & Hofstee, 1992), French (Rolland, 1993), Japanese, Chinese, and Filipino samples (Bond, 1979; Bond et al., 1975; Guthrie & Bennett, 1971; all cited in McCrae et al., 1998).

Cross-cultural research of the past decade on the validity of the FFM in different countries and cultures has continued to support claims of universality. De Fruyt and Mervielde (1998), for example, confirmed the validity of the FFM in the Dutch language, and Trull and Geary (1997) confirmed its validity in Chinese. De Raad, Perugini, and Szirmak (1997) reported support for the FFM in Dutch, Italian, Hungarian, American English, and German; Hofstee, Kiers, De Raad, Goldberg et al. (1997) also provided support for the FFM in Dutch, American English, and German. McCrae, Costa, and Yik (1996) provided support for the FFM in the Chinese personality structure, and Digman and Shmelyov (1996) documented its utility in Russia. Other studies have documented its validity in other countries and cultures, including Italy (Caprara, Barbaranelli, & Comrey, 1995; Caprara & Perugini, 1994); Australia and South Africa (Heaven, Connors, & Stones, 1994); Hong Kong (Ng, Cooper, & Chandler, 1998); Canada, Finland, Poland, and Germany (Paunonen, Jackson,

Trzebinski, & Forsterling, 1992); Germany, Portugal, Israel, China, Korea, and Japan (McCrae & Costa, 1997); and others (see review in McCrae et al., 1998). Collectively, these studies provide convincing and substantial evidence to support the claim that the FFM—consisting of Extroversion, Neuroticism, Openness, Conscientiousness, and Agreeableness—represents a universal taxonomy of personality that is applicable to all humans.

The universality of the FFM suggests that all humans share a similar personality structure that can be characterized by the five traits or dimensions that comprise the FFM. To explain this universality, some writers (for example, MacDonald, 1998) have suggested an evolutionary approach. This approach posits a universality both of human interests and in the neurophysiological mechanisms underlying trait variation. Personality structure is viewed as a universal psychological mechanism, a product of natural selection that serves both social and nonsocial functions in problem solving and environmental adaptation. Based on this theory, one would expect to find similar systems in animals that serve similar adaptive functions, and one would expect personality systems to be organized within the brain as discrete neurophysiological systems.

In this view, traits such as Conscientiousness (emotional stability), Neuroticism (affect intensity), and the other components of the FFM are considered to reflect stable variations in systems that serve critical adaptive functions. Conscientiousness, for example, may serve to help individuals monitor the environment for dangers and impending punishments, and to persevere in tasks that are not intrinsically rewarding (MacDonald, 1998). Affect intensity functions measured by Neuroticism are adaptive in that they help mobilize behavioral resources by moderating arousal in situations requiring approach or avoidance.

According to MacDonald (1991, 1998), this evolutionary approach suggests a hierarchical model in which "behavior related to personality occurs at several levels based ultimately on the motivating aspects of evolved personality systems" (p. 130). In this model, humans possess evolved motive dispositions—for example, intimacy, safety—which are serviced by a universal set of personality dispositions that help individuals achieve their affective goals by managing personal and environmental resources. This resource management leads to concerns, projects, and tasks, which in turn lead to specific action units or behaviors through which the individual achieves the goals specified by the evolved motive dispositions (see Figure 15.1).

Note that this model—and the assumptions about universality of the FFM made by McCrae and Costa and others (for example, McCrae & Costa, 1997)—does not minimize the importance of cultural and individual variability. Culture can substantially influence personality through the resources, social structures, and social systems available in a specific environment to help achieve goals. Culture can therefore influence mean levels of personality, and values about the various personality traits. Culture is "undeniably relevant in the development of characteristics adaptations that guide the expression of personality in thoughts, feelings, and behaviors" (McCrae et al., 1998). Culture defines context, and provides differential meaning to the components of context, including who is involved, what is happening, where it is occurring, and the like.

Figure 15.1 Hierarchical model of motivation showing relationships between domain-specific and domain-general mechanisms

Level 1	EVOLVED MOTIVE DISPOSITIONS (Domain-Specific Mechanisms)
Level 2	PERSONAL STRIVINGS (Direct Psychological Effects of Domain-Specific Mechanisms)
Level 3	CONCERNS, PROJECTS, TASKS (Utilize Domain-General Mechanisms)
Level 4	SPECIFIC ACTION UNITS (Utilize Domain-General Mechanisms)

EXAMPLE:

Evolved Motive Disposition	INTIMACY
Personal Striving	INTIMATE RELATIONSHIP WITH A PARTICULAR PERSON
Concern, Project, Task	Arrange meeting — Improve appearance — Get promotion
Action Units	Find phone number — Begin dieting — Work on weekends

Source: Emmons (1989). Reprinted by permisison of Lawrence Erlbaum Associates, Inc.

Culture, therefore, plays a substantial role in producing the specific behavioral manifestations—the specific action units—that individuals will engage in to achieve what may be universal affective goals. A universal personality structure, however, is considered to be the mechanism by which such goals are achieved through a balance and interaction with culture.

The utility of the approach offered by the FFM, along with its underlying concept of a universal personality structure, continues to receive considerable support in the literature. Recent research has shown that the FFM can predict variations in behavior within individuals in longitudinal studies (Borkenau & Ostendorf, 1998) and is stable across different instruments and observers (McCrae & Costa, 1987). Some recent evidence even suggests that the FFM may apply to nonhuman primates as well. King and Figueredo (1997), presented 43 trait adjectives with representative items from the FFM to zoo trainers who work with chimpanzees in 12 different zoos. The trainers were asked to describe the chimpanzees in terms of the adjectives provided. The results showed no differences between the zoos, and the interrater reliability among the raters was high. Factor analysis of the ratings produced six factors, five of which corresponded to the FFM; the sixth corresponded to dominance. Of course, the findings from this study are not conclusive. A conservative interpretation would be that they merely indicate that human raters use their implicit theories of personality to rate nonhumans. Taken in conjunction with the growing literature concerning the relationship between biological and genetic factors and personality, however, they suggest that the FFM may be indicative of a universal personality structure that may be applicable not only to humans, but also to nonhuman primates and perhaps other mammals as well (McCrae et al., 1998).

The Measurement of Personality across Cultures

One of the most serious issues in all cross-cultural research on personality is whether or not personality can be measured reliably and validly across different cultures. If methods of assessing personality are not reliable or valid across cultures, then the results of research using these methods cannot be trusted to give accurate portrayals of personality similarities or differences across cultures.

Most personality measures used in cross-cultural research were originally developed in a single language and single culture, and validated in that language and culture. The psychometric evidence typically used to demonstrate a measure's reliability and validity in a single culture involves examination of internal, test–retest, and parallel forms reliabilities, convergent and predictive validities, and replicability of the factor structures that comprise the various scales of the test. To obtain all these types of psychometric evidence for the reliability and validity of a test, researchers must literally spend years conducting countless studies addressing each of these specific concerns. The best measures of personality—as well as all other psychological constructs—have this degree of psychometric evidence backing them.

To validate personality measures cross-culturally requires similar psychometric evidence from all cultures in which the test is to be used. In the strictest sense, therefore, researchers interested in cross-cultural studies on personality should select instruments that have been demonstrated to have acceptable psychometric properties. This is a far cry from merely selecting a test that seems to be interesting and translating it for use in another culture. At the very least, equivalence of its psychometric properties should be established empirically, not assumed or ignored.

Data addressing the psychometric evidence necessary to validate a test in a target culture would provide the safest avenue by which such equivalence can be demonstrated. If such data exist, they can be used to support contentions concerning psychometric equivalence. Even if those data do not offer a high degree of support (reliability coefficients are lower, or factor structures are not exactly equivalent), that does not necessarily mean that the test as a whole is not equivalent. There are, in fact, multiple alternative explanations of why such data may not be as strong in the target culture as in the culture in which the test was originally developed. Paunonen and Ashton (1998) outline and describe ten such possible interpretations, ranging from poor test translation and response style issues to different analytic methods. Thus, if a test is examined in another culture for its psychometric properties and the data are not as strong as they were in the original culture, each of these possibilities should be examined before concluding that the test is not psychometrically valid or reliable. In many cases, the problem may be minor and fixable.

Given these criteria, how have the various personality tests used in cross-cultural research fared? Paunonen and Ashton (1998) have reviewed the data concerning the California Psychological Inventory, the Comrey Personality Scales, the 16 Personality Factors Questionnaire, the Pavlovian Temperament Survey, the Personality Research Form, and the Nonverbal Personality Questionnaire. After reviewing each test's reliability, convergent validity, predictive validity, and factor structure invariance, these writers conclude that "(a) structured tests of personality can readily be adapted for use in a wide variety of cultures, and (b) there is an organization to many Western-derived personality traits that appears to be universal, or at least general to many of the world's cultures" (p. 165). Clearly, this conclusion is consonant with the notion of personality structure as universal in humans. Other recent studies (for example, Benet-Martinez & John, 1998) have also provided evidence for the psychometric equivalence of measures of the Five Factor Model. These data provide some degree of reassurance that the cross-cultural studies reviewed in this chapter have measured personality in psychometrically acceptable ways.

The Measurement of Personality to Assess Psychopathology across Cultures

One of the interesting ways in which personality tests are used cross-culturally involves the assessment not only of personality, but also of clinical states and psychopathology. The most widely used scale in such cross-cultural assessments is the Minnesota Multiphasic Personality Inventory (MMPI). Recently, Butcher, Lim, and Nezami (1998) reviewed the use of the MMPI in various countries and cultures, including six Asian cultures, six Spanish-speaking cultures, eight European cultures, and three cultures in the Middle East. They reported on the procedures most researchers used in adapting the MMPI for use in their particular cultural milieu, including translation and back-translation, bilingual test–retest evaluation, study of equivalency, and the like. They concluded:

> Clinical case studies involving the assessment of patients from different cultures have shown that MMPI-2 interpretations drawn from an American perspective generally produce congruent conclusions about clinical patients tested in other countries. . . . Computer-based MMPI-2 interpretations appear to have a high degree of accuracy when applied to patients from other countries. Computer-based reports derived on interpretive strategies developed for the United States were rated as highly accurate by clinicians when they were applied in Norway, Australia, and France. (p. 207)

Thus, clinical studies across cultures involving personality scales such as the MMPI have been shown to be quite reliable and valid in assessing psychopathology and abnormal behavior in other cultures as well. This finding is once again consistent with the premise of a universal underlying personality structure that can be reliably and validly assessed by methods typically developed and refined in the United States or Europe. If such a universal personality structure exists and can be measured via some means, then deviations from that personality structure in the form of psychopathology should also be measurable using those same means. In the next section, however, we explore the area of indigenous personalities, which, on the surface, appear antithetical to the notion of underlying universality in personality organization.

Culture and Indigenous Personalities

Indigenous personalities are conceptualizations of personality developed in a particular culture that are specific and relevant only to that culture. In general, not only are the concepts of personality rooted in and derived from the particular cultural group under question, but the methodologies used to test and examine those concepts are also particular to that culture. Thus, in contrast to much of the research described so far, using standardized personality measures to assess personality dimensions, studies of indigenous personalities often use their own, nonstandardized methodologies.

Over the years, many scientists have been interested in indigenous conceptions of personality, and have described many different personality constructs considered to exist only in specific cultures. Berry and colleagues (1992) examined three such indigenous personality concepts, each of which is fundamentally different from American or Western concepts. The African model of personality, for example, views personality as consisting of three layers, each representing a different aspect of the person. The first layer, found at the core of the person and personality, embodies a spiritual principle; the second layer involves a psychological vitality principle; the third layer involves a physiological vitality principle. The body forms the outer framework that houses all these layers of the person. In addition, family lineage and community affect different core aspects of the African personality (Sow, 1977, 1978, cited in Berry et al., 1992; see also Vontress, 1991).

Doi (1973) has postulated *amae* as a core concept of the Japanese personality. The root of this word means "sweet," and loosely translated, *amae* refers to the passive, childlike dependence of one person on another. It is said to be rooted in mother–child relationships. According to Doi, all Japanese relationships can be characterized by *amae,* which serves as a fundamental building block of Japanese culture and personality. This fundamental interrelationship between higher- and lower-status people in Japan serves as a major component not only of individual psychology but of interpersonal relationships, and it does so in ways that are difficult to grasp from a North American individualistic point of view.

Early work in this area produced findings of many other personality constructs thought to be culture-specific. Such constructs have included the national character or personality of Arab culture (Beit-Hallahmi, 1972), North Alaskan Eskimos (Hippler, 1974), the Japanese (Sakamoto & Miura, 1976), the Fulani of Nigeria (Lott & Hart, 1977), the Irulas of Palamalai (Narayanan & Ganesan, 1978), Samoans (Holmes, Tallman, & Jantz, 1978), South African Indians (1983), and the Ibo of Nigeria (Akin-Ogundeji, 1988). In more recent years, researchers using standardized personality tests have found that scales derived from such tests are not fully adequate to describe personality in some cultures, such as India (Narayanan, Menon, & Levine, 1995) and the Philippines (Church, Katigbak, & Reyes, 1996; Church, Reyes, Katigbak, & Grimm, 1997).

Indigenous personality measures—that is, measures developed for use in a particular culture—give us further ideas and insights about the nature of indigenous psychologies and personalities. Cheung and Leung (1998), for example, reviewed three measures of personality developed for use in Chinese cultures. Of them, the Chinese Personality Assessment Inventory (CPAI) most resembles the standardized personality measures familiar to Americans and Europeans. Factor analyses of its items, however, produced four major scales: Dependability, Chinese Tradition, Social Potency, and Individualism. While there is some overlap between the concepts underlying these scales and the FFM, there are also clear discrepancies (such as Chinese Tradition). It seems that there are aspects of personality that are relevant and important to Chinese culture that are probably not captured in traditional personality measures that assess the Big Five.

Clearly, this line of research suggests that not all aspects of personality in the various cultures of the world can be adequately defined and measured by concepts and traits such as those described in the FFM. Indeed, much of the work on indigenous psychology and personality has provided fuel for those who subscribe to the cultural psychology school—the view that culture and personality are mutually constituted. In this view, it makes no sense to consider personality as a universal construct; instead, it makes more sense to understand each culture's personalities as they exist and have developed within that culture.

The cultural psychology viewpoint rejects the notion of a universal organization to personality that may have genetic, biological, and evolutionary components. Its proponents argue that the research supporting universality and its possible biological substrates may be contaminated by the methods used. These methods, the argument goes, have been developed in American or European research laboratories by American or European researchers; because of this cultural bias, the findings support the FFM as a default by-product of the methods. Indigenous approaches, it is claimed, are immune from such bias because their methods are centered around concepts and practices that are local to the culture being studied (see, however, the replication of the FFM using nontraditional methods of assessing taxonomies of trait adjectives in multiple languages; De Raad, Perugini, Hrebickova, & Szarota, 1998).

Is there a middle ground? I believe there is. In the past, scientists interested in cross-cultural psychology have tended to think about universal and culture-specific aspects of psychological phenomena—personality, emotion, language, and the like—as mutually exclusive, dichotomous categories. Thus, personality is either universal or indigenous. A better and more fruitful approach might be to consider the question not of *whether* personality is universal *or* indigenous, but rather *how* personality is both universal *and* culture-specific. It is entirely possible that some aspects of personality may be organized in a universal fashion, either because of biological or genetic factors or because of culture-constant learning and responses to the environment. The fact that some aspects of personality may be organized universally, however, does not necessarily argue against the possibility that other aspects of personality may be culturally unique. It may be these culturally unique aspects that give personality its own special flavor in each specific cultural milieu, and allow researchers the possibility of studying aspects of personality that they might not observe in other cultures. Thus, a more beneficial way of understanding the relationship between culture and personality may be to see indigenous and universal aspects of personality as two sides of the same coin, rather than as two mutually exclusive dichotomies. If we come to understand the relationship between culture and personality (and biology, for that matter) in ways that allow for the coexistence of universality and indigenization, then we can tackle the problem of exactly how to conceptualize and study this coexistence.

⧈ Conclusion

In this chapter, we have discussed the major approaches to understanding and studying the relationship between culture and personality, and have examined many different types of studies on this topic. Cross-cultural studies of personality dimensions have shown many ways in which cultures may differ in mean levels of personality. More recent research on the organization of personality, however, suggests that the Five Factor Model—a constellation of personality traits comprising Neuroticism, Extroversion, Openness, Conscientiousness, and Agreeableness—may be universal to all humans. Some research has also provided support for the existence of these factors in nonhuman primates. Research on indigenous approaches to personality, however, have demonstrated culturally specific aspects of personality that cannot be accounted for by the FFM. These two seemingly disparate sets of findings suggest a conflict in our understanding of the relationship between culture and personality, represented by the cross-cultural psychology versus cultural psychology schools of thought. I have suggested that these two seemingly opposing viewpoints need not be seen as mutually exclusive; rather, it may be more beneficial to view them as different, coexisting aspects of personality. The challenge for future research is to capture this coexistence, examining the relative degree of contribution of biological and cultural factors in the development and organization of personality.

In our quest to understand the relationship between culture and personality, one of the biggest issues we will need to tackle concerns the influence of context, and the effects of context on that understanding. As we have seen, context is a major dimension of culture (Hall, 1966). High-context cultures place little value on cross-context consistency, allowing (and necessitating) behaviors and cognitions that differ according to context or situation. Low-context cultures, in contrast, discourage cross-context differences, emphasizing instead consistency and stability across contexts. American culture is relatively low-context, emphasizing stability. It is only within this type of cultural context that we can even conceive of personality as a set of enduring characteristics with stability and consistency across cultures (see the definition of personality at the beginning of this chapter). Thus, a person in this cultural context should exhibit similar personality characteristics despite considerable differences in context.

It is relatively easy to demonstrate the existence of context specificity effects in assessments of personality. Recently, I conducted a simple study with a small group of monolingual American students ($N = 40$). The study consisted of having students complete a personality test in two conditions. The personality test was the Big Five Inventory–54 (John, 1989), which assesses the five traits associated with the FFM (McCrae & Costa, 1987). Students completed this measure once in the usual way with general directions and a second time with context-specific directions ("Complete this test responding as if you were interacting with your best friend"). Even with this simple context manipulation, an analysis of the data indicated that students' responses differed substantially under the two conditions. Students gave significantly higher ratings in the second condition than the first on extroversion and agreeableness: $F(1,38) = 18.90$, $p < .001$ and $F(1,38) = 12.70$, $p < .001$, respectively. They gave significantly lower ratings in the second condition on neuroticism: $F(1,38) = 16.85$, $p < .001$. Thus, context-specificity in personality assessment can be obtained with American participants as well, further challenging our traditional notions of personality, and the very definition of personality. Ultimately, these concerns need to be addressed in future work as well.

Glossary

indigenous personalities Conceptualizations of personality developed in a particular culture that are specific and relevant only to that culture.

locus of control People's attributions of control over their behaviors and relationships as internal or external to themselves. People with an internal locus of control see their behavior and relationships with others as dependent upon their own behavior. People with an exter-

nal locus of control see their behavior and relationships as contingent upon forces outside of themselves and beyond their control.

personality A set of relatively enduring behavioral and cognitive characteristics, traits, or predispositions that people take with them to different situations, contexts, and interactions with others, and that contribute to differences among individuals.

Culture and Social Behavior

Humans are social animals, and much of our everyday lives involves interactions with and influences of others. Especially in North America, we struggle with the tension between being unique, separate individuals ("Every man for himself") and being fundamentally connected to one another ("No man is an island").

Culture exerts considerable influence in the social arena. How we interact with others, perceive others, and work with others—all are influenced by the culture in which we live. We have all learned particular ways of behaving, perceiving, and working based on our own cultural upbringing and milieu. We may believe our way is the way people of all cultures should behave and interact, but what is true for us is often not true for people of other cultural groups.

This chapter will review some of these cultural differences in social behavior, including ingroup and outgroup relationships; interpersonal attraction, love, and intercultural marriage; attributions; aggression; and conformity, compliance, obedience, and cooperation. The goal of this chapter is to highlight the many and profound ways in which people of different cultures behave differently in social contexts. At the same time, we will see cross-cultural similarities.

Culture and Ingroup/Outgroup Relationships

Culture influences social behavior in many different ways. We all live with others, forming attachments, bonds, and relationships. We are close to some people and distant from others. We make friends, acquaintances, and even enemies. Some of the people we see every day we know well, yet other people we see every day we don't know at all. Strangers, family members, friends, co-workers, acquaintances—the list of people in our everyday world is long.

One way social scientists have learned to understand our relationships with different people is by classifying them into categories that approximate the psychological categories we create. Especially important to understanding self–other relationships and pertinent to understanding cultural differences in social behavior is the category of ingroups versus outgroups.

Ingroups and Outgroups

The ingroups–outgroups classification is one of the oldest and best studied social classifications in social psychology and sociology (see Brewer & Kramer, 1985; Messick & Mackie, 1989; and Tajfel, 1982, for reviews and more complete descriptions of this distinction). Most of us intuitively know the difference between ingroups and outgroups. **Ingroup relationships** are relationships characterized by some degree of familiarity, intimacy, and trust. We feel close to the people around us we consider in our ingroup. Self–ingroup relationships develop through bonds that tie the ingroup together through common friendship or relationships or goals.

Outgroup relationships are just the opposite. Outgroup relationships lack the familiarity, intimacy, and trust characteristic of relationships with ingroup others. Ingroup relationships may be associated with feelings of closeness, but outgroup relationships may lack such feelings altogether and may even involve negative feelings of hostility, aggression, aloofness, or superiority. A bond exists that binds ingroup relationships together, but no such bond exists for relationships with people on the outside. These people simply exist and are barely in our consciousness. They do not have any special relationship with us.

The ingroup–outgroup distinction is dichotomous, allowing us to characterize or classify everyone in our world into one of these two categories. But social scientists know the world is not that simple. Our social relationships cannot be neatly classified into two categories. There are differing degrees of intimacy, familiarity, and closeness even within one category. Classification schemes like ingroups–outgroups are simply aids that help us understand our behavior with others while acknowledging that greater complexity exists in those relationships.

Much of socialization and enculturation—the time of growing and learning about the rules and standards of our society and culture—is spent learning which people constitute our ingroup and outgroup. From birth (and arguably before), we are busy building relationships with the people around us. As we go to school, make friends, find jobs, fall in love, and generally go through life, we develop relationships with many different people. Explicitly or implicitly, we categorize those relationships in our own minds according to the dimensions that define our ingroups and outgroups.

The ingroup–outgroup distinction is applicable to all cultures and societies of the world. People of all cultures must learn to differentiate among the people they have relationships with. However, people of different cultures differ in exactly how these relationships develop, and with whom. The people we generally consider to belong to our ingroup may not be the same people that members of another culture consider to be in their ingroup. The same is true for outgroups. And even when the same people can be classified as ingroup or outgroup across cultures, the particular shapes, forms, and meanings of those relationships may be entirely different. Recognizing these similarities and differences forms the basis for understanding how culture can influence ingroup and outgroup relationships and guide our social behaviors.

Cultural Differences in Ingroup/Outgroup Relationships

Cultural differences in the structure and format of ingroup/outgroup relationships.   I have already touched on how people of different cultures can differ in their self–ingroup and –outgroup relationships. My own observations suggest that people of different cultures may not consider the same types of people and relationships when defining ingroups and outgroups. Just because we consider a certain type of person (a friend at school, a work colleague) an ingroup (or outgroup) member, we cannot assume that people from another culture will interpret and act on those relationships in exactly the same way.

Cultures differ in the formation and structure of self–ingroup and self–outgroup relationships in other ways as well. In North American culture, ingroup and outgroup membership is stable, no matter what we are talking about, to whom we are talking, or where we are talking. Our friends are our friends no matter what. But to someone in another culture, some people may constitute an ingroup in one circumstance or situation, but *the same people* may constitute an outgroup in another. It is not uncommon for businesspeople in many Asian cultures, for example, to consider each other outgroups and competitors when talking about domestic business issues. But when the discussion turns to international business competition, those same outgroup competitors may band together to form an ingroup. This type of switching of ingroups and outgroups is not limited to Asian or collectivistic cultures; it is present in many, if not all, cultures. When former President Bush visited Japan in 1991 with the chief executive officers of many different American companies, they all represented ingroup "Americans," even though those companies and officers would consider each other outgroup rivals in relation to domestic issues. As with many cultural differences, cultures differ in terms of degree but not necessarily presence or absence of this switching phenomenon.

Cross-cultural research has amply demonstrated that people of different cultures perceive relationships differently. Forgas and Bond (1985), for example, asked participants in Hong Kong and Australia about 27 social episodes related to university student life. They asked participants to group the episodes into categories based on their perceived similarity, to label their groupings, and to identify subgroups of the most similar episodes within those groups. They then subjected the data to a statistical technique known as multidimensional scaling, which identifies the kinds of dimensions that best underlie the groupings made by each group of participants. Four dimensions best described how the Hong Kong Chinese participants cognitively represented the episodes: (1) power distance, (2) task versus social orientation, (3) evaluation, and (4) involvement. For the Australian sample, however, a different set of four dimensions emerged: (1) competitiveness, (2) social versus task orientation, (3) involvement, and (4) self-confidence. These differences are clearly related to differences in the cultural values of the two societies. The Hong Kong Chinese cultural values of strong communal feelings, collectivism, and social usefulness, together with an acceptance of authority, influence their perceptions of the social events. For the Australians, competitiveness, self-confidence, freedom, and hedonistically based evaluations dominate their perceptions. These data demonstrate clearly how the same social episodes can be perceived very differently in different cultures.

Another recent study also demonstrated interesting psychological differences in how people perceive their ingroups. In this study (Harrison, Stewart, Myambo, & Teveraishe, 1995), adolescents in Zimbabwe and the United States completed a 33-item test that measured six aspects of social relationships: (1) reliable alliance, (2) enhancement or worth, (3) affection, (4) instrumental help and guidance, (5) companionship and social integration, and (6) intimacy. The researchers added three other dimensions: (7) conflict, (8) satisfaction, and (9) discipline. The participants completed this test about their relationship with six target individuals: mother, father, favorite relative, teacher, best friend, and favorite sibling. The results indicated that the Zimbabweans perceived social support as being provided by a variety of persons in their social network. The Americans, however, perceived social support as being provided primarily by parents and best friends. Also, the Zimbabweans perceived their social support network as providing them with intimacy; the Americans, on the other hand, perceived their social support network as basically providing them with affection. Again, these differences highlight the different ways in which people of different cultures can perceive ingroups and outgroups, and the different psychological meanings attributed to them. These differences are related to differences in cultural values: Zimbabwean culture places a higher value on relationships, whereas American culture places a higher value on individuality and uniqueness.

Cultural differences in the meaning of ingroup/outgroup relationships.
Some scientists have done a considerable amount of work on cultural differences in self–ingroup and –outgroup relationships. Triandis and his colleagues (1988) have done an especially nice job of elucidating how self–ingroup and self–outgroup relationships differ across cultures by using the cultural dimension of individualism versus collectivism to understand cultural differences in social behavior.

As we have seen throughout this book, individualism–collectivism (IC) is one of the most important social psychological dimensions of culture. Many writers across the social science disciplines have used this dimension to understand differences in social behaviors across the cultures they have studied (for example, Hofstede, 1980, 1983; Kluckholn & Strodtbeck, 1961; Mead, 1961; Triandis, 1972). IC refers to the degree to which a culture promotes individual needs, wishes, desires, and values over group and collective ones. Individualistic cultures encourage their members to become unique individuals; hierarchical power and status differences are minimized, while equality is emphasized. Collectivistic cultures stress the needs of a group; individuals are identified more through their group affiliation than by individual position or attributes. Hierarchical differences and vertical relationships are emphasized, and role, status, and appropriate behaviors are more clearly defined by position.

Self–ingroup and self–outgroup relationships differ in individualistic and collectivistic cultures, and these differences in the meaning of ingroup and outgroup relationships produce differences in the types of behaviors people engage in when interacting with others. In individualistic cultures, such as the United States, people often belong to multiple ingroups. Many Americans belong to several ingroups—music groups, sport groups, church groups, social groups, and so forth. Children may belong to football teams during football season, basketball teams during basketball season, and baseball teams during baseball season. They may take swimming lessons, take piano or violin lessons, belong to Boy or Girl Scouts, and generally just be the busiest people around. In contrast, members of collectivistic cultures, including many Asian and South American cultures, belong to fewer ingroups. They do not belong to all the different sports, music, and social groups that people in individualistic cultures do.

This difference between individualistic and collectivistic cultures in ingroup membership has important consequences for the degree of commitment people have to different groups. In general, in exchange for belonging to fewer groups, people in collectivistic cultures have greater commitments to the groups to which they belong. They also identify more with the groups to which they belong; that is, the groups themselves become an integral part of each individual's self-concept and identity. This makes sense because, by definition, collectivistic cultures depend on groups to a much greater degree, and subjugating personal goals in favor of collective goals is a necessity.

Members of individualistic cultures do not necessarily collapse their sense of self-identity and self-concept into the groups to which they belong. They have fewer commitments to their ingroups and move much more easily from ingroup to ingroup. While groups take on special importance in collectivistic cultures, the same degree of importance does not attach to group membership in individualistic cultures.

It follows that collectivistic cultures require a greater degree of harmony, cohesion, and cooperation within their ingroups and place greater burdens on individuals to identify with the group and conform to group norms. Sanctions usually exist for nonconformity. Individualistic cultures depend less on groups and more on the uniqueness of their individuals. The pursuit of personal goals rather than collective ones is of primary importance. As a result, individualistic cultures require less harmony and cohesion within groups and place less importance on conformity of individuals to group norms.

These differences in the meaning of self–ingroup relationships between individualistic and collectivistic cultures have consequences for behavior. In collectivistic cultures, for example, we would expect people to make more individual sacrifices for their ingroups in pursuit of group goals. We would expect to see people trying harder to cooperate with each other, even if it means that the individual must suppress his or her own feelings, thoughts, behaviors, or goals to maintain harmony and cohesion. We would expect people to try to find ways of agreeing with each other, downplaying and minimizing interpersonal differences for the sake of harmony.

Self–ingroup relationships in individualistic cultures have different consequences for behavior. In these cultures, we would expect people to make fewer sacrifices of their own individual goals, needs, and desires for the sake of a common good. We would expect people to be more expressive of their own feelings, attitudes, and opinions, without as much fear or worry about the consequences for group harmony or cohesion. We would expect people to bring up interpersonal concerns, problems, and conflicts more freely.

Not only do self–ingroup relationships differ between individualistic and collectivistic cultures, but self–outgroup relationships also differ. In collectivistic cultures, the primary focus of attention is on ingroup relationships. For that reason, relationships with outgroup people are marked by a relative lack of concern. To the degree that members of collectivistic cultures focus on harmony, cohesion, and cooperation in ingroup relations, they tend to exhibit distancing, aloofness, and even discrimination with regard to self–outgroup relationships. The opposite is true in individualistic cultures. People of individualistic cultures are more likely to treat outgroup persons more equally, with relatively less distinction between ingroups and outgroups. Members of individualistic cultures engage in positive, relationship-building behaviors with outgroup others that members of collectivistic cultures would reserve only for ingroup others. These concepts are summarized in Table 16.1.

Recent cross-cultural research on ingroup and outgroup relationships.

Recent research continues to support many of these notions originally proposed by Triandis and his colleagues (1988). In Chapter 11, for example, we discussed two studies that found differences in emotional expressions among the United States, Japan, Poland, and Hungary that supported these ideas concerning cultural differences in self–ingroup and self–outgroup relationships. In another study, Goodwin and Lee (1994) asked British and Singapore Chinese university students to complete a questionnaire designed to assess the degree to which they would discuss or do 35 behaviors that are typically considered taboo. The items ranged from discussion of sexual fantasies to crying in front of friends. Participants answered these items in relation to interactions with close friends of both sexes. The results indicated that the British participants were more likely than the Chinese participants to discuss taboo subjects with their close friends. These findings are consistent with the greater maintenance of harmony and cohesion in ingroup relationships in more collectivistic cultures.

Table 16.1 Self–Ingroup and Self–Outgroup Relationship Differences as a Function of Individualism and Collectivism

Type of Culture	Characteristics
In individualistic cultures . . .	1. People have more ingroups.
	2. People are not as attached to any single ingroup, because there are numerous ingroups to which they can be attached.
	3. Survival of the individuals and the society is more dependent on the successful and effective functioning of individuals rather than groups.
	4. People make relatively fewer distinctions between ingroups and outgroups.
In collectivistic cultures . . .	1. People have fewer ingroups.
	2. People are very attached to the ingroups to which they belong.
	3. Survival of the individuals and the society is more dependent on the successful and effective functioning of the groups rather than individuals.
	4. People make greater distinctions between ingroup and outgroup others.

Source: Adapted from Triandis et al., 1988.

In another study, Wheeler, Reis, and Bond (1989) asked participants in the United States and Hong Kong to complete the Rochester Interaction Record (RIR) for a period of two weeks. The RIR involves the self-description of every interaction that lasts for more than 10 minutes in which interactants attended to and adjusted their behavior between each other. Each interaction is described in terms of when it occurred, its length, who the interactants were, their sex breakdown, and eight scales involving ratings of disclosure, quality, satisfaction, and the nature of the interaction. The results indicated that the Hong Kong Chinese students had longer but fewer interactions, with fewer people, than did the American students. The Chinese students also reported a higher percentage of group and task interactions, and indicated great self- and other-disclosure. These findings are certainly consonant with the previous discussion concerning the type, number, and quality of self–ingroup interactions in collectivistic versus individualistic cultures.

Summary

People in all cultures and societies grow up learning to make distinctions among others in terms of ingroups and outgroups. Culture exerts considerable influence not only over the structure and format of those self–ingroup and self–outgroup relationships but also over the very meaning of those relationships. And cultural differences in the meaning of those relationships produces real, observable differences in the behaviors, thoughts, and feelings of the individual when interacting with ingroup and outgroup others.

How we conceptualize and act on our relationships with others can differ dramatically from culture to culture. Therefore, in interacting with others, if we try to interpret their social behaviors within our own limited cultural framework, it is very possible that we will misunderstand and misinterpret those behaviors. Good intentions may be seen as bad; innocuous behaviors may be seen as threatening or aggressive.

Culture, Person Perception, and Attractiveness

Person perception refers to the process of forming impressions of others. Social scientists have long realized the influence of impressions and perceptions of others on our interactions. Questions concerning the degree to which impressions influence actual behaviors and the extent to which people's expectations color their impressions of others fall within the purview of person perception. Social scientists are also interested in whether bad first impressions can be overcome. Research on person perception has outlined several key factors that contribute to the formation of our impressions of others, including appearance, schemas, stereotypes, and selectivity in person perception.

Knowledge Based on U.S. Research

Appearance, especially physical attractiveness, influences judgments of personality. Research with American subjects has consistently shown that people tend to ascribe desirable personality characteristics to those who are good-looking, seeing them as more sensitive, kind, sociable, pleasant, likable, and interesting than those who are unattractive (Dion, 1986; Patzer, 1985). Attractive people are also judged to be more competent and intelligent (Ross & Ferris, 1981).

In the past few years, two meta-analytic studies of the correlates of attractiveness have been conducted, aggregating data involving judges in the United States and Canada. In one (Eagly, Ashmore, Makhijani, & Longo, 1991), attractiveness ratings were shown to be strongly correlated with social competence, adjustment, potency, and intellectual competence, and negatively with modesty. In the other (Feingold, 1992), attractiveness was correlated with social skills, sociability, mental health, dominance, intelligence, and sexual warmth, and again negatively with modesty. These meta-analyses, which were conducted and reported independently, demonstrated quite consistent agreement in findings involving North American participants with regard to the psychological meanings attributed to attractive faces.

Other aspects of appearance also influence our perceptions of others. For example, greater height, which is generally considered attractive, has been associated with leadership ability, competence, and high salary (Deck, 1968;

Patzer, 1985). Adults with baby-face features tend to be judged as warm, kind, naive, and submissive; adults with more mature facial features tend to be judged as strong, worldly, and dominant (Berry & McArthur, 1985, 1986). People who are neat dressers are thought to be conscientious (Albright, Kenny, & Malloy, 1988). People with poor eye contact are often judged as dishonest (DePaulo, Stone, & Lassiter, 1985).

Research on person perception in the United States has also focused on the ways impressions are formed and the way information about others is stored. Much attention has been given to the study of **cognitive schemas** as organizational tools. A schema is a conceptual framework that people use to make sense of the world and people around them. **Social schemas** are organized clusters of ideas about categories of social events and people that have been shown to influence person perceptions (Markus & Zajonc, 1985). Much attention has also been given to the study of stereotypes—widely held beliefs about people's underlying psychological characteristics or personality traits—and their influence on our impressions of others. Finally, social psychologists have studied the influence of selectivity on our perceptions of others to either confirm or disconfirm beliefs and stereotypes.

Cross-Cultural Studies on Attractiveness

Although the effects of attractiveness and physical appearance on the formation of positive impressions is well documented in the mainstream psychological literature, cultures clearly differ on the meaning and definition of attractiveness. Beauty is a relative judgment, and people of different cultures can have quite different concepts of what is beautiful and what is not. Cultural differences in the definition of attractiveness, in turn, can influence the formation of impressions. Daibo, Murasawa, and Chou (1994), for example, compared judgments of physical attractiveness made by Japanese and Koreans. They showed male and female university students in both countries slides of Japanese and Korean females and asked them to rate the attractiveness and likability of each person using 13 bipolar adjective scales. Three poses of each person were shown: front view, profile, and three-quarter view. Facial physiognomy—that is, the anatomical characteristics of the face—were also measured separately by an anatomist, and these measurements were correlated with the psychological judgments provided by the respondents. In Japan, attractiveness ratings were positively correlated with large eyes, small mouths, and small chins. In Korea, however, attractiveness ratings were correlated with large eyes, small and high noses, and thin and small faces. Koreans tended to attach other affective and psychological judgments, such as maturity and likability, to judgments of attractiveness. The Japanese, however, did not. These findings show not only that the two cultures have different standards for beauty, but that beauty has culturally specific psychological meanings.

A study by Wheeler and Kim (1997) demonstrated similar effects. These researchers showed photos of Korean males and females to Korean university students, who made judgments of social competence, intellectual competence, concern for others, integrity, adjustment, potency, sexual interest/warmth, and modesty. Consistent with research involving North American judges, this study found that Korean students rated attractive faces as more socially and intellectually competent, better adjusted, more sexually interesting, and less modest. Contrary to previous research with North Americans, however, the Koreans did not rate attractive faces as more potent. They did rate them as having more integrity and concern for others, which was not found in previous mainstream studies. Wheeler and Kim concluded that, while all cultures appear to stereotype on the basis of physical attractiveness, the contents of the stereotypes probably depend on cultural values.

Another study also demonstrated cultural differences in the psychological meaning derived from attractive faces. Matsumoto and Kudoh (1993) asked American and Japanese subjects to judge Caucasian and Japanese faces that were either smiling or neutral on three dimensions: attractiveness, intelligence, and sociability. The Americans consistently rated the smiling faces higher on all three dimensions, congruent with our traditional notions of person perception and impression formation. The Japanese, however, only rated the smiling faces as more sociable. There was no difference in their ratings of attractiveness between smiles and neutrals, and they rated the neutral faces as more intelligent.

Despite the abundance of cross-cultural research demonstrating cultural differences in judgments of attractiveness and its inferred psychological meaning, at least one convincing study has reported judgments of attractiveness that are consistent across cultures. Cunningham, Roberts, Barbee, Druen, and Wu (1995) conducted a series of three studies, all using basically the same methodology. In the first study, White Americans and Asian and Hispanic immigrants judged faces of Asian, Hispanic, Black, and White women. In the second study, Taiwanese respondents rated the same stimuli. In the third study, Black and White Americans rated Black female faces. The stimuli were photographs whose subjects ranged from college students to contestants in beauty contests in other cultures. In all three studies, the researchers obtained attractiveness ratings from the judges, as well as 28 separate measurements of facial features. The results across all three studies indicated extremely high correlations among the judge groups in their attractiveness ratings. Moreover, the attractiveness ratings by all groups correlated with the same facial characteristics, which included the nature of the eyes, nose, cheeks, chins, and smiles.

There is no clear-cut answer as to why some studies have found differences across cultures while others have found cross-cultural similarity. Clearly, methodological differences across the studies need to be ruled out before making any definitive statements concerning the possible influence of culture on ratings of attractiveness. For example, the differences in the results across studies may be attributable to the nature of the samples tested, or the nature of the stimuli used. Also, differences in the findings across cultures may be associated with degree of exposure to other cultures' standards of beauty via mass media (magazines, movies, television), and these effects are not handled consistently in all cross-cultural research. Regardless of the research findings, however, we know from personal experience that there are enough individual differences within any culture in judgments of attractiveness to suggest that beauty really is in the eye of the beholder.

Cross-Cultural Research on Other Aspects of Person Perception

Many cross-cultural studies challenge our traditional notions of person perception in North American psychology. For example, cross-cultural studies of nonverbal behavior—gaze, proximity, touching behaviors, verbal utterances, facial expressions—all speak to the impact of culture on communication. Differences in these behaviors arising from differences in cultural upbringing undoubtedly influence our perception of people of different cultures. We are often unaware of or unprepared to deal with cultural differences, and it is easy to form negative perceptions of others because of cultural differences in these nonverbal behaviors.

The recognition of faces is yet another area of research related to person perception. Numerous studies have amply demonstrated that people tend to recognize others of their own perceived race more accurately than the faces of other perceived races. While most studies examining and demonstrating this effect have involved comparisons of Whites and Blacks (for example, Bothwell, Brigham, & Malpass, 1989; Brigham & Malpass, 1985; Shapiro & Penrod, 1986), this finding has also been replicated using Asian faces and respondents (Ng & Lindsay, 1994). A number of hypotheses have been offered to explain such effects. For example, differences in facial anatomical features may make certain types of faces more easily recognizable than others. The *contact hypothesis* suggests that recognition accuracy is directly related to the amount of contact one has with others; as people generally have more contact with others of their same perceived race, this exposure leads to higher recognition rates. Another hypothesis suggests that nonfamiliar faces, especially of other perceived races, all "look alike" and thus are less discernible than own-race faces. Another hypothesis suggests that racial attitudes, including prejudice against others, may cause individuals to process faces of other races differently than own-race faces. Although cross-cultural research has amply demonstrated own-race superiority in facial recognition, research is far behind in examining which of these hypotheses, or others, either singly or in combination, may account for this phenomenon.

Even when different cultures agree on overall dimensional judgments of others, they may disagree on the behavioral consequences of those judgments. For example, Bond and Forgas (1984) presented Chinese and Australian subjects with a description of a target person varying across the dimensions of extroversion, agreeableness, conscientiousness, and emotional stability. Across both cultures, conscientiousness was linked with intentions of trust, while extroversion and agreeableness were linked to intentions of association. However, the Chinese subjects were much more likely than the Australians to form behavioral intentions of trust and to form behavioral associations based on agreeableness.

Certainly, as the research on attractiveness suggests, there are similarities as well as differences in person perception processes across cultures. Bernieri and Gillis (1995), for example, reported striking similarities between American and Greek participants' judgments of rapport when viewing 50 videorecorded dyadic interactions. Thus, ample evidence exists to suggest that cultures are both similar and different in both the process and the meaning of person perception and impression formation. This area of social psychology is indeed germane to our understanding of cultures, stereotypes, and ethnocentrism because it forms the basis for such intergroup and interpersonal processes. Future research has the daunting task of trying to unravel how similarities and differences in these processes coexist, and why.

Culture and Interpersonal Attraction: Love, Intimacy, and Intercultural Marriages

As our world gets smaller and smaller, the frequency of interacting with people of ethnic and cultural backgrounds different from our own increases. As these intercultural interactions increase, so does the likelihood that people will become attracted to each other, fall in love, get married, and have families. Indeed, whereas intercultural and interracial relationships were a rarity in the past, they are now more and more frequent. With this increase in intercultural and interracial relationships comes increased tension, frustrations, worries, and joys.

Driven by new concerns arising from our increasingly intercultural world, the amount of cross-cultural research of the last few years on this topic has also increased. Psychologists use the term *interpersonal attraction* to encompass a variety of experiences, including liking, friendship, admiration, lust, and love. U.S. research on interpersonal attraction and love has produced a number of interesting findings, mainly focusing on the factors that contribute to attraction. At the same time, cross-cultural research gives us important clues to cultural differences in attraction and love, and an increasing number of studies on intercultural relationships point to the pitfalls and possible solutions.

Interpersonal Attraction and Love in the United States

Studies conducted by psychologists as early as the 1950s (for example, Festinger, Schachter, & Back, 1950) showed that proximity influences attraction: People who live close to each other are more likely to like one another. Findings from more recent studies support these early findings. In the late 1970s, for instance, Ineichen (1979) showed that people who live close together are more likely to get married.

In the United States, physical attractiveness is an important ingredient of interpersonal relationships (Patzer, 1985), but attractiveness may be more important in male preference for females than the reverse (Buss, 1988). Most people surveyed in the United States prefer physically attractive partners in romantic relationships. But a **matching hypothesis** also suggests that people of approximately equal physical characteristics are likely to select each other as partners. Likewise, a **similarity hypothesis** suggests that people similar in age, race, religion, social class, education, intelligence, attitudes, and physical attractiveness tend to form intimate relationships (Brehm, 1985; Hendrick & Hendrick, 1983). Certainly, there is something safe about similarities in a relationship that make similar partners particularly attractive for romance and love. Finally, a **reciprocity hypothesis** suggests that people tend to like others who like them (Byrne & Murnen, 1988).

Few people in the United States would discount the importance of love in the development and maintenance of long-term relationships such as friendship and marriage, and love has been a particularly well studied topic in American psychology. Hatfield and Berscheid's (Berscheid, 1988; Hatfield, 1988) theory of love and attachment proposes that romantic relationships are characterized by two kinds of love. One is **passionate love**, involving absorption of another that includes sexual feelings and intense emotion. The second is **companionate love**, involving warm, trusting, and tolerant affection for another whose life is deeply intertwined with one's own. Sternberg's (1988) theory is similar to Hatfield and Berscheid's but divides companionate love into two separate components: intimacy and commitment. *Intimacy* refers to warmth, closeness, and sharing in a relationship. *Commitment* refers to an intention to maintain a relationship in spite of the difficulties that arise. In Sternberg's theory, eight different forms of love can exist, depending on the presence or absence of each of the three factors: passionate love, intimacy, and commitment. When all three factors are present, Sternberg calls that relationship **consummate love**.

Another well-studied area of interpersonal attraction is intimacy. In research conducted in the United States, intimacy is closely associated with *self-disclosure*—the degree to which people will disclose information about themselves to others (for example, Adamopoulos, 1991; Altman & Taylor, 1973; Helgeson, Shaver, & Dyer, 1987). In the United States, high levels of self-disclosure characterize intimate relationships. According to social penetration theory, relationship development is based on four stages of increasing disclosure, with partners able to describe themselves fully in the final stage.

Interpersonal Attraction, Love, and Intimacy across Cultures

Cross-cultural studies have amply demonstrated cultural differences in attitudes about love and romance around the world. For example, Ting-Toomey (1991) compared ratings of love commitment, disclosure maintenance, ambivalence, and conflict expression by 781 subjects from France, Japan, and the United States. Love commitment was measured by ratings of feelings of attachment, belongingness, and commitment to the partner and the relationship; disclosure maintenance by ratings of feelings concerning the private self in the relationship; ambivalence by ratings of feelings of confusion or uncertainty regarding the partner or the relationship; and conflict expression by ratings of frequency of overt arguments and seriousness of problems. The French and the Americans had significantly higher ratings than the Japanese on love commitment and disclosure maintenance. The Americans also had significantly higher ratings than the Japanese on relational ambivalence. The Japanese and the Americans, however, had significantly higher ratings than the French on conflict expression.

Simmons, vom Kolke, and Shimizu (1986) examined attitudes toward love and romance among American, German, and Japanese students. The results indicated that romantic love was valued more in the United States and Germany than in Japan. These researchers explained this cultural difference by suggesting that romantic love is more highly valued in less traditional cultures with few strong, extended family ties, and less valued in cultures where kinship networks influence and reinforce the relationship between marriage partners.

Many other studies document cultural differences in attitudes about love and romance. Furnham (1984), for instance, administered the Rokeach Value Survey to groups of South Africans, Indians, and Europeans. The Europeans valued love more than did the South Africans and the Indians. The South Africans, however, placed a higher value on equality and peace. Murstein, Merighi, and Vyse (1991) compared American and French college students' attitudes about love. They found that Americans tended to prefer friendships that slowly evolve into love, as well as relationships in which the lovers are caught up in an excited, panicky state; the French rated higher on love as characterized by altruistic generosity.

Dion and Dion (1993) tested respondents who were classified into one of four ethnocultural groups—Anglo-Celtic, Chinese, Other Asian, and European—on a 54-item love attitude scale. The results indicated that the Chinese and Other Asian respondents were more friendship oriented in their love relationships than were respondents of the other two groups. Asian women also expressed more altruism than did Anglo-Celtic women. Ellis and colleagues (1994) used a semantic differential technique to examine the subjective meaning of love and power in Spaniards, Mexicans, Hispanic Americans, and Anglo-Americans. This technique involves multiple-item ratings on three scales: evaluation (positive–negative), potency (strong–weak), and activity (active–passive). The results indicated that the Mexicans rated love as less positive and less potent than the other three groups. They also found that the psychological judgments of love and power along the three dimensions were correlated for Spaniards, but not for the other three groups. Finally, Elbedour, Shulman, and Kedem (1997) examined and compared perceptions of intimacy in friendships among Israeli Jewish and Bedouin adolescents. Overall, the data indicated that intimacy was perceived to reflect a balance between closeness and individuality. But Jewish adolescents reported less of a need to control or to be similar to each other in friendships, whereas Bedouin adolescents reported more emphasis on control and conformity to friends.

Despite differences in the definitions and importance of attraction, love, and romance, however, some research suggests amazing cross-cultural similarity in sex differences with regard to mate selection. In one of the best-known studies on this topic (Buss, 1989), more than 10,000 respondents in 37 different cultures drawn from 33 countries completed two questionnaires, one dealing with factors in choosing a mate and the second dealing with preferences concerning potential mates. In 36 of the 37 cultures, females rated financial prospects as more important than did males; in 29 of those 36 cultures, females also rated ambition and industriousness as more important than did males. In all 37 cultures, males preferred younger mates, while females preferred older mates; in 34 of the cultures, males rated good looks as more important than did females; and in 23 of the cultures, males rated chastity as more important than did females. Buss (1989) concluded that females value cues related to resource acquisition in potential mates more highly than males do, whereas males value reproductive capacity more highly than do females. These findings were predicted, in fact, on the basis of an evolutionary-based framework that generated hypotheses related to evolutionary concepts of parental involvement, sexual selection, reproductive capacity, and certainty of paternity or maternity. The degree of agreement in sex differences across cultures has led Buss (1989) and his colleagues to view these mate selection preferences as universal, arising from different evolutionary selection pressures on males and females.

A more recent study by Hatfield and Sprecher (1995) has replicated and extended the findings by Buss and his colleagues. In this study, male and female students in the United States, Russia, and Japan were surveyed concerning their preferences in a marital partner using a 12-item scale. The items all referred to positive traits: physically attractive, intelligent, athletic, ambitious, good conversationalist, outgoing and sociable, status or money, skill as a lover, kind and understanding, potential for success, expressive and open, and sense of humor. Across all three cultures, the data indicated that the only scale on which men gave higher ratings than women was physical attractiveness. Women gave higher ratings than men on all the other scales except good conversationalist. There were also some interesting cultural differences. For example, Americans preferred expressivity, openness, and sense of humor more than did the Russians, who in turn preferred these traits more than did the Japanese. Russians desired skill as a lover most, while Japanese preferred it least. The Japanese gave lower ratings than the other two cultures on kind and understanding, good conversationalist, physical attractiveness, and status. In this study, however, no mention was made of the possibility of cultural response sets, which may render the cultural differences reported ambiguous.

Another recent study highlights cross-cultural similarity in yet another important aspect of intimate relationships: anger expressions and possible conflict resolutions. In this study (Kubany et al., 1995), 160 Filipino college students rated their feelings and reactions to four different types of statements: self-attributed distress ("I feel anxious"), self-attributed anger ("I'm getting angry"), partner attributed distress ("You've been making me feel upset all week"), and partner attributed anger ("You're getting me angry"). The results indicated that "You" messages were rated as more aversive, more likely to evoke animosity, less likely to evoke compassion, more like to evoke antagonistic behavior, and less likely to evoke conciliatory behavior. Also, compared to statements of distress, anger statements were rated as more aversive, more likely to evoke animosity, less likely to evoke compassion, more likely to evoke antagonistic behavior, and less likely to evoke conciliatory behavior. According to Kubany and colleagues (1995), these findings replicate similar studies conducted in the United States, and suggest that

> explicitly communicated anger and blame may operate similarly as instigators of animosity and antagonism—across cultures and across languages. It may be that words of anger generally tend to evoke animosity and antagonism because words of anger, by definition and from experience with "angry" people, connote or communicate unfriendliness and adversarial antagonism. Similarly, the experience of being blamed may tend to instigate animosity and antagonistic inclinations in people everywhere. On intuitive grounds alone, it seems unlikely that many people like to be blamed for negative outcomes, and the experience of being blamed may generally tend to instigate a hostile counterresponse. (pp. 76–77)

Thus, although there may be cross-cultural differences in views about love and intimacy, there may be something universal about how we express ourselves, particularly our anger, that can help resolve or perpetuate conflicts in those types of relationships.

Intercultural Marriages

Given the cultural differences in attitudes toward love, interpersonal attraction, and marriage, it is no wonder that intercultural and interracial marriages and relationships bring with them their own special problems and issues. As the frequency of interacting with people from many diverse cultures and ethnicities increases in our everyday lives, so too will the number of such relationships.

While theories about love and attraction are prevalent and popular in American psychology, I know of no research across cultures that directly tests their validity. That is, are the components and psychological meanings of love the same or different across cultures? There is sufficient information from cross-cultural research, however, to suggest how the concepts of attraction, love, and intimacy differ across cultures.

It is important to consider first how different cultures may view love. In the United States, people generally feel that love is a necessary and sometimes sufficient ingredient for long-term romantic relationships and marriage. "Love conquers all," as the saying goes. But love does not enjoy the same consideration for long-term relationships and marriage in many cultures as it does in the United States. I remember talking to a person from another culture about the "divorce rate problem" of the United States. We were discussing sociological data indicating that the frequency of divorce is higher than it is has ever been in American history and that it continues to rise. He commented to me that there is no such problem in his country. "The reason for this difference," he said, "is quite clear. You Americans marry the person you love; we love the person we marry."

These types of differences were exemplified in a recent study by Levine, Sato, Hashimoto, and Verma (1995). These researchers asked students in 11 different countries to rate the importance of love for both the establishment and maintenance of a marriage. The countries included were India, Pakistan, Thailand, Mexico, Brazil, Japan, Hong Kong, the Philippines, Australia, England, and the United States. The responses of the participants were correlated with indices of individualism versus collectivism, gross domestic product/ living costs, marriage rates, fertility rates, and divorce rates. The results indicated that the individualistic countries were more likely to rate love as essential to the establishment of a marriage, and to agree that the disappearance of love is a sufficient reason to end a marriage. Countries with large GDPs also showed this tendency—not surprising, given the high correlation between affluence and individualism. Also, countries with high marriage and divorce rates, and low fertility rates, assigned greater importance to romantic love. Divorce rates were highly correlated with the belief that the disappearance of love warranted the dissolution of a marriage.

Arranged marriages are quite common in many cultures of the world, including Japan, China, and India. Sometimes marriages are arranged by parents far before the age at which the couple can even consider marriage. In other cases, marriage meetings are held between prospective couples, who may then date for a while to decide whether to get married or not. Love is often not part of this equation but is something that should grow in the marriage relationship.

When any two people get married, conflict is inevitable because any two people come from two different worldviews and perspectives. This situation is exacerbated in intercultural marriages, because the two people bring not only their individual differences but also their cultural differences and values (see Kiev, 1973). Studies of intercultural marriages (see Franklin, 1992, for a review) have generally shown that conflicts in intercultural marriages arise in several major areas, including the expression of love and intimacy, the nature of commitment and attitudes toward the marriage itself, and approaches to child rearing when couples have children. Other potential sources of conflict include differences in perceptions of male–female roles (McGoldrick & Preto, 1984; Romano, 1988), differences in domestic money management (Ho, 1984; Hsu, 1977; Kiev, 1973; McGoldrick & Preto, 1984), differences in perceptions of relationships with extended family (Cohen, 1982; Markoff, 1977), and differences in the definitions of marriage itself (Markoff, 1977).

It is no wonder that couples in intercultural marriages experience conflicts around intimacy and love expression. As described in Chapter 11, people of different cultures vary considerably in their expression of basic emotions such as anger, frustration, or happiness. And as we have seen, cultures differ on the degree to which emotions such as love and intimacy are seen as important ingredients of a successful marriage. These differences arise from a fundamental difference in attitudes toward marriage. Americans tend to view marriage as a lifetime companionship between two individuals in love. People of many other cultures view marriage more as a partnership formed for succession (that is, for producing offspring) and for economic and social bonding. Love rarely enters the equation in the beginning for people in these cultures, although they usually tend to develop a love relationship with the marriage partner over time. With such fundamental differences in the nature of marriage across cultures, it is no wonder that intercultural marriages are often among the most difficult of relationships.

Sometimes the differences between two people involved in an intercultural marriage do not arise until they have children. Oftentimes, major cultural differences emerge around issues of child rearing. This is no surprise, either, because of the enormous differences in socialization practices and the role of parenting in the development of culture, as was discussed in Chapter 7. Although it has been a common belief that children of intracultural marriages have stronger ethnic identities than children of intercultural marriages, recent research does not tend to support this claim (for example, Parsonson, 1987). Children tend to develop strong or weak ethnic identities based not on their parents' similarity or difference, but on their upbringing, especially with regard to attitudes, values, and behaviors regarding their single or dual cultures. Children with stronger ethnic identities, however, are more likely to want to marry within their own ethnic group (Parsonson, 1987).

How can intercultural couples overcome these additional obstacles in their relationships to build successful marriages? Of course, communication is important in any relationship, and such communication is especially important in intercultural relationships (Atkeson, 1970). Many of the skills discussed in Chapter 14 come into play here. Couples involved in an intercultural relationship need to develop intercultural sensitivity and a constructive method of dealing with conflict to make their relationships successful.

Ho (1984) has suggested that three types of adjustments help to resolve differences: capitulation, compromise, and coexistence. *Capitulation* refers to the ability and willingness to give up one's own cultural behaviors and accept the other's position occasionally. *Compromise* refers to finding a mutual point, with both partners partially giving up their positions and partially accepting each other's. *Coexistence* refers to the process by which both partners live with their respective differences by accepting each other "as they are" in their marriage.

Tseng (1977) offers some additional ways of dealing with intercultural relationships. Tseng's "alternating way" is one in which partners take turns in adapting their cultural behaviors. A "mixing way" is one in which partners take some behaviors and customs from both cultures and randomly introduce them into their marriage. "Creative adjustment" is when partners invent a completely new set of behavior patterns after deciding to give up their respective cultural norms.

It seems to me that there is yet another way of negotiating the trials and tribulations of intercultural marriage, which I will call the "context constructionistic" way. Cultural differences between two people will manifest themselves in specific contexts. One way for two people from different cultures to deal with these differences is to discuss the perspectives of both cultures in relation to each context in which there is a conflict or difference. The couple can then discuss the pros and cons of both perspectives in relation to their lives as a whole—work, family, children, and cultural and ethnic "balance"—and make functional decisions based on these discussions. In some cases, a couple may choose to go with one cultural perspective, in other cases, with the other perspective. The couple may choose to alternate perspectives, or to be creative and establish their own unique perspective on the situation, blending their cultural knowledge. In this fashion, the everyday negotiation of intercultural marriage is an interesting and exciting journey in which the couple as a unit must engage, rather than a "problem" to be dealt with.

In many ways, intercultural marriages are the prime example of intercultural relationships. For them to be successful, both partners need to be flexible, compromising, and committed to the relationship. If these three ingredients are in the pot, couples will often find ways to make their relationships work. Despite the difficulties, anecdotal evidence suggests intercultural marriages are not necessarily associated with higher divorce rates than intracultural marriages. Perhaps it all comes down to how much both spouses are willing to work to negotiate differences, compromise, and stay together.

Culture and Attributions

Attributions are the inferences people make about the causes of events and their own and others' behaviors. Attributions represent the ways we understand the world around us and the behavior of others. You might attribute a friend's failure to show up for a date to irresponsibility, too much traffic, or just forgetting. You might attribute your success on an exam to your effort or to luck. Attributions allow us to examine the biases people have when explaining others' behavior, which in turn affect their own behavior.

The study of attributions has a rich history in social psychology. Researchers have studied the types of attributions people make, especially in relation to the locus of causality. An important concept in attribution research is the distinction between internal and external attributions. Internal attributions specify the cause of behavior within a person; external attributions locate the cause of behavior outside a person. Researchers have also studied the causal properties of attributions, including locus, stability, controllability, and globality. Attributions have been widely studied in achievement situations, ranging from academic settings to sports and occupational contexts. These studies have led to development of several major theories of attribution. And research on attribution bias has led to several popular concepts in American social psychology, including fundamental attribution error, defensive attributions, and self-serving bias.

Traditional American Patterns of Attributions

One of the most popular models of attribution in American psychology is Kelley's (1967, 1973) covariation model. This model assumes that people attribute behavior to causes that are present when the behavior occurs and absent when the behavior does not occur. According to this theory, people consider three types of information when making attributions: consistency, distinctiveness, and consensus. **Consistency** refers to whether a person's behavior in a situation is the same over time. **Distinctiveness** refers to whether a person's behavior is unique to the specific target of the behavior. **Consensus** refers to whether other people in the same situation tend to respond in the same manner. Behaviors that have high consistency but low distinctiveness or consensus produce internal attributions. Behaviors that have high consistency, high distinctiveness, and high consensus produce external attributions.

Another major theory of attribution in American psychology is Weiner's (1974; Weiner et al., 1972) theory, which focuses on the concept of stability. According to Weiner, stability cuts across the internal–external dimension, creating four types of attributions for success and failure (stable and unstable, internal and external). For example, if you failed to get a job you wanted, you might attribute your failure to stable internal factors (lack of ability or initiative), stable external factors (too much competition), unstable internal factors (lack of effort), or unstable external factors (bad luck). Using Weiner's model of attribution, the types of emotions and behaviors that will probably occur in consequence to these attribution types can be predicted.

Studies conducted on attributional styles of people in the United States have shown a number of different ways we may be biased in interpreting the world around us and the behavior of others. **Fundamental attribution error** refers to a bias toward explaining the behavior of others using internal attributions but explaining our own behaviors using external attributions (Jones & Nisbett, 1971; Watson, 1982). It is not uncommon to hear students attribute a friend's bad grade to low intelligence or ability (internal). At the same time, however, they may attribute their own bad grades to a teacher's choice of test questions or to bad luck (external).

Self-serving bias is the tendency to attribute one's successes to personal factors and one's failures to situational factors (Bradley, 1978). If you fail an exam, for instance, you may attribute your failure to a poorly constructed test, lousy teaching, distractions, or a bad week at home (external). If you ace an exam, however, you are more likely to attribute your success to effort, intelligence, or ability (internal).

Defensive attributions refer to the tendency to blame victims for their misfortune. Some scientists have suggested that we engage in defensive attributions because they make us feel less likely to be victimized in a similar way (Thornton, 1984). If you attribute others' misfortunes (for example, burglary, rape, loss of a job) to the victim rather than to circumstance, it is easier to believe that the same misfortunes will not happen to you.

These attributional styles and theories have an impact both on our own behavior and on our understanding of the behavior of others; many of you can probably recognize some of these attributional tendencies in your own behavior. However, these attributional styles and biases have been documented in research conducted almost exclusively in the United States with American participants. Cross-cultural research suggests that attributional styles and biases may be culture-bound.

Attributional Styles across Cultures

Research concerning attributions about academic achievement. Much of the early cross-cultural research on attributions focused on attributions concerning success and failure in academic achievement situations, for several reasons. The participants in most studies are students, and academic achievement is a relevant and meaningful topic on which to obtain data. Such data are also relevant and meaningful across cultures, as many people in many cultures go to school. All students have experience with similar situations, unlike other types of success and performance. And obtaining attributional data from students is relatively easy.

Many cross-cultural studies have found considerable differences in the nature of attributions about academic performance across cultures, and these findings often differ from what has typically been found to be true of Americans. Table 16.2 summarizes a selective representation of these studies. Hau and Salili (1991), for example, asked junior and senior high school students in Hong Kong to rate the importance and meaning of 13 specific causes of academic performance. Effort, interest, and ability—all internal attributions— were rated the most important causes, regardless of success or failure. Research from the United States would have predicted that these dimensions would be important in making attributions of success but not failure, because of self-serving bias.

Two studies with Taiwanese subjects also challenge our notions about self-serving attributions. Crittenden (1991) found that Taiwanese women used more external and self-effacing attributions about themselves than did American women. Crittenden suggested that the Taiwanese women did this to enhance their public and private self-esteem by using an attributional approach that conformed to a feminine gender role. Earlier, Bond, Leung, and Wan (1982) found that self-effacing Chinese students were better liked by their peers than those who adopted this attributional style less often.

Table 16.2 Selected Cross-Cultural Studies Examining Attributions Regarding Academic Achievement

Citation	Participants	Attributions about . . .	Major Findings
Hau and Salili, 1991	Hong Kong Chinese	Perceived performance in an examination taken the previous week	Most important causal attributions were effort, interest in study, study skill, and ability in study.
Hall et al., 1986	Black and white U.S. junior high school students	Test performance	Attributions of success or failure did not predict active or nonattending behaviors.
Graham and Long, 1986	Black and white U.S. junior high school students	Hypothetical and actual performance in an exam	Blacks did not revise their expectancies downward as much as whites when the causes of success were perceived as unstable. Blacks were less certain that failure would occur again. Blacks anticipated relatively higher praise when success was due to external uncontrollable causes. Middle-SES white children attributed high exam performance to good luck less than did low-SES white and middle-SES black children. Middle-SES white children attributed poor performance to difficulty of the exam, whereas middle-SES black children perceived poor instruction from their teacher as a dominant cause of failure.
Graham, 1984	Black and white U.S. sixth graders	Induced failure performance on a puzzle	Black children attributed their failure more to insufficient effort, reported higher expectancies, perceived themselves as more competent, and persisted longer at the task.

Study	Participants	Situation	Findings
Crittenden, 1991	Taiwanese and American university students	Hypothetical situations that may happen to a college student involving relationships and achievement events	Taiwanese students saw likability as less highly correlated with productivity traits than Americans. Students in both cultures expressed preference for internal rather than external attributions, and for self-effacing rather than self-enhancing patterns. Taiwanese liked the external and self-effacing patterns slightly more than internal and self-enhancing patterns.
Bong, Leung, and Wan, 1982	Hong Kong Chinese students	Confederate's competent or incompetent performance on an intellectual task	Self-effacing confederate was better liked but rated less competent than a self-enhancing confederate. Incompetent confederates who made self-enhancing attributions were perceived as more anxious than other confederates.
Mizokawa and Ryckman, 1990	Six groups of Asian Americans—Chinese, Japanese, Korean, Filipino, Vietnamese, and other Southeast Asian—in 4th through 11th grades	Success and failure in school achievement situations	Koreans had the highest effort attribution scores, and Southeast Asians the lowest. Japanese and Korean students attributed more success than failure to ability. Chinese and Vietnamese students evenly attributed success and failure to ability. Southeast Asians attributed failures to lack of ability. Koreans attributed successes to ability, but failures to other factors.
Yan and Geier, 1994	American, Chinese, Japanese, Korean, and Southeast Asian university undergraduates	School-related successes and failures	Americans attributed academic achievement more often to ability than did Asians; they also attributed success more to effort than they attributed failure to lack of effort. Asians attributed effort equally for success and failure; students in the four Asian groups appeared more similar than different in their attributions.

(continued on next page)

Table 16.2 Selected Cross-Cultural Studies Examining Attributions Regarding Academic Achievement *(continued)*

Citation	Participants	Attributions about . . .	Major Findings
Ng, McClure, Walkey, and Hunt, 1995	New Zealand and Singapore university students	Success and failure in examinations	The most frequent attribution for both success and failure was effort for both groups; the second most frequent attribution for New Zealanders was ability, for Singaporeans luck. Singaporeans gave higher attributional importance ratings than New Zealanders to mood, study technique, examination skill, luck, God and supernatural factors, and family; the New Zealanders gave higher ratings to effort.
Wong, Derlega, and Colson, 1988	White and black U.S. university undergraduates	Performance of either a white or black 4-year-old being taught a lesson on home and family safety	Both white and black participants generated more attributional questions and provided more causal explanations to account for the performance of a black than a white target person, reflecting greater concern for causal understanding of performance by minority children. Both black and white participants expected the white student to do better than the black student in three different achievement situations.
Kashima and Triandis, 1986	Japanese and American university students in the United States	Success or failure in a memory task	Japanese attributed failure more to themselves and success less to themselves than did Americans.
Salili, 1994	British and Chinese children in Hong Kong, and Chinese undergraduates and adults	Importance ratings of success or failure in participant-generated situations	British females considered success in personal social life significantly more important than did British males and Chinese. Chinese students considered success in academic work and outstanding achievement significantly more important than did Britons. Chinese men rated success in extracurricular activities more important than did Chinese women and all Britons.

Other cross-cultural studies on attributions concerning academic performance pepper the literature with findings that challenge American notions of attribution. Kashima and Triandis (1986) showed that Japanese people use a much more group-oriented, collective approach to attribution with regard to attention and memory achievement tasks. Compared to their American counterparts, Japanese subjects attributed failure to themselves more and attributed success to themselves less. Kashima and Triandis (1986) interpreted this finding as suggestive of American and Japanese cultural differences in degree of responsibility taking.

Research has gone beyond the mere documentation of cultural differences in attributional styles to suggest several possible negative consequences. Wong, Derlaga, and Colson (1988), for example, asked 40 white and 40 black undergraduates to read stories about the performance of either a black or a white child. The students were then asked to (1) explain why the child failed or succeeded, (2) describe questions in their mind concerning the child's performance, and (3) predict the child's performance on other tasks. All subjects, regardless of race, generated more questions and causal explanations for the performance of a black than a white child. And all subjects expected the white child to do better than the black child on other tasks.

In the same vein, Tom and Cooper (1986) examined the attributions of 25 white elementary school teachers for the performance of students varying in social class, race, and gender. The results indicated that the teachers were more likely to take account of the successes of middle-class, white students and discount their failures, relative to students of other social classes or race.

However, the consequences of cultural differences in attributional style are not entirely negative. Hall, Howe, Merkel, and Lederman (1986) asked teachers to make causal attributions about the performance of black and white students. They found that the teachers believed that black females exerted the greatest amount of effort (and that black males exerted the least). Graham and her colleagues (for example, Graham, 1984; Graham & Long, 1986) have reported considerable overlap in the attributions of the black and white subjects in their studies and that these attributions are often equally adaptive. They have also found that attributions are influenced by social factors such as class as well as race and culture.

Collectively, these studies paint a rather consistent and persuasive picture about the nature of attributional processes with regard to academic performance and achievement. More recent research has gone beyond academic performance to assess attributions with regard to a wide range of other topics.

Research concerning attributions in nonacademic areas. Are the data presented so far limited to attributions concerning academic achievement, or are they representative of more global ways in which people around the world interpret the events around them? Cross-cultural research in the past decade has demonstrated that cultural differences in attributional styles are not limited to academic achievement and performance, but exist in relation to a wide range of life situations.

Table 16.3 provides a brief summary of selected cross-cultural studies examining attributional processes in relation to nonacademic achievement and performance. A perusal of these studies also indicates widespread differences in the nature of attributions around the world. For example, Moghaddam, Ditto, and Taylor (1990) examined the attributional processes of high- and low-distressed Indian female immigrants to Canada in relation to the degree to which they have adjusted to life in Canada. They found that the Indian women were more likely to attribute both successes and failures to internal causes. American research would have hypothesized that the subjects would attribute only successes to internal causes and attribute failures to external causes, again because of self-serving bias.

Forgas, Furnham, and Frey (1989) documented broad cross-national differences in the importance of different types of specific attributions for wealth. Their study included 558 subjects from the United Kingdom, Australia, and the Federal Republic of Germany. The British considered family background and luck the most important determinants of wealth. The Germans also considered family background the most important determinant. The Australians, however, rated individual qualities the most important determinant of wealth.

Romero and Garza (1986) reported differences between Hispanic and Anglo women in their attributions concerning occupational success and failure. In their study, Chicana and Anglo-American female university students provided data concerning their attributions about an Anglo, Black, or Chicana female's success or failure in a teaching job. They found that Chicanas tended make more attributions on the basis of luck, ethnicity, or gender. In making attributions about failure, Anglo females tended to attribute less competence to the actor than did the Chicana females.

As Table 16.3 indicates, cultural differences in the nature of attributional processes exist across a wide range of events, including occupational performance, wealth and economic success, crime, physical and psychological disorders, sports, and moral and immoral behaviors. Collectively, these studies indicate quite convincingly that attributional styles differ substantially across cultures, and that they do not conform to the attributional biases we are familiar with from research involving Americans.

Summary

As these studies exemplify, attributional styles are quite different across cultures. But we need to go beyond the mere documentation of differences to discover why those differences occur. It may be that the way Americans conceptualize attributions, success, and failure has a lot to do with the differences found in cross-cultural research. Duda and Allison (1989) have suggested that our definitions of success and failure are ethnocentrically biased. How Americans view success and failure—that is, in terms of personal achievement on the basis of competition with others—is different from how people of other cultures define them. They also suggest that the meanings of the specific elements in theories and research on attribution may differ among cultures (for example,

Table 16.3 Selected Cross-Cultural Studies Examining Attributions Regarding Nonacademic Topics

Citation	Participants	Attributions about . . .	Major Findings
Schuster, Forsterlung, and Weiner, 1989	Taxi drivers and civil servants in Germany, Belgium, India, South Korea, and England	An unsuccessful attempt to find employment	Indian respondents rated all causes as more external, variable, and uncontrollable than did participants in other countries.
Romero and Garza, 1986	Chicana and Anglo female university students	A description of occupational success or failure of an Anglo, Black, or Chicana female	Chicanas showed greater tendency to attribute the actor's occupational outcome to luck, ethnicity, or gender. In the failure condition, the Anglo females attributed less competence to the actor than did the Chicana females.
Forgas, Furnham, and Frey, 1989	Individuals in Britain, Australia, and Germany	Wealth and economic success	British considered family background, individual effort, exploitation, and luck the most important. Germans considered family background, exploitation, individual ability, and effort as most important. Australians considered individual effort and ability, family background, social rewards, and membership in special trades or professions the most important.
Na and Loftus, 1998	Korean and American law students and under-graduates	Law, prisoners, and crimes	Korean undergraduates had less positive attitudes toward law than did American undergraduates. Koreans were more lenient toward criminals and made more external attributions of crimes than did Americans.

(continued on next page)

Table 16.3 Selected Cross-Cultural Studies Examining Attributions Regarding Nonacademic Topics *(continued)*

Citation	Participants	Attributions about . . .	Major Findings
Furnham and Akande, 1997	British and South Africans	Underlying factors for overcoming cognitive disorders (dyslexia, fear of flying, amnesia, and "learning difficulties")	South Africans endorsed self-reliance, external control, and professional help more than Britons as methods of overcoming cognitive disorders.
Edman and Kameoka, 1997	Filipino and American women	Physical illness	Filipino women attributed the cause of illnesses to spiritual-social explanations more frequently than did Americans.
McGowan, McGowan, and Omifade, 1997	West African and African American athletes	Ruminations of success and failure	African Americans tended to attribute failure to factors that were more internal, stable, and personally controllable than did West Africans.
Lee, Hallahan, and Herzog, 1996	Sports articles and editorials of newspapers in Hong Kong and the United States	Events described in articles	Attributions from Hong Kong were more situational and less dispositional than those from the United States.
Si, Rethorst, and Willimczkik, 1995	Chinese and German individuals	Achievement outcomes in sports	Chinese participants perceived the causes for subjective success and failure as more internal and more controllable than did the Germans.
Kawanishi, 1995	Anglo-Americans and Japanese	Stress and coping	Japanese were more likely to attribute successful coping with stress to luck, and to see the cause of stress as their own responsibility.

Morris and Peng, 1994	American and Chinese students	Social and physical events	Causal perceptions of social but not physical events differed between the two groups. English-language newspapers were more dispositional and Chinese-language newspapers more situational in explanations of the same crimes. Chinese survey respondents differed in weightings of personal disposition and situational factors as causes of recent murders and in counterfactual judgments about how murders might have been averted by changed situations.
Al-Zharany and Kaplowitz, 1993	American and Saudi university students	Moral or immoral behaviors associated with success or failure	Americans favored internal attributions. Saudis showed more outgroup derogatory bias and intergroup bias.
Moghaddam, Ditto, and Taylor, 1990	Indian immigrant women in Canada	Adjustment to life in Canada	Indian women were likely to attribute both successes and failure to internal causes.

effort, work, luck). Different meanings assigned to these elements have implications for the meanings of the attributions associated with them. Finally, Duda and Allison suggest that the use of bipolar dimensions in research may be extremely limited. Cultural differences in the dimensions that are important for understanding and predicting attributions may lead to entirely different expectations of attribution styles.

As some of the research reviewed here involving children indicates, cultural differences in attributional styles appear quite early in life. Culture-specific attributional styles may be a natural part of enculturation and socialization, as children are exposed to these cultural styles from an early age. Bornstein and associates (1998), for example, examined attributions of mothers of 20-month-olds in Argentina, Belgium, France, Israel, Italy, Japan, and the United States with regard to success and failure in seven parenting tasks. They found only a few cross-cultural similarities, but many differences, especially with regard to degree of competence and satisfaction in parenting. Child age could not be a factor, as it was controlled in the study, and child gender was found not to influence the data either. These types of findings provide us with ideas about how and why parents transmit valuable cultural information to their children, resulting in specific styles of attribution (among many other psychological effects).

In another study, Chandler and Spies (1996) examined cultural differences in ratings of 11 attributes of achievement in seven countries. The attributes rated were bias, help, luck, ability, competence, effort, task, chance, knowledge, skills, and mood; the dimensions they were rated on were internal–external, global–specific, controllable–uncontrollable, stable–unstable, and predictable–unpredictable. The results indicated cultural differences on 9 of the 11 attributes across the seven countries, suggesting that different cultures attribute different psychological meanings to the various attributional components. Such data, in turn, help us understand how and why certain attributions may be used in certain countries and cultures, depending on the particular cultural values and mores in those countries. The results from this study suggest one of the reasons why many of the attributional styles that have been consistently found in research with Americans are not necessarily true for people in other parts of the world: Even though the components of the attribution process may be the same across cultures, the way in which these components are used differs across cultures.

As the field is already peppered with ample evidence of cultural differences in attributional styles, future research needs to go beyond merely documenting differences to exploring how and why these differences occur. More research is needed to explore the developmental processes associated with cultural differences in attributions; other studies will need to investigate the possible mediators of cultural differences in attributional styles. Research will also need to examine the linkage between culture as measured on the individual level and attributional styles, reducing the reliance on the use of countries as culture, with its inherent stereotypic description of culture underlying country.

At the same time, more theoretical work is needed on the nature of the attributional process itself, and its meaning to individuals and cultures. For example, although the research reviewed here is quite convincing in documenting cultural differences in attributional styles, it seems to me that there may be a basic commonality across cultures in the core values underlying the attributional differences. That is, all cultures may encourage an attributional style that has at its core "enhancement of the self" as an underlying value. Yet because people of different cultures come to define the self in different ways (see Chapter 3), the specific nature of the attributions that a person learns and uses will be different, reflecting these differences in the definition of self, despite commonality in the core theme or value. If, for example, bolstering one's self-impression about one's abilities and efforts enhances the self, as traditional American research has documented in relation to successful events, then this attributional style may operationalize the core value of "self-enhancement." But in another culture, bolstering one's self-worth may actually be detrimental to the core self; in such a culture, restraint in such attributions may actually be operationalizing the core value of "self-enhancement," even though the outward manifestation of the attribution does not reflect such enhancement. Thus, people of different cultures may appear to differ in their attributional styles on one level, yet on another level may be entirely similar in their core values and principles. Future research needs to take into account such possibilities and delve more deeply into the nature of attributions, especially with regard to the meaning of attributional styles to the individual and culture.

Nevertheless, cultural differences in attributions are especially important in furthering our understanding of intercultural interactions. The consequences of incorrect attributions are potentially severe. Interpreting the causes of behavior accurately, especially with regard to intentions and good will, is important to the success of *any* type of social interaction. Intercultural interactions are no exception. We should not be too quick to attribute another person's behavior to ill will or negative feelings, when that behavior may actually be rooted in a cultural dynamic that fosters that behavior with no ill will. If we leave room for the influence of cultural factors in our attributions of others' behavior as well as our own, we will have taken an important step toward improving intercultural understanding and relationships.

Culture and Aggression

Aggression may be defined as any act or behavior that hurts another person, either physically or psychologically. Although some research suggests that the tendency to be aggressive is biologically and perhaps even genetically based, most psychologists would agree that there is a large learning and environmental component to aggression. That is, the tendency to be aggressive appears to be learned as one is socialized and enculturated into society and culture. The most prevalent models of aggression suggest that aggression occurs when provocation of some sort leads to some kind of negative emotions, which prime a person to either fight or flee. Which response the individual chooses depends on genetics and biological predispositions, previously learned response patterns, and the specific characteristics of the context and situation (Geen, 1994).

That culture may influence group-level tendencies toward aggression is well documented in the literature. Many cross-cultural psychologists and anthropologists have examined cultures such as the Yanomami of Venezuela and Brazil (for example, Sponsel, 1998)—a cultural group well known for its aggressive tendencies, both within the group and toward outsiders, and often referred to as the "fierce people." Landau (1984) compared levels of stress, social support systems, and the rates of murder and other crimes in 13 countries and found a correlation among these variables. Robbins, DeWalt, and Pelto (1972) showed that countries with hotter and more humid climates are associated with higher murder rates, and this tendency has also been documented for the states of the United States (Anderson & Anderson, 1996).

Indeed, many studies document cross-cultural differences in aggression. For example, Terav and Keltikangas (1998) examined justifications for aggression and withdrawal in Finland and Estonia. Participants were presented with a description of two everyday social problems and a list of problem-solving strategies, and were asked to provide a justification for each strategy. The results indicated that the Estonian participants more often chose instrumental justifications for their aggressive behavior, suggesting that aggression was a means to an end. The Finnish participants, however, more often reported that aggression was fun. The authors concluded that aggression is considered more deviant in Finland than in Estonia.

Bond and associates (1985) studied aggressive insults and criticisms in Hong Kong and the United States. They hypothesized that such insults and criticisms by a boss of a subordinate would be perceived as less aggressive in Hong Kong, because this culture is relatively higher on Hofstede's (1980) dimension of power distance than the United States. Therefore, aggressive behaviors would be more acceptable in relationships where status and power are unequal. Their data did indicate that the Chinese perceived such insults as less illegitimate, and saw less reason to dislike the superior who delivered them.

Cultural differences in aggression appear not only across countries, but within countries as well. Cohen, Nisbett, Bowdle, and Schwartz (1996), for example, conducted three experiments comparing white males who were born in either the northern or southern part of the United States. A confederate in the experiment insulted the participants, whose reactions were recorded. The northerners appeared relatively unaffected by the insult. The southerners, however, perceived more threat to their masculine reputation; they were more upset, more physiologically and cognitively primed for aggression, and more likely to engage in aggressive and dominant behavior. Cortisol and testosterone levels were measured, and both were found to be elevated in the southern sample. The authors attributed these findings to the southern culture of "honor" that manifested itself in cognitions, emotions, and behaviors among southerners but not northerners.

Some studies have suggested that groups tend to be more aggressive than individuals. Jaffe and Yinon (1983), for example, showed that groups of Israeli participants were more willing to administer shocks to subjects in an experiment than were individuals. Other studies, however, have suggested that being in groups does not necessarily lead to more aggression. Rather, people are more sure of themselves in groups. If the group's cultural norms favor aggression, then aggressive behaviors are more likely to occur. However, if the group's cultural norms favor nonaggression, then behaviors are more likely to be restrained (Rabbie, 1982).

Not only are there cultural differences in instigation of aggression; there appear to be such differences in being the target of aggression. Harris (1996), for example, assessed experiences as both target and instigator of aggression in Anglo and Hispanic university students. The Anglo students reported experiencing significantly more lifetime aggression as both target and aggressor than did the Hispanic participants.

A number of studies indicate that cultural differences in aggression appear early in life. Osterman and colleagues (1994), for example, documented differences in perceptions of aggression among 8-year-olds in two samples from Finland, two from the United States, and one from Poland. Another study (Farver et al., 1997) documented differences in 4-year-old children in the United States, Sweden, Germany, and Indonesia. In this study, children told two stories using toys with aggressive and neutral cues. American children's narratives had significantly more aggressive content, aggressive words, unfriendly characters, and mastery of situations with aggression than did those of the other three cultures. Zahn-Waxler and associates (1996) documented similar tendencies in a comparison of 4-year-old American and Japanese children. They found that American children showed more anger, more aggressive behavior and language, and greater underregulation of emotion than did Japanese children across different contexts of assessment.

Some studies have searched for some of the learning and environmental sources of cultural differences in aggression. Yamaguchi and Li (1995), for example, examined the relationship between aggressive motives and child-rearing conditions in Japanese and Chinese college students. They found that child-rearing practices were indeed related to aggression, albeit in different ways for the two samples. In another study, Osterwell and Nagano-Nakamura (1992) asked Japanese and Israeli mothers of kindergarten children about their children's fights and quarrels. They reported considerable differences in the mothers' perceptions, which surely must affect the children's attitudes toward aggression through socialization and enculturation. The Japanese mothers saw aggression as natural—a fact of life with both positive and negative elements, but that should be kept under control so as not to harm others. The Israeli mothers saw aggression as dangerous to both aggressor and aggressee. Thus, the Japanese viewed aggression as a natural and necessary aspect of development, whereas the Israelis perceived it as justified mainly as self-defense and as expressing negative emotional states.

However, not all cross-cultural studies document differences in tendencies or attitudes toward aggression. A few studies have reported cultural similarities as well. Tomada and Schneider (1997), for example, examined elementary school children in Italy, and compared their results with previous findings in the United States. American studies had shown that overt physical and verbal aggression is more prevalent among boys, whereas covert aggression within interpersonal relationships is more prevalent among girls. Although the data did not perfectly support this difference in the Italian sample, the authors concluded that the distinction between overt and covert aggression is useful in describing sex differences in aggression across cultures.

In a different vein, a study by Ramirez (1993) examined the degree of acceptance of various forms of aggressive behavior in four regions in Spain. Not only were these four regions surprisingly similar in their attitudes of acceptance of aggression, but these data were related to similar data collected in Finland and Poland. These findings suggest a possible cross-cultural or universal aspect to attitudes about aggression.

Thus, cross-cultural research has shown that aggressive tendencies, attitudes, and norms differ across cultures, and that these differences are firmly established at a relatively early age. The available evidence also points to aspects of child rearing and maternal values and attitudes as possible sources of cultural differences in aggression. At the same time, some studies have shown that at least some aspects of aggression, such as sex differences and attitudes concerning acceptance, may be similar across cultures. What we do not know at this point is which aspects of aggression are similar across cultures, and which are different. Nor do we know what specific sources of learning—child rearing, parental views on aggression, or others—contribute to aggressive behavior, or the relative contribution of psychological as opposed to biological or genetic factors. Future research will need to address these issues, going beyond documenting cultural similarities and differences in aggression to delve into the more difficult question of how and why these similarities and differences occur.

Culture and Conformity, Compliance, Obedience, and Cooperation

Few words and concepts are associated with such negative connotations in American social psychology and social behavior as conformity, compliance, and obedience to the group. These words often stir up forceful images of robots and automatons lacking any individuality. Without doubt, these images strike at the heart of the "rugged individualism" that is not only central but vital to American culture and sense of self. **Conformity** refers to people yielding to real or imagined social pressure. **Compliance** is generally defined as people yielding to social pressure in their public behavior, even though their private beliefs may not have changed. **Obedience** is a form of compliance that occurs when people follow direct commands, usually from someone in a position of authority. Whether we like it or not, these issues are very real in all of our lives. Research on these topics in the United States has shown that not only do conformity, compliance, and obedience exist, but their effects are pervasive.

In contrast to the often negative connotations of conformity, compliance, and obedience, cooperation is a construct with generally positive connotations. **Cooperation** refers to people's ability to work together toward common goals. It is a hallmark value of many cultures, especially collectivistic cultures, as it is necessary for the successful functioning of ingroups.

Research on these topics has been conducted quite extensively around the world. In the United States, several studies serve as landmark classics in this area of social psychology, including those by Asch and Milgram.

Research in the United States

Two of the best-known studies on conformity, compliance, and obedience are the Asch and Milgram studies. In his earliest experiments, Asch (1951, 1955, 1956) examined a subject's response to a simple judgment task after other "subjects" (actually experimental confederates) had all given the same incorrect response. For example, a subject would be placed in a room with others, shown objects (lines, balls, and so forth), and asked to make a judgment about the objects (such as relative sizes). The answer was often obvious, but subjects were asked to give their answers only after a number of experimental confederates had given theirs. The basic finding from these simple experiments was that, more often than not, subjects would give the wrong answer, even though it was obviously wrong, if the people answering before them had given that same wrong answer. Across studies and trials, group size and group unanimity were major influencing factors. Conformity peaked when the group contained seven people and was unanimous in its judgments (even though the judgments were clearly wrong).

In Asch's studies, compliance resulted from subtle, implied pressure. But in the real world, compliance can occur in response to explicit rules, requests, and commands. We can only imagine how forceful and pervasive group pressure to conform and comply are in the real world if they can operate in a simple laboratory environment among people unknown to the subject on a task that has relatively little meaning.

In Milgram's (1974) famous study, subjects were brought into a laboratory ostensibly to study the effects of punishment on learning. Subjects were instructed to administer shocks to another subject (actually an experimental confederate) when the latter gave the wrong response or no response. The shock meter was labeled from "Slight Shock" to "DANGER: Severe Shock," and the confederate's behaviors ranged from simple utterances of pain through pounding on the walls, pleas to stop, and then deathly silence. (No shock was actually administered.) Milgram reported that 65% of the subjects obeyed the commands of the experimenter and administered the most severe levels of shock.

The Asch experiments were rather innocuous in the actual content of the compliance (for example, judgments of the length of lines). The Milgram studies, however, clearly highlighted the potential negative and harmful effects of compliance and obedience. To this day, it stands as one of the best-known studies in American social psychology. Replication is unlikely to be attempted today because of restrictions based on ethics and university standards of conduct, but its findings speak for themselves on the power of group influence.

Cross-Cultural Research on Conformity and Compliance

In thinking about cultural differences in conformity, compliance, and obedience, we need to be aware of the American cultural bias against these terms. We need to understand that our negative feelings are firmly rooted in our own individualistic culture. If we can see that these feelings are rooted in our cultural upbringing, it then follows that different cultures may have different feelings about conformity, obedience, and compliance. Whereas these behaviors are viewed negatively in American culture, they may very well be positively valued social behaviors in other cultures.

A number of cross-cultural studies do indeed show that people of other cultures view conformity, obedience, and compliance differently than Americans. Some studies have shown that Asian cultures in particular not only engage in conforming, compliant, and obedient behaviors to a greater degree than Americans, but that they also *value* conformity to a greater degree. For example, Punetha, Giles, and Young (1987) administered an extended Rokeach Value Survey to three groups of Asian subjects and one group of British subjects. The British subjects clearly valued individualistic items, such as independence and freedom, whereas the Asian subjects endorsed societal values including conformity and obedience.

Studies involving other Asian and American comparisons have generally produced the same results. Hadiyono and Hahn (1985) reported that Indonesians endorsed conformity more than Americans did. Argyle, Henderson, Bond, Iizuka, and Contarello (1986) found that Japanese and Hong Kong Chinese endorsed obedience more than did British and Italian subjects. Buck, Newton, and Muramatsu (1984) found that Japanese were more conforming than Americans. Nor is valuing conformity and obedience limited to Asian cultures. Cashmore and Goodnow (1986) demonstrated that Italians were more conforming than Anglo-Australians, and El-Islam (1983) documented cultural differences in conformity in an Arabian sample.

Two cross-cultural studies on child-rearing values speak to the strength of these values in socialization and enculturation. Not only Asian but also Puerto Rican subjects were found to value conformity and obedience in child rearing (Burgos & Dias-Perez, 1986; Stropes-Roe & Cochrane, 1990). A number of anthropological works on Japanese culture (for example, Benedict, 1946; Doi, 1985) confirm the importance of obedience and compliance in Japanese child rearing.

Recently, Bond and Smith (1996) conducted a meta-analysis of studies examining the effects of conformity across studies involving the types of tasks originally used by Asch. Meta-analysis is a technique that allows a researcher to examine findings across a large number of studies, and to relate those findings either to characteristics of the studies or to other data relevant to those studies. Their analysis involved 133 studies conducted in 17 different countries. They found that the magnitude of the effect of conformity was very large in some countries and very small in others, with a mean effect of moderate value. When they analyzed the relationship between the magnitude of the effect and characteristics of the studies, they found that conformity was higher when the majority that tried to influence the conforming participant was larger, and when there was a greater proportion of female participants. Conformity was also greater when the majority did not consist of outgroup members, and when the stimuli were more ambiguous. Of particular note was the finding that effect size was significantly related to individualism–collectivism, with conformity higher in collectivistic countries than in individualistic ones.

That conformity is related to cultural values of individualism or collectivism makes sense. Traditional American culture fosters individualistic values, endorsing behaviors and beliefs contrary to conformity. To conform in American culture is to be "weak" or somehow deficient. But many other cultures foster more collectivistic, group-oriented values; in those cultures, concepts of conformity, obedience, and compliance enjoy much higher status and a positive orientation. In these cultures, conformity is viewed not only as "good" but as necessary for the successful functioning of the culture, its groups, and the interpersonal relationships of its members.

Culture and Obedience

Like conformity, obedience is a value that has different connotations and meanings in different cultures. In Milgram's (1974) study, you will recall, about 65 % of the participants obeyed the instructions of the experimenter and administered a high level of shock to a confederate (who in reality received no shock). Smith and Bond (1999) review nine other studies that used the Milgram paradigm, conducted in the United States and eight other countries. The results of these studies indicated a broad range in the percentage of participants obeying the experimenter, ranging from a low of 16 % among female students in Australia to a high of 92 % in the Netherlands. These differences may reflect real cultural differences in obedience, but they may also reflect other types of differences, including differences in the meaning of the particular tasks used in the studies, the specific instructions given to the participants, and the nature of the confederate who supposedly received the shocks.

We need to ask ourselves why the best-known studies of conformity and obedience conducted in the United States are so negative in their orientation. Although the Asch studies are rather innocuous, the Milgram studies are clearly a powerful indictment of the potential negative consequences of obedience. Have any studies been conducted by American social psychologists that might show positive outcomes of conformity, compliance, or obedience? If not, perhaps we need to examine the possible biases of American social scientists in approaching these topics.

Culture and Cooperation

A number of studies in the cross-cultural literature highlight the important differences between cultures in their values and attitudes about cooperation, and in their cooperative behaviors. Domino (1992), for example, compared children from the People's Republic of China with children from the United States on a social values task. The task required the child to decide between two alternatives offering tokens to the child and an unspecified classmate. Basically, the choices involved receiving more tokens for oneself or receiving fewer tokens and allowing the classmate to receive more. Six different types of outcome preferences were distinguished: including individualism, competition, equality, group enhancement or cooperation, competition and individualism, and equality and individualism. Across a series of trials, the most common preferences of American children were individualism (receiving many tokens for oneself) and competition (receiving as many more tokens than the other as possible). In contrast, the most common preferences of Chinese children were equality (equal division of tokens) and group enhancement (most number of tokens collectively for both individuals, irrespective of division). Domino (1992) interpreted these findings as supportive of the notion that the process of socialization in China is geared to promoting group solidarity and group consciousness.

In another study, Mann, Mitsui, Beswick, and Harmoni (1994) compared 11- and 12-year-old Australian and Japanese children in their endorsement of rules governing respect for others. The children completed two questionnaires about their endorsement of seven rules in relation to six target persons: father, mother, best friend, teacher, adult neighbor, and same-age neighbor. The results indicated that Japanese children showed greater correspondence between endorsed and self-reported respect than did Australian children. The Japanese also differentiated more than the Australians did in their respect for parents and teacher versus friends and neighbors. These findings indicated that Japanese social rules governing respect are highly person- and situation-related, consistent with the strong distinction between ingroups and outgroups in collectivistic cultures, and consistent with Hall's (1976) analysis of Japan as a high-context culture.

Cultural differences are apparent not only in the levels of respect and cooperation afforded others, but also in the process of engaging in cooperative tasks. Filardo (1996), for example, videotaped European American and African American eighth graders participating in a cooperative, problem-solving board game that involved group decision making. Transcripts of these videotapes were coded by research assistants in terms of the activities that occurred as well as the ways in which participants interacted. The results indicated that, overall, African Americans were more active than their European

American counterparts, and engaged in more performance outputs that expressed "a lack of consideration for the point of view of the listener or a view of the parties as having asymmetrical rights with respect to one another or as expecting compliance" (p. 75). European Americans engaged in more brief, unelaborated expressions of agreement with another group member's previous utterance or action.

While research seems to indicate that collectivistic cultures are more conforming and obedient, they also seem to be more cooperative. The onus is on future cross-cultural research to examine the ways in which conformity and obedience, on the one hand, and cooperation, on the other, coexist in a delicate balance within a culture and society, as well as the specific contexts in which these behaviors occur. It seems to me that conforming or cooperating occurs within a context of recognizing the possible ramifications and consequences of nonconforming or noncooperating, and future studies should take into account what these ramifications are. It may be that, given equivalent consequences, people's conformity or cooperation will be more similar than different across cultures.

 ## Conclusion

Humans are social animals. By nature we bond with others, live with others, work and play with others. Our whole lives are spent in some kind of interaction or relationship with other people. No matter how we look at it, we cannot ignore the fact that we are fundamentally connected with other people in our world. Our behaviors, thoughts, and feelings are all influenced by others, and we in turn influence those around us.

As we grow in our own cultures and societies, we learn certain ways of behaving, interacting, feeling, and interpreting in relation to the world around us. By the time we are adults, we are so well practiced at these ways that we often don't think about how or why we do the things we do. Our attributions, interpersonal and romantic relationships, and group behaviors are all strongly influenced by the culture in which we live. The research reviewed in this chapter—on ingroup/outgroup behaviors, person perception, intimate relationships, attributions, and conformity and obedience—underscores the profound and pervasive impact of culture.

We need to recognize that culture plays a major role in shaping our behaviors with others. And we need to recognize that what is true for us in our own social behavior may not be true for other people from other cultures. While we may frown on conformity to group norms or obedience to authority, many cultures view them as positive aspects of social behavior. While we may believe that our successes are due to internal attributes and our failures to external ones, people from other cultures may attribute successes and failures to themselves equally. While we may accept or even encourage expressing negative feelings toward ingroup others, people from other cultures may find such expressions reprehensible or even dangerous.

These are a few examples of how culture can influence social behavior. Just as how we think and feel and act is valid for us within our culture, how people from other cultures think and feel and act is equally valid for them based on their cultural background, no matter how different their behaviors are from ours. Validity, of course, is a different question from acceptance or liking, but it is the first step toward those goals as well.

As we close this chapter, I cannot help feeling that, despite the great differences across cultures in people's social behaviors, there are considerable underlying similarities as well. As I suggested at the end of the section on attributions, there must be some kind of underlying core value or psychological principle operating in all of us that helps us enhance our sense of self, or foster our psychological and cultural goals. Culture produces differences in how we define those goals, and in their behavioral manifestations. Yet, at the core of it all, perhaps there is some culture-constant belief or value that we all operate on as human beings. The seminal review by Amir and Sharon (1988) on the cross-cultural validity of social psychological laws speaks to this point. Their review of studies examining social psychological principles across cultures indicated that original findings are often replicated across studies in statistical main effects—that is, in broad ways transcending culture. Somehow, cross-cultural psychology and research should attempt to engage this core, seeking similarities as well as differences at various levels of our psychological lives.

Glossary

aggression Any act or behavior that hurts another person, either physically or psychologically.

attributions The inferences people make about the causes of events and their own and others' behaviors.

cognitive schemas Conceptual frameworks that people use to make sense of the world and people around them.

companionate love Love that involves warm, trusting, and tolerant affection for another whose life is deeply intertwined with one's own.

compliance People yielding to social pressure in their public behavior, even though their private beliefs may not have changed.

conformity People yielding to real or imagined social pressure.

consensus One of the dimensions thought to influence the nature of attributions; it refers to whether other people in the same situation tend to respond in the same manner.

consistency One of the dimensions thought to influence the nature of attributions; it refers to whether a person's behavior in a situation is the same over time.

consummate love Love that is characterized by passionate love, intimacy, and commitment.

cooperation People's ability to work together toward common goals.

defensive attributions The tendency to blame victims for their misfortune.

distinctiveness One of the dimensions thought to influence the nature of attributions; it refers to whether a person's behavior is unique to the specific target of the behavior.

fundamental attribution error An attributional bias to explain the behavior of others using internal attributions but explain our own behaviors using external attributions.

ingroup relationships Relationships characterized by some degree of familiarity, intimacy, and trust. We feel close to people around us we consider to be in our ingroup. Self–ingroup relationships develop through bonds that tie the ingroup together through common friendship or relationships or goals.

matching hypothesis A hypothesis about love relationships that suggests that people of approximately equal physical characteristics are likely to select each other as partners.

obedience A form of compliance that occurs when people follow direct commands, usually from someone in a position of authority.

outgroup relationships Relationships that lack the familiarity, intimacy, and trust characteristic of relationships with ingroup others.

passionate love Love that involves absorption of another and includes sexual feelings and intense emotion.

person perception The process of forming impressions of others.

reciprocity hypothesis A hypothesis about love relationships that suggests that people tend to like others who like them.

self-serving bias The tendency to attribute our successes to personal factors and our failures to situational factors.

similarity hypothesis A hypothesis about love relationships that suggests that people similar in age, race, religion, social class, education, intelligence, attitudes, and physical attractiveness tend to form intimate relationships.

social schemas Organized clusters of ideas about categories of social events and people that have been shown to influence person perceptions.

Culture and Organizations

We all spend a major portion of our lives in organizations. In fact, most of you reading this book are probably doing so within the educational system—an organization that plays an important part in many people's lives and is an important agent of socialization in the development and maintenance of culture. The companies that we work for are also organizations. And many of the extracurricular activities we engage in are supported by organizations, such as the YMCA, churches, sport clubs, and the like. Other organizations provide structure and services, such as government and hospitals.

In the past, it was probably easier than it is now to study organizations in relative isolation from issues of culture. Previously, the American workforce was less racially, ethnically, and culturally diverse than it is today. With less cultural diversity, the expectations of the members of any work organization were generally similar. Communication, lines of authority, and hierarchical structure were established with less conscious awareness of differences among people. Members of organizations had implicit, tacit knowledge about how to behave around one another and how to work together, because they all started with relatively similar cultural backgrounds.

Organizations were more isolated from issues of culture in yet another way, as many companies in the past were entirely or primarily domestic. Most of the work-related issues companies dealt with were confined to the United States and its culture. And most of the companies that competed or cooperated with one another were based in the same country and culture. This national work environment has now become a thing of the past. Not only is the American workforce culturally diverse, but many companies today operate in an international arena.

The American workplace now includes unprecedented numbers of **multinational and international corporations**—work organizations that have subsidiaries, satellite offices, and work units in more than one country. These companies need to deal increasingly with people of diverse and varied backgrounds. Today, transfers from one business unit to another within the same company can mean a transfer from one country to another. Clearly, this internationalization of business brings with it more intercultural issues and challenges.

Even domestic companies that are not multinational in their structure must face the challenge of internationalization, with its associated intercultural issues. New trade laws and treaties (such as the North American Free Trade Agreement, or NAFTA) have brought more business competitors from distant cultures, as well as increased opportunities for opening markets in other countries and cultures. Advances in communication and transportation allow companies and individuals to work more easily today than ever before over vast physical and cultural distances.

Technological changes in communication—telephones, facsimile machines, videoteleconferencing, and electronic mail—have forced the issue of culture to the forefront of our work lives. The business world has become a global village, in which the exchange of goods, services, and resources knows few boundaries. This global village raises issues within our borders as well as across borders. Many of these issues are cultural. Our ability to deal with these issues in an ever-changing business world will determine our success or failure.

Although there are many different types of organizations in the world, this chapter will focus on one particular type—work organizations—because they have been the topic of many intercultural studies and provide the context for our knowledge of the effects of culture on organizations. The information gained in understanding the relationship between culture and work organizations can be useful in understanding other organizations as well.

In this chapter, we will begin by defining organizational culture, and distinguish it from organizational climate. We will examine cross-cultural research analyzing organizational culture first through organizational structure and then through work-related values, using Hofstede's four major dimensions of culture. Finally, we will examine cross-cultural research on a variety of work-related behaviors, including motivation and productivity, leadership and management, decision making, and intercultural issues related to business.

Organizational Culture and Organizational Climate

An organization is a structure created by people to achieve certain objectives. Organizations are generally composed of people who work collectively to address the overall goals of the organization. Different people or groups may have different specific goals within the organization, but theoretically they should collectively address a common goal (for example, building a car, selling groceries). Different people or groups may be specialized according to role, objective, or task, and rank or status within a hierarchy may differentiate them from one another.

Like people, each organization is unique; like groups of people and cultures, groups of organizations have similarities we may characterize as culture. In recent years, it has become fashionable to refer to this aspect of organizations as "organizational culture" or "corporate culture" (O'Reilly, 1989; O'Reilly, Chatman, & Caldwell, 1991). It is important to define *organizational culture* and to distinguish it from another widely used term, *organizational climate*.

Although various definitions of organizational culture have been offered, most are comparable to the definition of culture presented earlier in this book (Chapter 2)—but applied to an organization instead of a social group or society. As you will recall, we have defined culture as *a dynamic system of rules—explicit and implicit—established by groups in order to ensure their survival, involving attitudes, values, beliefs, norms, and behaviors, shared by a group but harbored differently by each specific unit within the group, communicated across generations, relatively stable but with the potential to change across time.* **Organizational culture**, therefore, refers to *a dynamic system of rules that are shared among members of an organization.* The rules involve various psychological constructs, such as attitudes, values, beliefs, norms, and behaviors. Organizational culture is thus larger than the behavioral practices we observe in everyday work. It refers to deeper-seated values and beliefs held to be important not only by individual employees, but by the organization itself.

This definition of organizational culture allows us to define, analyze, and understand organizational culture not as a single, unitary construct, but rather as a dynamic, multifaceted construct that exists on many different levels. This is important because, as you will see in the remainder of this chapter, most writers talk about organizational culture as if there is only one such entity in an organization. In our work on this topic (for example, Colvin, Matsumoto, Taylor, & Takeuchi, 1998), we have differentiated three levels of organizational culture: individual, intraorganizational, and interorganizational.

On the *individual* level, culture is manifested in the cultures that individuals bring with them to the workplace, based on the cultural milieu in which they were raised and socialized. At the *intraorganizational* level, culture exists within an organization—that is, among people within departments and units, and among departments and units within a company. This level is most congruent with contemporary views of organizational culture. It includes the explicit and implicit rules governing shared daily practices, such as human resource policies regarding pay, raises, promotion, and termination, as well as unspoken rules of how to deal with your manager. Finally, the *interorganizational* level recognizes that companies do not exist in a vacuum. Instead, they coexist with other companies, both within a country and across countries, on which they depend for survival and existence. Culture at this level includes many explicit (in the form of domestic and international business laws) and implicit (informal dos and don'ts) rules that govern how companies deal with each other and coexist for mutual prosperity and wealth.

Organizational climate refers to a shared perception of "the way things are around here" (Reichers & Schneider, 1990)—a shared perception of organizational policies, practices, and procedures. In addition, the term contains nuances of an emotional climate—that is, how people generally feel in their normal, everyday business practices. Climate can probably be best understood as a manifestation of organizational culture (Reichers & Schneider, 1990; Schein, 1985), which generally refers to a deeper, less consciously held set of values, attitudes, and meanings.

The concept of organizational climate is a long-standing one in the field of industrial and organizational psychology. Reichers and Schneider (1990), in their review of these two constructs, point out that writing appeared as early as 1939 on organizational climate and its relationship to work behaviors. Organizational culture, on the other hand, is a relatively new concept. It first appeared in the literature in 1979 and has become an important catchphrase for the 1980s and 1990s. Most of the cross-cultural research on organizations has focused on culture, not climate, and that will be our focus in this chapter. Hopefully, future research will begin to examine in more detail how organizational climate is related to culture, and how it differs across national and social cultures.

Culture and Organizational Structure

One way in which scientists have traditionally tried to understand organizational culture is by analyzing organizational structures. The assumption is that differences in underlying values, beliefs, norms, and behaviors between organizations should manifest themselves in observable differences in how companies structure and organize themselves to do their work. Thus, by examining differences in structure, we should be able to gain an understanding of the organizational cultures underlying those structures.

This approach has not been without merit. Some writers, for example, have suggested that organizations differ along certain stable dimensions. Robbins (1987) suggests that organizations differ in complexity, formalization, and centralization. **Complexity** refers to the degree to which organizations foster differentiation of tasks and activities within themselves. **Formalization** refers to the degree to which organizations provide structure and rules for their operations. **Centralization** refers to the degree to which organizations concentrate their operations and decision-making capabilities in a limited number of business units or people.

Berry and associates (1992) point out that a number of factors determine how organizations deal with these three dimensions. These factors include the size of the organization, the technology available to it, its resources, and its history. In addition, we need to take into account the culture of the people comprising the organization—its employees—and their worldview or ways of understanding and interacting with the world and with other people.

Given all these factors, it is no wonder that organizations differ on these dimensions according to the national culture in which they exist. Several writers have used these differences to describe the "national character" of organizations, clearly referring to what we would call organizational culture. Lammers and Hickson (1979), for example, suggest three different types of national character in organizations: the Latin type, the Anglo-Saxon type, and the Third World type. The **Latin type** is characterized as a classic bureaucracy, with centralized power and decision making and many hierarchical levels. The **Anglo-Saxon type** is more or less the opposite, with less centralization, more diffusion of power and decision making, and less hierarchy in the bureaucracy. The **Third World type** is characterized by greater centralization of decision making, less formalization of rules, and a more paternalistic or traditional family orientation.

Lammers and Hickson's (1979) study is but one attempt to examine cultural differences in organizational structure. All the different types of organizations of the world cannot be pigeonholed into three (or any number of) limited classifications, just as it would be impossible to pigeonhole all people into neat categories of classification (no matter how hard psychologists and the census bureau may try!). But general tendencies toward differences in organizational structure can be observed across countries, and these differences are most likely related to cultural differences in the people comprising the organizations and the countries in which they exist. As with people, each organization needs to be understood on its own terms. Many other countries, not only the United States, are dealing with increasing diversity in their populations. This diversity challenges us to begin questioning the validity of broad generalizations about people and organizations based solely on structure.

Cultural Differences in Work-Related Values

Another way in which scientists have tried to understand organizational culture is through research on employees' work-related values. This approach represents an evolution in the field's understanding of organization culture, from conceptualizing it in terms of structural components to describing culture in terms of its functional components. Much of how we understand corporate culture today is based on this functional approach, which has its roots in assessing corporate culture by examining the work-related values of company employees.

People of different cultural backgrounds come to work with different values related to their work. These values include individual orientation and attitudes toward work itself, toward the organization and company loyalty, toward personal relationships with other members of the company, and so forth. Cultural similarities and differences in value orientations related to work can be a source of overall growth and financial gain or of conflict, frustration, and organizational stumbling.

The best-known study of work-related values was conducted by Hofstede (1980, 1984) in the 1960s and 1970s. His study involved employees at International Business Machines (IBM), a multinational corporation with branch offices and subsidiaries in many different countries. In his original study (1980), Hofstede reported data collected from workers in 40 different countries. In a later study (1984), he reported data from an additional 10 countries. Altogether, more than 116,000 questionnaires were distributed to workers in these various countries, spanning upwards of 20 different languages and including a total of seven different occupational levels.

The questionnaire itself contained approximately 160 items, of which 63 were related to work values. The questions clustered around four major themes: satisfaction, perception, personal goals and beliefs, and demographics. On the basis of the data he obtained, Hofstede identified four major dimensions of work-related values and computed overall scores for each country on each of these four dimensions. This approach allowed him to order the countries according to their score on each dimension. This ecological approach, using country or group scores as the units of analysis, is useful for identifying and characterizing national tendencies; however, a one-to-one correspondence with those same tendencies does not necessarily exist on the individual level within a country.

Hofstede called the four major dimensions in his study power distance (PD), uncertainty avoidance (UA), individualism (IN), and masculinity (MA). IN was introduced in Chapter 2 as the construct individualism versus collectivism (IC), and all four dimensions have been referred to frequently throughout this book. Indeed, Hofstede's study was a major impetus to viewing and understanding cultures using a dimensional approach. Moreover, the findings of this study have served as the foundation for much of the work that has been done since on culture and organizations. Each of the dimensions he identified is related to concrete differences in attitudes, opinions, beliefs, and behaviors within work organizations, and each forms the basis for understanding certain societal norms that exist in each of the countries in Hofstede's studies. These dimensions also have consequences for organizational structure and interorganizational behavior.

Power Distance

Status and power are sociological concepts associated with groups of individuals. In companies and organizations, vertical or hierarchical relationships based on status and power differences are common. Indeed, differentiating people according to their roles, functions, and positions is vital to the successful operation of an organization. Work organizations are no different in this respect from any other organizations. The various statuses afforded different individuals within a hierarchy come with certain benefits, rights, privileges, and power not afforded others. The "chain of command" within a company identifies the players and their roles. Each company decides these issues based on their importance for its continued functioning in the marketplace.

The basic hierarchical relationship is that between a boss and his or her immediate subordinate. In most cases, an employee is involved in a hierarchical relationship both with someone of higher status and with others of lower status. People within each culture develop ways of interacting with others according to the status differential that exists between the individual and the person with whom he or she is interacting. Power distance (PD) refers to the degree to which different cultures encourage or maintain power and status differences between interactants. Cultures high on PD develop rules, mechanisms, and rituals that serve to maintain and strengthen the status relationships among their members. Cultures low on PD minimize those rules and customs, ignoring if not eliminating the status differences between people.

In Hofstede's original study (1980), the Philippines, Mexico, Venezuela, and India had the highest scores on this dimension. These findings suggest that the cultures underlying these countries maintained strong status differences. New Zealand, Denmark, Israel, and Austria had the lowest scores on PD, suggesting that the cultures underlying these countries did the most to minimize status and power differentials. Spain, Pakistan, Japan, and Italy were right in the middle of the scores. The United States had slightly lower scores, reflecting some degree of minimizing of power differences.

The findings for the United States are somewhat surprising. American culture seems to value minimizing power differences among people—treating all people as equals. Mulder (1976, 1977) has suggested a kind of PD imbalance in American culture. According to Mulder, people of lower status try to minimize power differences when interacting with someone of higher status, but people of higher status try to maintain power differences with subordinates. In a company, subordinates attempt to minimize power differences when interacting with their bosses, while their bosses try to maintain the power differential with their subordinates.

According to Hofstede, cultural differences on PD are related to individual differences in behaviors that have consequences for their work. Table 17.1 summarizes PD-related characteristics Hofstede gleaned from his own research and that of others. For example, managers in organizations in high-PD cultures are seen as making decisions autocratically and paternalistically, whereas managers in low-PD cultures are seen as making decisions only after more extensive consultation with their subordinates.

The concrete behaviors listed in Table 17.1 are related to societal norms, which in turn have important consequences for organizational structure. In general, cultures high on PD foster organizations with greater centralization of organization and process, taller organizational pyramids, larger proportions of supervisory personnel, larger wage differentials, lower qualifications for lower strata of employees, and greater valuation of white-collar as opposed to blue-collar jobs. All these characteristics of work organizations and of interpersonal relationships within companies can be considered as natural consequences of social and cultural differences on power distance.

Table 17.1 Summary of Connotations of Power Distance (PD) Differences Found in Survey Research

Low-PD Countries	High-PD Countries
Parents put less value on children's obedience.	Parents put high value on children's obedience.
Students put high value on independence.	Students put high value on conformity.
Authoritarian attitudes in students are a matter of personality.	Students show authoritarian attitudes as a social norm.
Managers seen as making decisions after consulting with subordinates.	Managers seen as making decisions autocratically and paternalistically.
Close supervision negatively evaluated by subordinates.	Close supervision positively evaluated by subordinates.
Stronger perceived work ethic: strong disbelief that people dislike work.	Weaker perceived work ethic: more frequent belief that people dislike work.
Managers more satisfied with participative superior.	Managers more satisfied with directive or persuasive superior.
Subordinates' preference for manager's decision-making style clearly centered on consultative, give-and-take style.	Subordinates' preference for manager's decision-making style polarized between autocratic-paternalistic and majority rule.
Managers like seeing themselves as practical and systematic; they admit a need for support.	Managers like seeing themselves as benevolent decision makers.
Employees less afraid of disagreeing with their boss.	Employees fear to disagree with their boss.
Employees show more cooperativeness.	Employees reluctant to trust each other.
Managers seen as showing more consideration.	Managers seen as showing less consideration.
Students have positive associations with "power" and "wealth."	Students have negative associations with "power" and "wealth."
Mixed feeling about employees' participation in management.	Ideological support for employees' participation in management.
Mixed feelings among managers about the distribution of capacity for leadership and initiative.	Ideological support among managers for a wide distribution of capacity for leadership and initiative.
Informal employee consultation possible without formal participation.	Formal employee participation possible without informal consultation.
Higher-educated employees hold much less authoritarian values than lower-educated ones.	Higher- and lower-educated employees show similar values about authority.

Source: Hofstede (1980), p. 92. Reprinted by permission of the publisher.

Uncertainty Avoidance

Uncertainty is a fact of life. No one can predict with 100% accuracy what the future holds for any of us. While this is true for individuals, it is especially true for companies. Today's profits can easily turn into tomorrow's losses, and vice versa. How a market will react to a new product, revisions in old products, corporate restructuring, mergers and acquisitions, and all the other changes that occur within organizations and in the business world is a major source of uncertainty. With this uncertainty can come confusion, stress, and anxiety.

Every society and every organization develops its own ways of dealing with the anxiety and stress associated with uncertainty. Oftentimes, these ways involve development of rituals, informal or written, concerning a code of conduct among employees, as in intracompany policies regarding communication or interpersonal relationships. These rules may also govern behavior between companies within a society, or across cultures, as in domestic and international laws governing business and interbusiness relationships.

Uncertainty avoidance (UA) describes the degree to which different societies and different cultures develop ways to deal with the anxiety and stress of uncertainty. Cultures high on UA develop highly refined rules and rituals that are mandated and become part of the company rubric and normal way of operation. Companies in these cultures may be considered rule-oriented. In Hofstede's survey, Greece, Portugal, Belgium, and Japan were the four countries with the highest scores on this dimension. Cultures low on UA are less concerned with rules and rituals to deal with the stress and anxiety of uncertainty. Companies in these cultures have a more relaxed attitude concerning uncertainty and ambiguity and mandate fewer rules and rituals for their employees. In Hofstede's study, Sweden, Denmark, and Singapore had the lowest scores on UA.

Cultural differences on UA are directly related to concrete differences in jobs and work-related behaviors. Table 17.2 lists the characteristics of people associated with cultures high or low on UA. For example, cultures high on UA tend to be associated with greater job stress than cultures low on UA. This finding is ironic, given that cultures high on UA place greater emphasis on developing ways of dealing with the stress and anxiety produced by uncertainty. Perhaps the ways that are developed are so complex that they produce increased stress in the workers who have to abide by those rules and rituals!

Cultural differences on UA have concrete consequences for organizations and organizational structure. Organizations located in cultures high on UA generally have more structured activities, more written rules, a greater number of specialists, more managers involved in details, more task-oriented managers, and more conformity in managerial style than do organizations in cultures low on UA. Organizations in high-UA cultures also tend to have lower labor turnover, less ambitious employees, less risk-taking behaviors and ventures, and more ritualistic behavior.

Table 17.2 Summary of Connotations of Uncertainty Avoidance (UA) Differences Found in Survey Research

Low-UA Countries	High-UA Countries
Lower anxiety level in population.	Higher anxiety level in population.
Greater readiness to live by the day.	More worry about the future.
Lower job stress.	Higher job stress.
Less emotional resistance to change.	More emotional resistance to change.
Less hesitation to change employers.	Tendency to stay with the same employer.
Loyalty to employer is not seen as a virtue.	Loyalty to employer is seen as a virtue.
Preference for smaller organizations as employers.	Preference for larger organizations as employers.
Smaller generation gap.	Greater generation gap.
Lower average age in higher level jobs.	Higher average age in higher level jobs: gerontocracy.
Managers should be selected on other criteria than seniority.	Managers should be selected on the basis of seniority.
Stronger achievement motivation.	Less achievement motivation.
Hope of success.	Fear of failure.
More risk-taking.	Less risk-taking.
Stronger ambition for individual advancement.	Lower ambition for individual advancement.
Prefers manager career over specialist career.	Prefers specialist career over manager career.
A manager need not be an expert in the field he manages.	A manager must be an expert in the field he manages.
Hierarchical structures of organizations can be by-passed for pragmatic reasons.	Hierarchical structures of organizations should be clear and respected.
Preference for broad guidelines.*	Preference for clear requirements and instructions.
Rules may be broken for pragmatic reasons.	Company rules should not be broken.
Conflict in organizations is natural.*	Conflict in organizations is undesirable.
Competition between employees can be fair and right.	Competition between employees is emotionally disapproved of.
More sympathy for individual and authoritative decisions.	Ideological appeal of consensus and of consultative leadership.
Delegation to subordinates can be complete.*	However, initiative of subordinates should be kept under control.
Higher tolerance for ambiguity in perceiving others (higher LPC).	Lower tolerance for ambiguity in perceiving others (lower LPC).
More prepared to compromise with opponents.	Lower readiness to compromise with opponents.

*Based on studies by Laurent (1978).

Table 17.2 Summary of Connotations of Uncertainty Avoidance (UA) Differences Found in Survey Research *(continued)*

Low-UA Countries	High-UA Countries
Acceptance of foreigners as managers.	Suspicion toward foreigners as managers.
Larger fractions prepared to live abroad.	Fewer people prepared to live abroad.
Higher tolerance for ambiguity in looking at own job (lower satisfaction scores).	Lower tolerance for ambiguity in looking at own job (higher satisfaction scores).
Citizen optimism about ability to control politicians' decisions.	Citizen pessimism about ability to control politicians' decisions.
Employee optimism about the motives behind company activities.	Employee pessimism about the motives behind company activities.
Optimism about people's amount of initiative, ambition, and leadership skills.	Pessimism about people's amount of initiative, ambition, and leadership skills.

Source: G. Hofstede, *Culture's Consequences: International Differences in Work-Related Values,* pp. 132–133. Copyright © 1980 Sage Publications. Reprinted by permission of Sage Publications, Inc.

Individualism–Collectivism

Individualism–collectivism (IC) has been used to explain, understand, and predict cultural differences in a variety of contexts. IC refers to the degree to which a culture fosters individualistic tendencies as opposed to group or collectivistic tendencies. Individualistic cultures tend to foster development of autonomous, unique, and separate individuals. In these cultures, the needs, wishes, desires, and goals of individuals take precedence over group or collective goals. Collectivistic cultures foster interdependence of individuals within groups. In these cultures, individuals sacrifice their own personal needs and goals for the sake of a common good.

IC is a very important dimension in relation to work organizations. Collectivistic cultural values foster more compliance with company policies and more conformity in group, section, or unit behavior. Collectivism also fosters a greater degree of reliance on group work and group orientation to company and organizational tasks. Harmony within groups, sections, or business units is valued more in collectivistic cultures; members are more likely to engage in behaviors that ensure harmony and to refrain from behaviors that threaten harmony.

In his original research, Hofstede named this dimension individualism (IN) rather than IC. Yet it was clear that he discussed this dimension from the perspective of IC, and we use that term here for consistency. In Hofstede's study, the United States, Australia, Great Britain, and Canada had the highest scores on IC. Workers in these countries were characterized as being the most individualistic of all workers in the study. It is interesting to note that each of these countries has a strong historical link to Great Britain. Peru, Pakistan, Colombia, and Venezuela had the lowest scores on IC and were the most collectivistic.

IC differences between countries and cultures are associated with concrete differences in worker attitudes, values, beliefs, and behaviors about work and their companies. Table 17.3 summarizes the differences Hofstede gleaned from his and other people's studies. For example, people in individualistic cultures tend to regard their personal time as important and to make clear distinctions between their time and company time. People in individualistic cultures place more importance on freedom and challenge in their jobs, and initiative is generally encouraged on the job. In collectivistic cultures, freedom, independence, and initiative are normally frowned upon.

IC cultural differences across countries and societies produce clear consequences for organizational structure and work in general (Hofstede, 1980). For example, organizations in individualistic cultures are not expected to look after their employees across their life span. Organizations in collectivistic cultures are expected to do so, as they are morally responsible for the welfare of their employees for most of their lives. As a result, employees in individualistic cultures tend to have a more calculating or analytic view of their relationship to their companies, while employees of collectivistic cultures tend to view their relationship with their companies as moral in nature. Likewise, in individualistic cultures, employees are expected to defend their own personal interests; employees in collectivistic cultures can expect their companies to have their best interests at heart.

On the level of organizational policy, companies in individualistic cultures generally have policies, rules, and guidelines that allow and encourage individual initiative and freedom; collectivistic cultures do not. Promotion and organizational advancement in individualistic cultures are generally based on accomplishment or achievement; in collectivistic cultures, promotions are generally based on seniority regardless of accomplishment.

Masculinity

Biological differences between men and women are a given. The question that every society, culture, and individual has to deal with is the degree to which the biological differences translate, or should translate, to practical differences in social roles, functions, or positions. Traditionally, American culture has expected men to be more assertive, dominant, and the primary wage earner and women to be more nurturing, caring, and primarily concerned with family and child care issues (see also Chapter 8). This picture has been changing rapidly in the United States and continues to be a source of conflict, controversy, and confusion. Values concerning equity and equality have infused the workplace, and many American companies are still in transition toward providing gender equity in the workplace.

Each culture and society must deal with the issue of sex roles and gender differences. A fourth dimension emerged in Hofstede's study, which he labeled masculinity (MA). This label is somewhat misleading because almost all the employees who completed the questionnaire were male. Many of the items

Table 17.3 Summary of Connotations of Individualism (IC) Differences Found in Survey and Related Research

Low-IC Countries	High-IC Countries
Importance of provisions by company (training, physical conditions).	Importance of employees' personal life (time).
Emotional dependence on company.	Emotional independence from company.
Large company attractive.	Small company attractive.
Moral involvement with company.	Calculative involvement with company.
Moral importance attached to training and use of skills in jobs.	More importance attached to freedom and challenge in jobs.
Students consider it less socially acceptable to claim pursuing their own ends without minding others.	Students consider it socially acceptable to claim pursuing their own ends without minding others.
Managers aspire to conformity and orderliness.	Managers aspire to leadership and variety.
Managers rate having security in their position more important.	Managers rate having autonomy more important.
Managers endorse "traditional" points of view, not supporting employee initiative and group activity.	Managers endorse "modern" points of view on stimulating employee initiative and group activity.
Group decisions are considered better than individual decisions.	However, individual decisions are considered better than group decisions.
Duty in life appeals to students.	Enjoyment in life appeals to students.
Managers choose duty, expertness, and prestige as life goals.	Managers choose pleasure, affections, and security as life goals.
Individual initiative is socially frowned upon: fatalism.	Individual initiative is socially encouraged.
More acquiescence in responses to "importance" questions.	Less acquiescence in responses to "importance" questions.
People thought of in terms of ingroups and outgroups; particularism.	People thought of in general terms; universalism.
Social relations predetermined in terms of ingroups.	Need to make specific friendships.
More years of schooling needed to do a given job.	Fewer years of schooling needed to do a given job.
More traffic accidents per 1000 vehicles.	Fewer traffic accidents per 1000 vehicles.
More traditional time use pattern.	More modern time use pattern.

Source: G. Hofstede, *Culture's Consequences: International Differences in Work-Related Values,* pp. 166–167. Copyright © 1980 Sage Publications. Reprinted by permission of Sage Publications, Inc.

identified with this dimension, in fact, had more to do with materialism than relationships, and Hofstede interpreted this factor as associated with masculinity. Still, this dimension can be conceptually useful in understanding gender differences in the workplace. According to Hofstede, MA refers to the degree to which cultures foster or maintain differences between the sexes in work-related values. Cultures high on MA—such as Japan, Austria, Venezuela, and Italy—were associated with the greatest degree of sex differences in work-related values. Cultures low on MA—such as Denmark, Netherlands, Norway, and Sweden—had the fewest differences between the sexes.

As with each of the other dimensions Hofstede generated, cultural differences on MA were associated with very concrete differences between workers and organizations. Table 17.4 summarizes these differences. For example, managers in cultures high on MA valued leadership, independence, and self-realization; cultures low on MA placed less importance on these constructs. Employees in high-MA cultures regarded earnings, recognition, advancement, and challenge relatively more important than did employees in low-MA cultures. And fewer women were in mixed-sex jobs in organizations in high-MA cultures than in low-MA cultures.

Cultural differences on MA have interesting consequences for both organizational structure and employee relationships (Hofstede, 1980). For example, young men in high-MA cultures generally expect to make a career in their jobs, and those who don't see themselves as failures. In high-MA cultures, organizational interests, needs, and goals are viewed as a legitimate reason to interfere in the personal and private lives of employees. High-MA cultures generally have fewer women in more qualified and better-paid jobs, and those women who are in more qualified jobs tend to be very assertive. Job stress is generally higher in organizations located in high-MA cultures.

Recent Research on Organizational Culture

Hofstede's original research described above was an important catalyst for the field, redefining corporate culture in terms of culture as cross-cultural psychologists and anthropologists have typically defined it, and allowing for measurement-driven assessments of it in actual work settings. Not only did his work have far-reaching consequences in the area of organizational psychology; the specification and quantification of the four dimensions of culture was a major plus for many other areas of psychology as well. Harry Triandis (1998), for example, attributes much of his initial interest in and attention to the concept of individualism–collectivism to Hofstede's work, and by now we are well familiar with the major contributions Triandis has made to all areas of cross-cultural and mainstream psychology from this perspective.

Subsequent research on organizational culture has focused, to a large extent, on the deep-seated values that employees may have. These values are generally assumed to occur as a result of their relationship with their companies,

Table 17.4 Summary of Connotations of Masculinity (MA) Differences Found in Survey and Related Research

Low-MA Countries	High-MA Countries
Relationship with manager, cooperation, friendly atmosphere, living in a desirable area, and employment security relatively more important to employees.	Earnings, recognition, advancement, and challenge relatively more important to employees.
Managers relatively less interested in leadership, independence, and self-realization.	Managers have leadership, independence, and self-realization ideal.
Belief in group decisions.	Belief in the independent decision maker.
Students less interested in recognition.	Students aspire to recognition (admiration for the strong).
Weaker achievement motivation.	Stronger achievement motivation.
Achievement defined in terms of human contacts and living environment.	Achievement defined in terms of recognition and wealth.
Work less central in people's lives.	Greater work centrality.
People prefer shorter working hours to more salary.	People prefer more salary to shorter working hours.
Company's interference in private life rejected.	Company's interference in private life accepted.
Greater social role attributed to other institutions than corporation.	Greater social role attributed to corporation.
Employees like small companies.	Employees like large corporations.
Entire population more attracted to smaller organizations.	Entire population more attracted to larger organization.
Lower job stress.	Higher job stress.
Less skepticism as to factors leading to getting ahead.	Skepticism as to factors leading to getting ahead.
Students more benevolent (sympathy for the weak).	Students less benevolent.
Managers have more of a service ideal.	Managers relatively less attracted by service role.
"Theory X" strongly rejected.	"Theory X" (employees dislike work) gets some support.
More women in jobs with mixed sex composition.	Fewer women in jobs with mixed sex composition.
Smaller or no value differences between men and women in the same jobs.	Greater value differences between men and women in the same jobs.
Sex role equality in children's books.	More sex role differentiation in children's books.

Source: G. Hofstede, *Culture's Consequences: International Differences in Work-Related Values,* pp. 200–201. Copyright © 1980 Sage Publications. Reprinted by permission of Sage Publications, Inc.

or because of the particular sociocultural milieu within which the employees and the companies exist. Research in this area in the past two decades has expanded our knowledge of dimensions of corporate culture in several ways.

Bond and Hofstede's Confucian Dynamism

Although the four dimensions Hofstede originally described in his work seemed applicable to companies and cultures around the world, some scientists raised questions about their adequacy in the Asian business world. While dimensions such as IC, PD, UA, and MA are indeed important markers of culture in Asia, other values seem to be at work in Asian companies that are not fully described by Hofstede's original four dimensions. To investigate this possibility further, Michael Bond and his colleagues, in collaboration with Hofstede (Chinese Culture Connection, 1987; Hofstede & Bond, 1988), have studied the work-related values and psychological characteristics of workers and organizations in Asian countries. No doubt much of the impetus for this line of research has been the surge in industry and business success of the "five dragons" of Asia: Japan, Hong Kong, Korea, Taiwan, and China.

Through their work, these researchers have identified a fifth important dimension of work-related values: **Confucian dynamism**. Many of the principles and values found to be important to Asian companies are thought to be rooted in Confucian thought and principles, including:

- Unequal status relationships lead to a stable society.
- The family is typical of all social organizations.
- Virtue in life consists of working hard, acquiring useful skills and as much education as possible, not being a spendthrift, and persevering when faced with difficult tasks.

These principles translate to abstract values that play an important role not only in interpersonal relationships in business but also as organizational goals and principles. These values include persistence and perseverance, relationships ordered by status, preservation of this order, thrift, and a sense of shame. Also important are values that enforce personal steadiness and stability; protection of face and outward stance; respect for tradition, custom, history, and heritage; and reciprocation of favors, greetings, and gifts. Many writers have suggested that these values stand at the core of many Asian cultures, permeating work and organizational life as an important cultural dimension above and beyond those originally identified by Hofstede.

Other Research on Organizational Culture

Since the original publication of Hofstede's work, a number of scientists have taken up the call to study in more depth corporate culture from the standpoint of work-related values. In general, these studies not only confirm the importance of Hofstede's original work, but expand and improve our knowledge in this area.

Hofstede (1996a) himself, since his original study, has gone on to collect more data from IBM subsidiaries around the world, expanding on the original database that served as the foundation for the first set of findings. In addition, he has done a considerable amount of work to link the four dimensions of culture with characteristics of the countries to which they are related, such as geography, climate, educational levels, and the like. He has analyzed specific companies in terms of the kinds of cultural values they harbor, and has conducted many case studies analyzing the success and failure of organizational development activities in these companies. In many of these cases, he has shown how developmental or training activities that are not congruent with the underlying cultural values of the organization face a difficult path at best, and at worst are doomed to fail. His point is that understanding the psychological dimensions underlying companies is a necessary component of successful plan development for training and other organizational activities.

Research by other scholars has shed additional light on the nature of cultural differences in work-related values around the world. Trompenaars (1993), for example, reported data from about 15,000 respondents, ranging across 30 companies in 50 different countries. A 79-item survey sampling seven different dimensions was administered to all participants. Analysis of the data indicated that seven factors were particularly relevant to predicting intercultural differences among the countries, and to the conduct of international business. These factors are universalism versus particularism, individualism versus collectivism, neutral versus emotional, specific versus diffuse, achievement versus ascription, time orientation, and attitude toward the environment. Universalism versus particularism refers to the degree to which people emphasize relationships with others (particularism) as opposed to using standards that are independent of specific social relationships. Achievement versus ascription refers to the characteristics that determine a person's status. Status afforded because of an accomplishment (such as academic or athletic achievement) is achieved status. Status afforded because of a nonaccomplishment characteristic (such as a hereditary title) is ascribed status.

Smith, Dugan, and Trompenaars (1996), following up on these ideas, sampled 8,841 employees from 43 different countries on these dimensions and others. They submitted their data to a statistical technique known as multidimensional scaling, which identifies dimensions that may underlie the ratings provided by the participants and reduces the data to a smaller set of dimensions that seem to account for the data. Three dimensions were found to be important in differentiating among the cultures in this study: achievement versus ascription, individualism–collectivism, and a combination dimension that included elements of the first two along with elements of power distance, Confucian dynamism, egalitarianism, and integration. These authors argued that Hofstede's original IC and PD dimensions may be better described as representing different orientations to continuity in group membership (loyal versus utilitarian involvement) and toward obligations in social relationships (conservative versus egalitarian commitment).

Hofstede (1996b), however, reanalyzed Trompenaars' (1993) data on the country or ecological level rather than the individual level. Using factor analyses and correlational techniques, he found that only two of Trompenaars' seven dimensions could be confirmed statistically: individualism/achievement and universalism/diffuse. Moreover, Hofstede (1996b) reported that both these dimensions were correlated with his own Individualism index. Thus, it appears possible that the set of dimensions on the individual employee level may differ slightly from the dimensions found on the ecological or country level.

Recently, some research has been conducted on dimensions other than those proposed by Hofstede. Furnham and associates (1993), for example, had 1,688 participants from 13 countries complete seven scales designed to measure Protestant work ethics. The results indicated highly significant differences between countries, and these differences were consistent across measures. Participants from industrialized countries tended to have lower scores than those from Third World countries. In addition, scores for the countries were highly positively correlated with Hofstede's dimension of power distance, and negatively correlated with individualism.

Collectively, the findings from recent research suggest that many of Hofstede's original cultural dimensions may be appropriate for describing ecological level differences in cultural values across countries. In addition, a fifth dimension—Confucian dynamism—may be especially important for Asian companies and cultures. Other dimensions may be important for understanding cultural differences on the individual, rather than the ecological, level.

Measuring Organizational Culture

Although the research on organizational culture has been influential in all fields of cross-cultural psychology, its practical applications have been especially apparent in actual work settings. Much of the emphasis on corporate culture in the fields of business and management today is based on this research. Many people quickly realized the relevance of the topic to their everyday work lives, and the importance of understanding organizational culture from a business standpoint. For this reason, researchers of the past 10 to 15 years have been hard at work developing methods of assessing organizational culture that can be directly applied to the corporate business world.

A number of applied scales assessing organizational culture have been developed over the past decade. Rosseau (1990) reviewed seven such scales: the Norms Diagnostic Index (Allen & Dyer, 1980), the Kilmann–Saxton Culture-Gap Survey (Kilmann & Saxton, 1983), the Organizational Culture Inventory (Human Synergistics, 1986), the Organizational Value Congruence Scale (Enz, 1986), the Organizational Culture Profile (O'Reilly, Chatman, & Caldwell, 1988), the Organizational Beliefs Questionnaire (Sashkin & Fulmer, 1985), and the Corporate Culture Survey (Glaser, 1983). Other scales have been developed since the time of this review, including Beach's (1993) Organizational

Culture Survey. Like much of the research on work-related values, all of these scales focus on cultural norms, attitudes, or values held by employees. The Organizational Culture Inventory, for example, focuses on behavioral norms that facilitate fitting into the organization and meeting the expectations of coworkers. Likewise, the Organizational Culture Profile measures values regarding what is important, how to behave, and what attitudes are appropriate.

One limitation of these approaches is that they are focused almost exclusively on the level of the individual. Although this level of culture is clearly pervasive and important in any social group, including organizations, it is not the only level of culture that needs to be understood. As discussed earlier in this chapter, organizational culture is a dynamic, multilevel construct that exists not only at the level of individual employees, but also across departments and business units within an organization and among organizations in a larger national and international business milieu. Thus, while it is important to capture individual-level culture, a complete picture of organizational culture needs to address the intra- and interorganizational levels as well.

For example, companies generally develop their own sets of rules, attitudes, values, beliefs, and attitudes regarding intraorganization functioning. Rules exist for communication and interaction among department units within companies. Policies exist for human resources, promotion, raises, and pay. Policies exist for training, length of employment, and many other intraorganizational factors. Laws exist that govern how businesses can work with each other, and international business laws exist to dictate how corporations can interact across national borders. All of these constitute levels of corporate culture above and beyond the culture that individuals bring with them to work.

Until recently, no assessment technique has captured all three levels of organizational culture (individual, intraorganizational, and interorganizational). In the past two years, however, Colvin and her colleagues (Colvin et al., 1997; Colvin, Matsumoto, Taylor, & Takeuchi, 1998; Matsumoto et al., 1997) have developed such a measure, called the Multi-Level Organizational Culture Profile (MLOCP). Based on contemporary research in the area of business, management, and industrial/organizational psychology, these researchers identified the most salient characteristics of five types of organizational classifications: start-up companies, bureaucracies, total quality management (TQM) companies, learning organizations, and world-class organizations (see, for example, Hodgetts, Luthans, & Lee, 1994). For each type, they identified characteristics at each level of corporate culture, and organized them into five domains: cultural factors (individual); human resources, performance, and organizational structure (intraorganizational); and environmental factors (interorganizational). Each domain consists of approximately 20 items that survey values, attitudes, norms, and practices pertinent to that domain. Company representatives describe the company by rating the degree to which each item is characteristic of their company, and scores are generated for each item and across items within each domain. Sample items from each of the five domains surveying the three levels of organizational culture are provided in Table 17.5.

Table 17.5 Sample Items from Colvin et al.'s MLOCP

HUMAN RESOURCE SYSTEMS *Indicate the extent to which you agree that your company . . .*	Disagree	Tend to Disagree	Neither Agree nor Disagree	Tend to Agree	Agree
1. has a formalized training and career development system	..1..	..2..	..3..	..4..	..5..
2. relies on external suppliers to provide training	..1..	..2..	..3..	..4..	..5..
3. spends an adequate amount of its HR budget on training	..1..	..2..	..3..	..4..	..5..
4. provides continuous performance feedback to employees	..1..	..2..	..3..	..4..	..5..
5. formally evaluates HR practices such as selection/training	..1..	..2..	..3..	..4..	..5..

CULTURAL FACTORS *Indicate the extent to which you agree that your company values . . .*	Disagree	Tend to Disagree	Neither Agree nor Disagree	Tend to Agree	Agree
1. innovation	..1..	..2..	..3..	..4..	..5..
2. participation in decision-making	..1..	..2..	..3..	..4..	..5..
3. team contributions	..1..	..2..	..3..	..4..	..5..
4. commitment to the job and the organization	..1..	..2..	..3..	..4..	..5..
5. life-long employment	..1..	..2..	..3..	..4..	..5..

ORGANIZATIONAL STRUCTURE *Indicate the extent to which you agree that your company . . .*	Disagree	Tend to Disagree	Neither Agree nor Disagree	Tend to Agree	Agree
1. on average, has a small span of control	..1..	..2..	..3..	..4..	..5..
2. has jobs that are highly specialized	..1..	..2..	..3..	..4..	..5..
3. is a mechanistic organization	..1..	..2..	..3..	..4..	..5..
4. uses a just-in-time production strategy	..1..	..2..	..3..	..4..	..5..
5. makes decisions that are bound by rules, policies, and procedures	..1..	..2..	..3..	..4..	..5..

ENVIRONMENTAL FACTORS *Indicate the extent to which you agree that your company . . .*	Disagree	Tend to Disagree	Neither Agree nor Disagree	Tend to Agree	Agree
1. has a global orientation	..1..	..2..	..3..	..4..	..5..
2. is unaffected by changes in the environment.............................	..1..	..2..	..3..	..4..	..5..
3. exists within a regulated industry	..1..	..2..	..3..	..4..	..5..
4. competes intensely with other organizations	..1..	..2..	..3..	..4..	..5..
5. is bound by few state and federal laws	..1..	..2..	..3..	..4..	..5..

PERFORMANCE *Indicate the extent to which you agree that your company defines organizational effectiveness in terms of . . .*	Disagree	Tend to Disagree	Neither Agree nor Disagree	Tend to Agree	Agree
1. profitability	..1..	..2..	..3..	..4..	..5..
2. market share	..1..	..2..	..3..	..4..	..5..
3. productivity..	..1..	..2..	..3..	..4..	..5..
4. meeting its customer satisfaction goals	..1..	..2..	..3..	..4..	..5..
5. survival	..1..	..2..	..3..	..4..	..5..

In an initial study using the MLOCP, Colvin and colleagues (1997) asked human resource managers at 31 American companies to describe their company using the MLOCP. In addition, they were asked to complete a number of quantitative and open-ended questions concerning their company. Correlations were then computed between each of the items on all five domains and the company's self-classification as a start-up, bureaucracy, TQM, learning, or world-class organization (ranked in this order). The results indicated that a substantial number of items in each domain were significantly correlated with organizational type. World-class organizations, for example, were associated with risk taking, change, and team contributions (cultural values); long-term business plans and formal upward communication systems (organizational structure); an adequate HR training budget and job rotation (HR systems); adaptability to change in the environment and development of strategic alliances with other organizations (environment); and profitability, market share, and productivity (performance).

In a subsequent study using the MLOCP, Matsumoto and colleagues (1998) compared the original 31 American companies with 41 Japanese companies. Two sets of analyses were conducted. First, the researchers correlated each of the items in each of the domains with organizational type, separately for each country, replicating the earlier findings. For the American companies, the following dimensions were found to be predictive of organizational type: dynamic collectivism, strategic environmental positioning, systematic flexibility in HR, horizontal hierarchies, and achievement through meeting dynamic customer needs. For Japanese companies, the dimensions predictive of organizational type were quality and adaptability through fairness, reactive orientations to the environment, skilled and flexible employees, autocratic structure, and non-immediacy in performance.

The second analysis involved a direct comparison of American and Japanese responses on each of the items. The researchers found statistically significant differences in each domain, with some items being rated higher by Americans, and some rated higher by Japanese. For example, in the cultural factors domain, Americans rated higher than Japanese on commitment to job and organization, workforce diversity, respect for authority, and ethical behavior; the Japanese rated higher on lifelong employment and conformity. In the domain of performance, Americans rated higher on public image and obtaining new investors and sources of funding; the Japanese rated higher on profitability, low employee turnover, and stability. These findings are generally congruent with previous comparisons of Japanese and American businesses (for example, Ebrahimpour & Johnson, 1992), but go beyond them by incorporating assessments and comparisons of multiple levels of cultural variables in the same set of companies.

The advantage of multilevel assessments of culture is that they give researchers and persons in applied positions—such as trainers, organizational consultants, and business executives—the tools with which to understand organizational culture as an organized and integrated system that involves both macro- and micro-level factors. Such an approach incorporates individuals within a larger social system, addressing both systemic and individual differences. Multilevel assessment of organizational culture, therefore, represents an evolution not only in our theoretical understanding of organizational cultures, but also in the methods by which we can study and characterize them.

Some Practical Implications of Organizational Culture

Our increased awareness of the nature and function of organizational culture has brought about a growing interest in the practical implications of organizational culture in business and places of work. An increasing number of studies have examined these implications in the past ten years, and they provide important information concerning real-life issues involving organizational culture. Some studies, for example, have examined the role of organizational culture in producing or mitigating stress perceived by employees (for example, Peterson, 1997; Peterson & Smith, 1997; Thompson, Stradling, Murphy, & O'Neill, 1996). Peterson (1997) suggests that not only does the specific work that people do create stress; so does the culture in which they work. Some organizational cultures may produce stress by their very nature (Thompson et al., 1996) or through the historical evolution of cultural values in the company (Peterson & Smith, 1997).

One topic that has gained prominence not only in the scientific literature but also in applied work is the issue of cultural fit between person and company. Given the work conducted in the past two decades on organizational culture, and the work that has been done for years on individual culture, a logical question concerns the match between employees and the cultures they come from and a company and its organizational culture. Do "mismatches" create conflicts? Do successful "matches" lead to more productive companies?

To address these types of questions, Bochner and Hesketh (1994) examined Hostede's dimensions of power distance (PD) and individualism (IN) in 263 employees of a multinational company, representing 28 different countries. Participants completed a questionnaire that measured more concrete work-related attitudes, such as superior–subordinate relationships, decision-making styles, work ethic, task orientation, psychological contracts, and individual-versus group-level achievements. The researchers classified respondents according to their country's rankings on PD and IN in Hofstede's previous data, and examined differences between high- and low-PD and high- and low-IN countries. They found that respondents in high-PD cultures were less open with their superiors, had more contact with them, and described supervision as being more close and direct. These respondents were also more task-oriented, and showed a greater tendency to believe that some people are inherently lazy and find work noxious. The results for IN indicated that collectivists had more informal contact with fellow workers, knew staff better, and were more likely to work on a team than alone. The researchers also classified respondents in terms of ingroups or outgroups, and found that when people of opposing work-related values interact daily and cooperatively, difficulties still arise, even though the interactions occur on an equitable basis. In particular, there were major differences between these two groups in perceived discrimination, attitudes toward multiculturalism, and counternormative behavior.

Abrams, Ando, and Hinkle (1998) examined cross-cultural differences in organizational identification and subjective norms as predictors of workers' turnover intentions. In their study, employees of companies in Great Britain and Japan completed questionnaires related to turnover intentions, attitudes toward leaving the organization, subjective norms regarding perceived approval for leaving, and organizational identification. In the British sample, turnover intentions were predicted by organizational identification; workers with stronger identifications with the company had lower turnover intentions. In the Japanese sample, however, turnover intentions were associated with both organizational identification and subjective norms. These findings suggest that, while social identity is strongly associated with employee turnover in both cultures, subjective normative aspects of group membership play a larger role in predicting turnover in Japan than they do in Great Britain.

Research has also documented positive aspects of employee–company cultural congruence. Meglino, Ravlin, and Adkins (1989), for example, questioned 191 production workers, 17 supervisors, and 13 managers on job satisfaction and organization commitment; they also collected objective data concerning attendance, performance, and efficiency. Two measures of employees' values congruence were computed and correlated with all psychological and behavioral data. Correlational analyses indicated that workers who were more satisfied and committed had values that were congruent with those of their supervisor.

These findings raise important questions concerning the nature of personnel selection in all companies and cultures today, especially in the United States with its diverse workforce population. Adding to the complexity of these issues are the cultural and ethnic differences in career choices of today's young adults (Kim, 1993) and perceived past and future barriers to career development (Luzzo, 1993). Finding an appropriate match between employer and employee is a daunting task for both individuals and organizations, as neither side profits from an unsuitable relationship or unhappy employees.

The literature of the past few years includes a number of approaches to personnel selection and training, all of which demonstrate an increasing sensitivity to cultural issues. For example, Love, Bishop, Heinish, and Montei (1994) have described the adaptations and modifications they made to a selection system for hiring American workers in a Japanese–American joint venture assembly plant. During the 1980s, the number of such joint ventures between the United States and Japan increased dramatically, particularly in the automotive industry. Today, there are many such ventures, not only with Japanese companies but with companies from many different cultures. In addition, an increasing number of American companies are establishing themselves in other countries and cultures, raising the same issues overseas. In their work, Love and colleagues (1994) modified job analysis procedures and traditional selection systems to accommodate Japanese culture and management philosophy. They then engaged in a series of steps to validate their system cross-culturally to ensure compatibility with Japanese management demands regarding productivity, team orientation, quality standards, and formal employee performance evaluations. It is particularly interesting to note the reason why the selection system could not be compared with performance criteria data on individuals:

> After submitting a formal proposal to develop a performance appraisal system, in part for validation purposes, and meeting with management, it quickly became obvious that Japanese management philosophy prohibits such a practice. Differentiating between employees on the basis of job performance is an affront to Japanese cultural beliefs which prefer a homogeneous workforce (Maher & Wong, 1994). In particular, Japanese managers suggested that individual performance appraisals would damage the "team" concept, held in high esteem throughout the plant. (p. 843)

Thus, organizational culture and the fit between employee and company are real-life issues that have important implications in our everyday lives. Organizations have begun to struggle with the issue of cultural match between employee and company, and new ways of assimilating newcomers into organizations are constantly being developed from a cultural perspective (see, for example, Hess, 1993). Although most research approaches this issue from the organization's point of view, some writing has also addressed efforts by employees to assess the fit between themselves and the culture of the organization to which they are applying (for example, Pratt, 1993). Systematic research on these issues is still young, and we have much to learn. What constitutes a "successful" or "unsuccessful" match? How do we make these assessments? In some cultures, as Love et al. discovered, making such assessments may be counter to the prevailing cultural norms. And how valid is the suggestion that all personnel selection decisions should be informed by matches? Are there optimal levels of mismatches that may spur on maximal performance? For example, although individualism is usually associated with creativity and initiative, at least one study has shown that innovation and entrepreneurship is highest under conditions of balanced individualism and collectivism, and lowest in either highly individualistic or highly collectivistic corporations (Morris, Avila, & Allen, 1993). Could such an effect exist within organizations as well?

Summary

Clearly, the research indicates that culture plays an important role in influencing work organizations as a whole, as well as their individual members. Culture influences organizational goals, structures, and functions. Culture also influences employee attitudes, values, behaviors, and interpersonal dynamics. The dimensions that Hofstede, Bond, and others have identified are extremely useful in helping us understand how and why these cultural differences exist. Researchers have developed a number of ways of measuring organizational culture, and we know that differences in organizational culture have many important ramifications on our work lives.

As we leave this section on organizational culture, I would like to comment on the widespread perception that individuals may lose a part of themselves and a part of their individual culture when they become employees of an organization with its own culture. Certainly, many people approach this topic with considerable fear and apprehension. Research on organizational climate or corporate culture, however, has not provided support for such a loss of cultural identity or values. Berry and associates (1992) reviewed several studies that examined correlations between organizational climate and actual employee attitudes and productivity. In general, these studies found very little correlation.

Undoubtedly, employees need to learn organizational rules concerning proper behavior, but these rules are learned relatively late in their personal development. After all, people have been learning the rules of their culture since birth. Organizational culture may refer more to "values related shared daily practices in the workplace" (Berry et al., 1992, p. 322) than to shared values of life, which is more akin to our understanding of culture. Thus, it may be more accurate to suggest that employees of an organization all learn to engage temporarily in the organizational culture while they are within the organization. That is, they learn to work and function within a "temporary culture" that is added to the cultural milieu within which they normally operate. This temporary culture exists as an entity separate from more basic cultural values and does not necessarily change the fundamental self outside of the work environment. Rather, it is a limited and contextualized version of culture that people move into and out of in their daily lives. Thus, although a tangible climate exists within corporations and organizations, it does not replace or detract from our individual cultures.

Culture and the Meaning of Work

In the rest of this chapter, we turn our attention from cultural influences on organizations to the ways in which culture influences specific work-related behaviors in individuals. We begin by examining how people of different cultures define work differently, or derive different meanings from work.

People construe themselves and their existence in relation to work differently across cultures, and these differences are related to meaningful dimensions of cultural variability. As discussed in Chapter 3, people who are members of collectivistic cultures tend to have interdependent construals of self; that is, they tend to see people around them as fundamentally interrelated with themselves and as integral parts of their self-identity. Thus, people of collectivistic cultures may view their work groups and the work organizations (companies) to which they belong as a fundamental part of themselves. Work, work colleagues, and the company become synonymous with the self. The bonds between these people and their work colleagues, and between themselves and their company, are stronger and qualitatively different from those of people in individualistic cultures.

Individualistic cultures, by contrast, tend to foster a view of self as independent, unique, and autonomous from others. People in individualistic cultures thus have an easier time separating themselves from their jobs. They make greater distinctions between "work time" and "personal time," and between company-based expense accounts and personal expenses. They also make greater distinctions between social and work activities, with regard to both their work colleagues and their business associates (potential clients, customers, and so forth).

Cultural differences in the meaning of work can manifest themselves in other aspects of work as well. For example, in American culture, it is easy to think of work simply as a means to accumulate money (pay or salary) and make a living. In other cultures, especially collectivistic ones, work may be seen more as fulfilling an obligation to a larger group. In this situation, we would expect to find less movement of individuals from one job to another because of the individual's social obligations toward the work organization to which he or she belongs and to the people comprising that organization. In individualistic cultures, it is easier to consider leaving one job and going to another because it is easier to separate jobs from the self. A different job will just as easily accomplish the same goals.

Of course, the fact that people come from different cultures does not necessarily mean that they think about work entirely differently. For example, in a study involving British and Japanese employees (Abrams et al., 1998), we saw that organizational identification was an important predictor of turnover attitudes in both cultures. Thus, people of different cultures exhibit important similarities as well as differences. Nonetheless, cultural differences in the meaning of work appear to be related to cultural differences in a number of work-related behaviors, including motivation and productivity, leadership and management styles, and decision-making processes.

Culture, Motivation, and Productivity

One important issue all companies, work organizations, and businesses must address is the degree to which their employees will be productive in various types of work settings. All companies want to maximize productivity while minimizing personnel costs and the expenditure of other resources, thereby ensuring the greatest profit margins. This concern has led to an important area of research on productivity as a function of group size.

Early research on group productivity in the United States typically showed that individual productivity tends to decline in larger groups (Latané, Williams, & Harkins, 1979). These findings contributed to the coining of the term **social loafing.** Two factors appear to contribute to this phenomenon. One is reduced efficiency resulting from a lack of coordination among workers' efforts, resulting in lack of activity or duplicate activity. The second factor is a reduction in effort by individuals when they work in groups as compared to when they work by themselves. Latané (1981) and his colleagues (Latané et al., 1979) conducted a number of studies investigating group size, coordination, and effort. They found that in larger groups, both lack of coordination and reduced effort resulted in decreased productivity. Latané (1981) attributed these findings to a diffusion of responsibility in groups. As group size increases, the responsibility for getting a job done is divided among more people, and group members ease up because their individual contribution is less recognizable.

Early cross-cultural research on groups and their productivity, however, found exactly the opposite phenomenon in other cultures. Earley (1989) examined social loafing in an organizational setting among managerial trainees in the United States and in the People's Republic of China. Subjects in both cultures worked on a task under conditions of low or high accountability and low or high shared responsibility. The results clearly indicated social loafing for the American subjects, whose individual performances in a group were less than when working alone, but not for the Chinese.

Shirakashi (1985) and Yamaguchi, Okamoto, and Oka (1985) conducted studies involving Japanese participants in several tasks. They found that not only did social loafing not occur, but exactly the opposite occurred. Working in a group enhanced individual performance rather than diminished it. Gabrenya, Wang, and Latané (1985) also demonstrated this **social striving** in a sample of Chinese schoolchildren.

Several authors have speculated as to why social striving is observed in other cultures. These explanations center around the culture's degree of collectivism or group orientation. Cultures that are more collectivistic (such as China and Japan) foster interpersonal interdependence and group collective functioning more than does the individualistic American culture. Groups tend to be more productive in these cultures precisely because they foster coordination among ingroup members. These cultures also place higher values on individual contributions in group settings.

Interestingly, this trend may also be occurring in the United States, at least partially as a result of the influence of Asian, especially Japanese, business practices that focus on teamwork, cooperation, and quality (see Ebrahimpour & Johnson, 1992; Hodgetts et al., 1994). As a result of studying successful business practices overseas, many American companies have tried to adapt and adopt some of these practices, including increasing teamwork, in their daily work behaviors. Although many of the early efforts were unsuccessful and difficult, the past decade has seen considerable improvement and progress in this area.

Indeed, several studies involving American participants have begun to challenge the traditional notion of social loafing (for example, Harkins, 1987; Harkins & Petty, 1982; Shepperd & Wright, 1989; Weldon & Gargano, 1988; Zaccaro, 1984). Jackson and Williams (1985), for instance, reported that Americans working collectively improved performance and productivity. In a more recent study, Westaby (1995) asked participants in the United States and Japan to complete a paper-and-pen tracing task, either individually or in the presence of a group. Although the author expected that the Japanese would perform better in the group situation, the effect of group presence was actually the same for Americans and Japanese. Participants of both cultures had higher productivity and job quality in the presence of a group than when working alone. Further analyses indicated that, although Japanese participants had higher productivity than American participants in general (regardless of social context), there was no difference in the quality of the work. Thus, our notions of social loafing and group productivity are now being challenged not only cross-culturally but also within American culture.

Other recent research continues to complement our knowledge of cultural influences on social loafing, social striving, and group-related work behaviors. Wagner (1995), for example, had 492 students complete questionnaires assessing the degree to which they perceived a shared responsibility with others, identifiability with others, individualism and collectivism, and cooperation. They participated in groups of different sizes, producing a group report that required cooperation among group members. The results indicated that individualists who felt independent and less reliant were less apt to engage in cooperative behavior, whereas collectivists who felt interdependent and reliant on groups were more likely to behave cooperatively. These findings suggest that there may be a relationship between individualistic cooperation and social loafing, but that the same relationship cannot explain cooperation in collectivists.

Finally, as more recent research has uncovered social striving effects among work groups with American participants, an increasing number of scientists are turning their efforts to understanding the mechanisms underlying such social striving in an individualistic culture. Some scholars have suggested that one way in which work groups and teams can become more productive in an individualistic culture is through the use of constructive thought patterns that help to transform self-managing teams into self-leading teams (for example, Manz, 1992; Neck & Manz, 1994). The idea is that employees become empowered to influence strategic issues concerning what they do and why, in addition to how they do their work. Again, these suggestions highlight the notion that different bases may underlie productivity or nonproductivity in different cultural groups.

With increased American interest in the organizational and management styles of other countries, this topic is sure to receive even more attention in the future. A central question is bound to revolve around the best combination of ingredients (such as group size, nature of the individuals, nature of the tasks) to maximize social striving among all participants and to minimize social loafing. Recent economic necessities have forced many companies and organizations to consider spending less on personnel, resulting in "downsizing" or, more recently, "rightsizing." With fewer people doing more work, people in successful business organizations have been forced to reevaluate and redefine their own identities within their work groups in a more collectivistic way, for the success of the business unit and their own survival. The research conducted to date seems to suggest that groups from all types of cultures may experience social striving or social loafing. Which outcome occurs depends on a host of factors, including group size, identifiability, shared responsibility, and culture. Exactly which factors influence which outcomes in what ways is not yet clear, and more research is clearly needed. The picture that emerges so far is that the specific ingredients that result in striving or loafing are different in different cultural milieus.

Culture, Leadership, and Management Styles

Given that organizations and the people who are members of them differ so much across cultures, it is no surprise that leadership and management styles of people in power in those organizations also differ. But before we can understand these differences, we need to realize that the definition of leadership and management differs across cultures.

Cultural Differences in the Definition of Leadership and Management

In many industrialized cultures, **leadership** can be defined as the "process of influence between a leader and followers to attain group, organizational, or societal goals" (Hollander, 1985, p. 486). Leaders may be autocratic, dictatorial, democratic, and so on. In common language, we speak of "strong" and "effective" leaders as opposed to "weak" and "ineffective" ones. In many work situations, especially in the United States, we expect leaders to have vision, authority, and power and to give subordinates tasks that have meaning in a larger picture. In American culture, leaders are expected to be decision makers, "movers and shakers" of organizations and people.

In other cultures, leaders may share many of these same traits, but their leadership and managerial styles are not necessarily seen as dynamic or action-oriented. For example, some of the most effective leaders and managers in organizations in India are seen as much more nurturing, taking on a parental role within the company and in relation to their subordinates (Sinha, 1980). These leaders are seen as much more participative, guiding and directing their subordinates' tasks and behaviors as opposed to merely giving directives. Still, leaders and managers in India need to be flexible, at times becoming very authoritative in their work roles. Thus, the optimal leadership style in India, according to Sinha, is somewhere between a totally participative and totally authoritative style.

Another way leadership and managerial styles differ across cultures is in the boundaries of that leadership. In American culture, for example, workers make a clear distinction between work and personal life. When 5:00 P.M. arrives and the bell to end work rings, many American workers consider themselves "off" from work and on their personal time. The boundary between work and their personal lives is very clear. Leaders, bosses, and others in the company should have nothing to say about how members of the company live their personal lives (for example, where they should live or whom they should marry). In other cultures, however, the boundaries between work and personal life are less clear. In many countries, the individual's existence at work becomes an integral part of the self. Thus, the distinction between work and company, on the one hand, and one's personal life, on the other, is fuzzy and blurred. Needless to say, leaders in such cultures can request overtime work from their subordinates and expect to receive it with much less griping than in American culture.

As the distinction between work and self becomes blurred, so do the boundaries of jurisdiction for leaders. For example, leaders and managers in India and Japan are expected to look after their subordinates in terms of their work and existence within the company; but it is not uncommon for leaders to be concerned with their subordinates' personal, private lives as well. Subordinates in these cultures will not hesitate to consult with their bosses about problems at home and to seek advice and help from them about those problems. Leaders, more often than not, will see helping their subordinates with this part of their lives as an integral and important part of their jobs. In India and Japan, it is not uncommon for bosses to find marriage partners for their subordinates and to look after them inside as well as outside the company. The bond between them extends well beyond the company.

As with many other cultural differences, differences in the definition and boundaries of leaders and managers are related to individualism–collectivism (IC). As we have seen, people in collectivistic cultures identify themselves more with their work organizations and companies; they see their work and their company as an integral part of themselves. People in individualistic cultures see themselves as unique and autonomous beings; the distinction between themselves and their company is clear-cut. Thus, leaders and managers in collectivistic cultures see their responsibilities as extending beyond the work environment to a much greater extent than do managers in individualistic cultures.

Cross-Cultural Research on Leadership and Management

Given these cross-cultural differences in the definition of leadership, it is not surprising that many cross-cultural studies report differences in specific leadership behaviors (see, for example, Black & Porter, 1991, on managerial differences in the United States and Hong Kong; Okechuku, 1994, on managers' ratings of subordinates in Canada, Hong Kong, and China). Smith, Peterson, and Misumi (1994), for instance, obtained effectiveness ratings of work teams in electronics assembly plants in Japan, Great Britain, and the United States, as well as ratings of ten event management processes used by superiors. The results indicated that, for the Japanese, work performance was dependent on the relatively frequent use of manuals and procedures, and on relatively frequent guidance from supervisors. American and British supervisors, however, favored more contingent responses, suggesting that the preferred managerial response depends on the specific event or task that they are faced with.

Many other studies have documented cross-cultural differences in leadership and managerial style. Schmidt and Yeh (1992) found cross-national differences in leader influence strategies in Japan, Taiwan, Australia, and Great Britain. Howell and colleagues (1995) found cultural differences in decision making and contingent punishment in Japan, Korea, Taiwan, Mexico, and the United States. Gerstner and Day (1994) asked students from eight different countries to rate 59 traits of a business leader; they found that the ratings correlated highly with Hofstede's indices of IN, PD, and UA.

Some studies have attempted to identify culture-specific leadership and managerial styles. Many authors, for example, have tried to describe the Japanese management style (see, for example, the review by Keys & Miller, 1984), in hopes of adapting Japanese leadership and managerial practices to American industry. Similarly, Jou and Sung (1990) have described four managerial styles prevalent in Taiwan. No doubt much of this attention to Japan and other Asian countries was due to the widespread success of Asian companies and economies, including those of South Korea, Hong Kong, Taiwan, and mainland China. In the past five to ten years, however, the American economy and businesses appear to be doing relatively better in the world economy, while many Asian economies are struggling. These dynamic trends in the global economy are associated with an evolution in studies of managerial styles across cultures, and many authors are now questioning the long-term effectiveness of Asian managerial and leadership approaches of the past (see, for example, Keys, Denton, & Miller, 1994).

Not all cross-cultural research on this topic, however, has shown cultural differences; a substantial amount of literature documents cultural similarities in leadership behaviors as well. For example, Smith and colleagues (1992) examined work teams in Japan, Hong Kong, the United States, and Great Britain, and found that leaders who were rated high in behaviors related to task performance and group maintenance all achieved higher work quality. Smith (1998) also found consistent themes in a survey of managers' handling of day-to-day work events in Brazil, Mexico, Colombia, and Argentina. Many other studies (see review by Bond & Smith, 1996) show similar cross-cultural consistencies in some aspects of managerial behavior.

How are we to make sense of the literature that shows both similarities and differences across cultures in leadership and managerial behaviors? Misumi (1985) suggests that management involves general and universal functions that all effective leaders must carry out, but that the specific ways in which they are carried out may differ. Misumi (1985) contrasts functions related to task performance (P) and group maintenance (M), and suggests that both domains involve universal leadership goals that are consistent across cultures and companies. Different specific behaviors may be used to accomplish these managerial goals, however, depending on situations, companies, and cultures. This approach invites us to examine and understand human behavior on multiple levels—one level involving cross-cultural universals or similarities in functions and goals, the other involving differences in culture- and context-specific instrumental behaviors.

Intracultural and cross-cultural research has accomplished much in the way of documenting cross-cultural consistencies and differences in leadership behaviors. Less frequent in the literature, however, are studies that examine leadership and managerial effectiveness in intercultural settings. What happens, for example, when managers from other countries and cultures—Japan, Korea, Hong Kong, France, or Germany, for example—come to the United States and are placed in a situation in which they must manage and lead American subordinates? What happens when Americans are sent to other countries? Such situations occur frequently in today's global marketplace and are often central to the effective and successful functioning of companies. Yet research has been slow to address these complex questions. One study (Thomas & Toyne, 1995) suggests that American subordinates may respond best when managers from other cultures demonstrate moderate levels of adaptation to the American culture and employee; high or low levels of adaptation have less positive effects on the subordinates. More research on this important topic is obviously necessary to capture the essence of effective intercultural management, a situation that promises to become even more important in the future.

Culture and Decision-Making Processes

Making decisions is one of the most important things a company, or any organization, does. As with many other types of behaviors, culture influences how a company makes decisions.

Many organizations in the United States use a democratic decision-making procedure. In a democratic procedure, every person involved has a say in the decision, usually by way of a vote; once votes are tallied, the decision of the majority prevails. This procedure has advantages and disadvantages. A major advantage to this procedure is that everyone has an equal say in the process. Democratic decision making is associated with an individualistic cultural viewpoint, which tends to see each person as a separate, autonomous being.

One disadvantage to this process concerns the consequences of close votes. If a proposal wins only a bare majority (51%), then a large minority (up to 49%) may be less than enthusiastic in implementing the decision. This scenario can lead, and has indeed led, to sabotage and disruption in many organizations.

The democratic process can also lead to considerable red tape and bureaucracy. Many organizations, in fact, are not so much democracies as oligarchies (Ferrante, 1992). An **oligarchy** is an organizational structure characterized by rule or decision-making power of a few. Decisions are typically made by people "at the top," who then impose their decisions on subordinates. Sometimes the sheer size of organizations necessitates that they be oligarchies if decisions are to be made at all. If everyone were to be involved in all types of decisions, the bureaucratic process would simply be too unwieldy and time-consuming. This top-down approach to business decisions is characteristic of many American companies.

Cross-cultural research and the intercultural experiences of many business-persons reveal interesting differences in organizational decision making across cultures. One of the most studied cultures is that of Japan, because of its economic successes over the past few decades. (Similar decision-making procedures in other cultures are reviewed in Berry et al., 1992.) The Japanese process of decision making is known as the **ringi** system. In a Japanese company, there is no formal system by which every person is ensured a vote. Instead, a proposal is circulated among all people who will be affected by it, regardless of status, rank, or position. Initiatives for proposals can come from top, middle, or lower management, or from subordinates within a business section. Even before a proposal is formally circulated among all interested parties, there is often considerable discussion and debate about the proposal. All views are taken into account, so that the proposal, when written and formally circulated, addresses concerns and negative consequences raised by as many parties as possible. There is considerable consultation about the proposal on as broad a basis as possible, and consensus is achieved before the proposal is ever formally implemented. This broad-based, consensus-building procedure is called **nemawashi**. If proposals do not achieve consensus by this procedure, they do not appear formally. Proposals that have gone through this procedure and have received the blessing of all those affected are then put in the form of a formal proposal on paper. A routing of the proposal involves all section chiefs and managers before it gets to the person or persons on top, who then put their formal stamp of approval on it. Needless to say, by the time something gets to that stage, it has met with the approval of many people throughout the organization.

Like all decision-making procedures, the Japanese system has advantages and disadvantages. One of the major disadvantages is the time-consuming nature of the process. In fact, the inability of Japanese managers to make a decision on the spot in international negotiations is often a source of frustration for American negotiators, who are used to dealing with single decision makers. The Japanese negotiator, however, must contact all the people within the company affected by the impending decision prior to making that decision. An advantage of the Japanese system, however, is the speed with which decisions can be implemented. Although the Japanese typically take much more time making a decision, they can usually implement it relatively quickly. No doubt, having everyone briefed in advance about the proposal aids in speedy implementation. Also, people in a collectivistic culture are more likely to get behind a decision that is for the good of the company, whatever their personal feelings about it.

Cross-cultural studies of organizational decision making point out other important and interesting differences between cultures. Yates and Lee (1995), for example, found that people of East Asian cultures were more confident than Americans that their decisions were correct. To explain these findings, the authors suggest that people of East Asian cultures tend to select what may appear to be the first adequate solution to a problem that is identified, rather than considering a wide range of alternatives before deciding. Smith, Wang, and Leung (1997) obtained similar results in their study of 121 managers from mainland China, who reported strong reliance on widespread beliefs as a source of guidance when making decisions and handling various work events. Radford and associates (1991, 1993) found comparable differences between Australian and Japanese students. The Australians preferred careful, individual thought when making decisions; the Japanese preferred other strategies that involved more interpersonal dimensions. On an organizational level, Hall, Jiang, Loscocco, and Allen (1993) compared decision-making patterns in small businesses in China and the United States. They found that, in general, the Chinese organizations were more centralized than their American counterparts.

Weatherly and Beach (1998) conducted four studies that examined the relationship between organizational culture and decision making involving managers and employees from a number of commercial organizations. They found that the decisions made by an organization are generally influenced by the degree to which features of the options are compatible with features of the organization's own culture; the higher the degree of compatibility, the more likely it is that the decision will endorse that option. They also found that an organization's employees are more likely to endorse a management decision if features of the decision are compatible with features of the organizational culture. This study is important because it places organizational decision making within the larger context of organizational culture at multiple levels.

One particular problem that has plagued decision making in groups is "groupthink"—a collective pattern of thinking that hinders effective group decisions. Groupthink is generally characterized by direct pressure, self-censorship, illusions of invulnerability, unanimity, or morality, mind guarding, collective rationalization, and shared stereotypes (Janis, 1983). These types of processes may underlie social loafing and general apathy toward work and productivity. Such destructive thought patterns, however, can be transformed into constructive ones, or "teamthink" (Neck & Manz, 1994). Teamthink involves the encouragement of divergent views, open expression of concerns and ideas, awareness of limitations and threats, recognition of members' uniqueness, and discussion of collective doubts. These constructive patterns lead to more effective decision making. Such a process may be critical for many organizations in many cultures, and especially for increasingly diversified companies in the United States, because it may be one way of maintaining individuality while serving the collective common good of the organization.

In summary, while cross-cultural research has contributed considerably to our knowledge of cultural similarities and differences in decision-making processes, much more work remains to be done. Once again, the findings on decision making suggest there are both culture-specific and universal aspects to this organizational behavior. Although the particular ways in which decisions are made may vary across cultures, the underlying rationale for those decision processes—including views of decision making as extensions of the underlying organizational culture—may be similar. Future research should pursue these ideas of coexisting and complementary similarities and differences.

Intercultural Issues Regarding Business and Work

As companies become increasingly dependent on other companies in other countries and cultures for business survival and success, people today are facing an ever-larger number of intercultural issues in the workplace. Add to these organizational developments the increasingly porous and flexible nature of national borders, and the result is a large number of people of different cultural backgrounds, lifestyles, values, and behaviors living and working together. These social trends and changes bring their own particular set of issues, challenges, and opportunities regarding intercultural interactions in the workplace and other work-related situations.

For multinational corporations, international business is not just international; it is inter*cultural*. As we have seen throughout this chapter, business organizations are affected in many different ways by the cultures in which they reside. Organizational structures differ, organizational decision-making procedures differ, and people differ—in their definitions of work, work-related values, identification between self and company, and rules of interacting with other workers. Today's international business world requires that business organizations, and the people within them, gain intercultural competence as well as business competence.

In this final section of the chapter, we will discuss three broad areas in which intercultural issues have come to the fore in recent decades: international negotiation, overseas assignments, and working with an increasingly diverse workforce population.

International Negotiation

Improving communications technologies and changes in trade and tariff laws have resulted in an increasing interdependence among countries for economic and business survival. Not only multinational corporations but domestic companies too need to negotiate with companies in other countries to obtain resources, sell products, and conduct other business activities.

In the United States, Americans generally approach negotiation with a certain set of assumptions, summarized in Table 17.6 (Kimmel, 1994). In the United States, negotiation is a business, not a social activity. The objective of the negotiation is to get a job done, which usually requires a mixture of problem solving and bargaining. Communication is direct and verbal, with little deliberate or intentional use of nonverbal behaviors in the communication process.

Along with the 11 basic assumptions summarized in Table 17.6, Kimmel (1994) lists eight cultural values related to the American negotiation process:

1. *Time* is a commodity to be used efficiently to accomplish goals.
2. *Individual control.* You control your own destiny, and should do something about your life.

Table 17.6 U.S. Assumptions about Negotiating

Topic	Description
Conception of the negotiation process	Negotiation is a business, not a social activity. The object is to get a job done, which usually requires a mixture of problem-solving and bargaining activities. Most negotiations are adversarial, and negotiators are trying to get as much as possible for their side. The flow of a negotiation is from prenegotiation strategy sessions to opening sessions to give-and-take (bargaining) to final compromises to signing and implementation of agreements. All parties are expected to give up some of their original demands. Success can be measured in terms of how much each party achieves its bottom-line objectives.
Type of issues	Substantive issues are more important than social and emotional issues. Differences in positions are seen as problems to be solved.
Protocol	Negotiations are scheduled occasions that require face-to-face interactions among the parties involved. Efficiency of time centering on substantive tasks is valued over ceremony and social amenities. During negotiation, standardized procedures of interaction should be followed; social interactions are informal and should occur elsewhere.
Reliance on verbal behaviors	Communication is direct and verbal. What is said is more important than how it is said, or what is not said. Communications tend to be spontaneous and reactive after presentation of initial positions.
Nature of persuasive arguments	Tactics such as bluffing are acceptable in the bargaining process. Current information and ideas are more valid than history or tradition.
Individual negotiator's latitude	The representatives who negotiate have a great deal of latitude in reaching agreements for their companies.
Bases of trust	Negotiators trust the other parties until they prove untrustworthy. Trust is judged by the behavior of others.
Risk-taking propensities	Negotiators are open to different or novel approaches to problem issues. Brainstorming is good. Avoiding uncertainty is not important in the negotiation process. Fixed ideological positions and approaches are not acceptable.
Value of time	Time is very important. Punctuality is expected. A fixed time is allotted for concluding a negotiation.
Decision-making system	Majority voting and/or authoritative decisions are the rule. Certain team members are expected to be authorized to make binding decisions.
Forms of satisfactory agreement	Oral commitments are not binding. Written contracts that are exact and impersonally worded are binding. There is the expectation of contractual finality. Lawyers and courts are the final arbitrators in any arguments after contracts have been signed.

Source: Adapted from Kimmel, 1994.

3. *Specialization* is desirable in work and social relationships; there is little desire for consistency or harmony.
4. *Pragmatism.* There are few absolute truths; what works is good.
5. *Democracy.* Everyone with an interest in an issue should have a say in the process.
6. *Equal opportunity.* People should have equal opportunities to develop their abilities.
7. *Independence.* Authority is resisted, and everyone has a right to privacy.
8. *Competition.* One must compete with others to get ahead; achievements are rewarded through upward mobility and income.

Negotiation processes in other cultures, however, challenge many of these traditionally American assumptions. In the arena of international negotiation, negotiators come as representatives not only of their companies but of their cultures as well. They bring all the issues of culture—customs, rituals, rules, and heritage—to the negotiating table. Factors that we are not even aware of play a role in these negotiating sessions, such as the amount of space between the people, how to greet each other, what to call each other, and what kinds of expectations we have of each other. The "diplomatic dance" that has been observed between American and Arab negotiators is but one example. People from Arab cultures tend to interact with others at a much closer distance than Americans are accustomed to. As the Arabs move closer, Americans unconsciously edge backward, whereupon the Arabs unconsciously edge forward, until they are almost chasing each other around the room.

Many studies have examined the Japanese approach to negotiation (see, for example, Allerheiligen, Graham, & Lin, 1985; Goldman, 1994; Graham, 1983, 1984, 1993; Graham & Andrews, 1987), which challenges virtually all of the American assumptions. Graham and Andrews (1987), for example, videotaped American and Japanese participants during negotiation, then reviewed the videotapes with them to discuss negotiation processes and outcomes. One of the main concerns expressed by participants in both cultures involved language and communication processes. Indeed, even small cultural differences can have big effects on international business. In the Japanese language, for example, the word for yes (*hai*) is also used as a conversation regulator, signaling to others that you are listening to what they are saying (but not necessarily agreeing). American negotiators, hearing this word used as a regulator, often interpret it to mean yes. As you can imagine, considerable conflict can and does arise when, after using this word throughout the conversation, the Japanese take a contradictory position. To the Japanese, they were merely saying "um hmm," but to the Americans, it sounded like "yes." Such misunderstandings can lead to conflict, mistrust, the breakdown of negotiations, and the loss of business and good faith relations (see Okamoto, 1993).

One interesting cultural difference between American and Japanese approaches to negotiation is in entertainment. American businesspeople are used to "sitting down at the table and hammering out a deal." Japanese businesspeople may want to have dinner, have drinks, and play golf. The Japanese are more willing to engage in these activities because they are interested in developing a relationship with their business partners as people; it also gives them a good opportunity to make judgments about the character or integrity of potential partners, which is an important aspect of their business decisions. American businesspeople are primarily concerned with "the deal" and what is right for the company's bottom line. Many American business negotiators not used to the Japanese style of negotiating become impatient with these activities, feeling as though they never get to talk business. By the same token, many Japanese negotiators, put on the spot by American negotiators, feel as though they have been thrust into a situation and forced to make a decision they cannot possibly make. Needless to say, these cultural differences in negotiation styles have led to many a breakdown in international business negotiations.

Cross-cultural research on international negotiation has spanned other countries and cultures as well, including Brazil (Allerheiligen et al., 1985; Graham, 1983, 1984), China (Allerheiligen et al., 1985), Russia (Graham et al., 1992), Taiwan (Graham et al., 1988), Germany and Britain (Campbell et al., 1988), and Mexico and Canada (Adler et al., 1987). Many of these studies, like those on the Japanese process, demonstrate how people of different cultures approach negotiation from often quite different viewpoints. For example, Tse and colleagues (1994) examined Chinese and Canadian negotiation practices. They found that the Chinese sought to avoid conflict more than the Canadians did, and when conflict did occur, they opted for withdrawal or consultation with superiors more than the Canadians did. Context may also play an important role in the negotiation process, as people of collectivistic cultures tend to make a larger distinction between ingroup and outgroup members than do people of individualistic cultures. Thus, negotiation processes involving collectivistic cultures may differ drastically depending on the exact nature of the relationship between the negotiators (ingroup versus outgroup) and the exact context of the negotiation (formal meeting during the day at a company versus informal meeting after work in a bar).

The available research tells us little about the degree to which negotiators adjust their cultural practices depending on whom they are negotiating with, and on what parameters such adjustment occurs. Nor has cross-cultural research done much to elucidate the ingredients of a "successful" negotiation. Future studies are needed to examine these important questions regarding international/intercultural negotiations.

Overseas Assignments

Many multinational corporations with subsidiaries and business partners in other countries are finding it increasingly necessary to send workers abroad for extended periods of time. Worker exchanges and overseas assignments are used to train employees and business units in another country in skills that are found only there. Such overseas assignments can give rise to myriad problems, not only because of all the cultural differences discussed in this chapter, but also because of limited language skills and differing expectations of the person on assignment and his or her hosts.

American companies today would not hesitate to send "the most qualified person" on assignment, either for negotiation or long-term, regardless of sex, race, or ethnicity. Many other cultures, however, are not accustomed to women in important positions in business, and may not be totally receptive to people of different perceived races or ethnicities. In many contexts, a woman would not be taken as seriously as a man, and racial/ethnic stereotypes may dominate interactions. Resulting frustrations might include not being looked at during a conversation, or having questions directed to a man when a woman is the recognized leader or expert on an assignment team.

Many of the most pressing problems for people on overseas assignments occur not at work but in other aspects of living in a foreign country. Major differences in lifestyle, customs, and behaviors often overshadow cultural differences at work. If an individual goes on overseas assignment with his or her family, there is the added problem of their adjustment to the new culture, especially if school-age children are involved. The entire spectrum of intercultural adjustment and acculturation becomes important. Even when workers do well in their work environment, they may do poorly in their home and community adjustment. And while employees may find a safe haven during the workday in a milieu with which they are somewhat familiar, their families are often left bearing the brunt of intercultural adaptation. Interested readers should recall the material presented in Chapter 14 on intercultural communication and the development of intercultural sensitivity.

On the positive side, people who go on overseas assignments have a tremendous opportunity to learn new skills and new ways of doing their work that can help them when they return. They may learn a new language and customs, broadening their perspectives. They may make new friends and business acquaintances, and this type of networking may have business as well as personal payoffs in the future. Foreign assignment is an important aspect of today's international business world that promises to play an even larger role in the global village of the future. Completing these assignments to the best of our abilities requires us to understand all the influences of culture, both in and out of the workplace. In the future, these types of skills will be even more valuable than they are today. Little systematic, formal research exists on this topic in the published literature (despite an abundance of anecdotal and case study data that are proprietary to many companies). Future research on this important topic will help in the design of intercultural adjustment programs for company employees, allowing them to be more effective in their overseas assignments.

Working with an Increasingly Diverse Workforce Population

Organizations all around the world are dealing with an increasingly diverse workforce population. For example, American companies are increasingly hosting workers from other countries. Joint ventures between American and Asian and European companies have increased over the past ten years—most visibly in automobile manufacturing, but also in computers and semi-conductors, communication technology, and many other fields. One result is an influx of workers from these countries and cultures to the United States.

Many of the problems that arise when American workers go overseas also arise when foreign workers come to the United States. Often, managers from another culture come to oversee and supervise production or assembly, bringing with them all the expectations, customs, and rituals of their home country. Not surprisingly, they find that those ways of doing business do not work in the United States, because the people are different and the system is different. Similarly, many of the problems experienced by American families abroad are also experienced by the families of workers who come to the United States. To make the transition easier, many Japanese companies in the Los Angeles area have established little Japanese villages and apartments where the Japanese lifestyle and customs can be preserved. These controversial enclaves serve to maintain barriers between people, raising problems of their own.

One recent study highlights some of the problems and issues that may arise in these situations. In this study, Graham (1993) spent six months as a hidden participant/observer at a Japanese automobile plant near Lafayette, Indiana (Subaru/Isuzu Automotive). During this time, the author was able to document worker resistance to Japanese management practices in the form of sabotage, protest, agitation, and confrontation. The results of this study brought into question the validity and worth of simply "transferring" the Japanese management model to the American milieu. The data also failed to support the contention that participation schemes (such as teamwork) automatically increase worker control or that decentralized authority structures increase worker autonomy.

A recent study focused on cultural differences in ways of handling disagreement. In this study (Smith, Dugan, Peterson, & Leung, 1998), managers and supervisors from a variety of organizations in 23 countries completed a questionnaire about how they handled disagreements in their work unit. The responses were aggregated for each country, and the country mean values on the questionnaire were correlated with the country's scores on Hofstede's dimensions described earlier. The results indicated that power distance (PD) significantly predicted the frequency of disagreements between work groups. In handling disagreements, people in low-PD cultures tended to rely on subordinates and coworkers. People of individualistic countries relied more on their own personal experience and training, whereas people of collectivistic cultures relied more on formal rules and procedures. Although this study involved participants in different countries, these types of psychological differences based on PD and IC may be important in understanding cultural differences within a single multicultural organization.

Despite the potential problems associated with receiving foreign workers, many of the advantages of overseas assignments also apply to receiving people from abroad. The ability to reap these benefits depends on the openness of the host organization to learn and on the goodwill and intent of the employee and the company to engage in a mutually beneficial partnership.

Even without international joint ventures and worker exchanges, many American companies are dealing with increasing diversity solely on the basis of the increasing diversity of the American population. The United States is home to people of many different races, ethnicities, and cultures. Within this "mixed salad" of cultures are generational differences, from recent immigrants to second-, third-, and multi-generation Americans of wide-ranging ethnic and cultural backgrounds. The problems that can occur when two cultures clash can be magnified many times over when people from multiple cultures are thrust together to interact toward a common goal.

Many of the issues raised in dealing with people across countries and cultures are relevant for domestic work organizations dealing with an increasingly diverse American workforce as well. People come to work with different expectations, and different expectations can lead to intercultural clashes. Cultural differences in the management of time and people, in identification with work, and in making decisions all provide areas for conflict. People in the United States come to work with differences in work-related values and the degree to which they respect or minimize power and status differences between them. People come to work with different views regarding sex differences and how to manage uncertainty.

Many successful companies have met these challenges by making explicit what kinds of communication styles, decision making, productivity, and worker behaviors are important for the success of the company. Many companies today actively train their employees in intercultural issues ranging from communication to expectations (see, for example, Goldman, 1992); the most successful of these programs undoubtedly have important positive, practical implications in many arenas of people's lives. Many companies have created temporary organizational cultures in which their employees can move and adapt without fear of losing themselves or their own personal cultures. They have designed ways not only of avoiding problems but also of handling problems effectively and constructively when they do arise. While negotiating all of these issues requires additional work and effort by companies and people alike, organizations that can do so successfully are likely to realize long-term benefits to the bottom line.

Conclusion

The cultural differences that people bring with them to the workplace, both internationally and domestically, present us with challenges unprecedented in the modern industrialized period of history. To meet these challenges, business, government, and private organizations look to research and education about cultural diversity as it relates to work. Intercultural communication and competence training and business consulting with regard to managing diversity have become major growth industries.

Too often, the idea of managing diversity rests on the underlying assumption that diversity is an unwanted by-product of our work environment—a nuisance variable that must be dealt with in order to maximize efficiency. As we move toward a greater appreciation of cultural similarities and differences, however, we may gain a better appreciation for the different approaches to work, management, and leadership that have worked for different cultures. As we confront the challenges of diversity in the future, we need to move away from the notion of managing a nuisance variable to viewing it as a potential resource for tapping into products, services, and activities that will make companies more efficient, productive, and profitable than ever before. By tapping into diversity rather than managing it, perhaps we can increase international and intercultural cooperation not only in business but among people in general.

Glossary

Anglo-Saxon type of organization A work organization more or less opposite to the Latin type, with less centralization, more diffusion of power and decision making, and less hierarchy in the bureaucracy.

centralization The degree to which organizations concentrate their operations and decision-making capabilities in a limited number of business units or people.

complexity The degree to which organizations foster differentiation of tasks and activities within themselves.

Confucian dynamism A dimension of work-related values important to Asian companies and thought to be rooted in Confucian thought and principles.

formalization The degree to which organizations provide structure and rules for their operations.

Latin type of organization A work organization that is characterized as a classical bureaucracy, with centralized power and decision making and many hierarchical levels.

leadership The "process of influence between a leader and followers to attain group, organizational, or societal goals" (Hollander, 1985).

multinational and international corporations Work organizations that have subsidiaries, satellite offices, and work units in more than one country.

nemawashi The broad-based, consensus-building procedure that occurs within the Japanese ringi system of decision making.

oligarchy An organizational structure characterized by rule or decision-making power of a few. Decisions are typically made by people "at the top" who impose their decisions on subordinates.

organizational climate A shared perception of organizational policies, practices, and procedures, and how people feel about them.

organizational culture A dynamic system of rules involving attitudes, values, beliefs, norms, and behaviors that are shared among members of an organization.

ringi The Japanese process of decision making, which involves circulating a proposal among all people who will be affected by it, addressing concerns and negative consequences raised by as many parties as possible, consulting on as broad a basis as possible about the proposal, and achieving consensus before the proposal is ever formally implemented.

social loafing The common finding in research on group productivity in the United States that individual productivity tends to decline in larger groups.

social striving The opposite of social loafing; the finding in many cultures that working in a group enhances individual performance rather than diminishes it.

Third World type of organization A work organization characterized by greater centralization of decision making, less formalization of rules, and a more paternalistic or traditional family orientation.

Conclusion

Implications for Mainstream Psychology and Everyday Life

As we have seen throughout this book, the influence of culture on our lives is enormous. Culture influences the language we speak, our perceptions of the world around us, our behaviors and attitudes, the structures of our homes, our system of education, our government, and our health. Across all the topics covered in this book, culture plays a major, albeit sometimes silent and invisible, role in determining how we act and how we perceive the actions of others.

In the past, mainstream academic psychology, and many psychologists, never gave much thought to culture as a serious variable in theory and in research. Culture is to psychology what air is to us or water is to fish—all around us but invisible. We don't think about it often, but it is there, and influences everything about us. Only when we come into contact with others from different cultures, as occurs more and more often in our diverse and shrinking world, do we think twice about culture. Today, we realize that culture is a major source of psychological differences that need to be accounted for in both theoretical and empirical work.

Thus, we are in the middle of a cultural revolution of sorts in psychology, and cross-cultural studies in all aspects of psychology are much more commonplace today than ever before. When we study cultures, it is easy to get lost in the mass of "facts," especially about cultural differences. The facts derived from cross-cultural research in psychology, anthropology, and other disciplines would indeed fill the volumes of an encyclopedia on cultural differences. It would be interesting to have such an encyclopedia—a *Farmer's Almanac of Culture*, if you will—to help us understand the breadth and scope of culture's influence on our lives.

But even when we are surrounded by all those differences, or perhaps *especially* when we are surrounded by those differences, we must not forget that there are important similarities as well. The study of human behavior across cultures informs us of those similarities as well as differences. This book has sought to highlight the major similarities and differences among cultures across a broad range of psychological phenomena.

What does it all mean—to academic psychology, and to each one of us individually? Where do we go from here? In this final chapter, I would like to discuss the implications of this cultural revolution in psychology, both for mainstream academic psychology and for individuals in a diverse and interdependent world. The profound implications in both domains give rise to challenges that make this era of psychology so exciting.

Implications for Mainstream Psychology

As discussed in the introductory chapter of this book, all research is associated with certain parameters that limit the knowledge and data that are generated from that research. The research that forms the basis for much of mainstream psychology has been based largely on studies using American university students as research subjects. And many of those studies were conducted many years ago, when the American population was much more homogeneous than it is today.

For many years, there was no need to question the validity or veracity of the knowledge generated in American psychology. The knowledge gathered from those studies formed the basis of many theories and models in psychology that were indeed applicable at the time. Geographically, the United States was relatively isolated, with only Canada to the north and Mexico to the south, separated from the rest of the world by vast oceans on both east and west. With so much space and so many resources within the continental United States, Americans had little need for interdependence with others for their survival and welfare, and little interaction with different peoples. Moreover, the rest of the world tended to treat American academia as the ultimate ivory tower, glamorizing it as it does so many other American things (celebrities, sports, popular culture). American psychology, like many other academic fields, was and still is a major driving force for psychology in many other parts of the world, in terms of academic training, research, and theory.

This picture is currently changing, however. The American university student population, mirroring the population as a whole, has become increasingly diverse in race, sex, class, and lifestyle—that is, in culture. The same is true of university faculty who teach psychology. Borders between countries are becoming more porous, and instantaneous communication by phone, fax, and electronic mail enables us to interact with people in far places and disparate cultures much more easily today than ever before. With modern transportation, a few hours' plane ride can take us physically to those distant countries and cultures. Americans are also much more interdependent economically with people of other countries and cultures than ever before. Because of all these factors, Americans are increasingly coming in contact with people of very different cultures in their everyday lives, and the American population is diversifying at a rapid pace. Finally, academic psychology has become much more prominent in other parts of the world, including Europe and Asia.

It is against this backdrop that cross-cultural psychology is such a welcome and timely addition to mainstream academic, predominantly American, psychology. As mentioned in Chapter 1, cross-cultural research actually has quite a long history in psychology, but it is only recently that it has become so important to psychology as a whole. And although research in cross-cultural psychology has produced evidence of both similarities and differences in psychological processes and behaviors, it is the cultural differences that have greater consequences for mainstream academic psychology.

Cultural differences challenge mainstream theoretical notions about the nature of people, and force us to rethink our basic theories of personality, perception, cognition, emotion, development, social psychology, and other psychological processes. We are on the verge of witnessing encyclopedic-type compendia of cultural differences in almost all subfields of psychology, with ample evidence from many cultures that the truths of mainstream Americans are not necessarily applicable to the rest of the world. Many such studies and findings have been reviewed in this book.

In fact, it has become almost too easy to produce a research finding documenting a cultural difference in some aspect of psychological behavior. Indeed, the challenge facing cross-cultural psychology today and in the future is not simply to continue compiling cultural differences in various facets of psychological research. Instead, the greatest challenge of the near future is to develop theoretical models and conceptual frameworks that can explain how cultures are both similar and different, and why. The overwhelming evidence cross-cultural psychology has already gathered, and will continue to gather, brings with it an obligation to make some sense of it all.

The Challenge for Cross-Cultural Psychology

Fortunately, a small but growing number of cross-cultural psychologists have been interested in discovering how cultures come to create similarities and differences, and why. Many have turned their efforts to studying the developmental processes underlying enculturation—the process of learning the rules, values, attitudes, beliefs, behaviors, and opinions of one's first, original culture—and have made important inroads toward understanding how we acquire culture and how it influences our lives (see Chapter 7). Another important inroad involves the relationship between culture and self-concept as a mediator of psychological differences across cultures (see Chapter 3). A third avenue has been the use of meaningful dimensions of cultural variability, such as individualism–collectivism (IC), to predict and explain cultural similarities and differences.

As discussed throughout the book, many researchers have used IC to predict and explain cultural differences in a wide variety of psychological constructs (also see review by Triandis, 1995). This construct is a major plus for cross-cultural research and thinking because it allows us to go beyond nationality, race, or ethnicity in predicting and explaining differences, focusing instead on functional psychological predictions and interpretations of data. Constructs such as IC give researchers and theoreticians alike a basis on which they can understand the psychological impact of culture on both the macro-social and individual levels.

Recent advances in cross-cultural methods include the development of ways to measure IC tendencies on the individual level (reviewed in Chapter 2), and these methods have had a large and positive impact on theory building in cross-cultural psychology. Triandis (Triandis, Leung, Villareal, & Clack, 1985) refers to IC at the individual level as *idiocentrism* and *allocentrism*, and their measurement is a major plus for research. It allows researchers to ascertain empirically that their samples differ on this construct, providing an important methodological check and eliminating reliance on anecdotes, impressions, or stereotypes when interpreting findings. It also allows researchers to assess numerically the degree of within-culture variability on this important construct. Using this index, researchers can determine how much of the difference between groups is attributable to individual-level differences in IC.

Say, for example, that a researcher intends to compare two cultures and has participants complete an individual-level measurement of IC. Group differences on the dependent variable can be tested through normal procedures (for example, *t*-test, ANOVA, chi-square). In addition, the relationship between IC and the dependent variable can be assessed through correlational procedures. If correlations are found, their influence on the group differences obtained earlier can be tested using multiple regression or analysis of covariance (ANACOVA). The degree of contribution of IC to the group differences can be computed by comparing effect sizes of the group differences between the original and ANACOVA analyses.

In fact, this was the approach adopted in a recent study of cultural display rules of emotional expression in the United States, Japan, Russia, and South Korea (Matsumoto, Takeuchi, Andayani, Kouznetsouva, & Krupp, in press). In that study, participants in the four countries completed an individual-based measure of IC, as well as an inventory of the rules governing their displays of seven different emotions in four separate social contexts. The analyses indicated that not only were there cross-national differences both in display rules and in IC, but that IC and display rules were correlated with each other, between and within the countries. We then used an effect-size comparison technique based on findings from ANACOVAs testing the display rule ratings across the four countries using IC scores as covariates. These comparisons indicated that individual-level IC accounted for approximately 30 % of the differences between countries in display rules.

As discussed briefly in Chapter 2, many methods of IC measurement are available to choose from, and the field is embracing these measures in cross-cultural comparisons. These developments are a major plus, as they relate culture to functional psychology, giving us a basis for understanding how and why similarities and differences occur. They allow for valuable methodological checks in our research, and for statistical assessments of the contribution of measured culture to observed differences (as in the study just described). The innovative and promising approach allows researchers to specify the exact degree of contribution of specific cultural dimensions on their variables of interest, and it allows theorists to incorporate these estimates of contribution into their models and theory building. In some cases, such as with display rules, this process may force us to consider the contribution of other factors to psychological processes.

In fact, the field has perhaps been too preoccupied with IC to the exclusion of other important dimensions. Clearly, no one dimension can capture "culture." In the study of display rules described here, for example, IC accounted for only about 30% of the variance between countries. What accounts for the other 70%? I believe that another cultural dimension, power distance (PD) or status differentiation, is just as important as IC, if not more so. Future endeavors should include developing individual-level measures of this important cultural construct, and integrating it into cross-cultural research. In any case, it is this approach—specifying meaningful dimensions of cultural variability and actually measuring them—that promises to enable cross-cultural psychology to meet the challenge of developing theoretical models to explain cultural similarities and differences.

The Challenge for Mainstream Psychology

If the challenge for cross-cultural psychology is to develop theoretical models to explain cultural similarities and differences, the challenge for mainstream psychology is to integrate these cultural frameworks into mainstream academic psychology.

Research on bilingualism reviewed in Chapter 12 has demonstrated that bilinguals seem to access two cultural frames of references, depending on which language they are speaking. Many of you who are bilingual may recognize this phenomenon. Although there are certainly areas of overlap and similarity, bilinguals have reported having different personalities, judging emotions differently, appraising events and the environment around them differently, and attributing the causes of events differently depending on the language used when performing these tasks. Not only do multiple cultural frameworks exist in their minds, but bilinguals have the added ability to monitor *which* cultural framework to adopt in each social context. Thus, they have a meta-cognitive process that allows them to engage with their "multiple personalities" in a healthy and constructive way. This ability is related to the development of intercultural sensitivity (see, for example, Bennett, 1993, reviewed in Chapter 14).

Most Americans are monolingual; most of the rest of the world is multilingual. Thus, the information obtained from research with Americans, and theories derived from Americans by Americans, may be based on a theory of mind that is not really applicable to the rest of the world. We may not stop to think about whether those theories make sense or not, because they are bounded within our own cultural framework. It is only when we look outside of ourselves that we can experience, understand, and appreciate those boundaries.

Lillard (1998a) has suggested these notions in a recent review discussing ethnopsychologies. She suggests that theories of mind and folk psychologies (a set of basic beliefs about minds and behavior) are actually quite variable according to culture, although we don't often realize it. Four reasons why such folk theories differ around the world are (1) external differences reflect internal differences in psychological meaning, (2) every culture fosters certain optional construals in their own psychologies, (3) preconditions for social cognition and attitudes vary across cultures, and (4) nuances in psychological meaning can exist despite apparent similarities. She reviewed a number of aspects of theories of mind that vary across cultures, including the structure of mind, attributional processes, and specific processes such as perception, emotion, and thought. That these various ethnopsychologies even exist suggests that mainstream American approaches to psychology do not do justice to the actual diversity of psychological processes and functions in the world.

Created largely within a monolingual, monocultural milieu, mainstream psychology has a lot of catching up to do if it is to be truly inclusive of as many people as possible in a world of diversity. The assimilation of cross-cultural findings and theories into mainstream psychology suggests a fundamental revision in ways of thinking about self and personality that have important consequences for all areas of psychology. No information or ideas that we have currently need to be thrown out; they just need to be placed within the proper context to be applicable to more people. Cross-cultural work needs to be assimilated into mainstream psychology, and mainstream psychology needs to accommodate to these ideas. The end product will be qualitatively different than the psychology to which we are currently accustomed.

What is needed is a fundamental revision in the very nature of psychology—one that incorporates culture as a normal part of its working variables, in research as well as theory. That is, we need to move from a psychology of the past to a *cultural psychology* of the future. In a cultural psychology, culture is not an afterthought or an exotic extension of mainstream psychology; rather, it is an integral part of mainstream psychology. And in fact, some writers have begun to take up the challenge of creating that cultural psychology (see, for example, Cole, 1996, and review by Takahashi & Hatano, 1997).

How do we take up this challenge? The fight, if you will, is not in the laboratory or the field; it is in us. The greatest challenge facing cross-cultural psychology now is to think less about producing finding after finding of cultural differences, and to think more about ways of integrating them collectively into a cohesive, comprehensive theory incorporating mainstream as well as cross-cultural psychology. This challenge applies equally to all the subfields of psychology, which are Humpty Dumpty–like splintered fragments of a larger collective. Although the need for specificity and fragmentation is understandable, so is the need for integration and synthesis. We need to look outside of psychology to help us "put the pieces back together"; otherwise, we can never envision the whole, only its parts. This integration may require us to consult with anthropology, sociology, business, medicine, and other disciplines. In developing theoretical models to integrate cultural similarities and differences, we need to go outside of psychology to know more about psychology. These almost Herculean efforts will be what is required to put Humpty Dumpty back together.

This new approach need not be forced down anyone's throat, nor need the revisions be horrendously traumatic. Little steps will turn to big steps, and big steps will be a journey. In the end, it is the walking, not the destination, that is the desired end. Are cross-cultural psychologists up to the task? Are psychologists up to the task?

Implications for Our Everyday Lives

Finding an Intercultural Process Model to Engage with Diversity

As we learn more about both cultural similarities and differences, we need to touch base with the reasons why we study cultures in the first place. Without revisiting our motivations, the mass of facts about both similarities and differences will remain just that—a mass of facts. We need a way to take those facts and use them—to allow those facts to become means to an end, and not an end in themselves. When we revisit our motivations, we should quickly realize that the ultimate reason we study culture is to improve our lives and our relationships with others in a diverse world. This goal should be the primary reason we study culture and its influence on human behavior. If we are not able to take the information gathered so far and use it in some productive way, the great opportunity provided by this information will slip through our hands and be wasted.

Recall the two goals of psychology discussed in Chapter 1. One goal of psychology is to produce knowledge; the second is to use the knowledge that is produced to intervene in people's lives and help make them better. The knowledge that is produced in psychology is used by therapists, counselors, consultants, and teachers to intervene directly in people's lives. As our world becomes increasingly diverse in culture, heritage, and tradition, accurate information about cultural influences on psychology becomes increasingly important in our ability to deliver meaningful and effective intervention programs for the people whose lives we touch.

How can we, in our everyday lives, approach this final task? One way would be to create a Farmer's Almanac of culture in your mind, documenting the cultural similarities and differences found in specific cultures and building your own reference book that you can retrieve at any time. This is a formidable task, as there is so much about culture to learn and so little time, energy, and storage space available. Despite the difficulties, however, this approach is not without merit, and certainly many people develop such almanacs in their minds about a small number of cultures with which they become intimately familiar. Many individuals who spend extended periods of time immersed in different cultures—through travel, business, or homestay programs—do build such an almanac, albeit unconsciously. The strength of this approach lies both in increasing our capacity to be culturally relative and in guiding our behavior in daily interactions with people from diverse backgrounds.

But none of us can create a Farmer's Almanac of culture for all the cultures we might possibly come in contact with in our lives, and many of us do not have the opportunity to travel and immerse ourselves in other cultures to become culturally fluent in this fashion. Instead, the vast majority of us will need to rely on a *process* of intercultural growth that we can rely on to engage with the multitude of diversities that exist in our world today.

In fact, we discussed such a process in Chapter 14 when we described a model of intercultural sensitivity. This model depicts the various stages in which people engage with cultural differences, ranging from denial and minimization of those differences on one end, to acceptance, adaptation, and integration on the other. One assumption of this model is that being more appreciative and more multicultural is preferable to being in denial or minimizing differences. Although some people may actually debate this assumption, I would argue that this assumption is valid—not only in today's diverse world, but especially in tomorrow's even more diverse world.

How do we move from one end of the spectrum in that model to the other—from denial and minimization to integration? The road from one end to the other is not an easy one, because the existence of differences makes it relatively easy for all of us to engage in denial or to minimize the importance of those differences in our lives. As we discussed in Chapter 4, our own ethnocentric and stereotypic ways of thinking, which are themselves inevitable consequences of normal, psychological functioning, make it easy for us to create negative value judgments about those differences. And it is only normal that we have at least slightly negative emotional reactions when engaging with cultural differences. These negative reactions, and the negative value judgments we are apt to make because of our ethnocentrism and stereotypic thinking, make it difficult for us to engage in healthier and more constructive methods of interacting, and keep us from truly appreciating those differences and integrating with people who exhibit those differences.

As we discussed in Chapter 14, the process of intercultural communication is complex, and conflicts based on intercultural misunderstandings are inevitable. Thus, if we are to go beyond these ethnocentric and stereotypic biases when engaging with intercultural differences, it is extremely important to be able to control our own negative emotional reactions when engaging with those differences. This point is related to the points made earlier in Chapter 4 about the role of emotion and mood in the process of person perception and stereotyping. Those who can regulate their emotional reactions will then be able to engage in a more constructive intercultural process such as that outlined in the model of intercultural sensitivity described in Chapter 14, and open the door to more successful intercultural interactions. Those who cannot will have that door closed to them. Emotions, therefore, are central to this process, and hold the key to successful intercultural experiences.

Regulating Emotions: A Key to Personal Growth

Many of us who have experience dealing with children know that even very young children can engage in morally altruistic behaviors. They may offer their favorite blanket, toy, or food to another youngster in distress, or lend a helping hand to Mom or Dad or a sibling at play. When something happens to hurt, anger, frustrate, or upset them, however, it is a very different story. They begin to cry or throw a temper tantrum. Their thinking and worldview revert back to a more primitive way of dealing with and understanding their world. It becomes impossible for them to engage in moral or altruistic acts of kindness, because their way of thinking is locked into a more infantile mode of operation. As mentioned in Chapter 4, many psychologists refer to this process as *regression*.

Regression is not the sole domain of children and adolescents. Adults of all ages also regress at times. We all know of instances and individuals who, when hurt, upset, frustrated, or angry, cannot think straight; they rant and rave and revert back to a more primitive way of thinking, acting, and feeling. Although the outward manifestations of these processes may differ between adults and children (adults may not just pick up their toys and storm out of the room), there is considerable similarity in the underlying psychological processes.

When a negative emotion is aroused, people can easily be overcome by those feelings, which then "take over" their way of being. Even people who are usually adept at thinking critically about things, and who often act in perfectly moral and altruistic ways, may not be able to think or act in such a manner when overcome by negative emotions.

A critical moment arises in an intercultural interaction episode when negative emotions are aroused because of inevitable cultural differences. Those individuals who can somehow control or regulate those negative feelings—who can somehow put them on hold and not act directly upon them or allow them to overcome their way of thinking, acting, and feeling—will be able to engage in other processes that can help them expand their appraisal and attribution of the causes of the differences. Once emotions are held in check and not immediately acted upon, individuals can then think critically about the origins of those differences, perhaps going beyond their own cultural lenses and framework to entertain the possibility of other causes of the differences that they may not have even been aware of. If this type of critical thinking can occur, then individuals will have an active choice of accepting or rejecting alternative hypotheses concerning the causes of those differences. Hopefully, they will have the openness and flexibility to accept rival hypotheses if it turns out their initial reactions were inaccurate.

Thus, the three key ingredients of personal growth are:

1. Emotional regulation
2. Critical thinking (generation of rival hypotheses)
3. Openness/flexibility to accept rival hypotheses

For example, suppose you meet someone for the first time. You try to look directly at her and shake her hand, but she looks directly away from you, seemingly refusing to acknowledge your presence or shake your hand. Your immediate reaction may well be negative. At this point, it may be easy to form a negative impression about this person, based upon a negative attribution about the cause of the difference in behavior from what you expected. If you are able to put that reaction on hold, however, and then to engage in critical thinking about possible causes of that behavior, you might consider a number of alternative hypotheses. Whereas direct eye contact may be a sign of respect in your culture, avoiding eye contact may be a sign of respect in her culture. Whereas shaking hands is an accepted form of greeting in your culture, such contact may be limited to intimate partners in her culture. Once you have generated these and other possible hypotheses, you will then have the choice of accepting or rejecting them. If you choose to accept an alternative cause of the unexpected behavior, hopefully you will have the openness and flexibility to change your mind regarding your initial negative reaction.

This model is inherently a growth model. By engaging in critical thinking about cultural differences and being open and flexible to new ways of thinking, you allow your ways of perceiving people to continue to grow. You continually add more and more complexity to your method of interacting with diversity. This complexity allows you to move from denial and minimization to adaptation and integration on the intercultural sensitivity model discussed earlier. This entire process is possible, however, only when you can regulate your emotions and not allow negative emotions to get the best of you.

Conversely, if our negative emotional reactions to inevitable cultural differences continue to overwhelm us and dictate how we think, feel, and act, we cannot engage in critical thinking about those differences. Rather, we regress to a previous way of thinking about those differences that is rooted in our ethnocentric and stereotypic ways of viewing the world. Instead of creating rival hypotheses that stimulate growth in our ways of thinking, we will instead only reinforce our preexisting, limited ways of thinking. Openness to new ideas and rival hypotheses is not even an option, because these new ideas don't exist. Instead, there is only a regurgitation of stereotypes and ethnocentric attitudes. This scenario is a nongrowth model.

In summary, then, the three main ingredients of personal growth in relation to cultural differences are emotion regulation, critical thinking, and openness and flexibility. Of these, emotion regulation is the key ingredient, as it is the gatekeeper of the growth process. If we cannot put our inevitable negative emotions in check, it is impossible to engage in what is clearly higher-order thinking about cultural differences.

Using Critical Thinking

Once we can deal with our emotional reactions, exactly how can we think critically about cultural differences? In this section, I present seven guidelines for this critical thinking process. These guidelines are not universal in the sense that they have been "proven" by cross-cultural research. Instead, they are my feeble attempt at taking all the information presented in this book, along with my experience and the experiences of others interacting with people of different backgrounds, and synthesizing this information into a coherent set of guidelines that I have found useful. Others may have their own guidelines, and those may be at variance with mine. I offer these not as an end-all prescription for successful human relations, but as a platform from which to launch meaningful discussions with others about this important topic. Whether people agree or disagree with these guidelines is a question secondary to the more important issue of their contribution to our ability to talk about these emotionally charged issues.

Recognize that culture is a psychological construct.   I have focused on a definition of culture as a psychological construct emphasizing the subjective (Triandis, 1972) rather than objective aspects of culture. I believe it is these subjective aspects of culture, existing in our minds as mental blueprints or programming, that are most important to understanding the contribution of culture to human behavior. Culture refers to the degree to which a group of people share attitudes, values, beliefs, and behaviors. It is communicated from one generation to the next. As such, culture is a functional entity—one we cannot see but only infer from observations of human behavior.

Culture is not race. Being born of a particular race does not mean that you automatically harbor the cultural values associated with that race. Culture is not nationality. Being a citizen of a country does not mean that you automatically adopt the culture associated with that country. Culture is not birthplace. Being born in a certain place does not automatically mean that you harbor the culture of your birthplace.

When we think of intercultural relations and cultural diversity, both within the United States and abroad, we mostly think of differences according to race, ethnicity, or nationality. Yet I have not used these terms and concepts in this book. This lack of focus on race, ethnicity, and nationality is a function of my view that the important aspect of people is their underlying psychological culture, not the color of their skin or the citizenship on their passport.

Some people may interpret my position as suggesting that race, nationality, and other personal characteristics are not important. That is not true. Future cross-cultural research and thinking in this area must meet the formidable challenge of integrating these concepts with psychological definitions of culture to examine their joint influence and interactive effects on human behaviors. In adopting the approach taken in this book, I hoped to highlight the important role of subjective, psychological culture in producing similarities and differences in behaviors and to bring a fresh way of thinking to old and nagging problems.

As we learn more about what culture is and is not, we need to recognize the fuzzy nature of the definition of culture, based in function rather than biology or geopolitics. By recognizing that culture is a psychological construct—our learned mental programming—we can avoid the use of race and nationality in understanding cultural differences among people. Defining culture as a meaningful psychological construct also allows us to consider the remaining guidelines.

Recognize individual differences within a culture.

Defining culture as a sociopsychological construct is not enough. With a functional definition of culture, we need to recognize individual differences within cultures. Within any culture, people differ according to how strongly they adhere to or comply with the values, standards, and mores of that culture. While some people may be true representatives of their culture, others may not be as adequately described by their culture. Yet they are all members of the culture. Even within the individualistic American culture, for example, we can find people who harbor more collectivistic cultural values. Describing all individuals within this cultural group as individualistic ignores actual cultural differences that exist among individual members.

Recognizing individual differences within cultures helps us develop flexibility in our ethnocentrism and stereotypes. One of the keys to improving intergroup and interpersonal relationships is to develop a healthy flexibility with regard to ethnocentrism and stereotypes. Recognizing individual differences in culture and how these differences are related to behaviors is one of the first steps to eliminating reliance on negative and detrimental stereotypes.

Understand our own cultural filters and ethnocentrism.

We are not always aware of our own cultural filters as we perceive, think about, and interpret events around us and the behavior of others. We are not always aware of the cultural bases of our behaviors and actions. Often, the way we see the world (worldview) is fundamentally different from the way others see the world.

One important first step in gaining an understanding of cultural influences on behavior is to recognize that we have our own perceptual filters and cultural bases for behavior. We need to stop and think about how our own cultural upbringing contributed to how we interact with the world and with others. This comparison comes to the forefront when we travel outside our culture. By clashing with the cultures of others, we are forced to think about differences in cognition and behavior. In doing so, we may come to a better understanding of our own filters and biases.

Allow for the possibility that conflicts are cultural.

One fallacy of cross-cultural study is the assumption that if you study cultures, there will be no intercultural conflicts. This is not the case. In interacting with others, conflicts and misunderstandings will undoubtedly occur. All too often, we are too quick to attribute the cause of the conflict or misunderstanding to some fault or shortcoming in the other person, or the other person's culture. And because we have a limited understanding of culture, equating it with race or nationality, we may make negative attributions about that race or nationality, when in fact the differences arose because of culture.

With a better understanding of cultural influences on behavior, we can allow for the possibility that many conflicts and misunderstandings are due to cultural differences. By doing so, we avoid personalizing the source of conflict and misunderstanding in our interactions and focus on the reasons the misunderstanding may have arisen in the first place. Of course, some conflicts do arise because of personal differences, ignorance, stupidity, or close-mindedness. But we can consider that culture may be a contributing factor and give people the benefit of the doubt.

Recognize that cultural differences are legitimate. Simply attributing conflicts and misunderstandings to culture is not enough; we need to recognize and respect legitimate differences between our cultural upbringing and that of others. This is often a very difficult task because, within our own cultural context, we see a failure to behave in culturally appropriate ways as "bad" or "wrong." Therefore, our natural tendency is to label the same behaviors of others as "bad" or "wrong." But a person from another culture may view those same behaviors as "good" or "acceptable" or "normal." In fact, behaviors that seem bad or ignorant or stupid to us may be performed by a person of sincerity and trustworthiness. And no matter how much we want to label them as bad or ignorant or stupid, the other person's cultural ways, values, and beliefs have just as much legitimacy to them as ours have to us. A step in the right direction is to respect that legitimacy and that difference and find a way to work from that level of respect.

Have tolerance, be patient, and presume good intent. How can we find ways to work things out? Once we recognize that conflicts arise because of differences in culture, and that cultural differences in others are legitimate, where do we go from there? One answer lies in examining how we traditionally deal with these conflicts.

American culture is based on preservation of an individualistic sense of self. In finding ways to maintain self-integrity, we often attribute negative characteristics to others, lashing out at them when we feel our cultural norms have been violated. This style of making attributions is related to the individualistic American culture. It is neither bad nor good; it is just the way things are.

When we are too quick to attribute negative characteristics to others, however, we deny the possibility that their intent may have been good—that it was only the behavioral manifestations of that good intent that we were at odds with. By being tolerant of transgressions and presuming good intent in intercultural interaction, we allow that possibility to exist. If we practice tolerance and presume good intent, we will be able to operate on the level of psychological culture discussed throughout this book, finding ways to explore and react to underlying intent rather than focusing solely on behaviors we find offensive.

Learn more about cultural influences on behavior.   As we turn toward the future, we must continue to learn how culture influences human behavior. By recognizing the impact of culture on behavior, we face an incredible challenge and opportunity. The diverse world that faces us, both within the United States and as part of an interdependent global village, provides a rich and complex arena for human behavior. Psychology has yet to explore this arena fully. These challenges bring new opportunities and new hopes, not only for science but also for people and their lives.

As we come in contact with people of different cultures from around the world, whether through our travels or theirs, we are exposed to many different ways that culture manifests itself in behavior. As our understanding grows, we will come to appreciate even more the important role that culture plays in helping us meet the challenges of survival successfully and with integrity. Cultures will continue to change, because culture itself is not a static, fixed entity. That cultures change over time is apparent today in Europe, Russia, Asia, and indeed the United States. These changes ensure that there will never be a shortage of things to learn about cultural influences on human behavior. The important thing is that we must want to learn it.

Achieving Intercultural Success or Stagnation

So we return to the question posed earlier in this section of this chapter: How can we move from one end of the intercultural sensitivity model (denial and minimization) to the other (adaptation, acceptance, and integration)? As we have seen, the key to such movement is a personal growth process model in which our ways of thinking, person perception, and worldview are constantly being updated by the new and exciting cultural differences with which we engage in our everyday lives. The key to this process is the ability to regulate and control our emotional reactions. If we can do so, then the world's cultural diversity is an exciting research laboratory, where we can constantly test our hypotheses, explore new hypotheses, throw out theories that don't work, and create theories of the world that do. The world becomes an exciting place to be, and intercultural episodes and conflicts provide a stage for forging new relationships, new ideas, and new people—a stage for intercultural success for those individuals who can engage in the process. I call these individuals *voyagers*, because to them, life is an enjoyable journey (see Figure 18.1).

On the other hand, some people cannot control their emotional reactions. Instead of engaging in the critical thinking necessary for personal growth, they only reinforce their ethnocentric and stereotypic worldviews. Instead of expanding their knowledge and thinking patterns, they crystallize and reinforce their preexisting, limited ways of dealing with the world. Theirs is a no-growth model of stagnation, and these individuals are not engaged in a journey. Their

Figure 18.1 Steps to interpersonal and intercultural success or stagnation

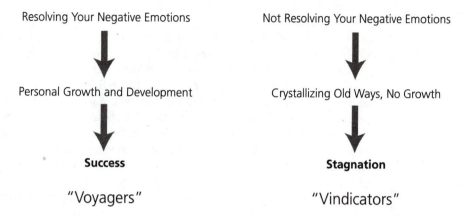

worldviews are established solely to vindicate their preexisting ethnocentric and stereotypic ways of thinking, not to challenge those ways and grow. Therefore, I call these people *vindicators*.

The world of the voyager is neither a panacea nor utopia. These processes do not ensure that we will all live happily ever after, or that we will like and enjoy all cultural differences we come into contact with. After critically thinking about an episode or event, we may indeed come to the conclusion that someone is morally wrong, or just plain rude or selfish. Understanding differences and appreciating how they originate and their meaning to other people's lives does not mean that we have to like those differences, or accept them for our own life. What is important is not the conclusions we draw from this process, but engaging in the process itself. The distinction between a voyager and a vindicator lies not in their conclusions, but in the processes they engage in to draw their conclusions.

Conclusion

In Knowing Others, We Will Come to Know Ourselves

Human behavior is too rich and complex to be "captured" by understanding the world through the eyes of a single culture. One of the major goals of this book has been to examine how culture influences our behaviors and our lives and to challenge the many truths of our cultural world. Many cross-cultural studies in the literature speak to this breadth, and to this need. I hope that this book has been like an intercultural journey for you, with travel to many other lands and cultures and meetings with many diverse peoples, and that it has helped to foster that challenge of your knowledge and worldview.

In challenging the "traditional," we cannot and should not disregard its importance of the work that produced that knowledge. But we have so much more to learn, and as time progresses the need to learn increases. Improvements in communication bring previously distant points on the globe closer and closer together. The opening of national borders and the infusion of people from all walks of life and cultures into our workplaces and our families ensures that cross-cultural issues will remain a high priority in the years to come.

Can we keep up? Future cross-cultural research will help uncover universal and culture-specific aspects of human behavior. Scholars will increasingly have to include culture as a major determinant in theories of human behavior, and researchers will include culture as a variable in their studies. As new information is uncovered, we will undoubtedly improve our thinking about the nature of culture and cultural influences on the behavior of others. The real test of this knowledge is not in understanding the facts presented in this book, or in cognitively memorizing the intercultural process described here. It will be in our ability to control our emotional reactions at intercultural gaffes and to resolve the inevitable intercultural conflicts in our lives. In doing so, we have to know others well. In knowing others, we will come to know ourselves.

Advice for Those Breaking into This Field

In closing, I would like to offer some suggestions for people wanting to break into psychology in general, and cross-cultural psychology in particular. Other writers will have a great deal of excellent advice, but I would simply like to share the kinds of things that have helped me along in my career.

Get grounded in academic psychology.   Get a solid grounding in the methods of contemporary academic psychology. Take as many classes on research methods and statistics as you can. Challenge instructors of your content courses about methods and statistics. Work in a research laboratory as an apprentice with someone who is willing to take you under his or her wing and "show you the ropes." Volunteer. Do a lot of research, make a lot of mistakes, and take time to think a lot along the way. Polish your skills at not only doing research, but learning how to think logically, rationally, and critically. Learn how to use a computer and analyze your own data. Be able to do everything in a study from start to finish, and do it well.

Get exposed to the variety of human behavior.   Get a lot of life experience. Have friends. Take time for love and relationships. Work in a clinical setting. Experience interacting with people with different psychopathologies. Experience the range of human emotions—from the ultimate joys of accomplishment to the depths of anguish and despair of loss. As a psychologist, understand people from an emotional standpoint, not only from a cognitive/research standpoint. You can't learn about the taste of strawberries by reading about it in a book; you have to experience it for yourself.

Get experience in an unfamiliar culture.   Travel, but not just as a tourist. Learn about the customs, ways, and lifestyles of different people. Learn how they think, experience emotions, and experience life. Learn another language, and get to the point where you are fluent in it. Learn to accept, appreciate, and respect cultural diversity. Become multicultural yourself. It is an entirely different plane of being.

Put it all together.   Finally, put it all together. Take your life experiences with the range of human behavior, your knowledge and appreciation of culture, and the academic skills you have learned, and integrate them into a meaningful career and life that teaches the rest of us something that we don't already know. Make the world a better place. The next frontier for psychology is culture, and the next generation of psychologists armed with these skills will be those who are ready for that journey.

As you leave this book, it is my sincere hope that you leave as a voyager and not as a vindicator, and that you will use the knowledge and information you have learned not only in your academic preparation in psychology, but also in your everyday, personal lives. Good luck in that journey.

References

Abebimpe, V. R. (1981). Overview: White norms and psychiatric diagnosis of black patients. *American Journal of Psychiatry, 139,* 888–891.

Abrams, D., Ando, K., & Hinkle, S. (1998). Psychological attachment to the group: Cross-cultural differences in organizational identification and subjective norms as predictors of workers' turnover intentions. *Personality and Social Psychology Bulletin, 24*(10), 1027–1039.

Abrams, K. K., Allen, L. R., & Gray, J. J. (1993). Disordered eating attitudes and behaviors, psychological adjustment, and ethnic identity: A comparison of black and white female college students. *International Journal of Eating Disorders, 14,* 49–57.

Abramson, R. P., & Pinkerton, D. S. (1995). *Sexual nature, sexual culture.* Chicago, IL: University of Chicago Press.

Acioly, N. M., & Schliemann, A. D. (1986). *Intuitive mathematics and schooling in understanding a lottery game.* Paper presented at the Tenth PME Conference, London.

Adamopoulos, J. (1991). The emergence of interpersonal behavior. In S. Ting-Toomey & F. Korzenny (Eds.), *Cross-cultural interpersonal communication* (pp. 155–270). Newbury Park, CA: Sage.

Adler, N. E., Boyce, T. Chesney, M. A., Cohen, S., Folkman, S., Kahn, R. L., & Syme, S. L. (1994). Socioeconomic status and health. *American Psychologist, 49,* 15–24.

Adler, N. J., Schwartz, T., & Graham, J. L. (1987). Business negotiations in Canada (French and English speakers), Mexico and the United States. *Journal of Business Research, 15,* 411–429.

Adorno, T. W., Frenkel-Brunswick, E., Levinson, D. J., & Sanford, R. N. (1950). *The authoritarian personality.* New York: Harper & Row.

Ainsworth, M. D., Blehar, M. C., Waters, E., & Wall, S. (1978). *Patterns of attachment: A psychological study of the strange situation.* Hillsdale, NJ: Erlbaum.

Ajwani, J. K. (1982). A correlational study of Cattel's personality factor B. and I.Q. as measured by his culture fair test. *Indian Psychological Review, 22*(1), 9–11.

Akan, G. E. & Grilo, C. M. (1995). Sociocultural influences on eating attitudes and behaviors, body image, and psychological functioning: A comparison of African American, Asian American, and Caucasian college women. *International Journal of Eating Disorders, 18* (2), 181–187.

Akin-Ogundeji, O. (1988). An African perspective on personality: A case study of the Ibo. *Journal of Human Behavior and Learning, 5*(1), 22–26.

Alarcon, R. D. (1995). Culture and psychiatric diagnosis. *Cultural Psychiatry, 18*(3), 449–465.

Alarcon, R. D., & Leetz, K. L. (1998). Cultural intersections in the psychotherapy of borderline personality disorder. *American Journal of Psychotherapy, 52*(2), 176–190.

Albert, A.A., & Porter, J. R. (1986). Children's gender role stereotypes. A comparison of the United States and South Africa. *Journal of Cross-Cultural Psychology, 17,* 45–65.

Albright, L., Kenny, D. A., & Malloy, T. E. (1988). Consensus in personality judgments at zero acquaintance. *Journal of Personality and Social Psychology, 55,* 387–395.

Al-Issa, I. (Ed.). (1995). *Handbook of culture and mental illness: An international perspective.* Madison, CT: International Universities Press, Inc.

Allen, L., & Santrock, J. W. (1993). *Psychology: The context of behavior.* Dubuque, IA: Brown & Benchmark.

Allerheiligen, R., Graham, J. L., & Lin, C. (1985, Fall). Honesty in interorganizational negotiations in the United States, Japan, Brazil, and the Republic of China. *Journal of Macromarketing,* 4–16.

Altarriba, J (Ed.). (1993). *Cognition and culture: A cross-cultural approach to cognitive psychology.* Amsterdam, Netherlands: North-Holland/Elsevier Science Publishers.

Altarriba, J., & Santiago-Rivera, A. L. (1994). Current perspectives on usiing linguistic and cultural factors in counseling the Hispanic client. *Professional Psychology: Research and Practice, 25*(4), 388–397.

Altman, I., & Taylor, D. A. (1973). *Social penetration: The development of interpersonal relationships.* New York: Holt, Rinehart, & Winston.

Altman, S. A. (1962). A field study of the sociobiology of rhesus monkeys, *Macacca mulatta. Annals of the New York Academy of Sciences, 102,* 338–435.

Al-Zaharani, S. S. A., & Kaplowitz, S. A. (1993). Attributional biases in individualistic and collectivistic cultures: A comparison of Americans with Saudis. *Social Psychology Quarterly, 56,* 223–233.

Amelang, M., & Borkenau, P. (1982). Ueber die faktorielle Struktur und externe Validtaet einiger Fragebogen-Skalen zur Erfassung von Dimensionen der Extraversion und emotionalen Labilitaet [The factional structure and external validity of some questionnaire scales for measurement of the dimensions of extraversion and emotional lability]. *Zeitschrift fuer Differentielle und Diagnostische Psychologie, 3*(2), 119–145.

American Psychiatric Association (APA). (1987). *Diagnostic and statistical manual of mental disorders* (3rd ed.). [DSM-III-R]. Washington, DC: Author.

American Psychiatric Association (APA). (1994). *Diagnostic and statistical manual of mental disorders* (4th ed.). [DSM-IV]. Washington, DC: Author.

Amir, Y. & Sharon, I. (1988). Are social psychological laws cross-culturally valid? *Journal of Cross Cultural Psychology, 18*(4), 383–470.

Anderson, C. A., & Anderson, K. B. (1996). Violent crime rate studies in philosophical context: A destructive testing approach to heat and southern culture of violence effects. *Journal of Personality, 70*(4), 740–756.

Angyal, A. (1951). *Neurosis and treatment: A holistic theory.* New York: Wiley.

Anshel, M. H., Williams, L. R. T., & Hodge, K. (1997). Cross-cultural and gender differences on coping style in sport. *International Journal of Sport Psychology, 28*(2), 141–156.

APS Observer. (1997, October). *Human capital inititaitive: Reducing violence: A research agenda* (Report No. 5).

Arbona, C. (1995). Culture, ethnicity, and race: A reaction. *The Counseling Psychologist, 23*(1), 74–78.

Archer, D. (Producer and director). (1991). *A world of gestures: Culture and nonverbal communication* [Videotape]. Berkeley: University of California Extension Center for Media and Independent Learning.

Argyle, M., Alkema, F., & Gilmour, K. (1978). The communication of friendly and hostile attitudes by verbal and non-verbal signals. *European Journal of Social Psychology, 1*(3), 385–402.

Argyle, M., & Cook, M. (1976). *Gaze and mutual gaze.* Cambridge, England: Cambridge University Press.

Argyle, M., Henderson, M., Bond, M. H., Iizuka, Y., & Contarello, A. (1986). Cross-cultural variations in relationship rules. *International Journal of Psychology, 21,* 287–315.

Argyle, M., Salther, G., Nicholson, H., Williams, M., & Burgess, P. (1970). The communication of inferior and superior attitudes by verbal and non-verbal signals. *British Journal of Sociology and Clinical Psychology, 9,* 222–231.

Asch, S. E. (1951). Effects of group pressure upon the modification and distortion of judgments. In

H. Guetzkow (Ed.), *Groups, leadership and men: Research in human relations* (pp. 177–190). Pittsburgh: Carnegie Press.

Asch, S. E. (1955). Opinions and social pressures. *Scientific American, 193,* 31–35.

Asch, S. E. (1956). Studies of independence and conformity: A minority of one against a unanimous majority. *Psychological Monographs, 70*(9, Whole No. 416).

Atkeson, P. (1970). Building communication in intercultural marriage. *Psychiatry: Journal for the Study of Interpersonal Processes, 33*(3), 396–408.

Atkinson, D. R., Casa, A., & Abreu, J. (1992). Mexican American acculturation, counselor ethnicity and cultural sensitivity, and perceived counselor competence. *American Psychologist, 39,* 515–520.

Atkinson, D. R., Furlong, M. J., & Poston, W. C. (1986). Afro-American preferences for counselor characteristics. *Journal of Counseling Psychology, 33,* 326–330.

Atkinson, D. R., Ponce, F. Q., & Martinez, F. M. (1984). Effects of ethnic, sex, and attitude similarity on counselor credibility. *Journal of Counseling Psychology, 31*(40), 588–590.

Atkinson, J. W. (1964). *An introduction to motivation.* Princeton, NJ: Van Nostrand Reinhold.

Au, T. K. (1983). Chinese and English counterfactuals: The Sapir-Whorf hypothesis revisited. *Cognition, 15,* 155–187.

Au, T. K. (1984). Counterfactuals: In reply to Alfred Bloom. *Cognition, 17,* 289–302.

Aune, K., & Aune K. (1995). Culture differences in the self-reported experience and expression of emotions in relationships. *Journal of Cross-Cultural Psychology, 27,* 67–81.

Averill, J. R. (1980). Emotion and anxiety: Sociocultural, biological, and psychological determinants. In A. O. Rorty (Ed.), *Explaining emotions* (pp. 37–72). Berkeley: University of California Press.

Bachman, J.G., & O'Malley, P.M. (1984). Black-white differences in self-esteem: Are they affected by response styles? *American Journal of Sociology, 90*(3), 624–639.

Baddeley, A. D., & Hitch, G. (1974). Working memory. In G. Bower (Ed.), *Recent advances in learning and motivating.* New York: Academic Press.

Bahrick, H. P., & Hall, L. K. (1991). Lifetime maintenance of high school mathematics content. *Journal of Experimental Psychology: General, 120,* 20–33.

Bakan, D. (1966). *The duality of human existence.* Boston, MA: Beacon Press.

Balint, M. (1959). *Thrills and regression.* London, England: Hogarth Press.

Bard, P., & Mountcastle, V. B. (1948). Some forebrain mechanisms involved in the expression of rage with special reference to suppression of angry behavior. *Research Publications of the Association for Research on Nervous and Mental Disease, 27,* 362–404.

Barna, L. M. (1997). Stumbling blocks in intercultural communication. In L. Samovar & R. Porter (Eds.), *Intercultural communication: A reader* (pp. 370–379). Belmont, CA: Wadsworth.

Barnlund, D. C., & Araki, S. (1985). Intercultural encounters: The management of compliments by Japanese and Americans. *Journal of Cross-Cultural Psychology, 16*(1), 9–26.

Barnlund, D. C., & Yoshioka, M. (1990). Apologies: Japanese and American styles. *International Journal of Intercultural Relations, 14,* 193–206.

Barry, H. (1980). Description and uses of the Human Relations Area Files. In H. C. Triandis & J. W. Berry (Eds.), *Handbook of cross-cultural psychology, Vol. 2: Methodology* (pp. 445–478). Boston: Allyn & Bacon.

Barry, H., Josephson, L., Lauer, E., & Marshall, C. (1976). Agents and techniques for child training. *Ethnology, 16,* 191–230.

Bartlett, F. C. (1932). *Remembering.* Cambridge, England: Cambridge University Press.

Baumrind, D. (1971). Current patterns of parental authority. *Developmental Psychology Monograph, 4* (No. 1, Pt. 2).

Beach, L. R. (1993). Image theory: Personal and organizational decisions. In G. A. Klein & J. Orasanu (Eds.), *Decision making in action: Models and methods* (pp. 148–157).Norwood, NJ: Ablex Publishing Corp.

Bechtold, D. W. (1988). Cluster suicide in American Indian adolescents. *American Indian and Alaska Native Mental Health Research, 1*(3), 26–35.

Beiser, M. (1985). A study of depression among traditional Africans, urban North Americans, and Southeast Asian refugees. In A. Kleinman & B. Good (Eds.), *Culture and depression. Studies in the anthropology and cross-cultural psychiatry of affect and disorder* (pp. 272–298). Berkeley: University of California.

Beit-Hallahmi, B. (1972). National character and national behavior in the Middle East conflict: the case of the "Arab personality." *International Journal of Group Tensions, 2*(3), 19–28.

Ben-David, A. (1996). Therapists' perceptions of multicultural assessment and therapy with immigrant families. *Journal of Family Therapy, 18,* 23–41.

Benedict, R. (1946). *The chrysanthemum and the sword.* Boston: Houghton Mifflin.

Benet-Martinez, V., & John, O. P. (1998). Los Cinco Grandes across cultures and ethnic groups: Multi trait-multi method analyses of the Big Five in Spanish and English. *Journal of Personality and Social Psychology, 75*(3), 729–750.

Bennett, M. J. (1979). Overcoming the golden rule: Sympathy and empathy. *Communication Yearbook, 3,* 407–422.

Bennett, M. J. (1988). Foundations of knowledge in international educational exchange: Intercultural communication. In J. Reid (Ed.), *Building the professional dimension of educational exchange.* Washington, D.C.: NAFSA.

Bennett, M. J. (1993). Towards ethnorelativism: A developmental model of intercultural sensitivity. In R. Michael Paige (Ed.), *Education for the intercultural experience.* Yarmouth, ME: Intercultural Press.

Beratis, S. (1986). Suicide in southwestern Greece 1979–1984. *Acta Psychiatrica Scandinavica, 74*(5), 433–439.

Berger, C. (1979). Beyond initial interaction. In H. Giles & R. St. Claire (Eds.) *Language and social psychology* (pp. 122–144). Oxford, UK: Basil Blackwell.

Berger, C. R., & Calabrese, R. J. (1975). Some explorations in initial interaction and beyond: Toward a development theory of interpersonal communication. *Human Communication Research, 10,* 179–196.

Bergling, K. (1981). *Moral development: The validity of Kohlberg's Theory.* Stockholm: Almgrist & Wilsell International.

Berkman, L. F., & Syme, S. L. (1979). Social networks, host resistance, and mortality: A nine-year follow-up study of Alameda County residents. *American Journal of Epidemiology, 109,* 186–204.

Berko, J. (1958). The child's learning of English morphology. *Word, 14,* 150–177.

Berko-Gleason, J. (Ed.). (1989). *The development of language* (2nd ed.). Columbus, OH: C. E. Merrill.

Berlin, B., & Kay, P. (1969). *Basic color terms: Their universality and evolution.* Berkeley: University of California Press.

Bernal, H. (1993). A model for delivering culture-relevant care in the community. *Public Health Nursing, 10*(4), 228–232.

Bernieri, F. & Gillis, J.S. (1995). The judgement of rapport: A cross-cultural comparison between Americans and Greeks. *Journal of Nonverbal Behavior, 19*(2), 115–131.

Berry, D. S., & McArthur, L. Z. (1985). Some components and consequences of a babyface. *Journal of Personality and Social Psychology, 48,* 312–323.

Berry, D. S., & McArthur, L. Z. (1986). Perceiving character in faces: The impact of age-related craniofacial changes in social perception. *Psychological Bulletin, 100,* 3–18.

Berry, J. W. (1966). Temne and Eskimo perceptual skills. *International Journal of Psychology, 1,* 207–229.

Berry, J. W. (1969). On cross-cultural comparability. *International Journal of Psychology, 4,* 119–128.

Berry, J. W. (1976). Sex differences in behavior and cultural complexity. *Indian Journal of Psychology, 51,* 89–97.

Berry, J. W., Poortinga, Y. H., Segall, M. H., & Dasen, P. R. (1992). *Cross-cultural psychology: Research and applications.* New York: Cambridge University Press.

Berscheid, E. (1988). Some comments on love's anatomy: Or, whatever happened to old-fashioned lust? In R. J. Sternberg & M. L. Barnes (Eds.), *Anatomy of love.* New Haven, CT: Yale University Press.

Best, D., House, A., Barnard, E. A., & Spicker, S. B. (1994). Parent-child interactions in France, Germany, and Italy: The effects of gender and culture. *Journal of Cross-Cultural Psychology, 25*(2), 181–193.

Betancourt, H., & Lopez, R. S. (1993). The study of culture, ethnicity, and race in American psychology. *American Psychologist, 48*(6), 629–637.

Bickerton, D. (1981). *The roots of language.* Ann Arbor, MI: Karoma Publishers.

Biehl, M., Matsumoto, D., Ekman, P., Hearn, V., Heider, K., Kudoh, T., & Ton, V. (1997). Matsumoto and Ekman's Japanese and Caucasian facial expressions of emotion (JACFEE): Reliability data and cross-national differences. *Journal of Nonverbal Behavior, 21,* 3–21.

Bigler, R. S. & Liben, L. S. (1993). A cognitive-developmental approach to racial stereotyping and reconstructive memory in Euro-American children. *Child Development, 64* (5), 1507–1518.

Binion, V. J. (1990). Psychological androgyny: A black female perspective. *Sex Roles, 22,* 487–507.

Birenbaum, M. & Kraemer, R. (1995). Gender and ethnic-group differences in causal attributions for success and failure in mathematics and language examinations. *Journal of Cross-Cultural Psychology, 26*(3), 342–359.

Bissilat, J., Laya, D., Pierre, E., & Pidoux, C. (1967). La notion de lakkal dans la culture Djerma-Songhai [The concept of lakkal in Djerma-Songhai culture]. *Psychopathologie Africaine, 3,* 207–264.

Black, J. S., & Porter, L. W. (1991). Managerial behavior and job performance: A successful manager in Los Angeles may not succeed in Hong Kong. *Journal of International Business Studies, 22,* 99–113.

Blau, Z. S. (1981). *Black children–white children: Competence, socialization, and social structure.* New York: Free Press.

Bletzer, K.V. (1991). Biobehavioral characteristics of a culture-bound syndrome perceived as life-threatening illness. *Qualitative Health Research, 1* (2), 200–233.

Blinco, M. A. P. (1992). A cross-cultural study of task persistence of young children in Japan and the United States. *Journal of Cross-Cultural Psychology, 21*(3), 407–415.

Block, J. (1983). Differential premises arising from differential socialization of the sexes: Some conjectures. *Child Development, 54,* 1335–1354.

Bloom, A. H. (1981). *The linguistic shaping of thought: A study in the impact of language on thinking in China and the West.* Hillsdale, NJ: Erlbaum.

Bloom, A. H. (1984). Caution—the words you use may affect what you say: A response to Au. *Cognition, 17*(3), 275–287.

Bochner, S. (1982). *Cultures in contact: Studies in cross-cultural interaction.* Oxford, England: Pergamon.

Bochner, S. (1994). Cross-cultural differences in the self concept. *Journal of Cross-Cultural Psychology, 25,* 273–283.

Bochner, S., & Hesketh, B. (1994). Power distance, individualism/collectivism, and job-related attitudes in a culturally diverse work group. *Journal of Cross-Cultural Psychology, 25*(2), 233–257.

Bochner, S., & Osako, T. (1977). Ethnic role salience in racially homogeneous and heterogeneous societies. *Journal of Cross-Cultural Psychology, 8*(4), 477–492.

Bochner, S., & Perks, W. R. (1971). National role evocation as a function of cross-national interaction. Journal of *Cross-Cultural Psychology, 2*(2), 157–164.

Bond, M. H. (1979). Dimensions used in perceiving peers: Cross-cultural comparisons of Hong Kong, Japanese, American and Filipino university students. *International Journal of Psychology, 14*(1), 47–56.

Bond, M. H. (1979). Winning either way: The effect of anticipating a competitive interaction on person perception. *Personality and Social Psychology Bulletin, 5*(3), 316–319.

Bond, M. H. (1986). *The psychology of the Chinese people.* New York: Oxford University Press.

Bond, M. H. (1991). Chinese values and health: A cultural-level examination. *Psychology and Health, 5*(2), 137–152.

Bond, M. H., & Forgas, J. P. (1984). Linking person perception to behavior intention across cultures: The role of cultural collectivism. *Journal of Cross-Cultural Psychology, 15,* 337–352.

Bond, M. H., Leung, K., & Wan, K. C. (1982). The social impact of self-effacing attributions: The Chinese case. *Journal of Social Psychology, 118*(2), 157–166.

Bond, M. H., Nakazato, H., & Shiraishi, D. (1975). Universality and distinctiveness in dimensions of Japanese person perception. *Journal of Cross Cultural Psychology, 6*(3), 346–357.

Bond, M. H., & Smith, P. B. (1996). Cross-cultural social and organizational psychology. *Annual Review of Psychology, 47,* 205–235.

Bond, M. H., & Tak-Sing, C. (1983). College students' spontaneous self concept: The effect of culture among respondents in Hong Kong, Japan, and the United States. *Journal of Cross-Cultural Psychology, 14,* 153–171.

Bond, M. H., Wan, K. C., Leong, K., & Giacalone, R. A. (1985). How are responses to verbal insult related to cultural collectivism and power distance? *Journal of Cross-Cultural Psychology, 16*(1), 111–127.

Bond, M. H., & Wang, S. (1983). China: Aggressive behavior and the problems of mainstreaming order and harmony. In A. P. Goldstein & M. H. Segall (Eds.), *Aggression in global perspective* (pp. 58–74). New York: Pergamon.

Boor, M. (1976). Relationship of internal-external control and national suicide rates. *Journal of Social Psychology, 100*(1), 143–144.

Borkenau, P., & Ostendorf, F. (1998). The Big Five as states: How useful is the five-factor model to describe intraindividual variations over time? *Journal of Research in Personality, 32*(2), 202–221.

Born, M., Bleichrodt, N., & Van der Flier, H. (1987). Cross-cultural comparison of sex-related differences on intelligence tests: A meta-analysis. *Journal of Cross-Cultural Psychology, 18,* 283–314.

Bornstein, H. M. (1989). Cross-cultural developmental comparisons: The case of Japanese-American infant and mother activities and interactions. What we know, what we need to know, and why we need to know. *Developmental Review, 9*, 171–204.

Bornstein, M. H., Haynes, O. M., Azuma, H., et al (1998). A cross-national study of self-evaluations and attributions in parenting: Argentina, Belgium, France, Israel, Italy, Japan and the United States. *Developmental Psychology, 34*(4), 662–676.

Bothwell, R. K., Brigham, J. C. & Malpass, R. S. (1989). Cross-racial identification. *Personality and Social Psychology Bulletin, 15* (1), 19–25.

Bouchard, T. J., Jr., & McGue, M. (1981). Familial studies of intelligence: A review. *Science, 212,* 1055–1059.

Boucher, J. D., & Brandt, M. E. (1981). Judgement of emotion: American and Malay antecedents. *Journal of Cross Cultural Psychology, 12*(3), 272–283.

Boucher, J. D., & Carlson, G. E. (1980). Recognition of facial expression in three cultures. *Journal of Cross-Cultural Psychology, 11*(3), 263–280.

Boucher, J. D., Landis, D., & Clark, K. A. (1987). *Ethnic conflict: International perspectives.* Newbury Park, CA: Sage.

Bowen, M. (1966). The use of family theory in clinical practice. *Comprehensive Psychiatry, 7,* 345–374.

Bowlby, J. (1969). *Attachment and loss, Vol. 1: Attachment.* New York: Basic Books.

Bradley, G. W. (1978). Self-serving biases in the attribution process: A re-examination of the fact or fiction question. *Journal of Personality and Social Psychology, 35,* 56–71.

Brandt, M. E., & Boucher, J. D. (1985). Judgement of emotions from antecedent situations in three cultures. In I. Lagunes & Y. Poortinga (Eds.), *From a different perspective: Studies of behavior across cultures* (pp.348–362). Netherlands: Swets & Zeitlinger.

Brandt, M. E., & Boucher, J. D. (1986). Concepts of depression in emotion lexicons of eight cultures. *International Journal of Intercultural Relations, 10,* 321–346.

Brehm, S. S. (1985). *Intimate relationships.* New York: Random House.

Brewer, M. B., & Campbell, D. T. (1976). *Ethnocentrism and intergroup attitudes.* New York: Wiley.

Brewer, M. B., & Kramer, R. M. (1985). The psychology of intergroup attitudes and behavior. *Annual Review of Psychology, 36,* 219–243.

Brigham, J. C. & Malpass, R. S. (1985). The role of experience and contact in the recognition of faces of own and other race persons. *Journal of Social Issues, 41* (3), 139–155.

Brislin, R. (1970). Back translation for cross-cultural research. *Journal of Cross-Cultural Psychology, 1,* 185–216.

Brislin, R. (1993). *Understanding culture's influence on behavior.* Fort Worth, TX: Harcourt Brace Jovanovich.

Bronstein, P. (1984). Differences in mothers' and fathers' behaviors toward children: A cross-cultural comparison. *Developmental Psychology, 20*(6), 995–1003.

Bronstein, P. A., & Paludi, M. (1988). The introductory psychology course from a broader human perspective. In P. A. Bronstein & K. Quina (Eds.), *Teaching a psychology of people: Resources for gender and sociocultural awareness* (pp. 21–36). Washington, DC: American Psychological Association.

Brook, D. W., Gordon, C., & Meadow, H. (1998). Ethnicity, culture, and group psychotherapy. *Group, 22*(2), 53–80.

Broota, K.D., & Ganguli, H.C. (1975). Cultural differences in perceptual selectivity. *Journal of Social Psychology, 95,* 157–163.

Brown, R., & Lenneberg, E. (1954). A study in language and cognition. *Journal of Abnormal and Social Psychology, 49,* 454–462.

Bruner, J. S., Oliver, R. R., & Greenfield, P. M. (1966). *Studies in cognitive growth.* New York: Wiley.

Buck, E. B., Newton, B. J., & Muramatsu, Y. (1984). Independence and obedience in the U. S. and Japan. *International Journal of Intercultural Relations, 8,* 279–300.

Buck, R. (1984). *The communication of emotion.* New York: Guilford Press.

Bugental, D. E., Kaswan, J. W., & Love, L. R. (1970). Perception of contradictory meanings conveyed by verbal and nonverbal channels. *Journal of Personality and Social Psychology, 16*(4), 647–655.

Burger, J. M., & Hemans, L. T. (1988). Desire for control and the use of attribution processes. *Journal of Personality, 56,* 531–546.

Burgos, N. M., & Diaz-Perez, Y. I. (1986). An explanation of human sexuality in the Puerto Rican culture. Special issue: Human sexuality, ethnoculture, and social work. *Journal of Social Work and Human Sexuality, 4,* 135–150.

Burleson, B. R. (1997). A different voice on different cultures: Illusion and reality in the study of sex differences in personal relationships. *Personal Relationships, 4*(3), 229–241.

Buss, D. M. (1988). The evolution of human intra-sexual competition: Tactics of mate attraction. *Journal of Personality and Social Psychology, 54,* 616–628.

Buss, D. M. (1989). Sex differences in human mate preferences: Evolutionary hypotheses tested in 37 cultures. *Behavioral and Brain Sciences, 12,* 1–49.

Butcher, J. N, Lim, J., & Nezami, E. (1998). Objective study of abnormal personality in cross-cultural settings: The Minnesota Multiphasic Personality Inventory (MMPI-2). *Journal of Cross Cultural Psychology, 29*(1), 189–211.

Buunk, B., & Hupka, R. B. (1987). Cross-cultural differences in the elicitation of sexual jealousy. *Journal of Sex Research, 23*(1), 12–22.

Byrne, D., & Murnen, S. K. (1988). Maintaining loving relationships. In R. J. Sternberg & M. L. Barnes (Eds.), *The psychology of love.* New Haven, CT: Yale University Press.

Calhoun, J. B. (1950). The study of wild animals under controlled conditions. *Annals of the New York Academy of Sciences, 51,* 113–122.

Campbell, N. C. G., Graham, J. L., Jolibert, A., & Meissner, H. G. (1988). Marketing negotiations in France, Germany the United Kingdom and the United States. *Journal of Marketing, 52,* 49–62.

Cannon, W. B. (1927). The James-Lange theory of emotions: A critical examination and an alternative theory. *American Journal of Psychology, 39,* 106–124.

Caprara, G. V., Barbaranelli, C. & Comrey, A. L. (1995). Factor analysis of the NEO-PI Inventory and the Comrey Personality Scales in an Italian sample. *Personality and Individual Differences, 18*(2), 193–200.

Caprara, G. V., & Perugini, M. (1994). Personality described by adjectives: The generalizability of the Big Five to the Italian lexical context. *European Journal of Personality, 8*(5), 357–369.

Carlo, G., Koller H. S., Eisenberg N., DaSilva, S. M., & Frohlich, B. C. (1996). A cross-national study on the relations among prosocial moral reasoning, gender role orientations, and prosocial behaviors. *Developmental Psychology, 32*(2), 231–240.

Carrell, L. J. (1997). Diversity in the communication curriculum: Impact on student empathy. *Communication Education, 46*(4), 234–244.

Carroll, J. B., & Casagrande, J. B. (1958). The function of language classifications in behavior. In E. E. Maccoby, T. M. Newcomb, & E. L. Hartley (Eds.), *Readings in social psychology* (pp. 18–31). New York: Holt.

Carson, R. C., Butcher, J. N., & Coleman, J. C. (1988). *Abnormal psychology and modern life* (8th ed.). Glenview, IL: Scott, Foresman.

Carter, K. A., and Dinnel, D. L. (1997). *Conceptualization of self-esteem in collectivistic and individualistic cultures.* Bellingham: Western Washington University Press.

Cashmore, J. A., & Goodnow, J. J. (1986). Influences on Australian parents' values: Ethnicity versus sociometric status. *Journal of Cross-Cultural Psychology, 17,* 441–454.

Caudill, W., & Weinstein, H. (1969). Maternal care and infant behavior in Japan and America. *Psychiatry: Journal for the Study of Interpersonal Processes, 32*(1), 12–43.

Cederblad, M. (1988). Behavioural disorders in children from different cultures. *Acta Psychiatrica Scandinavia Supplementum, 344,* 85–92.

Cerroni-Long, E. L. (1985). Culture as communication: Defining the parameters of analysis. *Communication and Cognition, 18*(4), 379–392.

Chandler, T. A., & Spies, C. J. (1996). Semantic differential comparisons of attributions and dimensions among respondents from seven nations. *Psychological Reports, 79,* 747–758.

Chandra, S. (1975). Some patterns of response on the Queensland test. *Australian Psychologist, 10* (2), 185–192.

Chao, K. R. (1996). Chinese and European American mothers' beliefs about the role of parenting in children's school success. *Journal of Cross-Cultural Psychology, 27*(4), 403–423.

Chen, G. M. (1990). Intercultural communication competence: Some perspectives of research. *Howard Journal of Communications, 2*(3), 243–261.

Chen, G. M. (1995). Differences in self-disclosure patterns among Americans versus Chinese: A comparative study. *Journal of Cross-Cultural Psychology, 26,* 84–91.

Cheng, D., Leong, F. T. L., & Geist, R. (1993). Cultural differences in psychological distress between Asian and Caucasian American college students. *Journal of Multicultural Counseling and Development, 21,* 182–190.

Cheung, F. M., & Leung, K. (1998). Indigenous personality measures: Chinese examples. *Journal of Cross Cultural Psychology, 29*(1), 233–248.

Chinese Culture Connection. (1987). Chinese values and the search for culture-free dimensions of culture. *Journal of Cross-Cultural Psychology, 18,* 143–164.

Chisholm, J. (1983). *Navajo infancy*. New York: Aldine.

Chomsky, N. (1965). *Aspects of the theory of syntax*. Cambridge, MA: MIT Press.

Chomsky, N. (1967). *Current issues in linguistic theory*. The Hague: Mouton.

Chomsky, N. (1969). *Deep structure, surface structure, and semantic interpretation*. Bloomington: Indiana University Linguistics Club.

Church, A. T. & Katigbak, M. S. (1988). Imposed-etic and emic measures of intelligence as predictors of early school performance of rural Philippine children. *Journal of Cross Cultural Psychology, 19* (2), 164–177.

Church, A. T., Katigbak, M. S., & Reyes, J. A. S. (1996). Toward a taxonomy of trait adjectives in Filipino: Comparing personality lexicons across cultures. *European Journal of Personality, 10*(1), 3–24.

Church, A. T., & Lonner, W. J. (Eds.), (1998). Personality and its measurement in cross cultural perspective. *Journal of Cross-Cultural Psychology, 29*(1).

Church, A. T., Reyes, J. A. S., Katigbak, M. S., & Grimm, S. D. (1997). Filipino personality structure and the Big Five model: A lexical approach. *Journal of Personality, 65*(3), 477–528.

Claeys, W. (1967). The factorial intelligence structure of the Congolese at the beginning of their university studies. *Psychologica Belgica, 7*, 7–15.

Clark, M. L., & Person, W. (1982). Racial stereotypes revisited. *International Journal of Intercultural Relations, 6*, 381–392.

Clymer, C. E. (1995). The psychology of deafness: Enhancing self-concept in the deaf and hearing impaired. *Family Therapy, 22*(2), 113–120.

Clymer, K. J. (1995). *Quest for freedom: The United States' and India's independence*. Columbia: Columbia University Press.

Cogan, J. C., Bhalla, S. K., Sefa-Dedeh, A., & Rothblum, E. D. (1996). A comparison study of United States and African students on perceptions of obesity and thinness. *Journal of Cross-Cultural Psychology, 27*, 98–113.

Cohen, D., Nisbett, R. E., Bowdle, B. F., & Schwartz, N. (1996). Insult, aggression, and the southern culture of honor: An "experimental ethnography." *Journal of Personality and Social Psychology, 70*(5), 945–960.

Cohen, N. (1982). Same or different? A problem of identity in cross-cultural marriages. *Journal of Family Therapy, 4*(2), 177–199.

Cole, M. (1996). *Cultural psychology: A once and future discipline*. Cambridge: Harvard University Press.

Cole, M., Gay, J., Glick, J. A., & Sharp, D. W. (1971). *The cultural context of learning and thinking: An exploration in experimental anthropology*. New York: Basic Books.

Cole, M., & Scribner, S. (1974). *Culture and thought: A psychological introduction*. New York: Wiley.

Collett, P. (1971). On training Englishmen in the non-verbal behavior of Arabs: An experiment in inter-cultural communication. *International Journal of Psychology, 6*, 209–215.

Comas-Diaz, L. (1992). The future of psychotherapy with ethnic minorities *Psychotherapy, 29*, 88–94.

Comas-Diaz, L., & Jacobsen, F. M. (1991). Ethnocultural transference and countertransference in the therapeutic dyad. *American Journal of Orthopsychiatry, 61*, 392–402.

Conroy, M., Hess, D. R., Azuma, H., & Kashiwagi, K. (1980). Maternal strategies for regulating children's behavior. *Journal of Cross-Cultural Psychology, 11*(2), 153–172.

Cook, P. (1994). Chronic illness beliefs and the role of social networks among Chinese, Indian, and Anglo Celtic Canadians. *Journal of Cross-Cultural Psychology, 25*(4), 452–465.

Cousins, S. D. (1989). Culture and self-perception in Japan and the United States. *Journal of Personality and Social Psychology, 56*, 124–131.

Crandall, C. S., & Martinez, R. (1996). Culture, ideology, and antifat attitudes. *Personality and Social Psychology Bulletin, 22*(11), 1165–1176.

Crittenden, K. S. (1991). Asian self-effacement or feminine modesty? Attributional patterns of women university students in Taiwan. *Gender and Society, 5*, 98–117.

Crook, T. H., Youngjohn, J. R., Larrabee, G. J., & Salama, M. (1992). Aging and everyday memory: A cross-cultural study. *Neuropsychology, 6* (2), 123–136.

Cunningham, M.R., Roberts, A.R, Barbee, A.P., Druen, P. B., & Wu, C. (1995). "Their ideas of beauty are, on the whole, the same as ours": Consistency and variability in the cross-cultural perception of female physical attractiveness. *Journal of Personality and Social Psychology, 68*(2), 261–279.

Dabul, A. J., Bernal, M. E., & Knight, G. P. (1995). Allocentric and idiocentric self-description and academic achievement among Mexican American and Anglo American adolescents. *The Journal of Social Psychology, 135*(2), 621–630.

Daibo, I., Murasawa, H., & Chou, Y. (1994). Attractive faces and affection of beauty: A comparison in preference of feminine facial beauty in Japan and Korea. *The Japanese Journal of Research on Emotions, 1*(2), 101–123.

Dalal, K. A., Sharma, R., & Bisht, S. (1983). Causal attributions of ex-criminal tribal and urban children in India. *The Journal of Social Psychology, 119,* 163–171.

Damond, M. E., Breur, N. L., & Pharr, A. E. (1993). The evaluation of setting and a culturally specific HIV/AIDS curriculum: HIV/AIDS knowledge and behavior intent of African American adolescents. *Journal of Black Psychology, 19,* (2), 169–189.

Darwin, C. (1872). *The expression of emotion in man and animals.* London: John Murray.

Darwin, C. (1998). In P. Ekman (Ed.), *The expression of the emotions in man and animals* (3rd ed.). New York: Oxford University Press.

Dasen, P. R. (1975). Concrete operational development in three cultures. *Journal of Cross-Cultural Psychology, 6,* 156–172.

Dasen, P. R. (1982). Cross-cultural aspects of Piaget's theory: The competence-performance model. In L. L. Adler (Ed.), *Cross-cultural research at issue.* New York: Academic Press.

Dasen, P. R., Dembele, B., Ettien, K., Kabran, L., Kamagate, D., Koffi, D. A., & N'Guessean, A. (1985). N'glouele, l'intelligence chez les Baoule [N'glouele: Intelligence among the Ivory Coast Baoule]. *Archives de Psychologie, 53,* 293–324.

Dasen, P. R., Lavallee, M., & Retschitzki, J. (1979). Training conservation of quantity (liquids) in West African (Baoule) children. *International Journal of Psychology, 14,* 57–68.

Dasen, P. R., Ngini, L., & Lavallee, M. (1979). Cross-cultural training studies of concrete operations. In L. Eckensberger, Y. Poortinga, & W. Lonner (Eds.), *Cross-cultural contributions to psychology* (pp. 94–104). Amsterdam: Swets & Zeitlinger.

Dasgupta, S. D. (1998). Gender roles and cultural continuity in the Asian Indian immigrant community in the U.S. *Sex Roles, 38* (11–12), 953–974.

David, K. H., & Bochner, S. (1967). Teacher ratings of I.Q. and porteus maze scores of Pitjandjara children. *Perceptual and Motor Skills, 25* (2), 639–640.

Davies, I. R. L., Sowden, P. T., Jerrett, D. T., & Corbelt, G. G. (1998). A cross-cultural study of English and Setswana speakers on a colour triads task: A test of the Sapir-Whorf hypothesis. *British Journal of Psychology, 89*(1), 1–15.

Davis, F. G. (1991). *Who is black? One nation's definition.* University Park: Pennsylvania State University Press.

Deck, L. P. (1968). Buying brains by the inch. *Journal of College and University Personnel Associations, 19,* 33–37.

De-Fruyt, F., & Mervielde, I. (1998). The assessment of the Big Five in the Dutch language domain. *Psychologica Belgica, 38*(1), 1–22.

Degler, C. (1971). *Neither black nor white: Slavery and race relations in Brazil and the United States.* New York: Macmillan.

Delgado, M. (1995). Hispanic natural support systems and alcohol and other drug services: Challenges and rewards for practice. *Alcoholism Treatment Quarterly, 12,* 17–31.

DePaulo, B. M., Stone, J., & Lassiter, G. D. (1985). Deceiving and detecting deceit. In B. R. Schlenker (Ed.), *The self and social life* (pp. 323–370). New York: McGraw-Hill.

Depaulo, E. M., Rosenthal, R., Eisenstat, R. A., Rogers, P. L., & Susan, F. (1978). Decoding discrepant nonverbal cues. *Journal of Personality and Social Psychology, 36*(3), 313–323.

De Raad, B., Hendriks, A. J., & Hofstee, W. K. (1992, October). Towards a refined structure of personality traits. *European Journal of Personality, 6*(4), 301–319.

De Raad, B., Perugini, M., & Szirmak, Z. (1997). In pursuit of a cross-lingual reference structure of personality traits: Comparisons among five languages. *European Journal of Personality, 11*(3), 167–185.

De Raad, B., Perugini, M., Hrebickova, M., & Szarota, P. (1998, January). Lingua franca of personality: Taxonomies and structures based on the psycholexical approach. *Journal of Cross Cultural Psychology, 29*(1), 212–232.

Desjarlais, R. R. (1991). Dreams, divination, and Yolmo ways of knowing. *Dreaming: Journal of the Association for the Study of Dreams, 1* (3), 211–224.

De Valois, R. L., Abramov, I., & Jacobs, G. H. (1966). Analysis of response patterns of LGN cells. *Journal of the Optical Society of America, 56,* 966–977.

De Valois, R. L., & Jacobs, G. H. (1968). Primate color vision. *Science, 162,* 533–540.

Devereux, C. E., Jr., Bronfenbrenner, U., & Suci, G. (1962). Patterns of parent behaviour in the United States of America and the Federal Republic of Germany: A cross-national comparison. *International Social Science Journal, 14,* 488–506.

Devine, P. G., & Malpass, R. S. (1985). Orienting strategies in differential face recognition. *Personality and Social Psychology Bulletin, 11* (1), 33–40.

Dhawan, N., Roseman, I. J., Naidu, R. K., Komilla, T., & Rettek, S. I. (1995). Self-concepts across two cultures. *Journal of Cross-Cultural Psychology, 26*(6), 606–621.

Diaz-Loving, R. (1998, January). Contributions of Mexican ethnopsychology to the resolution of the etic-emic dilemma in personality. *Journal of Cross Cultural Psychology, 29*(1), 104–118.

Diener, E., Diener, M. (1995, April). Cross-cultural correlates of life satisfaction and self-esteem. *Journal of Personality and Social Psychology, 68*(4), 653–663.

Digman, J. M., Shmelyov, A. G. (1996, August). The structure of temperament and personality in Russian children. *Journal of Personality and Social Psychology, 71*(2), 341–351.

DiMartino, C. E. (1994). Appraising social dilemmas: A cross-cultural study of Sicilians, Sicilian Americans, and Americans. *Journal of Cross-Cultural Psychology, 25*(2), 165–180.

Dinges, N. G., & Hull, P. (1992). Personality, culture, and international studies. In D. Lieberman (Ed.), *Revealing the world: An interdisciplinary reader for international studies.* Dubuque, IA: Kendall-Hunt.

Dion, K. K. (1986). Stereotyping based on physical attractiveness: Issues and conceptual perspectives. In C. P. Herman, M. P. Zanna, & E. T. Higgins (Eds.), *Ontario symposium on personality and social psychology* (Vol. 3). Hillsdale, NJ: Erlbaum.

Dion, K., & Dion, K. (1993). Gender and ethnocultural comparisons in styles of love. *Psychology of Women Quarterly, 17,* 463–473

Doi, K. (1982). Two dimensional theory of achievement motivation. *Japanese Journal of Psychology, 52,* 344–350.

Doi, K. (1985). The relation between the two dimensions of achievement motivation and personality of male university students. *Japanese Journal of Psychology, 56,* 107–110.

Doi, T. (1973). *The anatomy of dependence.* Tokyo: Kodansha.

Domino, G. (1992). Cooperation and competition in Chinese and American children. *Journal of Cross-Cultural Psychology, 23*(4), 456–467.

Domino, G., & Lin, W. (1993). Cancer metaphors: Taiwan and the United States. *International Journal of Psychology, 28*(1), 45–56.

Draguns, J. (1997). Abnormal behavior patterns across cultures: Implications for counseling and psychotherapy. *International Journal of Intercultural Relations, 21*(2), 213–248.

Duda, J. L., & Allison, M. T. (1989). The attributional theory of achievement motivation: Cross-cultural considerations. *International Journal of Intercultural Relations, 13,* 37–55.

Durie, M. H. (1997). Maori, cultural identity and its implications for mental health services. *International Journal of Mental Health, 26* (3), 23–35.

Durkheim, E. (1938/1964). *The rules of sociological method.* Reprint. London: The Free Press of Glenscoe.

Durrett, M. E., Otaki, M., & Richards, P. (1984). Attachment and mothers' perception of support from the father. *Journal of the International Society for the Study of Behavioral Development, 7,* 167–176.

Dyal, J. A. (1984). Cross-cultural research with the locus of control construct. In H. M. Lefcourt (Ed.), *Research with the locus of control construct* (Vol. 3, pp. 209–306). New York: Academic Press.

Eagly, A., Ashmore, R. D., Makhijani, M. G., & Longo, L. C. (1991). What is beautiful is good, but . . . : A meta-analytic review of research on the physical attractiveness stereotype. *Psychological Bulletin, 110*(1), 109–128.

Earley, P. C. (1989). Social loafing and collectivism: A comparison of the United States and the People's Republic of China. *Administrative Science Quarterly, 34,* 565–581.

Eberhardt, J. L., & Randall, J. L. (1997). The essential notion of race. *Psychological Science, 8*(3), 198–203.

Ebrahimpour, M., & Johnson, J. L. (1992). Quality, vendor evaluation and organizational performance: A comparison of U.S. and Japanese firms. *Journal of Business Research, 25,* 129–142.

EchoHawk, M. (1997). Suicide: The scourge of Native American people. *Suicide and Life Threatening Behavior, 27*(1), 60–67.

Edman, J. L. & Kameoka, A. K. (1997). Cultural differences in illness schemas: An analysis of Filipino and American illness attributions. *Journal of Cross-Cultural Psychology, 28*(3), 252–265.

Edwards, P. K. (1981). Race, residence, and leisure style: Some policy implications. *Leisure Sciences, 4*(2), 95–112.

Efron, D. (1941). *Gesture and environment.* New York: King's Crown.

Ekman, K. L. (1982). A comparative study of value priorities in a sample of United States Air Force personnel and their spouses. *Dissertation Abstracts International, 43*(6-B), 2037.

Ekman, P. (1972). Universal and cultural differences in facial expression of emotion. In J. R. Cole (Ed.), *Nebraska symposium on motivation, 1971* (pp. 207–283). Lincoln: University of Nebraska Press.

Ekman, P. (1973). Universal facial expressions in emotion. *Studia Psychologica, 15*(2), 140–147.

Ekman, P. (1994). Strong evidence for universals in facial expressions: A reply to Russell's mistaken critique. *Psychological Bulletin, 115*, 268–287.

Ekman, P., & Friesen, W. V. (1969). The repertoire of nonverbal behavior: Categories, origins, usage, and coding. *Semiotica, 1*, 49–98.

Ekman, P., & Friesen, W. V. (1971). Constants across cultures in the face and emotion. *Journal of Personality and Social Psychology, 17*, 124–129.

Ekman, P., & Friesen, W. V. (1986). A new pan-cultural expression of emotion. *Motivation and Emotion, 10*, 159–168.

Ekman, P., Friesen, W. V., & Bear, J. (1984, May). International language of gestures. *Psychology Today*, pp. 64–69.

Ekman, P., Friesen, W. V., & Ellsworth, P (1972). *Emotion in the human face.* New York: Garland.

Ekman, P., Friesen, W., LeCompete, W. L., Ricci-Bitti, P. E., Tomita, M., Tzavaras, A., O'Sullivan, M., Diacoyanni-Tarlatzis, I., Krause, R., Pitcairn, T., Scherer, K., Chan. A., & Heider, K. (1987). Universals and cultural differences in the judgements of facial expressions of emotion. *Journal of Personality and Social Psychology, 53*(4), 712–717.

Ekman, P., & Heider, K. G. (1988). The universality of a contempt expression: A replication. *Motivation and Emotion, 12*, 17–22.

Ekman, P., Levenson, R., & Friesen, W. V. (1983). Autonomic nervous system activity distinguishes among emotions. *Science, 221*, 1208–1210.

Ekman, P., O'Sullivan, M., & Matsumoto, D. (1991a). Confusions about context in the judgment of facial expression: A reply to 'contempt and the relativity thesis.' *Motivation and Emotion, 15*, 169–176.

Ekman, P., O'Sullivan, M., & Matsumoto, D. (1991b). Contradictions in the study of contempt: What's it all about? *Motivation and Emotions, 15*, 293–296.

Ekman, P., Sorenson, E. R., & Friesen, W. V. (1969). Pan-cultural elements in facial displays of emotion. *Science, 164*, 86–94.

Elbedour, S., Shulman, S., & Kedem, P. (1997). Adolescent intimacy. *Journal of Cross-Cultural Psychology, 28*, 5–22.

Eley, T. C. (1997). General genes: A new theme in developmental psychopathology. *Current Directions in Psychological Science, 6*(4), 90–95.

El-Islam, M. F. (1983). Cultural change and intergenerational relationships in Arabian families. *International Journal of Family Psychiatry, 4*, 321–329.

Ellis, B., Kimmel, H., Diaz-Guerrero, R., Canas, J., & Bajo, M. (1994). Love and power in Mexico, Spain, and the United States. *Journal of Cross-Cultural Psychology, 25*(4), 525–540.

Enz, C. (1986). *Power and shared values in the corporate culture.* Ann Arbor, MI: University of Michigan Press.

Erikson, E. H. (1950). *Childhood and society.* New York: Norton.

Erikson, E. H. (1963). *Childhood and society* (2nd ed.). New York: Norton.

Ervin, S. M. (1964). Language and TAT content in bilinguals. *Journal of Abnormal and Social Psychology, 68*, 500–507.

Espin, O. M. (1993). Feminist theory: Not for or by white women only. *Counseling Psychologist, 21*, 103–108.

Evans, J. L., & Segall, M. H. (1969). Learning to classify by color and function: A study of concept discovery by Ganda children. *Journal of Social Psychology, 77*, 35–55.

Exline, R. V., Jones, P., & Maciorowski, K. (1977). *Race, affiliative-conflict theory and mutual visual attention during conversation.* Paper presented at the American Psychological Association meeting in San Francisco.

Eysenck, H. J. (1983). Is there a paradigm in personality research? *Journal of Research in Personality, 17*(4), 369–397.

Eysenck, S. B. G., & Abdel-Khalek, A. M. (1989). A cross cultural study of personality: Egyptian and English children. *International Journal of Psychology, 24*, 1–11.

Eysenck, S. B. G., Baban, P., Derevenco, P., & Pitariu, H. (1989). A cross cultural study of personality: Romanian and English adults. *Revue Roumaine des Science Sociales Serie de Psychologie, 33*(1), 75–80.

Eysenck, S. B. G., & Chan, J. (1982). A comparative study of personality in adults and children: Hong Kong vs. England. *Personality and Individual Differences, 3,* 153–160.

Eysenck, S. B. G., Makaremi, A., & Barrett, P. T. (1994). A cross-cultural study of personality: Iranian and English children. *Personality and Individual Differences, 16*(2), 203–210.

Fabrega, H. (1989). Language, culture, and the neurobiology of pain: A theoretical exploration. *Behavioral Neurology, 2* (4), 235–260.

Farver, J. M., Welles-Nystroem, B., Frosch, D. L., Wimbarti, S., & Hoppe-Graff,S. (1997). Toy stories: Aggression in children's narratives in the United States, Sweden, Germany, and Indonesia. *Journal of Cross-Cultural Psychology, 28*(4), 393–420.

Farver, M. J. & Howes, C. (1988). Cross-cultural differences in social interaction: A comparison of American and Indonesian children. *Journal of Cross-Cultural Psychology, 19*(2), 203–215.

Feather, N. T. (1986). Value systems across cultures: Australia and China. *International Journal of Psychology, 21,* 697–715.

Fehr, B. J. (1977). *Visual interactions in same and interracial dyads.* Unpublished master's thesis, University of Delaware.

Fehr, B. J. (1981). *The communication of evaluation through the use of interpersonal gaze in same and interracial female dyads.* Unpublished doctoral dissertation, University of Delaware.

Fehr, B. J., & Exline, R. V. (1987). Social visual interaction: A conceptual and literature review. In A. W. Siegman & S. Feldstein (Eds.), *Nonverbal behavior and communication* (2nd ed.) (pp. 225–326). Hillsdale, NJ: Erlbaum.

Feingold, A. (1992). Good-looking people are not what we think. *Psychological Bulletin, 111*(2), 304–341.

Feist, J., & Brannon, L. (1988). *Health psychology: An introduction to behavior and health.* Belmont, CA: Wadsworth.

Ferrante, J. (1992). *Sociology: A global perspective.* Belmont, CA: Wadsworth.

Festinger, L., Schachter, S., & Back, K. (1950). *Social pressures in informal groups: A study of human factors in housing.* New York: Harper.

Filardo, E. K. (1996). Gender patterns in African American and White adolescents' social interactions in same-race, mixed-gender groups. *Journal of Personality and Social Psychology, 71*(1), 71–82.

Fishman, J. A. (1960). A systematization of the Whorfian hypothesis. *Behavioral Science, 5,* 323–339.

Fletcher, J. M., Todd, J., & Satz, P. (1975). Culture fairness of three intelligence tests and a short form procedure. *Psychological Reports, 37,* (3, Pt 2), 1255–1262.

Flores, E., Eyre, S. L., & Millstein, S. G. (1998). Sociocultural beliefs related to sex among Mexican American adolescents. *Hispanic Journal of Behavioral Sciences, 20* (1), 60–82.

Forgas, J. P., & Bond, M. H. (1985). Cultural influences on the perceptions of interaction episodes. *Personality and Social Psychology Bulletin, 11*(1), 75–88.

Forgas, J. P., Furnham, A., & Frey, D. (1989). Cross-national differences in attributions of wealth and economic success. *Journal of Social Psychology, 129,* 643–657.

Forgas, P. J. (1992). On mood and peculiar people: Affect and person typicality in impression formation. *Journal of Personality & Social Psychology, 62*(5), 863–875.

Forgas, P. J. (1994). The role of emotion in social judgments: an introductory review and an Affect Infusion Model (AIM). *European Journal of Social Psychology, 24,* 1–24.

Forgas, P. J., & Bower, H. G. (1987). Mood effects on person-perception judgments. *Journal of Personality and Social Psychology, 53*(1), 53–60.

Forgas, P. J., & Fiedler, K. (1996). Us and them: Mood effects on intergroup discrimination. *Journal of Personality and Social Psychology, 70,* 28–40.

Forgas, P. J., & Moylan, J. S. (1991). Affective influences on stereotype judgements. *Cognition and Emotion, 5*(5/6), 379–395.

Forgas, P. J., & O'Driscoll, M. (1984). Cross-cultural and demographic differences in the perception of nations. *Journal of Cross-Cultural Psychology, 15*(2),

Forston, R. F., & Larson, C. U. (1968). The dynamics of space: An experimental study in proxemic behavior among Latin Americans and North Americans. *Journal of Communication, 18,* 109–116.

Franz, C. E., & White, K. M. (1985). Individuation and attachment in personality development: Extending Erickson's theory. *Journal of Personality, 53*(2): 224–256.

Freedman, D. (1974). *Human infancy: An evolutionary perspective.* Hillsdale, NJ: Erlbaum.

Freud, S., & Strachey, J. (1961). *Beyond the pleasure principle.* New York: W.W. Norton and Co, Inc.

Friedman, H. S. (1978). The relative strength of verbal versus nonverbal cues. *Personality and Social Psychology Bulletin, 4*(1), 147–150.

Friedman, M., & Rosenman, R. H. (1974). *Type A behavior and your heart.* New York: Knopf.

Friesen, W. V. (1972). *Cultural differences in facial expressions in a social situation: An experimental test of the concept of display rules.* Unpublished doctoral dissertation, University of California, San Francisco.

Furnham, A. (1984). Value systems and anomie in three cultures. *International Journal of Psychology, 19,* 565–579.

Furnham, A., & Akande, A. (1997). Cross-Cultural Differences in Attributions for Overcoming Specific Psychological Problems. *Journal of Social Behavior and Personality, 12*(3), 727–742.

Furnham, A., & Alibhai, N. (1983). Cross-cultural differences in the perception of female body shapes. *Psychology Medicine, 13,* 829–837.

Furnham, A., & Baguma, P. (1994). Cross-cultural differences in the evaluations of male and female body shapes. *International Journal of Eating Disorders, 15,* 81–89.

Furnham, A., Bond, M., Heaven, P., Hilton, D., Lobel, T., Masters, J., Payne, M., Rajamanikam, R., Stacey, B., & Van Daalen, H. (1991). A comparison of protestant work ethic beliefs in thirteen nations. *The Journal of Social Psychology, 133,* (2), 185–197.

Gabrenya, W. K., Jr., Wang, Y., & Latané, B. (1985). Social loafing on an optimizing task: Cross-cultural differences among Chinese and Americans. *Journal of Cross-Cultural Psychology, 16,* 223–242.

Galati, D. & Sciaky, R. (1995). The representation of antecedents of emotions in northern and southern Italy. *Journal of Cross-Cultural Psychology, 26*(2), 123–140.

Galloway, C. M. (1984). Nonverbal behavior in teacher-student relationships: An intercultural perspective. In. A. Wolfgang (Ed.), et al. *Nonverbal behavior: Perspectives, applications, intercultural insights* (pp. 411–430). Lewiston, NY: Hogrefe & Huber Publishers.

Garcia Coll, C. T. (1990). Developmental outcomes of minority infants: A process oriented look at our beginnings. *Child Development, 61,* 270–289.

Garcia Coll, C. T., Sepkoski, C., & Lester, B. M. (1981). Cultural and biomedical correlates of neonatal behavior. *Developmental Psychobiology, 14,* 147–154.

Gardner, H., & Hatch, T. (1989). Multiple intelligences go to school: Educational implications of the theory of multiple intelligences. *Educational Researcher, 18,* 4–10.

Garratt, G. A., Baxter, J. C., & Rozelle, R. M. (1981). Training university police in black-American nonverbal behaviors. *Journal of Social Psychology, 113,* 217–229.

Garro, L. C. (1986). Language, memory, and focality: A reexamination. *American Anthropologist, 88*(1), 128–136.

Geary, C. D. (1996). International differences in mathematical achievement: Their nature, causes, and consequences. *Current Directions in Psychological Science, 5*(5), 133–137.

Geen, R. G. (1994). Social Psychological. In M. Hersen & R. T. Ammerman (Eds.), *Handbook of aggressive and destructive behavior in psychiatric patients* (pp. 51–64). New York: Plenum Press.

Geen, T. R. (1992). Facial expressions in socially isolated nonhuman primates: Open and closed programs for expressive behavior. *Journal of Research in Personality, 26,* 273–280.

Geertz, C. (1973). *The interpretation of cultures.* New York: Basic Books.

Geertz, C. (1975). From the natives point of view: On the nature of anthropological understanding. *American Scientist, 63,* 47–53.

Georgas, J. (1989). Changing family values in Greece: From collectivist to individualist. *Journal of Cross-Cultural Psychology, 20,* 80–91.

Georgas, J. (1991). Intrafamily acculturation of values in Greece. *Journal of Cross-Cultural Psychology, 22,* 445–457.

Gerber, E. (1975). *The cultural patterning of emotions in Samoa.* Unpublished doctoral dissertation, University of California, San Diego.

Gergen, K. J., Gulerce, A., Lock, A., & Misra, G. (1996). Psychological science in cultural context. *American Psychologist,* 496–503.

Gerstner, C. R., & Day, D. V. (1994, Summer). Cross cultural comparison of leadership prototypes. *Leadership Quarterly, 5*(2), 121–134.

Gilligan, C. (1982). *In a different voice: Psychological theory and women's development.* Cambridge, MA: Harvard University Press.

Gim, R. H., Atkinson, D. R., & Kim, S. J. (1991). Asian-American acculturation, counselor ethnicity and cultural sensitivity, and ratings of counselors. *Journal of Counseling Psychology, 38,* 57–62.

Gitter, A. G., Black, H., & Fishman, J. E. (1975). Effect of race, sex, nonverbal communication and verbal communication on perception of leadership. *Sociology and Social Research, 60*(1), 46–57.

Gladwin, H., & Gladwin, C. (1971). Estimating market conditions and profit expectations of fish sellers at Cape Coast, Ghana. In G. Dalton (Ed.), *Studies in economic anthropology. Anthropological Studies No. 7* (pp. 122–143). Washington, DC: American Anthropological Association.

Gladwin, T. (1970). *East is a big bird: Navigation and logic on Puluwat Atoll.* Cambridge, MA: Harvard University Press.

Glaser, S. R. (1983). Assessing organizational culture: An interpretive approach. Paper presented at the annual meeting of the Speech Communication Association (Washington, DC, November 10–13).

Gleason, H. A. (1961). *An introduction to descriptive linguistics.* New York: Holt, Rinehart & Winston.

Goldman, A. (1992). Intercultural training of Japanese for U.S.–Japanese interorganizational communication. *International Journal of Intercultural Relations, 16,* 195–215.

Goldman, A. (1994). The centrality of "Ningensei" to Japanese negotiating and interpersonal relationships: implications for U.S.–Japanese communication. *International Journal of Intercultural Relations, 18*(1), 29–54.

Goldstein, A. P., & Segall, M. H. (Eds.). (1983). *Aggression in global perspective.* Elmsford: Pergamon Press.

Goodwin, R., & Lee, I. (1994). Taboo topics among Chinese and English friends. *Journal of Cross-Cultural Psychology, 25*(3), 325–338.

Goody, J. R. (1968). *Literacy in traditional societies.* Cambridge, England: Cambridge University Press.

Goody, J. R. (1977). *The domestication of the savage mind.* Cambridge, England: Cambridge University Press.

Gottfredson, L. S. (1994). The science and politics of race-norming. *American Psychologist, 49* (1), 955–963.

Graham, H. L., Evenko, L. I., & Rajan, M. N. (1992). A empirical comparison of Soviet and American business negotiations. *Journal of International Business Studies, 23,* 387–418.

Graham, J. L. (1983). Brazilian, Japanese, and American Business Negotiations. *Journal of International Business Studies,* Spring/Summer, 1983, 47–61.

Graham, J. L. (1993). The Japanese negotiation style: Characteristics of a distinct approach. *Negotiation Journal,* April, 123–140.

Graham, J. L. (1994, Spring). The influence of culture on the process of business negotiations: An exploratory study. *Journal of International Business Studies,* 81–96.

Graham, J. L., & Andrews, J. D. (1987). A holistic analysis of Japanese and American business negotiations. *Analysis of Business Negotiations, 24*(4), 63–77.

Graham, S. (1984). Communicating sympathy and anger to black and white children: The cognitive (attributional) consequences of affective cues. *Journal of Personality and Social Psychology, 47*(1), 40–54.

Graham, S. (1992). Most of the subjects were white and middle-class: Trends in published research on African Americans in selected APA journals, 1970–1989. *American Psychologist, 47,* 629–639.

Graham, S., & Long, A. (1986). Race, class, and the attributional process. *Journal of Educational Psychology, 78,* 4–13.

Greenfield, M. P. (1997). You can't take it with you. *American Psychologist, 52,* 1115–1124.

Greenfield, P. M., Reich, L. C., & Oliver, R. R. (1966). On culture and equivalence II. In J. S. Bruner, R. R. Oliver, & P. M. Greenfield (Eds.), *Studies in cognitive growth* (pp. 270–318). New York: Wiley.

Grisaru, N., Budowski, D., & Witztum, E. (1997). Possession by the "Zar" among Ethiopian immigrants to Israel: Psychopathology or culture-bound syndrome? *Psychopathology, 30*(4), 223–233.

Grossmann, K., Grossmann, K. E., Spangler, S., Suess, G., & Unzner, L. (1985). Maternal sensitivity and newborn attachment orientation responses as related to quality of attachment in northern Germany. In I. Bretherton & E. Waters (Eds.), *Growing points of attachment theory. Monographs of the Society of Research in Child Development, 50* (1–2 Serial No. 209).

Gudykunst, W. B. (1993). Toward a theory of effective interpersonal and intergroup communication: An anxiety/uncertainty management (AUM) perspective. In R. L. Wiseman, & J. Koester (Eds.); et al. *International and intercultural communication annual: Intercultural communication competence, 17* (pp.33–71). Newbury Park: Sage.

Gudykunst, W. B. (1997). Cultural variability in communication. *Communication Research, 24*(4), 327–348.

Gudykunst, W. B., Gao, G., Nishida, T., Bond, M. H., et al. (1989). A cross cultural comparison of self-monitoring. *Communication Research Reports, 6*(1), 7–12.

Gudykunst, W. B., Gao, G., Schmidt, K. L., Nishida, T., Bond, M. L., Leung, K., Wang, G., & Barraclough, R.A. (1992). The influence of individualism-collectivism, self-monitoring, and predicted-outcome value on communication in ingroup and outgroup relationships. *Journal of Cross-Cultural Psychology, 23*(2), 196–213.

Gudykunst, W. B., Matsumoto, Y., Ting-Toomey, S., Nishida, T., Kim, K., & Heyman, S. (1996). The influence of cultural individualism-collectivism, self construals, and individual values on communication styles across cultures. *Human Communication Research, 22*(4), 510–543.

Gudykunst, W. B., & Nishida, T. (1984). Individual and cultural influences on uncertainty reduction. *Communication Monographs, 51*, 23–36.

Gudykunst, W. B., & Nishida, T. (1986a). Attributional confidence in low- and high-context cultures. *Human Communication Research, 12*, 525–549.

Gudykunst, W. B., & Nishida, T. (1986b). The influence of cultural variability on perceptions of communication behavior associated with relationship terms. *Human Communication Research, 13*, 147–166.

Gudykunst, W. B., & Shapiro, R. B. (1996). Communication in everyday interpersonal and intergroup encounters. *International Journal of Intercultural Relations, 20*(1), 19–45.

Gudykunst, W. B., Sodetani, L. L., & Sonoda, K. T. (1987). Uncertainty reduction in Japanese-American/Caucasian relationships in Hawaii. *The Western Journal of Speech Communication, 51*, 256–278.

Gudykunst, W. B., & Ting-Toomey, S. (1988). Culture and affective communication. Special Issue: Communication and affect. *American Behavioral Scientist, 31*, 384–400.

Gudykunst, W. B., Yang, S. M., & Nishida, T. (1985). A cross-cultural test of uncertainty reduction theory: Comparisons of acquaintances, friends, and dating relationships in Japan, Korea, and the United States. *Human Communications Research, 11*(3), 407–454.

Gudykunst, W. B., Yang, S., & Nishida, T. (1987). Cultural differences in self-consciousness and self-monitoring. *Communications Research, 14*(1), 7–34.

Gudykunst, W. B., Yoon, Y., & Nishida, T. (1987). The influence of individualism-collectivism on perceptions of communication in ingroup and outgroup relationships. *Communication Monographs, 54*, 295–306.

Guilford, J. P. (1985). The structure of intellect model. In B. B. Wolman (Ed.), *Handbook of intelligence: Theories, measurements, and applications.* New York: Wiley.

Guinn, B. (1998). Acculturation and health locus of control among Mexican American adolescents. *Hispanic Journal of Behavioral Sciences, 20*(4), 492–499.

Guisinger, S., & Blatt, S. J. (1994). Individuality and relatedness: Evolution of a fundamental dialectic. *American Psychologist, 49*, 104–111.

Gumpez, J. J., & Levinson, S. C. (Eds.). (1996). *Rethinking linguistic relativity.* Cambridge, England: Cambridge University Press.

Guthrie, G. M., & Bennet, A. B. (1971). Cultural differences in implicit personality theory. *International Journal of Psychology, 6*(4), 305–312.

Hadiyono, J. E. P., & Hahn, M. W. (1985). Personality differences and sex similarities in American and Indonesian college students. *Journal of Social Psychology, 125*, 703–708.

Hadley, R. F. (1997). Cognition, systematicity and nomic necessity. *Mind and Language, 12*(2), 137–153.

Haghighatgou, H., & Peterson, C. (1995). Coping and depressive symptoms among Iranian students. *Journal of Social Psychology, 135*(2), 175–180.

Hall, C. C. I., Evans, B. J., & Selice, S. (Eds.). (1989). *Black females in the United States: A bibliography from 1967 to 1987.* Washington, DC: American Psychological Association.

Hall, E. T. (1963). A system for the notation of proxemic behavior. *American Anthropologist, 65*, 1003–1026.

Hall, E. T. (1966). *The hidden dimension.* New York: Doubleday.

Hall, E. T. (1973). *The silent language.* New York: Anchor.

Hall, E. T. (1976). *Beyond culture.* New York: Anchor.

Hall, J. (1998). *Expressiveness and expression accuracy.* Unpublished manuscript.

Hall, J. A. (1978). Gender effects in decoding nonverbal cues. *Psychological Bulletin, 85*, 845–857.

Hall, K. R. L., & Devore, I. (1965). Baboon social behavior. In I. Devore (Ed.), *Primate behavior.* New York: Holt, Rinehart & Winston.

Hall, R. H., Jiang, S., Loscocco, K. A., & Allen, J. K. (1993). Ownership patterns and centralization: A China and U.S. comparison. *Sociological Forum, 8*(4), 595–608.

Hall, V. C., Howe, A., Merkel, S., & Lederman, N. (1986). Behavior, motivation, and achievement in desegregated junior high school science classes. *Journal of Educational Psychology, 78,* 108–115.

Hamid, P. N. (1994). Assertiveness and personality dimensions in Chinese students. *Psychological Reports, 75*(1), 127–130.

Hamid, P. N. (1994). Self-monitoring, locus of control, and social encounters of Chinese and New Zealand students. *Journal of Cross-Cultural Psychology, 25*(3), 353–368.

Hamilton, L. H., Brooks-Gunn, J., & Warren, M. P. (1985). Sociocultural influences on eating disorders on professional female ballet dancers. *International Journal of Eating Disorders, 4* (4), 465–477.

Hamilton, V. L., Blumenfeld, P. C., Akoh, H., & Miura, K. (1991). Group and gender in Japanese and American elementary classrooms. *Journal of Cross-Cultural Psychology, 22,* 317–346.

Hammer, M. R., Nishida, H., & Wiseman, R. L. (1996). The influence of situational prototypes on dimensions of intercultural communication competence. *Journal of Cross-Cultural Psychology, 27*(3), 267–282.

Hampel, R., & Krupp, B. (1977). The cultural and the political framework of prejudice in South Africa and Great Britain. *The Journal of Social Psychology, 103,* 193–202.

Hanna, G. S., House, B., & Salisbury, L. H. (1968). WAIS performance of Alaskan native university freshmen. *Journal of Genetic Psychology, 112* (1), 57–61.

Harkins, S. G. (1987). Social loafing and social facilitation. *Journal of Experimental Social Psychology, 23,* 1–18.

Harkins, S. G., & Petty, R. E. (1982). Effects of task difficulty and task uniqueness on social loafing. *Journal of Personality and Social Psychology, 43,* 1214–1229.

Harlow, H. F., & Harlow, M. K. (1969). Effects of various mother-infant relationships on rhesus monkey behavior. In B. M. Foss (Ed.), *Determinants of infant behavior* (Vol. 4). London: Methuen.

Harris, A. C. (1996). African Americans and Anglo American gender identities: An empirical study. *Journal of Black Psychology, 22* (2), 182–194.

Harris, M. B. & Koehler, K. M. (1992). Eating and exercise behaviors and attitudes of southwestern Anglos and Hispanics. *Psychology and Health, 7,* 165–174.

Harrison, A. O., Stewart R.B., Myambo, K., Teveraishe, C. (1995). Perceptions of social networks among adolescents from Zimbabwe and the United States. *Journal of Black Psychology, 21*(4), 382–407.

Harrison, A. O., Wilson, M. N., Pine, C. J., Chan, S. Q., & Buriel, R. (1990). Family ecologies of ethnic minority children. *Child Development, 61,* 347–362.

Hart, I. (1971). Scores of Irish groups on the Cattell Culture Fair Test of Intelligence and the California Psychological Inventory. *Irish Journal of Psychology, 1* (1), 30–25.

Hasegawa, T., & Gudykunst, W. B. (1998). Silence in Japan and the United States. *Journal of Cross Cultural Psychology, 29*(5), 668–684.

Hatfield, E. (1988). Passionate and companionate love. In R. J. Sternberg & M. L. Barnes (Eds.), *The psychology of love* (pp. 191–217). New Haven, CT: Yale University Press.

Hatfield, E., & Sprecher, S. (1995). Men's and women's preferences in maritial partners in the United States, Russia, and Japan. *Journal of Cross-Cultural Psychology, 26*(6), 728–750.

Hau, K., & Lew, W. J. (1989). Moral development of Chinese students in Hong Kong. *International Journal of Psychology, 24*(5), 561–569.

Hau, K., & Salili, F. (1991). Structure and semantic differential placement of specific causes: Academic causal attributions by Chinese students in Hong Kong. *International Journal of Psychology, 26,* 175–193.

Hauser, M. D. (1993, July). Right hemisphere dominance of the production of facial expression in monkeys. *Science, 261,* 475–477.

Hayashi, S. (1997). The effects of self-perception and attitudes to cultures on international students' feeling of adjustment. *The Japanese Journal of Psychology, 68*(5), 346–354.

Hays, J. R., & Smith, A. L. (1980). Comparison of WISC-R and Culture Fair Intelligence Test scores for three ethnic groups of juvenile delinquents. *Psychological Reports, 46* (3, Pt 1), 931–934.

Healey, M. C., & Prince, A. (1998). Alternative tactics in the breeding behaviour of male coho salmon. *Behaviour, 135*(8–9), 1099–1124.

Heaven, P. C. L., Connors, J., & Stones, C. R. (1994). Three or five personality dimensions? An analysis of natural language terms in two cultures.

Personality and Individual Differences, 17(2), 181–189.

Heelas, P., and Lock, A. (1981). *Indigenous psychologies: An anthropology of the self.* London, England: Academic Press.

Heider, E. R., & Oliver, D. (1972). The structure of the color space in naming and memory for two languages. *Cognitive Psychology, 3,* 337–354.

Helgeson, V. S., Shaver, P., & Dyer, M. (1987). Prototypes of intimacy and distance in same-sex and opposite-sex relationships. *Journal of Social and Personal Relationships, 4,* 195–233.

Henderson, N. D. (1982). Human behavior genetics. *Annual Review of Psychology, 33,* 403–440.

Hendrick, C., & Hendrick, S. (1983). *Liking, loving, and relating.* Pacific Grove, CA: Brooks/Cole.

Henriques, G. R., Calhoun, L. G., & Cann, A. (1996). Ethnic differences in women's body satisfaction: An experimental investigation. *The Journal of Social Psychology, 136*(6), 689–697.

Herrnstein, R.J., & Murray, C. (1994). *The bell curve: Intelligence and class structure in American life.* New York: Free Press.

Hess, J. A. (1993). Assimilating newcomers into an organization: A cultural perspective. *Journal of Applied Communication Research,* May, 189–210.

Heyes, C. M. (1993). Imitation, culture and cognition. *Animal Behaviour, 46*(5), 999–1010.

Hiatt, L. R. (1978). Classification of the emotions. In L. R. Hiatt (Ed.), *Australian aboriginal concepts* (pp. 182–187). Princeton, NJ: Humanities Press.

Hiatt, R. A., Pasick, R. J., Perez Stable, E. J., McPhee, S. J., et al. (1996). Pathways to early cancer detection in the multiethnic population of the San Francisco Bay area. *Health Education Quarterly, 23,* S10–S27.

Higginbotham, H. N. (1979). Culture and mental health services. In A. J. Marsella, G. DeVos, & F. L. K. Hsu (Eds.), *Perspectives on cross-cultural psychology* (pp. 307–332). New York: Academic Press.

Hill, R. F., & Fortenberry, J. D. (1992). Adolescence as a culture-bound syndrome. *Social Science and Medicine, 35,* 73–80.

Hinde, R. A., & Rowell, T. E. (1962). Communication by posture and facial expressions in the rhesus monkey (*Macaca mulatta*). *Proceedings of the Zoological Society of London, 138,* 1–21.

Hippler, A. E. (1974). The North Alaska Eskimos: A culture and personality perspective. *American Ethnologist, 1*(3), 449–469.

Hippler, A. E. (1980). Editorial. *International Association of Cross-Cultural Psychology Newsletter, 14,* 2–3.

Hirschfield, L. A. (Series Ed.). (1996). Learning, development, and conceptual change. *Race in the making: Cognition, culture, and the child's construction of human kinds.* Cambridge, MA: The MIT Press.

Ho, D. Y (1998). Indigenous psychologies: Asian perspectives. *Journal of Cross Cultural Psychology, 29*(1), 88–103.

Ho, M. K. (1984). Social group work with Asian/Pacific-Americans. *Social Work with Groups, 7*(3), 49–61.

Hoch, E. M. (1990). Experiences with psychotherapy training in India. *Psychotherapy and Psychosomatics, 53*(1–4), 14–20.

Hodgetts, R. M., Luthans, F., & Lee, S. M. (1994). New paradigm organizations: from total quality to learning to world-class. *Organizational Dynamics, 22*(3), 5–19.

Hoek, H. W., van Harten, P. N., van Hoeken, D., & Susser, E. (1998). Lack of relation between culture and anorexia nervosa: Results of an incidence study on Curacao. *New England Journal of Medicine, 338*(17), 1231–1232.

Hofstede, G. (1980). *Culture's consequences: International differences in work-related values.* Beverly Hills, CA: Sage.

Hofstede, G. (1983). Dimensions of national cultures in fifty countries and three regions. In J. B. Deregowski, S. Dziurawiec, & R. C. Annis (Eds.), *Expiscations in cross-cultural psychology* (pp. 335–355). Lisse: Swets & Zeitlinger.

Hofstede, G. (1984). *Culture's consequences: International differences in work-related values.* Newbury Park, CA: Sage.

Hofstede, G. (1996a). The cultural relativity of organizational practices and theories. In J. Billsberry et al. (Eds.), *The effective manager: Perspectives and illustrations.* London: Sage Publications, Inc.

Hofstede, G. (1996b). Riding the waves of commerce: A test of Trompenaars' "model" of national culture differences. *International Journal of Intercultural Relations, 20*(2), 189–198.

Hofstede, G. (1997). *Culture and organizations.* New York: McGraw Hill.

Hofstede, G., & Bond, M. (1988). Confucius & economic growth: New trends in culture's consequences. *Organizational Dynamics, 16*(4), 4–21.

Hofstee, W. K. B., Kiers, H. A., De Raad, B., Goldberg, L. R., et al. (1997). A comparison of Big Five structures of personality traits in Dutch, English, and German. *European Journal of Personality, 11*(1), 15–31.

Hollander, E. (1985). Leadership and power. In G. Lindzey & E. Aaronson (Eds.), *The handbook of social psychology* (Vol. 2) (3rd ed., pp. 485–537). New York: Random House.

Holloway, S. D., & Minami, M. (1996). Production and reproduction of culture: The dynamic role of mothers and children in early socialization. In D. W. Schwalb, B. J. Schwalb, et al. (Eds.), *Japanese childrearing: Two generations of scholarship* (pp. 164–176). New York: Guilford Press.

Holmes, L. D., Tallman, G., & Jantz, V. (1978, Fall). Samoan personality. *Journal of Psychological Anthropology, 1*(4), 453–469.

Hoosain, R. (1986). Language, orthography and cognitive process: Chinese perspectives for the Sapir-Whorf hypothesis. *International Journal of Behavioral Development, 9*(4), 507–525.

Hoosain, R. (1991). *Psycholinguistic implications for linguistic relativity: A case study of Chinese.* Hillsdale, N J: Lawrence Erlbaum Associates, Inc.

Howell, J. P., Dorfman P. W., Hibino, S., Lee, J. K., & Tale, U. (1995). Leadership in Western and Asian countries: Commonalities and differences in effective leadership processes and substitutes across cultures. Las Cruces: New Mexico State University.

Howell, S. (1981). Rules not words. In P. Heelas & A. Lock (Eds.), *Indigenous psychologies: The anthropology of the self* (pp. 133–143). San Diego, CA: Academic Press.

Hsu, L. (1977). An examination of Cooper's test for monotonic trend. *Educational and Psychological Measurement, 37*(4), 843–845.

Huang, L. N., & Ying, Y. (1989). Japanese children and adolescents. In J. T. Gibbs & L. N. Huang (Eds.), *Children of color.* San Francisco: Jossey-Bass.

Hudson, W. (1960). Pictorial depth perception in subcultural groups in Africa. *Journal of Social Psychology, 52,* 183–208.

Hughes, B., & Paterson, K. (1997). The social model of disability and the disappearing body: Towards a sociology of impairment. *Disability and Society, 12*(3), 325–340.

Hui, C. H. (1984). *Individualism-collectivism: Theory, measurement, and its relation to reward allocation.* Unpublished doctoral dissertation, University of Illinois.

Hui, C. H. (1988). Measurement of individualism-collectivism. *Journal of Research in Personality, 22,* 17–36.

Hui, C. H., & Triandis, H. C. (1986). Individualism-collectivism: A study of cross cultural research-ers. *Journal of Cross-Cultural Psychology, 17,* 225–248.

Hull, P. V. (1987). Bilingualism: *Two languages, two personalities? Resources in education, educational resources clearinghouse on education.* Ann Arbor: University of Michigan Press.

Hull, P. V. (1990a). *Bilingualism: Two languages, two personalities?* Unpublished doctoral dissertation, University of California, Berkeley.

Hull, P. V. (1990b, August). *Bilingualism and language choice.* Paper presented at the Annual Convention of the American Psychological Association, Boston.

Hunt, E., & Agnoli, F. (1991). The Whorfian hypothesis: A cognitive psychology perspective. *Psychological Review, 98,* 377–389.

Husen, T. (1967). *International study of achievement in mathematics.* New York: Wiley.

Ineichen, B. (1979). The social geography of marriage. In M. Cook & G. Wilson (Eds.), *Love and attraction.* New York: Pergamon Press.

Isaac, M., Janca, A., & Orley, J. (1996). Somatization: A culture-bound or universal syndrome? *Journal of Mental Health UK, 5*(3), 219–222.

Itoi, R., Ohbuchi, K. I., & Fukuno, M. (1996). A cross-cultural study of preference of accounts: Relationship closeness, harm severity, and motives of account making. *Journal of Applied Social Psychology, 26* (10), 913–934.

Iwao, S., & Triandis, C. H. (1993). Validity of auto- and heterostereotypes among Japanese and American students. *Journal of Cross-Cultural Psychology, 24*(4), 428–444.

Izard, C. E. (1971). *The face of emotion.* New York: Appleton-Century-Crofts.

Izard, C. E. (1994). Innate and universal facial expressions: Evidence from developmental and cross-cultural research. *Psychological Bulletin, 115*(2), 288–299.

Izard, C. E., & Haynes, O. M. (1988). On the form and universality of the contempt expression: A challenge to Ekman and Friesen's claim of discovery. *Motivation and Emotion, 12*(1), 1–16.

Jackson, J. M., & Williams, K. D. (1985). Social loafing on difficult tasks: Working collectively can improve performance. *Journal of Personality and Social Psychology, 49,* 937–942.

Jacob, E. (1997). Context and cognition: Implications for educational innovators and anthropologists. *Anthropology and Education Quarterly, 28* (1), 3–21.

Jacobsen, L. (1996). PPR bistand til sprogskolerne—et omrade uden lovdaekning./Psychological support in language schools: An unlegislated area. *Psykologisk—Paedagogisk Radgivning, 33*(1): 46–61.

Jaffe, Y., & Yinon, Y. (1983). Collective aggression: The group-individual paradigm in the study of collective antisocial behavior. In H. H. Blumberg, A.P. Hare, V. Kent, & M. F. Davies (Eds.), *Small groups and social interaction: Vol. 1.* (pp. 267–175). Chichester: Wiley.

Jahoda, G. (1984). Do we need a concept of culture? *Journal of Cross-Cultural Psychology, 15*(2), 139–151.

James, W. (1890). *The principles of psychology* (Vol. 2). New York: Holt.

Janicki, M. G., & Krebs, D. L. (1998). Evolutionary approaches to culture. In C. B. Crawford & D. L. Krebs et al., (Eds.), *Handbook of evolutionary psychology: Ideas, issues and applications* (pp. 163–207). Mahwah, NJ: Lawrence Erlbaum Associates, Inc.

Janis, I. L. (1983). *Group think.* Boston: Hougton Mifflin.

Jeanquart-Barone, S., & Sekaran, U. (1996). Institutional racism: An empirical study. *Journal of Social Psychology, 136*(4), 477–482.

Jencks, C., Smith, M., Acland, H., Bane, M. J., Cohen, D., Gintis, H., Heyns, B., & Michaelson, S. (1972). *Inequality: A reassessment of the effect of family and schooling in America.* New York: Harper & Row.

Jensen, A. R. (1968). Social class, race and genetics: Implications for education. *American Educational Research Journal, 5* (1), 1–42.

Jensen, A. R. (1969). How much can we boost IQ and scholastic achievement? *Harvard Educational Review, 39,* 1–123.

Jensen, A. R. (1971). Twin differences and race differences in I.Q.: A reply to Burgess and Jahoda. *Bulletin of the British Psychological Society, 24* (84), 195–198.

Jensen, A. R. (1973). Personality and scholastic achievement in three ethnic groups. *British Journal of Educational Psychology, 43* (20), 115–125.

Jensen, A. R. (1977). Cumulative deficit in IQ of Blacks in the rural South. *Developmental Psychology, 13* (93), 184–191.

Jensen, A. R. (1980). *Bias in mental testing.* New York: Free Press.

Jensen, A. R. (1981). *Straight talk about mental tests.* London: Methuen.

Jensen, A. R. (1983). Effects of inbreeding on mental-ability factors. *Personality and Individual Differences, 4* (1): 71–87.

Jensen, A. R. (1984). The black-white difference on the K-ABC: Implications for future tests. *Journal of Special Education, 18* (3), 377–408.

Jensen, A. R., & Johnson, F. W. (1994). Race and sex differences in head siza and I. Q. *Intelligence, 18*(3), 309–333.

Jensen, A. R., & Munro, E. (1979). Reaction time, movement time, and intelligence. *Intelligence, 3* (2), 121–126.

Jensen, A. R., & Reed, T. E. (1990). Simple Reaction time as a suppressor variable in the chronometric study of intelligence. *Intelligence, 14*(4), 375–388.

Jensen, A. R., & Whang, P. A. (1993). Reaction times and intelligence: A comparison of Chinese-American and Anglo-American children. *Journal of Biosocial Science, 25* (3), 397–410.

Jensen, S. M. (1970). A technical description of the Danish Binet test under revision. *Skolepsykologi, 7* (4), 241–248.

Jilek, A. L., Jilek, M., Kaaya, J., Mkombachepa, L., & Hillary, K. (1997). Psychosocial study of epilepsy in Africa. *Social Science and Medicine, 45*(5), 783–795.

John, O. (1989). The BFI-54. Unpublished test, Institute of Personality and Social Research, Department of Psychology, University of California, Berkeley.

Johnson, D. L., Johnson, C. A., & Prince Williams, D. (1967). The Draw A Man Test and Raven Progressive Matrices performance of Guatemalan boys and Latino children. *Revista Interamericana de Psicologia, 1* (2), 143–157.

Johnson, T. M. (1987). Premenstrual syndrome as a Western culture-specific disorder. *Culture, Medicine and Psychiatry, 11*(3), 337–356.

Jones, E. E., & Harris, V. A. (1967). The attribution of attitudes. *Journal of Experimental Social Psychology, 3,* 1–24.

Jones, E. E., & Nisbett, R. E. (1971). The actor and the observer: Divergent perceptions of the causes of behavior. In E. E. Jones, D. E. Kanouse, H. H. Kelley, R. E. Nisbett, S. Valins, & B. Weiner (Eds.), *Attribution: Perceiving the causes of behavior* (pp. 79–94) Morristown, NJ: General Learning Press.

Joseph, R. A., Markus, H. R., & Tafarodi, R. W. (1992). Gender differences in the source of self-esteem. *Journal of Personality and Social Psychology, 63,* 1017–1028.

Joshi, S. M. & MacLean, M. (1997). Maternal expectations of child development in India, Japan, and England. *Journal of Cross-Cultural Psychology, 28*(2), 219–234.

Jou, J. Y. H., & Sung, K. (1990). Chinese value system and managerial behavior. *International Journal of Psychology, 25,* 619–627.

Kahneman, D., & Tversky A. (1973). On the psychology of prediction. *Psychological Review, 80* (4), 237–251.

Kane, C.M. (1994). Differences in the manifest dream content of Anglo-American, Mexican-American, and African-American college women. *Journal of Multicutural Counseling and Development, 22,* 203–209.

Karlins, M., Coffman, T. L., & Walters, G. (1969). On the fading of social stereotypes: Studies in three generations of college students. *Journal of Personality and Social Psychology, 13*(1), 1–16.

Karno, M., Jenkins, J. H., De la Silva, A., Sanatana, F., Telles, C., Lopez, S., & Mintz, J. (1987). Expressed emotion and schizophrenic outcome among Mexican-American families. *Journal of Nervous and Mental Disease, 175,* 145–151.

Kashima, E. S. & Kashima, Y. (1998). Culture and language: The case of cultural dimensions and personal pronoun use. *Journal of Cross-Cultural Psychology, 29,* 461–486.

Kashima, Y., Kim, U., Gelfand, M. J., Yamaguchi, S., Choi, S., & Yuki, M. (1995). Culture, gender, and self: A perspective from individualism-collectivism research. *Journal of personality and Social Psychology, 69,* 925–937.

Kashima, Y., & Triandis, H. C. (1986). The self-serving bias in attributions as a coping strategy: A cross-cultural study. *Journal of Cross-Cultural Psychology, 17,* 83–97.

Katigbak, M. S., Church, A. T., & Akamine, T. X. (1996). Cross cultural generalizability of personality dimensions: Relating indigenous and imported dimensions in two cultures. *Journal of Personality and Social Psychology, 70*(1), 99–114.

Katz, D., & Braly, K. (1933). Racial stereotypes of one hundred college students. *Journal of Abnormal & Social Psychology, 28,* 280–290.

Kawanishi, Y. (1995). The effects of culture on beliefs about stress and coping: Causal attribution of Anglo-American and Japanese persons. *Journal of Contemporary Psychotherapy, 25*(1), 49–60.

Kay, P., & Kempton, W. (1984). What is the Sapir-Whorf hypothesis? *American Anthropologist, 86,* 65–89.

Keating, C. (1976). Nonverbal aspects of communication. *Topics in Culture Learning, 4,* 12–13.

Keats, D. M. (1982). Cultural bases of concepts of intelligence: A Chinese versus Australian comparison. In P. Sukontasarp, N. Yongsiri, P. Intasuwan, N. Jotiban, & C. Suvannathat (Eds.), *Proceedings of the Second Asian Workshop on Child and Adolescent Development* (pp. 67–75). Bangkok: Burapasilpa Press.

Keats, D. M., & Fang, F. X. (1987). Cultural factors in concepts of intelligence. In C. Kagitcibasi et al., (Ed.), *Growth and progress in cross-cultural psychology* (pp. 236–247). Berwyn, PA: Swets North America.

Keitner, G. I., Fodor, J., Ryan, C. E., et al. (1991). A cross-cultural study of major depression and family functioning. *Canadian Journal of Psychiatry, 36*(4), 254–258.

Keller, H., Chasiotis, A., & Runde, B. (1992). Intuitive parenting programs in German, American, and Greek parents of 3–month-old infants. *Journal of Cross-Cultural Psychology, 23*(4), 510–520.

Kelley, H. H. (1967). Attributional theory in social psychology. *Nebraska Symposium on Motivation, 15,* 192–241.

Kelley, H. H. (1973). The processes of causal attribution. *American Psychologist, 28,* 107–128.

Kelley, M. & Tseng, H. (1992). Cultural differences in child rearing: A comparison of immigrant Chinese and Caucasian American mothers. *Journal of Cross-Cultural Psychology, 23*(4), 444–455.

Keltikangas-Jaervinen, L. & Terav, T. (1996). Social decision-making strategies in individualist and collectivist cultures: A comparison of Finnish and Estonian adolescents. *Journal of Cross Cultural Psychology, 27* (6), 714–732.

Kemper, T. (1978). *A social interactional theory of emotions.* New York: Wiley.

Kendon, A. (1987). On gesture: Its complementary relationship with speech. In A. W. Siegman & S. Feldstein (Eds.), *Nonverbal behavior and communication* (pp. 65–97). Hillsdale, NJ: Erlbaum.

Keys, J. B., Denton, L. T., & Miller, T. R. (1994). The Japanese management theory jungle revisited. *Journal of Management, 20*(2), 373–402.

Khaleefa, O. H., Erdos, G. & Ashria, I. H. (1996). Creativity in an indigenous Afro-Arab Islamic culture: The case of Sudan. *Journal of Creative Behavior, 30* (4). 268–282.

Kiev, A. (1972). *Transcultural psychiatry.* New York: Free Press.

Kiev, A. (1973). The psychiatric implicaitons of interracial marriage. In I. R. Stuart, and L. E. Abt (Eds.), *Interracial marriage: Expectations and realities* (pp. 162–176). New York: Grossman Publishers.

Kilmann, R. H. & Saxton, M. J. (1983). *Kilmann-Saxton culture gap survey.* Tuxedo, NY: Organizational Design Consultants, Inc.

Kim, E. Y. (1993). Career choice among second-generation Korean-Americans: Reflections of a cultural model of success. *Anthropology and Education Quarterly, 24*(3), 224–248.

Kim, M., Hunter, J. E., Ahara, A. M., Horvath, A., Bresnahan, M., & Yoon, H. (1996). Individual vs. culture-level dimensions of individualism and collectivism: Effects on preferred conversational styles. *Communication Monograph, 63,* 29–49.

Kim, U., and Berry, J. W. (1993). Introduction. In K. Uichol & J. W. Berry (Eds.), *Indigenous psychologies: Research and experience in cultural context. Cross-cultural research Indigenous and methodology series, Vol. 17,* 1–29. Newbury Park, CA: Sage Publications, Inc.

Kim, Y. Y., & Gudykunst, W. B. (Eds.). (1988). Cross cultural adaptation: Current approaches. *International and intercultural communication annual, 11.* Newbury Park: Sage.

Kimayer, L. (1984). Culture, affect, and somatization: Parts 1 and 2. *Transcultural Psychiatric Research Review, 21,* 159–188, 237–262.

Kimmel, P. R. (1994). Cultural perspectives on international negotiations. *Journal of Social Issues, 50*(1), 179–196.

King, J. E., & Figueredo, A. J. (1997). The Five-Factor Model plus dominance in chimpanzee personality. *Journal of Research in Personality, 31*(2), 257–271.

Kitayama, S., & Karasawa, M. (1997). Implicit self-esteem in Japan: Name letters and birthday numbers. *Personality and Social Psychology Bulletin, 23*(7), 736–742.

Kitayama, S., & Markus, H. R. (1991). Culture and the self: Implications for cognition, emotion, and motivation. *Psychological Review, 98,* 224–253.

Kitayama, S., & Markus, H. R. (Eds.). (1994). *Emotions and culture: Empirical studies of mutual influence.* Washington: American Psychological Association.

Kitayama, S., & Markus, H. R. (in press, a). A cultural perspective to self-conscious emotions. In J. P. Tangney & K. Fisher (Eds.), *Shame, guilt, embarrassment, and pride: Empirical studies of self-conscious emotions.* New York: Guilford Press.

Kitayama, S., & Markus, H. R. (in press, b). Culture and self: Implications for internationalizing psychology. In J. D'Arms, R. G. Hastie, & H. K. Jacobson (Eds.). *Becoming more international and global: Challenges for American higher education.* Ann Arbor: University of Michigan Press.

Kitayama, S., Markus, H. R., Kurokawa, M., & Negishi, K. (1993). *Social orientation of emotions: Cross-cultural evidence and implications.* Unpublished manuscript. University of Oregon.

Kitayama, S., Markus, H. R., & Matsumoto, H. (1995). Culture, self, and emotion: A cultural perspective on "self-conscious" emotions. In J. P. Tangney & K. Fisher (Eds.), *Self-conscious emotions: The psychology of shame, guilt, embarrassment, and pride* (pp. 439–464). New York: Guilford Press.

Kitayama, S., Matsumoto, H., Markus, H. R., & Norasakkunkit, V. (1997). Individual and collective processes in the construction of the self: Self-enhancement in the United States and self-criticism in Japan. *Journal of Personality and Social Psychology, 72,* 1245–1267.

Kleinman, A. (1978). Culture and depression. *Culture and Medical Psychiatry, 2,* 295–296.

Kleinman, A. (1982). Neurasthenia and depression: A study of somatization and culture in China. *Culture, Medicine and Psychiatry, 6*(2), 117–190.

Kleinman, A. (1988). *Rethinking psychiatry: From cultural category to personal experience.* New York: Free Press.

Klingelhofer, E. L. (1967). Performance of Tanzanian secondary school pupils on the Raven Standard Progressive Matrices Test. *Journal of Social Psychology, 72* (2), 205–215.

Kluckholn, F., & Strodtbeck, F. (1961). *Variations in value orientations.* Evanston, IL: Row, Peterson.

Kohlberg, L. (1976). Moral stages and moralization: The cognitive-developmental approach. In J. Lickona (Ed.), *Moral development behavior: Theory, research and social issues.* New York: Holt, Rinehart & Winston.

Kohlberg, L. (1984). *The psychology of moral development: The nature and validity of moral stages* (Vol. 2). New York: Harper & Row.

Kosmitzki, C. (1996). The reaffirmation of cultural identity in cross-cultural encounters. *Personality and Social Psychology Bulletin, 22,* 238–248.

Koss, J. D. (1990). Somatization and somatic complaint syndromes among Hispanics: Overview and ethnopsychological perspectives. *Transcultural Psychiatric Research Review, 27,* 5–29.

Kral, M. J. (1998). Suicide and the internalization of culture: Three questions. *Transcultural Psychiatry, 35*(2), 221–233.

Kranzler, J. H., & Jensen, A. R. (1989). Inspection time and intelligence: A meta-analysis. *Intelligence, 13*(4), 329–347.

Krause, I. B. (1989). Sinking heart: A Punjabi communication of distress. *Social Science and Medicine, 29*(4), 563–575.

Kreutzer, V. O. (1973). A study of the use of underachieving students as tutors for emotionally disturbed children. *Dissertation Abstracts International, 34*(6-A), 3145.

Kroeber, A. L., & Kluckholn, C. (1952). *Culture: A critical review of concepts and definitions* (Vol. 47, No. 1). Cambridge, MA: Peabody Museum.

Kubany, E. S., Bauer, G. B., Pangilinan, M. E., Muraoka, M. Y., et-al. (1995). Impact of labeled anger and blame in intimate relationships: Cross-cultural extensions of findings. *Journal of Cross-Cultural Psychology, 26*(1), 65–83.

Kudoh, T., & Matsumoto, D. (1985). A cross-cultural examination of the semantic dimensions of body postures. *Journal of Personality and Social Psychology, 48*, 1440–1446.

Kush, C. J. (1996). Field-dependence, cognitive ability, and academic achievement in Anglo American and Mexican American Students. *Journal of Cross-Cultural Psychology, 27*(5), 561–575.

LaFrance, M., & Mayo, C. (1976). Racial differences in gaze behavior during conversations: Two systematic observational studies. *Journal of Personality and Social Psychology, 33*(5), 547–552.

Lambert, E. W., Mermigis, L., & Taylot, M. D. (1986). Greek Canadians' attitudes toward own group and other Canadian ethnic groups: A test of the multiculturalism hypothesis. *Canadian Journal of Behavioral Science, 18*(1), 35–51.

Lammers, C. J., & Hickson, D. J. (Eds.). (1979). *Organizations alike and unlike: International and interinstitutional studies in the sociology of organizations.* London: Routledge & Kegan Paul.

Landau, M. S. (1984). The effects of spatial ability and problem presentation format on mathematical problem solving performance of middle school students. *Dissertation Abstracts International, 45*(2-A), 442–443.

Lange, C. (1887). *Ueber Gemuthsbewegungen.* Leipzig: Theodor Thomas.

Langer, E. J. (1989). *Mindfulness.* Reading, MA: Addison-Wesley.

Langman, P. F. (1997). White culture, Jewish culture, and the origins of psychotherapy. *Psychotherapy, 34*(2), 207–218.

Latané, B. (1981). The psychology of social impact. *American Psychologist, 36*, 343–356.

Latané, B., Williams, K., & Harkins, S. (1979). Many hands make light the work: The causes and consequences of social loafing. *Journal of Personality and Social Psychology, 37*, 322–332.

Laurendeau-Bendavid, M. (1977). Culture, schooling, and cognitive development: A comparative study of children in French Canada and Rwanda. In P. R. Dasen (Ed.), *Piagetian psychology: Cross-cultural contributions* (pp. 123–168). New York: Gardner/Wiley.

Laurent, A. (1978). *Matrix organizations and Latin cultures.* Working Paper 78–28. Brussels: European Institute for Advanced Studies in Management.

Lazarus, R. S. (1991). *Emotion and adaptation.* New York: Oxford University Press.

Lederer, G. (1982). Trends in authoritarianism: A study of adolescents in West Germany and the United States since 1945. *Journal of Cross-Cultural Psychology, 13*(3), 299–314.

Lee, F., Hallahan, M. & Herzog, T. (1996). Explaining real-life events: How culture and domain shape attributions. *Personality and Social Psychology Bulletin, 22*(7), 732–741.

Lee, H. O., & Boster, F. J. (1992). Collectivism-individualism in perceptions of speech rate: A cross-cultural comparison. *Journal of Cross-Cultural Psychology, 23*, 377–388.

Lee, S., (1995). Reconsidering the status of anorexia nervosa as a culture-bound syndrome. *Social Science and Medicine, 42*, 21–34.

Lee, V. K., & Dengerink, H. A. (1992). Locus of control in relation to sex and nationality: A cross-cultural study. *Journal of Cross-Cultural Psychology, 23*(4), 488–497.

Lee, W. M. L., & Mixson, R. J. (1995). Asian and Caucasian client perceptions of the effectiveness of counseling. *Journal of Multicultural Counseling and Development, 23*(1), 48–56.

Leenaars, A. A., Anawak, J., & Taparti, L. (1998). Suicide among the Canadian Inuit. In R. J. Kosky & H. S. Hadi (Eds.): *Suicide prevention: The global context* (pp. 111–120). New York: Plenum Press.

Leff, J. (1973). Culture and the differentiation of emotional states. *British Journal of Psychiatry, 123*, 299–306.

Leff, J. (1977). International variations in the diagnosis of psychiatric illness. *British Journal of Psychiatry, 131*, 329–338.

Leff, J. (1981). *Psychiatry around the globe: A transcultural view.* New York: Dekker.

Leff, J. (1986). The epidemiology of mental illness. In J. L. Cox (Ed.), *Transcultural psychiatry* (pp. 23–36). London: Croom Helm.

Leung, K. (1988). Some determinants of conflict avoidance. *Journal of Cross-Cultural Psychology, 19,* 125–136.

Leung, K. (1989). Cross-cultural differences: Individual-level vs. culture-level analysis. *International Journal of Psychology, 24,* 703–719.

Leung, K., & Bond, H. M. (1989). On the empirical identification of dimensions for cross-cultural comparisons. *Journal of Cross-Cultural Psychology, 20*(2), 133–151.

Leung, K., & Van De Vijver, F. (1996). Cross-cultural research methodology. In F. T. L. Leong, J. T. Austin, et al. (Eds.), *The psychology research handbook: A guide for graduate students and research assistants* (pp.351–358). Thousand Oaks, CA: Sage.

Levin, H. M. (1996). Accelerated schools after eight years. In L. Schauble & R. Glaser (Eds.), *Innovations in learning: New environments for education* (pp. 329–352). Mahwah, N. J.: Lawrence Erlbaum Associates, Inc.

Levine, J. B. (1991). The role of culture in the representation of conflict in dreams: a comparison of Bedouin, Irish, and Israeli children. *Journal of Cross-Cultural Psychology, 22,* 472–490.

Levine, R. A. (1977). Child rearing as cultural adaptation. In P. H. Leiderman, S. R. Tulkin, & A. Rosenfeld (Eds.), *Culture and infancy* (pp. 15–27). New York: Academic Press.

Levine, R., Sato, S., Hashimoto, T., & Verma, J. (1995). Love and marriage in eleven cultures. *Journal of Cross-Cultural Psychology, 26*(5), 554–571.

Levy, G., Lysne, M., Underwood, L. (1995). Children's and adults' memories for self-schema consistent and inconsistent content. *Journal of Social Psychology, 135* (1), 113–115.

Levy, R. I. (1973). *Tahitians.* Chicago: University of Chicago Press.

Levy, R. I. (1983). Introduction: Self and emotion. *Ethos, 11,* 128–134.

Levy, R. I. (1984). The emotions in comparative perspective. In K. Scherer & P. Ekman (Eds.), *Approaches to emotion* (pp. 397–412). Hillsdale, NJ: Erlbaum.

Levy-Bruhl, L. (1910). *Les fonctions mentales dans les societes inferieures.* Paris: Alcan. (Trans: 1928, *How natives think.* London: Allen & Unwin.)

Levy-Bruhl, L. (1922). *Mentaliete primitive.* Paris: Alcan. (Trans. 1923, *Primitive mentality.* London: Allen & Unwin.)

Levy-Bruhl, L. (1949). *Les camets de Lucien Levy-Bruhl.* [The notebooks of Lucien Levy-Bruhl.] Paris: Press Universitaires de France.

Lewotin, R. C., Rose, S., & Kamin, L. J. (1984). *Not in our genes: Biology, ideology and human nature.* New York: Pantheon Books.

Lillard, A. (1998a). Ethnopsychologies: Cultural variations in theories of mind. *Psychological Bulletin, 123,* 3–32.

Lillard, A. (1998b). Ethnopsychologies: Reply to Wellman (1998) and Gauvain (1998). *Psychological Bulletin, 123,* 43–46.

Lin, P., & Schwanenflugel, P.(1995). Cultural familiarity and language factors in the structure of category knowledge. *Journal of Cross-Cultural Psychology, 26*(2), 153–168.

Linton, R. (1936). *The study of man: An introduction.* New York: Appleton.

Little, D. T., Oettingen, G., Stetsenko, A., & Baltes, B. P. (1995). Children's action-control beliefs about school performance: How do American children compare with German and Russian children? *Journal of Personality and Social Psychology, 69*(4), 686–700.

Liu, L. G. (1985). Reasoning counterfactually in Chinese: Are their any obstacles? *Cognition, 21*(3), 239–270.

Livesly, W. J., & Bromley, D. B. (1973). *Person perception in childhood and adolescence.* London: Wiley.

Lonner, W. J., & Ibrahim, F. A. (1989). Assessment in cross-cultural counseling. In P. B. Pedersen, J. Dragus, W. Lonner, & J. E. Trimble (Eds.), *Counseling across cultures* (3rd ed.) (pp. 299–334). Honolulu: University of Hawaii Press.

Lott, D. F., Hart, B. L. (1977, Summer). Aggressive domination of cattle by Fulani herdsmen and its relation to aggression in Fulani culture and personality. *Ethos, 5*(2), 174–186.

Love, K. G., Bishop, R. C., Heinisch, D. A., & Montei, M. S. (1994). Selection across two cultures: Adapting the selection of American assemblers to meet Japanese job performance demands. *Personnel Psychology, 47,* 837–846.

Lucy, J. A. (1992). *Language diversity and thought: A reformation of the linguistic relativity hypothesis.* Cambridge, England: Cambridge University Press.

Lueptow, L. B., Garovich, L., & Lueptow, M. B. (1995). The persistence of gender stereotypes in the face of changing sex roles: Evidence contrary to the sociocultural model. *Ethology and Sociobiology, 16*(6), 509–530.

Luria, A. R. (1976). *Cognitive development: Its cultural and social foundations* (M. Lopes & L. Solotaroff, trans.). Cambridge, MA: Harvard University Press. [Original work published 1974]

Lutz, C. (1980). *Emotion words and emotional development on Ifaluk Atoll.* Unpublished doctoral dissertation, Harvard University.

Lutz, C. (1982). The domain of emotion words in Ifaluk. *American Ethnologist, 9,* 113–128.

Lutz, C. (1983). Parental goals, ethnopsychology, and the development of emotional meaning. *Ethos, 11,* 246–262.

Lutz, C. (1988). *Unnatural emotions: Everyday sentiments on a Micronesian atoll and their challenge to Western theory.* Chicago: University of Chicago Press.

Lutz, C. (1992). Culture and consciousness: A problem in the anthropology of knowledge. In F. S. Kessel & P. M. Cole (Eds.), *Self & conciousness: multiple perspectives* (pp. 64–87). Hillsdales, NJ: Lawrence Erlbaum Associates, Inc.

Luzzo, D. A. (1993). Ethnic differences in college students' perceptions of barriers to careers development. *Journal of Multicultural Counseling and Development, 21,* 227–236.

Lynn, R., Paspalanova, E., Steinsky, D., & Tzenova, B. (1998). Intelligence in Bulgaria. *Psychological Reports, 82* (3, Pt 1), 912–914.

Ma, K. H. & Cheung, C. (1996). A cross-cultural study of moral stage structure in Hong Kong Chinese, English, and Americans. *Journal of Cross-Cultural Psychology, 27*(6), 700–713.

Ma, S. M. (1998). *Immigrant subjectives in Asian American and Asian Diaspora literatures.* New York: State University of New York Press.

Maccoby, E. E., & Jacklin, C. N. (1974). *The psychology of sex differences.* Stanford, CA: Stanford University Press.

Maccoby, E. E., & Martin, J. A. (1983). Socialization in the context of the family: Parent-child interaction. In E. M. Hetherington (Ed.), *Handbook of child psychology, Vol. 4: Socialization, personality, and social development* (4th ed.), (pp. 1–101). New York: Wiley.

Macdonald, K (1991). A perspective on Darwinian psychology: The importance of domain-general mechanisms, plasticity, and individual differences. *Ethology and Sociobiology, 12*(6), 449–480.

Macdonald, K (1998). Evolution, culture, and the five-factor model. *Journal of Cross Cultural Psychology, 29*(1), 119–149.

MacLachlan, M. (1997). *Culture and health.* Chichester, England: John Wiley and Sons, Inc.

Maehr, M., & Nicholls, J. (1980). Culture and achievement motivation: A second look. In N. Warren (Ed.), *Studies in cross-cultural psychology* (Vol. 2) (pp. 221– 267). London: Academic Press.

Maher, T. E., & Wong, Y. Y. (1994). The impact of cultural differences on the growing tensions between Japan and the United States. *SAM Advanced Management Journal, 59,* 40–46.

Maio, R. G., & Esses, M. V. (1998). The social consequences of affirmative action: Deleterious effects on perceptions of groups. *Personality and Social Psychology Bulletin, 24*(1), 65–74.

Major, B., Spencer, S., Schmader, T., Wolfe, C., & Crocker, J. (1998). Coping with negative stereotypes about intellectual performance: the role of psychological disengagement. *Personality and Social Psychology Bulletin, 24*(1), 34–50.

Malpass, R. (1993, August). *A discussion of the ICAI.* Symposium presented at the Annual Convention of the American Psychological Association, Toronto, Canada.

Malpass, R. S. (1974). Racial bias in eyewitness identification. *Personality and Social Psychology Bulletin, 1* (1), 42–44.

Malpass, R. S. (1981). Effective size and defendant bias in eyewitness identification lineups. *Law and Human Behavior, 5* (4), 299–309.

Malpass, R. S., & Kravitz, J. (1969). Recognition for faces of own and other race. *Journal of Personality and Social Psychology, 13* (4), 330–334.

Mann, L., Mitsui, H., Beswick, G., & Harmoni, R. V. (1994). A study of Japanese and Australian children's respect for others. *Journal of Cross-Cultural Psychology, 25*(1), 133–145.

Manrai, L. A., & Manrai, A. K. (1995). Effects of cultural-context, gender, and acculturation on perceptions of work versus social/leisure time usage. *Journal of Business Research, 32* (2), 115–128.

Manson, S. M., & Shore, J. H. (1981). Psychiatric epidemological research among American Indian and Alaska Natives: Some methodological issues. *White Cloud Journal, 2,* 48–56.

Manson, S. M., Shore, J. H., & Bloom, J. D. (1985). The depressive experience in American Indian communities: A challenge for psychiatric theory and diagnosis. In A. Kleinman & B. Good (Eds.), *Culture and depression: Studies in the anthropology and cross-cultural psychiatry of affect and disorder* (pp. 331–368). Berkeley: University of California Press.

Manz, C. C. (1992). Self-leading work teams: Moving beyond self-management myths. *Human Relations, 45*(11), 1119–1140.

Marin, G., Gamba, R. J., & Marin, B. V. (1992). Extreme response style and acquiescence among Hispanics: The role of acculturation and education. *Journal of Cross Cultural Psychology, 23*(4), 498–509.

Markham, R., & Wang, L. (1996). Recognition of emotion by Chinese and Australian children. *Journal of Cross-Cultural Psychology, 27*(5), 616–643.

Markoff, R. (1977). Intercultural marriage: Problem areas. In W. S. Tsent, J. F. McDermott Jr., and T. W. Maretzk (Eds.), *Adjustment in intercultural marriage* (pp. 51–61). Honolulu: University of Hawaii Press.

Marks, D. (1997). Models of disability. *Disability and Rehabilitation an International Multidisciplinary Journal, 19*(3), 85–91.

Markus, H. R. (1977). Self-schemata and processing information about the self. *Journal of Personality and Social Psychology, 35,* 63–78.

Markus, H. R., & Kitayama, S. (1991a). Cultural variation in self-concept. In G. R. Goethals & J. Strauss (Eds.), *Multidisciplinary perspectives on the self.* New York: Springer-Verlag.

Markus, H. R., & Kitayama, S. (1991b). Culture and the self: Implications for cognition, emotion, and motivation. *Psychological Review, 98,* 224–253.

Markus, H. R., & Kitayama, S. (1998). The cultural psychology of personality. *Journal of Cross Cultural Psychology, 29*(1), 63–87.

Markus, H. R., & Zajonc, R. (1985). The cognitive perspective in social psychology. In G. Lindzey & E. Aaronson (Eds.), *Handbook of social psychology* (3rd ed.) (Vol. 1) (pp. 137–230). New York: Random House.

Marmot, M. G., & Syme, S. L (1976). Acculturation and coronary heart disease in Japanese Americans. *American Journal of Epidemiology, 104,* 225–247.

Marsella, A. J. (1979). Cross-cultural studies of mental disorders. In A. J. Marsella, G. DeVos, & F. L. K. Hsu (Eds.), *Perspectives on cross-cultural psychology* (pp. 233–262). New York: Academic Press.

Marsella, A. J. (1980). Depressive experience and disorder across cultures. In H. C. Triandis & J. Draguns (Eds.), *Handbook of cross-cultural psychology, Vol. 6: Psychopathology* (pp. 237–289). Boston: Allyn & Bacon.

Marsella, A. J., Sartorius, N., Jablensky, A., & Fenton, F. R. (1985). Cross-cultural studies of depressive disorders. In A. Kleinman & B. Good (Eds.), *Culture and depression* (pp. 299–324). Berkeley: University of California Press.

Martin, J. N., & Hammer, M. R. (1989). Behavioral categories of intercultural communication competence: Everyday communicators' perceptions. *International Journal of Intercultural Relations, 13*(3), 303–332.

Martin, W. E., & Farris, K. K. (1994). A cultural and contextual decision path approach to career assessment with Native Americans: A psychological perspective. *Journal of Career Assessment, 2* (3), 258–275.

Masters, R. D., & Sullivan, D. G. (1989). Nonverbal displays and political leadership in France and the United States. *Political Behavior, 11*(2), 123–156.

Mathews, H. F., Lannin, D. R., & Mitchell, J. P., (1994). Coming to terms with advanced breast cancer: Black women's narratives from eastern North Carolina. *Social Science Medicine, 38*(6), 789–800.

Matsumoto, D. (1987). *Sport science approaches to training in U. S. Judo.* Paper presented at the Fourth Annual National Judo Coaches Conference, United States Olympic Training Center, Colorado Springs, CO.

Matsumoto, D. (1989). Cultural influences on the perception of emotion. *Journal of Cross-Cultural Psychology, 20,* 92–105.

Matsumoto, D. (1990). Cultural similarities and differences in display rules. *Motivation and Emotion, 14*(3), 195–214.

Matsumoto, D. (1991). Cultural influences on facial expressions of emotion. *Southern Communication Journal, 56,* 128–137.

Matsumoto, D. (1992a). American Japanese cultural differences in the recognition of universal facial expressions. *Journal of Cross-Cultural Psychology, 23,* 72–84.

Matsumoto, D. (1992b). More evidence for the universality of a contempt expression. *Motivation and Emotion, 16*(4), 363–368.

Matsumoto, D. (1993). Ethnic differences in affect intensity, emotion judgments, display rule attitudes, and self-reported emotional expression in an American sample. *Motivation and Emotion, 17*(2), 107–123.

Matsumoto, D. (1994). *Cultural influences on research methods and statistics.* Pacific Grove, CA: Brooks/Cole.

Matsumoto, D. (1996a). *Culture and psychology.* Pacific Grove, CA: Brooks Cole.

Matsumoto, D. (1996b). *Unmasking Japan: Myths and realities about the emotions of the Japanese.* Stanford, CA: Stanford University Press.

Matsumoto, D., & Assar, M. (1992). The effects of language on judgments of universal facial expressions of emotion. *Journal of Nonverbal Behavior, 16,* 85–99.

Matsumoto, D., Colvin, C., Taylor, S., Goh, A., & Murayama, M. (1998, August). American-Japanese differences in organizational culture. In C. Colvin (Chair), *Cultural analysis of organizational typologies.* Symposium conducted at the 24th International Congress of Applied Psychology, San Francisco.

Matsumoto, D., & Ekman, P. (1988). Japanese and Caucasian facial expressions of emotion (JACFEE). Slides available from David Matsumoto, Department of Psychology, San Francisco State University, 1600 Holloway Avenue, San Francisco, CA 94132.

Matsumoto, D., & Ekman, P. (1989). American-Japanese cultural differences in intensity ratings of facial expressions of emotion. *Motivation and Emotion, 13,* 143–157.

Matsumoto, D., & Fletcher, D. (1994). *Cultural influences on disease.* Manuscript submitted for publication.

Matsumoto, D., & Hearn, V. (1991). *Culture and emotion: Display rule differences between the United States, Poland, and Hungary.* Manuscript submitted for publication.

Matsumoto, D., Kasri, F., & Kooken, K. (1999). American-Japanese cultural differences in judgements of expression intensity and subjective experience. *Cognition and Emotion, 13*(2), 201–218.

Matsumoto, D., Kasri, F., Milligan, E., Singh, U., & The, J. (1997). *Lay conceptions of culture: Do students and researchers understand culture in the same way?* Unpublished paper, San Francisco State University.

Matsumoto, D., & Kishimoto, H. (1983). Developmental characteristics in judgments of emotion from nonverbal vocal cues. *International Journal of Intercultural Relations, 7,* 415–424.

Matsumoto, D., & Kudoh, T. (1987). Cultural similarities and differences in the semantic dimensions of body postures. *Journal of Nonverbal Behavior, 11,* 166–179.

Matsumoto, D., & Kudoh, T. (1993). American-Japanese cultural differences in attributions of personality based on smiles. *Journal of Nonverbal Behavior, 17*(4), 231–243.

Matsumoto, D., Kudoh, T., Scherer, K, & Wallbott, H. (1988). Antecedents of and reactions to emotions in the United States and Japan. *Journal of Cross-Cultural Psychology, 19*(3), 267–286.

Matsumoto, D., Kudoh, T., & Takeuchi, S. (1996). Changing patterns of individualism and collectivism in the United States and Japan. *Culture and Psychology, 2,* 77–107.

Matsumoto, D., Pun, K. K., Nakatani, M., Kadowaki, D., Weissman, M., McCarter, L., Fletcher, D., & Takeuchi, S. (1994). *Cultural differences in attitudes and concerns about osteoporosis in older Japanese and Japanese-American women: Differential implications for patient management.* Manuscript submitted for publication.

Matsumoto, D., Takeuchi, S., Andayani, S., Koutnetsouva, N., & Krupp, D. (1998). The contribution of individualism-collectivism to cross-national differences in display rules. *Asian Journal of Social Psychology, 1,* 147–165.

Matsumoto, D., Wallbott, H. G., & Scherer, K. R. (1987). Emotions in intercultural communication. In M. K. Asante & W. B. Gudykunst (Eds.), *Handbook of international and cultural communication.* Newbury Park, CA: Sage.

Matsumoto, D., Weissman, M., Preston, K., Brown, B., & Kupperbusch, C. (1997). Context-specific measurement of individualism–collectivism on the individual level: The IC Interpersonal Assessment Inventory (ICIAI). *Journal of Cross-Cultural Psychology, 28,* 743–767.

Matsuyama, Y., Hama, H., Kawamura, Y., & Mine, H. (1978). Analysis of emotional words. *The Japanese Journal of Psychology, 49,* 229–232.

Mauro, R., Sato, K., & Tucker, J. (1992). The role of appraisal in human emotions: A cross-cultural study. *Journal of Personality and Social Psychology, 62*(2), 301–317.

May, P. A., & Dizmang, L. H. (1974). Suicide and the American Indian. *Psychiatric Annals, 4*(11), 22–28.

Mccargar, D. F. (1993). Teacher and student role expectations: Cross-cultural differences and implications. *Modern Language Journal, 77* (2), 192–207.

McClelland, D. C. (1961). *The achieving society.* Princeton, NJ: Van Nostrand.

McConatha, J. T., Lightner, E., & Deaner, S. L. (1994). Culture, age, and gender as variables in the expression of emotions. *Journal of Social Behavior and Personality, 9*(3), 481–488.

McCrae, R. R., & Costa, P. T. (1987). Validation of the Five-Factor model of personality across instruments and observers. *Journal of Personality and Social Psychology, 52*(1), 81–90.

McCrae, R. R., & Costa, P. T. Jr. (1997). Personality trait structure as a human universal. *American Psychologist, 52*(5), 509–516.

McCrae, R. R., Costa, P. T., Jr., Del-Pilar, G. H., & Rolland, J. P. (1998, January). Cross-cultural assessment of the five-factor model: The revised NEO personality inventory. *Journal of Cross Cultural Psychology, 29*(1), 171–188.

McCrae, R. R., Costa, P. T., & Yik, M. S. M. (1996). Universal aspects of Chinese personality structure. In M. H. Bond (Ed.); et al, *The handbook of Chinese psychology.* (pp. 189–207). Hong Kong: Oxford University Press.

McGoldrick, M. & Preto, N. G. (1984). Ethnic intermarriage: Implications for therapy. *Family Process, 23*(3), 347–364.

McGowan, R.W., McGowan, J.S. & Omifade, A. (1997). Cultural effects: attributions following ruminations of success and failure. *Psychological Reports,* 81, 155–159.

Mead, M. (1961). *Cooperation and competition among primitive people.* Boston: Beacon Press.

Meade, R.D. (1971). Future time perspectives of college students in America and in India. *Journal of Social Psychology, 83,* 175–182.

Meglino, B. M., Ravlin, E. C., & Adkins, C. L. (1989). A work values approach to corporate culture: A field test of the value congruence process and its relationship to individual outcomes. *Journal of Applied Psychology, 74*(3), 424–432.

Mehrabian, A. (1970). Authoritarianism, rigidity, and Eysenck's E and N dimensions in an authoritarian culture. *Psychological Reports, 27*(1), 326.

Mehrabian, A. (1981). *Silent messages: Implication of emotions and attitudes* (2nd ed.). Belmont, CA: Wadsworth.

Mehrabian, A., & Wiener, M. (1967). Decoding of inconsistent communications. *Journal of Personality and Social Psychology, 6*(1), 109–114.

Merton, R. (1968). *Social theory and social structures.* New York: Free Press.

Mesquita, B., & Frijda, N. H. (1992). Cultural variations in emotions: A review. *Psychological Bulletin, 112*(2), 179–204.

Messick, D. M., & Mackie, D. M. (1989). Intergroup relations. *Annual Review of Psychology, 40,* 45–81.

Milgram, S. (1974). *Obedience to authority.* New York: Harper & Row.

Miller, J. G. (1984). Culture and the development of everyday social explanation. *Journal of Personality and Social Psychology, 46,* 961–978.

Miller, J. G., & Bersoff, D. M. (1992). Culture and moral judgment: How are conflicts between justice and interpersonal responsibilities resolved? *Journal of Personality and Social Psychology, 62,* 541–554.

Mintz, J., Mintz, L., & Goldstein, M. (1987). Expressed emotion and relapse in first episodes of schizophrenia. *British Journal of Psychiatry, 151,* 314–320.

Mirande, M. (1985). *The Chicano experience: An alternative perspective.* Notre Dame: University of Notre Dame Press.

Miron, M. (1975). A study of cross-cultural factorial structure of intelligence. *Psychologia: An International Journal of Psychology in the Orient, 18* (2), 92–94.

Misumi, J., Iwai, N. An empirical study on persistence and change in leadership behavior. *Japanese Journal of Experimental Social Psychology, 25*(2), 95–106.

Miura, I. T., Okamoto, Y., Kim, C. C., Steere, M., et al. (1993). First graders' cognitive representation of number and understanding of place value. Cross-national comparisons: France, Japan, Korea, Sweden, and the United States.

Miyake, K. (1993). Temperament, mother-infant interaction, and early emotional development. *The Japanese Journal of Research on Emotions, 1*(1), 48–55.

Miyake, K., Chen, S., & Campos, J. J. (1985). Infant temperament, mother's mode of interaction, and attachment in Japan. An interim report. In I. Bretherton & E. Waters (Eds.), *Growing points of attachment theory. Monographs of the Society of Research in Child Development, 50* (1–2, Serial No. 209).

Mizokawa, D. T., & Ryckman, D. B. (1990). Attributions of academic success and failure: A comparison of six Asian-American ethnic groups. *Journal of Cross-Cultural Psychology, 21*(4), 434–451.

Moghaddam, F. M., Ditto, B., & Taylor, D. M. (1990). Attitudes and attributions related to psychological symptomatology in Indian immigrant women. *Journal of Cross-Cultural Psychology, 21,* 335–350.

Moghaddam, M. F., Taylor, M. D., Lambert, E. W., & Schmidt, E. A. (1995). attributions and discrimination: A study of attributions to the self, the group, and external factors among whites, blacks, and Cubans in Miami. *Journal of Cross-Cultural Psychology, 26*(2), 209–220.

Moore, J. T. (1988, March). *Pride against prejudice: The biography of Larry Doby.* Greenwood Publishing Group Incorporated.

Morelli, G. A., Oppenheim, D., Rogoff, B., & Goldsmith, D. (1992). Cultural variations in infant sleeping arrangements: Questions of independence. *Developmental Psychology, 28,* 604–613.

Morgan, L. H. (1877). *Ancient society: Or, researches in the line of human progress from savagery through barbarism to civilization.* Chicago: C. H. Kerr.

Morikawa, H., Shand, N., & Kosawa, Y. (1988). Maternal speech to prelingual infants in Japan and the United States: Relationships among functions, forms and referents. *Journal of Child Language, 15*(2), 237–256.

Morinaga, Y., Frieze, I. H., & Ferligoj, A. (1993). Career plans and gender-role attitude of college students in the United States, Japan, and Slovenia. *Sex Roles, 29*(5–6), 317–334.

Morinis, A. (1985). The ritual experience: Pain and the transformation of consciousness in ordeals of initiation. *Ethos, 13* (2), 150–174.

Morris, D., Collett, P., Marsh, P., & O'Shaughnessy, M. (1980). *Gestures: Their origins and distribution.* New York: Scarborough.

Morris, M. H., Avila, R. A., & Allen, J. (1993). Individualism and the modern corporation: Implications for innovation and entrepreneurship. *Journal of Management, 19*(3), 595–612.

Morris, M. W., & Peng, K. (1994). Culture and cause: American and Chinese attributions for social and physical events. *Journal of Personality and Social Psychology, 67*(6), 949–971.

Muela, S. H., Ribera, J. M., & Tanner, M. (1998). Fake malaria and hidden parasites—the ambiguity of malaria. *Anthropology and Medicine, 5*(1), 43–61.

Mukai, T. & McCloskey, L. (1996). Eating attitudes among Japanese and American elementary schoolgirls. *Journal of Cross-Cultural Psychology, 27*(4), 424–435.

Mulder, M. (1976). Reduction of power differences in practice: The power distance reduction theory and its applications. In G. Hofstede & M. S. Kassem (Eds.), *European contributions to organize theory* (pp. 79–94). Assen, Netherlands: Van Gorcum.

Mulder, M. (1977). *The daily power game.* Leyden, Netherlands: Martinus.

Munro, D. (1979). Locus-of-control attribution: Factors among Blacks and Whites in Africa. *Journal of Cross-Cultural Psychology, 10*(2), 157–172.

Munroe, R. H., Shimmin, H. S., & Munroe, R. L. (1984). Gender understanding and sex role preference in four cultures. *Developmental Psychology, 20*(4), 673–682.

Murase, T. (1986). Naikan therapy. In T. S. Lebra & W. P. Lebra (Eds.), *Japanese culture and behavior* (pp. 388–398). Honolulu: University of Hawaii Press.

Murdock, G. P., Ford, C. S., & Hudson, A. E. (1971). *Outline of cultural materials* (4th ed.). New Haven, CT: Human Relations Area Files.

Murphy, H. B. M. (1982). Culture and schizophrenia. In I. Al-Issa (Ed.), *Culture and psychopathology* (pp. 221–249). Baltimore, MD: University Park Press.

Murphy, J. M. (1976). Psychiatric labeling in cross-cultural perspective. *Science, 191,* 1019–1028.

Murstein, B., Merighi, J., & Vyse, S. (1991). Love styles in the United States and France: A cross-cultural comparison. *Journal of Social and Clinical Psychology, 10*(1), 37–46.

Myers, D. (1987). *Social psychology* (2nd ed.). New York: McGraw-Hill.

Myers, F. R. (1979). Emotions and the self: A theory of personhood and political order among Pintupi aborigines. *Ethos, 7,* 343–370.

Myers, J. K., Weissman, M. M., Tischler, G. L., Holzer, C. E., Leaf, P. J., Orvaschel, H., Anthony, J. C., Boyd, J. H., Burke, J. D., Kramer, M., & Stolzman, R. (1984). Six month prevalence of psychiatric disorders in three communities: 1980 to 1982. *Archives of General Psychiatry, 41,* 959–967.

Na, E. Y., & Loftus, E. F. (1998). Attitudes toward law and prisoners, conservative authoritarianism, attribution, and internal-external locus of control: Korean and American law students and undergraduates. *Journal of Cross-Cultural Psychology, 29*(5), 595–615.

Narayanan, L. Menon, S., & Levine, E. L. (1995, February). Personality structure: A culture-specific examination of the five-factor model. *Journal of Personality Assessment, 64*(1) 51–62.

Narayanan, S., Ganesan, V. (1978, May). The concept of self among the Irulas of Palamalai. *Journal of Psychological Reseraches, 22*(2), 127–134.

Neck, C. P., & Manz, C. C. (1994). From groupthink to teamthink: Toward the creation of constructive thought patterns in self-managing work teams. *Human Relations, 47*(8), 929–951.

Nemoto, T., Wong, F. Y., Ching, A., Chng, C. L., Bouey, P., Henrickson, M., & Smeber, R. E. (1998). HIV seroprevalence, risk behaviors, and cognitive factors among Asian and Pacific Islander American men who have sex with men: A summary and critique of empirical studies and methodological issues. *AIDS Education and Prevention, 10*(3), 31–47.

Nenty, H. J. (1986). Cross-culture bias analysis of Cattell Culture-Fair Intelligence Test. *Perspectives in Psychological Researches, 9* (1), 1–16.

Nenty, H.J., & Dinero, T. E. (1981). A cross-cultural analysis of the fairness of the Cattell Culture Fair Intelligence Test using the Rasch model. *Applied Psychological Measurement, 5* (3), 355–368.

Ng, D., McClure, J., Walkey, F., & Hunt, M. (1995). New Zealand and Singaporean attributions and achievement perceptions. *Journal of Cross-Cultural Psychology, 26*(3), 276–297.

Ng, H. S., Cooper, M., & Chandler, P. (1998). The Eysenckian personality structure: A "Giant Three" or "Big Five" model in Hong Kong? *Personality and Individual Differences, 25*(6), 1111–1131.

Ng, W. G., & Lindsay, R. L. (1994). Cross-race facial recognition: Failure of the contact hypothesis. *Journal of Cross-Cultural Psychology, 25*(2), 217–232.

Nichols, R. K., & McAndrew, T. F. (1984). Stereotyping and autostereotyping in Spanish, Malaysian, and American college students. *The Journal of Social Psychology, 124,* 179–189.

Niedenthal, P., & Beike, D. (1997). Interrelated and isolated self-concepts. *Personality and Social Psychology Review, 1*(2), 106–128.

Niyekawa-Howard, A. M. (1968). *A study of second language learning: The influence of first language on perception, cognition, and second language learning: A test of the Whorfian hypothesis.* Washington, DC: U.S. Dept. of Health, Education, and Welfare, Office of Education, Bureau of Research.

Noel, D. L. (1968). A theory of the origin of ethnic stratification. *Social Problems, 16*(2), 157–172.

Noesjirwan, J. (1977). Contrasting cultural patterns of interpersonal closeness in doctors' waiting rooms in Sydney and Jakarta. *Journal of Cross-Cultural Psychology, 8,* 357–368.

Noesjirwan, J. (1978). A laboratory study of proxemic patterns of Indonesians and Australians. *British Journal of Social and Clinical Psychology, 17,* 333–334.

Nomura, N., & Barnlund, D. (1983). Patterns of interpersonal criticism in Japan and United States. *International Journal of Intercultural Relations, 7*(1), 1–18.

Nurmi, J., Poole, E. M., & Seginer, R. (1995). Tracks and transitions: A comparison of adolescent future-oriented goals, explorations, and commitments in Australia, Israel, and Finland. *International Journal of Psychology, 30*(3), 355–375.

Nyborg, H., Eysenck, S. B. G., & Kroll, N. (1982). Cross cultural comparison of personality in Danish and English children. *Scandinavian Journal of Psychology, 23,* 291–297.

Ochs, E. (1988). *Culture and language development: Language acquisition and language socialization in a Samoan village.* Cambridge, England: Cambridge University Press.

Ochs, E., & Schieffelin, B. B. (Eds.). (1979). *Developmental pragmatics.* New York: Academic Press.

Ochs, E., & Schieffelin, B. B. (1983). *Acquiring conversational competence.* London & Boston: Routledge & Kegan Paul.

Oettingen, G. (1997). Culture and future thought. *Culture and Psychology, 3*(3), 353–381.

Ogbu, J. U. (1981). Origins of human competence: A cultural-ecological perspective. *Child Development, 52,* 413–429.

Okabe, R. (1983). Cultural assumptions of east and west: Japan and the United States. In W. Gudykunst (Ed.), *Intercultural communication theory: Current perspectives* (pp. 21–44). Beverly Hills, CA: Sage.

Okamoto, K. (1993). *Nihonjin no YES wa Naze No Ka? (Why is a Japanese yes a no?).* Tokyo, Japan: PHP Research Laboratory.

Okechuku, C. (1994). The relationship of six managerial characteristics to the assessment of managerial effectiveness in Canada, Hong Kong and People's Republic of China. *Journal of Occupational and Organizational Psychology, 67*(1), 79–86.

Olah, A. (1995). Coping strategies among adolescents: A cross-cultural study. *The Association for Professionals in Services for Adolescents,* 491–507.

Oliver, W. A. (1973). Childbirth expectancies and experiences as a function of locus of control and Lamaze training. *Dissertation Abstracts International, 33*(4-B), 1802–1803.

Omi, M., & Winant, H. (1994). *Racial formation in the United States: From the 1960s to the 1990s* (2nd ed.). New York: Routledge.

Opler, M. K., & Singer, J. L. (1959). Ethnic differences in behavior and psychopathology. *International Journal of Social Psychiatry, 2,* 11–23.

Oquendo, M. A. (1996a). Psychiatric evaluation and psychotherapy in the patient's second language. *Psychiatric Services, 47*(6), 614–618.

Oquendo, M. A. (1996b). Psychiatric evaluation in a second language: Commentary reply. *Psychiatric Services, 47*(9), 1002.

O'Reilly, C. A. (1989). Corporations, culture, and commitment: Motivation and social control in organizations. *California Management Review, 31,* 9–25.

O'Reilly, C. A., Chatman, J., & Caldwell, D. F. (1991). People and organizational culture: A profile-comparison approach to assessing person-organization fit. *Academy of Management Journal, 34,* 487–516.

Orpen, C. (1971a). Prejudice and adjustment to cultural norms among English-speaking South Africans. *The Journal of Psychology, 77,* 217–218.

Orpen, C. (1971b). The effect of cultural factors on the relationship between prejudice and personality. *The Journal of Psychology, 78,* 73–79.

Oster, H., & Ekman, P. (1979). Facial expressions of emotion. *Annual Reviews of Psychology, 30,* 527–554.

Osterman, K., Bjorkquist, K., Lagerspetz, K. (1994). Peer and self-estimated aggression and victimization in 8 year old children from five ethnic groups. *Aggressive Behavior, 20,* 411–428.

Osterweil, Z., Nagano-Nakamura, K. (1992). Maternal views on aggression: Japan and Israel. *Aggressive Behavior, 18,* 263–270.

O'Toole, A. J., Deffenbacher, K. A., Valentin, D., & Abdi, H. (1994). Structural aspects of face recognition and the other-race effect. *Memory and Cognition, 22* (2), 208–224.

O'Toole, A. J., Peterson, J., & Deffenbacher, K. A. (1996). An "other-race effect" for categorizing faces by sex. *Perception, 25* (6), 669–676.

Oyserman, D. (1993). The lens of personhood: Viewing the self and others in a multicultural society. *Journal of Personality and Social Psychology, 65*(5), 993–1009.

Oyserman, D., Gant, L., & Ager, J. (1995). A socially contextualized model of African American identity: Possible selves and school persistence. *Journal of Personality and Psychology, 69*(6), 1216–1232.

Paguio, L. P., Robinson, B. E., Skeen, P., & Deal, J. E. (1987, September). Relationship between fathers' and mothers' socialization practices and children's locus of control in Brazil, the Philippines, and the United States. *Journal of Genetic Psychology, 148*(3), 202–313.

Palmer, S. (1971). Characteristics of suicide in 54 non-literate societies. *Life Threatening Behavior, 1*(3), 178–183.

Pang, O. V. (1991). The relationship of test anxiety and math achievement to parental values in Asian American and European American middle school students. *Journal of Research and Development in Education, 24*(4), 1–10.

Papousek, H., & Papousek, M. (1997). Preverbal communication in humans and the genesis of culture. In U. C. Segerstrale & P. M. Molnar (Eds.), *Nonverbal communication: Where nature meets culture* (pp. 87–107). Hillsdale, NJ: Lawrence Erlbaum Associates, Inc.

Papps, F., Walker, M. Trimboli, A., & Trimboli, C. (1995). Parental discipline in Anglo, Greek, Lebanese, and Vietnamese cultures. *Journal of Cross-Cultural Psychology, 26*(1), 49–64.

Parkin, M. (1974). Suicide and culture in Fairbanks: A comparison of three cultural groups in a small city of interior Alaska. *Psychiatry: Journal for the Study of Interpersonal Processes, 37*(1), 60–67.

Parsonson, K. (1987). Intermarriages: Effects on the ethnic identity of the offspring. *Journal of Cross-Cultural Psychology, 18*(3), 363–371.

Pascual, L., Haynes, O. M., Galperin, Z. C., & Bornstein, H. M. (1995). Psychosocial determinants of whether and how much new mothers work: A study in the United States and Argentina. *Journal of Cross-Cultural Psychology, 26*(3), 314–330.

Patel, P. G. (1996). Linguistic and cognitive aspects of the orality-literacy complex in ancient India. *Language and Communication, 16* (4), 315–329.

Patterson, M. L. (1995). Invited article: A parallel process model of nonverbal communication. *Journal of Nonverbal Behavior, 19*(1), 3–29.

Patzer, G. L. (1985). *The physical attractiveness phenomena.* New York: Plenum Press.

Paunonen, S. V., & Ashton, M. C. (1998). The structured assessment of personality across cultures.

Journal of Cross Cultural Psychology, 29(1), 150–170.

Paunonen, S. V., Jackson, D. N., Trzebinski, J., & Forsterling, F. (1992). Personality structure across cultures: A multimethod evaluation. *Journal of Personality and Social Psychology, 62*(3), 447–456.

Pelto, P. J. (1968, April). The differences between "tight" and "loose" societies. *Trans-action*, pp. 37–40.

Pelto, P. J., & Pelto, G. H. (1975). Intra-cultural diversity: Some theoretical issues. *American Ethnologist, 2,* 1–18.

Peng, K., Nisbett, E. R., & Wong, Y. C. Nancy. (1997). Validity problems comparing values across cultures and possible solutions. *Psychological Methods, 2*(4), *329–344.*

Pennebaker, J. W., Rime, B., & Blankenship, V. E. (1996). Stereotypes of emotional expressiveness of northerners and southerners: A cross-cultural test of Montesquieu's hypothesis. *Journal of Personality and Social Psychology, 70*(2), 372–380.

Pe-Pua, R. (1989). Pagtatanong-Tanong: A cross-cultural research method. *International Journal of Intercultural Relations, 13,* 147–163.

Peterson, M. (1997). Work, corporate culture, and stress: implications for worksite health promotion. *American Journal of Health Behavior, 21*(4), 243–252.

Peterson, M. F., & Smith, P. B. (1997). Does national culture or ambient temperature explain cross-national differences in role stress? No Sweat! *Academy of Management Journal, 40*(4), 930–946.

Petrie, K., Dibble, C., Long-Taylor, M., & Ruthe, G. (1986). A New Zealand information subtest for the WAIS—R. *New Zealand Journal of Psychology, 15* (1), 23–26.

Pfeiffer, K. T. (1994). Alaskan native suicide. *Dissertation Abstracts International Section A: Humanities and Social Sciences, 54*(8-A), 3214.

Pfeiffer, W. M. (1982). Culture-bound syndromes. In I. Al-Issa (Ed.), *Culture and psychopathology* (pp. 201–218). Baltimore, MD: University Park Press.

Phinney, J. S. (1996). When we talk about American ethnic groups, what do we mean? *American Psychologist, 51*(9), 918–927.

Phinney, S. J., & Chavira, V. (1992). Ethnic identity and self-esteem: an exploratory longitudinal study. *Journal of Adolescence, 15,* 271–281.

Piaget, J. (1952). *The origins of intelligence in children.* New York: International Universities Press.

Piaget, J. (1954). *Construction of reality in the child.* New York: Basic-Books.

Piers, G., & Singer, M. B. (1971). *Shame and guilt: A psychoanalytic and a cultural study.* New York: W. W. Norton.

Pike, K. L. (1954). *Language in relation to a unified theory of the structure of human behavior, Pt. 1* (Preliminary ed.). Glendale, CA: Summer Institute of Linguistics.

Piker, S. (1998). Contributions of psychological anthropology. *Journal of Cross Cultural Psychology, 29*(1), 9–31.

Pittam, J., Gallois, C., Iwawaki, S., & Kroonenberg, P. (1995). Australian and Japanese concepts of expressive behavior. *Journal of Cross-Cultural Psychology, 26*(5), 451–473.

Pollack, R. H., & Silvar, S. D. (1967). Magnitude of the Mueller-Lyer illusion in children as a function of the pigmentation of the fundus oculi. *Psychonomic Science, 8,* 83–84.

Ponchillia, S. V.(1993). The effect of cultural beliefs on the treatment of native people with diabetes and visual impairment. *Journal of Visual Impairment and Blindness, 87* (9), 333–335.

Pontius, A. A. (1997). Lack of sex differences among east Ecuadorian school children on geometric figure rotation and face drawings. *Perceptual and Motor Skills, 85* (1), 72–74.

Poole, G., & Ting, K. (1995). Cultural Differences between Euro-Canadian and Indo-Canadian maternity patients. *Journal of Social Psychology, 135*(5), 631–644.

Poortinga, H. Y. (1989). Equivalence of cross-cultural data: An overview of basic issues. *International Journal of Psychology, 24,* 737–756.

Poortinga, H. Y. (1990). *Presidential address IACCP towards a conceptualization of culture for psychology.* Unpublished paper, Tilburg University, The Netherlands.

Poortinga, Y. H., Schoots, N. H., & van de Koppel, J. M. H. (1993). The understanding of Chinese and Kurdish emblematic gestures by Dutch subjects. *International Journal of Psychology, 28*(1), 31–44.

Poortinga, Y. H., van de Vijver, F. J. R., Joe, R. C., & van de Koppel, J. M. H. (1987). Peeling the onion called culture: A synopsis. In C. Kagitcibasi et al., (Eds.), *Growth and progress in cross-cultural psychology* (pp. 22–34). Berwyn, PA: Swets North America.

Pratt, G. (1993). Should I take this job? The organizational culture dimension to career decisions. *Educational Psychology in Practice, 8*(4), 222–224.

Price-Williams, D., & Ramirez III, M. (1977). Divergent thinking, cultural differences, and bilingualism. *The Journal of Social Psychology, 103*, 3–11.

Prince, R. (1980). Variations in psychotherapeutic procedures. In H. C. Triandis & J. Draguns (Eds.), *Handbook of cross-cultural psychology, Vol. 6: Psychopathology* (pp. 291–349). Boston: Allyn & Bacon.

Prince, V. (1985). Sex, gender, and semantics. *Journal of Sex Research, 21,* 92–96.

Pugh, J. F. (1991). The semantics of pain in Indian culture and medicine. *Culture, Medicine and Psychiatry, 15* (1), 19–43.

Puloka, M. H. (1997). A commonsense perspective on the Tongan folk healing. *International Journal of Mental Health, 26*(3), 69–93.

Punamaeki, R. L., & Joustie, M. (1998). The role of culture, violence, and personal factors affecting dream content. *Journal of Cross-Cultural Psychology, 29*(2), 320–342.

Punetha, D., Giles, H., & Young, L. (1987). Ethnicity and immigrant values: Religion and language choice. *Journal of Language and Social Psychology, 6,* 229–241.

Rabbie, J. M., & Horwitz, M. (1982). Conflicts and aggression among individuals and groups. In H. Hirsch, H. Brandstatter, & H. Kelley (Eds.), *Proceedings of the XXII International Congress of Psychology, Leipzig, DDR, No. 8. Social Psychology* Amersterdam: Noord-Holland Publishing Company.

Radford, M. H. (1991). Differences between Australian and Japanese students in reported use of decision processes. *International Journal of Psychology, 26*(1), 35–52.

Radford, M. H. B. (1989). Culture, depression, and decision-making behavior: A study with Japanese and Australian clinical and non-clinical populations. Unpublished doctoral dissertation, Flinters University of South Australia.

Radford, M. H. B., Mann, L., Ohta, Y., & Nakane, Y. (1993). Differences between Australian and Japanese students in decisional self-esteem, decisional stress, and coping styles. *Journal of Cross-Cultural Psychology, 24*(3), 284–297.

Ramirez, J. M. (1993). Acceptability of aggression in four Spanish regions and a comparison with other European countries. *Aggressive Behavior, 19*(3), 185–197.

Rao, V., & Rao, V. (1985). Sex-role attitudes across two cultures: United States and India. *Sex Roles, 13*(11–12), 607–624.

Rattan, M. S., & MacArthur, R. S. (1968). Longitudinal prediction of school achievement for Metis and Eskimo pupils. *Alberta Journal of Educational Research, 14* (1), 37–41.

Ratzlaff, C., Leroux, J., Vogt, A., Nishinohara, H., Yamamoto, A., Matsumoto, D. (1998, August). *ICAPS: A new scale of intercultural adjustment II.* Paper presented at the meeting of the American Psychological Association, Boston, MA.

Redmond, M. V., & Bunyi, J. M. (1993). The relationship of intercultural communication competence with stress and the handling of stress as reported by international students. *International Journal of Intercultural Relations, 17*(2), 235–254.

Reece, D. (1996). Covering and communication: The symbolism of dress among Muslim women. *Howard Journal of Communications, 7*(1), 35–52.

Reed, T. E., & Jensen, A. R. (1992). Conduction velocity in a brain nerve pathway of normal adults correlates with intelligence levels. *Intelligence, 16* (3–4), 259–272.

Reed, T. E., & Jensen, A. R. (1993). A somatosensory latency between the thalamus and cortex also correlates with level of intelligence. *Intelligence, 17* (4), 443–450.

Reichers, A. E. & Schneider, B. (1990). Climate and culture: An evolution of constructs. In B. Schneider (Ed.), *Organizational climate and culture* (pp. 5–39). San Francisco: Jossey-Bass.

Reid, P. T., & Trotter, K. H. (1993). Children's self-presentations with infants: Gender and ethnic comparisons. *Sex Roles, 29*(3–4), 1993.

Remland, M. S., Jones, T. S., & Brinkman, H. (1991). Proxemic and haptic behavior in three European countries. *Journal of Nonverbal Behavior, 15*(4), 215–232.

Remland, M. S., Jones, T. S., & Brinkman, H. (1995). Interpersonal distance, body orientation, and touch: Effects of culture, gender, and age. *Journal of Social Psychology, 135*(3), 281–297.

Resnik, H. L., & Dizmang, L. H. (1971). Observations on suicidal behavior among American Indians. *American Journal of Psychiatry, 127*(7), 882–887.

Riemann, R., Angleitner, A., & Strelau, J. (1997, September). Genetic and environmental influences on personality: A study of twins reared together using the self- and peer-report NEO-FFI scales. *Journal of Personality, 65*(3), 449–475.

Riesman, P. (1977). *Freedom in Fulani social life: An introspective ethnography* (M. Fuller, Trans.). Chicago: University of Chicago Press. (Original work published 1974.)

Rivers, W. H. R. (1905). Observations on the senses of the Todas. *British Journal of Psychology, 1,* 321–396.

Robbins, M. C., DeWalt, B. R., & Pelto, P. J. (1972). Climate and behavior: A biocultural study. *Journal of Cross-Cultural Psychology, 3*(4), 331–344.

Robbins, S. R. (1987). *Organization theory: Structure, design and applications.* Englewood Cliffs, NJ: Prentice-Hall.

Robertson, A., & Cochrane, R. (1976). Attempted suicide and cultural change: An empirical investigation. *Human Relations, 29*(9), 863–883.

Robins, L. N., Helzer, J. E., Weissman, M. M., Ovraschel, H., Gruenberg, E., Burke, J. D., & Reiger, D. (1984). Lifetime prevalence of specific psychiatric disorders in three sites. *Archives of General Psychiatry, 41,* 949–958.

Rodenhauser, P. (1994). Cultural barriers to mental health care delivery in Alaska. *Journal of Mental Health Administration, 21,* 60–70.

Rohner, R. P. (1984). Toward a conception of culture for cross-cultural psychology. *Journal of Cross-Cultural Psychology, 15,* 111–138.

Rolland, J. S. (1993). Mastering family challenges in serious illness and disability. In F. Walsh (Ed.); et al. *Normal family processes (2nd ed.). Guilford family therapy series.* (pp. 444–473). New York: The Guilford Press.

Romano, J. L. (1988). Stress management counseling: From crisis to intervention. *Counseling Psychology Quarterly, 1*(2–3), 211–219.

Romero, G. J., & Garza, R. T. (1986). Attributes for the occupational success/failure of ethnic minority and nonminority women. *Sex Roles, 14,* 445–452.

Rosch, E. (1973). On the internal structure of perceptual categories. In T. E. Moore (Ed.), *Cognitive development and the acquisition of language* (pp. 111–144). San Diego, CA: Academic Press.

Rosch, E. (1978). Principles of categorization. In E. Rosch & B. B. Lloyd (Eds.), *Cognition and categorization* (pp. 28–48). Hillsdale, NJ: Erlbaum.

Rose, M. H. (1995). Apprehending deaf culture. *Journal of Applied Communication Research, 23*(2), 156–162.

Roseman, I. J., Dhawan, N., Rettek, S. I., Nadidu, R. K., & Thapa, K. (1995). *Journal of Cross-Cultural Psychology, 26,* 23–48.

Rosenberg, E. L., & Ekman, P. (1994). Coherence between expressive and experiential systems in emotion. *Cognition and Emotion, 8*(3), 201–229.

Ross, B. M., & Millson, C. (1970). Repeated memory of oral prose in Ghana and New York. *International Journal of Psychology, 5,* 173–181.

Ross, J., & Ferris, K. R. (1981). Interpersonal attraction and organizational outcome: A field experiment. *Administrative Science Quarterly, 26,* 617–632.

Ross, L. (1977). The intuitive psychologist and his shortcomings: Distortions in the attribution process. In L. Berkowitz (Ed.), *Advances in experimental social psychology* (Vol. 10) (pp. 174–221). New York: Academic Press.

Rossiter, J. C. (1994). The effect of a culture-specific education program to promote breastfeeding among Vietnamese women in Sydney. *International Journal of Nursing Studies, 31*(4), 369–379.

Rotter, J. B. (1954). *Social learning and clinical psychology.* Englewood Cliffs, NJ: Prentice-Hall.

Rotter, J. B. (1966). Generalized expectancies for internal versus external control of reinforcement. *Psychological Monographs, 80* (Whole NO. 609).

Rousseau, D. M. (Normative beliefs in fund-raising organizations: Linking culture to organizational performance and individual responses. *Group and Organization Studies, 15*(4), 448–460.

Rubin, G. (1995). Maitrise des emotions, emprise et analite [Emotion control, mastery, and anality]. *Revue-Francaise-de-Psychanalyse 59* (3), 803–809.

Ruch, W. (1995). Will the real relationship between facial expression and affective experience please stand up: The case of exhilaration. *Cognition and Emotion, 9*(1), 33–58.

Russell, G. L., Fujino, D. C., Sue, S., Cheung, M., & Snowden, L. R. (1996). The effects of the therapist-client ethnic in the assessment of mental health functioning. *Journal of Cross-Cultural Psychology, 27*(5), 598–615.

Russell, J. A. (1991). Culture and the categorization of emotions. *Psychological Bulletin, 110,* 426–450.

Russell, J. A. (1994a). Is there universal recognition of emotion from facial expression? A review of the cross-cultural studies. *Psychological Bulletin, 115*(1), 102–141.

Russell, J. A. (1994b). Afterword. In J. Russell, J. Fernandez-Dols, A. Manstead, & J. Wellenkamp (Eds.), *Everyday conceptions of emotion* (pp.571–574). Netherlands: Kluwer Academic Publishers.

Russell, J. A. (1995). Facial expressions of emotion: What lies beyond minimal universality? *Psychological Bulletin, 118*(3), 379–391.

Russell, J. A. (1997). Reading emotions from and into faces: Resurrecting a dimensional-contextual perspective. In J. A. Russell, J. M. Fernandez-Dols, et al. (Eds.), *The psychology of facial expression. Studies in emotion and social interaction,* 2nd series (pp. 295–320). New York: Cambridge University Press; Paris: Editions De La Maison Des Sciences De L'Homme.

Russell, J. A., & Sato, K. (1995). Comparing emotion words between languages. *Journal of Cross-Cultural Psychology, 26*(4), 384–391.

Ryan, R. A. (1980). Strengths of the American Indian family: State of the art. In F. Hoffman (Ed.), *The American Indian family: Strength and stresses.* Isleta, NM: American Indian Social Research and Development Association.

Sachdev, P. S. (1990). Whakama: Culturally determined behavior in the New Zealand Maori. *Psychological Medicine, 20*(2), 433–444.

Sackett, P. R., & Wilk S. L. (1994). Within-group norming and other forms of score adjustment in preemployment testing. *American Psychologist, 49*(11), 929–954.

Sagi, A., Lamb, M. E., Lewkowicz, K. S., Shoham, R., Dvir, R., & Estes, D. (1985). Security of infant-mother, -father, and metapelet attachments among kibbutz reared Israeli children. In I. Bretherton & E. Waters (Eds.), *Growing point in attachment theory. Monographs of the Society for Research in Child Development, 50* (1–2 Serial No. 209).

Sakamoto, Y., & Miura, T. (1976, March). An attempt to understand Japanese personality from a family psychiatry point of view. *Australian and New Zealand Journal of Psychiatry, 10*(1-A), 115–117.

Salili, F. (1994). Age, sex, and cultural differences in the meaning and dimensions of achievement. *Personality and Social Psychology Bulletin, 20,* 635–648.

Salovey, P., & Birnbaum, D. (1989). Influence of mood on health related cognitions. *Journal of Personality and Social Psychology, 57,* 539–551.

Samovar, L. A., & Porter, R. E. (1985). *Intercultural communication: A reader.* Belmont, CA: Wadsworth.

Samovar, L. A., & Porter, R. E. (1995). *Communication between cultures.* Belmont, CA: Wadsworth.

Samovar, L. A., & Porter, R. E. (1997). *Intercultural communication: A reader.* Belmont, CA: Wadsworth.

Sampson, E. E. (1988). The debate on individualism: Indigenous psychologies and their role in personal and societal functioning. *American Psychologist, 43,* 15–22.

Santa, J. L., & Baker, L. (1975). Linguistic influences on visual memory. *Memory and Cognition, 3*(4), 445–450.

Santiago-Rivera, A. L., & Azara, L. (1995). Developing a culturally sensitive treatment modality for bilingual Spanish-speaking clients: Incorporating language and culture in counseling. *Journal of Counseling and Development, 74*(1), 12–17.

Sargent, C. (1984). Between death and shame: Dimensions of pain in Bariba culture. *Social Science and Medicine, 19* (12), 1299–1304.

Satoh, K. (1996). Expression in the Japanese kindergarten curriculum. *Early Child Development and Care, 123,* 193–202.

Saudino, K. J. (1997, August). Moving beyond the heritability question: New directions in behavioral genetic studies of personality. *Current Directions in Psychological Science, 6*(4), 86–90.

Scarr, S., & Weinberg, R. A. (1976). I.Q. test performance of black children adopted by white families. *American Psychologist, October,* 726–739.

Schachter, S., & Singer, S. S. (1962). Cognitive, social and physiological determinants of emotional state. *Psychological Review, 69,* 379–399.

Schaller, G. (1963). *The mountain gorilla.* Chicago: University of Chicago Press.

Schaller, G. (1964). *The year of the gorilla.* Chicago: University of Chicago Press.

Schein, E. H. (1985). *Organizational culture and leadership: A dynamic view.* The Jossey-Bass Management Series and The Jossey-Bass Social and Behavioral Science Series. San Francisco: Jossey-Bass Inc.

Scherer, K. R. (1997a). Profiles of emotion-antecedent appraisal: Testing theoretical predictions across cultures. *Cognition and Emotion, 11*(2), 113–150.

Scherer, K. R. (1997b). The role of culture in emotion-antecedent appraisal. *Journal of Personality and Social Psychology, 73*(4), 902–922.

Scherer, K. R., Matsumoto, D., Wallbott, H., & Kudoh, T. (1988). Emotional experience in cultural context: A comparison between Europe, Japan, and the USA. In K. Scherer (Ed.), *Facets of emotion: Recent research* (pp. 5–30). Hillsdale, NJ: Erlbaum.

Scherer, K. R., Summerfield, A., & Wallbott, H. (1983). Cross-national research on antecedents and components of emotion: A progress report. *Social Science Information, 22,* 355–385.

Scherer, K. R., & Wallbott, H. G. (1994). Evidence for universality and cultural variation of differential emotion response patterning. *Journal of Personality and Social Psychology, 66*(2), 310–328.

Schieffelin, B. B. (1981). *How Kaluli children learn what to say, what to do, and how to feel: An ethnographic study of the development of communicative competence.* Unpublished doctoral dissertation, University of California, San Diego.

Schieffelin, B. B. (1990). *The give and take of everyday life: Language socialization of Kaluli children.* New York: Cambridge University Press.

Schieffelin, B. B., & Ochs, E. (Eds.). (1986). *Language socialization across cultures.* Cambridge, England: Cambridge University Press.

Schimmack, U. (1996). Cultural influences on the recognition of emotion by facial expressions. *Journal of Cross-Cultural Psychology, 27,* 37–50.

Schneller, R. (1988). The Israeli experience of cross-cultural misunderstanding: Insights and lessons. In F. Poyatos et al. (Eds.), *Cross-cultural perspectives in nonverbal communication* (pp. 153–173). Goettingen, Germany: Hogrefe & Huber Publishers.

Schubert, J., & Cropley, A. J. (1972). Verbal regulation of behavior and IQ in Canadian Indian and white children. *Developmental Psychology, 7*(3), 295–301.

Schuster, B., Forsterlung, F., & Weiner, B. (1989). Perceiving the causes of success and failure: A cross-cultural examination of attributional concepts. *Journal of Cross-Cultural Psychology, 20,* 191–213.

Schwartz, N., Strack, F., Kommer, D., & Wagner, D. (1987). Soccer, rooms, and the quality of life: Mood effects on judgments of satisfaction with life in general and with specific domains. *European Journal of Social Psychology, 17*(1), 69–79.

Schwartz, S. (1990). Individualism-collectivism: Critique and proposed refinements. *Journal of Cross-Cultural Psychology, 21,* 139–157.

Schwartz, S., & Bilsky, W. (1987). Toward a universal psychological structure of human values. *Journal of Personality and Social Psychology, 53,* 550–562.

Schwartz, S. H. (1978). Temporal instability as a moderator of the attitude behavior relationship. *Journal of Personality and Social Psychology, 36*(7), 715–724.

Schwartz, S. H. (1994). Are there universal aspects in the structure and contents of human values? *Journal of Social Issues, 50*(4), 19–45.

Scribner, S. (1979). Modes of thinking and ways of speaking: Culture and logic reconsidered. In I. O. Freedle (Ed.), *New directions in discourse processing* (pp. 223–243). Norwood, NJ: Able.

Scrull, T. K. (1983). Organizational and retrieval processes in person memory: An examination of processing objectives, presentation format, and the possible role of self-generated retrieval cues. *Journal of Personality and Social Psychology, 44*(6), 1157–1170.

Seelye, H. N., & Brewer, B. M. (1970). Ethnocentrism and acculturation of north Americans in Guatemala. *The Journal of Social Psychology, 80,* 147–155.

Segall, M. H. (1979). *Cross-cultural psychology: Human behavior in global perspective.* Pacific Grove, CA: Brooks/Cole.

Segall, M. H. (1984). More than we need to know about culture, but are afraid to ask. *Journal of Cross Cultural Psychology, 15* (2), 153–162.

Segall, M. H., Campbell, D. T., & Hersokovits, J. (1963). Cultural differences in the perception of geometric illusions. *Sciences, 193,* 769–771.

Segall, M. H., Campbell, D. T., & Hersokovits, J. (1966). *The influence of culture on visual perception.* Indianapolis: Bobbs-Merrill.

Segall, M. H., Dasen, P. R., Berry, J. W., & Poortinga, Y. H. (1990). *Human behavior in global perspective: An introduction to cross-cultural psychology.* New York: Pergamon Press.

Seiffge-Krenke, I. & Shulman, S. (1990). Coping style in adolescence: A cross-cultural study. *Journal of Cross-Cultural Psychology, 21*(3), 351–377.

Shahim, S. (1992). Correlations for Wechsler Intelligence Scale for Children-Revised and the Weschler Preschool and Primary Scale of Intelligence for Iranian children. *Psychological Reports, 70,* 27–30.

Shane, S., Venkataraman, S., & MacMillan, I. (1995). Cultural differences in innovation championing strategies. *Journal of Management, 21* (5), 931–952.

Shapiro, P. N., & Penrod, S. (1986). Meta-analysis of facial identification studies. *Psychological Bulletin, 100*(2), 139–156.

Shayer, M., Demetriou, A., & Perez, M. (1988). The structure and scaling of concrete operational thought: Three studies in four countries and only one story. *Genetic Psychology Monographs, 114,* 307–376.

Shea, J. D. (1985). Studies of cognitive development in Papua New Guinea. *International Journal of Psychology, 20,* 33–61.

Shepperd, J., & Wright, R. (1989). Individual contributions to a collective effort: An incentive analysis. *Personality and Social Psychology Bulletin, 15,* 141–149.

Shirakashi, S. (1985). Social loafing of Japanese students. *Hiroshima Forum for Psychology, 10,* 35–40.

Shore, B. (1991). Twice born, once conceived: Meaning construction and cultural cognition. *American Anthropologist, 93,* (1), 9–27.

Shuter, R. (1977). A field study of nonverbal communication in Germany, Italy, and the United States. *Communication Monographs, 44,* 298–305.

Shweder, R. A. (1979a). Rethinking culture and personality theory: I. A critical examination of two classical postulates. *Ethos, 7*(3), 255–278.

Shweder, R. A. (1979b). Rethinking culture and personality theory: II. A critical examination of two more classical postulates. *Ethos, 7*(4), 279–311.

Shweder, R. A. (1980). Rethinking culture and personality theory: III. From genesis and typology to hermeneutics and dynamics. *Ethos, 8*(1), 60–94.

Shweder, R. A. (1994). Liberalism as destiny. In B. Puka et al. (Eds.), *Moral development: A compendium: Vol. 4. The great justice debate: Kohlberg criticism* (pp.71–74). New York: Garland Publishing, Inc.

Shweder, R. A., & Bourne, E. J. (1984). Does the concept of the person vary cross-culturally? In R. A. Shweder & R. A LeVine (Eds.), *Culture theory: Essays on mind, self, and emotion* (pp. 158–199). Cambridge, England: Cambridge University Press.

Shweder, R. A., Mahapatra, M., & Miller, J. G. (1987). Culture and moral development. In J. Kagan & S. Lamb (Eds.), *The emergence of morality in young children.* Chicago: University of Chicago Press.

Si, G., Rethorst, S., & Willimczik, K. (1995). Causal attribution perception in sports achievement: A cross-cultural study on attributional concepts in Germany and China. *Journal of Cross-Cultural Psychology, 26*(5), 537–553.

Simmons, C. H., vomKolke, A., & Shimizu, H. (1986). Attitudes toward romantic love among American, German and Japanese students. *Journal of Social Psychology, 126,* 327–336.

Simonds, P. E. (1965). The bonnet macaque in South India. In I. DeVore (Ed.), *Primate behavior: Field studies of monkeys and apes* (pp. 175–196). New York: Holt, Rinehart & Winston.

Simonton, D. K. (1996). Presidents' wives and First Ladies: On achieving eminence within a traditional gender role. *Sex Roles 35,* (5–6), 309–336.

Singelis, M. T., Triandis, C. H., Bhawuk, S. D., & Gelfand, J. M. (1995). Horizontal and vertical dimensions of individualism and collectivism: A theoretical and measurement refinement. *Cross-Cultural Research, 29*(3), 241–275.

Singelis, T. (1994). The measurement of independent and interdependent self-construals. *Personality and Social Psychology Bulletin, 20* (5), 580–591.

Singelis, T., & Sharkey, W. (1995). Culture, self-construal, and embarrassability. *Journal of Cross-Cultural Psychology, 26*(6), 622–644.

Skinner, B. F. (1957). *Verbal behavior. The century psychology series.* New York: Appleton-Century-Crofts.

Slavin, M. O., and Kriegman, D. (1992). *The adaptive design of the human psyche: Psychoanalysis, evolutionary biology, and the therapeutic process.* New York: The Guilford Press.

Slee, R., & Cook, S. (1994). Creating cultures of disability to control young people in Australian schools. *Urban Review, 26,* 15–23.

Smith, J. R., Griffith, E. J., Griffith, K. H., & Steger, J. M. (1980). When is a stereotype a stereotype? *Psychological Reports, 46,* 643–651.

Smith, P. B. (1998, October). *Leadership in high power distance cultures: An event management perspective.* Paper presented at the Third Latin-American Reunion of Cross-Cultural Psychology, Toluca, Mexico.

Smith, P. B., & Bond, M. H. (1999). *Social psychology: Across cultures* (2nd ed.) Boston, MA: Allyn and Bacon, Inc.

Smith, P. B., Dugan, S., Peterson, M. F., & Leung, K. (1998, August). Individualism: Collectivism and the handling of disagreement. A 23-country study. *International Journal of Intercultural Relations, 22*(3), 351–367.

Smith, P. B., Dugan, S., & Trompenaars, F. (1996). National culture and the values of organizational employees. *Journal of Cross-Cultural Psychology, 27*(2), 231–264.

Smith, P. B., Dugan, S., & Trumpenaars, F. (1997). Locus of control and affectivity by gender and occupational status: A 14-nation study. *Sex Roles, 36*(1–2), 51–77.

Smith, P. B., Peterson, M. F., & Misumi, J. (1994). Event management and work team effectiveness in Japan, Britain and USA. *Journal of Occupational and Organizational Psychology, 67,* 33–43.

Smith, P. B., Peterson, M., Misumi, J., & Bond, M. (1992). A cross-cultural test of the Japanese PM leadership theory. *Applied Psychology: An International Research, 41,* 5–20.

Smith, P. B., Wang, Z. M., & Leung, K. (1997). Leadership, decision-making, and cultural context: Event management within Chinese joint ventures. *Leadership Quarterly, 8*(4), 413–431.

Snarey, J. R. (1985). Cross-cultural universality of social development: A critical review of Kohlbergian research. *Psychological Bulletin, 97,* 202–232.

Sniderman, M. P., Northrup, A. D., Fletcher, F. J., Russell, H. P., & Tetlock, E. P. (1993). Psychological and cultural foundations of prejudice: The case of anti-Semitism in Quebec. *The Canadian Review of Sociology and anthropology, 30*(2), 242–270.

Snyder, C. R. (1974). Acceptance of personality interpretations as a function of assessment procedures. *Journal of Consulting and Clinical Psychology, 42*(1), 150.

Snyder, C. R., & Higgins, R. L. (1988). Excuses: Their effective role in the negotiation of reality. *Psychological Bulletin, 104,* 23–35.

Snyder, M. (1974). Self-monitoring of expressive behavior. *Journal of Personality and Social Psychology, 30*(4), 526–537.

Solis-Camara, P., & Fox, R. A. (1995). Parenting among mothers with young children in Mexico and the United States. *Journal of Social Psychology, 135*(5), 591–599.

Song, M. J., & Ginsburg, H. P. (1987). The development of informal and formal mathematical thinking in Korean and U. S. children. *Child Development, 58,* 1286–1296.

Soudijn, K. A., Hutschemaekers, G. J. M. & Van de Vijver, F. J. R. (1990). Culture conceptualizations. In F. J. R. Van de Vijver and G. J. M. Hutschemaekers (Eds.), *The investigation of culture: Current issues in cultural psychology* (pp. 19–39). Tilburg: Tilburg University Press.

Sow, I. (1977). *Psychiatrie dynamique africaine.* Paris: Payot.

Sow, I. (1978). *Les structures anthropologiques de la folie en Afrique noire.* Paris: Payot.

Sowell, T. (1983). *The economics and politics of race.* New York: Quill.

Spadone, R. a. (1992). Internal-external control and temporal orientation among Southeast Asians and White Americans. *The American Journal of Occupational Therapy, 46*(8), 713–718.

Spearman, C. E. (1927). *The abilities of man.* New York: Macmillan.

Spencer, H. (1876). *Principles of sociology.* New York: D. Appleton.

Spinks, P. M. (1983, June). A preliminary culture specific personality scale. *Journal of Cross Cultural Psychology, 14*(2), 201–219.

Spitzberg, B. (1997). A model of intercultural communication competence. In L. Samovar & R. Porter (Eds.), *Intercultural communication: A reader* (pp. 379–391). Belmont, CA: Wadsworth.

Sponsel, L. E. (1998). Yanomami: An arena of conflict and aggression in the Amazon. *Aggressive Behavior, 24*(2), 97–122.

Steele, S. (1990). *The content of our character: A new vision of race in America.* New York: Harper Collins

Steinberg, S. (1989). *The ethnic myth: Race, ethnicity, and class in America.* Boston: Beacon Press.

Stephan, W. G., Stephan, C. W., & Cabezas De Vargas, M. (1996). Emotional expression in Costa Rica and the United States. *Journal of Cross-Cultural Psychology, 27*(2), 147–160.

Steptoe, A., Sutcliffe, I., Allen, B., & Coombes, C. (1991). Satisfaction with communication, medical knowledge, and coping styles in patients with metastatic cancer. *Social Science and Medicine, 32*(6), 627–632.

Steptoe, A., & Wardle, J. (Eds.). (1994). *Psychosocial processes and health: A reader.* Cambridge, England: Cambridge University Press.

Sternberg, R. J. (1986). *Intelligence applied: Understanding and increasing your intellectual skills.* New York: Harcourt Brace Jovanovich.

Sternberg, R. J. (1988). Triangulating love. In R. J. Sternberg & M. L. Barnes (Eds.), *The psychology of love* (pp. 119–138). New Haven, CT: Yale University Press.

Sternberg, R. J., & Lubart, T. I. (1995). *Defying the crowd: Cultivating creativity in a culture of conformity.* New York: The Free Press.

Stevenson, H. W., et al. (1985). Cognitive performance and academic achievement of Japanese, Chinese, and American children. *Child Development, 56*(3), 718–734.

Stevenson, H. W., Lee, S. Y., & Stigler, S. Y. (1986). *Beliefs and achievements: A study in Japan, Taiwan, and the United States.* Unpublished manuscript.

Stevenson, W. H., Chen, C., & Lee, S. (1993). Mathematics achievement of Chinese, Japanese, and American children: Ten years later. *Science, 259,* 53–58.

Stewart, A. J., Malley, J. E. (1987). Role combination in women: Mitigating agency and communion. In F. J. Crosby et al., (Eds.), *Spouse, parent, worker: On gender and multiple roles* (pp. 44–62). New Haven, CT: Yale University Press.

Stewart, V. (1973). Tests of the "carpentered world" hypothesis by race and environment in American and Zambia. *International Journal of Psychology, 8,* 83–94.

Stiff, J. B., Hale, J. L., Garlick, R., & Rogan, R. G. (1990). Effects of cue incongruence and social normative influences on individual judgements of honesty and deceit. *The Southern Communication Journal, 55,* 206–229.

Stigler, J. W., & Baranes, R. (1988). Culture and mathematics learning. In E. Rothkpof (Ed.), *Review of research in education* (Vol. 15) (pp. 253–306). Washington DC: American Educational Research Association.

Stigler, J. W., Lee, S., & Stevenson, H. W. (1986). Digit memory in Chinese and English: Evidence for a temporally limited store. *Cognition, 23,* 1–20.

Stigler, W. J. & Perry, M. (1988). Mathematics learning in Japanese, Chinese, and American classrooms. *New Directions for Child Development, 41,* 27–58.

Streltzer, J. (1997). Pain. In W. Tseng & J. Streltzer (Eds.) *Culture and psychopathology: A guide to clinical assessment* (pp. 87–100). New York: Brunner/Mazel, Inc.

Strodtbeck, F. L. (1964). Considerations of meta-method in cross-cultural studies. *American Anthropologist, 66*(3), 223–229.

Stropes-Roe, M., & Cochrane, R. (1990). The child-rearing values of Asian and British parents and young people: An inter-ethnic and inter-generational comparison in the evolution of Kohn's 13 qualities. *British Journal of Social Psychology, 29,* 149–160.

Stryker, S. (1986). Identity theory: Developments and extensions. In K. Tardley & T. Honess (Eds.), *Self and identity* (pp. 89–107). New York: Wiley.

Suchman, R. G. (1966). Cultural differences in children's color and form perception. *Journal of Social Psychology, 70,* 3–10.

Sue, D., Sue, D., & Sue, S. (1990). *Understanding abnormal behavior* (3rd ed.). Boston: Houghton Mifflin.

Sue, S. (1977). Community mental health services to minority groups: Some optimism, some pessimism. *American Psychologist, 32,* 616–624.

Sue, S. (1991, August). *Ethnicity and mental health: Research and policy issues.* Invited address presented at the Annual Meeting of the American Psychological Association, San Francisco.

Sue, S., Akutsu, P. D., & Higashi, C. (1985). Training issues in conducting therapy with ethnic-minority-group clients. In P. Pedersen (Ed.), *Handbook of cross-cultural counseling and therapy.* New York: Greenwood Press.

Sue, S., & Morishima, J. K. (1982). *The mental health of Asian Americans.* San Francisco: Jossey-Bass.

Sue, S., & Zane, N. (1987). The role of culture and cultural techniques in psychotherapy: A reformation. *American Psychologist, 42,* 37–45.

Suggs, D. N., & Miracle, A. W. (Eds.). (1993). *Culture and human sexuality: A reader.* Pacific Grove: Brooks/Cole Publishing Co.

Super, C. M., & Harkness, S. (1986). The developmental niche: A conceptualization at the interface of child and culture. *International Journal of Behavioural Development, 9,* 545–569.

Super, C. M., & Harkness, S. (1994). The developmental niche. In W. Lonner & R. Malpass (Eds.), *Psychology and culture* (pp. 95–99). Boston: Allyn & Bacon.

Suzuki, T. (1978). *Japanese and the Japanese.* Tokyo: Kodansha.

Swartz, L. (1985). Anorexia nervosa as a culture-bound syndrome. *Social Science and Medicine, 20,* 725–730.

Tafarodi, R. W. & Swann, W. B., Jr. (1996). Individualism-collectivism and global self-esteem: Evidence for a cultural trade-off. *Journal of Cross-Cultural Psychology, 27*(6), 651–672.

Tajfel, H. (1982). Social psychology of intergroup relations. *Annual Review of Psychology, 33,* 1–39.

Takahashi, K. (1990). *Affective relationships and their lifelong development.* (Vol. 10). Hillsdale, NJ: Lawrence Erlbaum.

Takahashi, K., & Hatano, G. (1997). A landmark toward the construction of cultural psychology. *Human Development, 40,* 355–359.

Takahashi, K., & Majima, N. (1994). Transition from home to college dormitory: The role of preestablished affective relationships in adjustment to a new life. *Journal of Research on Adolescence, 4*(3), 367–384.

Takahashi, Y. (1997). Culture and suicide: From a Japanese psychiatrist's perspective. *Suicide and Life Threatening Behavior, 27*(1), 137–145.

Takaki, R. (1998). *Strangers from a different shore: A history of Asian Americans* (rev. ed.). Boston: Back Bay Books.

Takano, Y. (1989). Methodological problems in cross-cultural stidies of linguist relativity. *Cognition, 31,* 141–162.

Takano, Y., & Noda, A. (1993). A temporary decline of thinking ability during foreign language processing. *Journal of Cross-Cultural Psychology, 24*(4), 445–462.

Takano, Y., & Noda, A. (1995). Interlanguage dissimilarity enhances the decline of thinking ability during foreign language processing. *Language Learning, 45*(40), 657–681.

Takano, Y., & Osaka, E. (1997). "Japanese collectivism" and "American individualism": Reexamining the dominant view. *The Japanese Journal of Psychology, 68*(4), 312–327.

Takeuchi, D., Higginbotham, N., Marsella, A., Gomes, K., Kwan, L., Ostrowski, B., et al. (1987). Native Hawaiian mental health. In A. B. Robillard, & A. J. Marsella (Eds.), *Contemporary issues in mental health research in the Pacific Islands* (pp. 149–176). Honolulu: University of Hawaii Press.

Talamantes, M. A., Lawler, W. R., & Espino, V. (1995). Hispanic American elders: Caregiving norms surrounding dying and the use of hospice services. *Hospice Journal, 10*(2), 35–49.

Tanaka-Matsumi, J., & Draguns, J. G. (1997). Culture and psychopathology. In J. W. Berry, M. H. Segall, & C. Kagitcibasi (Eds.), *Handbook of cross-cultural psychology. Vol. 3: Social behavior and applications* (2nd ed.) (pp. 449–491). Boston, MA: Allyn and Bacon.

Taylor, J. (1992). *Paved with good intentions: The failure of race relations in contemporary America.* New York: Carroll & Graf.

Tedlock, B. (1987). Zuni and Quiche dream sharing and interpreting. *Dreaming: Anthropological and psychological interpretations. School of American research advanced seminar series* (pp. 105–131). Cambridge, UK: Cambridge University Press.

Terav, T., & Keltikangas, J. L. (1998). Social decision-making strategies among Finnish and Estonian adolescents. *Journal of Social Psychology, 138*(3), 381–391.

Terrell, M. D. (1992, August). *Stress, coping, ethnic identity and college adjustment.* Paper presented at the annual meeting of the American Psychological Association, Washington, D.C.

Tharp, R. G. (1991). Cultural diversity and treatment of children. *Journal of Consulting and Clinical Psychology, 5*(3), 381–392.

Thomas, A., & Chess, S. (1977). *Temperament and development.* New York: Brunner/Mazel.

Thomas, A., & Sillen, S. (1972). *Racism and psychiatry.* New York: Brunner/Mazel.

Thomas, D. C., & Toyne, B. (1995). Subordinates' Responses to Cultural Adaptation by Japanese Expatriate Managers. *Journal of Business Research, 32,* 1–10.

Thompson, N., Stradling, S., Murphy, M., & O'Neill, P. (1996). Stress and Organizational Culture. *British Journal of Social Work, 26*(5), 647–665.

Thornton, B. (1984). Defensive attribution of responsibility: Evidence for an arousal-based motivational bias. *Journal of Personality and Social Psychology, 46,* 721–734.

Thurstone, L. L. (1938). *Primary mental abilities.* Chicago: University of Chicago Press.

Ting-Toomey, S. (1991). Intimacy expressions in three cultures: France, Japan, and the United States. *International Journal of Intercultural Relations, 15,* 29–46.

Ting-Toomey, S. (1997). Managing intercultural conflicts effectively. In L. Samovar & R. Porter (Eds.), *Intercultural communication: A reader* (pp. 392–404). Belmont, CA: Wadsworth.

Tolman, A., & Reedy, R. (1998). Implementation of a culture-specific intervention for a Native American community. *Journal of Clinical Psychology in Medical Settings, 5*(3), 381–392.

Tom, D., & Cooper, H. (1986). The effect of student background on teacher performance attributions: Evidence for counterdefensive patterns and low expectancy cycles. *Basic and Applied Social Psychology, 7,* 53–62.

Tomada, G., & Schneider, B. H. (1997). Relational aggression, gender, and peer acceptance: Invariance across culture, stability over time, and concordance among informants. *Developmental Psychology, 33*(4), 601–609.

Tomasello, M. (1993). On the interpersonal origins of self-concept. In U. Neisser (Ed), et al., *The perceived self: Ecological and interpersonal sources of self-knowledge. Emory symposia in cognition, 5* (pp. 174–184). New York: Cambridge University Press.

Tomkins, S. S. (1962). *Affect, imagery, and consciousness, Vol. 1: The positive affects.* New York: Springer.

Tomkins, S. S. (1963). *Affect, imagery, and consciousness, Vol. 2: The positive affects.* New York: Springer.

Torrey, E. F. (1972). *The mind game: Witchdoctors and psychiatrists.* New York: Emerson Hall.

Trankina, F. J. (1983). Clinical issues and techniques in working with Hispanic children and their families. In G. J. Powell (Ed.), *The psychological development of minority group children* (pp. 307–329). New York: Brunner/Mazel.

Triandis, H. C. (1972). *The analysis of subjective culture.* New York: Wiley.

Triandis, H. C. (1989). The self and social behavior in differing cultural contexts. *Psychological Review, 96,* 506–520.

Triandis, H. C. (1994). *Culture and social behavior.* New York: McGraw-Hill.

Triandis, H. C. (Series Ed.). (1995). *New directions in social psychology: Individualism & collectivism.* Boulder: Westview Press.

Triandis, H. C. (1996). The psychologist measurement of cultural syndromes. *American Psychologist, 51*(4), 407–415.

Triandis, H. C. (1998). Vertical and horizontal individualism and collectivism: Theory and research implications for international comparative management. In Joseph L. C. Cheng & Richard B. Peterson (Eds.), *Advances in international comparative management, Vol. 12* (pp. 7–35). Stamford: JAI Press, Inc.

Triandis, H. C., Bontempo, R., Betancourt, H., Bond, M., Leung, K., Brenes, A., Georgas, J., Hui, C. H., Marin, G., Setiadi, B., Sinha, J. B., Verma, J., Spangenberg, J., Touzard, H., & de Montonollin, G. (1986). The measurement aspects of individualism and collectivism across cultures. *Australian Journal of Psychology, 38,* 257–267.

Triandis, H. C., Bontempo, R., Villareal, M. J., Asai, M., & Lucca, N. (1988). Individualism and collectivism: Cross-cultural perspectives on self-ingroup relationships. *Journal of Personality and Social Psychology, 4,* 323–338.

Triandis, H. C., & Lambert, W. W. (1958). A restatement and test of Schlosberg's theory of emotion with two kinds of subjects from Greece. *Journal of Abnormal and Social Psychology, 56,* 321–328.

Triandis, H. C., Leung, K., Villareal, M., & Clack, F. (1985). Allocentric versus idiocentric tendencies: Convergent and discriminate validation. *Journal of Research in Personality, 19,* 395–415.

Triandis, H. C., McCusker, C., & Hui, C. H. (1990). Multimethod probes of individualism and collectivism. *Journal of Personality and Social Psychology, 59,* 1006–1020.

Trommsdorff, G., & Iwawaki, S. (1989). Students' perceptions of socialization and gender role in Japan and Germany. *International Journal of Behavioral Development, 12* (4), 485–493.

Trompenaars, F. (1993). *Riding the waves of culture.* London: Brealey.

Tronick, E. Z., Morelli, G. A., & Ivey, P. K. (1992). The Efe forager infant and toddlers pattern of social relationships: Multiple and simultaneous. *Developmental Psychology, 28,* 568–577.

Trull, T. J., & Geary, D. C. (1997). Comparison of the Big-Five factor structure across samples of Chinese and American adults. *Journal of Personality Assessment, 69*(2), 324–341.

Tse, D. K., Francis, J., & Walls, J. (1994). Cultural differences in conducting intra- and inter-cultural negotiations: A Sino-Canadian comparison. *Journal of International Business Studies, 25*(3), 537.

Tseng, W. (1977). Family diagnosis and classification. *Annul Progress in Child Psychiatry and Child Development,* 434–454.

Tseng, W., & McDermott, J. F. (1981). *Culture, mind and therapy: An introduction to cultural psychiatry.* New York: Brunner/Mazel.

Tullett, A. D. (1997). Cognitive style: Not culture's consequence. *European Psychologist, 2* (3), 258–267.

Tulviste, P. (1978). On the origins of the theoretic syllogistic reasoning in culture and in the child. *Acta at commentationes Universitatis Tortuensis, 4,* 3–22.

Turner, V. (1993). Body, brain, and culture. *Brain, culture, and the human spirit: Essays from an emergent evolutionary perspective* (pp. 77–108). Lanham, MD: Universoty Press of America.

Tuss, P., Zimmer, J., & Ho, H. (1995) Causal attributions of under achieving fourth-grade students in China, Japan, and the United States. *Journal of Cross-Cultural Psychology, 26*(4), 408–425.

Tversky, A. & Kahneman, D. (1981). The framing of decisions and the psychology of choice. *Science, 211* (4481), 453–458.

Tylor, E. B. (1865). *Researches into the early history of mankind and development of civilization.* London: John Murray.

The USA's new immigrants. (1997, October 13). *USA Today,* p. A11.

U.S. Bureau of the Census. (1985). Persons of Spanish origin in the United States: March 1985. *Current Population Reports* (Series P-20, No. 403). Washington, DC: Government Printing Office.

Uziel-Miller, N. D., Lyons, J. S., Kissiel, C., & Love, S. (1998). Treatment needs and initial outcomes of a residential recovery program for African American women and their children. *American Journal on Addictions, 7,* 43–50.

Valadez, J. R. (1998). Applying to college: Race, class, gender differences. *Professional School Counseling, 1* (5), 14–20.

Van den Berghe, P. L. (1981). *The ethnic phenomenon.* New York: Elsevier.

Van de Vijver, F. J. R., & Leung, K. (1997a). Methods and data analysis of comparative research. In J. W. Berry, Y. H. Poortinga, & J. Pandey (Eds.), *Handbook of cross-cultural psychology* (2nd ed., Vol. 1, pp. 257–300). Boston: Allyn & Bacon.

Van de Vijver, F. J. R., & Leung, K. (1997b). *Methods and data analysis for cross-cultural research.* Newbury Park, CA: Sage.

Van-Geert, P. (1995). Green, red, and happiness: Towards a framework for understanding emotion universals. *Journal of Culture and Psychology, 1*(2), 259–268.

van Hooff, J. A. R. A. M. (1967). The facial displays of the catarrhine monkeys and apes. In D. Morris (Ed.), *Primate ethology* (pp. 7–68). London: Weidenfeld and Nicolson.

Verkuyten, M. & Hagendoorn, L. (1998). Prejudice and self-categorization: The variable role of authoritarianism and in-group stereotypes. *Personality and Social Psychology Bulletin, 24*(1), 99–110.

Vinacke, W. E. (1949). The judgment of facial expressions by three national-racial groups in Hawaii: I. Caucasian faces. *Journal of Personality, 17,* 407–429.

Vinacke, W. E., & Fong, R. W. (1955). The judgment of facial expressions by three national-racial groups in Hawaii: II. Oriental faces. *Journal of Social Psychology, 41,* 184–195.

Vogt, A. L., LeRoux, J., Ratzlaff, C., Nishinohara, H., Yamamoto, A., & Matsumoto, D. (1998, April). *A new scale of intercultural adjustment.* Paper presented at the meeting of the Western Psychological Association, Irvine, CA.

Von-Raffler Engel, W. (1981). Developmental kinesics: How children acquire communicative and non-communicative nonverbal behavior. *Infant Mental Health Journal, 2*(2), 84–94.

Vontress, C. E. (1991). Traditional healing in Africa: Implications for cross-cultural counseling. *Counseling and Development, 70,* 242–249.

Vornberg, A. J., & Grant, T. R. (1976). Adolescent cultural acquaintance experiences and ethnic group attitudes. *Adolescence, 6*(44), 601–608.

Vrij, A., & Winkel, F. W. (1991). Cultural patterns in Dutch and Surinam nonverbal behavior: an analysis of simulated police/citizen encounters. *Journal of Nonverbal Behavior, 15*(3), 169–184.

Vrij, A., & Winkel, F. W. (1992). Crosscultural police-citizen interactions: The influence of race, beliefs, and nonverbal communication on impression formation. *Journal of Applied Social Psychology, 22*(19), 1546–1559.

Vrij, A., & Winkel, F. W. (1994). Perceptual distortions in cross-cultural interrogations: The impact of skin color, accent, speech style, and spoken fluency on impression formation. *Journal of Cross-Cultural Psychology, 25*(2), 284–295.

Wagner, D. A. (1977). Ontogeny of the Ponzo illusion: Effects of age, schooling and environment. *International Journal of Psychology, 12,* 161–176.

Wagner, D. A. (1980). Culture and memory development. In H. Triandis & A. Heron (Eds.), *Handbook of cross-cultural psychology, Vol. 4: Developmental psychology.* Boston: Allyn & Bacon.

Wagner, J. A., III, (1995). Studies of individualism-collectivism: Effects on cooperation in groups. *Academy of Management Journal, 38*(1), 152–172.

Wainryb, C., & Turiel, E. (1994). Dominance, subordination, and concepts of personal entitlements in cultural contexts. *Child Development, 65* (6), 1701–1722.

Walker, C. E. (1977). Continuing professional developmental: The future for clinical psychology. *Clinical Psychologist, 30*(2), 6–7, 22.

Walker, L. J. (1984). Sex differences in the development of moral reasoning: A critical review. *Child Development, 57,* 522–526.

Walkey, H. F., & Chung, C. R. (1996). *Journal of Cross-Cultural Psychology, 27*(3), 283–292.

Wallbott, H., & Scherer, K. (1986). How universal and specific is emotional experience? Evidence from 27 countries on five continents. *Social Science Information, 25,* 763–795.

Wallbott, H., & Scherer, K. (1988). Emotion and economic development: Data and speculations concerning the relationship between emotional experience and socioeconomic factors. *European Journal of Social Psychology, 18,* 267–273.

Wallbott, H., & Scherer, K. (1995). Cultural determinants in experiencing shame and guilt . In J. Tangney & K. Fischer (Eds.), *Self-conscious emotions.* New York: The Gullford Press.

Walters, T. K. (1994). Acculturative stress, social support, and trauma in a community sample of Cambodian refugees. *Dissertation Abstracts International: Section B: The Sciences and Engineering, 54*(8-B), 4374.

Wassenaar, D. R., Van der Veen, M., & Pillay, A. L. (1998). Women in cultural transition: Suicidal behavior in South African Indian women. *Suicide and Life Threatening Behavior, 28,* 82–93.

Watkins, D., Akande, A., Cheng, C., & Regmi, M. (1996). Cultural and gender differences in the self-esteem of college students: A four-country comparison. *Social Behavior and Personality, 24*(4), 321–328.

Watkins, D., & Cheung, S. (1995). Culture, gender, and response bias: An analysis of responses to the Self-Description Questionnaire. *Journal of Cross-Cultural Psychology, 26*(5), 490–504.

Watkins, D., & Regmi, M. (1996). Within-culture and gender differences in self-concept. An investigation with rural and urban Nepalese school children. *Journal of Cross-Cultural Psychology, 27*(6), 692–699.

Watson, D. (1982). The actor and the observer: How are their perceptions of causality divergent? *Psychological Bulletin, 92,* 682–700.

Watson, O. M. (1970). *Proxemic behavior: A cross-cultural study.* The Hague: Mouton.

Watson, O. M., & Graves, T. D. (1966). Quantitative research in proxemic behavior. *American Anthropologist, 68,* 971–985.

Weatherly, K. A., & Beach, L. R. (1998). Organizational culture and decision making. In L. R. Beach et al. (Eds.), *Image theory: Theoretical and empirical foundations* (pp. 211–225). Mahwah, NJ: Lawrence Erlbaum Associates, Inc.

Weber, G. G. (1997). Cross-cultural menopause: A study in contrasts. *A clinician's guide to menopause. Clinical practice* (pp. 45–62). Washington, DC: Health Press International.

Weiner, B. (1974). *Achievement motivation and attribution theory.* Morristown, NJ: General Learning Press.

Weiner, B., Frieze, I., Kukla, A., Reed, L., Rest, S., & Rosenbaum, R. M. (1972). Perceiving the causes of success and failure. In E. E. Jones, D. E. Kanouse, H. H. Kelley, R. E. Nesbett, S. Valins, & B. Weiner (Eds.), *Perceiving the causes of behavior.* Morristown, NJ: General Learning Press.

Weiss, S. C., (1980). Porteus Maze performances on nonliterate and literate Campas from Eastern Peru. *Journal of Social Psychology, 112* (2), 303–304.

Weldon, E., & Gargano, G. M. (1988). Cognitive loafing: The effects of accountability and shared responsibility on cognitive effort. *Personality and Social Psychology Bulletin, 14,* 159–171.

Westaby, J. D. (1995, August). Presence of others and task performance in Japan and the United States: A laboratory investigation. *International Journal of Psychology, 30*(4), 451–460.

Wheeler, L., & Kim, Y. (1997). What is beautiful is culturally good: The physical attractiveness stereotype has different content in collectivistic cultures. *Personality and Social Psychology Bulletin, 23*(8), 795–800.

White, G. M. (1980). Conceptual universals in interpersonal language. *American Anthropologist, 88,* 759–781.

Who, S. (1983). *Primary health care: The Chinese experience.* World Health Organization.

Whorf, B. L. (1956). *Language, thought and reality* (J. Carroll, Ed.). Cambridge, MA: MIT Press.

Wierzbicka, A. (1986). Human emotions: Universal or culture-specific? *American Anthropologist, 88,* 584–594.

Wierzbicka, A. (1994). Semantic universals and primitive thought: The question of the psychic unity of humankind. *Journal of Linguistic Anthropology, 4*(1), 23.

Wierzbicka, A. (1995). The relevance of language to the study of emotions. *Psychological Inquiry, 6*(3), 248–252.

Williams, J. E., Satterwhite, R. C., & Best, D. L. (1999). Pancultural gender stereotypes revisited: The five factor model. *Sex Roles, 40*(7–8), 513–525.

Williams, J., & Best, D. (1982). *Measuring sex stereotypes: A thirty-nation study.* Beverly Hills, CA: Sage.

Williams, J., & Best, D. (1990). *Measuring sex stereotypes: A multination study.* Beverly Hills, CA: Sage.

Williams, J., & Best, D. (1994). Cross-cultural views of women and men. In W. Lonner & R. Malpass (Eds.), *Psychology and culture.* Boston: Allyn & Bacon.

Williams, L. Anshel, M., & Quek, J. (1997). Cognitive style in adolescent competitive athletes as a function of culture and gender. *Journal of Sport Behavior, 20*(2), 232–245.

Willman, E., Feldt, K., & Amelang, M. (1997). Prototypical behavior patterns of social intelligence: An intercultural comparison between Chinese and German subjects. *International Journal of Psychology, 32*(5), 329–346.

Winegar, L. (1995). Emotion and facial expression: A semantic perspective. *Culture and Psychology, 1,* 227–258.

Wing, D. M., Crow, S. S., & Thompson, T. (1995). An ethnonursing study of Muscogee (Creek) Indians and effective health care practices for treating alcohol abuse. *Family and Community Health, 18*(2), 52–64.

Winton, W. M. (1986). The role of facial response in self-reports of emotion: A critique of Laird. *Journal of Personality and Social Psychology, 50,* 808–812.

Wiseman, R. L., Hammer, M. R., & Nishida, H. (1989). Predictors of intercultural communication competence. *International Journal of Intercultural Relations, 13,* 349–370.

Wittgenstein, L. 1968. *Philosophical investigations.* (G. E. M. Anscombe, trans.). New York: Macmillan. [Originally published 1953]

Wittmer, J. (1971). Old order Amish and non-Amish youth: A personality comparison utilizing the 16 PF. *Personality, 2*(4), 305–313.

Wober, M. (1974). Toward an understanding of the Kiganda concept of intelligence. In J. W. Berry & P. R. Dasen (Eds.), *Culture and cognition* (pp. 261–280). London: Methuen.

Wohl, J. (1989). Integration of cultural awareness into psychotherapy. *American Journal of Psychotherapy, 43*(30), 343–355.

Wolf, R. M. (1965). The measurement of environments. In C. W. Harris (Ed.), *Proceedings of the 1964 Invited Conference on Testing Problems.* Princeton, NJ: Educational Testing Service.

Wolff, B. B., & Langley, S. (1968). Cultural factors and the response to pain: A review. *American Anthropologist, 70* (3), 494–501.

Wolpoff, M., & Caspari, R. (1997). *Race and human evolution: A fatal attraction.* New York: Simon & Schuster.

Wong, P. T. P., Derlaga, V. J., & Colson, W. (1988). The effects of race on expectancies and performance and attributions. *Canadian Journal of Behavioral Science, 20,* 29–39.

Wood, P. B., & Chesser, M. (1994). Black stereotyping in a university population. *Sociological Focus, 27*(1), 17–34.

Wood, P. C., Hillman, S. B., & Sawilowsky, S. S. (1995). Comparison of self-esteem scores: American and Indian adolescents. *Psychological Reports, 76,* 367–370.

World Health Organization. (1973). *Report of the International Pilot Study of Schizophrenia, Vol. 1.* Geneva: Author.

World Health Organization. (1979). *Schizophrenia: An international follow-up study.* New York: Wiley.

World Health Organization. (1981). *Current state of diagnosis and classification in the mental health field.* Geneva: Author.

World Health Organization. (1991). *World health statistics quarterly.* Geneva: Author.

Wylie, R. C. (1979). *The self concept, Vol. 2: Theory and research on selected topics.* Lincoln: University of Nebraska Press.

Yamaguchi, S. (1994). Collectivism among the Japanese: A perspective from the self. In U. Kim & H. Triandis (Eds.), *Individualism and collectivism: Theory, method, and applications. Cross-cultural research and methodology series, Vol. 18,* (pp. 175–188). Thousand Oaks, CA: Sage Publications, Inc.

Yamaguchi, S., Kuhlman, D. M., & Sugimori, S. (1995). Personality correlates of allocentric tendencies in individualist and collectivist cultures. *Journal of Cross-Cultural Psychology, 26*(6), 658–672.

Yamaguchi, S., Okamoto, K., & Oka, T. (1985). Effects of coactor's presence: Social loafing and social facilitation. *Japanese Psychological Research, 27,* 215–222.

Yamamoto, J., & Kubota, M. (1983). The Japanese-American family. In G. J. Powell (Ed.), *The psychological development of minority group children* (pp. 307–329). New York: Brunner/Mazel.

Yamamoto, K., Soliman, A., Parsons, J., & Davies, O. L. (1987). Voices in unison: Stressful events in the lives of children in six countries. *Child Psychology and Psychiatry, 28*(6), 855–864.

Yamauchi, H., & Li, Y. (1995). Comparative study of aggressive motives of Japanese and Chinese college students. *Psychologia: An International Journal of Psychology in the Orient, 38*(4), 209–219.

Yan, W. & Gaier, L. E. (1994). Causal attributions for college success and failure: An Asian-American comparison. *Journal of Cross-Cultural Psychology, 25,* 146–158.

Yang, K. S. (1982). Causal attributions of academic success and failure and their affective consequences. *Chinese Journal of Psychology* [Taiwan], *24,* 65–83. (The abstract only is in English.)

Yao, L. E. (1985). A comparison of family characteristics of Asian American and Anglo American high achievers. *International Journal of Comparative Sociology, 26 (3–4),* 198–206.

Yap, P. M. (1974). *Comparative psychiatry. A theoretical framework.* Toronto: University of Toronto.

Yee, H. A., Fairchild, H. H., Weizmann, F., & Wyatt, E. G. (1993). Addressing psychology's problems with race. *American Psychologist, 48*(11), 1132–1140.

Yrizarry, N., Matsumoto, D., & Wilson-Cohn, C. (1998). American-Japanese differences in multi-scalar intensity ratings of universal facial expressions of emotion. *Motivation and Emotion, 22*(4), 315–327.

Yu, E. S. H. (1974). Achievement motive, familism, and hsiao: A replication of McClellend-Winterbottom studies. *Dissertation Abstracts International, 35,* 593A (University Microfilms No. 74-14, 942).

Yum, J. O. (1987). Korean philosophy and communication. In D. L. Kincaid (Ed.), *Communication theory: Eastern and western perspectives.* New York: Academic Press.

Zaccaro, S. J. (1984). The role of task attractiveness. *Personality and Social Psychology Bulletin, 10,* 99–106.

Zahn-Waxler, C., Friedman, J. R., Cole, M. P., Mizuta, I., & Hiruma, N. (1996). Japanese and United States preschool children's responses to conflict and distress. *Child Development, 67,* 2462–2477.

Zhang, M., Yan, H., & Phillips, M. R. (1994). Community-based psychiatric rehabilitation in Shanghai: Facilities, services, outcome, and culture-specific characteristics. *British Journal of Psychiatry, 165*(24), 70–79.

Zimmerman, S. (1995). Perceptions of intercultural communication competence and international student adaptation to an American campus. *Communication Education, 44*(4), 321–335.

Zuckerman, M. (1990). Some dubious premises in research and theory on racial differences: Scientific, social, and ethical issues. *American Psychologist, 45*(12), 1297–1303.

Name Index

Abdel-Khalek, A. M., 391
Abebimpe, V. R., 256
Abramov, I., 326
Abrams, D., 467, 470
Abrams, K. K., 239, 240
Abramson, R. P., 34
Abreu, J., 267
Acioly, N. M., 188
Adamopoulos, J., 415
Adkins, C. L., 467
Adler, N. E., 233
Ager, J., 72
Agnoli, F., 329
Ainsworth, M. D., 177
Akan, G. E., 239
Akande, A., 221, 430
Akoh, H., 44
Akutsu, P. D., 267
Alarcon, R. D., 262, 265
Albert, A. A., 216
Albright, L., 411
Alibhai, N., 231
Allen, J. K., 468, 478
Allen, L. R., 224, 239, 240
Allison, M. T., 428
Altarriba, J., 269
Altman, I., 415
Altman, S. A., 348
Al-Zahrani, S., 431

Amir, Y., 14, 442
Ando, K., 467
Andrews, J. D., 481
Anshel, M. H., 221
Archer, D., 354
Argyle, M., 341, 348, 438
Asai, M., 42
Asch, S. E., 437
Assar, M., 333
Atkinson, D. R., 267
Atkinson, J. W., 61, 62
Au, T. K., 328
Aune, K., 279
Averill, J. R., 310
Avila, R. A., 468
Azuma, H., 180

Baban, P., 391
Back, K., 414
Baddeley, A. D., 89
Baguma, P., 232
Bahrick, H. P., 89
Baltes, B. P., 190
Baranes, R., 185, 186, 188, 320
Barbee, A. P., 412
Bard, P., 306
Barnard, E. A., 181
Barry, H., 19, 220
Bartlett, F. C., 149

Baumrind, D., 179
Baxter, J. C., 356
Beach, L. R., 478
Bear, J., 352, 353
Beike, D., 70, 71
Beiser, M., 263
Ben-David, A., 269
Benedict, R., 386, 438
Benet-Martinez, V., 398
Bennett, M. J., 378
Berkman, L. F., 234
Berko, J., 315
Berko-Gleason, J., 315
Berlin, B., 325
Bernal, M. E., 68
Bernieri, F., 414
Berry, D. S., 213, 411
Berry, J. W., 18, 19, 23, 35, 48, 218,
    219, 220, 221, 222, 229, 256,
    377, 399, 448, 469, 477
Berscheid, E., 415
Bersoff, D. M., 200
Best, D. L., 86, 181, 212–215, 216,
    217
Betancourt, H., 10, 11, 31
Bhalla, S. K., 239
Bhawuk, S. D., 45
Bickerton, D., 316
Bilsky, W., 46

Binion, V. J., 212
Birdwhistell, R., 273
Birenbaum, M., 190
Bishop, R. C., 467
Bisht, S., 204
Bissilat, J., 168
Blankenship, V. E., 280
Blatt, S. J., 70, 71
Blau, Z. S., 164
Blehar, M. C., 177
Bleichrodt, N., 219
Blinco, M. A. P., 204
Block, J., 220
Bloom, A. H., 327, 328
Bloom, J. D., 263
Blumenfeld, P. C., 44
Bochner, S., 59, 79, 81, 102, 167,
    466
Bond, M. H., 58, 62, 136, 176, 237,
    391, 394, 405, 413, 423, 425,
    438, 439, 460, 475
Bontempo, R., 42
Born, M., 219
Bornstein, H. M., 182, 184, 432
Boster, F. J., 43
Bouchard, T. J., Jr., 163
Boucher, J. D., 282, 298, 299, 308
Bourne, E. J., 58, 60, 365
Bower, H. G., 88
Bowlby, J., 177
Bradley, G. W., 422
Braly, K., 84, 85
Brandt, M. E., 298, 299, 308
Brannon, L., 231, 234, 235
Brehm, S. S., 415
Breuer, N. L., 248
Brewer, B. M., 81
Brewer, M. B., 42, 198, 404
Brinkman, H., 221, 351
Brislin, R., 79, 91, 125, 211, 220
Bromley, D. B., 60
Bronfenbrenner, U., 180
Bronstein, P. A., 181, 200
Brook, D. W., 269
Brooks-Gunn, J., 239, 240
Broota, K. D., 146
Brown, B., 46, 47
Brown, R., 325, 329
Bruner, J. S., 148
Buck, E. B., 438
Buck, R., 88, 290
Budowski, D., 259
Bunyi, J. M., 377, 378
Burger, J. M., 88
Burgos, N. M., 438

Buriel, R., 174
Burleson, B. R., 221
Bush, G., 405
Buss, D. M., 415, 417
Butcher, J. N., 254
Byrne, D., 415

Cabezas De Vargas, M., 279
Caldwell, D. F., 447, 462
Calhoun, J. B., 350
Calhoun, L. G., 232
Campbell, D. T., 141, 198
Campos, J. J., 178
Cann, A., 232
Cannon, W. B., 306
Carlo, G., 201
Carlson, G. E., 282
Carrell, L. J., 377
Carroll, J. B., 324
Carson, R. C., 254, 259, 261, 264
Casa, A., 267
Casagrande, J. B., 324
Cashmore, J. A., 438
Caspari, R., 30
Cederblad, M., 183
Chan, J., 390, 391, 393
Chan, S. Q., 174
Chandler, P., 394
Chao, K. R., 189
Chasiotis, A., 181
Chatman, J., 447, 462
Chavira, V., 193
Chen, C., 186
Chen, G. M., 321, 376
Chen, S., 178
Cheng, C., 221
Cheng, D., 258
Chess, S., 175
Cheung, C., 200
Cheung, M., 267
Cheung, S., 221
Chisholm, J., 176
Chomsky, N., 316
Chou, Y., 411
Chung, C. R., 83, 86
Church, A. T., 167, 386, 392, 400
Churchill, W., 353
Clack, F., 42, 492
Clymer, C. E., 33
Cochrane, R., 438
Cogan, J. C., 239
Cole, M., 149, 152
Cole, M. P., 204
Coleman, J. C., 254
Collett, P., 353, 356

Colson, W., 426, 427
Comas-Diaz, L., 224, 266, 267
Conroy, M., 180
Contarello, A., 438
Cook, M., 348
Cook, P., 244
Cook, S., 33
Cooper, H., 427
Cooper, M., 394
Costa, P. T., 394, 395, 396, 402
Cousins, S. D., 59
Crandall, C. S., 239, 240
Crittenden, K. S., 423, 425
Crocker, J., 102
Crow, S. S., 248
Cunningham, M. R., 412

Dabul, A. J., 68
Daibo, I., 411
Dalal, K. A., 204
Damond, M. E., 248
Darwin, C., 272–273
Dasen, P. R., 18, 23, 48, 168, 195,
    196, 221
Dasgupta, S. D., 222
DaSilva, S. M., 201
David, B. G., 167
Davies, O. L., 257
Deaner, S. L., 280
Deck, L. P., 410
De-Fruyt, F., 394
Delgado, M., 248
Demetriou, A., 195
Denton, L. T., 475
DePaulo, B. M., 341, 411
De Raad, B., 394, 400
Derlaga, V. J., 426, 427
De Valois, R. L., 326
Devereux, C. E., Jr., 180, 181
Devore, I., 348
Dhawan, N., 59
Diaz-Perez, Y. I., 438
DiMartino, C. E., 204
Dinges, N. G., 333
Dion, K. K., 410, 416
Ditto, B., 428, 431
Doi, K., 62, 438
Doi, T., 65, 70, 399
Domino, G., 244, 440
Druen, P. B., 412
Duda, J. L., 428
Dugan, S., 389, 393, 461, 484
Durie, M. H., 268
Durkheim, E., 50
Durrett, M. E., 178

Dvir, R., 178

Earley, P. C., 471
Eberhardt, J. L., 31
Ebrahimpour, M., 465, 471
Edman, J. L., 244, 430
Efron, D., 338
Eisenberg, N., 201
Ekman, P., 128, 148, 238, 273, 274,
    275, 277, 278, 279, 282, 283,
    284, 285, 286, 287, 288, 338,
    339, 347, 352, 353
Elbedour, S., 416
El-Islam, M. F., 438
Ellis, B., 416
Ellsworth, P., 273
Erikson, E. H., 177, 201–204
Ervin, S. M., 322
Espin, O. M., 225
Espino, V., 248
Esses, M. V., 94
Estes, D., 178
Evans, B. J., 224
Evans, J. L., 148
Exline, R. V., 348, 349
Eysenck, S. B. G., 390, 391, 393,
    394

Fairchild, H. H., 30
Farver, M. J., 204, 435
Fehr, B. J., 348, 349
Feist, J., 231, 234, 235
Ferligoj, A., 221
Ferrante, J., 203, 476
Ferris, K. R., 410
Festinger, L., 414
Fiedler, K., 88
Figueredo, A. J., 396
Fishman, J., 328–329
Fletcher, D., 118, 235, 236, 237,
    238
Fletcher, F. J., 82
Fong, R. W., 273
Ford, C. S., 19
Forgas, J. P., 405, 413, 428, 429
Forgas, P. J., 84, 86, 88, 89, 90, 368,
    405
Forsterling, F., 395, 429
Forston, R. F., 351
Fortenberry, J. D., 260
Freedman, D., 176
Freidman, M., 234
Freud, S., 70
Frey, D., 428, 429
Friedman, J. R., 204

Friesen, W. V., 238, 273, 274, 277,
    279, 282, 283, 287, 338, 339,
    347, 352, 353
Frieze, I. H., 221
Frijda, N. H., 300
Frohlich, B. C., 201
Fujino, D. C., 267
Fukuno, M., 221
Furlong, M. J., 267
Furnham, A., 231, 232, 416, 428,
    429, 430, 462

Gabrenya, W. K., Jr., 471
Gaier, L. E., 190, 425
Galati, D., 299
Gallois, C., 279
Galperin, Z. C., 182
Ganguli, H. C., 146
Gant, L., 72
Gao, G., 391
Garcia Coll, C. T., 176, 184
Gardner, H., 169
Gargano, G. M., 471
Garratt, G. A., 356
Garza, R. T., 428, 429
Gay, J., 149
Geary, C. D., 186, 187
Geary, D. C., 394
Geertz, C., 23, 54
Geist, R., 258
Gelfand, J. M., 45
Georgas, J., 43
Gerber, E., 308, 309
Gergen, K. J., 3, 13, 14
Giles, H., 438
Gilligan, C., 58, 199, 200
Gillis, J. S., 414
Gim, R. H., 267
Ginsburg, H. P., 186
Gladwin, C., 188
Gladwin, H., 188
Gladwin, T., 188
Gleason, H. A., 324
Glick, J. A., 149
Goethals, G. R., 64
Goldberg, L. R., 394
Goldman, A., 481, 485
Goldsmith, D., 181
Goldstein, M., 256
Goodnow, J. J., 438
Goodwin, R., 408
Goody, J. R., 198
Gordon, C., 269
Graham, J. L., 481, 482, 484
Graham, S., 10, 424, 427

Grant, T. R., 102
Graves, T. D., 349, 351
Gray, J. J., 239, 240
Greenfield, M. P., 123, 164
Greenfield, P. M., 148
Griffith, E. J., 84
Griffith, K. H., 84
Grilo, C. M., 239
Grisaru, N., 259
Grossmann, K., 178
Grossmann, K. E., 178
Gudykunst, W. B., 43, 320, 321,
    360, 370, 371, 372, 373, 375,
    376, 380, 391
Guilford, J. P., 161
Guinn, B., 244
Guisinger, S., 70, 71
Gulerce, A., 13

Hadiyono, J. E. P., 438
Hagendoorn, L., 96
Haghighatgou, H., 257
Hahn, M. W., 438
Hall, C. C. I., 224
Hall, E. T., 41, 159, 349, 351, 372,
    402
Hall, J. A., 350, 351
Hall, K. R. L., 348
Hall, L. K., 89
Hall, R. H., 478
Hall, V. C., 424, 427
Hama, H., 308
Hamid, P. N., 388
Hamilton, L. H., 239, 240
Hamilton, V. L., 44
Hammer, M. R., 376, 380
Hampel, R., 95
Harkins, S. G., 470, 471
Harkness, S., 192
Harlow, H. F., 177
Harlow, M. K., 177
Harris, A. C., 221, 224, 435
Harris, M. B., 239
Harris, V. A., 60
Harrison, A. O., 174, 406
Hashimoto, T., 419
Hatano, G., 494
Hatch, T., 169
Hatfield, E., 415, 417
Hau, K., 200, 423, 424
Haynes, O. M., 182
Hearn, V., 281, 282
Hegel, G. W. F., 197
Heider, K. G., 283, 326
Heinisch, D. A., 467

Hemans, L. T., 88
Henderson, M., 438
Henderson, N. D., 163
Hendrick, C., 415
Hendrick, S., 415
Henriques, G. R., 232
Herrnstein, R. J., 165–167
Hersokovits, J., 141
Hesketh, B., 466
Hess, D. R., 180
Hess, J. A., 468
Hiatt, L. R., 308
Hiatt, R. A., 249
Hickson, D. J., 449
Higashi, C., 267
Higginbotham, H. N., 263, 266, 267
Higgins, R. L., 88
Hill, R. F., 260
Hillary, K., 244
Hillman, S. B., 389
Hinde, R. A., 348
Hinkle, S., 467
Hippler, A. E., 198, 400
Hippocrates, 231
Hiruma, N., 204
Hitch, G., 89
Ho, H., 190
Hoch, E. M., 268
Hodge, K., 221
Hodgetts, R. M., 463, 471
Hoek, H. W., 259
Hofstede, G., 27, 41, 42, 43, 44, 69,
    118, 215, 217–218, 236, 285,
    320, 407, 434, 450, 451, 452,
    455, 456, 457, 458, 459, 460,
    461, 462
Hofstee, W. K. B., 394
Hollander, E., 473
Holloway, S. D., 185
House, A., 181
Howe, A., 427
Howell, S., 309
Howes, C., 204
Hudson, A. E., 19
Hudson, W., 145, 146
Hughes, B., 33
Hui, C. H., 42, 44, 45, 46
Hull, P., 333
Hunt, E., 329
Hunt, M., 426
Husen, T., 186

Ibrahim, F. A., 263
Iizuka, Y., 438
Ineichen, B., 414

Isaac, M., 258
Itoi, R., 221
Ivey, P. K., 178
Iwao, S., 83
Iwawaki, S., 216, 279
Izard, C., 273, 282, 285

Jacklin, C. N., 218
Jackson, D. N., 394
Jackson, J. M., 471
Jacobs, G. H., 326
Jacobsen, F. M., 266, 267
James, W., 63, 306
Janca, A., 258
Jencks, C., 163
Jensen, A., 162, 163
Jiang, S., 478
Jilek, A. L., 244
Jilek, M., 244
Joe, C. R., 117
John, O. P., 398, 402
Johnson, J. L., 465, 471
Jones, E. E., 60, 422
Jones, P., 349
Jones, T. S., 221, 351
Joseph, R. A., 58, 63
Josephson, L., 220
Joshi, S. M., 181

Kaaya, J., 244
Kameoka, A. K., 244, 430
Kane, C. M., 158
Kaplowitz, S., 431
Karasawa, M., 390
Karno, M., 256
Kashima, E. S., 320
Kashima, Y., 69, 320, 426, 427
Kashiwagi, K., 180
Kasri, F., 20, 128, 284
Katigbak, M. S., 167, 400
Katz, D., 84, 85
Kawamura, Y., 308
Kay, P., 325, 327
Keats, D. M., 167, 168
Kedem, P., 416
Keller, H., 181
Kelley, H. H., 422
Kelley, M., 180, 181
Kemper, T., 310
Kempton, W., 327
Kendon, A., 352, 353
Kenny, D. A., 411
Keys, J. B., 475
Kiers, H. A., 394
Kiev, A., 259, 419

Kim, E. Y., 467
Kim, K., 380
Kim, M., 321, 360
Kim, S. J., 267
Kimmel, P. R., 479, 480
King, J. E., 396
King, M. L., 99
Kishimoto, H., 354
Kissiel, C., 248
Kitayama, S., 41, 56, 57, 63, 64, 66,
    67, 69, 296, 297, 387, 389,
    390
Kleinman, A., 66, 254, 255, 256,
    257, 258, 260
Kluckholn, C., 18, 23, 39, 41, 407
Knight, G. P., 68
Koehler, K. M., 239
Kohlberg, L., 199
Koller, H. S., 201
Komilla, T., 59
Kosmitzki, C., 72
Koss, J. D., 258
Kraemer, R., 190
Kramer, R. M., 42, 404
Krause, I. B., 259
Kroeber, A. L., 18, 23, 39
Kroll, N., 391
Kroonenberg, P., 279
Krupp, B., 95, 492
Kubota, M., 183
Kudoh, T., 69, 287, 292, 303, 342,
    354, 412
Kuhlman, D. M., 391
Kupperbusch, C., 47
Kurokawa, M., 66, 67
Kush, C. J., 189

Labarre, W., 386
LaFrance, M., 349
Lamb, M. E., 178
Lambert, E. W., 82, 102, 273
Lammers, C. J., 449
Lange, C., 306
Langman, P. F., 265
Lannin, D. R., 244
Larson, C. U., 351
Lassiter, G. D., 411
Latané, B., 470, 471
Lauer, E., 220
Laurendeau-Bendavid, M., 197
Laurent, A., 454
Lavallee, M., 195
Lawler, W. R., 248
Laya, D., 168
Lazarus, R. S., 87

Lederman, N., 427
Lee, H. O., 43
Lee, I., 408
Lee, S., 72, 186, 187, 259
Lee, S. M., 463
Leetz, K. L., 265
Leff, J., 255, 256, 257, 263, 264, 308
Lenneberg, E., 325, 329
Leong, F. T. L., 258
Lester, B. M., 176
Leung, K., 42, 44, 118, 136, 423, 425, 477, 484, 492
Levenson, R., 238
Levin, M., 151
Levine, J. B., 158, 159
Levine, R., 419
Levine, R. A., 183
Levy, R. I., 299, 307, 309, 310
Levy-Bruhl, L., 198
Lewkowicz, K. S., 178
Lightner, E., 280
Lillard, A., 494
Lin, P., 327
Lin, W., 244
Little, D. T., 190
Livesly, W. J., 60
Lock, A., 13
Long, A., 424, 427
Lonner, W. J., 263, 386, 392
Lopez, R. S., 10, 11, 31
Loscocco, K. A., 478
Love, K. G., 467
Love, S., 248
Lucca, N., 42
Luria, A. R., 153, 198
Luthans, F., 463
Lutz, C., 65, 157, 307, 308, 309, 310
Luzzo, D. A., 467
Lyons, J. S., 248

Ma, K. H., 200
Maccoby, E. E., 179, 218
Maciorowski, K., 349
Mackie, D. M., 42, 404
MacLean, M., 181
Maehr, M., 61, 62
Mahapatra, M., 200
Maio, R. G., 94
Majima, N., 204
Major, B., 102
Malloy, T. E., 411
Malpass, R., 19, 151
Mann, L., 390

Manson, S. M., 263
Manz, C. C., 472, 478
Markham, R., 282
Marks, D., 33
Markus, H. R., 41, 54, 56, 57, 58, 63, 64, 66, 67, 69, 296, 297, 387, 389, 411
Marmot, M. G., 234, 236
Marsella, A. J., 251, 254, 256, 257, 260, 263
Marsh, P., 353
Marshall, C., 220
Martin, J. A., 179
Martin, J. N., 376
Martinez, R., 239, 240
Mathews, H. F., 244
Matsumoto, D., 20, 41, 43, 46, 47, 64, 68, 69, 72, 118, 126, 128, 136, 235, 236, 237, 238, 243, 279, 280, 281, 282, 283, 284, 285, 286, 287, 290, 292, 300, 303, 333, 354, 389, 412, 447, 463, 465, 492
Matsuyama, Y., 308
Mayo, C., 349
McAndrew, T. F., 83, 84
McArthur, L. Z., 411
McCabe, A., 321
McClelland, D. C., 61
McCloskey, L., 240
McClure, J., 426
McConatha, J. T., 280
McCrae, R. R., 394, 395, 396, 397, 402
McCusker, C., 45
McDermott, J. F., 229, 266, 267, 268
McGowan, J. S., 430
McGowan, R. W., 430
McGue, M., 163
Mead, M., 41, 273, 276, 386, 407
Meade, R. D., 159
Meadow, H., 269
Meglino, B. M., 467
Mehrabian, A., 341, 342
Merkel, S., 427
Mermigis, L., 82
Merton, R., 93
Mervielde, I., 394
Mesquita, B., 300
Messick, D. M., 42, 404
Milgram, S., 437, 439
Miller, J. G., 60, 61, 200, 365
Miller, T. R., 475
Milligan, E., 20

Millson, C., 149
Minami, M., 185, 321
Mine, H., 308
Mintz, J., 256
Mintz, L., 256
Misra, G., 13
Misumi, J., 474, 475
Mitchell, J. P., 244
Miura, K., 44
Miyake, K., 178, 179
Mizokawa, D. T., 425
Mizuta, I., 204
Mkombachepa, L., 244
Moghaddam, M. F., 102, 428, 431
Montei, M. S., 467
Morelli, G. A., 178, 181
Morgan, L. H., 197
Morinaga, Y., 221
Morishima, J. K., 255
Morris, D., 353
Morris, M. H., 468
Mountcastle, V. B., 306
Moylan, J. S., 88
Muela, S. H., 244
Mukai, T., 240
Mulder, M., 41, 451
Munro, D., 388, 393
Munroe, R. H., 216
Munroe, R. L., 216
Muramatsu, Y., 438
Murasawa, H., 411
Murase, T., 268
Murnen, S. K., 415
Murphy, J. M., 254, 255
Murphy, M., 466
Murray, C., 165–167
Myambo, K., 406
Myers, D., 63
Myers, F. R., 309
Myers, J. K., 256

Naidu, R. K., 59
Nakane, Y., 390
Neck, C. P., 472, 478
Negishi, K., 66, 67
Newton, B. J., 438
Ng, D., 426
Ng, H. S., 394
Ngini, L., 195
Nicholls, J., 61, 62
Nichols, R. K., 83, 84
Niedenthal, P., 70, 71
Nisbett, E. R., 123
Nisbett, R. E., 422

Nishida, T., 320, 321, 370, 371, 373, 376, 380, 391
Niyekawa-Howard, A. M., 327
Noda, A., 334
Noesjirwan, J., 351
Norasakkunkit, V., 389
Northrup, A. D., 82
Nurmi, J., 204
Nyborg, H., 391

Ochs, E., 316
O'Driscoll, M., 84, 86
Oettingen, G., 190
Ogbu, J. U., 174
Ohbuchi, K. I., 221
Ohta, Y., 390
Oka, T., 471
Okamoto, K., 471, 481
Olah, A., 204
Oliver, R. R., 148, 326
Omifade, A., 430
O'Neill, P., 466
Opler, M. K., 255
Oppenheim, D., 181
Oquendo, M. A., 264
O'Reilly, C. A., 447, 462
Orley, J., 258
Orpen, C., 96
Osaka, E., 69
Osako, T., 81
O'Shaughnessy, M., 353
Oster, H., 148
O'Sullivan, M., 283
Otaki, M., 178
Oyserman, D., 71, 72

Paludi, M., 200
Pang, O. V., 190
Papps, F., 181
Parsons, J., 257
Parsonson, K., 420
Pascual, L., 182
Paterson, K., 33
Patzer, G. L., 410, 411, 415
Paunonen, S. V., 394, 397, 398
Pelto, P. J., 22, 23, 25, 41
Peng, K., 123
Pennebaker, J. W., 280
Perez, M., 195
Perks, W. R., 102
Perlman, I., 339
Perry, M., 190
Peterson, C., 257
Peterson, M. F., 466, 474, 484

Petty, R. E., 471
Pfeiffer, W. M., 260, 261
Pharr, A. E., 248
Phillips, M. R., 268
Phinney, J. S., 31, 32
Phinney, S. J., 193
Piaget, J., 61, 193–197
Pidoux, C., 168
Pierre, E., 168
Pillay, A. L., 221
Pine, C. J., 174
Pinkerton, D. S., 34
Pitariu, H., 391
Pittam, J., 279
Pollack, R. H., 145
Ponchillia, S. V., 247
Poole, E. M., 204
Poole, G., 244
Poortinga, Y. H., 18, 23, 25, 48, 117, 122, 124, 128, 129, 221, 354
Porter, J. R., 216
Poston, W. C., 267
Pratt, G., 468
Preston, K., 46
Price-Williams, D., 331
Prince, R., 211, 268
Puloka, M. H., 259
Punetha, D., 438

Quek, J., 221

Radford, M. H. B., 258, 389, 478
Ramirez, M., III, 331
Randall, L. J., 31
Ravlin, E. C., 467
Redmond, M. V., 377, 378
Reedy, R., 266, 268
Regmi, M., 68, 221
Reich, L. C., 148
Reid, P. T., 221
Remland, M. S., 221, 351
Retschitzki, J., 195
Rettek, S. I., 59
Reyes, J. A. S., 400
Ribera, J. M., 244
Richards, P., 178
Riesman, P., 309
Rime, B., 280
Rivers, W. H. R., 143
Robbins, S. R., 448
Roberts, A. R., 412
Robins, L. N., 256
Rodenhauser, P., 268
Roemer, M. I., 247
Rogoff, B., 181

Rohner, R. P., 23
Romero, G. J., 428, 429
Rosch, E., 147, 326
Rose, M. H., 30, 33
Roseman, I. J., 59, 302, 304
Rosenman, R. H., 234
Ross, B. M., 149
Ross, J., 410
Ross, L., 60, 365
Rossiter, J. C., 248
Rothblum, E. D., 239
Rowell, T. E., 348
Rozelle, R. M., 356
Ruch, W., 107
Runde, B., 181
Russell, G. L., 267
Russell, H. P., 82
Russell, J. A., 65, 272, 283, 284, 285, 288, 307, 308, 309
Ryan, R. A., 225
Ryckman, D. B., 425

Sachdev, P. S., 259
Sagi, A., 178
Salili, F., 423, 424, 426
Santiago-Rivera, A. L., 269
Santrock, J. W., 224
Sapir, E., 323–329
Sato, S., 419
Satterwhite, R. C., 215
Sawilowsky, S. S., 389
Scarr, S., 164
Schachter, S., 306, 414
Schaller, G., 348
Scherer, K., 27, 43, 282, 292, 293, 294, 295, 296, 302, 303, 304
Schieffelin, B. B., 316
Schimmack, U., 286
Schliemann, A. D., 188
Schmader, T., 102
Schmidt, E. A., 102
Schoots, N. H., 354
Schuster, B., 429
Schwanenflugel, P., 327
Schwartz, S., 23, 46, 215
Sciaky, R., 299
Scribner, S., 149, 150, 153
Seelye, H. N., 81
Sefa-Dedeh, A., 239
Segall, M. H., 18, 23, 48, 118, 140, 141, 144, 148, 221
Seginer, R., 204
Seiffge-Krenke, I., 204
Selice, S., 224
Sepkoski, C., 176

Shahim, S., 167
Shapiro, R. B., 370
Sharkey, W., 68
Sharma, R., 204
Sharon, I., 442
Sharp, D. W., 149
Shayer, M., 195
Shea, J. D., 197
Shepperd, J., 471
Shimizu, H., 416
Shimmin, H. S., 216
Shirakashi, S., 471
Shoham, R., 178
Shore, J. H., 263
Shulman, S., 204, 416
Shuter, R., 351
Shweder, R. A., 58, 60, 200, 296, 365, 387
Sillen, S., 256
Silvar, S. D., 145
Simmons, C. H., 416
Simonds, P. E., 348
Singelis, T. M., 45, 68, 69
Singer, J. L., 255
Singer, S. S., 306
Singh, U., 20
Sinha, J., 473
Skinner, B. F., 315, 364
Slee, R., 33
Smith, J. R., 84
Smith, P. B., 389, 393, 439, 461, 466, 474, 475, 477, 484
Snarey, J. R., 200
Sniderman, M. P., 82
Snowden, L. R., 267
Snyder, C. R., 88
Sodetani, L. L., 370
Soliman, A., 257
Song, M. J., 186
Sonoda, K. T., 370
Sorenson, E. R., 274, 282
Sow, I., 399
Sowell, T., 99
Spangler, S., 178
Spearman, C. E., 161
Spencer, H., 197
Spencer, S., 102
Spicker, S. B., 181
Spitzberg, B. H., 375
Steele, S., 99
Steger, J. M., 84
Steinberg, S., 99
Stephan, C. W., 279
Stephan, W. G., 279

Sternberg, R. J., 155, 169, 415
Stetsenko, A., 190
Stevenson, W. H., 186, 187
Stewart, R. B., 406
Stewart, V., 145
Stigler, J. W., 185, 186, 187, 188, 190, 320
Stone, J., 411
Stradling, S., 466
Strodtbeck, F., 41, 407
Stropes-Roe, M., 438
Stryker, S., 54
Suchman, R. G., 148
Suci, G., 180
Sue, D., 256
Sue, S., 224, 255, 256, 265, 266, 267
Suess, G., 178
Sugimori, S., 391
Summerfield, A., 292, 293
Super, C. M., 192
Susser, E., 259
Suzuki, T., 317, 319
Swann, W. B., Jr., 390, 393
Swartz, L., 259
Syme, S. L., 234, 236
Szirmak, Z., 394

Tafarodi, R. W., 58, 390, 393
Tajfel, H., 42, 404
Takahashi, K., 204, 242, 494
Takaki, R., 72
Takano, Y., 69, 328, 334
Takeuchi, S., 69, 447, 463
Tak-Sing, C., 58
Talamantes, M. A., 248
Tanner, M., 244
Taylor, D. A., 415
Taylor, D. M., 428, 431
Taylor, D. R., 99
Taylor, M. D., 82, 102
Terrell, M. D., 229
Tetlock, E. P., 82
Teveraishe, C., 406
Tharp, R. G., 269
Thomas, A., 175, 256
Thomas, D. C., 476
Thompson, N., 466
Thompson, T., 248
Thornton, B., 423
Thurstone, L. L., 161
Ting, K., 244
Ting-Toomey, S., 43, 380, 381, 415
Tolman, A., 266, 268
Tom, D., 427

Tomkins, S. S., 88, 273
Torrey, E. F., 268
Toyne, B., 476
Trankina, F. J., 183
Triandis, H. C., 23, 24, 25, 39, 42, 44, 45, 46, 59, 69, 83, 118, 234, 235, 236, 237, 273, 406, 407, 408, 409, 426, 427, 458, 492, 499
Trimboli, A., 181
Trimboli, C., 181
Trommsdorff, G., 216
Trompenaars, F., 389, 393, 461, 462
Tronick, E. Z., 178
Trotter, K. H., 221
Trull, T. J., 394
Trzebinski, J., 395
Tseng, H., 180, 181
Tseng, W., 229, 266, 267, 268
Tulviste, P., 153
Turiel, E., 221
Tuss, P., 190
Tylor, E. B., 197

Unzner, L., 178
Uziel-Miller, N. D., 248

Van de Koppel, J. M. H., 354
Van der Flier, H., 219
Van der Veen, M., 221
Van de Vijver, F. J. R., 117, 136
Van Harten, P. N., 259
Van Hoeken, D., 259
Van Hooff, J., 348
Verkuyten, M., 96
Verma, J., 419
Villareal, M. J., 42, 492
Vinacke, W. E., 273
Vom Kolke, A., 416
Vontress, C. E., 399
Vornberg, A. J., 102
Vrij, A., 81, 354, 355

Wagner, D. A., 144, 149
Wagner, J. A., III, 472
Wainryb, C., 221
Walker, L. J., 200
Walker, M., 181
Walkey, H. F., 83, 86, 426
Wall, S., 177
Wallbott, H., 27, 43, 282, 292, 293, 294, 295, 296, 303
Wan, K. C., 423, 425
Wang, L., 282

Wang, S., 176
Wang, Y., 471
Wang, Z. M., 477
Warren, M. P., 239, 240
Wassenaar, D. R., 221
Waters, E., 177
Watkins, D., 68, 221
Watson, O. M., 349, 351
Weatherly, K. A., 478
Weinberg, R. A., 164
Weiner, B., 422, 429
Weissman, M., 46, 47
Weizmann, F., 30
Weldon, E., 471
White, G. M., 309
Whorf, B. L., 317, 323–329
Wierzbicka, A., 66, 288, 296
Williams, J. E., 86, 212–215, 216, 217
Williams, K. D., 470, 471
Williams, L. R. T., 221

Wilson, M. N., 174
Wing, D. M., 248
Winkel, F. W., 81, 354, 355
Wiseman, R. L., 376, 380
Wittgenstein, L., 122
Witztum, E., 259
Wober, M., 168
Wohl, J., 265, 269
Wolf, R. M., 164
Wolfe, C., 102
Wolpoff, M., 30
Wong, P. T. P., 426, 427
Wong, Y. C., 123
Wood, P. C., 389
Wright, R., 471
Wu, C., 412
Wyatt, E. G., 30
Wylie, R. C., 63

Yamaguchi, S., 69, 391, 435, 471
Yamamoto, J., 183

Yamamoto, K., 257
Yan, H., 268
Yan, W., 190, 425
Yang, K. S., 62
Yang, S. M., 271, 391
Yao, L. E., 189
Yap, P. M., 259, 260
Yee, H. A., 30
Yoon, Y-C., 321
Young, L., 438
Yu, E. S. H., 62

Zaccaro, S. J., 471
Zahn-Waxler, C., 139, 204, 435
Zajonc, R., 411
Zane, N., 266, 267
Zhang, M., 268
Zimmer, J., 190
Zimmerman, S., 377, 380
Zuckerman, M., 30, 31, 119, 120

Subject Index

Abnormal behavior, 251–270. *See also* Psychological disorders
  assessment of, 261–264, 398–399
  cross-cultural research on, 254–261
  culture-bound syndromes and, 258–260
  culture-specific interventions for, 267–268
  defining, 252–254
  indigenous healing systems and, 264
  treatment of, 264–269
Aborigines, Australian, 141
Academic achievement. *See also* Education
  attributions about, 423–427
  biological factors related to, 186–187
  cross-national differences in, 185–186
  environmental factors related to, 187
  language differences and, 187
  parental/familial values and, 189–190
  school systems and, 187–188
  student attitudes and, 190
  teaching styles and, 190–191

Accommodation, 195, 205
Acculturation, 175, 205
Achievement motivation, 61–62, 73
Adaptors/manipulators, 339, 357
Adjective Check List (ACL), 213, 214
Affirmative action policies, 94
Affluence, 27
African Americans
  gender differences among, 224
  intelligence tests and, 162, 166
  nonverbal behaviors among, 349
African cultures
  attachment studies in, 178–179
  concept of intelligence in, 168
  indigenous personality model for, 399
  pain perception in, 160
  problem-solving process and, 152–153
  social support in, 406
  visual perception and, 145, 146
Aggression, 433, 442
  cross-cultural research on, 433–436
  gender differences and, 220–221
  visual behaviors and, 348–349
Agreeableness, 394
Alcoholism, 248

Allocentric tendencies, 45, 50, 391–392, 492
Ambivalent attachment, 177, 206
America. *See* United States
American Indian Depression Schedule (AIDS), 263
American Psychiatric Association (APA), 261
Amok (culture-bound syndrome), 258–259, 260
Analysis of covariance (ANACOVA), 492
Analysis of variance (ANOVA), 114, 126–127
Analyzing data, 113–114
Androgyny, 224
Anger, 275, 293, 299, 303
  expressing in intimate relationships, 417–418
Anglo-Saxon type of organization, 449, 486
Animals
  personality characteristics in, 396–397
  visual behavior among, 348
Animism, 194, 206
Anorexia nervosa, 259
Anthropological medicine, 138–139
Anti-Semitism, 82

Applied psychologists, 2
Appraisal, 87, 103
  of emotions, 301–305
Arabic cultures, 249, 351, 356
Arranged marriages, 419
Asian Americans
  cardiovascular disease among,
    234
  cultural reaffirmation effect in,
    72–73
  gender role differences among,
    224
  mental health services and, 265–
    266
  parenting styles of, 180
  student attitudes among, 190
Asian cultures
  achievement motivation in, 62
  attractiveness studies in, 411–
    412
  Confucian dynamism in, 460
  false uniqueness effect in, 63–64
  health-related attitudes among,
    244
  individualism–collectivism
    studies of, 44
  nonverbal behaviors in, 349
  positive emotions in, 66, 67
  self-construals among, 58
Assimilation, 195, 206
Assumptions, 4, 16
  of similarities, 373
Attachment, 177–179, 206
  cross-cultural studies on, 178–
    179
  types of, 177
Attention structure, 348, 357
Attractiveness
  cross-cultural studies on, 411–
    413
  interpersonal attraction and, 415
  personality judgments based on,
    410
Attributional confidence, 373
Attributions, 88, 103, 421–433
  causality of emotions and, 303–
    304
  cross-cultural research on, 423–
    433
  defensive, 423
  defined, 421, 442
  emotional expression and, 286,
    287
  stereotypes and, 88, 90
  traditional American patterns of,
    422–423

Australian Aborigines, 141
Authoritarian parents, 179, 206
Authoritarian personality, 96
Authoritative parents, 179, 206
Autonomy vs. shame and doubt
    stage, 202
Auto-stereotypes, 83–84
Avanga (culture-bound syndrome),
    259
Avoidant attachment, 177, 206

Back translation, 124–125, 136
Banding process, 170
Basic trust vs. mistrust stage, 201–
    202
Behavior
  abnormal, 251–270
  aggressive, 433–436
  biological bases of, 137–140
  cultural influences on, 502
  eating and dieting, 239–240
  ethnocentrism and, 77–79, 97
  interpretations of, 98
  nonverbal, 337–358
  social, 403–443
  suicidal, 240–242
Bell Curve, The (Herrnstein and
    Murray), 165–167
Bem Sex Role Inventory, 224
Bias
  confirmation, 154
  mood-congruent, 88
  researcher, 128–129
  self-serving, 422
Bicultural individuals, 72
Bilingualism, 330–335
  linguistic relativity and, 330–
    331, 332–333
  misperceptions about, 333–335
  United States and, 331–332
Biographic research, 108
Biological factors
  behavior influenced by, 137–140
  IQ scores and, 162–163, 187
  math achievement and, 186–187
  personality and, 393–394
Blind spot, 140, 172
Body conceptions, 231–232
Bottom-up approach, 11
Businesses. *See* Organizations

California Psychological Inventory
    (CPI), 333
Capitulation, 420
Cardiovascular disease, 234–235

Carpentered world theory, 142–
    143, 144, 172
Case studies, 108
Categorization, 87, 103, 172
  cultural influences on, 147–149
  of emotions, 308–309
  stereotypes and, 87–88, 148
Cattell Culture Fair Intelligence
    Test, 164, 165
Causal interpretations, 127–128
Centralization, 448, 486
Centration, 194, 206
Channels, 362, 383
Child rearing, 179–184. *See also*
    Parenting
  cross-cultural research on, 180–
    182
  economic factors in, 182–183
  extended families and, 183–184
  intercultural marriages and, 420
  traditional knowledge about, 179
Children
  attachment and, 177–179
  temperament of, 175–177
China. *See also* Asian cultures
  achievement motivation in, 62
  concept of intelligence in, 168
  personality construct of, 400
  teaching styles in, 190–191
Chinese Culture Connection, 460
Chinese Personality Assessment
    Inventory (CPAI), 400
Chi-square, 126
Civil Rights Act (1991), 170
Classification process. *See*
    Categorization
Classism, 93
Climate, 27
Clinical psychologists, 268–269
Coexistence, 420
Cognition, 147–157, 172
  categorization and, 147–149
  creativity and, 155–156
  decision making and, 154–155
  decoding process and, 365
  face recognition and, 151–152
  gender and, 218–219
  memory and, 149–151
  problem solving and, 152–154
Cognitive development, 193–198,
    206
  Piaget's stage theory of, 193–197
Cognitive schemas, 411, 442
Cognitive template, 60, 73
Collaborative learning, 192

Collectivistic cultures, 41. *See also* Individualistic cultures
creativity and, 156
emotions and, 281, 286
empirical studies on, 43–44
health issues related to, 234–238
ingroup/outgroup relationships and, 406–408, 409
interdependent construal of self in, 57–58
meaning of work in, 469–470
methods used for measuring, 44–47
theoretical studies on, 42–43
Colors
categorization of, 147–148
perception of, 324–326
Commitment, 415
Communication. *See also* Language; Nonverbal behaviors
channels, signals, and messages, 361–362
components of, 360–362
defining, 360
encoding and decoding processes in, 361
intercultural, 345–346, 360, 368–382
intracultural, 360, 366–368
role of culture in process of, 362–365
verbal and nonverbal behaviors in, 340–343, 360–361
Communication technology, 27
Companionate love, 415, 442
Complexity, 448, 486
Compliance, 436–437, 442
cross-cultural research on, 438–439
domestic research on, 437–438
Componential intelligence, 169
Comprehensive health systems, 247
Compromise, 420
Concept
defined, 87, 103
of emotion, 307–311
Concept formation, 87
cultural diversity and, 147–149
stereotypes and, 87–88
Conceptual definitions of variables, 112, 122–124
Concrete operations stage, 194
Confirmation bias, 154
Conflict
intercultural, 371, 380–382, 419–420, 500–501

in intimate relationships, 417–418, 419–420
managing, 380–381
Conformity, 436, 442
cross-cultural research on, 438–439
domestic research on, 437–438
gender differences and, 219–220
Confucian dynamism, 460, 486
Conscientiousness, 394
Consciousness, 157–160
dreams and, 157–158
pain perception and, 160
time orientation and, 158–159
Consensus, 422, 442
Conservation, 194, 206
Consistency, 422, 442
Construals of self. *See* Self-construals
Constructive marginality, 379
Consumers of knowledge, 107–108
Consummate love, 415, 442
Contact cultures, 349
Contact hypothesis, 413
Contempt, 275, 283
Context, 371–373, 421
Contextual intelligence, 169
Contextualization, 41, 50
Context variables, 118
Conventional morality, 199, 206
Cooperation, 437, 442
culture and, 440–441
Coping, 87
with cultural discrepancies, 238–239
Corporations. *See also* Organizations
multinational and international, 446, 486
Correlation, 114
Correlational interpretations, 127–128
Counting systems, 187, 320
Countries, cultures vs., 119
Creative adjustment, 420–421
Creativity
cultural influences on, 155–156
intelligence and, 169
Critical thinking, 499–502
Cross-cultural approach, 9–10, 16
Cross-cultural communication. *See* Intercultural communication
Cross-cultural comparisons, 38–39, 50
Cross-cultural psychology, 2, 11–14
career advice related to, 504–505

contemporary challenge for, 491–493
evolution of, 13
Cross-cultural research, 8–11, 16, 105–106, 115–136. *See also* Research
approaches to, 11
conceptual definitions of variables in, 122–124
cultural response sets and, 126
definitions of culture and, 119–120
design issues in, 117–119
environment, settings, and procedures in, 125–126
equivalence issues in, 115, 121–122
evaluation guidelines, 130–134
hypothesis-testing in, 116–118
intercultural research vs., 365–366
interpreting findings from, 127–130
language and translation issues in, 124–125
limitations in, 15–16
measuring culture in, 38–47
methodology issues in, 117–127
operationalization of variables in, 123–124
sampling adequacy in, 120–121
statistical analysis of, 126–127
Cross-cultural studies
on abnormal behavior, 254–261
on aggression, 433–436
on attachment, 178–179
on attractiveness, 411–413
on attributions, 423–433
on conformity and compliance, 438–439
on emotions, 278–282, 283–287, 292–296, 298–300, 301–305, 307–310
on gender, 212–225
on health, 235–238
on ingroup/outgroup relationships, 408–409
on intelligence, 161–167
on interpersonal attraction, 415–418
on language, 317–323, 332–333
on leadership and management, 474–476
on math achievement, 185–186
on moral reasoning, 200–201

Cross-cultural studies *(continued)*
  on nonverbal behaviors, 346–356
  on organizational culture, 460–462
  on parenting styles, 180–182
  on personality, 388–394, 397–398
  on person perception, 411–414
  on Piaget's stage theory, 195–196
  on temperament, 176–177
Cross-cultural validation study, 118–119
Cultural display rules, 160, 276–278, 312
  cross-cultural research on, 278–282, 347
Cultural diversity. *See also* Cross-cultural studies
  abnormal behavior and, 251–270
  aggressive behavior and, 433–436
  attributional styles and, 423–433
  biological characteristics and, 137–140
  categorization and, 147–149
  child-rearing practices and, 179–184
  clinical training in, 268–269
  creativity and, 155–156
  decision making and, 154–155
  developmental processes and, 193–204
  dreams and, 157–158
  educational systems and, 185–192
  emotions and, 285–290, 294–298, 299–300, 301–305, 307–310
  face recognition and, 151–152
  gender and, 212–225
  health and, 229–250
  intelligence and, 161–171
  language and, 317–323
  leadership styles and, 473–474
  legitimacy of, 501
  memory and, 149–151
  pain perception and, 160
  problem solving and, 152–154
  suicidal behavior and, 240–242
  time orientation/perspective and, 158–159
  visual perception and, 141–147
  work-related values and, 449–458

Cultural identity, 71
Cultural-level analyses, 118
Cultural psychology, 13, 16, 494
Cultural reaffirmation effect, 72–73
Cultural relativism, 252, 270
Cultural response sets, 126, 136
Culture, 24–26, 50
  as abstract concept, 20–21
  aspects of life affected by, 19
  attributions and, 421–433
  biological bases of behavior and, 137–140
  cognition and, 147–157
  common usages of word, 18–19
  communication process and, 362–365
  consciousness and, 157–160
  cyclical and dynamic nature of, 21–22
  definitions of, 23–26, 119–120
  developmental processes and, 193–204
  disability and, 33
  education and, 185–192
  emotion and, 271–312
  enculturation process and, 173–193
  ethnicity and, 31–32
  ethnocentrism and, 38
  factors influencing, 26–27
  gender and, 32–33, 209–227
  health and, 229–250
  importance of defining, 17–18
  individual differences and, 28, 500
  individualism–collectivism dimension of, 41, 42–47
  intelligence and, 161–171
  language and, 313–336
  laypersons' conceptions of, 20
  measuring in research, 38–47
  nationality and, 32
  nonverbal behavior and, 337–358
  objective elements of, 39
  organizations and, 445–487
  perception and, 140–147
  personality and, 28–29, 385–402
  popular culture and, 34–35
  as psychological construct, 499–500
  psychology and influence of, 47–49
  race and, 30–31, 119–120, 499
  self-concept and, 53–73

  sexual orientation and, 33–34
  social behavior and, 403–443
  stereotypes and, 38
  subjective elements of, 39–41
Culture-affiliation hypothesis, 332, 336
Culture-bound syndromes, 258–260, 270
Culture-free intelligence tests, 164, 165
Culture-specific interventions, 267–268
Culture-specific principles, 10, 16
  pancultural principles vs., 35–37
Cycle of reciprocity, 21, 22

Data
  analyzing, 113–114, 126–127
  evaluating, 133
  nonequivalent, 129–130
Decentering, 125, 136
Decision making
  cultural influences on, 154–155
  organizational, 476–478
Decoding process, 361, 363–365, 383
Decoding rules, 290, 291, 312, 363–365
Defensive attributions, 423, 442
Democratic decision-making process, 476
Depression, 256–257, 263
Depth perception, 146
Descriptive definitions, 18
Descriptive statistics, 114
Developmental niche, 192–193
Developmental processes, 193–204
  cognitive development, 193–198
  moral reasoning, 199–201
  socioemotional development, 201–204
Diagnostic and Statistical Manual of Mental Disorders (DSM-IV), 261–262
Diagnostic Interview Schedule (DIS), 263
Difficult temperament, 175, 206
Dimensions, 40–41
Disability, culture and, 33
Discrepant messages, 342
Discriminant analysis, 114
Discrimination, 93–95, 103
  institutional, 94–95, 97
  reducing, 100–101

relationship between prejudice and, 93

Disease. *See also* Health
attitudes and beliefs related to, 242–245
body conceptions and, 231–232
cross-cultural research on, 235–238
cultural differences in defining, 230–231
culturally sensitive treatment approaches for, 247–249
health care systems for, 246–247
individualism and, 234–235
psychosocial determinants of, 232–233
social isolation and, 233–234

Disgust, 275, 303

Display rules. *See* Cultural display rules

Distinctiveness, 422, 442

Domains, 40–41

Dreams, cultural influences on, 157–158

Drug abuse, 248

Dynamic nature of culture, 24

Easy temperament, 175, 206

Eating disorders, 239–240

Ecological-level analyses, 44, 118

Economic factors
child-rearing practices and, 182–183
emotional experience and, 296
health and, 233, 236–237

Education. *See also* Academic achievement
categorization and, 148–149
enculturation and, 185–192
math achievement and, 185–187
memory and, 150
parental/familial values and, 189–190
school systems and, 187–188
student attitudes and, 190
teaching styles and, 190–191

Effect size estimates, 127

Egocentrism, 194, 206

Emblems, 339, 353–354, 357

Emics, 35–37, 50, 258

Emotion antecedents, 298–301, 312
cultural differences in, 299–300
cultural similarities in, 298–299
latent vs. manifest content and, 300–301

Emotion appraisal, 301–305, 312
cultural differences in, 303–305
cultural similarities in, 301–303

Emotions, 271–312
American view of, 305–307
antecedents of, 298–301
appraisal of, 301–305
concept and language of, 307–311
controlling or regulating, 101, 381–382, 497–498
cross-cultural research on, 278–282, 283–287, 292–296, 298–300, 301–305, 307–310
cultural display rules and, 276–278, 347
cultural shaping of, 296, 297
experience of, 290–298
expressed, 255–256
facial expressions of, 272–276, 347
functionalist approach to, 296–298
importance of, 271–272
indigenous, 65–66
intensity of, 283–284
labeling of, 308–309
location of, 309–310
meaning of, 310
nonverbal behaviors and, 339
perception of, 282–290, 291
physiological symptoms and, 294, 295
recognition of, 282–283, 285–286
social connotation of, 64–66, 67
stereotypes and, 88–89, 279–280
universality of, 272–276, 287–290, 292–294

Empathy, 379

Encoding process, 361, 383

Enculturation, 30, 50, 173–193, 206
attachment and, 177–179
educational system and, 185–192
Erikson's socioemotional development theory and, 203–204
ethnocentrism as consequence of, 77–79
parenting and, 179–184
socialization and, 173–175
temperament and, 175–177

Ensembled individualism, 70

Entrepreneurial health systems, 247

Environment
IQ scores and, 163–164
math achievement and, 187
for research, 113, 125–126

Equivalence, 115, 136
cross-cultural research and, 121–122, 129–130
dealing with non-equivalent data, 129–130

Erikson's theory of socioemotional development, 201–204
enculturation processes and, 203–204

Ethnic identity, 193

Ethnicity. *See also* Race
culture and, 31–32
gender differences and, 223–225

Ethnic role salience, 82

Ethnocentrism, 76–83
decoding rules and, 363–364
definitions of, 38, 50, 76–77, 103
enculturation and, 77–79
flexible vs. inflexible, 80–81
intercultural sensitivity and, 378–379
psychological factors contributing to, 81–83
recognizing in oneself, 79–81, 97, 500
stereotype formation and, 90–91

Ethnographic studies, 38, 50, 119, 136, 307

Ethnopsychologies, 494

Etics, 35–37, 50, 258

Experiential intelligence, 169

Expressed emotion, 255–256

Expression of Emotion in Man and Animals, The (Darwin), 273

Extended families, 183–184

External locus of control, 388–389

Extroversion, 394

Eyewitness testimony, 151

Eysenck Personality Questionnaire (EPQ), 390–391

Face recognition
cultural influences on, 151–152
person perception and, 413

Facial Action Coding System (FACS), 279

Facial expressions. *See also* Nonverbal behaviors
attributions based on, 286, 287

Facial expressions *(continued)*
  categorization of, 147
  cross-cultural research on, 278–282, 347–348
  cultural display rules and, 276–278, 347
  illustrated, 275
  intensity of, 283–284
  perception of, 283–290, 291
  recognition of, 282–283, 285–286
  universality of, 272–276, 287–290
Factor analysis, 124
False uniqueness effect, 63–64, 73
Families
  child-rearing practices in, 179–185
  educational influence of, 189–190
  extended, 183–184
  nonverbal behaviors in, 343
Fear, 275, 293, 303, 306
Feelings. *See* Emotions
Filial piety, 62, 73
Five Factor Model (FFM) of personality, 394–397
Flexible ethnocentrism, 80–81, 103
Focal points, 325
Foreign language effect, 334
Foreign language processing difficulties, 334
Formalization, 448, 486
Formal operations stage, 194–195
Front-horizontal foreshortening theory, 143, 144, 172
Functionalist approach to emotion, 296, 298
Fundamental attribution error, 60, 73, 365, 422, 442

g (general intelligence) factor, 161
Gaze behaviors, 348–350
Gender, 33, 211–212, 226
  cross-cultural research on, 212–225
  cultural influences on, 222–223
  ethnicity and, 223–225
  mainstream psychology and, 210–211
  mate selection and, 417
  parenting styles and, 181
  psychological differences and, 218–222
  self-concept and, 216–217

Gender identity, 212, 226
Gender role ideologies, 216, 226
Gender roles, 33, 212, 226
  ethnicity and, 224–225
  ideologies associated with, 216, 226
Gender stereotypes, 212, 226
  on aggressiveness, 220–221
  on conformity and obedience, 219–220
  cross-cultural research on, 212–216
General Collectivism Index (GCI), 44
Generalizable statements, 91
Generalizations, 4, 16
  stereotypes as, 98–100
Generations
  cultural rules communicated through, 26
  stereotypes perpetuated through, 91
Generativity vs. stagnation stage, 202–203
Genetic definitions, 18
Genetics. *See also* Biological factors
  IQ scores and, 162–163
  personality and, 393–394
Gesticulation, 352
Gestures, 339, 352–354, 358
Goodness of fit, 176, 206
Grammar, 314, 336
Great divide theories, 198, 206
Greek culture, 44
Greeting behaviors, 344
Gross domestic product (GDP), 236
Groups
  definition of culture applied to, 24–25
  ensuring the survival of, 25
Groupthink, 478
Guilt, 303

Happiness, 66, 275, 293, 299, 303
Hardiness, 230, 250
Health, 229–250. *See also* Mental health
  attitudes and beliefs related to, 242–245
  body conceptions and, 231–232
  cross-cultural research on, 235–238
  cultural differences in defining, 230–231

cultural discrepancies and, 238–239
culturally sensitive treatment approaches and, 247–249
eating disorders and, 239–240
economic factors and, 233, 236–237
health care delivery systems and, 246–247
indigenous healing systems and, 264
individualism and, 234–235
model of cultural influences on, 245–246
psychosocial determinants of, 232–233
social isolation and, 233–234
Health care delivery systems, 246–247
Health psychology, 232
Heart disease, 234–235
Hetero-stereotypes, 83–84
High-context (HC) communications, 372
Historical definitions, 18
Horizontal collectivism, 45
Horizontal individualism, 45
Horizontal-vertical illusion, 142, 143, 144
Hypotheses, 4–5, 16
  evaluating, 130
Hypothesis-testing research, 108–115
  analyzing data from, 113–114
  cross-cultural, 116–118
  developing questions for, 110
  interpreting findings from, 114–115
  methodology for, 110–113

Identifiable characteristics, 91
Identity
  ethnic, 193
  gender, 212
  sexual, 211
Identity vs. role confusion stage, 202
Idiocentric tendencies, 45, 51, 492
Illness. *See* Disease
Illustrators, 339, 358
Imitation, 192, 315
Immigrants
  acculturation of, 175
  cultural reaffirmation effect in, 72–73
  intelligence testing of, 162

INDCOL scale, 44–45
Independent construal of self, 56, 57, 73
    achievement motivation and, 61–62
    evaluating the research on, 66–70
    happiness and, 66
    indigenous emotions and, 65–66
    self-enhancement and, 63–64
    self-perception and, 58–60
    social connotation of emotions and, 64–66
    social explanation and, 60–61
Indigenous emotions, 65–66, 73
Indigenous healing systems, 264, 270
Indigenous personalities, 387, 399–401, 402
Individualism
    cardiovascular disease and, 234–235
    culture and, 28, 500
Individualism–collectivism (IC), 41, 42–47, 51
    cooperation and, 440–441
    emotions and, 281, 286
    empirical work on, 43–44
    health issues related to, 234–238
    ingroup/outgroup relationships and, 406–408, 409
    leadership/management styles and, 474
    measuring, 44–47
    self-concept and, 53–73
    theoretical work on, 42–43
    work-related values and, 455–456, 466
Individualism-Collectivism Interpersonal Assessment Inventory (ICIAI), 46–47
Individualistic cultures, 41. See also Collectivistic cultures
    creativity and, 156
    emotions and, 281, 286
    empirical studies on, 43–44
    health issues related to, 234–238
    independent construal of self in, 56, 57
    ingroup/outgroup relationships and, 406–408, 409
    meaning of work in, 470
    methods used for measuring, 44–47
    theoretical studies on, 42–43

Industry vs. inferiority stage, 202
Inferential statistics, 114, 126–127
Inflexible ethnocentrism, 80–81, 103
Ingroup relationships, 42, 403–410. See also Outgroup relationships
    cross-cultural research on, 408–409
    cultural differences in, 405–408
    defined, 404, 443
    emotional expression and, 280–281
    individualism–collectivism and, 406–408, 409
Initiative vs. guilt stage, 202
Institutional discrimination, 93–95, 97, 103
Instructional learning, 192
Integrity vs. despair stage, 203
Intelligence, 161–171
    cross-cultural research on, 161–167
    cultural differences in concepts of, 167–168
    recent developments in theories about, 168–169
    traditional definitions of, 161
    types of, 169
Intelligence tests, 161–167
    biological factors and, 162–163
    environmental factors and, 163–164
    equivalence and, 123
    ethnic minorities and, 162
    political controversy surrounding, 164
    selection issues and, 169–171
Intercultural communication, 345–346, 360, 368–382, 383
    competence in, 374–378
    conflict and, 371, 380–382
    context and, 371–373
    emotion regulation and, 381–382
    micromomentary analysis of, 369
    sensitivity in, 378–380
    stumbling blocks to, 373–374
    uncertainty and, 368, 370–371
Intercultural communication competence (ICC), 374–378, 383
    models of, 375–376
    research on, 376–378
Intercultural marriages, 418–421

Intercultural research, 366
Intercultural sensitivity (IS), 378–380, 383
Intercultural success, 502–503
Interdependent construal of self, 57–58, 73
    achievement motivation and, 61–62
    evaluating the research on, 66–70
    happiness and, 66
    indigenous emotions and, 65–66
    self-enhancement and, 63–64
    self-perception and, 58–60
    social connotation of emotions and, 64–66
    social explanation and, 60–61
Internal locus of control, 388–389
International Association for the Evaluation of Education Achievement (IEA), 186
International Association of Cross-Cultural Psychology, 11–12
International Classification of Diseases, Tenth Edition (ICD-10), 262
International corporations, 446
International negotiations, 479–482
International Pilot Study of Schizophrenia (IPSS), 254–255
Interorganizational-level culture, 447
Interpersonal attraction, 414–421
    cross-cultural studies on, 415–418
    domestic research on, 414–415
    intercultural marriages and, 418–421
    intimate relationships and, 414–415
Interpersonal communication, 260
Interpersonal space, 350–352
Interpretation
    of behavior, 98
    of research findings, 114–115, 127–130, 133–134
Intimacy vs. self-absorption stage, 202
Intimate relationships, 350, 415
    cross-cultural studies on, 415–418
    intercultural marriages and, 418–421

Intimate relationships *(continued)*
interpersonal attraction and, 414–415
Intracultural communication, 360, 366–368, 383
micromomentary analysis of, 367
Intraorganizational-level culture, 447
Introspection, 309, 312
IQ (intelligence quotient), 162–167. *See also* Intelligence tests
biological factors and, 162–163, 187
environmental factors and, 163–164
selection issues and, 169–170
Irreversibility, 194, 206

Japan. *See also* Asian cultures
achievement motivation in, 62
attitudes toward health and disease in, 243–244
construals of self in, 58
cultural display rules in, 277
decision-making process in, 477
false uniqueness effect in, 63–64
indigenous emotions of, 65
individualism–collectivism studies in, 44
infant attachment patterns in, 179
language of, 318–320, 321, 327
parenting styles in, 180
personality construct of, 399
positive emotions in, 66, 67
suicide in, 240–241
teaching styles in, 190–191
Journal of Cross-Cultural Psychology, 12
Joy, 293

Kinship sentiments, 95
Knowledge
accuracy and applicability of, 13–14
consumers of, 107–108
generating in psychology, 3–4, 5
relationship between methods and, 6–8
Kohlberg's theory of morality, 199–200
Koro (culture-bound syndrome), 259, 260

Labeling of emotions, 308–309
Language, 313–336. *See also* Communication; Nonverbal behaviors
acquisition of, 315–317
bilingualism and, 330–335
counting systems and, 187, 320
cross-cultural research and, 124–125, 317–323
emotions and, 307–311
features of, 314–315
intercultural communication and, 373–374
lexicons of, 314, 317–320
linguistic relativity and, 323–329
perception and, 324–326
pragmatics of, 315, 320–321
psychological testing and, 264
Sapir–Whorf hypothesis and, 323–329
Language acquisition device (LAD), 316–317, 336
Latah (culture-bound syndrome), 259, 260
Latent content, 300–301
Latin type of organization, 449
Leadership, 473–476
cross-cultural research on, 474–476
cultural differences in, 473–474
definition of, 473, 486
Learning. *See also* Education
of language, 315–317
Lexicon, 314, 317–320, 336
Linguistic relativity, 323–329. *See also* Sapir–Whorf hypothesis
bilingualism and, 330–331, 332–333
research challenging, 325–326, 328
research supporting, 324–325, 326–327
Locus of control, 388–389, 402
Logical thinking, 153–154
Long-term memory, 89
Love
cross-cultural studies on, 415–418
intercultural marriages and, 418–421
types of, 415
Low-context (LC) communications, 372

Machismo, 225, 226
Management, 473–476
cross-cultural research on, 474–476
cultural differences in, 473–474
Manifest content, 300–301
Marriage. *See also* Intimate relationships
arranged, 419
intercultural, 418–421
Masculinity (MA), 41, 51
health issues related to, 236–238
work-related values and, 217–218, 449–458, 459
Matching hypothesis, 415, 443
Mate selection, 417
Math achievement. *See also* Academic achievement
biological factors related to, 186–187
cross-national differences in, 185–186
environmental factors related to, 187
language differences and, 187, 320
Media stereotypes, 91
Medical delivery systems, 246–247
Medical model, 230, 250
Memory, 89
culture and, 149–151
stereotypes and, 89
Mental health, 251–270. *See also* Psychological disorders
assessment of abnormal behavior, 261–264
culture-bound syndromes and, 258–260
defining abnormality, 252–254
indigenous healing systems and, 264
suicidal behavior and, 240–242
treatment methods and, 264–269
Mental processes. *See* Cognition
Messages, 361–362, 383
Meta-analysis, 439
Methodology, research
conceptual definitions of variables and, 122–124
cultural response sets and, 126
definitions of culture and, 119–120
design issues, 117–119

environment, setting, and procedures, 113, 125–126
equivalence issues, 121–122
evaluating, 133
language and translation issues, 124–125
operationalization, 112–113, 123–124
research paradigm and, 110–111
sampling procedure, 111–112, 120–121
statistical analysis, 126–127
Mexican Americans, 224–225
Micronesia, 65
Mindfulness, 381
Minnesota Multiphasic Personality Inventory (MMPI), 398–399
Minority group-affiliation hypothesis, 332–333, 336
Monocultural individuals, 72
Monolingualism, 331
Mood-congruent bias, 88
Moral reasoning, 199–201
cross-cultural studies on, 200–201
Kohlberg's theory of morality, 199–200
Morphemes, 315, 336
Mortality
social isolation and, 233–234
socioeconomic status and, 233
Motivation
achievement, 61–62
employee productivity and, 470–473
hierarchical model of, 396
visual perception and, 146
Mueller-Lyer illusion, 141–142, 143, 144, 145
Multicultural identities, 71–73
Multicultural psychology, 13
Multi-Level Organizational Culture Profile (MLOCP), 463–465
Multinational and international corporations, 446, 486. See also Organizations
Multiple regression, 114

Naikan therapy, 267–268
National health systems, 247
Nationality, culture vs., 32
Native Americans
culture-specific interventions for, 268

language studies among, 324
mental health services and, 265–266
Natural resources, 27
Negotiation process, 479–482
American assumptions related to, 479–481
Nemawashi procedure, 477, 486
Neuroticism, 394
Noncontact cultures, 349
Nonequivalent data, 129–130
Nonverbal behaviors, 337–358. See also Communication; Language
classification of, 338–340
communication process and, 340–343, 360–361
cross-cultural research on, 346–356
cultural influences on, 343–346, 362–363
definition of, 337, 358
facial expressions, 272–276, 347–348
gaze and visual behaviors, 348–350
gestures, 352–354
interpersonal space and, 350–352
misinterpretations of, 374
need for training in, 355–356
types of, 337
Normative definitions, 18
North American Free Trade Agreement (NAFTA), 446

Obedience, 437, 443
culture and, 439–440
domestic research on, 437–438
gender differences and, 219–220
Obesity, 239–240
Object classification, 324
Objective elements of culture, 39, 51
Observational studies, 113
Oligarchy, 476, 486
On the Origin of Species (Darwin), 273
Openness, 394
Operationalization, 39, 51, 112–113, 136
Optical illusions, 141–144, 172
Oral traditions, 149, 150
Organizational climate, 448, 486

Organizational culture, 447–448, 458–469
contemporary research on, 458–469
cross-cultural research on, 460–462
definition of, 447, 486
measuring, 462–466
practical implications of, 466–468
Organizations, 445–487
climate in, 448, 486
culture in, 447–448, 458–469
decision-making processes in, 476–478
discrimination patterns in, 94–95
intercultural issues for, 479–485
leadership and management styles in, 473–476
meaning of work in, 469–470
motivation and productivity in, 470–473
national character in, 449
negotiation processes in, 479–482
overseas assignments within, 482–483
structure of, 448–449
workforce diversity in, 483–485
work-related values in, 449–458, 459
Osteoporosis, 243
Other-referents, 318–320
Outgroup relationships, 42, 403–410. See also Ingroup relationships
cross-cultural research on, 408–409
cultural differences in, 405–408
defined, 404, 443
emotional expression and, 280–281
individualism–collectivism and, 406–408, 409
Overseas assignments, 482–483

Pain perception, 160
Pancultural principles, 35–37
Paradigms, research, 110–111, 136
Parenting, 179–184. See also Child rearing
cross-cultural research on, 180–182

Parenting *(continued)*
economic factors in, 182–183
educational success and, 189–190
extended families and, 183–184
intercultural marriages and, 420
styles of, 179
teenage, 184
Participants, research, 111–112
demographic equivalence of, 121–122
sampling adequacy and, 120–121
Passionate love, 415, 443
Pathogens, 230, 250
Perception, 140–147, 172. *See also* Person perception
cultural influences on, 141–147
of emotions, 282–290, 291
experience and, 140–141
gender differences and, 218–219
language and, 324–326
optical illusions and, 141–142
pain, 160
Perfectly controlled and comprehensive study (PCCS), 289–290
Permissive parents, 179, 206
Personality, 385–402
approaches to studying culture and, 386–388
cross-cultural research on, 388–394, 397–398
culture distinguished from, 28–29
defining, 386–388, 402
Five Factor Model of, 394–397
indigenous conceptions of, 387, 399–401
locus of control and, 388–389
measurement of, 390–391, 397–399
prejudice and, 96–97
psychopathology and, 398–399
self-esteem and, 389–390
Personal relationships, 350–351
Person perception, 410–414, 443
attractiveness and, 410, 411–413
cross-cultural studies on, 411–414
domestic research on, 410–411
physical appearance and, 410–411
Phonemes, 315, 336
Phonology, 314, 336
Physical health. *See* Health

Physiological symptoms
emotional experience and, 294, 295
somatization and, 257–258
Piaget's stage theory, 193–197
cross-cultural studies on, 195–196
Pluralism, 379
Ponzo illusion, 142, 143, 144–145
Popular culture, 34–35
Population density, 27
Postconventional morality, 199, 206
Postures, 354
Power distance (PD), 41, 51
creativity and, 156
health issues related to, 236–238
work-related values and, 450–452, 466, 484
Pragmatics, 315, 320–321, 336
Preconceptions, 374. *See also* Stereotypes
Preconventional morality, 199, 206
Prejudice, 92–93, 103
factors contributing to, 95–97
methods for reducing, 97–100
origins of, 95–97
relationship between discrimination and, 93
Preoperational stage, 194
Present State Examination (PSE), 263
Primacy effect, 149
Principles of Psychology (James), 206
Problem-solving process, 152–154
Procedures, research, 113, 125–126
Productivity, 470–473
Proxemics, 350–352
Psychological definitions, 18
Psychological disorders, 251–270
cross-cultural research on, 254–261
culture-bound syndromes, 258–260
culture-specific interventions for, 267–268
defining abnormality, 252–254
depression, 256–257
diagnosing, 261–262
indigenous healing systems and, 264
measurement instruments for, 262–264, 398–399
psychotherapeutic approaches and, 264–265

schizophrenia, 254–256
somatization, 257–258
treatment of, 264–269
Psychological factors
biology and, 137–139
ethnocentrism and, 81–83
gender and, 218–222
health and, 232–233
stereotypes and, 86–90
Psychologists, 2–3
clinical training of, 268–269
emotions as viewed by, 306–307
Psychology
career advice related to, 504–505
clinical training in, 268–269
contemporary challenge for, 493–495
creating knowledge in, 3–4, 5
cross-cultural research and, 8–11
cultural revolution in, 12–13, 490–495
influence of culture on, 47–49
intelligence defined in, 161
process of research in, 4–8
two goals of, 2–3, 495
types of research in, 108–109
Psychopathology, 398–399. *See also* Psychological disorders
Psychotherapy, 264–265
Public relationships, 351

Questions, research, 110

Race. *See also* Ethnicity
culture and, 30–31, 119–120, 499
stereotypes based on, 98–99
visual perception and, 145
Racism, 93, 96
Reciprocity cycle, 21, 22
Reciprocity hypothesis, 415, 443
Regression, 100, 382, 497
Regulators, 340, 358
Reliability, 106–107, 112–113, 136
Replication, 4, 16, 107, 136
Research, 106–115, 134–135. *See also* Cross-cultural research
analyzing data from, 113–114
consumers of, 107–108
evaluation guidelines for, 130–134
hypothesis-testing, 108–115
interpreting findings from, 114–115, 127–130
measuring culture in, 38–47

methodology used for, 110–113
parameters and conditions of, 109–115
process of, 4–8
questions for, 110
reliability of, 106–107
replication of, 107
types of, 108–109
validity of, 106
Researcher bias, 128–129
Research paradigms, 110–111, 136
Ringi system, 477, 486
Rochester Interaction Record (RIR), 409
Romantic love, 416
Running amok, 259

Sadness, 275, 293, 299, 303
Sample, research, 111, 136
Sampling procedure, 111–112, 136
cross-cultural research and, 120–121
Sapir–Whorf hypothesis, 160, 323–329, 336
bilingualism and, 330–331
color perception and, 324–326
explained, 323–324
object classification and, 324
research challenging, 325–326, 328
research supporting, 324–325, 326–327
Schedule for Affective Disorders and Schizophrenia (SADS), 263
Schizophrenia, 254–256, 263
Scholastic achievement. See Academic achievement
School systems, 187–188. See also Education
Science
creation of knowledge in, 3–4
process of research in, 4–8
Scientific philosophy, 9, 16
Secure attachment, 177, 206
Selective attention, 86–87, 103
Self-concept, 54, 73
cognitive, emotional, motivational processes and, 58–66
cultural influences on, 54–56
emotions and, 64–66, 310
gender differences in, 216–217
independent vs. interdependent, 56–58

Self-construals
achievement motivation and, 61–62
communication styles and, 321
evaluating research on, 66–70
happiness and, 66
independent, 56, 57
indigenous emotions and, 65–66
interdependent, 57–58
self-enhancement and, 63–64
self-perception and, 58–60
social connotation of emotions and, 64–66
social explanation and, 60–61
Self-contained individualism, 70
Self-disclosure, 415
Self-enhancement, 63–64
Self-esteem, 63, 389–390
Self-perception, 58–60
Self-referents, 318–320
Self-serving bias, 42, 443
Self-worth, 389
Semantic memory, 89, 103
Semantics, 314, 336
Sensorimotor stage, 194
Sensory memory, 89
Serial position effect, 149, 172
Setting, research, 113, 125–126
Sex, 32, 211, 227. See also Gender
Sexism, 93
Sex roles, 32–33, 211, 227. See also Gender roles; Gender stereotypes
Sexual identity, 211, 227
Sexual orientation, 33–34
Shame, 295–296, 303
Sharing, psychological, 25
Short-term memory, 89
Signals, 361, 383
Similarity hypothesis, 415, 443
"Sinking heart" condition, 259
Slow-to-warm-up temperament, 175–176, 206
Smiling faces, 287
Social behavior, 403–443
aggression and, 433–436
attributions and, 421–433
conformity, compliance, and obedience in, 436–441
ingroup/outgroup relationships and, 403–410
interpersonal attraction and, 414–421
person perception and, 410–414

Social class. See also Economic factors
health and, 232–233
IQ scores and, 164
Social consultive relationships, 351
Social factors
health and, 232–233
math achievement and, 187
prejudice and, 95–97
Social isolation, 233–234
Socialist health systems, 247
Socialization, 173–193, 206
attachment and, 177–179
educational system and, 185–192
enculturation and, 173–175
ethnocentrism as consequence of, 77–79
parenting and, 179–184
temperament and, 175–177
Socialization agents, 175, 206
Social loafing, 470–472, 487
Socially disengaged emotions, 64, 66, 67, 73
Socially engaged emotions, 64–65, 66, 67, 73
Social schemas, 411
Social striving, 471, 487
Socioeconomic status (SES), 121. See also Economic factors
emotional experience and, 296
health and, 233
Socioemotional development, 201–204
Erikson's theory of, 201–203
Sociotypes, 83
Somatization, 257–258, 270
Spatial reasoning, 218–219
Stagnation, intercultural, 502–503
Statistics, 113–114
analysis of, 126–127
types of, 114
Status differentiation (SD), 41, 51
Stereotypes, 83–92
appraisal and, 87
attribution and, 88, 90
categorization and, 87–88, 148
concept formation and, 87–88
content of, 84–86
decoding process and, 364–365
defined, 38, 51, 83, 103
development of, 86–90
emotions and, 88–89, 279–280
ethnocentrism and, 90–91
examining limitations in, 97–100
gender, 212

Stereotypes *(continued)*
  intercultural communication
    and, 374
  memory and, 89
  recognizing, 97
  selective attention and, 86–87
  types of, 83–84
Stoicism, 160
Structural definitions, 18
Student attitudes, 190
Subjective elements of culture, 39–
    41, 51
Subjective experience of emotion,
    312
Substance abuse, 248
Substantive processing, 88
Suicidal behavior, 240–242
Survey research, 108
Survival, ensuring, 25
Susto (culture-bound syndrome),
    259, 260
Syllogisms, 153
Symbolizing three dimensions in
    two theory, 144, 172
Syndromes, culture-bound, 258–
    260, 270
Syntax, 314, 336
System of rules, 24

Tasks, sorting, 148–149
Teaching styles, 190–191
Teamthink, 478
Technology, 27
Teenage parents, 184
Temperament, 175–177, 207
  cross-cultural studies on, 176–
    177
  traditional knowledge about,
    175–176
Thematic Apperception Test
    (TAT), 145, 332
Theories, 4, 16
  accuracy and applicability of,
    13–14
  evaluating, 130
  psychological research and, 5–6
Third World type of organization,
    449, 487
Thought processes. *See* Cognition
Tightness, 41, 51
Time orientation and perspective,
    158–159

Tolerance, 501–502
Top-down approach, 11
Translation issues, 124–125
Trappist monks, 235
Trust
  formation of, 177–178
  socioemotional development
    and, 201–202
Twin studies, 163
Type A personality, 232, 234

Uncertainty avoidance (UA), 41, 51
  creativity and, 156
  health issues related to, 236–238
  work-related values and, 453–
    455
Uncertainty reduction, 368, 370–
    371
Uninvolved parents, 179, 207
Uniqueness, 63–64
United States
  attitudes toward health and
    disease in, 243–244
  attribution patterns in, 422–423
  conformity, compliance,
    obedience studies in, 437–438
  construals of self in, 56
  cross-cultural research in, 15
  cultural diversity in, 14–15
  emotions as viewed in, 305–307
  false uniqueness effect in, 63–64
  individualism-collectivism
    studies in, 44
  interpersonal attraction studies
    in, 414–415
  language conventions used in,
    322–323
  negotiation-process assumptions
    in, 479–481
  nonverbal behaviors in, 343–
    344, 349, 350–351
  person perception studies in,
    410–411
  positive emotions in, 66, 67
  teaching styles in, 191
  treatment of abnormal behavior
    in, 265–267
Universality studies, 273, 312
Universal principles, 10, 16

Validity, 106, 112–113, 136
Value judgments, 129, 136

Variables
  conceptual definitions of, 112,
    122–124
  context, 118
  operationalization of, 112–113,
    123–124
Verbal behaviors. *See also* Language;
    Nonverbal behaviors
  communication process and,
    340–343, 360
  cultural influences on, 362–363
Vertical collectivism, 45
Vertical individualism, 45
Vindicators, 503
Visual behaviors, 348–350
Visual perception, 140. *See also*
    Perception
  cultural influences on, 141–147
Vocal characteristics, 354
Voyagers, 502, 503

Wechsler Adult Intelligence Scale
    (WAIS), 112, 122–123
Welfare-oriented health systems,
    247
Whakama (culture-bound
    syndrome), 259
Within-group norming, 170
Witiko (culture-bound syndrome),
    259
Words. *See also* Language
  cross-cultural research on, 317–
    320
Work. *See also* Organizations
  cultural meaning of, 469–470
  decision-making processes and,
    476–478
  diversity of workforce at, 483–
    485
  leadership and management
    styles at, 473–476
  motivation and productivity at,
    470–473
  organizational culture and, 446–
    448, 458–469
  values related to, 449–458
World Health Organization
    (WHO), 254–256
World Health Statistics Quarterly,
    235

Zar (culture-bound syndrome), 259

TO THE OWNER OF THIS BOOK:

I hope that you have found *Culture and Psychology,* 2nd edition, useful. So that this book can be improved in a future edition, would you take the time to complete this sheet and return it? Thank you.

School and address: _____

_____

Department: _____

Instructor's name: _____

1. What I like most about this book is: _____

_____

_____

2. What I like least about this book is: _____

_____

_____

3. My general reaction to this book is: _____

_____

_____

4. The name of the course in which I used this book is: _____

_____

5. Were all of the chapters of the book assigned for you to read? _____

    If not, which ones weren't? _____

6. In the space below, or on a separate sheet of paper, please write specific suggestions for improving this book and anything else you'd care to share about your experience in using this book.

_____

_____

_____

OPTIONAL:

Your name: _____ Date: _____

May we quote you, either in promotion for *Culture and Psychology,* 2nd edition, or in future publishing ventures?

Yes: _____ No: _____

Sincerely yours,

David Matsumoto